# Social Science Research

## A Cross Section of Journal Articles for Discussion and Evaluation

*Seventh Edition*

Turner C. Lomand

Editor

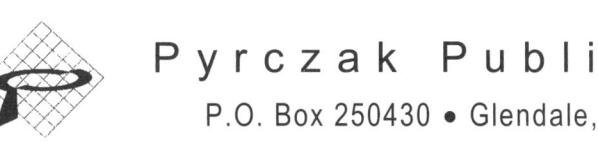

P y r c z a k   P u b l i s h i n g

P.O. Box 250430 • Glendale, CA 91225

"Pyrczak Publishing" is an imprint of Fred Pyrczak, Publisher, A California Corporation.

This edition was prepared in collaboration with Randall R. Bruce.

Although the editor and publisher have made every effort to ensure the accuracy and completeness of information contained in this book, we assume no responsibility for errors, inaccuracies, omissions, or any inconsistency herein. Any slights of people, places, or organizations are unintentional.

Project Director: Monica Lopez.

Editorial assistance provided by Cheryl Alcorn, Jenifer Dill, Karen Disner, Erica Simmons, and Sharon Young.

Cover design by Robert Kibler and Larry Nichols.

Printed in the United States of America by Malloy, Inc.

ISBN 978-1-936523-01-6

# Contents

*Continued* →

# Notes

# Introduction to the Seventh Edition

The research articles in this book will help students learn how to read and evaluate published research. The articles were selected because they are clearly written, employ straightforward research designs, deal with interesting topics, and, as a group, illustrate a variety of methodological techniques.

The articles represent a cross section of social science research. Although sociology, social work, social psychology, and criminal justice are most heavily represented, some works from other related disciplines are also included.

## Learning How to Read Research

Social science students, instructors, researchers, and practitioners all read far more research than they conduct. The ability to comprehend research reports is clearly a useful skill, but it is not a skill most individuals acquire naturally. It needs to be learned. Like most learned skills, an individual gets better through instruction and practice. A classroom teacher can provide instruction, but learning to fully comprehend research reports also requires practice. Structured practice is exactly what this collection of articles and the associated questions provide.

## Evaluating Research

All the research articles in this collection make a contribution to the advancement of knowledge in their fields. However, none of them are examples of perfect research. Perfect research eludes researchers for three primary reasons.

First, there is no perfect way to sample. Some groups, such as successful criminals, are difficult to locate. Even if they can be located, some of the people a researcher wants to include in a sample are unwilling or unable to participate. In addition, due to time and budgetary limitations, many researchers make do with samples of convenience such as the students in the classes they teach.

Second, there is no perfect way to measure the key variables of interest to social scientists. For example, if a researcher conducts interviews using a tape recorder, he or she can review the material as often as needed to obtain accurate transcripts and reliable interpretations. However, the presence of an audiotape recorder may influence what the respondents are willing to tell the researcher. Using alternatives such as taking notes or relying on the interviewer's memory are likely to lead to an incomplete record. In short, researchers often have to select among imperfect ways to measure the variables of interest.

Finally, interpreting and drawing implications from data involve subjectivity. Trained researchers may have honest differences of opinion on how to do this for a given set of data.

For the reasons stated above, important decisions in the social sciences should be based on the *body of relevant research*. Thus, before generalizing from the results of any given article in this book, students should examine the results of other published research on the same topic.

## Reading Statistics

Most of the articles in this book employ relatively simple statistical procedures. There are exceptions, however. It is almost certain that every reader will encounter some statistical techniques with which he or she is not familiar. This happens not just to students but to professionals as well. Unless directed differently by an instructor, in these situations students should focus on the author's *interpretation* of the statistics in the narrative of the report.

## The Appendix

For most students, primary instruction in reading research articles comes from a classroom instructor. Appendix A may help in that instruction. It contains an excellent article that explains the purpose of each part of a standard research article: heading, abstract, introduction, method, results, and discussion.

## Factual and Discussion Questions

The *Factual Questions* at the end of each article address major points of the article, particularly methodological issues. These questions can be answered directly from the article itself. The lines in each article are numbered, which should help in documenting answers. These questions should help students recognize the types of information in research articles that are substantively important and should be noticed.

The *Questions for Discussion* draw attention to methodological issues on which there may be honest differences of opinion. There are no right or wrong answers to these questions. However, students should be prepared to provide reasons for their answers if they are discussed in class.

## Evaluation Criteria

At the end of each article are 13 basic evaluation criteria that require quality ratings. These may also be used as the basis for classroom discussions. Depending upon the objectives for a research methods class, some instructors may require students to apply a more detailed set of criteria when evaluating the articles.

## New to the Seventh Edition

Many of the articles from the Sixth Edition have been retained. The new articles that have been added to the Seventh Edition are Articles 1, 7, 12, 13, 15, 21, 27, 29, 30, 32, 33, and 36.

## Acknowledgment

Robert F. Szafran pioneered this reader in the social sciences. In his capacity as editor of the First Edition, he established many structural elements that guided the development of this edition. His contribution is greatly appreciated.

## Feedback

I welcome your feedback on this collection and am especially interested in receiving suggestions for improving the next edition of this book. You can write to me care of the publisher using the address on the title page of this book or by e-mailing messages to me via Info@Pyrczak.com.

Turner C. Lomand
Editor

# Article 1

# Conspiracy Beliefs About HIV/AIDS Among HIV-Positive African American Patients in Rural Alabama

ANDREW A. ZEKERI
Tuskegee University

TSEGAYE HABTEMARIAM
Tuskegee University

BERHANU TAMERU
Tuskegee University

DAVID NGAWA
Tuskegee University

VINAIDA ROBNETT
Tuskegee University

ABSTRACT. This is apparently the first survey examining endorsement of HIV/AIDS conspiracy beliefs and their relations to educational attainment among 205 HIV-positive African American patients receiving care at an AIDS Outreach Organization in Alabama. Thirty-one percent somewhat or strongly believed that "AIDS is a form of genocide against African Americans," 29% strongly agreed that "AIDS was created by the government to control the Black population," 56.1% agreed that the government is withholding a cure for AIDS, and 69.8% agreed that the government is withholding information about the disease from the public. Fifty-two percent agreed that "HIV is a man-made virus," and 43.1% that "AIDS was produced in the government's laboratory." Respondents with high school or college education were less likely to endorse conspiracy beliefs. Being open and sensitive to questions about conspiracy beliefs plus understanding the historical roots and social context from which such questions arise in African American communities is needed to counter such beliefs.

From *Psychological Reports*, 104, 388–394. Copyright © 2009 by Psychological Reports. Reprinted with permission.

The African American population has been hard hit by human immunodeficiency virus (HIV), which causes Acquired Immunodeficiency Syndrome (AIDS). African Americans make up about 12% of the national

5 population but represent about 50% of all people in the USA who were living with HIV/AIDS in 2005 (Centers for Disease Control and Prevention, 2006). Of AIDS cases among women, 63% are African American. HIV transmission and AIDS in the USA is dispro-

10 portionately striking among African Americans. Given this racial disparity in the HIV/AIDS infection rate, it is essential to identify factors that may make a difference in prevention and intervention. Some research on HIV/AIDS prevention has emphasized taking into ac-

15 count conspiracy beliefs (beliefs about large-scale discrimination by the government and the health-care system against African Americans) held by some in the African American community (e.g., Jones, 1993; Thomas & Quinn, 1993; Bird & Bogart, 2005; Bogart &

20 Thorburn, 2005, 2006).

Although such beliefs may have implications for HIV/AIDS surveillance, public policy, and prevention programs, research on conspiracy beliefs about HIV/AIDS among HIV-positive African Americans

25 has been limited. No published peer-reviewed assessments of conspiracy beliefs focusing on rural African Americans with AIDS were located, but much of the substantial literature has focused on more general populations. One unstudied population is African

30 Americans who are HIV-positive and live in rural areas of the southern USA; so empirical research is needed. Such beliefs could influence health-care utilization, medication adherence, and overall open communication and discussion with medical practitioners.

35 The purpose of this study was to conduct an empirical study on HIV/AIDS conspiracy beliefs among HIV-infected rural African American patients and to include a possible association with educational attainment.

40 Several prior studies have indicated a significant percentage of African Americans hold conspiracy beliefs regarding HIV/AIDS (e.g., Bogart & Thorburn, 2005, 2006; Whetten, Leserman, Whetten, Ostermann, Thielman, Swarts, & Stangl, 2006). In their study of

45 607 respondents in California, Herek and Capitanio (1994) reported that 20% of the 263 African Americans in their sample compared to 4% Euro-Americans believed that "the government is using AIDS to kill off minority groups." Furthermore, 43% of African Ameri-

50 cans and 37.1% Euro-Americans believed that information about AIDS is being held back. As anticipated, educational attainment and income were associated with these beliefs, as the African Americans who agreed that the government is using AIDS to kill off

55 minority groups were likely to have completed fewer years of formal education and to have lower income. Earlier, Klonoff and Landrine (1999) conducted a

door-to-door survey of 520 African Americans in San Bernardino County, California, reporting 26.5% of their respondents agreed with the statement, "HIV/AIDS is a man-made virus that the federal government made to kill and wipe out Black people." Respondents who agreed with this genocidal statement were most likely male college graduates. In a related study, Bogart and Thorburn (2005), in a random telephone survey of 500 African Americans in the USA, stated that over 20% of men and 12% of women somewhat or strongly agreed that "AIDS is a form of genocide against Blacks," while over 30% of men and 24% of women agreed that "AIDS was produced in a government laboratory." Similarly, in Parsons, Simmons, Shinhoster, and Kilburn's survey (1999) of 715 parishioners in Louisiana, almost 70% of their respondents did not believe that the government is telling the truth about AIDS, and 27.5% agreed that AIDS was "intended to wipe Blacks off the face of the earth."

A recent study of lack of trust of health-care providers and use of the government health services suggested that conspiracy beliefs may be widespread and reflected substantial mistrust (Whetten et al., 2006). In this study, 23% of 422 African Americans and 11% of the 189 Euro-Americans who were HIV-positive strongly and somewhat believed that the government created AIDS to kill minorities.

A positive relation of endorsement of HIV/AIDS conspiracy beliefs with educational attainment was hypothesized; that is, patients with better education (high school or college graduates) would be less likely to endorse such conspiracy beliefs. However, findings are contradictory or inconclusive. One study stated lower educational attainment was associated with belief that the government is using AIDS as a way of killing minority people (Herek & Capitanio, 1994), but in another study (Klonoff & Landrine, 1999) results were contradictory. Since some of these studies were conducted more than a decade ago, an additional survey should focus on the relation between education and endorsement of HIV/AIDS conspiracy beliefs to have a more current assessment for conclusions.

**Method**

*Participation*

Data were obtained from an AIDS Outreach Organization clinic in southeastern Alabama as part of an ongoing study of persons diagnosed with HIV. This clinic provides medical and social support services to HIV-positive persons who live in a 23-county area.

The survey was conducted in the summer of 2005 and fall of 2006. The Adherent Nurse requested participation of 300 HIV-positive African Americans who were patients of the clinic and taking antiretroviral medications. She obtained verbal informed consent from each patient and gave a self-administered questionnaire to be completed privately. She collected completed questionnaires and gave each participant a $15 Wal-Mart gift card in appreciation for participation. Of the 300 patients invited, 205 (68%) completed the questionnaire, 40 refused participation, and 55 partially completed the questionnaire. Lack of interest and not wanting to be used as a "guinea pig" were the excuses given by most nonrespondents. The analyses reported in the present paper are limited to the 205 respondents (118 men and 87 women) with completed questionnaires.

*Measures*

The nine conspiracy beliefs (cf. Table 1) were adapted from previous studies (Herek & Capitanio, 1994; Klonoff & Landrine, 1999; Parsons et al., 1999; Bird & Bogart, 2005; Bogart & Thorburn, 2005, 2006). Participants reported agreement with the statements of HIV/AIDS conspiracy beliefs using options of 1: *Disagree strongly*, 2: *Disagree somewhat*, 3: *No opinion*, 4: *Agree somewhat*, and 5: *Agree strongly*. These options were collapsed into two categories for the bivariate analyses presented in Table 1. Educational attainment was measured by four categories—1: *Did not graduate from high school*, 2: *Completed high school*, 3: *Some college or vocational school*, and 4: *Completed college*. Sex of the respondent (1: *Male* and 2: *Female*) and age in years were included.

*Analyses*

Frequency distributions and descriptive statistics provided information about patients' characteristics and beliefs about HIV/AIDS conspiracy. To estimate the relation of education with conspiracy beliefs, crosstabulations were made, then percentages were calculated to report in Table 1. Values of chi-squared statistics were calculated to test the statistical significance of the distributions by educational groups. $p = .05$ was considered significant.

**Results**

Of the 205 patients, 57.6% were men and 42.4% were women. Fifty-eight percent of the participants were single, 17% were married, and 11.2% were divorced. Less-than-high-school education was reported by 23%, while 31% reported completing high school. Only 15% of these patients reported having a 4-yr. college degree. One hundred and twenty-nine were 34 years old or younger, and 37% ($n = 76$) were 35 years or older.

Of these patients, 56% endorsed the belief about the government's role in withholding a cure for AIDS and 69.8% information about the disease from the public (Table 1); 52.7% endorsed extreme beliefs that "HIV is a man-made virus"; and 43.1% strongly agreed that "AIDS was produced in the government's laboratory." Thirty-seven percent of the patients agreed with the statement, "People who take the new medicine for HIV are human guinea pigs for the government." Thirty-one percent believed that "AIDS is a form of genocide against Blacks," and 28.8% said that "AIDS was

Table 1
*HIV-AIDS Conspiracy Beliefs Endorsed Overall and by Education (N = 205): Percent Agreeing Somewhat and Strongly*

| Belief item | Total | Did not graduate high school ($n = 47$) | | High school or college graduate ($n = 158$) | | $\chi^2$ | Effect Size |
|---|---|---|---|---|---|---|---|
| | | $f$ | % | $f$ | % | | |
| A lot of information is being held back from the public. | 69.8 | 38 | 80.8 | 105 | 66.4 | 12.91* | .49 |
| HIV is a man-made virus. | 52.7 | 32 | 68.1 | 76 | 48.1 | 11.95* | .44 |
| AIDS is a form of genocide against Blacks. | 30.7 | 21 | 46.8 | 41 | 25.9 | 9.44* | .48 |
| The government is not telling the truth about AIDS. | 46.3 | 28 | 59.6 | 67 | 42.4 | 7.05 | .39 |
| AIDS was created by the government to control the Black population. | 28.8 | 20 | 42.5 | 39 | 24.7 | 6.25 | .39 |
| There is a cure for AIDS, but it is being withheld from the poor. | 56.1 | 33 | 70.2 | 82 | 51.9 | 7.23 | .46 |
| The medicine that doctors prescribe to treat HIV is poison. | 28.9 | 23 | 48.9 | 37 | 22.8 | 13.67* | .51 |
| People who take the new medicine for HIV are human guinea pigs for the government. | 36.6 | 30 | 63.8 | 45 | 28.5 | 21.91* | .76 |
| AIDS was produced in a government lab. | 43.1 | 21 | 57.5 | 61 | 38.6 | 9.48* | .40 |

*$p < .05$.

created by the government to control the Black population." Twenty-nine percent ($n = 23$) endorsed "The medicine that doctors prescribe to treat HIV is poison."

Values of chi-square in Table 1 show that educa-
170 tional attainment was significant and differently distributed for endorsement of six specific beliefs. Respondents who were high school or college graduates were less likely than peers with less education to endorse the beliefs that "A lot of information about AIDS
175 is being held back from the public," "HIV is a man-made virus," "AIDS is a form of genocide against African Americans," "The medicine that doctors prescribe to treat HIV is poison," "People who take the new medicine for HIV are human guinea pigs for the gov-
180 ernment," and "AIDS was produced in the government's laboratory." The calculated effect sizes (Cohen, 1988) in Table 1 confirm education's effect is meaningful in this sample of 205.

**Discussion**

The present study confirms the association of six
185 different types of HIV/AIDS conspiracy beliefs with amount of education within this sample of HIV-infected African American patients living in rural Alabama. The study has three important findings. First, there is a high prevalence of conspiracy beliefs about
190 HIV/AIDS in this sample. These patients hold misconceptions about medications used to treat HIV infection. These findings are similar to those of previous studies on such beliefs and of medical care and mistrust in urban areas (Herek & Capitanio, 1994; Klonoff & Lan-
195 drine, 1999; Parsons et al., 1999; Bogart & Thorburn, 2005, 2006; Whetten et al., 2006). Extreme beliefs related to genocidal conspiracies were endorsed at size-

able rates. Earlier research is extended to a different group of African Americans. Data lend support to the
200 suggestion that many African Americans do not trust the government and the medical community. Despite increased scientific knowledge about HIV/AIDS in the early 21st century, the prevalence of specific conspiracy beliefs regarding HIV/AIDS for this sample has
205 not changed significantly. Such beliefs may challenge the efficacy of AIDS educational programs directed toward such groups.

Also, the hypothesis that education was significantly related to endorsement of six HIV/AIDS con-
210 spiracy beliefs was supported. Confirming Herek and Capitanio (1994), less-educated patients were more likely to endorse lack of efficacy of new treatments for HIV (e.g., "The medicine that doctors prescribe to treat HIV is poison") and the government's role in handling
215 the AIDS epidemic (e.g., "AIDS is a form of genocide against African Americans"). However, results are inconsistent with those of Klonoff and Landrine (1999), who found that individuals with more education (i.e., college versus high school graduates) were most likely
220 to endorse these statements. Such differences may reflect sampling procedures since the current sample were rural African Americans infected with HIV living in Alabama, while Klonoff and Landrine's sample were from urban areas of California. Geographic varia-
225 tion in beliefs may also account for this finding.

Further, in addition to the work of Bogart and Thorburn (2005), the current study empirically documents beliefs that "The medicine that doctors prescribe to treat HIV is poison" and "People who take the new

230 medicine for HIV are human guinea pigs for the government," as was suggested in the popular press.

### Limitations

Present results must be viewed within the context of several limitations. This clinic-based study only sampled African American patients engaged in HIV
235 medical care, a narrow selection that may prevent generalizability of findings to other groups and areas of the USA. This study was cross-sectional, and the sample size was small. No conclusions can be drawn.

### Suggestions for Medical Personnel

This study provides information about the preva-
240 lence of HIV/AIDS conspiracy beliefs among African Americans in rural Alabama who are HIV-infected and has clear implications for addressing this issue in medical settings. The results suggest distrust and concerns about potential harms associated with taking
245 medications, as well as less belief in the effectiveness of these medications, may be related to adherence to medical treatment (McGary, 1999). Strategies for [increasing] patients' understanding of medications used to treat HIV infection would need to be developed so
250 that respectfully presented information may require further research. The breadth and complexity of the association of educational attainment and endorsement of HIV/AIDS conspiracy beliefs present challenges.

### References

Bird, S. T., & Bogart, L. M. (2005). Conspiracy beliefs about HIV/AIDS and birth control among African Americans: Implications for the prevention of HIV, other STIs, and unintended pregnancy. *Journal of Social Issues, 61*, 109–126.

Bogart, L. M., & Thorburn, S. (2005). Are HIV/AIDS conspiracy beliefs a barrier to HIV prevention among African Americans? *Journal of Acquired Immune Deficiency Syndrome, 38*, 213–218.

Bogart, L. M., & Thorburn, S. (2006). Relationship of African Americans' sociodemographic characteristics to belief in conspiracies about HIV/AIDS and birth control. *Journal of the National Medical Association, 98*, 1144–1150.

Centers for Disease Control and Prevention. (2006). *HIV/AIDS surveillance report.* Vol. 17. Atlanta, GA: U.S. Department of Health and Human Services, pp. I–54.

Cohen, J. (1988). *Statistical power analysis for the behavioral sciences* (2nd ed.). Hillsdale, NJ: Erlbaum.

Herek, G. M., & Capitanio, J. P. (1994). Conspiracies, contagion, and compassion: Trust and public reactions to AIDS. *AIDS Education and Prevention, 6*, 365–375.

Jones, J. H. (1993). *Bad blood: The Tuskegee syphilis experiment.* New York: Free Press.

Klonoff, E. A., & Landrine, H. (1999). Do blacks believe that HIV/AIDS is a government conspiracy against them? *Preventive Medicine, 28*, 451–457.

McGary, H. (1999). Distrust, social justice, and health care. *The Mount Sinai Journal of Medicine, 66*, 236–240.

Parsons, S., Simmons, W., Shinhoster, F., & Kilburn, J. (1999). A test of the grapevine: An empirical examination of conspiracy theories among African Americans. *Sociological Spectrum, 19*, 201–222.

Thomas, S. B., & Quinn, S. C. (1993). The burdens of race and history on black Americans' attitudes toward needle exchange policy to prevent HIV disease. *Journal of Public Health Policy, 14*, 320–347.

Whetten, K., Leserman, J., Whetten, R., Ostermann, J., Thielman, N., Swarts, M., & Stangl, D. (2006). Exploring lack of trust in care providers and the government as a barrier to health service use. *American Journal of Public Health, 96*, 716–721.

**Acknowledgments**: The authors acknowledge the staff of Montgomery Aids Outreach and the Director for data collection. Authors also thank the anonymous reviewers for their insightful comments on their earlier draft.

**Address correspondence to**: Andrew A. Zekeri, Department of Psychology and Sociology. Tuskegee University, Tuskegee, AL 36088. E-mail: zekeri@tuskegee.edu

# Exercise for Article 1

## Factual Questions

1. Did the researchers have a hypothesis?

2. This study was conducted in which state in the United States?

3. What value of $p$ was used for significance?

4. Of the total sample, what percentage held the belief that HIV is a man-made virus?

5. Of the "high school or college graduate" subgroup, how many participants held the belief that HIV is a man-made virus?

6. Was the difference between the two groups on the first belief item in Table 1 statistically significant?

## Questions for Discussion

7. In your opinion, was the use of verbal informed consent a good idea? Explain. (See lines 109–111.)

8. Do you think that the 68% completion rate is adequate? Explain. (See lines 114–116.)

9. What is your understanding of the meaning of the term *effect size*? (See lines 181–183 and Table 1.)

10. To what extent do you agree with the researchers' statement of limitations? (See lines 232–238.)

11. Were any of the results especially surprising to you? Explain.

## Quality Ratings

Directions: Indicate your level of agreement with each of the following statements by circling a number from 5 for strongly agree (SA) to 1 for strongly disagree (SD). If you believe an item is not applicable to this research article, leave it blank. Be prepared to explain your ratings. When responding to criteria A and B, keep in mind that brief titles and abstracts are conventional in published research.

A. The title of the article is appropriate.

> SA   5   4   3   2   1   SD

B. The abstract provides an effective overview of the research article.

> SA   5   4   3   2   1   SD

C. The introduction establishes the importance of the study.

> SA   5   4   3   2   1   SD

D. The literature review establishes the context for the study.

> SA   5   4   3   2   1   SD

E. The research purpose, question, or hypothesis is clearly stated.

> SA   5   4   3   2   1   SD

F. The method of sampling is sound.

> SA   5   4   3   2   1   SD

G. Relevant demographics (for example, age, gender, and ethnicity) are described.

> SA   5   4   3   2   1   SD

H. Measurement procedures are adequate.

> SA   5   4   3   2   1   SD

I. All procedures have been described in sufficient detail to permit a replication of the study.

> SA   5   4   3   2   1   SD

J. The participants have been adequately protected from potential harm.

> SA   5   4   3   2   1   SD

K. The results are clearly described.

> SA   5   4   3   2   1   SD

L. The discussion/conclusion is appropriate.

> SA   5   4   3   2   1   SD

M. Despite any flaws, the report is worthy of publication.

> SA   5   4   3   2   1   SD

# Article 2

# Adolescent Internet Usage in Taiwan: Exploring Gender Differences

CHIEN-HUANG LIN
National Central University, Taiwan

SHU-FEN YU
National Central University, Taiwan

ABSTRACT. The purpose of this study was to explore gender differences in adolescent Internet accessibility, motives for use, and online activities in Taiwan; 629 5th- and 6th-graders were surveyed. Findings revealed that the gap in gender differences with regard to Internet use has decreased in this generation. Even though the Internet is the most recent form of major media in the world, it has become the second most important medium as perceived by boys and girls. No gender difference was found in adolescents' motives for using the Internet. The ranking of relative importance of motives for adolescents going online was searching for information, followed by socializing, and boredom avoidance for both boys and girls. However, a gender difference in online activities seems to persist. Searching for homework information and playing games were the most popular online activities for all adolescents. However, while girls tended to view the Internet more as a means of searching for information and e-mailing friends, boys tended to use it more for playing games and downloading software.

## Introduction

The preteens and teens of today are the first widely "wired" generation. According to a report released by eMarketer (2004), the number of preteens and teens online in the United States grew steadily from 26.6 [5] million in 2000 to 34.3 million in 2003, when nearly one-half of all youngsters were online. The report further points out that preteens and teens comprise over 20% of the American online population. A recent survey (Forrester Research, 2005) revealed that consumers [10] between the ages of 12 and 17 in North America were often online daily and averaged almost 11 hours per week. The trend is similar in Taiwan. According to a survey by Taiwan Network Information Center (2008), the Internet population in Taiwan has reached 15 million. Among them, Internet users under the age of 20 [15] accounted for about 2.86 million. Moreover, the two groups with the highest rates of Internet usage were 12- to 15-year-olds (98%) and 16- to 20-year-olds (95.6%). It appears that the Internet has become not only part of adolescents' daily life but one of the most important [20] media.

The popularity of the Internet among adolescents raises many challenges to the academic community as well as to market researchers. Due to their greater buying power, most research has focused on the Internet [25] behavior of adults while research on adolescents has been relatively neglected. Monitoring adolescent Internet behavior is important, in part, because they may encounter undesirable content, such as pornography or online harassment. Additionally, many online games [30] contain a large amount of violence. Though the advantages provided by the Internet are indispensable for modern life, its possible negative influences cannot be dismissed. More knowledge about adolescents' behaviors may provide parents and teachers with the infor- [35] mation necessary to guide them in their Internet use and help them avoid the dangers.

The purpose of this study was to explore gender differences in adolescent Internet accessibility, motives for use, and online activities in Taiwan. [40]

### Theoretical Background and Hypotheses

*Accessibility to the Internet*

Some studies have indicated that while males tend to highlight the value of using the Internet as well as their proficiency, females tend to express more negative attitudes toward computers and the Internet (e.g., [45] Durndell & Haag, 2002; Kadijevich, 2000; Whitley, 1997). In part because of such findings, computers and the Internet may be considered a masculine domain. Two factors may help explain this phenomenon. One is the ability to master computers and the Internet; it is [50] undeniable that males had more opportunities to use technology products such as the Internet. The result was that males have used the Internet more often and for a longer time than have females (Clemente, 1998; Kraut et al., 1998; Bruce, 1988). The other factor could [55] be embedded in the contents of the Internet, much of which was not targeted at females when the Internet first gained prominence. Clemente (1998) pointed out that, at least in the mid-1990s, the Internet simply did not have what most females wanted or needed. Giac- [60] quinta, Bauer, and Levin (1993) concluded much the same about the limited participation of women in early home computing: "Clearly, for the majority of these women, the design, marketing, and interpretation of home computer hardware and software did not address their needs or the reality of their lives. Mothers view time in the home very differently; time required to master computer activities is a burden rather than an escape or pastime" (p. 90). Since its content did not satisfy the needs of women, they tended to view the Internet as less important and used it less often than did males.

Recently, some researchers (e.g., Schumacher & Morahan-Martin, 2001) have argued that the gap has narrowed now that females have acquired more experience with the Internet and more content related to women's interests has become available. Empirical studies support this view. Hunley et al. (2005) reported that the amount of time spent on the computer was similar across genders. Tsai and Lin (2004) found no significant gender differences in adolescents' Internet self-efficacy, suggesting that both genders were competently mastering it. Nevertheless, education policies might play an important role in bridging the remaining gap. For example, in order to equip youngsters with the skills necessary to master technology and information resources in 2001, the Ministry of Education in Taiwan required computer and Internet classes starting in the 5th grade in every public elementary school. Since then, both boys and girls at school have had equal opportunity to access the Internet. For this new generation, the gender gap should have narrowed.

H1: There is no gender difference in accessibility to the Internet and its importance.

*Motives for Using the Internet*

Most studies investigating the motives for using media have focused on television (e.g., Rubin, 1977; Condry, 1989) and computers (e.g., Livingstone & Bovill, 1999). Rubin (1977) found that while "Viewing for arousal" was the most important reason to watch television for 9-year-olds, "Viewing to pass time" was the major motive among 13- to 17-year-olds. Investigating children's motives for using computers, Livingstone and Bovill (1999) reported that computers were most often used for playing games, word processing, drawing, and doing math or number work. Research specifically examining the motives for using the Internet, however, has only examined adults (e.g., Ferguson & Perse, 2000; Papacharissi & Rubin, 2000; Perse & Dunn, 1998). Ferguson and Perse (2000) found that entertainment was the most salient motive for visiting the Web, followed by passing time, acquiring social information, and relaxation. Similarly, Papacharissi and Rubin (2000) reported that information seeking and entertainment were equally important motives for using the Internet. As far as we know, only one study has investigated adolescent motives. Surveying 8- to 13-year-old children in the Netherlands, Valkenburg and Soeters (2001) found that boys and girls did not differ significantly in their motives for going online. They further pointed out that affinity to computers,

seeking information, and entertainment were the three most important motives for children to use the Internet. Their study showed that while older children more often reported going online for information, younger children mentioned using the Internet to avoid boredom more often than did older children. However, since motives can vary by age and conditions in a country, such as culture and economic development, these findings may not be applicable to Taiwan. This study uses the following research questions:

1. What are adolescents' motives for using the Internet?

2. Is there a gender difference in their motives for using the Internet?

*Online Activities Among Adolescents*

Although the literature suggests that the gender difference in computer use is closing, there continues to be a gender gap in online activities and in the content that is accessed (Clemente, 1998). Due to the importance of school and recreation in adolescent life, it seems reasonable that searching for homework information and online entertainment would be their most popular Internet activities. The Internet provides users with information about almost anything in mere moments. Moreover, in order to train teens how to master the Internet, certain school homework assignments in Taiwan require them to look for information online. These factors make the Internet an excellent tool in the eyes of teens. In addition to providing information, entertainment also attracts adolescents. A wide variety of games on the Internet appeals to adolescents' desires (e.g., for social contact, viewing violence, role-playing, and exploration).

Some findings from marketing reports and academic research support the idea that searching for information and playing games are the most common online activities for adolescents. For example, Hunley et al. (2005) pointed out that girls most often used the computer for homework. Surveying 6- to 11-year-old children, eMarketer (2005) found that game playing (42.6%) and searching for homework information (23.1%) were the most popular online activities for adolescents. Similarly, a study conducted by Mediamark Research (2005) reported game playing (42.6%) and "Did stuff for school/homework (23.1%)" as the top online activities for children ages 6 to 11. However, the report also indicated that boys (28.9%) were more likely to play games than were girls (11.1%). A Griffiths, Davies, and Chappell study (2004) also supported that boys tended to play games more often than did girls. Similarly, investigating adolescent perception and attitudes toward the Internet, Tsai and Lin (2004) found that while males tended to consider the Internet more as a "toy," females tended to view it as a tool or as technology with which to accomplish a task. Hunley et al. (2005) found that 46% of 10th-grade adolescents reported that searching for information on the Internet for school purposes was their main reason for going online. These findings may indicate that females tend to hold a more pragmatic view of the Internet, while males tend to focus more on enjoyment.

180     A greater focus on socializing may be another cause for gender differences. Literature suggests that girls view close relationships as more important (Gilligan, 1982; Buhrmester, 1996). Tsai and Lin's study (2004) indicated that female adolescents expressed

185 greater confidence in using the Internet for general or communication purposes. Conducting a survey of Internet users over 15 years of age in the United States, Hoffman, Kalsbeek, and Novak (1996) found that females were more likely to use the Internet for e-

190 mailing, while males were more likely to download software. It is possible that female adolescents tend to use e-mail to fulfill their need for social contact with friends. As to why males more often download software, online games may be behind this behavior. Some

195 games, especially those on children's Web sites, require the player to download software. Since male adolescents tend to spend more time playing online games, it may lead to their spending more time downloading materials. In one final point of difference, girls more

200 frequently surf for information about idols (Valkenburg & Soeters, 2001).

Based on the above findings, the following hypotheses about adolescent Internet behavior are proposed.

205 H2: Searching for information and playing games are the two most popular Internet activities among adolescents.

H3: Girls search for information on the Internet more often than do boys.

210 H4: Boys play games more often.

H5: Girls use e-mail more often.

H6: Boys download software more often.

H7: Girls use the Internet to surf for information about idols more often.

### Method

*Sample*

215     The experience with the Internet of 634 5th- and 6th-grade Taiwanese school children in this study ranged from six months to two years. The sampling process was as follows: First, 10 municipal elementary schools were drawn randomly from Taipei City, Tai-

220 wan. Then, one class of each 5th and 6th grade was drawn randomly from the chosen schools. All students in the chosen classes were then asked to fill out a questionnaire. Finally, 629 effective questionnaires were obtained. Our sample consisted of 337 5th-graders and

225 290 6th-graders; 347 were boys and 282 girls.

*Questionnaire and Measurements*

Before the survey, a focus group of 5 5th- and 5 6th-graders with an even number of each gender was conducted in order to develop the questions about online activities and motives that were to be used in the

230 questionnaire of this study, which consisted of four parts. In the first part, subjects were asked to report on the accessibility of computers and the Internet at home, their experience with the Internet (i.e., how long they had been using it), the amount of time spent on the

235 Internet weekly, and the location of the Internet. The second part asked subjects to indicate their three most frequent online activities from nine items: searching for homework information, playing games, e-mailing, downloading software, visiting children's Web sites,

240 chatting with friends, reading news, visiting idols' Web sites, and others. The third part aimed at detecting subjects' motives for using the Internet. Subjects were requested to rate how much each of the following statements was similar to their own reasons for using

245 the Internet on a 1–5 Likert scale, where 1 represents "Strongly disagree," and 5 stands for "Strongly agree." These statements were developed from the focus group:

1. I use the Internet because the content is interesting.

250 2. I use the Internet because it has become a habit for me.

3. I use the Internet because my parents or teachers ask me to search for information.

4. I use the Internet for killing time.

255 5. I use the Internet for learning new things.

6. I use the Internet because it enables me to escape loneliness and have the company of others.

7. I use the Internet because my parents use it.

8. I use the Internet for finding subjects to talk about

260 with friends.

9. I use the Internet for approaching my idols (to chat with and e-mailing them, or searching for news about idols).

10. I use the Internet because I have nothing else to do.

265     These statements were entered into a principal components analysis with varimax rotation. The analysis yielded three factors with eigenvalues higher than 1.0, which explained 53.27% of the variance. The three factors were labeled socializing (items 6, 8, and 9; ei-

270 genvalues = 1.96), boredom-avoidance (items 4 and 10; eigenvalues = 1.79), and information acquisition (items 1, 2, 3, 5, 7; eigenvalues = 1.58).

The last part of the questionnaire asked the subjects about their grade, sex, and views on the importance of

275 media today. Five types of media (i.e., television, newspapers, radio, magazines, and the Internet) were included. Subjects were asked to rate each on a 1–5 Likert scale, where 1 stands for "Very unimportant," and 5 stands for "Very important."

## Results

*Gender Differences in Internet Accessibility*

280  To investigate gender differences in Internet accessibility in Taiwan, we conducted a series of cross-tabulations on each of the categories. The frequencies and percentages are shown in Table 1. Over 94% reported having computers, and around 90% had Internet

285  access at home. Regarding their experience with the Internet, subjects were classified into two major groups. Around 35% of the boys and girls had less than one year of experience with the Internet, while 42% had at least 2 years of experience. This phenomenon

290  probably resulted from the fact that computer and Internet courses had been taught in Taiwanese schools starting in the 5th grade.

Table 1
*Gender Difference in the Internet Accessibility*

|  | Boys | | Girls | | |
| --- | --- | --- | --- | --- | --- |
|  | Frequency | % | Frequency | % | $\chi^2$ |
| Home with computer |  |  |  |  | .01 |
|   Yes | 329 | 94.8 | 267 | 94.7 |  |
|   No | 18 | 5.2 | 15 | 5.3 |  |
| Home with Internet |  |  |  |  | .11 |
|   Yes | 314 | 90.5 | 253 | 89.7 |  |
|   No | 33 | 9.5 | 29 | 10.3 |  |
| Internet access location |  |  |  |  | 23.88** |
|   Home | 255 | 73.5 | 221 | 78.4 |  |
|   School | 38 | 11.0 | 40 | 14.2 |  |
|   Public library | 10 | 2.9 | 9 | 3.2 |  |
|   Internet coffee shop | 31 | 8.9 | 2 | 0.7 |  |
|   Friend's house | 4 | 1.2 | 6 | 2.1 |  |
|   Other | 9 | 2.6 | 4 | 1.4 |  |
| Experience with Internet |  |  |  |  | .27 |
|   Less than one year | 120 | 34.7 | 97 | 34.8 |  |
|   1 to 2 years | 74 | 21.4 | 64 | 22.9 |  |
|   Over 2 years | 152 | 43.9 | 118 | 42.3 |  |
| Weekly online time |  |  |  |  | 8.83* |
|   Less than an hour | 137 | 39.5 | 134 | 47.5 |  |
|   1 to 5 hours | 143 | 41.2 | 109 | 38.7 |  |
|   5 to 10 hours | 30 | 8.6 | 25 | 8.9 |  |
|   Over 10 hours | 37 | 10.7 | 14 | 5.0 |  |

*Note.* $N = 625$ to $629$; $*p < .05$, $**p < .001$.

It is interesting to note that gender differences appeared in the categories of weekly online time and the

295  Internet access locations. Most subjects' weekly online time fell either into the category of "Less than an hour (boys: 39.5%; girls: 47.5%)" or "1 to 5 hours (boys: 41.2%; girls: 38.7%)." Ten percent of the boys reported spending over 10 hours surfing on the Internet weekly:

300  This percentage indicates that boys tend to spend more time than girls on the Internet ($\chi^2$ $(3, N = 629) = 8.83$, $p < .05$). Furthermore, Table 1 indicates that while girls tend to go online mostly at home and school, boys visit Internet coffee shops with greater frequency than do

305  girls ($\chi^2$ $(5, N = 629) = 23.88, p < .001$).

Table 2 shows the mean scores of the importance of media as perceived by the subjects. A series of *t*-tests on the mean scores of media with gender as the between-subjects factor was conducted. Results re-

310  vealed no gender difference in subjects' view of the importance of television and the Internet. In contrast, for media such as newspapers ($t(626) = 2.67, p < .01$), radio ($t(626) = 2.52, p < .05$), and magazines ($t(627) = 2.57, p < .05$) there was a significant difference, with

315  boys tending to view these media as more important than do girls. Furthermore, both genders held the same hierarchy of importance of media types. To examine the difference in their views of media types, a one-way analysis of variation (ANOVA) on the mean scores of

320  media as the between-subjects factor was conducted for each gender. The results of pairwise comparisons showed that the differences among ratings for television, Internet, and newspapers reached a significant level for both genders. Thus, for both boys and girls,

325  television was ranked as the most important media, followed by the Internet, radio, and newspapers and magazines.

Table 2
*Gender Difference in the Perceived Importance of Media*

| Media | Boys | | Girls | | |
| --- | --- | --- | --- | --- | --- |
|  | M | SD | M | SD | t |
| Television | 4.14 | 2.24 | 3.98 | 1.91 | .99 |
| Internet | 3.94 | 2.25 | 3.65 | 1.78 | 1.79 |
| Newspapers | 3.58 | 2.19 | 3.16 | 1.72 | 2.67** |
| Radio | 3.37 | 2.40 | 2.93 | 2.01 | 2.52* |
| Magazines | 3.31 | 2.38 | 2.87 | 1.95 | 2.57* |

*Note.* $N = 629$; $*p < .05$, $**p < .01$.

In sum, the results show that girls as well as boys had equivalent access to the Internet at home. There

330  was no discernable difference in their experience in and opportunities for using the Internet. Only the amount of time spent on the Internet and Internet access locations showed gender differences. This implies that the gap between genders in Internet use has de-

335  creased in this generation. Both boys and girls not only had the same opportunity to access the Internet, but also viewed it as the second most important media. Thus, hypothesis 1 is supported.

*Motives for Using the Internet*

Table 3 shows mean scores of motives for using the

340  Internet. To examine the differences between the three categories of motives (i.e., information acquisition, socializing, and boredom avoidance), a one-way ANOVA on the mean scores of motives as the between-subjects factor was conducted for boys and

345  girls separately. The results of the pairwise comparisons showed that while the differences among the three categories reached a significant level for girls, only the differences between the ratings of information and socializing as well as the differences between the ratings

350  of information and boredom avoidance reached significant levels for boys. This implies that the major motive for girls was to go online for information acquisition, followed by socializing and boredom avoidance. Though boys also reported that searching for informa-

355  tion was their main motivation for going online, social-

izing and boredom avoidance tied as their second ranked motive.

Table 3
*Gender Difference in Motives for Using the Internet*

| Motive | Boys | | Girls | | |
|---|---|---|---|---|---|
| | M | SD | M | SD | t |
| Information acquisition | 3.63 | .71 | 3.66 | .63 | –.49 |
| Sociability | 2.73 | .96 | 2.69 | .83 | .47 |
| Boredom avoidance | 2.61 | 1.24 | 2.44 | 1.07 | 1.83 |

*Note. N = 629*

360   To investigate the gender differences in the motives for Internet usage, a series of *t*-tests on the mean scores of children's motives for using the Internet with gender as the between-subjects factor was conducted. The *t* scores ranged from –.49 for information acquisition to 1.83 for boredom avoidance, and none of them reached a significant level. This implies that there were no gen-
365   der differences in motives for using the Internet.

On a less general level aside from the data presented in Table 3, gender differences appeared in specific motives that fall under the three broad categories of motives. In the information acquisition category,
370   girls more frequently than boys mentioned the motive of going online as a way to approach their idols, $t (627) = -2.14$, $p < .05$. Furthermore, under the category of socializing, a greater number of boys reported that the Internet allows them to have the company of others, $t$
375   $(627) = 2.71$, $p < .001$. The last specific motive with a gender difference barely reached the significant level. In the boredom avoidance category, more boys than girls reported that they used the Internet because they had nothing else to do, $t (626) = 1.94$, $p = .053$.

*Gender Differences in Online Activities*
380   To investigate gender differences in online activities, we conducted a series of cross-tabulations on each of the surveyed activities. Table 4 shows the frequencies and percentages. As expected, searching for information for homework and playing games were
385   among the top three online activities for both boys and girls. While the percentage of time girls spent searching for homework information was higher than that of boys ($\chi^2(1, N = 629) = 11.49$, $p < .01$), boys reported playing more games than did girls ($\chi^2(1, N = 629) =$
390   $24.27$, $p < .001$). Furthermore, survey results showed that girls spent a higher percentage of their time using e-mail than did boys ($\chi^2(1, N = 629) = 30.47, p < .001$). The percentage of downloading software among boys was almost double that of girls ($\chi^2(1, N = 629) = 50$,
395   $p < .001$). It is also interesting to note that girls tend to visit their idols' Web sites more often than do boys ($\chi^2(1, N = 634) = 17.79$, $p < .001$). Thus, hypotheses 2 to 7 are supported.

Table 4
*Gender Difference in Online Activities*

| | Boys | | Girls | | |
|---|---|---|---|---|---|
| | Frequency | % | Frequency | % | $\chi^2$ |
| Searching for information | 185 | 53.3 | 188 | 66.7 | 11.49* |
| Playing games | 210 | 60.5 | 115 | 40.8 | 24.27** |
| E-mailing | 109 | 31.4 | 150 | 53.2 | 30.47** |
| Downloading software | 177 | 51.0 | 66 | 23.4 | 50.00** |
| Visiting children's Web sites | 65 | 18.7 | 66 | 23.4 | 2.06 |
| Chatting | 56 | 16.1 | 47 | 16.7 | .03 |
| Reading news | 48 | 13.8 | 36 | 12.8 | .15 |
| Visiting idols' Web sites | 1 | 0.3 | 10 | 3.5 | 9.61* |

*Note. N = 629; *p < .01 **p < .001.*

### Discussion

The purpose of this study was to explore gender
400   difference in adolescent Internet usage in Taiwan, with a focus on Internet accessibility, motives, and online activities. The results supported the view that the gap in gender differences in Internet use has decreased in this generation. Both genders appear now to have
405   equivalent resources and experience in accessing the Internet. Even though the Internet is the most recent form of major media, it has become the second most important medium in the opinion of adolescents. Furthermore, no gender differences were found in adoles-
410   cents' motives for using the Internet. The ranking of the relative importance of motives for adolescents going online was searching for information, followed by socializing, and boredom avoidance for both boys and girls.

415   However, some gender differences in online activities among adolescents seem to have persisted. Searching for homework information and playing games were the two most popular online activities for all adolescents. While girls viewed the Internet more as a tool for
420   searching for information and e-mailing friends, boys tended to use it for entertainment purposes (i.e., playing games and downloading software). These findings are consistent with those of Hunley et al. (2005).

However, the findings here seem to raise more is-
425   sues than they resolve. Since this study should be considered exploratory, it may serve as a reference for future research. The results of this study reveal that adolescents today use the Internet almost daily. Unfortunately, the high frequency of Internet usage may in-
430   crease the number of adolescents exposed to harassment (British Broadcasting Corporation, 2002) and pornography (Cameron et al., 2005; Valkenburg & Soeters, 2001). Finkelhor, Mitchell, and Wolak (2000) found that youths were exposed to unwanted sexual
435   material (25%), sexual solicitation (19%), and harassment (6%). Future research could explore the relationship between the amount of time spent on the Internet and the experiences of encountering harassment or pornographic contents. Studies could also focus on
440   adolescents' responses to these experiences and the effect they have on them.

The responses from adolescents in this study established that playing games is one of the most popular online activities. A study by Griffiths et al. (2004) pointed out that adolescent online game players tended to sacrifice time that could be spent on their education. This study also found that compared to adults, adolescent gamers were more interested in violent games. This raises the possibility that this exposure might have a deleterious effect on their problem resolution methods. Future studies might examine the relationship between playing violent games and the use of violence in real life. Results of this study also show that socializing and boredom avoidance are two major motives for adolescents' online activities. Future research might examine the relationship between their motives and the kinds of online games adolescents play.

Parents, educators, policy makers, and scholars have long been concerned with the possible negative influence of media messages on children. Finkelhor et al. (2000) found that some youth are taking risks on the Internet, such as engaging in sexual conversations, seeking out X-rated sites, posting their own pictures, or harassing other Internet users. This study further pointed out that the rates are not high compared to other more risky behaviors, such as using drugs, drinking alcohol, or stealing, but they do reflect a new dimension of deviance that needs to be understood and addressed. As the number of adolescents online and the importance of the Internet continue to increase, so does the need for appropriate guidance (Dorman, 1997). However, until now research regarding parental mediation has focused only on television (e.g., Atkin, Greenberg, & Baldwin, 1991; Krcmar, 1996; Nathanson, 1999), and parental mediation patterns concerning adolescent Internet usage still remain unknown. There is a need to provide guidance for parents in teaching their children how to take advantage of the Internet without becoming a victim of it.

## References

Atkin, D., Greenberg, B. S., & Baldwin, T. F. (1991). The home ecology of children's television viewing: Parental mediation and the new video environment. *Journal of Communication, 41*, 40–52.

British Broadcasting Corporation. (2002). Youngsters targeted by digital bullies. Retrieved May 5, 2003, from: http://news.bbc.co.uk/hi/english/uk/newsid_1929000/1929944.stm

Bruce, M. (1988). Home interactive telematics: New technology with a history. In F. Van Rijn & R. Williams (Eds.), *Concerning home telematics: Proceedings of the IFIP TC 9 Conference on Social Implications of Home Interactive Telematics* (pp. 83–93).

Buhrmester, D. (1996). Need fulfillment, interpersonal competence, and the developmental contexts of early adolescent friendship. In W. M. Bukowski, A. F. Newcomb, & W. W. Hartup (Eds.), *The company they keep: Friendship in childhood and adolescence* (pp. 158–185), Cambridge: Cambridge University Press.

Cameron, K. A., Salazar, L. F., Bernhardt, J. M., Burgess-Whitman, N., Wingood, G. M., & DiClemente, R. J. (2005). Adolescents' experience with sex on the Web: Results from online focus groups. *Journal of Adolescence, 28*, 535–540.

Clemente, P. C. (1998). *State of the Net: The new frontier*. New York: McGraw-Hill.

Condry, J. C. (1989). *The psychology of television*. Hillsdale, NJ: Erlbaum.

Dorman, S. M. (1997). Internet safety for schools, teachers, and parents. *Journal of School Health, 67*, 355.

Durndell, A., & Haag, Z. (2002). Computer self-efficacy, computer anxiety, attitudes towards the Internet and reported experience with the Internet, by gender, in an East European sample. *Computers in Human Behavior, 18*, 521–535.

eMarketer. (2004). The online population among American adolescents and children increases dramatically. Retrieved January 9, 2006, from: http://www.emarketer.com/Report.aspx?kids_may04

eMarketer. (2005). What do kids love to do? Retrieved December 10, 2005, from: http://www.emarketer.com/Article.aspx?1003699

Ferguson, D. A., & Perse, E. M. (2000). The World Wide Web as a functional alternative to television. *Journal of Broadcasting & Electronic Media, 44*, 155–174.

Finkelhor, D., Mitchell, K., & Wolak, J. (2000). Online victimization: A report on the nation's youth. National Center for Missing & Exploited Children. Retrieved November 28, 2005, http://www.unh.edu/ccrc/youth_Internet-infopage.html

Forrester Research. (2005). Entertainment grabs youth's online time: Gaming sites get the greatest play with consumers. Retrieved December 8, 2005, http://www.forrester.com/Research/Document/Excerpt/0,7211,373352,00.html

Giacquinta, J. B., Bauer, J., & Levin, J. E. (1993). *Beyond technology's promise: An examination of children's educational computing at home*. Cambridge, UK: Cambridge University Press.

Gilligan, C. (1982). *In a different voice: Psychological theory and women's development*. Cambridge, MA: Harvard University Press.

Griffiths, M. D., Davies, M. N. O., & Chappell, D. (2004). Online computer gaming: A comparison of adolescent and adult gamers. *Journal of Adolescence, 27*, 87–96.

Hoffman, D. L., Kalsbeek, W. D., & Novak, T. P. (1996). Association for Computing Machinery. *Communications of the ACM, 39*(12), 36–46.

Hunley, S. A., Evans, J. H., Delgado-Hachey, M., Krise, J., Rich, T., & Schell, C. (2005). Adolescent computer use and academic achievement. *Adolescence, 40*(158), 307–318.

Kadijevich, D. (2000). Gender differences in computer attitude among ninth-grade students. *Journal of Educational Computing Research, 22*, 145–154.

Kraut, R., Lundmark, V., Patterson, M., Kiesler, S., Mukopadhyay, T., & Scherlis, W. (1998). Internet paradox: A social technology that reduces social involvement and psychological well-being? *American Psychologist, 53*(9), 1017–1031.

Krcmar, M. (1996). Family communication patterns, discourse behavior, and child television viewing. *Human Communication Research, 23*, 251–277.

Livingstone, S., & Bovill, M. (1999). *Young people, new media. Report of the research project children, young people, and the changing media environment*. London: London School of Economics and Political Science.

Mediamark Research. (2005). Mediamark Research Inc. releases its first-ever survey of children ages 6–11. Retrieved January 9, 2006, from: http://www.mediamark.com/mri/docs/press/pr_11-21-05_KidsStudy.htm

Nathanson, A. I. (1999). Identifying and explaining the relationship between parental mediation and children's aggression. *Communication Research, 26*, 124–143.

Papacharissi, Z., & Rubin, A. M. (2000). Predictors of Internet use. *Journal of Broadcasting & Electronic Media, 44*, 175–196.

Perse, E. M., & Dunn, D. G. (1998). The utility of home computers and media use: Implications of multimedia and connectivity. *Journal of Broadcasting & Electronic Media, 42*, 435–456.

Rubin, A. M. (1977). Television usage, attitudes and viewing behaviors of children and adolescents. *Journal of Broadcasting, 21*, 355–369.

Schumacher, J., & Morahan-Martin, J. (2001). Gender, Internet and computer attitudes and experiences. *Computers in Human Behavior, 17*, 95–110.

Taiwan Network Information Center. (2008). 2008 Internet Broadband Usage in Taiwan. Retrieved March 7, 2008, from: http://www.twnic.net.tw/download/200307/0801.pdf

Tsai, C., & Lin, C. (2004). Taiwanese adolescents' perceptions and attitudes regarding the Internet: Exploring gender differences. *Adolescence, 39*(156), 725–734.

Valkenburg, P. M., & Soeters, K. E. (2001). Children's positive and negative experiences with the Internet: An exploratory survey. *Communication Research, 28*(5), 652–675.

Whitley, B. E. (1997). Gender differences in computer-related attitudes and behavior: Meta-analysis. *Computers in Human Behavior, 13*, 1–22.

**About the authors**: *Chien-Huang Lin*, Department of Business Administration, National Central University, Taiwan. *Shu-Fen Yu*, Department of Information and Communication, Ming Chuan University, Department of Business Administration, National Central University, Taiwan.

**Address correspondence to**: Shu-Fen Yu, Department of Information and Communication, Ming Chuan University, 250 Sec. 5, Chung Shan N. Rd., Taipei 111, Taiwan, R.O.C. E-mail: sfyu@mcu.edu.tw

# Exercise for Article 2

## Factual Questions

1. What is the third hypothesis?

2. How many of the participants were 6th-graders?

3. What did the researchers conduct in order to develop the questions for their survey?

4. What percentage of the girls spent over 10 hours online?

5. Was there a significant difference between boys and girls in the perceived importance of the Internet? If yes, at what probability level?

6. Was there a significant difference between boys and girls in the frequency of playing games on the Internet? If yes, at what probability level?

## Questions for Discussion

7. Is it important to know that the selection of school and classes was done at random? Explain. (See lines 218–221.)

8. Table 2 presents the results of *t* tests. What is your understanding of the general purpose of such tests?

9. The researchers summarize the results in four tables. How helpful are the tables in helping you comprehend the results?

10. Do you agree with the researchers that the findings raise more issues than they resolve? (See lines 424–425.)

11. In your opinion, is this survey sufficiently important that it should be replicated with a sample from the United States? Explain.

## Quality Ratings

Directions: Indicate your level of agreement with each of the following statements by circling a number from 5 for strongly agree (SA) to 1 for strongly disagree (SD). If you believe an item is not applicable to this research article, leave it blank. Be prepared to explain your ratings. When responding to criteria A and B, keep in mind that brief titles and abstracts are conventional in published research.

A. The title of the article is appropriate.

   SA   5   4   3   2   1   SD

B. The abstract provides an effective overview of the research article.

   SA   5   4   3   2   1   SD

C. The introduction establishes the importance of the study.

   SA   5   4   3   2   1   SD

D. The literature review establishes the context for the study.

   SA   5   4   3   2   1   SD

E. The research purpose, question, or hypothesis is clearly stated.

   SA   5   4   3   2   1   SD

F. The method of sampling is sound.

   SA   5   4   3   2   1   SD

G. Relevant demographics (for example, age, gender, and ethnicity) are described.

   SA   5   4   3   2   1   SD

H. Measurement procedures are adequate.

   SA   5   4   3   2   1   SD

I. All procedures have been described in sufficient detail to permit a replication of the study.

   SA   5   4   3   2   1   SD

J. The participants have been adequately protected from potential harm.

   SA   5   4   3   2   1   SD

K. The results are clearly described.

   SA   5   4   3   2   1   SD

L. The discussion/conclusion is appropriate.

   SA   5   4   3   2   1   SD

M. Despite any flaws, the report is worthy of publication.

   SA   5   4   3   2   1   SD

# Article 3

# A Survey of the Health, Sleep, and Development of Children Adopted from China

MICHAEL A. RETTIG
Washburn University

KELLY McCARTHY-RETTIG
Desoto School District

ABSTRACT. The health, development, and sleeping patterns of 240 children adopted from China were examined using a survey research approach. Eighty percent of the children were 18 months of age or younger when adopted, and 98% of the children were girls. Sixty-two percent of the children were reported to have been developmentally delayed at the time of adoption; of this number, 91% were reported to have had delays in motor development. Of the families, 52% reported that children experienced sleep problems, but only 9% of the total sample experienced significant sleep difficulties. Implications for social workers are also discussed.

From *Health & Social Work, 31*, 201–207. Copyright © 2006 by the National Association of Social Workers. Reprinted with permission.

International adoption is an increasingly popular method for parents seeking to increase the size of their families. For example, Arsonson (2003) reported that there were more than 15,000 international adoptions in the United States in 1998. This was an increase of more than 2,000 from 1997. One of the main sources of international adoption is China. According to the National Adoption Information Clearinghouse (2003), there have been more than 32,000 visas issued for children being adopted from China since 1995. Given the large number of children coming to this country from China and the general concerns about the psychological and behavioral impact of adoption, it is reasonable to investigate health and developmental outcomes after the adoption.

Information on the postadoptive outcomes of children adopted from China is relevant to social workers, adoption agencies, and other professionals assisting families with international adoption. It is important that these professionals be aware of any potential problems so that families can be prepared for possible child care issues. For example, Shapiro and colleagues (2001) indicated that studies of children of international adoption have shown potential problems with psychological adjustment. These problems may be due to medical or nutritional deprivation, lack of a primary caregiver, or inconsistencies in caregivers. Howe (1997) noted that nearly 25% of adopted children will display some type of behavioral or mental health concern later in life, so it is important to be aware of postadoptive outcomes.

## Related Literature

We conducted a search for relevant literature using ERIC and Internet search engines. This search focused on studies relevant to children adopted from China and on reports investigating health, sleep, or developmental problems. Several reports relevant to this investigation were identified.

One potential area of concern regarding international adoptions involves medical concerns. Arsonson (2003), for example, identified and discussed 17 potential medical problems, including malnutrition, rickets, eczema, scabies, lead poisoning, bacterial intestinal infections, tuberculosis, hepatitis B and C, asthma, anemia, and visual or hearing problems. Despite the relatively large number of potential medical problems, Arsonson noted that the children typically have limited long-term medical issues and that these are fairly easily addressed with diagnosis and proper treatment.

Another potential area of concern involves the fact that earlier research has indicated that it is typical for children to present with developmental delays at the time of their adoption (Johnson & Traister, 1999; Miller & Hendrie, 2000; Miller, Kiernan, Mathers, & Klein-Gitelman, 1995). In the Miller and associates study, the mean age of children at arrival was 14 months, and they were seen within three months of arrival. These researchers found that approximately 74% of children showed delays in one or more areas of development at the time of their arrival in the United States. Miller and Hendrie assessed the health and developmental status of 452 children in two different groups. Of the 452 children, 98% were girls. They found that 75% of the children had significant developmental delays in at least one area and that the delays were related to length of time children spent in orphanages. The longer the time spent in an orphanage, the greater the developmental delays. Delays in gross motor skills were most common (55%), followed by delays in language (43%), socioemotional (28%), and cognitive skills (32%). Miller and Hendrie also found that a number of children had medical problems, including anemia (35%), elevated lead levels (14%), tuberculosis (3.5%), and hepatitis B surface antibody (22%). Each of these studies pointed to the need for continued long-term follow-up of the children.

75    A study conducted by Tessler and colleagues (1999) looked at intercountry adoption from a sociological perspective and examined the nature of families adopting children as well as some health and developmental outcomes. Children in this study were adopted

80    from China, Korea, Thailand, Peru, and the United States. Of the 361 families, 332 had adopted children from China. Similar to methods used in this study, the Tessler team set up a Web site and e-mail address through which families could complete questionnaires.

85    They received responses from 526 parents in 361 households in 38 states. Tessler and colleagues found that 97% of the children adopted were girls, and the mean age at adoption was two years. The children came from 15 different provinces across China. Sixty-

90    four percent of the adopted Chinese children were the only child in the family. A number of parents reported that the children lagged in development, especially in gross motor skills. However, they also reported that the children caught up quickly, learned English quickly,

95    adapted easily to new foods, and accepted their new families.

Shapiro and colleagues (2001) indicated that adoptive parents might be unprepared for a child's developmental problems or for possible problems with at-

100    tachment. Haugaard and colleagues (1999) pointed out that professionals and parents involved in the adoption process would benefit from knowing about specific child characteristics that can indicate which transracial children are at the greatest or least risk of short- or

105    long-term problems. Vonk and Angaran (2003) indicated that parents who adopt across race need training in cultural competence to be prepared for the demands of raising the child. They indicated in their survey of adoption agencies that only about half the agencies

110    provided training to facilitate transracial adoption.

*Sleep Problems*

A review of literature regarding the sleeping patterns of internationally adopted children revealed limited information. However, this also seems to be a potential area of concern given that approximately 25%

115    of children can experience sleep problems (Zuckerman, Stevenson, & Bailey, 1987) and that subpopulations of children, such as those with diagnosed disabilities or other developmental delays, may display greater difficulty with sleeping (Mindell, 1993). Zuckerman and

120    associates indicated that as many as 30% of children can have sleep problems during the first four years of life, with the highest incidence occurring from one to two years of age. They also found that many of these sleep problems do not disappear with age. In their

125    study, children who experienced sleeping problems at eight months of age also experienced sleep difficulties at three years of age.

According to the American Academy of Child and Adolescent Psychiatry (2000), children can experience

130    a variety of different sleep disorders. These can include nightmares, bedwetting, teeth grinding, or difficulty falling asleep. A subgroup of sleep disorders are referred to as parasomnias. These sleep disorders include sleep terrors, sleep talking, and sleepwalking. Para-

135    somnias usually occur during the first third of the night, and individuals have little memory of them.

Hopkins-Best (1998) indicated that sleep issues are among the most commonly reported problems of families of internationally adopted children. She noted that

140    sleeping alone, as is common in the United States, is different from many cultures that focus on a family bed. Although family beds may be more common in China than in the United States, it is uncertain what the sleeping conditions are for children in orphanages.

145    One study that addressed the sleep problems of internationally adopted children directly was conducted by Bishop (2001). This study examined the sleeping patterns of 17 internationally adopted girls (from China and Cambodia) compared with 15 children in nonadop-

150    tive families (seven boys and eight girls). The mean age of the adopted children was nine months; the mean age for the nonadopted children was 14 months. Bishop used a questionnaire to measure the children's sleeping patterns. The results indicated that there was only one

155    significant difference found in the sleep patterns of the two groups of children. The internationally adopted children had longer-duration night wakings than the nonadopted children. Overall, the hypothesis that the adopted children would display more sleep problems

160    than the nonadopted children was not supported.

**Method**

*Participants*

Participants in this survey were 240 families who had adopted children from China. Families responded from 35 states. All of the children were adopted between 1992 and 2001. Families responded by e-mail or

165    regular mail.

*Procedures*

A snowball sampling method was used. The national Families with Children from China (FCC) Web site (www.fwcc.org) was accessed to obtain member contact information. Families receiving the survey

170    were asked to forward it to other families with children adopted from China.

The survey questions were based in part on the interest regarding the health, development, and sleeping habits of children adopted from China and on the re-

175    search questions and format used by Tessler and colleagues (1999). A short introductory letter explaining the survey's purpose and providing contact information was included, as well as information on how to respond. The letter indicated that the results would be

180    made available through publication and that we would ask the FCC site to include this summary as a link.

A pilot test of the survey was sent electronically to 10 FCC families in the immediate geographic area. E-mail addresses for these families were obtained from
185  the local FCC group. Feedback on the questions and methods being used was requested from these 10 families. Families who did not respond within three weeks were sent a follow-up survey. On the basis of this pilot test of the survey, three questions were revised and two
190  additional questions were added to the survey, for a total of 23 questions.

    Although not all families who have adopted children from China are members of FCC, it is the largest such organization, and we felt that a large number of
195  families could be reached through it. A list of FCC contacts in several states was compiled, and e-mails were sent asking for permission to contact members. We asked, and hoped, that the contacts would forward the survey to local FCC members. Some of these con-
200  tacts indicated either that they were not comfortable forwarding the survey or that some local FCC groups had policies about not forwarding e-mails. E-mails were sent to families across the country from April to July 2001.
205      An electronic database was set up to collect and summarize the information obtained from the surveys. E-mail addresses were used as a primary key to be sure that there were no duplicate survey returns. The surveys were examined using the database's sort capabili-
210  ties, and reports were generated for each research question.

### Results

    Responses were obtained from 240 families by e-mail or regular mail, and all responses were obtained between April and August 2001. Responses came from
215  35 states, including 17 states east of the Mississippi River and 18 states west of the Mississippi River. Mothers responded to the survey in 89% of the returns; fathers, 11%. Children came from 22 different provinces: 19% were adopted from Guangdong, 17% from
220  Hunan, and 14% from Jiangxi; fewer than 10% were adopted from each of the other provinces.

    As indicated in Table 1, most of the children in this sample (68%) were adopted in their first year of life, and 80% were 18 months of age or younger when
225  adopted. The vast majority of children adopted were girls (98%) (Table 1). Of the 240 responses, only two indicated that the adopted child was a boy.

    The years in which these children were adopted ranged from 1992 to 2001; 38 children were adopted
230  between 1992 and 1995, 90 between 1996 and 1998, and 112 between 1999 and 2001. Almost half the families in this survey reported having other children. Of these, 44% were biological children, 38% were adopted children, 15% were both biological and adopted chil-
235  dren, and 3% were stepchildren (Table 2).

Table 1
*Characteristics of Children Adopted from China*

| Survey questions | % Responses |
| --- | --- |
| Age of child when adopted | |
|   0–1 year | 68 |
|   1–2 years | 20 |
|   2–3 years | 5 |
|   3–4 years | 3 |
|   4–5 years | 1 |
|   > 5 years | 1 |
| Gender | |
|   Male | 2 |
|   Female | 98 |
| Length of stay in orphanage | |
|   1–4 months | 11 |
|   5–9 months | 43 |
|   10–15 months | 29 |
|   16–24 months | 10 |
| Developmental delays in children | |
|   No | 38 |
|   Yes | 62 |
| Domains of developmental delay | |
|   Motor | 91 |
|   Language | 35 |
|   Social | 35 |
|   2 of 3 areas | 35 |
|   All 3 areas | 18 |

*Note.* Rounding error accounts for totals less than 100%.

Table 2
*Characteristics of Participants in Survey about Children Adopted from China*

| Survey questions | % Responses |
| --- | --- |
| Survey Respondents | |
|   Mothers | 89 |
|   Fathers | 11 |
| Time period of adoption | |
|   1992–1995 | 16 |
|   1996–1998 | 38 |
|   1999–2001 | 46 |
| Other children in the family | |
|   No | 52 |
|   Yes | 48 |
| If other children in family | |
|   Biological children | 44 |
|   Adopted children | 38 |
|   Both biological and adopted | 15 |
|   Stepchildren | 3 |

    As there have been reports raising concerns about the length of stay in orphanages, we included a question asking how long children had been in an orphanage before adoption. Most of the children in this study
240  (43%) had been in an orphanage for five to nine months (Table 1). One child was reported to have been in an orphanage for 12 years.

    Families were also asked whether they had visited the orphanage in China. Only 45% of families reported
245  visiting the child's orphanage. Of these 109 families, 81 were families who adopted children in the age range of birth to one year. Only 24% of families reported that their children spent time living with a foster family before adoption.

Table 3
*Problems with Sleep, Eating, Social Interactions, Bonding, or Acceptance Among Children Adopted from China*

| Area | % of families reporting problems | Extent of problems reported (%) | | |
|---|---|---|---|---|
| | | Minor | Some | Many |
| Sleep | 52 | 68 | 14 | 17 |
| Eating | 19 | 60 | 28 | 11 |
| Interacting with others | 16 | 11 | 4 | 1 |
| Bonding | 13 | 10 | 2 | 1 |
| Acceptance | 9 | 7 | 2 | —[a] |

[a]Only two families (less than 1%) reported having many problems in this area.

250 Families were asked how much they had been told or knew about their children before adoption and whether this information was correct. Forty-five percent of families reported knowing something about their child, and 17% reported knowing nothing about
255 their child. Of the families who did get some prior information, 33% reported that this information was accurate, and 15% reported that the information was partly correct.

Families were asked whether the children were de-
260 velopmentally delayed when adopted and if so, in what areas (language, social, motor, or any combination). Sixty-two percent of families reported that children were developmentally delayed at their arrival in the United States (Table 1). The families reporting devel-
265 opmental delays indicated that motor delays were the most common.

Families were asked whether children had any serious medical conditions at the time of adoption. Thirty-two families, or 13% of the total sample, reported that
270 children had medical problems. Of these 32 children, 84% were 0 to two years old when adopted. Three children had positive tuberculosis tests, five tested positive for hepatitis B or C, three had hearing or ear problems, two had visual problems, two had seizures,
275 and two had asthma. Other problems mentioned included high lead levels, rickets, dental decay, dyspraxia, and scabies.

The survey asked whether there had been any problems with the children's sleeping or eating behaviors as
280 well as whether there had been any problems with social interactions, bonding, or acceptance. For each of these items, a scale including the following responses was used: "no problems (less than 25% of the time)," "minor problems (25% of the time)," "some problems
285 (50% of the time)," and "many problems (75% or more of the time)."

Nearly 52% of families reported that children had some degree of sleep problems and that most of these were minor (Table 3). Only 9% of the total sample
290 reported many sleep problems (75% of the time or more). A number of families included comments about their children's sleep patterns, stating that children did not want to sleep alone, that children had night terrors, or that the sleeping problems faded as the children got
295 older.

A relatively small number of families reported problems with diet or eating. The responses indicated that only 19% experienced problems in this area. The majority of children were eating dairy products, al-
300 though a few families reported that children were lactose intolerant.

Families were asked whether there had been any problems with children interacting with others, bonding with family members, or being accepted by friends or
305 family. Survey responses indicated that 16% of the families reported problems with social interactions. Only 13% of the sample reported problems with bonding, and again most of these were minor. Very few problems were reported with acceptance of the child
310 (9%). Only two of the 240 families reported having many problems with the acceptance of their child by friends or family members.

Parents were also asked whether their children had been identified as gifted or in need of special education
315 services because of a disability. Seven percent of families reported that children had been identified as gifted; only 4% had been referred for special education services owing to disabilities. These figures need to be viewed with caution given that many of the children in
320 this survey were not yet of school age.

## Discussion

What are the postadoptive outcomes of internationally adopted children and, specifically, of children adopted from China? This central question and related questions in this investigation were what we hoped to
325 address with this research. The answers to these questions are important to social workers helping children and families through the adoption process. They are also important for our society as a whole, given the thousands of children being adopted from all over the
330 world.

The focus of this investigation was to obtain information to help children, families, schools, and society to be prepared for possible postadoptive outcomes. These outcomes may often be very positive. Anecdotal
335 comments included in the completed surveys indicated that many of the children are healthy, happy, smart, and social. Given that the children are often adopted into good home environments with loving, well-educated, professional parents, one could easily assume

340 that the long-term outlook for these children is very good.

The results of this study are consistent with those obtained in other studies. First, the majority of children adopted from China are young girls 18 months of age 345 or younger, from a variety of provinces. Consistent with other studies, many of the children displayed developmental delays at the time of adoption. An important point of distinction in future studies is whether the determination of developmental delay was made 350 through an agency or clinic or based on the parents' opinion. In this survey, parents made this determination. None of the families reported a formal determination of developmental delay. However, it is possible that children will display some delays in development, 355 especially in motor skills, at the time of adoption. These delays will very likely be temporary and fade as children get older.

Only 13% of children in this survey were reported as having serious medical problems. As Arsonson 360 (2003) has noted, these medical conditions are usually easily diagnosed, and treatment can begin immediately with very few long-term effects.

Several children were reported to have problems with sleeping. Slightly more than half of the surveys 365 (125 families) reported children having some degree of sleeping problems. Most of these problems were minor, with only 9% of the total sample reporting serious sleep problems. The extent and nature of the sleeping problems was not examined as closely as in research 370 studies focusing specifically on this topic. However, a number of families reported children having a difficult time falling asleep, experiencing night terrors, or not wanting to sleep alone. A more detailed examination of children's sleep problems is warranted and must take 375 into consideration cultural differences between the United States and China. The length of stay in an orphanage or whether children lived in a foster family (and, if so, how long) may be variables to be examined in other studies investigating sleep disorders.

### Limitations

380 The sampling technique and procedures used in this study were not effective. This contributed to the study's small sample size and makes generalization of the findings difficult. Given that thousands of children have been adopted from China in the past 10 years, the 385 total number of returns was far short of what we had hoped and represents approximately 1% of all children adopted from China. However, the research questions addressed in this survey are important, and an effective way to reach these families must be found. It is impor- 390 tant to the children, their families, and society that we know as much as possible about any potential problems both before and after the adoption.

### Implications for Social Workers and Other Professionals

International adoption presents challenges to the adoptive child, the adoptive parents, and the adoptive 395 extended family. One of the most important things needed to assist in successful postadoptive outcome is information.

Issues that need to be addressed by social workers and families involve information on the child. Children 400 adopted from China may experience abandonment issues that may lead to sleep, bonding, or attachment problems. The children may feel a sense of loss that their native family and country could not take care of them. There may be attachment issues inasmuch as 405 children may have been cared for by several different caregivers in orphanages or foster families before coming to their homes in the United States. There may also be identity problems as children work to discover why they are in their new world. Some problems children 410 experience may be transitional ones that will fade over time, but others may not. Such problems may include sleep, eating, or behavioral problems. Social workers can help families understand that such problems may occur and that these problems may be expected in chil- 415 dren coming from institutional settings (Johnson & Dole, 1999).

The overall lack of information on children and their history is an issue for families. Adoptive families are unlikely to know anything about a child's medical 420 history or prior family background. Even a child's exact birth date may be in question. Parents may also be concerned about the child's developmental delays and what can be done about them as well as about problems that children may experience with diet or sleeping. 425 Social workers can help provide needed information.

A number of suggestions can be made to social workers and educational professionals who work with adoptive children and their families. These suggestions are consistent with those of Judge (1999). First, adop- 430 tive children should receive complete medical and developmental examinations soon after their arrival in the United States. For many children, this may simply be precautionary, but it is important that information be obtained so that when intervention is warranted, it can 435 begin as soon as possible. This examination should also include a follow-up on any information provided on immunizations. Such examinations would appear to be needed for all children adopted internationally.

Second, the children's emotional health should be 440 addressed. Children may experience a sense of loss or attachment issues, and they should be provided with considerable emotional support. It is important that parents provide a consistent, predictable, and well-structured environment (Judge, 1999). Although this is 445 a good suggestion for any family, it is very important for adopted children adapting to their new world. Parents should be encouraged to spend as much time as possible with the child, attend promptly to the child's needs, and provide a supportive, empathic home envi- 450 ronment. Social workers should be prepared to provide families with resource information on sleep disorders or, even thumb sucking, as needed.

It is important to help families identify and locate local, state, and national resources and support groups
455 (Judge, 1999). This could include the FCC, which has many local chapters. It may also involve the use of more experienced parents who can discuss their adoption experiences and help new adoptive families learn what they can expect (Judge, 1999). For example, one
460 local community has an informal mothers' group that meets once a month. This group is made up only of mothers with internationally adopted children who can share their knowledge and experiences. The mothers and families have formed an important bond that also
465 allows the children an opportunity to get together on a regular basis.

In addition, families need to be encouraged to make an effort to learn about the child's native culture and to be prepared for the child's questions about Chinese
470 culture, language, and the adoption. Families should be encouraged to speak in an honest and matter-of-fact manner about the adoption, read books about adoption and China, and be prepared for the child's questions. Social workers could provide families with a list of
475 children's books that address adoption or Chinese culture. Parents should make an effort to learn about and celebrate Chinese holidays such as the Moon Festival or Chinese New Year, as this can be an important way for children to learn about their native country.

## References

American Academy of Child and Adolescent Psychiatry. (2000). *Children's sleep problems*. Retrieved July 2004 from www.aacap.org/publications/factsfam/sleep.html

Arsonson, J. E. (2003). *An update on health issues in children adopted from China*. Retrieved May 1999 from www.orphandoctor.com/medical/regional/China/healthissues.html

Bishop, C. T. (2001). *Sleep habits of internationally adopted children*. Unpublished master's thesis, St. Joseph's University, Philadelphia.

Haugaard, J. J., Palmer, M., & Wojslawowicz, J. (1999). International adoption: Children primarily from Asia and South America. *Adoption Quarterly*, *3*, 83–93.

Hopkins-Best, M. (1998). *Toddler adoption: The weaver's craft*. Indianapolis: Perspectives Press.

Howe, D. (1997). Parent-reported problems in 211 adopted children: Some risk and protective factors. *Journal of Child Psychology and Psychiatry and Allied Disciplines*, *38*, 401–411.

Johnson, D. E., & Dole, K. (1999). International adoptions: Implications for early intervention. *Infants & Young Children*, *11*, 34–45.

Johnson, D. E., & Traister, M. (1999). Micronutrient deficiencies, growth failure and developmental delays are more prevalent than infectious diseases in U.S. adopted Chinese orphans. *Pediatric Research*, *45*, 126A.

Judge, S. L. (1999). Eastern European adoptions: Current status and implications for intervention. *Topics in Early Childhood Special Education*, *19*, 244–252.

Miller, L. C, & Hendrie, N. W. (2000). Health of children adopted from China. *Pediatrics*, *105*, E76.

Miller, L. C., Kiernan, M. T., Mathers, M. I., & Klein-Gitelman, M. (1995). Developmental and nutritional status of internationally adopted children. *Archives of Pediatrics & Adolescent Medicine*, *149*, 40–44.

Mindell, J. (1993). Sleep disorders in children. *Health Psychology*, *12*, 151–162.

National Adoption Information Clearinghouse. (2003). *HealthFinder*. Retrieved April 2003 from http://www.calib.com/naic

Shapiro, V., Shapiro, J., & Paret, I. (2001). International adoption and the formation of new family attachment. *Smith College Studies in Social Work*, *71*, 389–418.

Tessler, R., Gamache, G., & Liu, L. (1999). *West meets East: Americans adopt Chinese children*. Westport, CT: Bergin & Garvey.

Vonk, M. E., & Angaran, R. (2003). Training for transracial adoptive parents by public and private adoption agencies. *Adoption Quarterly*, *6*, 53–62.

Zuckerman, B., Stevenson, J., & Bailey, V. (1987). Sleep problems in early childhood: Continuities, predictive factors, and behavioral correlates. *Pediatrics*, *80*, 664–671.

**Acknowledgments:** Special thanks to Megan, Ryan, and Kate Li Rettig.

**About the authors:** *Michael A. Rettig*, Ph.D., is professor, Department of Education, Washburn University, 1700 SW College Avenue, Topeka, KS 66621 (E-mail: Michael.rettig@washburn.edu). *Kelly McCarthy-Rettig*, MS, is a teacher in the Desoto School District, Desoto, KS.

# Exercise for Article 3

## Factual Questions

1. Did the review of literature regarding the sleeping patterns of internationally adopted children reveal much information?

2. From how many states did families respond?

3. For what words does FCC stand?

4. Of the 240 responses, how many indicated that the adopted child was a boy?

5. According to the researchers, why should the findings regarding identification of children as gifted or in need of special education services be viewed with caution?

6. According to the researchers, were the findings of this study consistent with those obtained in other studies?

## Questions for Discussion

7. The researchers state that they used "snowball sampling." What do you think this term means? (See line 166.)

8. What is your opinion on defining "no problems" as being "less than 25% of the time"? (See lines 281–283.)

9. In your opinion, how important are the limitations discussed by the researchers? (See lines 380–392.)

10. In your opinion, to what extent are the implications directly based on the data generated by this survey? (See lines 393–479.)

11. In a future study, do you think it would be useful to include a comparison group such as children adopted from within the United States? Why? Why not?

12. If you were to conduct a survey on the same topic, what changes, if any, would you make in the research methodology?

## *Quality Ratings*

Directions: Indicate your level of agreement with each of the following statements by circling a number from 5 for strongly agree (SA) to 1 for strongly disagree (SD). If you believe an item is not applicable to this research article, leave it blank. Be prepared to explain your ratings. When responding to criteria A and B, keep in mind that brief titles and abstracts are conventional in published research.

A. The title of the article is appropriate.

SA 5 4 3 2 1 SD

B. The abstract provides an effective overview of the research article.

SA 5 4 3 2 1 SD

C. The introduction establishes the importance of the study.

SA 5 4 3 2 1 SD

D. The literature review establishes the context for the study.

SA 5 4 3 2 1 SD

E. The research purpose, question, or hypothesis is clearly stated.

SA 5 4 3 2 1 SD

F. The method of sampling is sound.

SA 5 4 3 2 1 SD

G. Relevant demographics (for example, age, gender, and ethnicity) are described.

SA 5 4 3 2 1 SD

H. Measurement procedures are adequate.

SA 5 4 3 2 1 SD

I. All procedures have been described in sufficient detail to permit a replication of the study.

SA 5 4 3 2 1 SD

J. The participants have been adequately protected from potential harm.

SA 5 4 3 2 1 SD

K. The results are clearly described.

SA 5 4 3 2 1 SD

L. The discussion/conclusion is appropriate.

SA 5 4 3 2 1 SD

M. Despite any flaws, the report is worthy of publication.

SA 5 4 3 2 1 SD

# Article 4

# Bullies Move Beyond the Schoolyard: A Preliminary Look at Cyberbullying

JUSTIN W. PATCHIN
University of Wisconsin, Eau Claire

SAMEER HINDUJA
Florida Atlantic University

ABSTRACT. Bullying in a school setting is an important social concern that has received increased scholarly attention in recent years. Specifically, its causes and effects have been under investigation by a number of researchers in the social and behavioral sciences. A new permutation of bullying, however, has recently arisen and become more common: Tech-savvy students are turning to cyberspace to harass their peers. This exploratory article discusses the nature of bullying and its transmutation to the electronic world, and the negative repercussions that can befall both its victims and instigators. In addition, findings are reported from a pilot study designed to empirically assess the nature and extent of online bullying. The overall goal of the current work is to illuminate this novel form of deviance stemming from the intersection of communications and computers and to provide a foundational backdrop on which future empirical research can be conducted.

From *Youth Violence and Juvenile Justice*, 4, 148–169. Copyright © 2006 by Sage Publications, Inc. Reprinted with permission.

The home, neighborhood, and school are all recognized as important social and physical contexts within which adolescents develop. Bullying—an all too common form of youthful violence—has historically af-
5 fected only children and teenagers while at school, while traveling to or from school, or in public places such as playgrounds and bus stops. Modern technology, however, has enabled would-be bullies to extend the reach of their aggression and threats beyond this
10 physical setting through what can be termed *cyberbullying*, where tech-savvy students are able to harass others day and night using technological devices such as computer systems and cellular phones. Computers occupy a significant proportion of the homes in which
15 children reside and are frequently used for social, entertainment, academic, and productivity needs (National Telecommunications and Information Administration [NTIA], 2002). Moreover, cellular phones are gaining widespread popularity and use among the
20 younger age groups because they are perceived as a status symbol, allow for conversations with friends in different physical spaces, and provide a virtual tether of sorts for parents, allowing for supervision from afar.

Though they are intended to positively contribute to
25 society, negative aspects invariably surface as byproducts of the development of new technologies such as these. The negative effects inherent in cyberbullying, though, are not slight or trivial and have the potential to inflict serious psychological, emotional, or social harm.
30 When experienced among members of this highly impressionable and often volatile adolescent population, this harm can result in violence, injury, and even death (e.g., Meadows et al., 2005; Vossekuil, Fein, Reddy, Borum, & Modzeleski, 2002) and later criminality for
35 both the initiator and recipient of bullying (e.g., Olweus, Limber, & Mihalic, 1999; Patchin, 2002). One particularly horrendous anecdotal account deserves mention. In May of 2001, viciously offensive messages denigrating and humiliating a high school sophomore
40 girl who suffered from obesity and multiple sclerosis were posted anonymously to an online message board associated with a local high school in Dallas, Texas (Benfer, 2001). In time, the bullying crossed over to the physical world as the victim's car was vandalized,
45 profanities were written on the sidewalk in front of her home, and a bottle filled with acid was thrown at her front door, which incidentally burned her mother. This example vividly depicts how bullying online can lead to physical harm offline.[1]
50     Little research to date has been conducted on cyberbullying. However, research on the correlates of traditional bullying can assist in comprehending the reality and growth of this new phenomenon. To begin, the desire to be and remain popular takes on almost
55 lifelike proportions among kids and teenagers during certain stages of their life, and their self-esteem is largely defined by the way that others view them. Although it is unclear exactly when self-esteem increases or decreases during a child's life (Twenge & Campbell,
60 2001), it unquestionably shapes a child's development in profound ways. According to the social acceptance model, self-esteem stems from the perceptions that others have of the individual (Cooley, 1902). When individuals perceive themselves to be rejected or otherwise
65 socially excluded, a number of ill effects can result (Leary, Schreindorfer, & Haupt, 1995). Much research has validated this theory (Leary & Downs,

1995; Leary, Haupt, Strausser, & Chokel, 1998; Leary, Tambor, Terdal, & Downs, 1995) and has pointed to the following potentially negative outcomes: depression (Quellet & Joshi, 1986; Smart & Walsh, 1993), substance abuse (Hull, 1981), and aggression (Coie & Dodge, 1988; French & Waas, 1987; Hymel, Rubin, Rowden, & LeMare, 1990; Paulson, Coombs, & Landsverk, 1990; Stewart, 1985). In addition, low self-esteem tends to be found among chronic victims of traditional bullying (Hoover & Hazler, 1991; Neary & Joseph, 1994; Rigby & Slee, 1993).[2] It is expected that cyberbullying can similarly cripple the self-esteem of a child or adolescent, and without a support system or prosocial outlets through which to resolve and mitigate the strain, the same dysphoric and maladaptive outcomes may result. Despite these solemn possibilities, there has been very little empirical attention to date devoted toward better understanding the electronic variant of this deviance (exceptions include Berson, Berson, & Ferron, 2002; Finn, 2004; Ybarra & Mitchell, 2004).

This research seeks to fill this gap by exploring cyberbullying and examining its potential to become as problematic as traditional bullying—particularly with society's increasing reliance on technology. Its goal is to illuminate this novel form of deviance stemming from the intersection of communications and computers and to provide a foundational backdrop on which future empirical research can be conducted. First, what is known about traditional bullying will be summarized to provide a comparative point of reference. Second, data collected from various media sources will be presented to describe the technology that facilitates electronic bullying and to portray its prevalence. Third, preliminary findings from a pilot study of adolescent Internet users will be presented, highlighting the characteristics of this group and their involvement (both as victims and offenders) in the activity. Finally, suggestions for future empirical research will be offered as guidance for additional exploration of this subject matter.

### Traditional Bullying

*Bullying Defined*

A variety of scholars in the disciplines of child psychology, family and child ecology, sociology, and criminology have articulated definitions of bullying that generally cohere with each other. To begin, the first stages of bullying can be likened to the concept of harassment, which is a form of unprovoked aggression often directed repeatedly toward another individual or group of individuals (Manning, Heron, & Marshal, 1978). Bullying tends to become more insidious as it continues over time and is arguably better equated to violence rather than harassment. Accordingly, Roland (1989) states that bullying is "long-standing violence, physical or psychological, conducted by an individual or a group directed against an individual who is not

able to defend himself in the actual situation" (p. 21).[3] Stephenson and Smith (1989) contend that bullying is

> a form of social interaction in which a more dominant individual [the bully] exhibits aggressive behavior, which is intended to and does, in fact, cause distress to a less dominant individual [the victim]. The aggressive behavior may take the form of a direct physical and/or verbal attack or may be indirect as when the bully hides a possession that belongs to the victim or spreads false information about the victim. (p. 45)

Providing perhaps the most panoptic definition, Nansel et al. (2001) asserted that bullying is aggressive behavior or intentional "harm doing" by one person or a group, generally carried out repeatedly and over time and that involves a power differential. Many characteristics can imbue an offender with perceived or actual power over a victim and often provide a sophistic license to dominate and overbear. These include, but are not limited to, popularity, physical strength or stature, social competence, quick wit, extroversion, confidence, intelligence, age, sex, race, ethnicity, and socioeconomic status (Olweus, 1978, 1993, 1999; Rigby & Slee, 1993; Roland, 1980; Slee & Rigby, 1993). Nonetheless, research on the relevance of these differences between bullies and their victims has been inconclusive. For example, differences in physical appearance was not predictive of one's likelihood of being a bully or a victim (Olweus, 1978), but physical shortness (Voss & Mulligan, 2000) and weakness (Leff, 1999) were found to be relevant in other research.

Although the harassment associated with bullying can occur anywhere, the term *bullying* often denotes the behavior as it occurs among youth in school hallways and bathrooms, on the playground, or otherwise proximal or internal to the school setting. Bullies can also follow their prey to other venues such as malls, restaurants, or neighborhood hangouts to continue the harassment. In the past, interaction in a physical context was required for victimization to occur. This is no longer the case thanks to the increased prevalence of the Internet, personal computers, and cellular phones. Now, would-be bullies are afforded technology that provides additional media over which they can manifest their malice. The following sections outline the scope, breadth, and consequences of traditional bullying as a reference point from which cyberbullying can subsequently be viewed and understood.

*Extent and Effects of Traditional Bullying*

It is unclear exactly how many youth are bullied or bully others on any given day. In 1982, 49 fifth-grade teachers from Cleveland, Ohio, reported that almost one-fourth (23%) of their 1,078 students were either victims or bullies (Stephenson & Smith, 1989). More recently, a nationally representative study of 15,686 students in grades 6 through 10 identified that approximately 11% of respondents were victims of bullying, 13% were bullies, and 6% were both victims and bullies during a year (Nansel et al., 2001). Additional research conducted by the Family Work Institute substantiated these findings through interviews with 1,000 youth in grades 5 through 12. Their study found that 12% of youth were bullied five or more times during the previous month (Galinsky & Salmond, 2002). Finally, the Bureau of Justice Statistics reports that 8% of youth between the ages of 12 and 18 had been victims of bullying in the previous 6 months (Devoe et al., 2002). That said, conservative estimates maintain that at least 5% of those in primary and secondary schools (ages 7–16) are victimized by bullies each day (Björkqvist, Ekman, & Lagerspetz, 1982; Lagerspetz, Björkqvist, Berts, & King, 1982; Olweus, 1978; Roland, 1980).

Many young people are able to shrug off instances of being bullied, perhaps because of peer or familial support or higher self-efficacy. Nonetheless, others are not able to cope in a prosocial or normative manner or reconcile the pain experienced through more serious episodes or actions. Suicidal ideation, eating disorders, and chronic illness have beset many of those who have been tormented by bullies, whereas other victims run away from home (Borg, 1998; Kaltiala-Heino, Rimpelä, Marttunen, Rimpelä, & Rantanen, 1999; Striegel-Moore, Dohm, Pike, Wilfley, & Fairburn, 2002). In addition, depression has been a frequently cited consequence of bullying (e.g., Hawker & Boulton, 2000) and seems to perpetuate into adulthood, evidencing the potentially long-term implications of mistreatment during adolescence (Olweus, 1994). Finally, in extreme cases, victims have responded with extreme violence, such as physical assault, homicide, and suicide (Patchin, 2002; Vossekuil et al., 2002).

Following the fatal shootings at Columbine High School in Littleton, Colorado, in 1999, the educational system was challenged to address bullying because the two teenagers involved in the massacre were reported to have been ostracized by their classmates. Additional school violence research of 37 incidents involving 41 attackers from 1974 to 2000 found that 71% (29) of the attackers "felt bullied, persecuted, or injured by others prior to the attack" (Vossekuil et al., 2002, p. 21). It was also determined that the victimization played at least some role in their subsequent violent outburst. Other less serious but equally as negative outcomes can result from repeated bullying. For example, students who are constantly harassed may attempt to avoid the problems at school as much as possible, leading to tardiness or truancy (BBC News, 2001; Richardson, 2003; Rigby & Slee, 1999). Truancy has been identified as a significant antecedent to delinquency, dropout, and other undesirable outcomes in the juvenile justice literature (Farrington, 1980; Garry, 1996; Gavin, 1997; Nansel et al., 2001). Based on these findings, it is clear that victims of bullies are at risk to have a discontinuous developmental trajectory for many years.

The aggressors in the bullying dyad also appear to be more likely to engage in antisocial activities later in life (Tattum, 1989). For example, approximately 60% of those characterized as bullies in grades six through nine were convicted of at least one crime by the age of 24, compared to 23% who were not characterized as either bullies or victims (Olweus et al., 1999). Further underscoring the relationship between bullying and future criminality, Olweus and colleagues (1999) found that 40% of bullies had three or more convictions by the age of 24, compared to 10% of those who were neither instigators nor victims of bullying.

Based on this brief review, it is clear that both bully victims and offenders are at an increased risk for developmental problems that can continue into adulthood. As such, it is imperative that researchers seek to better understand the antecedents and consequences of bullying behavior, for practitioners to develop and implement antibullying programs in schools, and for societal institutions to better understand the ways in which bullying behaviors are carried out, both in traditional and nontraditional settings.

### Cyberbullying

Because of the advent and continued growth of technological advances, the transmutation of bullying has occurred—from the physical to the virtual. Physical separation of the bully and the victim is no longer a limitation in the frequency, scope, and depth of harm experienced and doled out. As instances of bullying are no longer restricted to real-world settings, the problem has matured. Although a migration to the electronic realm is a seemingly logical extension for bullies, little is currently known regarding the nature and extent of the phenomenon. In short, we define *cyberbullying* as willful and repeated harm inflicted through the medium of electronic text. Based on the literature reviewed above, the constructs of malicious intent, violence, repetition, and power differential appear most salient when constructing a comprehensive definition of traditional bullying and are similarly appropriate when attempting to define this new permutation. To be sure, cyberbullies are malicious aggressors who seek implicit or explicit pleasure or profit through the mistreatment of other individuals. Violence is often associated with aggression and corresponds to actions intended to inflict injury (of any type). One instance of mistreatment, although potentially destructive, cannot accurately be equated to bullying, and so cyberbullying must also involve harmful behavior of a repetitive nature. Finally, because of the very nature of the behavior, cyberbullies have some perceived or actual power over their victims. Although power in traditional bullying might be physical (stature) or social (competency or popularity), online power may simply stem from proficiency. That is, youth who are able to navigate the electronic world and utilize technology in a way that allows them to harass others are in a position of power relative to a victim.

A brief editorial published in 2003 in *Journal of the American Academy of Child and Adolescent Psychiatry* pointed to the lack of academic references to this topic despite its anticipated proliferation (Jerome & Segal, 2003). Despite this call for research, very little scholarly attention has been devoted to the topic. In a notable exception, Ybarra and Mitchell (2004) conducted telephone surveys of 1,498 regular Internet users between the ages of 10 and 17, along with their parents, and found that 19% of youth respondents were either on the giving or receiving end of online aggression in the previous year. The vast majority of offenders (84%) knew their victim in person, whereas only 31% of victims knew their harasser in person. This fact is noteworthy; it appears that power and dominance are exerted online through the ability to keep the offender's identity unknown (Ybarra & Mitchell, 2004). When comparing those who were only aggressors to those who had no involvement in online harassment, the former were significantly more likely to be the target of offline bullying, to display problematic behavior, to have low school commitment, and to engage in alcohol and cigarette use. When comparing those who had experience being both an offender and a victim with those who had no involvement in online harassment, the significant differences were the same as above—with the exception of low school involvement. It is interesting to note that real-world variables that play a contributive role in traditional forms of delinquency and crime—such as general deviance, low commitment to prosocial institutions such as school, and substance abuse—are also significantly related to bullying on the Internet.

There are two major electronic devices that young bullies can employ to harass their victims from afar. First, using a personal computer, a bully can send harassing e-mails or instant messages; post obscene, insulting, and slanderous messages to online bulletin boards; or develop Web sites to promote and disseminate defamatory content. Second, harassing text messages can be sent to the victim via cellular phones.

### Personal Computers

Research by the U.S. Department of Commerce noted that almost 90% of youth between the ages of 12 and 17 use computers, and by age 10, youth are more likely than are adults to use the Internet (NTIA, 2002). Demonstrating the broad reach of instant messaging and chat programs, 20 million kids between the ages of 2 and 17 logged onto the Internet in July 2002, and 11.5 million used instant messaging programs (NetRatings, 2002). Similarly, according to a study of 1,081 Canadian parents conducted in March 2000, 86% stated that their kids used the Internet, 38% had their own e-mail address, 28% used ICQ (an instant messaging program short for "I seek you"), and 28% regularly spent time in chat rooms (Network, 2001). Indeed,

America Online (AOL, 2002, 2003)—the most popular Internet service provider, with more than 35 million users—states that members join in on more than 16,000 chat sessions and send more than 2.1 billion instant messages per day across their network. As a point of reference, 1.9 billion phone calls are made each day in the United States. Finally, the Internet relay channels provide a venue for many other users on a daily basis. For example, on the morning of an average Saturday in May 2005, there were more than 1 million users online in more than 800 chat rooms (Gelhausen, 2005).

Pew Internet and American Life Project (2001) conducted an extensive research endeavor in 2001 to ascertain demographic and behavioral characteristics of teenagers who use the Internet. A telephone survey was administered to 754 children between the ages of 12 and 17 in November and December of 2000. Though not generalizable to the population of online teenagers across the United States because of many methodological limitations, the study paints an interesting picture of the user population and their activities while connected to the Internet. About 17 million youth aged 12 to 17 regularly use the Internet. This figure represents approximately three-fourths (73%) of those in this age bracket.

According to the Pew Internet and American Life Project (2001), approximately 29% of youth younger than 12 regularly go online. Among teenagers, approximately 95% of girls and 89% of boys have sent or received e-mail, and 56% of girls and 55% of boys have visited a chat room. Almost three-fourths of teenagers (74%; 78% of girls and 71% of boys) in the study use instant messaging to communicate with their friends, with 69% using the technology several times a week. Almost half (46%) of respondents who report using instant messaging programs spend between 30 and 60 minutes per session doing so, whereas 21% state that they spend more than 1 hour in the activity in an average online session. Testifying to the benefits of textual communication over verbal communication, 37% used it to say something they would not have said in person. Underscoring the potential for harassment and negative treatment online, 57% have blocked messages from someone with whom they did not wish to communicate, and 64% had refused to answer messages from someone with whom they were angry.

### Cellular Phones

In the United States, more than 150 million individuals, including half of the youth between 12 and 17 years of age, own cellular phones (Fattah, 2003). It is estimated that 74% of Americans between the ages of 13 and 24 will have a wireless device by 2006 (O'Leary, 2003). Cell phone usage is much higher among teenagers and young adults in Europe compared to the United States, 60% to 85% compared to 25% (O'Leary, 2003). Research estimates that by 2007 nearly 100 million individuals will use the text messag-

ing service on their wireless device (Fattah, 2003). Statistics compiled in November 2001 by UPOC (2001)—
405 a wireless communications firm in the United States—found that 43% of those who currently use text messaging are between the ages of 12 and 17. To note, the text messaging capabilities of cellular phones are being exploited to a greater degree in European and Asian
410 countries. In 2002, approximately 90 billion text messages were sent through the two major telecommunication service providers in China, which equals approximately 246 million per day (CD, 2003). In Europe and Asia, more than 30 billion text messages are sent be-
415 tween individuals each month (Katz, 2002). It is predicted that 365 billion text messages will be sent across western Europe in 2006, up from 186 billion in 2002 (GSMBox, 2002).

*Issues Specific to Cyberbullying*

Gabriel Tarde's (1903) laws of imitation suggests
420 that new technologies will be applied to augment traditional activities and behaviors. Certain characteristics inherent in these technologies increase the likelihood that they will be exploited for deviant purposes. Cellular phones and personal computers offer several advan-
425 tages to individuals inclined to harass others. First, electronic bullies can remain virtually anonymous. Temporary e-mail accounts and pseudonyms in chat rooms, instant messaging programs, and other Internet venues can make it very difficult for adolescents to
430 determine the identity of aggressors. Individuals can hide behind some measure of anonymity when using their personal computer or cellular phone to bully another individual, which perhaps frees them from normative and social constraints on their behavior. Fur-
435 ther, it seems that bullies might be emboldened when using electronic means to effectuate their antagonistic agenda because it takes less energy and fortitude to express hurtful comments using a keyboard or keypad than using one's voice.

440 Second, supervision is lacking in cyberspace. Although chat hosts regularly observe the dialog in some chat rooms in an effort to police conversations and evict offensive individuals, personal messages sent between users are viewable only by the sender and the
445 recipient and are therefore outside regulatory reach. Furthermore, there are no individuals to monitor or censor offensive content in e-mail or text messages sent via computer or cellular phone. Another contributive element is the increasingly common presence of
450 computers in the private environments of adolescent bedrooms. Indeed, teenagers often know more about computers and cellular phones than do their parents and are therefore able to operate the technologies without worry or concern that a probing parent will dis-
455 cover their participation in bullying (or even their victimization; NTIA, 2002).

In a similar vein, the inseparability of a cellular phone from its owner makes that person a perpetual

target for victimization. Users often need to keep it
460 turned on for legitimate uses, which provides the opportunity for those with malicious intentions to send threatening and insulting statements via the cellular phone's text messaging capabilities. There may truly be no rest for the weary as cyberbullying penetrates the
465 walls of a home, traditionally a place where victims could seek refuge.

Finally, electronic devices allow individuals to contact others (both for prosocial and antisocial purposes) at all times and in almost all places. The fact that most
470 adolescents (83%) connect to the Internet from home (Pew Internet and American Life Project, 2001) indicates that online bullying can be an invasive phenomenon that can hound a person even when not at or around school. Relatedly, the coordination of a bully-
475 ing attack can occur with more ease because it is not constrained by the physical location of the bullies or victims. A veritable onslaught of mistreatment can quickly and effectively torment a victim through the use of these communications and connectivity tools.

*Does Harm Occur?*

480 Of course, cyberbullying is a problem only to the extent that it produces harm toward the victim. In the traditional sense, a victim is often under the immediate threat of violence and physical harm and also subject to humiliation and embarrassment in a public setting.
485 These elements compound the already serious psychological, emotional, and social wounds inflicted through such mistreatment. One might argue that a victim of bullying in cyberspace—whether via e-mail, instant messaging, or cellular phone text messaging—can
490 quickly escape from the harassment by deleting the e-mail, closing the instant message, and shutting off the cellular phone and is largely protected from overt acts of violence by the offender through geographic and spatial distance. Such an argument holds much truth;
495 however, the fact remains that if social acceptance is crucially important to a youth's identity and self-esteem, cyberbullying can capably and perhaps more permanently wreak psychological, emotional, and social havoc.[4] It is not a stretch to say that physical harm,
500 such as being beaten up, might even be preferred by some victims to the excruciating pain they experience from nonphysical harm because the former can heal quicker. Furthermore, it is yet to be determined if there is a causal pathway between cyberbullying and tradi-
505 tional bullying, and so physical harm might very well follow as a logical outcome of a continually increasing desire on the part of the offender to most severely hurt the victim. To be sure, this must be explored in future studies.

510 With regard to public embarrassment, life in cyberspace is often intertwined with life in the real world. For example, many kids and teenagers spend days with their friends in school and nights with those same friends online through instant message programs and

515 chat channels. That which occurs during the day at school is often discussed online at night, and that which occurs online at night is often discussed during the day at school. There is no clean separation between the two realms, and so specific instances of cyberbully-
520 ing—disrespect, name calling, threats, rumors, gossip—against a person make their way around the interested social circles like wildfire.

Does the mistreatment experienced through online bullying lead to the same feelings that result from tradi-
525 tional bullying, such as self-denigration, loss of confidence and self-esteem, depression, anger, frustration, public humiliation, and even physical harm? This remains to be clearly depicted through empirical research but seems plausible based on the linchpin role of self-
530 esteem among children and teenagers previously described and on anecdotal evidence specifically related to online aggression (BBC News, 2001; Benfer, 2001; Blair, 2003; Meadows et al., 2005; ÓhAnluain, 2002; Richardson, 2003).
535 Because of the widespread availability of electronic devices, there is no lack of participants using the technologies. Their ubiquity provides a seemingly endless pool of candidates who are susceptible to being bullied or to becoming a bully. Unfortunately, however, little
540 is known in terms of how often these technologies are mobilized for deviant purposes. One empirical study has been conducted to date: In 2002, the National Children's Home (NCH, 2002)—a charitable organization in London—surveyed 856 youth between the ages of
545 11 and 19 and found that 16% received threatening text messages via their cellular phone, 7% had been bullied in online chat rooms, and 4% had been harassed via e-mail. Following the victimization, 42% told a friend, 32% told a parent or guardian, and 29% did not reveal
550 the experience to anyone. Because more information is clearly warranted, a study was designed to explore the nature and extent of cyberbullying.

### Current Study

*Method*

The current study involved an analysis of youthful Internet users in an effort to assess their perceptions of
555 and experiences with electronic bullying. It is difficult to individually observe the nature and extent of electronic bullying among adolescent Internet users because of the "private" nature of e-mails, cellular phone text messages, and instant messages and one-on-one
560 chat messages within online chat channels. To be sure, if the instances of cyberbullying occur in a public forum such as a popular chat channel and in the view of all chat room members, then direct observation and consequent analyses may be possible. Most of the time,
565 however, they occur through private (nonpublic), person-to-person communications. A survey methodology was therefore designed to collect data by requiring participants to recall and relate their cyberbullying practices and experiences via a questionnaire that was

570 linked from the official Web site of a popular music artist revered by the target age group. An electronic format was selected as it allows for efficiency in collecting data from a large number of participants (Couper, 2000; McCoy & Marks, 2001; Smith, 1997). The
575 survey was active between May 1, 2004, and May 31, 2004.

The context of the Internet must be considered when dealing with consent issues because forcing all online researchers to comply with traditional proce-
580 dures in this area is unduly onerous, particularly when possible harm is little to none. Because it is impossible to personally obtain informed consent from participants in much online survey research that solicits participants from postings on Web sites, implied consent has gener-
585 ally been accepted (Walther, 2002). This involves the presentation of informed consent information in electronic text (e.g., on a Web page), along with specific actions that must be performed prior to initiation of the survey. These actions often include the checking of a
590 check box (agreeing to participate) and clicking on a *submit* button to send the information to the server. From this, consent can be reasonably inferred (King, 1996). For the current study, researchers instructed participants who were younger than 18 to obtain per-
595 mission from their parent or guardian. Permission was demonstrated by the parent entering his or her initials in a specified box. Again, because of matters of anonymity associated with Internet research, it was impossible to actually verify that adolescents obtained proper
600 permission prior to completing the survey.

With survey research conducted over the Internet, questions also arise as to the reliability of the data (Cho & LaRose, 1999). Participants are self-selected, which introduces some bias as individuals are not randomly
605 chosen for inclusion in the study. Often, a convenience sample, where individuals are chosen because they are available (e.g., because they visit a particular Web site and see a solicitation for research participation), is employed. As a result, the sample obtained may not nec-
610 essarily be representative of all Internet users. Moreover, online demographic groups may not mirror those found in the real world (Witte, Amoroso, & Howard, 2000). Generalization to a larger population then becomes impossible with convenience sampling (Couper,
615 2000), but the technique has demonstrated utility for exploratory studies intended to probe a novel phenomenon. Researchers who seek to tap the resources of the World Wide Web will continue to face these challenging issues. Although these limitations are an unfor-
620 tunate cost of conducting Internet-based research, results from this preliminary study will help to inform a more methodologically rigorous investigation in the future.

The survey went through numerous iterations to op-
625 timize its design and presentation of questions. Prior research has determined that poor design can render dubious the quality of responses and may even affect

completion rate (Crawford, Couper, & Lamias, 2001; Krosnick, 1999; Preece, Rogers, & Sharp, 2002;
630 Schwarz, 1999). Specifics to the survey design bear mentioning. Demographic data were solicited at the beginning of the survey, which has been shown to decrease rates of attrition because individuals are not surprised by more personal questions at the resolution of
635 their participation (Frick, Bachtiger, & Reips, 2001). The survey in its entirety was presented to the respondent on one screen, which has also been shown to increase response rates (Crawford et al., 2001). Although our survey did consist of a vast number of questions,
640 findings related to the relationship between survey length and response rate have been mixed and inconclusive (Brown, 1965; Bruvold & Comer, 1988; Eicherner & Habermehl, 1981; Jobber & Saunders, 1993; Mason, Dressel, & Bain, 1961; Sheehan, 2001; Wit-
645 mer, Colman, & Katzman, 1999; Yammarino, Skinner, & Childers, 1991).

Incentives to participate in the form of cash or other prizes via a lottery have also been shown to increase response rate; human beings are motivated by the pos-
650 sibility of receiving something in return for their efforts, and this trait is manifested in survey participation as well (Cho & LaRose, 1999; Frick et al., 2001). As such, participants in the current study were entered into a random drawing to win one of three autographed
655 photographs of the musical artist from whose fan Web site they reached the survey. We also specified that the institutional review board at the researchers' university had approved the project to verify its legitimacy and strengthen the trust relationship between the research-
660 ers and the potential participants (Cho & LaRose, 1999).

A final point bears mentioning. As the Internet protocol (IP) address and timestamp were recorded with each participant's responses, we were able to eliminate
665 entries where all of the responses were completely the same. This might happen when a respondent fills out the questionnaire, clicks *submit*, goes back to the previous page where all of his or her responses are stored within the survey form, and then clicks *submit* again
670 (and continues in this pattern). To note, there were survey entries from the same IP address but with completely different responses to the questions posed. This was because some Internet service providers route multiple users through one IP address when connecting
675 from their internal network to the external Internet. To summarize, we browsed through all of the data and attempted to determine which entries were fraudulent and which were valid.

*Findings*

Because this was an Internet-based survey, anyone
680 could participate. Even though the survey was associated with a teen-oriented Web site, individuals from all ages also frequent the site and therefore completed the survey. As noted in Table 1, out of the 571 total re-

spondents, 384 were younger than 18 (67.3%; hence-
685 forth referred to as the youth sample). In both groups, the vast majority of respondents were female. This finding is likely attributable to the nature of the Web site on which the survey was linked (a female pop music star). Similarly, the vast majority of respondents
690 were Caucasian. There are several potential interpretations of this finding. First, individuals from different racial and ethnic backgrounds may be less interested in this particular entertainer than are others and may therefore be unlikely to visit the Web site to see the
695 survey solicitation. Alternatively, the overrepresentation of Caucasian respondents could be evidence of the oft-mentioned digital divide, where some populations are not privy to the access and use of technology such as computers and the Internet. As expected, most re-
700 spondents were between the ages of 12 and 20, and the average age of the youth sample was 14.1. Moreover, more than 70% of respondents from the complete sample were in grades 2 through 12. High school respondents (9th through 12th grade) represented the modal
705 category of respondents for both groups. As might be expected, the vast majority of all respondents came from English-speaking countries (the Web site and survey were written in English), and about 60% of respondents in both groups reported living in the United
710 States. It must be mentioned that because online identity is completely malleable (Hafner, 2001; Turkle, 1995), the demographic data obtained may not be completely accurate because of a lack of trust in our research project, mischief, or purposeful obfuscation.
715 Research performed over the Internet cannot entirely preempt this problem—at least in its current stage of technological development—and so a caveat is justified.

The remainder of the findings discussed relate only
720 to those respondents who were younger than 18 when they completed the survey (*n* = 384). Online bullying was specifically defined on the questionnaire for respondents as behavior that can include bothering someone online, teasing in a mean way, calling some-
725 one hurtful names, intentionally leaving persons out of things, threatening someone, and saying unwanted, sexually related things to someone. Table 2 presents the percentage of respondents who have been bullied ("Have you ever been bullied online?"), have bullied
730 others ("Have you ever bullied others while online?"), or have witnessed bullying online ("Have you ever seen other kids bullied online?"). Almost 11% of youth reported bullying others while online, more than 29% reported being the victim of online bullying, and more
735 than 47% have witnessed online bullying. Cyberbullying was most prevalent in chat rooms, followed by computer text messages and e-mail. Bullying using news groups or cellular phones was not as prominent for members of this sample. Indeed, although it is clear
740 that all who responded to the survey have access to a

Table 1
*Descriptive Statistics of Survey Respondents*

| | Complete sample[a] | | Youth sample[b] | |
|---|---|---|---|---|
| | *n* | % | *n* | % |
| Sex | | | | |
| Female | 452 | 78.3 | 325 | 84.6 |
| Male | 115 | 19.9 | 55 | 14.3 |
| Missing | 10 | 1.7 | 4 | 1.0 |
| Race | | | | |
| Caucasian | 429 | 74.4 | 289 | 75.3 |
| Hispanic | 43 | 7.5 | 32 | 8.3 |
| Asian or Pacific Islander | 43 | 7.5 | 28 | 7.3 |
| African American | 4 | 0.7 | 3 | 0.8 |
| Indigenous or aboriginal | 4 | 0.7 | 3 | 0.8 |
| Multiracial | 16 | 2.8 | 10 | 2.6 |
| Other race | 32 | 5.5 | 19 | 4.9 |
| Missing | 6 | 1.0 | 0 | 0.0 |
| Age | | | | |
| 9–11 | 37 | 6.4 | 37 | 9.6 |
| 12–13 | 110 | 19.1 | 110 | 28.6 |
| 14–15 | 135 | 23.4 | 135 | 35.2 |
| 16–17 | 102 | 17.7 | 102 | 26.6 |
| 18–20 | 128 | 22.2 | — | — |
| 21–25 | 41 | 7.1 | — | — |
| 26 and older | 18 | 3.1 | — | — |
| Missing | 6 | 1.0 | — | — |
| Grade | | | | |
| Grades 2–5 | 25 | 4.3 | 24 | 6.3 |
| Grades 6–8 | 149 | 25.8 | 149 | 38.8 |
| Grades 9–12 | 231 | 40.0 | 196 | 51.0 |
| Community college | 37 | 6.4 | 7 | 1.8 |
| University | 72 | 12.5 | 1 | 0.3 |
| Do not attend school | 52 | 9.0 | 4 | 1.0 |
| Missing | 11 | 1.9 | 3 | 0.8 |
| Country | | | | |
| United States | 349 | 60.5 | 227 | 59.1 |
| Canada | 62 | 10.7 | 46 | 12.0 |
| United Kingdom | 53 | 9.2 | 35 | 9.1 |
| Australia | 29 | 5.0 | 23 | 6.0 |
| Other or unknown | 84 | 14.6 | 53 | 13.8 |

a. *N* = 577; b. *N* = 384.

computer, it is unknown what proportion of respondents have access to a cellular phone.

Table 2
*Percentage of Youth Respondents Who Report Being a Bully, a Victim, or a Witness to Bullying*

| | Bully | Victim | Witness |
|---|---|---|---|
| Online | 10.7 | 29.4 | 47.1 |
| In a chat room | 7.6 | 21.9 | 42.4 |
| Via computer text message | 5.2 | 13.5 | 15.1 |
| Via e-mail | 1.8 | 12.8 | 13.8 |
| On a bulletin board | 1.0 | 2.9 | 13.8 |
| Via cell phone text message | 0.8 | 2.1 | 6.3 |
| In a newsgroup | 0.5 | 1.6 | 3.6 |

*Note. N* = 384.

As previously described, youth were asked a general question regarding their involvement in online 745 bullying. In addition, youth were asked to relate whether they experienced a number of behaviors that may be associated with bullying. Table 3 presents in-formation collected from these questions. Notably, 60.4% of respondents have been ignored by others 750 while online, 50.0% reported being disrespected by others, almost 30.0% have been called names, and 21.4% have been threatened by others. In addition, a significant proportion of youth were picked on by others (19.8%) or made fun of by others (19.3%) or had 755 rumors spread about them by others (18.8%).

Table 3
*Types of Online Bullying*

| | Percentage victimized |
|---|---|
| Ignored by others | 60.4 |
| Disrespected by others | 50.0 |
| Called names by others | 29.9 |
| Been threatened by others | 21.4 |
| Picked on by others | 19.8 |
| Made fun of by others | 19.3 |
| Rumors spread by others | 18.8 |

*Note. N* = 384.

Table 4
*Average Number of Bullying Experiences During Previous 30 Days for Youth Who Reported Being a Victim or a Bully*

| | Bully | | | Victim | | |
|---|---|---|---|---|---|---|
| | *n* | *M* | *Max* | *n* | *M* | *Max* |
| In a chat room | 39 | 1.23 | 10 | 83 | 3.36 | 50 |
| Via computer text message | 30 | 1.20 | 6 | 68 | 4.65 | 76 |
| Via e-mail | 18 | 0.39 | 2 | 61 | 4.07 | 107 |
| On a bulletin board | 16 | 1.50 | 9 | 31 | 2.42 | 10 |
| Via cell phone text message | 9 | 3.22 | 23 | 19 | 3.37 | 23 |
| In a newsgroup | 2 | 0.00 | 0 | 6 | 1.67 | 6 |

*Note. n* reflects the number of youth who reported experience in that behavior; *M* is the average number of times the experience occurred in the previous 30 days, and *Max* is the highest number of times the experience was reported during the previous 30 days.

In addition to asking respondents whether they have experienced bullying online, researchers also asked youth how frequently the bullying occurred during the previous 30 days. Table 4 presents summary statistics
760 reflecting the number of youth who reported involvement in the bullying experience, the average number of times the bullying occurred, and the maximum number of times the bullying occurred. For example, 83 youth reported being victimized in a chat room an average of
765 3.36 times during the previous 30 days. One youth reported being bullied in a chat room 50 times during the previous 30 days. Bullying via computer text messaging and e-mail also occurred frequently during the previous 30 days.

770    Table 5 demonstrates the negative effects associated with online bullying on victims. For example, 42.5% of victims were frustrated, almost 40.0% felt angry, and more than 27.0% felt sad. Almost one-third (31.9%) reported that it affected them at school,
775 whereas 26.5% reported that it affected them at home. Only 22.1% were not bothered by the bullying they experienced, and less than 44.0% stated that the bullying did not affect them.

Table 5
*Effects of Online Bullying*

| | Percentage yes |
|---|---|
| I felt frustrated | 42.5 |
| I felt angry | 39.8 |
| I felt sad | 27.4 |
| I was not bothered | 22.1 |
| It affected me at school | 31.9 |
| It affected me at home | 26.5 |
| It affected me with my friends | 20.4 |
| It did not affect me | 43.4 |

*Note.* Responses for youth who reported being bullied online (*N* = 113).

Table 6 describes the response taken by victims of
780 online bullying. Notably, almost 20% of victims were forced to stay offline, whereas almost 32% had to remove themselves from the environment in some capacity or way. Victims also revealed a hesitation to tell authority figures about their experiences. Even though
785 most confided in an online friend (56.6%), fewer than 9.0% of victims informed an adult.

Additional analyses were conducted to attempt to uncover correlates of online bullying. There were no statistically significant associations among age, race, or
790 gender and who is likely to be a victim of online bullying. The lack of relationship among race or gender and victimization may be more a function of the homogeneous nature of the data than any substantive finding and must be further tested. In accordance with intui-
795 tion, youth who participate in more activities online (represented by a variety score of 13 different activities) were more likely to experience online bullying. Also not surprising, youth who bully others were more likely to be victims of online bullying. In all, 75% of
800 youth who have bullied others online have been victims of bullying, whereas fewer than 25% of youth bullies have never been on the other end of such malicious actions ($\chi^2$ = 42.866; $p$ < .001). Future research should seek to better understand what additional factors
805 are associated with online bullying.

Table 6
*Response to Online Bullying*

| | Percentage yes |
|---|---|
| I tell the bully to stop | 36.3 |
| I get away | 31.9 |
| I do nothing | 24.8 |
| I stay offline | 19.5 |
| I bully others | 2.7 |
| I tell an online friend | 56.6 |
| I tell a friend | 25.7 |
| I tell nobody | 23.0 |
| I tell my mom and dad | 19.5 |
| I tell my brother or sister | 16.8 |
| I tell an adult | 8.8 |

*Note.* Responses for youth who reported being bullied online (*N* = 113).

## Discussion

The results of this study point to a number of key issues. First, bullying is occurring online and is impacting youth in many negative ways. Almost 30% of the adolescent respondents reported that they had been
810 victims of online bullying—operationalized as having been ignored, disrespected, called names, threatened, picked on or made fun of, or having had rumors spread by others. Admittedly, being ignored by another person may simply reflect obnoxious behavior that warranted
815 the outcome rather than actual and willful aggression. We were not able to parcel out the stimuli of instances when people were ignored but chose to include a

820 measure of it in the current analyses. This is because universal social acceptance is still largely desired by children and adolescents, even if as adults we understand that it is impossible to please everyone at all times. Being ignored would introduce dissonance and instability to the already tenuous relational and social equilibria sought by youths and may accordingly be 825 considered a passive–aggressive form of bullying. Along similar lines, although some of this harassment may be characterized as trivial (e.g., being ignored by others or being disrespected), more than 20% reported being threatened by others. Anger and frustration was a 830 commonly reported emotional response to the harassment. Finally, almost 60% of victims were affected by the online behaviors at school, at home, or with friends.

Several policy implications stem from the aforementioned findings. It is hoped that this harmful phe-835 nomena can be curtailed by proactively addressing the potentially negative uses of technology. Parents must regularly monitor the activities in which their children are engaged while online. Teachers, too, must take care to supervise students as they use computers in the 840 classrooms. Police officers must investigate those instances of cyberbullying that are potentially injurious and hold responsible parties accountable. Unfortunately, there are no methods to discern which harassment involves simple jest and which has the potential 845 to escalate into serious violence. Future research must analyze case studies and anecdotal stories of cyberbullying experiences to help determine when intervention by authority figures is most appropriate. Overall, parents, teachers, police officers, and other community 850 leaders must keep up with technological advances so that they are equipped with the tools and knowledge to identify and address any problems when they arise.

*Limitations of the Current Study*

The most notable limitations of this study relate to its administration because data were collected exclu-855 sively online. With regard to sampling, it is unquestionable that Internet users are dissimilar from those who do not go online. However, Walther (2002, p. 209) argues that concerns related to the generalizability of data collected from the Internet to a target population 860 assume that random samples of Internet users are sought in any study and that a sample obtained from the Internet is able to be generalized to other populations. We would have liked to obtain a random sample of all Internet users younger than 18 to ascertain the 865 extent and prevalence of online bullying, but such a task is impossible as no reliable sampling frame of individuals in cyberspace exists. Thus, we carefully targeted certain Web sites presumably visited by at least some adolescents who have personal experience 870 in the phenomenon. As it turned out, the sample was disproportionately Caucasian and female, and results therefore may be skewed toward these subgroups. As a result, any findings from the research should be very

875 cautiously applied to the larger group of Internet-using youth.

Another issue related to online data collection concerns misrepresentation of age by participants in this research. Undoubtedly, we cannot guarantee that respondents honestly indicated their age during participa-880 tion. Any qualms, though, can be overcome by considering the fallibility of traditional research methods, such as phone surveys or surveys distributed in highly populated settings (e.g., large college classes) or through the mail and even individual, face-to-face ad-885 ministration of questionnaires. A person can lie about his or her age in any of these contexts, and it is unreasonable to assume that a person would be more likely to do so in an online research setting (Walther, 2002).

*Directions for Future Research*

The current study provides the framework for fu-890 ture empirical inquiry on electronic bullying. Indeed, the authors are currently involved in a more comprehensive study that involves both Internet-based research and traditional paper-and-pencil surveys. As with any social scientific endeavor, replication is nec-895 essary to more fully understand the phenomena under consideration. There are several questions future research in this area must address. First, data must be collected to more accurately ascertain the scope, prevalence, and nuances of cyberbullying. For example, it is 900 important to discover whether cyberbullies are simply traditional bullies who have embraced new technologies to accomplish their intentions or if they are youth who have never participated in traditional, school-based bullying. Moreover, do personal computers en-905 able the stereotypical victims of bullies (i.e., those who are smart, physically small, and/or socially challenged) to retaliate using means that ensure their anonymity? It would also be important to determine whether commonly accepted stimuli for traditional bullying—the 910 need to (a) exert power and dominate, (b) compensate for victimization in another area of one's life, (c) cope with one's insecurities, and (d) attract attention and popularity—are similarly predictive in cyberspace-based instances of the deviance.

915 Also of interest is the extent to which electronic bullying results in harm to adolescents in their physical environments (e.g., at school or in their neighborhoods). Are threats made in cyberspace followed through on the playground? Are victims of cyberbully-920 ing the same individuals who are also victims of traditional bullying, or are they distinct groups? What about offenders? One could hypothesize that the victims of traditional bullying may turn to the Internet to exact revenge on their schoolyard aggressors. That is, the 925 victim becomes the offender by using his or her technological knowledge to inflict harm on the original bully.

In addition, it is useful to identify whether adults also participate in electronic harassment. Although they

930 may frequent chat rooms to a lesser degree than do children and adolescents, cellular phone use and even instant messaging programs are commonly utilized for both professional and personal purposes. Does electronic harassment occur to the same extent among 935 adults as compared to a population of adolescents? Does it occur in a more controlled and subtle manner or with the same degree of perceivably overt cruelty? Does it occur for fundamentally similar reasons across both groups, or are there factors endemic to youth or 940 adult life that condition and dictate bullying in an online context? These are just some of the important questions that need further examination.

Finally, future research efforts ought to more thoroughly examine the results of this preliminary investi- 945 gation using more rigorous methodology that ensures a more representative sample of responses. As indicated, the intent of this research is to generate scholarly interest in this unique form of adolescent harassment and therefore should be viewed simply as a small, but we 950 think significant, platform on which further research efforts should be built.

## Conclusion

The preceding review provides a description of bullying in cyberspace for the purposes of introducing it as a topic meriting academic inquiry and underscoring its 955 often inescapable pernicious nature. Indeed, 74% of the youth in this study reported that bullying occurs online, and almost 30% of the youth reported being victimized by others while online. Some may dismiss electronic bullying as normative behavior that does not physically 960 harm anyone. To be sure, some have this perception regarding traditional bullying, dismissing it as a rite of passage or an inevitable and even instructive element of growing up. Because of the familiarity and memorability of bullying as almost unavoidable in both the 965 schoolyard and neighborhood milieu during one's formative years, perhaps the reader may share those sentiments.

Because no consensus exists when considering whether cyberbullying merits increased attention be- 970 cause of society's continued progression into a wired world, perhaps it should just be considered another contemporary cultural challenge that kids often face when transitioning into adulthood. Conceivably, there is no need to panic when introduced to the concept that 975 online bullying does and will continue to take place as children seek to carve out an identity for themselves and cope with various pressures associated with their development. Alternatively, perhaps there is a need for alarm as both those who bully and those who are bul- 980 lied might yield readily to other criminogenic influences and proceed down a path of deviance online, offline, or both. Regardless, cyberbullying is very real, and it is hoped that this work has highlighted its relevance for the purposes of inspiring additional interest 985 in its etiology and consequences.

## End Notes

[1]The interested reader is encouraged to see Blair (2003) or ÓhAnluain (2002) for more examples.

[2]It should be mentioned that research has not identified a link between low self-esteem and the offenders of traditional bullying (Hoover & Hazler, 1991; Rigby & Slee, 1993).

[3]To be sure, females are also bullied to a substantive degree and must not be excluded from any analyses of the phenomenon.

[4]Cyberbullying repercussions have permanence because e-mails can be saved, instant messages and chat conversations can be logged, and Web pages can be archived for an offender, victim, or third party to read over in the future and thereby relive the experience.

## References

America Online. (2002). *AOL facts—2002*. Retrieved September 2, 2003, from http://www.corp.aol.com/whoweare/Factbook_F.pdf

America Online. (2003). *Who we are: Fast facts*. Retrieved September 2, 2003, from http://www.corp.aol.com/whoweare/fastfacts.html

BBC News. (2001). *Girl tormented by phone bullies*. Retrieved January 16, 2001, from http://news.bbc.co.uk/1/hi/education/1120597.stm

Benfer, A. (2001). *Cyber slammed*. Retrieved July 7, 2001, from http://www.dir.salon.com/mwt/feature/2001/07/03/cyber_bullies/index.html

Berson, I. R., Berson, M. J., & Ferron, J. M. (2002). Emerging risks of violence in the digital age: Lessons for educators from an online study of adolescent girls in the United States. *Journal of School Violence, 1*, 51–71.

Björkqvist, K., Ekman, K., & Lagerspetz, K. (1982). Bullies and victims: Their ego picture, ideal ego picture, and normative ego picture. *Scandinavian Journal of Psychology, 23*, 307–313.

Blair, J. (2003). New breed of bullies torment their peers on the Internet. *Education Week*. Retrieved February 5, 2003, from http://www.edweek.org/ew/ewstory.cfm?slug=21cyberbully.h22

Borg, M. G. (1998). The emotional reaction of school bullies and their victims. *Educational Psychology, 18*, 433–444.

Brown, M. (1965). Use of a postcard query in mail surveys. *Public Opinion Quarterly, 29*, 635–637.

Bruvold, N. T., & Comer, J. M. (1988). A model for estimating the response rate to a mailed survey. *Journal of Business Research, 16*, 101–116.

CD. (2003). *Thumbs down on mobile messaging*. Retrieved July 22, 2003, from http://www.chinadaily.com.cn/en/doc/2003-07/22/content_247257.htm

Cho, H., & LaRose, R. (1999). Privacy issues in Internet surveys. *Social Science Computer Review, 14*, 421–434.

Coie, J. D., & Dodge, K. A. (1988). Multiple sources of data on social behavior and social status in the school: A cross-age comparison. *Child Development, 59*, 815–829.

Cooley, C. H. (1902). *Human nature and the social order*. New York: Scribner.

Couper, M. P. (2000). Web-based surveys: A review of issues and approaches. *Public Opinion Quarterly, 64*, 464–494.

Crawford, S., Couper, M. P., & Lamias, M. (2001). Web surveys: Perceptions of burden. *Social Science Computer Review, 19*, 146–162.

Devoe, J. F., Ruddy, S. A., Miller, A. K., Planty, M., Peter, K., Kaufman, P. et al. (2002). *Indicators of school crime and safety*. Washington, DC: U.S. Department of Education, National Center for Education Statistics, U.S. Department of Justice, Bureau of Justice Statistics.

Eicherner, K., & Habermehl, W. (1981). Predicting the response rates to mailed questionnaires (comment on Herberlien & Baumgartner). *American Sociological Review, 46*, 1–3.

Farrington, D. (1980). Truancy, delinquency, the home, and the school. In L. Hersov & I. Berg (Eds.), *Out of school: Modern perspectives in truancy and school refusal* (pp. 49–63). New York: John Wiley.

Fattah, H. (2003). *America untethered*. Retrieved September 1, 2003, from http://www.upoc.com/corp/news/UpocAmDem.pdf

Finn, J. (2004). A survey of online harassment at a university campus. *Journal of Interpersonal Violence, 19*, 468–483.

French, D. C., & Waas, G. A. (1987). Social–cognitive and behavioral characteristics of peer-rejected boys. *Professional School Psychology, 2*, 103–112.

Frick, A., Bachtiger, M. T., & Reips, U.-D. (2001). Financial incentives, personal information, and dropout in online studies. In U.-D. Reips & M. Bosnjak (Eds.), *Dimensions of Internet science* (pp. 209–219). Lengerich, Germany: Pabst Science.

Galinsky, E., & Salmond, K. (2002). *Youth and violence: Students speak out for a more civil society*. New York: Families and Work Institute.

Garry, E. M. (1996). *Truancy: First step to a lifetime of problems*. Washington, DC: U.S. Department of Justice, Office of Juvenile Justice and Delinquency Prevention.

Gavin, T. (1997). *Truancy: Not just kids' stuff anymore.* Washington, DC: Federal Bureau of Investigation.

Gelhausen, A. (2005). *Summary of IRC networks.* Retrieved May 7, 2005, from http://irc.netsplit.de/networks/

GSMBox. (2002). *Ten years of SMS messages.* Retrieved August 10, 2003, from http://uk.gsmbox.com/news/mobile_news/all/94480.gsmbox

Hafner, K. (2001). *The well: A story of love, death & real life in the seminal online community.* New York: Carrol and Graf.

Hawker, D. S. J., & Boulton, M. J. (2000). Twenty years' research on peer victimization and psychological maladjustment: A meta-analysis review of cross-sectional studies. *Journal of Child Psychology and Psychiatry, 41*, 441–445.

Hoover, J., & Hazler, R. (1991). Bullies and victims. *Elementary School Guidance and Counseling, 25*, 212–219.

Hull, J. G. (1981). A self-awareness model of the causes and effects of alcohol consumption. *Journal of Abnormal Psychology, 90*, 586–600.

Hymel, S., Rubin, K. H., Rowden, L., & LeMare, L. (1990). Children's peer relationships longitudinal prediction of internalizing and externalizing problems from middle to late childhood. *Child Development, 61*, 2004–2021.

Jerome, L., & Segal, A. (2003). Bullying by Internet—Editorial. *Journal of the American Academy of Child and Adolescent Psychiatry, 42*, 751.

Jobber, D., & Saunders, J. (1993). A note on the applicability of the Brurold-Comer model of mail survey response rates to commercial populations. *Journal of Business Research, 26*, 223–236.

Kaltiala-Heino, R., Rimpelä, M., Marttunen, M., Rimpelä, A., & Rantanen, P. (1999). Bullying, depression, and suicidal ideation in Finnish adolescents: School survey. *British Medical Journal, 319*, 348–351.

Katz, A. R. (2002). *Text messaging moves from cell to home.* Retrieved August 15, 2003, from http://www.iht.com/articles/51152.html

King, S. (1996). Researching Internet communities: Proposed ethical guidelines for the reporting of results. *The Information Society, 12*, 119–128.

Krosnick, J. A. (1999). Survey research. *Annual Review of Psychology, 50*, 537–567.

Lagerspetz, K. M. J., Björkqvist, K., Berts, M., & King, E. (1982). Group aggression among schoolchildren in three schools. *Scandinavian Journal of Psychology, 23*, 45–52.

Leary, M. R., & Downs, D. L. (1995). Interpersonal functions of the self-esteem motive: The self-esteem system as a sociometer. In M. H. Kernis (Ed.), *Efficacy, agency, and self-esteem* (pp. 123–144). New York: Plenum.

Leary, M. R., Haupt, A. L., Strausser, K. S., & Chokel, J. T. (1998). Calibrating the sociometer: The relationship between interpersonal appraisals and state self-esteem. *Journal of Personality and Social Psychology, 74*, 1290–1299.

Leary, M. R., Schreindorfer, L. S., & Haupt, A. L. (1995). The role of self-esteem in emotional and behavioral problems: Why is low self-esteem dysfunctional? *Journal of Social and Clinical Psychology, 14*, 297–314.

Leary, M. R., Tambor, E. S., Terdal, S. J., & Downs, D. L. (1995). Self-esteem as an interpersonal monitor: The sociometer hypothesis. *Journal of Personality and Social Psychology, 68*, 518–530.

Leff, S. (1999). Bullied children are picked on for their vulnerability. *British Medical Journal, 318*, 1076.

Manning, M., Heron, J., & Marshal, T. (1978). Style of hostility and social interactions at nursery school and at home: An extended study of children. In A. Lionel, M. B. Hersov, & D. Shaffer (Eds.), *Aggression and antisocial behavior in childhood and adolescence* (pp. 29–58). Oxford, UK: Pergamon.

Mason, W., Dressel, R., & Bain, R. (1961). An experimental study of factors affecting response to a mail survey of beginning teachers. *Public Opinion Quarterly, 25*, 296–299.

McCoy, S., & Marks, P. V., Jr. (2001, August). *Using electronic surveys to collect data: Experiences from the field.* Paper presented at the AMCIS Annual Conference, Boston.

Meadows, B., Bergal, J., Helling, S., Odell, J., Piligian, E., Howard, C. et al. (2005, March 21). The Web: The bully's new playground. *People,* pp. 152–155.

Nansel, T. R., Overpeck, M., Pilla, R. S., Ruan, W. J., Simons-Morton, B., & Scheidt, P. (2001). Bullying behaviors among US youth: Prevalence and association with psychosocial adjustment. *Journal of the American Medical Association, 285*, 2094–2100.

National Children's Home. (2002). *1 in 4 children are the victims of "on-line bullying" says children's charity.* Retrieved September 1, 2003, from http://www.nch.org.uk/news/news5.asp?auto=195

National Telecommunications and Information Administration. (2002). *A nation online: How Americans are expanding their use of the Internet.* Retrieved June 13, 2004, from http://www.ntia.doc.gov/ntiahome/dn/anationonline2.pdf

Neary, A., & Joseph, S. (1994). Peer victimization and its relationship to self-concept and depression among schoolgirls. *Personality and Individual Differences, 16*, 183–186.

NetRatings, N. (2002). *IM programs draw US kids and teens online.* Retrieved July 30, 2003, from http://www.nua.com/surveys/index.cgi?f=VS&art_id=905358261&rel=true

Network, M. A. (2001). *Canada's children in a wired world: The parents' view—Final report.* Retrieved July 30, 2003, from http://www.media-awareness.ca/english/resources/special_initiatives/survey_resources/parents_survey/loader.cfm?url=/commonspot/security/getfile.cfm&PageID=31576

ÓhAnluain, D. (2002). *When text messaging turns ugly.* Retrieved September 4, 2002, from http://www.wired.com/news/school/0,1383,54771,00.html

O'Leary, N. (2003). *Cell phone marketers tap teens as the next frontier.* Retrieved February 17, 2003, from http://www.adweek.com/aw/magazine/article_display.jsp?vnu_content_id=1818786

Olweus, D. (1978). *Aggression in the schools: Bullies and whipping boys.* Washington, DC: Hemisphere Press.

Olweus, D. (1993). *Bullying at school.* Oxford, UK: Blackwell.

Olweus, D. (Ed.). (1994). *Bullying at school: Long-term outcomes for victims and an effective school-based intervention program.* New York: Plenum.

Olweus, D. (1999). Norway. In P. K. Smith, Y. Morita, J. Junger-Tas, D. Olweus, R. Catalano, & P. Slee (Eds.), *Nature of school bullying: A cross-national perspective* (pp. 28–48). London: Routledge.

Olweus, D., Limber, S., & Mihalic, S. (1999). *Bullying prevention program.* Boulder, CO: Center for the Study and Prevention of Violence.

Patchin, J. (2002). Bullied youths lash out: Strain as an explanation of extreme school violence. *Caribbean Journal of Criminology and Social Psychology, 7*, 22–43.

Paulson, M. J., Coombs, R. H., & Landsverk, J. (1990). Youth who physically assault their parents. *Journal of Family Violence, 5*, 121–133.

Pew Internet and American Life Project. (2001). *Teenage life online: The rise of the instant-message generation and the Internet's impact on friendships and family relationships.* Retrieved July 13, 2004, from http://www.pewinternet.org/pdfs/PIP_Teens_Report.pdf

Preece, J., Rogers, Y., & Sharp, S. (2002). *Interaction design: Beyond human–computer interaction.* New York: John Wiley.

Quellet, R., & Joshi, P. (1986). Loneliness in relation to depression and self-esteem. *Psychological Reports, 58*, 821–822.

Richardson, T. (2003). *Bullying by text message.* Retrieved February 20, 2003, from http://www.theadvertiser.news.com.au/common/story_page/0,5936,6012025%5E2682,00.html

Rigby, K., & Slee, P. T. (1993). Dimensions of interpersonal relating among Australian school children and their implications for psychological well-being. *The Journal of Social Psychology, 133*, 33–42.

Rigby, K., & Slee, P. T. (1999). Australia. In P. Smith, Y. Morita, J. Junger-Tas, D. Olweus, R. Catalano & P. Slee (Eds.), *The nature of school bullying: A cross-national perspective* (pp. 324–339). London: Routledge.

Roland, E. (1980). *Terror i skolen* [Terrorism in school]. Stavanger, Norway: Rogaland Research Institute.

Roland, E. (1989). Bullying: The Scandinavian research tradition. In D. P. Tattum & D. A. Lane (Eds.), *Bullying in schools* (pp. 21–32). Stroke-on-Trent, UK: Trentham.

Schwarz, N. (1999). Self-reports: How the questions shape the answers. *American Psychologist, 54*, 93–105.

Sheehan, K. B. (2001). E-mail survey response rates: A review. *Journal of Computer Mediated Communication, 6.* Retrieved January 18, 2006, from http://jcmc.indiana.edu/vol6/issue2/sheehan.html

Slee, P. T., & Rigby, K. (1993). The relationship of Eysenck's personality factors and self-esteem to bully/victim behaviour in Australian school boys. *Personality and Individual Differences, 14*, 371–373.

Smart, R., & Walsh, G. (1993). Predictors of depression in street youth. *Adolescence, 28*, 41–53.

Smith, C. B. (1997). Casting the net: Surveying an Internet population. *Journal of Computer Mediated Communication, 3.* Retrieved January 18, 2006, from http://jcmc.indiana.edu/vol3/issue1/smith.html

Stephenson, P., & Smith, D. (1989). Bullying in junior school. In D. P. Tattum & D. A. Lane (Ed.), *Bullying in schools* (pp. 45–58). Stroke-on-Trent, UK: Trentham.

Stewart, M. A. (1985). Aggressive conduct disorder: A brief review. 6th Biennial Meeting of the International Society for Research on Aggression (1984, Turku, Finland). *Aggressive Behavior, 11*, 323–331.

Striegel-Moore, R. H., Dohm, F.-A., Pike, K. M., Wilfley, D. E., & Fairburn, C. G. (2002). Abuse, bullying, and discrimination as risk factors for binge eating disorder. *The American Journal of Psychiatry, 159*, 1902–1907.

Tarde, G. (Ed.). (1903). *Gabriel Tarde's laws of imitation.* New York: Henry Holt.

Tattum, D. P. (1989). Violence and aggression in schools. In D. P. Tattum & D. A. Lane (Eds.), *Bullying in schools* (pp. 7–19). Stroke-on-Trent, UK: Trentham.

Turkle, S. (1995). *Life on the screen: Identity in the age of the Internet.* New York: Simon & Schuster.

Twenge, J. M., & Campbell, W. K. (2001). Age and birth cohort differences in self-esteem: A cross-temporal meta-analysis. *Personality and Social Psychology Review, 5*, 321–344.

UPOC. (2001). *Wireless stats.* Retrieved September 1, 2003, from http://www.genwireless.com/stats.html

Voss, L. D., & Mulligan, J. (2000). Bullying in school: Are short pupils at risk? Questionnaire study in a cohort. *British Medical Journal, 320*, 612–613.

Vossekuil, B., Fein, R. A., Reddy, M., Borum, R., & Modzeleski, W. (2002). *The final report and findings of the Safe School Initiative: Implications for the prevention of school attacks in the United States*. Retrieved August 29, 2003, from http://www.secretservice.gov/ntac/ssi_final_report.pdf

Walther, J. B. (2002). Research ethics in Internet enabled research: Human subjects issues and methodological myopia. *Ethics and Information Technology, 4*, 205.

Witmer, D. F., Colman, R. W., & Katzman, S. L. (1999). From paper-and-pencil to screen-and-keyboard. In S. Jones (Ed.), *Doing Internet research: Critical issues and methods for examining the Net* (pp. 145–161). Thousand Oaks, CA: Sage.

Witte, J. C., Amoroso, L. M., & Howard, P. E. N. (2000). Research methodology—Method and representation in Internet-based survey tools—Mobility, community, and cultural identity in Survey 2000. *Social Science Computer Review, 18*, 179–195.

Yammarino, F. J., Skinner, S., & Childers, T. L. (1991). Understanding mail survey response behavior. *Public Opinion Quarterly, 55*, 613–639.

Ybarra, M. L., & Mitchell, J. K. (2004). Online aggressor/targets, aggressors and targets: A comparison of associated youth characteristics. *Journal of Child Psychology and Psychiatry, 45*, 1308–1316.

**Acknowledgments**: We would like to thank the anonymous reviewers for helpful comments on an earlier draft.

**Address correspondence to**: Justin W. Patchin, Department of Political Science, University of Wisconsin, Eau Claire, 105 Garfield Avenue, Eau Claire, WI 54702-4004. E-mail: patchinj@uwec.edu

**About the authors**: *Justin W. Patchin* is an assistant professor of criminal justice at the University of Wisconsin, Eau Claire. His research areas focus on policy and program evaluation, juvenile delinquency prevention, and school violence. *Sameer Hinduja* is an assistant professor in the Department of Criminology and Criminal Justice at Florida Atlantic University. His research largely involves the integration of social science and computer science perspectives.

# Exercise for Article 4

## Factual Questions

1. The questionnaire was linked from what?

2. Did the researchers solicit demographic data at the beginning *or* at the end of the survey?

3. Were the majority of the respondents male *or* female?

4. Which ethnic/racial group constituted the vast majority of the respondents?

5. Are the results presented in Tables 2 through 6 based on the responses of all respondents *or* only respondents younger than 18?

6. What was the most frequent response to online bullying?

## Questions for Discussion

7. The introduction and literature review in lines 1–552 are longer than most others in this book. In your opinion, is this lengthy review an important part of this research report? Would the report have been as effective with a shorter review?

8. What is your opinion on the importance of the researchers' inability to verify if participants under 18 years of age actually obtained permission from their parents and guardians? (See lines 593–600 and 876–888.)

9. The researchers used an incentive to encourage participation in the survey. What is your opinion on the particular incentive used in this research? (See lines 647–656.)

10. The researchers make a number of suggestions for future research in lines 889–951. In your opinion, are some of the suggestions more important than others? Are some more interesting than others? Explain.

11. The researchers conclude by stating that they hope this research will inspire additional interest in the etiology and consequences of cyberbullying. Do you think that it will? Explain. (See lines 982–985.)

## Quality Ratings

Directions: Indicate your level of agreement with each of the following statements by circling a number from 5 for strongly agree (SA) to 1 for strongly disagree (SD). If you believe an item is not applicable to this research article, leave it blank. Be prepared to explain your ratings. When responding to criteria A and B, keep in mind that brief titles and abstracts are conventional in published research.

A. The title of the article is appropriate.

   SA   5   4   3   2   1   SD

B. The abstract provides an effective overview of the research article.

   SA   5   4   3   2   1   SD

C. The introduction establishes the importance of the study.

   SA   5   4   3   2   1   SD

D. The literature review establishes the context for the study.

   SA   5   4   3   2   1   SD

E. The research purpose, question, or hypothesis is clearly stated.

   SA   5   4   3   2   1   SD

F. The method of sampling is sound.

   SA   5   4   3   2   1   SD

G. Relevant demographics (for example, age, gender, and ethnicity) are described.

   SA   5   4   3   2   1   SD

H.  Measurement procedures are adequate.

SA   5   4   3   2   1   SD

I.  All procedures have been described in sufficient detail to permit a replication of the study.

SA   5   4   3   2   1   SD

J.  The participants have been adequately protected from potential harm.

SA   5   4   3   2   1   SD

K.  The results are clearly described.

SA   5   4   3   2   1   SD

L.  The discussion/conclusion is appropriate.

SA   5   4   3   2   1   SD

M.  Despite any flaws, the report is worthy of publication.

SA   5   4   3   2   1   SD

# Article 5

# "I Missed the Bus": School Grade Transition, the Wilmington Truancy Center, and Reasons Youth Don't Go to School

ARTHUR H. GARRISON
Delaware Criminal Justice Planning Council

ABSTRACT. Data from a 3-year truancy reduction program operating in Wilmington, Delaware, are analyzed to assess the association of truancy and reasons for truancy with school grade transition points from elementary to middle school and from middle school to high school. Data showed that there was a 95% increase in the number of truants between fifth and sixth grade and a 76% increase in the number of truants between eighth and ninth grade. There was an 87% increase in truancy among youth between 10 and 11 years old and 68% increase in truancy among youth 13 and 14 years old. The study includes analysis of truancy by various demographic variables and makes policy suggestions on how truancy can be reduced by focusing on the two key school transition points, the fifth and eighth grades.

From *Youth Violence and Juvenile Justice*, 4, 204–212. Copyright © 2006 by Sage Publications, Inc. Reprinted with permission.

Data from a truancy reduction center in Wilmington, Delaware, are used in this study to assess the association of truancy and reasons for truancy at school grade transition points. This research seeks to add to
5 the literature on the relationship between the reasons youth give for why they are truant and school grade transition. Research that has been conducted on why youth are truant generally includes poor school performance, lack of interest in school, or that youth do
10 not see any purpose or benefit in going to school (Ames & Archer, 1988; L. Anderman, Maehr, & Midfley, 1999; Chung, Elias, & Schneider, 1998).

One aspect of the newer research on truancy is how transition from one level of education to another (Akos,
15 2002; Alspaugh, 1998a, 1998b, 2000; Alspaugh & Harting, 1995; Arowosafe & Irvin, 1992; Mizelle & Mullins, 1997) can influence school performance and lead to truancy. School transition research has also examined the relationship between school grade transi-
20 tions and various protective factors (Entwisle & Alexander, 1993; Gutman & Midgley, 2000; Newman, Myers, Newman, Lohman, & Smith, 2000). School level transition has also been used to explain why both dropout and truancy patterns increase when youth

25 move from elementary to middle school and from middle school to high school (Alspaugh, 1998a, 1998b). Researchers have noted "potential dropouts from high school can be differentiated from graduates with 75% accuracy as early as third grade" (Phelan, 1992, p. 33;
30 see also Lloyd, 1978). Robins and Ratcliff (1980) found that youth truants in elementary school were 3 times more truant in high school than were youth who were not truant in elementary school. Research presented shows that patterns of truancy start as early as 6
35 years old in the second grade.

Part of the difficulty students have transitioning from elementary to middle school is in the change in the learning environment they encounter. In elementary school, the educational environment is one of task-goal
40 orientation in that students "engage in academic work in order to improve their competency or the intrinsic satisfaction that comes from learning" (E. Anderman & Midgley, 1997, p. 270). In addition to the change in the number of children in a class and the presence of mul-
45 tiple teachers for multiple subjects, middle schools have a performance-goal orientation learning environment. In a performance-goal orientation learning environment, students "engage in academic work to demonstrate or prove their competency, or to avoid the ap-
50 pearance of lack of ability relative to others" (E. Anderman & Midgley, 1997, p. 270).

In addition to the change in the educational environment, factors of puberty (Fenzel, 1989) and the students' perceptions about the transition and of being
55 able to fit in (Hertzog & Morgan, 1999; Pintrich & Schunk, 1996) play a role in the ability of students to adapt to the new school environment. Other factors affecting the transition include increased peer pressure, cliquishness among students, fear of bullying, being the
60 youngest in the new school, the need to fit in, and finding the right bus to go home (Akos, 2002; Schumacher, 1998). School transition research has shown that when youth transfer between school levels, a shift occurs in how the youth perceive and measure themselves. Far-
65 rington (1980) found that teacher labeling of elemen-

tary youth as "troublesome" was the best predictor of truancy in middle school.

The buildup of self-doubt or anxiety can develop while the youth is in the prior school transition grade (fifth grade—elementary before sixth grade—middle school) and continue into the school transition grade. Chung et al. (1998) concluded, "Students showing high levels of psychological distress prior to transition represent early adolescents at a greater risk than their peers for a continued stressful school transition" (p. 98). As the research by Midgley and Urban (1992) explained, after the "transition many students feel less positively about their academic potential and the value of schooling, they give up more quickly and put forth less effort, and their grades decline" (p. 5). Phelan (1992) concluded this alienation from school occurs when students "rightly or wrongly feel harassed or ignored by teachers [and] see no connection between school and their futures" (p. 33), and for "these children, this is the beginning of a downward trajectory that leads to school failure and school leaving" (Midgley & Urban, 1992, p. 5).

## Method

In an effort to reduce truancy in the city of Wilmington, a truancy reduction center was established in a local community center, West End Neighborhood House, to provide services to youth who were found truant by the Wilmington Police Department. Wilmington police officers brought youth who were found not in school during school hours to the West End Neighborhood House. Truant youth were turned over to a police officer who was assigned to the program at the community center (to maintain legal custody of the youth and release the patrol officer) and were interviewed by a social worker also assigned to the truancy center. Truant youth were interviewed, parents were contacted, and the schools they attended were also contacted to determine why the youth were not in school and to establish plans to address the reasons for the truancy.

This study involves a nonrandomized group of 756 youth who were truant and brought to the truancy reduction center by the Wilmington Police Department during the 3-school-year period of the program operation (1999–2002). The majority of youth were black (79.5%) and between 12 and 16 years old. The majority of the youth were enrolled in school (66.5%). The majority of the truant youth were not on probation (56.3%) or suspension (62.4%). The majority of the truant youth were not attending alternative schools (57.4%).

Information was collected from each youth as he or she was brought to the truancy reduction center by staff of the truancy center. The social worker interviewing each truant used a one-page questionnaire in which the date and time a truant was brought to the center were recorded, and demographic, home school assignment, age, race, sex, home address, the address where the youth was found truant, grade level, school district, whether the youth was suspended from school, and the stated reason the youth was truant were collected from each truant youth. Additional information including the number of days absent prior to being taken to the truancy center and whether the youth was on probation through the Delaware Family Court was collected through school contacts. This study provides results of cross-tabulation of age, race, sex, grade, and the reasons given for truancy.

## Finding

Although the majority of youth were in the early pubescent through teenage years, truancy showed a progressive pattern even at the younger ages. As shown in Figure 1, from the ages of 7 to 15, each year showed a progressive increase in the number of youth who were truant. There was an 87% increase in truancy among youth between 10 and 11 years old and a 68% increase in truancy among youth 13 and 14 years old.

The same pattern of progressive truancy was demonstrated when viewing truancy by grade progression. As shown in Figure 2, the number of truant youth increased with each grade progression up until the 9th grade. After youth reached the 10th grade, the number of truant youth decreased. The majority of truant youth, 76%, were in the middle school grades (6th through 8th) and the first year of high school (9th grade). Truancy between 5th grade and 6th grade (transition from elementary to middle school) increased by 95% and by 76% between 8th and 9th grade (transition from middle school to high school).

As shown in Table 1, the reasons "missed the bus" and "didn't feel like going" accounted for the majority (53.0%) of explanations given when asked about not being in school. Whether the youth were on probation, enrolled in school, or enrolled in an alternative school, these two reasons dominated. A third of the males (31.3%) and 26.7% of the females claimed they missed the bus. Less than a quarter (23.6%) of the males and 21.4% of the females stated they did not feel like going to school. Of the youth who were on school behavior probation ($n = 103$), 27.2% stated that they did not feel like going, whereas 26.2% of them stated that they missed the bus. Of those enrolled in school ($n = 503$), 32.8% stated that they missed the bus, and 25.0% stated that they did not feel like going. The majority of youth attending alternative schools provided the same two explanations but differed from other youth in that the main excuse was that they did not feel like going. Although 16.3% of the youth stated that they missed the bus, 24% stated that they did not feel like going to school.

The reasons of "missed the bus" and "didn't feel like going" accounted for the greatest number among youth between 9 and 15 years old. Use of the excuse "missed the bus" increased each year with youth be-

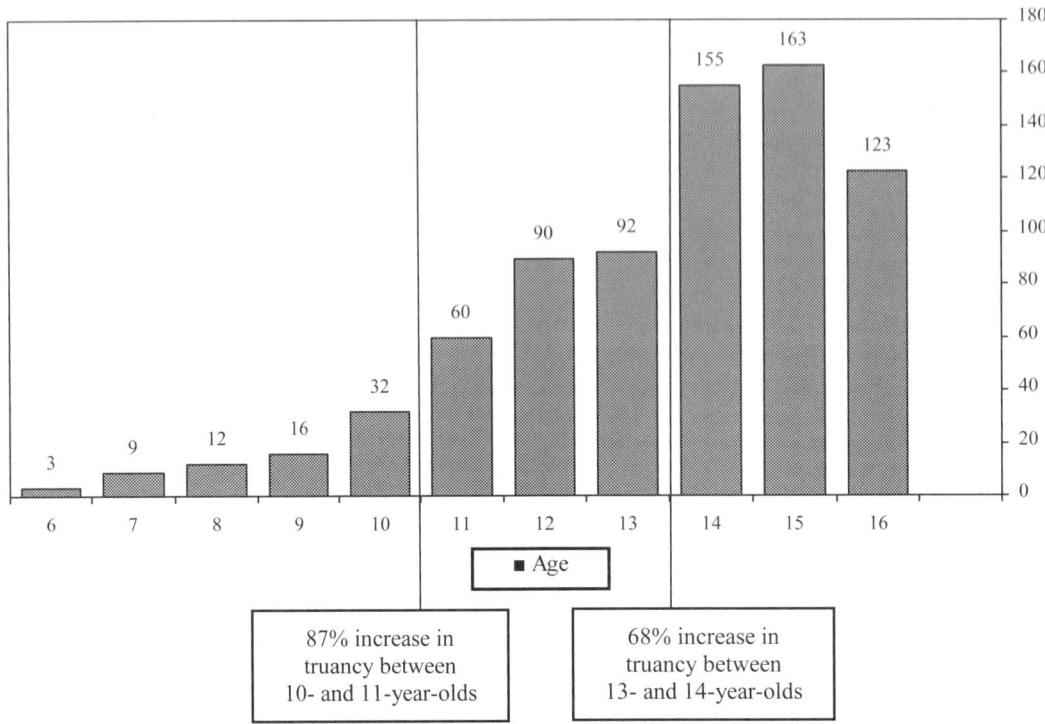

*Figure 1*. Number of youth truant by age.

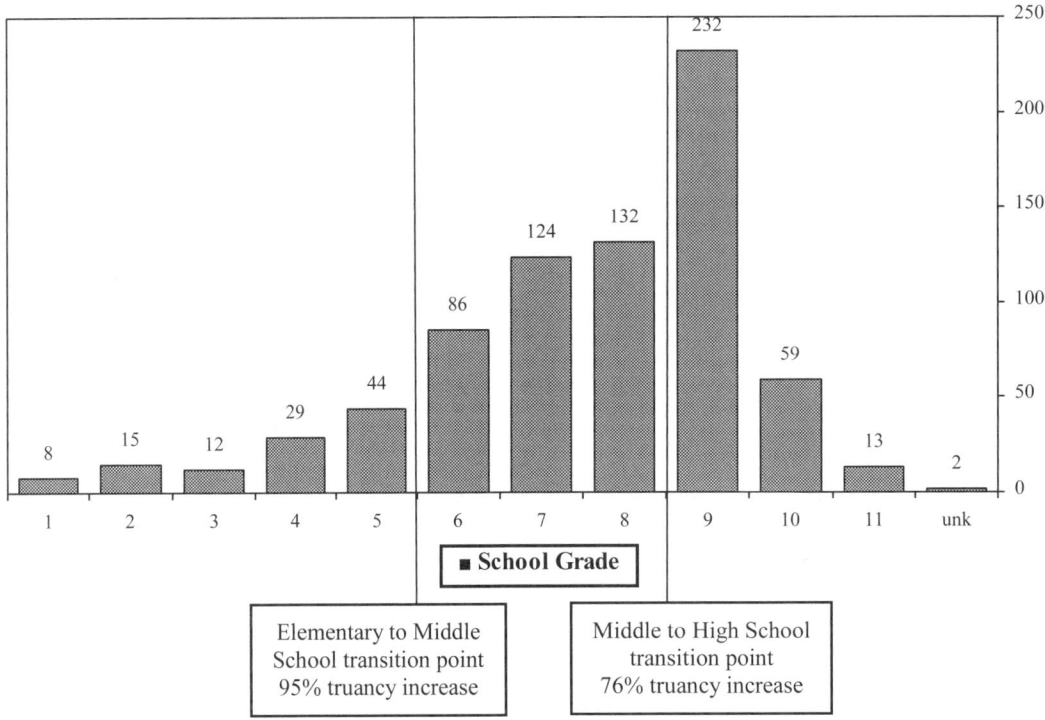

*Figure 2*. Number of youth truant by grade.

tween 9 and 14, after which use of the excuse decreased. The excuse "didn't feel like going" culminated with youth between 10 and 15, after which the excuse was used less often. The ages 9 through 15 and 10 through 15 are closely related to transition from elementary to middle school and from middle school to high school, respectively. As shown in Table 2, the two greatest increases in truancy are in the transfer grades (fifth to sixth and eighth to ninth).

The majority of youth who were truant were black (79.5%) and Hispanic (13.0%). Both Hispanic and black youth stated either to have "missed the bus" or that they "didn't feel like going" to school as explanations for truancy. Although 33.3% of Hispanic males stated they "didn't feel like going," only 22.0% of black males stated not wanting to go to school as an excuse. Overall, 53.0% of black youth stated that they either "missed the bus" or "didn't feel like going," and 54.0% of Hispanic youth provided the same two excuses. A greater majority of white youth (65.0%) provided the same two excuses.

The results of this study show that the majority of truant youth were in the transitional grades. The reason "didn't feel like going" increased consistently between the fifth and ninth grades. There was a 186% increase in the "didn't feel like going" explanation between the fifth and sixth grades and a 42% increase of the same excuse between the eighth and ninth grades. The number of youth truant increased by 95% between the fifth and sixth grades and 76% between the eighth and ninth grades. Use of the excuse "didn't feel like going" increased consistently between the fifth and ninth grades. Truancy occurred more with males than with females, and the age most vulnerable to truancy was between 11 and 15 years old. The most vulnerable grade to truancy was between the sixth and ninth grades.

The majority of truant youth were not "problem" youth (youth on school probation or attending alternative schools). In contrast to some research (Kee, 2001; McGiboney, 2001), youth have many reasons other than boredom and fear of other youth for not attending school. Only 2.8% of the youth stated they did not like school, and fear of other students was not reported as a reason for truancy.

A 186% increase in the "didn't feel like going" explanation between the fifth and sixth grade and a 42% increase of the same excuse between the eighth and ninth grade, as well as a 183% increase in the "missed the bus" explanation between the fifth and sixth grade and a 57% increase of the same excuse between the eighth and ninth grade, reflect the difficulty of school transition points. The use of the "missed the bus" explanation by elementary school youth (42%) and youth between 6 and 9 years old (50%) also demonstrates the problem of youth at very young ages being responsible for their own preparation and transportation to school. The use of the excuse "missed the bus" presupposes that they were responsible for catching the bus.

## Policy Implications and Conclusion

Truancy is one of the early risk factors to future academic failure and one of the first delinquent behaviors that leads to more serious delinquent and criminal behaviors. As shown by this study, truancy increased 95% between fifth and sixth grade and increased 87% among youth between 10 and 11 years old. Antitruancy programs should be designed for youth who begin fifth grade and continue through the sixth grade. Such programs should focus on the fears of youth who are about to enter middle school and should acclimate them to life in middle school. Programs such as visiting the middle school and spending time with teachers and other students in middle school could help alleviate the fears and anxieties that youth feel about the transfer. Similar programs should be established for youth starting their eighth year through the start of the ninth year. Research has shown that "students showing a high level of psychological distress during transition tended to have more adaptive difficulties in middle school," and youth who show "high levels of psychological distress prior to transition represent early adolescents at a greater risk…for continued stressful school transition" (Chung et al., 1998, p. 98). This study found that truancy begins at a very early age and has a progressive development through the early life and grade development of youth through to the middle of high school. Research has shown that there are various reasons for youth disengagement from school; thus, antitruancy programs should be progressively both age and grade appropriate when designed and developed.

Research on school transition suggests that some students develop self-esteem problems after transition. The reduction in self-esteem and not fitting in can lead to other adjustment problems including declined academic achievement, difficulties in peer relationships (Chung et al., 1998), alienation from teachers, and negative views on the utility of school. Such negative views can lead to truancy and dropping out. Programs designed to match youth who are at risk of maladjustment to school after transition with one teacher throughout the first year of transition and with one upperclassman could be a solution. Together, the teacher and the upperclassman could shepherd the youth through the first year. The teacher would focus on keeping the youth on task with school and help deal with any problems the student may have with other teachers. The upperclassman could guide a desperate youth through some of the social pitfalls that await a youth who is not fitting in.

To conclude, it is proposed that truancy can be explained, in part, by the transition from one school level to another. This study found that truancy increases at the two main transfer points in a youth's education, between elementary and middle school and between middle school and high school. Programs designed to address the stress of these two points can have an effect on reducing truancy as a whole.

Table 1
*Reasons Given for Not Going to School*

| Reason | n | % |
|---|---|---|
| Missed the bus | 227 | 30.0 |
| Didn't feel like going | 174 | 23.0 |
| Suspended | 91 | 12.0 |
| Not enrolled | 67 | 8.9 |
| No reason | 46 | 6.1 |
| Left early | 29 | 3.8 |
| Sick | 28 | 3.7 |
| Overslept | 21 | 2.8 |
| Doesn't like school | 21 | 2.8 |
| Medical appointment | 17 | 2.2 |
| Problems with other students | 14 | 1.9 |
| Court appointment | 9 | 1.2 |
| No transportation | 6 | 0.8 |
| Meeting parents | 4 | 0.5 |
| Lunch | 2 | 0.3 |
| Total | 756 | 100.0 |

Table 2
*Reason for Not Going to School, Cross-Tabulation to Grade of Truant*

| | Elementary | | | | | Middle | | | High | | | Unknown | Total |
|---|---|---|---|---|---|---|---|---|---|---|---|---|---|
| | 1 | 2 | 3 | 4 | 5 | 6 | 7 | 8 | 9 | 10 | 11 | | |
| Missed the bus | 4 | 6 | 6 | 11 | 12 | 34 | 42 | 37 | 58 | 14 | 3 | | 227 |
| Didn't feel like going | 2 | 4 | | 7 | 7 | 20 | 25 | 36 | 51 | 18 | 4 | | 174 |
| Suspended | | | 2 | 3 | 5 | 14 | 17 | 15 | 30 | 4 | 1 | | 91 |
| Not enrolled | 1 | | | 1 | 3 | 2 | 5 | 14 | 32 | 7 | 1 | 1 | 67 |
| No reason | 1 | 1 | 2 | 3 | 4 | 6 | 9 | 5 | 12 | 2 | 1 | | 46 |
| Left early | | | | | 2 | | 2 | 4 | 17 | 3 | 1 | | 29 |
| Sick | | 1 | | 1 | 4 | 2 | 6 | 2 | 8 | 4 | 1 | | 28 |
| Overslept | | 1 | | | 4 | 2 | 5 | 5 | 3 | | | 1 | 21 |
| Doesn't like school | | 1 | | | | | 4 | 4 | 8 | 4 | | | 21 |
| Medical appointment | | 1 | | 1 | | | 3 | 3 | 7 | 1 | | | 17 |
| Problems with other students | | | | 1 | 1 | 2 | 1 | 3 | 3 | 2 | 1 | | 14 |
| Court appointment | | | | | | 2 | 2 | 3 | 2 | | | | 9 |
| No transportation | | | 1 | 1 | 1 | | 2 | | 1 | | | | 6 |
| Meeting parents | | | 1 | | 1 | | 1 | 1 | | | | | 4 |
| Lunch | | | | | | 2 | | | | | | | 2 |
| Total | 8 | 15 | 12 | 29 | 44 | 86 | 124 | 132 | 232 | 59 | 13 | 2 | 756 |

# References

Akos, P. (2002). Student perceptions of the transition from elementary to middle school. *Professional School Counseling Journal*, 5, 339–345.

Alspaugh, J. (1998a). Achievement loss associated with the transition to middle school and high school. *The Journal of Educational Research*, 92, 20–25.

Alspaugh, J. (1998b). The relationship of school-to-school transitions and school size to high school dropout rates. *The High School Journal*, 81, 154–160.

Alspaugh, J. (2000). The effect of transition grade to high school, gender, and grade level upon dropout rates. *American Secondary Education*, 29, 2–9.

Alspaugh, J., & Harting, R. (1995). Transition effects of school grade-level organization on student achievement. *Journal of Research and Development in Education*, 28, 145–149.

Ames, C., & Archer, J. (1988). Achievement goals in the classroom: Students' learning strategies and motivation process. *Journal of Educational Psychology*, 80, 260–270.

Anderman, E., & Midgley, C. (1997). Changes in achievement goal orientations, perceived academic competence, and grades across the transition to middle-level schools. *Contemporary Educational Psychology*, 22, 269–298.

Anderman, L., Maehr, M., & Midfley, C. (1999). Declining motivation after the transition to middle school: Schools can make a difference. *Journal of Research and Development in Education*, 32, 131–147.

Arowosafe, D., & Irvin, J. (1992). Transition to a middle level school: What kids say. *Middle School Journal*, 24, 15–19.

Chung, H., Elias, M., Schneider, K. (1998). Patterns of individual adjustment changes during middle school transition. *Journal of School Psychology*, 36, 83–101.

Entwisle, D., & Alexander, K. (1993). Entry into school: The beginning school transition and educational stratification in the United States. *Annual Review of Sociology*, 19, 401–423.

Farrington, D. (1980). Truancy, delinquency, the home and the school. In L. Hersov & I. Berg (Eds.), *Out of school: Modern perspectives in truancy and school refusal* (pp. 49–63). Chichester, UK: Wiley.

Fenzel, L. (1989). Role strains and the transition to middle school: Longitudinal trends and sex differences. *Journal of Early Adolescence*, 9, 211–226.

Gutman, L., & Midgley, C. (2000). The role of protective factors in supporting the academic achievement of poor African American students during the middle school transition. *Journal of Youth and Adolescence*, 29, 223–248.

Hertzog, C., & Morgan, P. (1999). Making the transition from middle level to high school. *High School Magazine*, 6, 26–30.

Kee, T. (2001). Attribution style and school truancy. *Early Child Development and Care*, 169, 21–38.

Lloyd, D. (1978). Prediction of school failure from third-grade data. *Educational and Psychological Measurement*, 38, 1193–1200.

McGiboney, G. (2001). Truants welcome here: An alternative school designed specially for truants is boosting student attendance. *American School Board Journal*, 188, 43–45.

Midgley, C., & Urban, T. (1992). The transition to middle level schools: Making it a good experience for all students. *Middle School Journal*, 24, 5–14.

Mizelle, N., & Mullins, E. (1997). Transition into and out of middle school. In J. Irvin (Ed.), *What current research says to the middle level practitioner* (pp. 303–313). Columbus, OH: National Middle School Association.

Newman, B., Myers, M., Newman, P., Lohman, B., & Smith, V. (2000). The transition to high school for academically promising, urban, low-income African American youth. *Adolescence*, 35, 45–66.

Phelan, W. (1992). Building bonds to high school graduation: Dropout intervention with seventh and eighth graders. *Middle School Journal*, *24*, 33–35.

Pintrich, P., & Schunk, D. (1996). Motivation in education: Theory, research and applications. Englewood Cliffs, NJ: Prentice Hall.

Robins, L., & Ratcliff, K. (1980). The long-term outcome of truancy. In L. Hersov & I. Berg (Eds.), *Out of school: Modern perspectives in truancy and school refusal* (pp. 65–83). Chichester, UK: Wiley.

Schumacher, D. (1998). *The transition to middle school.* Retrieved February 24, 2004, from http://www.ericfacility.net/ericdigests/ed422119.html

**About the author**: *Arthur H. Garrison*, MS, is the director of criminal justice planning and senior researcher for the Delaware Criminal Justice Planning Council. He is also the project director for the Wilmington Hope Commission, which is a citywide initiative to design a strategy to reduce juvenile and adult violence in Wilmington, Delaware. He has written more than 20 program evaluations and has published more than 15 articles on a variety of juvenile and criminal justice issues. He has a master of science (1995) in criminal justice from West Chester University of Pennsylvania and a BA (1990) from Kutztown University of Pennsylvania.

# Exercise for Article 5

## Factual Questions

1. The youth were brought to the Neighborhood House by whom?

2. Who conducted the interviews?

3. Between what two ages was there the largest percentage increase in truancy?

4. What was the main excuse for truancy among students attending alternative schools?

5. How many of the truants were in fifth grade?

6. For all participants, how many indicated that they missed the bus?

## Questions for Discussion

7. The researcher states that the participants were a "nonrandomized group." What is your understanding of the meaning of this term? (See lines 105–109.)

8. Only truants who were caught by police participated in this survey. Could valuable information also be obtained by questioning a sample of all students about their truancy behavior? Explain.

9. Are you surprised at the dramatic drop in truancy after grade 9? Explain. (See Figure 2.)

10. The findings of this survey focus on (a) reasons given for being truant and (b) patterns of truancy across grade and age levels. Do you regard one of these types of findings as more important than the other? Explain.

11. This survey was conducted at one program. In your opinion, does this limit the generalizability of the results? Explain.

12. In your opinion, how important are the implications of this study? (See lines 236–292.)

13. If you were to conduct a survey on the same topic, what changes in the research methodology, if any, would you make?

## Quality Ratings

Directions: Indicate your level of agreement with each of the following statements by circling a number from 5 for strongly agree (SA) to 1 for strongly disagree (SD). If you believe an item is not applicable to this research article, leave it blank. Be prepared to explain your ratings. When responding to criteria A and B, keep in mind that brief titles and abstracts are conventional in published research.

A. The title of the article is appropriate.

SA   5   4   3   2   1   SD

B. The abstract provides an effective overview of the research article.

SA   5   4   3   2   1   SD

C. The introduction establishes the importance of the study.

SA   5   4   3   2   1   SD

D. The literature review establishes the context for the study.

SA   5   4   3   2   1   SD

E. The research purpose, question, or hypothesis is clearly stated.

SA   5   4   3   2   1   SD

F. The method of sampling is sound.

SA   5   4   3   2   1   SD

G. Relevant demographics (for example, age, gender, and ethnicity) are described.

SA   5   4   3   2   1   SD

H. Measurement procedures are adequate.

SA   5   4   3   2   1   SD

I. All procedures have been described in sufficient detail to permit a replication of the study.

SA   5   4   3   2   1   SD

J. The participants have been adequately protected from potential harm.

SA   5   4   3   2   1   SD

K.  The results are clearly described.

> SA  5  4  3  2  1  SD

L.  The discussion/conclusion is appropriate.

> SA  5  4  3  2  1  SD

M.  Despite any flaws, the report is worthy of publication.

> SA  5  4  3  2  1  SD

# Article 6

# Does Therapist Experience Influence Interruptions of Women Clients?

RONALD JAY WERNER-WILSON
Iowa State University

MEGAN J. MURPHY
Iowa State University

JENNIFER LYNN FITZHARRIS
Iowa State University

ABSTRACT. The feminist critique of marriage and family therapy and studies of interruptions in conversation influenced the topic of the present study. We replicated methodology from a study (Werner-Wilson, Price, Zimmerman, & Murphy, 1997) in which the researchers reported that student therapists interrupted women clients more frequently than male clients. Those results may have been related to therapist inexperience—since the therapists were students. In the present study, we compared interruptions from student therapists to those identified as "master" therapists who had extensive clinical experience. Analysis of Variance was used to compare videotaped sessions of therapists in marriage and family therapy training sessions to therapists from the American Association for Marriage and Family Therapy (AAMFT) Masters series. Results suggest that there is no statistically significant difference between the rate of interruptions used by students versus experienced therapists. Both groups interrupted women clients more often than men clients, a finding that replicates the earlier study by Werner-Wilson and colleagues (1997), which increases the generalizability about this pattern in marriage and family therapy.

From *Journal of Feminist Family Therapy*, 16, 39–49. Copyright © 2004 by The Haworth Press, Inc. Reprinted with permission.

One of the first empirical quantitative analyses of power in marriage and family therapy investigated interruptions, which were viewed as a sign of conversational power. That study reported that women clients were interrupted three times more often than men clients regardless of therapist gender (Werner-Wilson et al., 1997). The study published in 1997 included only student therapists so the findings could have been the result of limited professional training because therapist inexperience seems to be associated with a more directive interviewing style (Auerbach & Johnson, 1978). The present study represents a replication of the 1997 study with a sample of therapists that includes some who have significantly more experience, so interruptions could be compared between student therapists and those identified by the American Association for Marriage and Family Therapy as "master" therapists. This present study was influenced by two themes: language and therapeutic discourse as well as the feminist critique of marriage and family therapy.

## Relevant Literature

### The Feminist Critique

Feminists have brought to the forefront the importance of attending to social and political issues within the therapeutic context, such as examining the effects of race/ethnicity on client problems, openly discussing power and privilege one may or may not have within the context of a relationship, and making gender a central component of case conceptualization and intervention (Silverstein, 2003). Embedded within these suggestions is a central issue of power: How does power play out in relationships? Do therapists recognize power differences in the couples and families they treat? How do therapists attend to these power differences in the therapeutic context, that is, both between members of a couple and between themselves and their clients? Although feminists have long called for therapists to examine power in relationships, only recently have concrete suggestions been given regarding how therapists can address abstract concepts like power in therapy (Blanton & Vandergriff-Avery, 2001; Haddock, Zimmerman, & MacPhee, 2000).

In addition to offering ways of conceptualizing and intervening in family therapy, feminists have highlighted the differential treatment of men and women in therapy by their therapists. One of the themes of the feminist critique is associated with therapeutic process: women's voices are to be encouraged, heard, and validated in therapy. Feminist therapists actively encourage equal participation from women and men in therapy and in relationships (Cantor, 1990). From a feminist perspective, therapists should attend to gender issues rather than ignore gender hierarchies in relationships. If "therapeutic talk is, of course, all about the politics of influence" (Goldner, 1989, p. 58), then how well do therapists negotiate power in therapy? Are therapists replicating or challenging existing power inequalities in therapy? Furthermore, are therapists aware of their own stereotypes regarding gender and communication? One frequently heard stereotype is that women talk more than men (O'Donohue, 1996). Do therapists consciously mitigate their own gender-related biases? These questions seem relevant in light of recent studies that show a negative relationship between marital satisfaction and power inequality (Gray-Little, Baucom, & Hamby, 1996; Whisman & Jacobson, 1990).

65    Recent research seems to provide empirical support for this feminist critique of therapy. For example, Haddock and Lyness (2002) reported that male therapists frequently and negatively challenged female clients. The same pattern was not found for male clients. Other
70    research suggests that therapists scored low on taking a stance against client behaviors intended to control another (Haddock, MacPhee, & Zimmerman, 2001). Even though therapists may be aware of the importance of attention to power and gender issues in therapy, it
75    appears that they may not follow through in terms of how they communicate and/or intervene regarding conversational power. It could be argued that therapists have an ethical responsibility to challenge the hierarchies inherent in couples' relationships. Failure to do
80    so would be maintaining the status quo. Therefore, therapists' use of self seems particularly important given the power they have in relation to their clients to shape, end, or shift conversation (Avis, 1991).

*Language and Therapeutic Discourse*

    Given that therapists are responsible for monitoring
85    and perhaps intervening in the relational and communicational therapeutic context, it seems important to pay attention to interruptions—especially those employed by therapists—in therapeutic conversation. The language and communication literature is helpful in this
90    regard. In their pioneering investigation of interruptions as a power tactic in conversation, Zimmerman and West (1975) reported that males more frequently interrupt females in cross-sex pairs, whereas interruptions occur in equal numbers between same-sex con-
95    versational partners. Some studies have not found support for males interrupting more, regardless of partner sex (Hannah & Murachver, 1999; Turner, Dindia, & Pearson, 1995). Explanations of mixed results in studies of interruptions may result from different defini-
100   tions of "interruption," situational context, and whether activities are structured (Anderson & Leaper, 1998). In their meta-analysis of studies of interruption, Anderson and Leaper (1998) suggested that definitions of interruption may moderate gender differences, gender dif-
105   ferences are larger in unstructured activities, and situational factors may influence interruptions more than gender.

    In the language theory literature, two theories have been used to explain gender miscommunication: *two-*
110   *cultures theory* and *dominance theory.* The *two-cultures theory* of gender-linked language differences suggests that boys and girls grow up in different gender cultures, in which they learn different ways of communicating (Mulac, Erlandson, Farrar, Hallett, Molloy, &
115   Prescott, 1998). Boys use questions, for example, to control conversation, whereas girls use questions to sustain conversation. These cultural differences produce miscommunication when children grow up to be

120   adults, when they are interacting more with others from "different cultures." From this position, men do not view interruptions as a display of power; rather, men and women use language differently based on their previous experiences in their cultural sub-groups.

    The *dominance theory* of gender-linked language
125   differences suggests that men's domination of conversations via interruption and topic introduction is reflective of the power they hold in larger society. From this perspective, men use questions, interruptions, and other means of communication as a way to dominate conver-
130   sation and to keep women in a subordinate position. The result is that women speak less and men talk more, again isomorphic to patterns at a larger, societal level in which men have more power than women.

    Proponents of both theories seem to suggest that
135   there are communication differences between men and women, yet the theories posit different explanations for why these differences exist. Given that there have been few empirical investigations of interruptions in therapy, the first step should be to first examine whether there
140   are differences between rates of interruption in the therapeutic context. If gender differences related to interruption are discovered, then therapists may be compelled to address these differences, particularly if these differences impact power within the couple rela-
145   tionship.

    In recent years, researchers have begun to explore interruptions within the context of therapy. Although there are differences in results about the influence of therapist gender on use of interruptions, two different
150   studies (Stratford, 1988; Werner-Wilson et al., 1997) reported that women clients were much more likely than men clients to be interrupted by therapists. Stratford (1998) found that male therapists were more likely than female therapists to interrupt clients; Stratford also
155   reported that female clients were more likely than male clients to be interrupted. Werner-Wilson and his colleagues (1997) also reported that women clients were more likely than men clients to be interrupted in therapy but did not find a difference between women and
160   men therapists. Stratford (1988)—noting that therapist inexperience is associated with a more directive interviewing style (Auerbach & Johnson, 1978)—suggested that the difference in findings about therapist gender and interruptions might be due to differences in thera-
165   pist experience: Her study included experienced therapists while the Werner-Wilson et al. (1997) study included student therapists who have less experience. If Stratford's (1998) speculation is true, we might expect differences in interruption rates based on therapist ex-
170   perience level. The purpose of the present study is to investigate two related research questions:

1. Are women clients interrupted more than men clients?

2. Do student therapists interrupt women clients more
175   than experienced therapists?

## Method

*Participants*

The sample for the present study included clients and therapists from two sources: (a) doctoral student therapists and clients at a nonprofit marriage and family therapy clinic at a major southern university that was accredited by the American Association for Marriage and Family Therapy, and (b) "master" therapists from the Master Series video collection distributed by the American Association for Marriage and Family Therapy. "The Master Series presents the world's most respected marriage and family therapists conducting live, unedited therapy sessions at AAMFT annual conferences" (AAMFT Catalog, 1993, p. 4). Including these master therapists provides an opportunity to compare therapy process between two levels of clinical experience: doctoral students versus master therapists. In each case, the session was the initial consultation with either the student therapist or the master therapist and it featured both an adult woman client and an adult man client who were romantic partners. Table 1 provides descriptive information about cases included in the study.

*Procedures*

We replicated the approach used by Werner-Wilson and colleagues (1997) to investigate interruptions in the therapy process. We examined the first therapy session to control for treatment duration. Therapy sessions have predictable stages (e.g., social, engagement, information collection, intervention, closure), so we examined multiple time points in the session. Three five-minute segments were coded for every client from early, middle, and later stages in the session: (a) 10:00 to 15:00 minute segment; (b) 25:00 to 30:00 minute segment; and (c) 40:00 to 45:00 minute segment. Two senior-level undergraduate students, who were unaware of the purpose of this research, coded videotapes from the first therapy session.

Table 1
*Descriptive Information about Videotapes*

|  | Student Therapists | Master Therapists | Total |
|---|---|---|---|
| Therapist gender |  |  |  |
| Men | 52 | 14 | 66 |
| Women | 22 | 14 | 36 |
| Total | 74 | 28 | 102 |
| Modality |  |  |  |
| Marital | 60 | 16 | 76 |
| Family | 14 | 12 | 26 |
| Total | 74 | 28 | 102 |

*Coder training.* Coders learned the coding scheme by practicing on tapes not featured in the sample until they achieved 80 percent agreement. A graduate student, who was also unaware of the purpose of the present study, coded every sixth session; these tapes were used to calculate interrater reliability. The coders maintained an acceptable level of interrater reliability throughout the coding process: Intraclass correlations were .68.

*Coding scheme.* The transcripts were arranged with codes adjacent to each spoken turn to promote reliability by eliminating the need for coders to memorize codes: The coders viewed the video with the transcript and circled the appropriate code as they occurred during each speaking turn. A distinct set of codes was printed next to each speaker (e.g., therapist, woman client, man client) but each set of codes featured the same possible codes. For example, the therapist could interrupt either the woman or man client. Similarly, each client could interrupt either her/his partner or the therapist. In addition to enhancing reliability, this coding arrangement disguised the nature of the research project because coders identified conversational strategies used by each speaker, not just the therapist.

*Dependent Measures*

*Interruptions.* Interruptions—defined as a violation of a speaking turn, and operationalized as an overlap of speech that is disruptive or intrusive (West & Zimmerman, 1983; West & Zimmerman, 1977; Zimmerman & West, 1975)—were distinguished from other forms of overlap such as supportive statements that represent active listening skills. Statements that trailed off in tone or volume were not coded as interruptions because they represented invitations for reply. It is possible that people who talk more are interrupted more, so, following the procedure used by Werner-Wilson and colleagues (1997), we controlled for amount of client participation: A variable was constructed from the ratio of interruptions made by the therapist to number of speaking turns taken by the client. These ratios provided standardized measures to examine therapist interruptions.

## Results

Based on our review of the literature, it seemed important to consider the influence of client gender, therapist gender, modality, and client experience since each variable has been found to have an influence on some dimension of therapy process. Analysis of Variance (ANOVA) was conducted to examine the following main effects on the dependent variable (ratio of therapist interruptions to number of client speaking turns): client gender (man, woman), therapist gender (man, woman), modality (couple, family), and therapist experience (student, AAMFT master therapist). Based on our review of the literature, it also seemed important to investigate the following interaction effects:

- Client gender × Therapist gender (Stratford, 1998; Werner-Wilson, Zimmerman, & Price, 1999);
- Client gender × Modality (Werner-Wilson, 1997; Werner-Wilson et al., 1999);

270 • Therapist gender × Modality (Werner-Wilson et al., 1999); Therapist gender × Therapist experience (Stratford, 1998); Client gender × Therapist gender × Modality (Werner-Wilson et al., 1999);

• Client gender × Therapist gender × Modality × Therapist experience (Stratford, 1998).

275 There was a statistically significant difference for gender of client on the dependent variable (see Table 2). Neither therapist gender, modality, therapist experience, nor the interaction of any variables was significant (see Table 2). On average, therapists in the present 280 study interrupted women clients ($M = 0.064$) almost two times more often than men clients ($M = 0.037$).

Table 2
*Analysis of Variance for Therapist Behaviors: Interruption*

| Source | MS | F |
|---|---|---|
| Client Gender | 0.014 | 4.780* |
| Therapist Gender | 0.007 | 2.497 |
| Modality | 0.001 | 0.259 |
| Therapist Experience | 0.009 | 3.312 |
| Client Gender × Therapist Gender | 0.004 | 1.370 |
| Client Gender × Modality | 0.000 | 0.046 |
| Therapist Gender × Modality | 0.006 | 2.189 |
| Therapist Gender × Therapist Experience | 0.003 | 0.923 |
| Client Gender × Therapist Gender × Modality | 0.005 | 0.189 |
| Client Gender × Therapist Gender × Modality × Therapist Experience | 0.002 | 0.869 |

*$p < .05$, $n = 102$

## Discussion

### Gender As a Process Issue

285 Results from the present study continue to suggest that women clients are interrupted more often than men clients in conjoint couple and family therapy, although the rate was slightly lower in the present study than in the original study published in 1997. For some aspects 290 of the therapy process (e.g., therapy alliance, goal setting), there seems to be an interaction effect between client gender and therapy modality (Werner-Wilson et al., 1997; Werner-Wilson, Zimmerman, & Price, 1999) but this effect was not demonstrated in the present 295 study. Results from the present study also suggest that therapist experience—which was not measured in the 1997 study—does not significantly influence the number of interruptions directed toward women clients. In fact, master therapists interrupted women clients at a 300 higher rate than student therapists, although it was not statistically significant.

Our findings contribute to the literature in providing evidence that women clients are interrupted more frequently than men clients, regardless of therapist 305 gender or experience. Although the design of the current study could not directly test the validity of the two-cultures theory or the dominance theory (explain-

ing differences for men and women in language use), we tentatively suggest that these theories are too sim-310 plistic to adequately capture the complexity of interactions and power dynamics at play in relationships. Both theories, for example, posit that women may be more likely to be interrupted than men, *and* suggest that men use language in a way that is different from how 315 women use language. One might hypothesize, from either theory of language use, that men therapists would be somehow different from women therapists in how often they interrupt clients, yet results from the current study do not support this view. Simply put, a 320 more comprehensive theory that incorporates therapist and client markers of social standing may be more helpful for future researchers seeking to expand on the repeated finding in the therapy literature that women clients are more frequently interrupted than men cli-325 ents.

Findings from the present study suggest an ongoing need to consider the influence of gender as a process variable in marriage and family therapy. Most therapists would agree to the notion that men and women 330 should have relatively equal participation in therapy; it is likely that therapists are unaware that they tend to interrupt women far more frequently than men in therapy. The first step is for therapists to be aware of these patterns in therapy; the second step is for therapists to 335 use their positional power to assist men and women to equitably share the therapeutic floor.

## References

Anderson, K. J., & Leaper, C. (1998). Meta-analyses of gender effects on conversational interruption: Who, what, when, where, and how. *Sex Roles*, *39*, 225–252.

Auerbach, A., & Johnson, M. (1978). Research on therapists' level of experience. In A. Gorman & A. Razin (Eds.), *The therapists' contribution to effective psychotherapy: An empirical assessment*. New York: Pergamon Press.

Avis, J. M. (1991). Power politics in therapy with women. In T. J. Goodrich (Ed.), *Women and power: Perspectives for family therapy* (pp. 183–200). New York: Norton.

Blanton, P. W., & Vandergriff-Avery, M. (2001). Marital therapy and marital power: Constructing narratives of sharing relational and positional power. *Contemporary Family Therapy*, *23*, 295–308.

Cantor, D. W. (1990). Women as therapists: What we already know. In D. W. Cantor (Ed.), *Women as therapists: A multitheoretical casebook* (pp. 3–19). Northvale, NJ: Aronson.

Goldner, V. (1989). Generation and gender: Normative and covert hierarchies. In M. McGoldrick, C. M. Anderson, & F. Walsh (Eds.), *Women in families: A framework for family therapy* (pp. 42–60). New York: Norton.

Gray-Little, B., Baucom, D. H., & Hamby, S. L. (1996). Marital power, marital adjustment, and therapy outcome. *Journal of Family Psychology*, *10*, 292–303.

Haddock, S., A., & Lyness, K. P. (2002). Three aspects of the therapeutic conversation in couples therapy: Does gender make a difference? *Journal of Couple & Relationship Therapy*, *1*, 5–23.

Haddock, S. A., MacPhee, D., & Zimmerman, T. S. (2001). AAMFT Master Series Tapes: An analysis of the inclusion of feminist principles into family therapy practice. *Journal of Marital and Family Therapy*, *27*, 487–500.

Haddock, S. A., Zimmerman, T. S., & MacPhee, D. (2000). The Power Equity Guide: Attending to gender in family therapy. *Journal of Marital and Family Therapy*, *26*, 153–170.

Hannah, A., & Murachver, T. (1999). Gender and conversational style as predictors of conversational behavior. *Journal of Language and Social Psychology*, *18*, 153–174.

Mulac, A., Erlandson, K. T., Farrar, W. J., Hallett, T. S., Molloy, J. L., & Prescott, M. E. (1998). "Uh-huh. What's that all about?" Differing interpretations of conversational backchannels and questions as sources of miscommunication across gender boundaries. *Communication Research*, *25*, 642–668.

O'Donohue, W. (1996). Marital therapy and gender-linked factors in communication. *Journal of Marital and Family Therapy, 22,* 87–101.

Silverstein, L. B. (2003). Classic texts and early critiques. In L. B. Silverstein & T. J. Goodrich (Eds.), *Feminist family therapy: Empowerment in social context* (pp. 17–35). Washington, DC: APA.

Stratford, J. (1998). Women and men in conversation: A consideration of therapists' interruptions in therapeutic discourse. *Journal of Family Therapy, 20,* 393–394.

Turner, L. H., Dindia, K., & Pearson, J. C. (1995). An investigation of female/male verbal behaviors in same-sex and mixed-sex conversations. *Communication Reports, 8,* 86–96.

Werner-Wilson, R. J. (1997). Is therapeutic alliance influenced by gender in marriage and family therapy? *Journal of Feminist Family Therapy, 9,* 3–16.

Werner-Wilson, R. J., Price, S. J., Zimmerman, T. S., & Murphy, M. J. (1997). Client gender as a process variable in marriage and family therapy: Are women clients interrupted more than men clients? *Journal of Family Psychology, 11,* 373–377.

Werner-Wilson, R. J., Zimmerman, T. S., & Price, S. J. (1999). Are goals and topics influenced by gender and modality in the initial marriage and family therapy session? *Journal of Marital and Family Therapy, 25,* 253–262.

West, C., & Zimmerman, D. H. (1977). Women's place in everyday talk: Reflections on parent-child interaction. *Social Problems, 24,* 521–529.

West, C. & Zimmerman, D. H. (1983). Small insults: A study of interruptions in cross-sex conversations between unacquainted persons. In B. Thorne, C. Kramarae, & N. Henley (Eds.), *Language, gender and society* (pp. 103–117). Rowley, MA: Newbury House.

Whisman, M. A., & Jacobson, N. S. (1990). Power, marital satisfaction, and response to marital therapy. *Journal of Family Psychology, 4,* 202–212.

Zimmerman, D. H., & West, C. (1975). Sex roles, interruptions, and silences in conversation. In B. Thorne & N. Henley (Eds.), *Language & sex: Difference & dominance* (pp. 105–129). Rowley, MA: Newbury House.

**About the authors**: *Ronald Jay Werner-Wilson*, PhD, associate professor and Marriage and Family Therapy Program and Clinic director; *Megan J. Murphy*, PhD, assistant professor, and *Jennifer Lynn Fitzharris*, MS, are all affiliated with the Department of Human Development and Family Studies, Iowa State University, Ames, IA.

**Address correspondence to**: Ronald Jay Werner-Wilson, PhD, Department of Human Development and Family Studies, 4380 Palmer Building, Suite 1321, Iowa State University, Ames, IA 50011-4380. E-mail: rwwilson@iastate.edu

# Exercise for Article 6

## Factual Questions

1. The researchers state that recent studies show what type of relationship between marital satisfaction and power inequality?

2. The dominance theory suggests that men use questions, interruptions, and other means of communication as a way to do what?

3. Coding for interruptions in each therapy session was done for three segments. How long was each segment?

4. The researchers defined "interruptions" as a violation of a speaking turn. How was "interruptions" operationalized?

5. Was the difference between women clients and men clients being interrupted statistically significant? If yes, at what probability level?

6. Was the difference between men therapists and women therapists statistically significant? If yes, at what probability level?

## Questions for Discussion

7. The researchers discuss theories relating to their research in lines 108–145 and lines 302–325. In your opinion, are these discussions an important strength of this research report? Explain.

8. This study examined interruptions in only the initial consultation with a therapist. Would you be willing to generalize the results to subsequent sessions? Explain. (See lines 191–192.)

9. The researchers state that the undergraduate students who coded the videotapes were unaware of the purpose of this research. Speculate on why the researchers did not make them aware of the purpose. (See lines 207–210.)

10. In your opinion, is the "coder training" described in lines 211–219 an important part of this study? Explain.

11. The current study does not support the view that men therapists are different from women therapists in how often they interrupt clients. Does this result surprise you? Explain. (See lines 315–319.)

12. In your opinion, does this study make an important contribution to understanding how clients' gender *influences* therapists' behavior? Explain.

## Quality Ratings

Directions: Indicate your level of agreement with each of the following statements by circling a number from 5 for strongly agree (SA) to 1 for strongly disagree (SD). If you believe an item is not applicable to this research article, leave it blank. Be prepared to explain your ratings. When responding to criteria A and B, keep in mind that brief titles and abstracts are conventional in published research.

A. The title of the article is appropriate.

SA   5   4   3   2   1   SD

B. The abstract provides an effective overview of the research article.

SA   5   4   3   2   1   SD

C. The introduction establishes the importance of the study.

SA   5   4   3   2   1   SD

D.   The literature review establishes the context for the study.

SA   5   4   3   2   1   SD

E.   The research purpose, question, or hypothesis is clearly stated.

SA   5   4   3   2   1   SD

F.   The method of sampling is sound.

SA   5   4   3   2   1   SD

G.   Relevant demographics (for example, age, gender, and ethnicity) are described.

SA   5   4   3   2   1   SD

H.   Measurement procedures are adequate.

SA   5   4   3   2   1   SD

I.   All procedures have been described in sufficient detail to permit a replication of the study.

SA   5   4   3   2   1   SD

J.   The participants have been adequately protected from potential harm.

SA   5   4   3   2   1   SD

K.   The results are clearly described.

SA   5   4   3   2   1   SD

L.   The discussion/conclusion is appropriate.

SA   5   4   3   2   1   SD

M.   Despite any flaws, the report is worthy of publication.

SA   5   4   3   2   1   SD

# Article 7

# Motivational Signage Increases Physical Activity on a College Campus

M. ALLISON FORD
University of Mississippi, Oxford

DONALD TOROK
Florida Atlantic University, Davie

## ABSTRACT

*Objective*: The authors evaluated whether motivational signage influenced rates of stair use relative to elevator use on a college campus.

*Participants*: In March and April 2004, the authors observed students, faculty, staff, and any visitors accessing a college campus building.

*Methods*: During Phase I, the authors monitored ascending stair and elevator use at the same time each weekday (Monday–Friday). During Phase II, the authors placed motivational signs encouraging stair use at the bottom of the stairs and outside and inside the elevators. During the third week (Phase III), the authors removed the signs.

*Results*: The authors observed 18,389 ascending trips during the 3 weeks of the study. Motivational signs significantly contributed to an 18.6% increase in stair use in the second week, which was maintained in the following week.

*Conclusions*: The signage intervention successfully enhanced physical activity on a college campus by providing educational health tips that may have served as motivation to choose the stairs.

The prevalence of obesity in the United States is at an all-time high.[1] In 1991, only 4 states had obesity prevalence rates higher than 14% (15–19%). In 2002, 20 states had obesity prevalence rates of 15% to 19%,
5 29 states had rates of 20% to 24%, and 1 state had a rate > 25%.[1] The alarming increase in rates of obesity over the past decade is an epidemic.[1] Because obese individuals are at an increased risk for coronary heart disease, metabolic disorders (e.g., type 2 diabetes,
10 dyslipidemia, insulin resistance), stroke, osteoarthritis, and cancer, reversing this trend is a top health concern.[2] College is considered a critical period for weight gain among men and women.[3] The "Freshman 15" refers to the 15 pounds that students supposedly gain
15 during their first year of college; however, with obesity appearing at an earlier age among U.S. adolescents, this may turn into the Freshman 30 or 45. Because the transition to college life is a critical time for weight

gain in this population, we must take a closer look at
20 college students' physical activity behaviors.

Williams[4] cites physical activity as an important component of weight loss and weight maintenance. With rates of everyday physical activity and planned physical activity declining, researchers must examine
25 ways to reverse this trend.[2] Because educational level and health knowledge are important behavioral factors, the results of a recent study that revealed a decline in leisure-time physical activity in 19,298 university students worldwide are troubling.[5] The American College
30 of Sports Medicine recommends that every adult should accumulate 30 minutes of physical activity every day for health benefits.[6] The National Academies' Institute of Medicine physical activity recommendation for weight loss is a minimum daily expendi-
35 ture of 60 minutes.[7] With more than 60% of U.S. adults not getting sufficient levels of daily physical activity and an alarming 25% not active at all, finding ways to motivate individuals to increase levels of physical activity is critical.[7]
40 Over the past few years, several researchers[8–12] have evaluated motivational signage and its effectiveness on stair use versus elevator use in public locations. Andersen et al.[10] reported that signs with a motivational health message increased stair use at a Baltimore, MD,
45 mall from 5.4% to 7.2% for nonoverweight individuals and from 3.8% to 6.3% for overweight individuals. At a regional Midwest airport, Russell and Hutchinson[11] observed an increase in stair use from 8.2% to 14.9% with motivational signage. Coleman and Gonzaga[12]
50 reported a 4% increase in stair use at a United States-Mexico border community. All these community studies showed an increase in physical activity (as indicated by stair use) with motivational signage but low overall starting and ending levels (3.8% to 14.9%).
55 Using weight control signage at a community shopping center, Kerr[9] observed a significant increase in stair use among non-Caucasians.[9] In a worksite setting, Titze[13] observed a 5.3% increase in stair use after a short intervention that included motivational signs. Auweele et
60 al.[8] found that motivational signage and, interestingly, e-mail reminders increased rates of stair use among female employees at a Belgian worksite. Using motiva-

tional signage on a college campus, Russell et al.[14] reported a significant increase in stair use at a college
65  library. Most investigators have assessed stair and elevator use in large public areas, which generally comprise a transient population, but the observed changes in use may not necessarily reflect a sustained change in individual behavior. A college educational building
70  contains a more captive audience, allowing for an examination of repeat behaviors and better monitoring of intervention outcomes.

## Methods

This was a 3-phase observational study in which we monitored stair and elevator use without interacting
75  with the participants. The university's institutional review board approved the study. We excluded people who were pushing strollers or pulling carts, in wheelchairs, or holding large objects. Observers were the authors and trained students. Prior to the start of data
80  collection, we conducted a training session on the criteria and actions in which student observers should engage during data collection. During Phase I (baseline), we monitored ascending stair and elevator use for 10 hours per day on Monday through Thursday and 8
85  hours on Friday in a 4-story classroom building at a southern U.S. university. During Phase II, we placed motivational signs at the bottom of the stairs and outside and inside the elevators. Signs were 8" × 11" color posters containing slogans from the Centers for Disease
90  Control and Prevention's *Stairwell to Better Health* initiative.[15] The slogans were "Step up to a healthier lifestyle," "When you go up, your blood pressure goes down," "In one minute, a 150-pound person burns approximately 10 calories walking up the stairs and only
95  1.5 calories riding an elevator," and "Small steps make a big difference." We rotated signs daily. We recorded stair and elevator use during the same hours as Phase I. During Phase III, we removed the motivational signs and recorded stair and elevator use as we did in Phases
100  I and II.

## Results

Table 1 shows the demographics of the university population at the time of the study (spring semester 2004). We recorded 18,389 observations over the 3 weeks of the study. During Phase I, 23.6% used the
105  stairs and 76.4% used the elevator. Stair-use rates increased significantly in Phase II, with 28% (an 18.6% change) using the stairs. The significant increase in stair usage was maintained in Phase III, as 28.6% of the individuals took the stairs. A post hoc analysis of
110  variance revealed that more people took the stairs during the second and third weeks than during the first week, $F(2, 18,388) = 7.07, p = .017$.

Table 1
*Demographics of University (Population = 5,442)*

| Variable | % |
| --- | --- |
| Race/ethnicity | |
| Asian | 3.8 |
| Black | 24.3 |
| Hispanic | 17.3 |
| American Indian | 0.3 |
| White | 50.7 |
| Other | 3.7 |
| Age group (y) | |
| < 25 | 27.0 |
| 25–29 | 26.0 |
| 30–39 | 26.0 |
| 40–49 | 14.0 |
| 50–59 | 6.0 |
| 60 and older | 1.0 |

*Note.* In addition to students, we observed faculty, staff, and campus visitors.

## Comment

Our findings are consistent with other studies that show that motivational signage increases stair use over
115  a short duration of time.[7–11] One important finding was that the baseline rates of stair use were higher in this study than in other studies.[7–11] This higher rate may be because our participants' education level was assumed to be higher than the general population, as the setting
120  was an academic building on a university campus; higher education levels are associated with higher physical activity levels.[16] Because we conducted this study on a college campus, age may have also influenced our relatively higher baseline rates, although the
125  average age of this university's students is about 30 years.

In an earlier study, Kerr[9] did not observe long-term benefits of signs because he conducted that study at a shopping mall and the same people presumably did not
130  visit shopping malls on a daily basis. In addition, Russell and Hutchinson[11] observed increased stair use in an airport terminal, but their participants were also not likely a repeat audience. However, our study involved individuals who do frequent the same building. In fact,
135  all 3 phases had consistent weekly numbers: 6,182; 6,022; and 6,185, respectively.

Because we assessed stair and elevator use for 3 weeks using motivational signage as our only intervention, future researchers should follow up with a physi-
140  cal activity motivational intervention to assess whether the changes remained significant over a longer time period. Kerr[9] was unable to determine the long-term benefits of motivational signs because the shopping center setting did not necessarily reflect the same group
145  of people across a short time period. However, we were able to directly measure repeat behavior and thus the possible long-term benefits because our population comprised mostly student and faculty use, which would be regular during the school year. Participants' age and
150  level of education may again explain differences between ours and previous findings. For most, the earlier

in life someone makes a behavior change, the more likely they are to continue the change. In addition, a younger, more educated population may be more likely
155 to read motivational signs and adhere to their message than would the general population, which likely made up the group observed in the shopping center setting.

With obesity rates on the rise, knowing that motivational signs persuaded some college students to choose
160 using the stairs over the elevator is a positive finding. Certain cues, such as our motivational interventions, could encourage readiness to take action.[17] In fact, many health behavior models incorporate *cues to action* in the developmental stage (e.g., the health belief
165 model [HBM][18]). The HBM defines a *cue* as any strategy that activates a readiness-to-change behavior. We used motivational signs as cues to take the stairs rather than the elevator to enhance physical activity. The cues-to-action component of the HBM has not been a
170 focus of many studies using the model; however, our findings support the theory that cues (motivational signs) promote behavior change.[17]

Last, our study's design provides a mechanism to monitor repeat behavior and possible short-term health
175 benefits. Our intervention enhanced physical activity on a college campus by providing educational health tips. Future researchers could repeat this study and, as others[8] have done, send out e-mail reminders. The college campus is an ideal environment in which to repeat
180 this study using e-mail reminders because e-mail would be an easy way to provide cues to action regarding healthy habits such as taking the stairs. We recommend collecting data for a longer period postintervention to analyze longer-term effects.

### References

1. Centers for Disease Control and Prevention. *US Obesity Trends, 1985–2007.* http://www.cdc.gov/nccdphp/dnpa/obesity/trend/maps. Accessed August 1, 2008.
2. US Department of Health and Human Services. *Healthy People 2010* [conference edition]. Washington, DC: U.S. Government Printing Office; 2000.
3. Anderson DA, Shapiro JR, Lundgren JD. The freshman year of college as a critical period for weight gain: An initial evaluation. *Eat Behav.* 2003;4:363–367.
4. Williams PT. Vigorous exercise and the population distribution of body weight. *Int J Obes Relat Metab Disord.* 2004;28:120–128.
5. Haase A, Steptoe A, Sallis JF, Wardle J. Leisure-time physical activity in university students from 23 countries: Associations with health beliefs, risk awareness, and national economic development. *Prev Med.* 2004;39:182–190.
6. American College of Sports Medicine. *ACSM's Guidelines for Exercise Testing and Prescription.* 6th ed. Philadelphia, PA: Lippincott Williams & Wilkins; 2006.
7. Panel on Macronutrients; Panel on the Definition of Dietary Fiber; Subcommittee on Upper Reference Levels of Nutrients; Subcommittee on Interpretation and Uses of Dietary Reference Intakes; Standing Committee on the Scientific Evaluation of Dietary Reference Intakes; Institute of Medicine. *Dietary Reference Intakes for Energy, Carbohydrate, Fiber, Fat, Fatty Acids, Cholesterol, Protein, and Amino Acids (Macronutrients).* Washington, DC: National Academies Press; 2002.
8. Auweele YV, Boen F, Schapendonk W, Dornez K. Promoting stair use among female employees: The effects of a health sign followed by an e-mail. *J Sport Exerc Psychol.* 2005;27:188–196.
9. Kerr J. Six-month observational study of prompted stair climbing. *Prev Med.* 2001;33:422–427.
10. Andersen R, Franckowiak SC, Snyder J, Bartlett SJ, Fontaine KR. Can inexpensive signs encourage the use of stairs? Results from a community intervention. *Ann Intern Med.* 1998;129:363–369.
11. Russell WD, Hutchinson J. Comparison of health promotion and deterrent prompts in increasing use of stairs over escalators. *Percept Mot Skills.* 2000;91:55–61.
12. Coleman KJ, Gonzaga EC. Promoting stair use in a U.S.-Mexico border community. *Am J Public Health.* 2001;91:2007–2009.
13. Titze S. A worksite intervention module encouraging the use of stairs: Results and evaluations issues. *Soz Praventivmed.* 2001;46:13–19.
14. Russell WD, Dzewaltowski DA, Ryan GJ. The effectiveness of a point-of-decision prompt in deterring sedentary behavior. *Am J Health Promot.* 1999;13:257–259.
15. Centers for Disease Control and Prevention. *Stairwell to Better Health.* http://www.cdc.gov/nccdphp/dnpa/hwi/toolkits/stairwell/. Accessed August 4, 2008.
16. Caspersen CJ, DiPietro L. National estimates of physical activity among older adults. *Med Sci Sports Exerc.* 1991;23:S106.
17. Hochbaum GM . *Public Participation in Medical Screening Programs: A sociopsychological study.* Washington, DC: Government Printing office; 1958. PHS publication No. 572.
18. Glanz K, Rimer BK, Lewis FM. *Health Behavior and Health Education: Theory, Research and Practice.* 3rd ed. San Francisco, CA: Jossey-Bass; 2002.

**About the authors**: *Dr. Ford* is with the Department of Health, Exercise Science and Recreation Management, University of Mississippi, Oxford. *Dr. Torok* is with the Department of Exercise Science and Health Promotion, Florida Atlantic University, Davie.

**Address correspondence to**: Dr. M. Allison Ford, The University of Mississippi, Health, Exercise Science and Recreation Management, Turner 232, University, MS 38677. E-mail: ford@olemiss.edu

# Exercise for Article 7

## *Factual Questions*

1. Have most previous investigators assessed stair and elevator use in college educational buildings?

2. Who were the observers in this study?

3. The motivational signs were removed during which phase?

4. What percentage of the participants were in the under 25 age group?

5. What percentage of the participants were Asian?

6. Were the baseline rates of stair use higher in this study *or* higher in other studies?

## *Questions for Discussion*

7. Is it important to know that the researchers monitored stair and elevator use without interacting with the participants? Explain. (See lines 73–75.)

8. Are the signs described in sufficient detail? Explain. (See lines 88–96.)

9. Do you agree with the recommendation for collecting data for a longer postintervention period? Explain. (See lines 182–184.)

10. In the Contents of this book, this study is classified as an example of observational research. Do you agree with this classification? Explain.

11. If you were to conduct a study on the same topic, what changes, if any, would you make in the research methodology?

## *Quality Ratings*

Directions: Indicate your level of agreement with each of the following statements by circling a number from 5 for strongly agree (SA) to 1 for strongly disagree (SD). If you believe an item is not applicable to this research article, leave it blank. Be prepared to explain your ratings. When responding to criteria A and B, keep in mind that brief titles and abstracts are conventional in published research.

A. The title of the article is appropriate.

SA   5   4   3   2   1   SD

B. The abstract provides an effective overview of the research article.

SA   5   4   3   2   1   SD

C. The introduction establishes the importance of the study.

SA   5   4   3   2   1   SD

D. The literature review establishes the context for the study.

SA   5   4   3   2   1   SD

E. The research purpose, question, or hypothesis is clearly stated.

SA   5   4   3   2   1   SD

F. The method of sampling is sound.

SA   5   4   3   2   1   SD

G. Relevant demographics (for example, age, gender, and ethnicity) are described.

SA   5   4   3   2   1   SD

H. Measurement procedures are adequate.

SA   5   4   3   2   1   SD

I. All procedures have been described in sufficient detail to permit a replication of the study.

SA   5   4   3   2   1   SD

J. The participants have been adequately protected from potential harm.

SA   5   4   3   2   1   SD

K. The results are clearly described.

SA   5   4   3   2   1   SD

L. The discussion/conclusion is appropriate.

SA   5   4   3   2   1   SD

M. Despite any flaws, the report is worthy of publication.

SA   5   4   3   2   1   SD

# Article 8

# Shopping Center Fire Zone Parking Violators: An Informal Look

JOHN TRINKAUS
Baruch College (CUNY)

ABSTRACT. Data for 33 1-hr. observations at a shopping center in a suburban location showed about 700 violations of a traffic regulation prohibiting parking in a fire zone. Women driving vans were the least compliant—accounting for approximately 35% of the total.

From *Perceptual and Motor Skills*, *95*, 1215–1216. Copyright © 2002 by Perceptual and Motor Skills. Reprinted with permission.

To glean some information about the profile of motorists who fail to comply with rules on parking in designated fire zones in shopping centers (5), an informal enquiry was conducted, June through August of 2001,
5  at a shopping center located in a suburb of a large city in New York State. The center housed a bank, a large grocery food supermarket, three sit-down restaurants, and an assortment of 12 other shops and stores. The center was arranged in the form of a "U." The busi-
10  nesses—with sidewalks in front—lined the periphery, with parking (for about 450 vehicles) in the central area. Painted on the pavement in front of the establishments was a 6-ft.-wide continuous yellow zebra-striping, which, along with sign postings, delineated a
15  no-parking fire zone.

Three shops were located in one corner of the center—a dry cleaner, a bakery, and a laundromat—all of which opened early in the morning and appeared to do a brisk business seemingly with folks on their way to
20  work: people dropping off or picking up dry cleaning; those buying rolls, pastry, and coffee; and people leaving laundry to be done. It was the parking behavior of these people that was observed; in particular, those who pulled up in front of one of the three shops and
25  parked their vehicles in the fire zone.

Convenience sampling of the number of parkers, the type of vehicles driven (car or van), and the gender of the driver was conducted. Hour-long observations were made on weekdays, between the hours of 0700
30  and 0900: none during inclement weather. No note was made of commercial vehicles or those in which the driver remained behind the wheel while a passenger exited the vehicle and entered the shop to conduct business. As counting was done early in the day, there
35  were always many "legal" parking spaces available

(but necessitated walking approximately 75 to 150 feet further).

Thirty-three 1-hr. observations were made. A total of 916 parkings were noted: 693 (76%) in the fire zone
40  and 223 (24%) in designated lot spaces. Of the fire zone parkings, 396 (57%) were cars and 297 (43%) vans. Women were driving 222 (56%) of the cars, and men 174 (44%). Two hundred forty-one (81%) of the vans were driven by women, 56 (19%) by men. For
45  every three motorists who parked in the fire zone, there was approximately one motorist who parked in a designated lot space.

Recognizing such methodological limitations as the use of a relatively small sample of convenience, the
50  possibility of double counting, the lack of factoring for the intrinsic moral code of conduct of individual drivers, and the problem of verifiable replication of this enquiry, it seems that compliance with rules on parking in fire zones may leave something to be desired. As to
55  the finding that women driving vans appeared to be the least compliant with the parking regulation, it should be cautiously interpreted. For example, it may well be that the pattern observed could simply reflect a sample of the population of drivers and their vehicle types in
60  the geographical area or those normally frequenting the shopping center during the observation period. However, it does appear to track four other prior related informal enquiries by Trinkaus. Those who exceeded school zone limits (1), those who failed to observe stop
65  signs (2), those who delayed moving out at left-turning traffic signals (3), and those who blocked road intersections (4) all tended to be women driving vans.

Epilogue: To assess whether the parking behavior of drivers frequenting this shopping center might have
70  changed following the World Trade Center incident of September 11—more law abiding—five additional observations were made in late September. No note was made of vehicle type nor driver gender, but note was made of whether or not vehicles were adorned
75  with American flags or other patriotic trappings. A total of 129 parkings were observed: 94 (73%) in the fire zone and 35 (27%) in designated lot spaces. Of those that were parked in the fire zone, 22 (23%) were

80 decorated, while in designated lot spaces there were 3 (9%).

### References

1. Trinkaus, J. School-zone speed-limit dissenters: An informal look. *Perceptual and Motor Skills*, 1999, *88*, 1057–1058.
2. Trinkaus, J. Stop-sign dissenters: An informal look. *Perceptual and Motor Skills*, 1999, *89*, 193–194.
3. Trinkaus, J. Left-turning traffic procrastinators: An informal look. *Perceptual and Motor Skills*, 2000, *90*, 961–962.
4. Trinkaus, J. Blocking the box: An informal look. *Psychological Reports*, 2001, *89*, 315–316.
5. *Vehicle and traffic law.* (2000–2001) New York State, Stopping, standing, and parking. Article 32, Basic rules, Section 1200.

**Address correspondence to**: J. Trinkaus, One Linden Street, New Hyde Park, NY 11040.

# Exercise for Article 8

## Factual Questions

1. The observations were made in front of what types of shops?

2. How many one-hour observations were made?

3. What percentage of the fire zone parkings were made by individuals in vans?

4. The researcher mentions several "methodological limitations." What is the first one that is mentioned?

5. Five additional observations were made to assess what?

## Questions for Discussion

6. In your opinion, how important is it to know that the observations were made between 7 AM and 9 AM (i.e., between 0700 and 0900)? (See lines 28–30.)

7. Speculate on why the researcher did not make observations during inclement weather. (See lines 28–30.)

8. Do any of the findings surprise you? Do you find any especially interesting? Explain.

9. If you were conducting a study on the same topic, what changes in the research methodology, if any, would you make?

## Quality Ratings

Directions: Indicate your level of agreement with each of the following statements by circling a number from 5 for strongly agree (SA) to 1 for strongly disagree (SD). If you believe an item is not applicable to this research article, leave it blank. Be prepared to explain your ratings. When responding to criteria A and B, keep in mind that brief titles and abstracts are conventional in published research.

A. The title of the article is appropriate.

    SA   5   4   3   2   1   SD

B. The abstract provides an effective overview of the research article.

    SA   5   4   3   2   1   SD

C. The introduction establishes the importance of the study.

    SA   5   4   3   2   1   SD

D. The literature review establishes the context for the study.

    SA   5   4   3   2   1   SD

E. The research purpose, question, or hypothesis is clearly stated.

    SA   5   4   3   2   1   SD

F. The method of sampling is sound.

    SA   5   4   3   2   1   SD

G. Relevant demographics (for example, age, gender, and ethnicity) are described.

    SA   5   4   3   2   1   SD

H. Measurement procedures are adequate.

    SA   5   4   3   2   1   SD

I. All procedures have been described in sufficient detail to permit a replication of the study.

    SA   5   4   3   2   1   SD

J. The participants have been adequately protected from potential harm.

    SA   5   4   3   2   1   SD

K. The results are clearly described.

    SA   5   4   3   2   1   SD

L. The discussion/conclusion is appropriate.

    SA   5   4   3   2   1   SD

M. Despite any flaws, the report is worthy of publication.

    SA   5   4   3   2   1   SD

# Article 9

# Students' Ratings of Teaching Effectiveness: A Laughing Matter?

GARY ADAMSON
University of Ulster at Magee College

DAMIAN O'KANE
University of Ulster at Magee College

MARK SHEVLIN
University of Ulster at Magee College

ABSTRACT. Gump in 2004 identified a positive significant relationship between awareness of daily class objectives and ratings of the instructor's overall teaching effectiveness. The idea that rating of teaching effectiveness can be related to other nonteaching-related attributes of the lecturer was further examined. Correlations based on ratings of teaching effectiveness from 453 undergraduate students ($M = 21$ yr., $SD = 5.5$; 73% women) showed that another nonteaching-related variable, namely, how funny the instructor was perceived, was significantly related to indicators of teaching effectiveness.

The practice of having students evaluate teaching in universities is widespread in the UK and the USA, and the information from such surveys can be a useful guide for potential changes in course material and
5 method of delivery (QAA, 1997). For students' evaluation of teaching questionnaires to be used, there should be clear evidence that such measures are producing valid scores, that is, that such questionnaires are actually measuring teaching effectiveness.

10 Research suggests that ratings of teaching effectiveness are positively related to teaching and student-related variables such as awareness of daily class objectives (Gump, 2004), expected grades (Feldman, 1976; Marsh, 1987), the students' prior interest in the
15 topic (Marsh & Roche, 1997), and grading leniency (Greenwald & Gillmore, 1997). More alarmingly, Shevlin, Banyard, Davies, and Griffiths (2000) tested a model that specified ratings of the lecturers' charisma, measured by a single item, as a predictor of teaching
20 effectiveness, in particular "lecturer ability" and "module attributes." Using structural equation modeling, they found that the charisma ratings accounted for 69% of the variation of the lecturer ability factor and 37% of the module attributes factor.

25 The idea that ratings of teaching effectiveness can be related to other nonteaching-related attributes of the lecturer was further examined. An additional item, "The lecturer was funny," was included in a larger questionnaire designed to measure teaching effective-
30 ness. All items used a 5-point Likert response format

with anchors of 1 (Strongly Disagree) and 5 (Strongly Agree). This questionnaire was administered at a UK university to a sample of 453 undergraduate students who were enrolled in full-time courses within a de-
35 partment of social sciences ($M$ age = 21 yr., $SD$ = 5.5; 73% women). In total, six lecturers were rated (four men and two women) in this study.

Analysis showed items designed to reflect aspects of effective teaching were positively correlated with
40 rating how funny the lecturer was. Scores on the item "The lecturer was funny" were positively correlated with scores on the items "The lecturer helped me to develop an interest in the subject matter" ($r = .60$, $p < .01$), "I wanted to learn more about the topic"
45 ($r = .49$, $p < .01$), "The lectures were well organized" ($r = .40$, $p < .01$), and "The lecturer is successful in encouraging students to do supplementary reading on the subject matter of the module" ($r = .38, p < .01$).

The results suggest that students' perceptions of
50 funniness were moderately and significantly associated with ratings of teaching-related activity.

Whereas previous research has focused mainly on the dimensionality of measures of teaching effectiveness (Abrami, d'Apollonia, & Rosenfield, 1997), it is
55 suggested here that the validity of scores derived from any measure of teaching effectiveness ought to be ascertained prior to use of the measure.

## References

Abrami, P. C., d'Apollonia, S., & Rosenfield, S. (1997). The dimensionality of student ratings of instruction: What we know and what we do not. In R. P. Perry & J. C. Smart (Eds.), *Effective teaching in higher education: Research and practice.* New York: Agathon Press. pp. 321–367.

Feldman, K. A. (1976). Grades and college students' evaluations of their courses and teachers. *Research in Higher Education, 18*, 3–124.

Greenwald, A. G., & Gillmore, G. M. (1997). Grading leniency is a removable contaminant of student ratings. *American Psychologist, 52*, 1209–1217.

Gump, S. E. (2004). Daily class objectives and instructor's effectiveness as perceived by students. *Psychological Reports, 94*, 1250–1252.

Marsh, H. W. (1987). Students' evaluations of university teaching: Research findings, methodological issues, and directions for future research. *International Journal of Educational Research, 11*, 253–388.

Marsh, H. W., & Roche, L. A. (1997). Making students' evaluations of teaching effectiveness effective. *American Psychologist, 52*, 1187–1197.

Quality Assurance Agency for Higher Education. (1997). *Subject review handbook: October 1998 to September 2000.* (QAA 1/97) London: Quality Assurance Agency for Higher Education.

Shevlin, M., Banyard, P., Davies, M. D., & Griffiths, M. (2000). The validity of student evaluation of teaching in higher education: Love me, love my lectures? *Assessment and Evaluation in Higher Education, 25*, 397–405.

**Address correspondence to**: Dr. Mark Shevlin, School of Psychology, University of Ulster at Magee Campus, Londonderry, BT48 7JL, UK.

# Exercise for Article 9

## Factual Questions

1. What were the anchors for the statement, "The lecturer was funny"?

2. How many students participated in this study?

3. What was the average age of the students in this study?

4. What is the value of the correlation coefficient for the relationship between "The lecturer was funny" and "I wanted to learn more about the topic"?

5. The strongest correlation was between the lecturer being funny and what other item?

6. Do all the correlation coefficients reported in this study indicate direct (positive) relationships?

## Questions for Discussion

7. The researchers characterize being funny as a "nonteaching-related" attribute. Do you agree with this characterization (i.e., that being funny is not a teaching attribute)? (See lines 25–30.)

8. Six lecturers were rated by the students. Would you recommend using a larger number of lecturers in a future study on this topic? Explain. (See lines 36–37.)

9. After each correlation coefficient, this information appears: $p < .01$. What does this tell you about the correlation coefficients? (See lines 43–48.)

10. Would you characterize any of the correlation coefficients in lines 43–48 as representing very strong relationships?

11. The relationships reported in this study are positive. If you had planned this study, would you have anticipated finding any inverse (negative) relationships among the variables studied? Explain.

12. Do you think that this study shows a *causal* relationship between being funny and perceptions of other teaching attributes (i.e., does it provide evidence that being funny causes higher ratings on other items)? Explain.

13. This research report is shorter than others in this book. In your opinion, is its brevity a defect of the report? A strength of the report? Explain.

## Quality Ratings

Directions: Indicate your level of agreement with each of the following statements by circling a number from 5 for strongly agree (SA) to 1 for strongly disagree (SD). If you believe an item is not applicable to this research article, leave it blank. Be prepared to explain your ratings. When responding to criteria A and B, keep in mind that brief titles and abstracts are conventional in published research.

A. The title of the article is appropriate.

SA   5   4   3   2   1   SD

B. The abstract provides an effective overview of the research article.

SA   5   4   3   2   1   SD

C. The introduction establishes the importance of the study.

SA   5   4   3   2   1   SD

D. The literature review establishes the context for the study.

SA   5   4   3   2   1   SD

E. The research purpose, question, or hypothesis is clearly stated.

SA   5   4   3   2   1   SD

F. The method of sampling is sound.

SA   5   4   3   2   1   SD

G. Relevant demographics (for example, age, gender, and ethnicity) are described.

SA   5   4   3   2   1   SD

H. Measurement procedures are adequate.

SA   5   4   3   2   1   SD

I. All procedures have been described in sufficient detail to permit a replication of the study.

SA   5   4   3   2   1   SD

J. The participants have been adequately protected from potential harm.

SA   5   4   3   2   1   SD

K. The results are clearly described.

SA   5   4   3   2   1   SD

L.   The discussion/conclusion is appropriate.

SA   5   4   3   2   1   SD

M.   Despite any flaws, the report is worthy of publication.

SA   5   4   3   2   1   SD

# Article 10

# Relationships of Assertiveness, Depression, and Social Support Among Older Nursing Home Residents

DANIEL L. SEGAL
University of Colorado at Colorado Springs

ABSTRACT. This study assessed the relationships of assertiveness, depression, and social support among nursing home residents. The sample included 50 older nursing home residents (mean age = 75 years; 75% female; 92% Caucasian). There was a significant correlation between assertiveness and depression ($r = -.33$), but the correlations between social support and depression ($r = -.15$) and between social support and assertiveness ($r = -.03$) were small and nonsignificant. The correlation between overall physical health (a subjective self-rating) and depression was strong and negative ($r = -.50$), with lower levels of health associated with higher depression. An implication of this study is that an intervention for depression among nursing home residents that is targeted at increasing assertiveness and bolstering health status may be more effective than the one that solely targets social support.

From *Behavior Modification*, 29, 689–695. Copyright © 2005 by Sage Publications, Inc. Reprinted with permission.

Most older adults prefer and are successful at "aging in place"—that is, maintaining their independence in their own home. For the frailest and most debilitated older adults, however, nursing home placement is of-
5 tentimes necessary. About 5% of older adults live in a nursing home at any point in time, a figure that has remained stable since the early 1970s (National Center for Health Statistics, 2002). Depression is one of the most prevalent and serious psychological problems
10 among nursing home residents: About 15% to 50% of residents suffer from diagnosable depression (see review by Streim & Katz, 1996).

Social support is also an important factor in mental health among nursing home residents, and psychosocial
15 interventions often seek to bolster the resident's level of supportive relationships.

Assertiveness training plays an important role in traditional behavioral therapy with adults, and it has been recommended as a treatment component among
20 older adults with diverse psychological problems as well (Gambrill, 1986). Assertiveness may be defined as the ability to express one's thoughts, feelings, beliefs, and rights in an open, honest, and appropriate way. A

key component of assertiveness is that the communica-
25 tion does not violate the rights of others, as is the case in aggressive communications. It is logical that nursing home residents with good assertiveness skills would more often get what they want and need. Having basic needs met is a natural goal of all people, and failure to
30 do so could lead to depression or other psychological problems. Personal control has long been noted to improve mental health among nursing home residents (see Langer & Rodin, 1976), and assertiveness training would likely help residents express more clearly their
35 desires and needs.

Two studies have examined links between assertiveness, depression, and social support among older adult groups. Among 69 community-dwelling older adults, Kogan, Van Hasselt, Hersen, and Kabacoff
40 (1995) found that those who are less assertive and have less social support are at increased risk for depression. Among 100 visually impaired older adults, Hersen et al. (1995) reported that higher levels of social support and assertiveness were associated with lower levels of
45 depression. Assertiveness may rightly be an important skill among nursing home residents because workers at the institutional setting may not be as attuned to the emotional needs of a passive resident and the workers may respond poorly to the aggressive and acting-out
50 resident. However, little is known about the nature and impact of assertiveness in long-term care settings. The purpose of this study, therefore, was to assess relationships of assertiveness, social support, and depression among nursing home residents, thus extending the lit-
55 erature to a unique population.

## Method

Participants were recruited at several local nursing homes. Staff identified potential volunteers who were ostensibly free of cognitive impairment. Participants completed anonymously the following self-report
60 measures: Wolpe-Lazarus Assertiveness Scale (WLAS) (Wolpe & Lazarus, 1966), Geriatric Depression Scale (GDS) (Yesavage et al., 1983), and the Social Support List of Interactions (SSL 12-I) (Kempen & van Eijk, 1995). The WLAS consists of 30 yes/no

65 items and measures levels of assertive behavior. Scores can range from 0 to 30, with higher scores reflecting higher levels of assertiveness. The GDS includes 30 yes/no items and evaluates depressive symptoms spe-

70 cifically among older adults. Scores can range from 0 to 30, with higher scores indicating higher levels of depression. The SSL12-I is a 12-item measure of received social support that has good psychometric properties among community-dwelling older adults. Re-

75 spondents indicate on a 4-point scale the extent to which they received a specific type of support from a member of their primary social network (1 = seldom or never, 2 = now and then, 3 = regularly, 4 = very often). Scores can range from 12 to 48 with higher scores cor- responding to higher levels of support. The sample

80 included 50 older adult residents (mean age = 74.9 years, $SD$ = 11.9, age range = 50–96 years; 75% fe- male; 92% Caucasian).

## Results and Discussion

The mean WLAS was 18.1 ($SD$ = 4.1), the mean GDS was 9.0 ($SD$ = 5.5), and the mean SSL12-I was

85 29.2 ($SD$ = 7.3). The correlation between the WLAS and GDS was moderate and negative ($r = -.33$, $p <$ .05), with lower levels of assertiveness associated with higher depression. The correlation between the SSL12- I and GDS was small and nonsignificant ($r = -.15$, $ns$),

90 indicating a slight negative relationship between over- all support and depression. Similarly, the correlation between the SSL12-I and WLAS was small and non- significant ($r = -.03$, $ns$), indicating almost no relation- ship between overall support and assertiveness. Next,

95 correlations between a subjective self-rating of overall physical health status (0–100 scale, higher scores indi- cating better health) and the WLAS, GDS, and SSL12- I were calculated. As expected, the correlation between physical health and GDS was strong and negative

100 ($r = -.50$, $p < .01$), with poorer health associated with higher depression. The correlation between health and WLAS was positive in direction but small and nonsig- nificant ($r = .17$, $ns$), indicating little relationship be- tween health and assertiveness. Similarly, the correla-

105 tion between health and SSL12-I was also small and nonsignificant ($r = -.02$, $ns$), indicating no relationship between health and overall support. The slight relation- ship between health and assertiveness is an encourag- ing sign because it suggests that assertiveness (which is

110 primarily achieved through effective verbalizations) is not limited to only the least physically impaired nurs- ing home residents. Finally, gender differences on all dependent measures were examined (independent $t$ tests) and no significant differences were found (all $ps$

115 > .05).

Notably, the mean assertion and depression scores among nursing home residents are consistent with means on identical measures in community-dwelling older adults (assertion $M$ = 19.1; depression $M$ = 7.9;

120 Kogan et al., 1995) and visually impaired older adults (assertion $M$ = 18.3; depression $M$ = 10.4; Hersen et al., 1995), suggesting that the higher functioning group of nursing home residents are no more depressed and no less assertive than other samples of older persons.

125 Regarding social support, our nursing home sample appeared to show somewhat higher levels of overall support than community older adults in the normative sample ($N$ = 5,279, $M$ = 25.5) in the SSL12-I valida- tion study (Kempen & van Eijk, 1995). This may pos-

130 sibly be due to the nature of institutional living and the large numbers of support staff and health care person- nel.

The correlational results regarding the moderate negative association between assertion and depression

135 are consistent with data from community-dwelling older adults ($r = -.36$; Kogan et al., 1995) and visually impaired older adults ($r = -.29$; Hersen et al., 1995), suggesting a pervasive relationship among the vari- ables in diverse older adult samples and extending the

140 findings to nursing home residents. Contrary to the literature, the relationship between social support and depression among nursing home residents was weaker than the one reported in community-dwelling older adults ($r = -.50$; Kogan et al., 1995) and visually im-

145 paired older adults ($r = -.48$; Hersen et al., 1995). The relationship between assertiveness and overall support in this study was almost nonexistent, also contrary to earlier reports in which the relationship was moderate and positive in direction. Our results are consistent

150 with prior research showing no gender differences among older adults in assertiveness, depression, and social support using similar assessment tools (Hersen et al., 1995; Kogan et al., 1995). This study also suggests a strong negative relationship between health status and

155 depression among nursing home residents. An implica- tion of this study is that an intervention for depression among nursing home residents that is targeted at in- creasing assertiveness and bolstering health status may be more effective than the one that solely targets social

160 support.

Several limitations are offered concerning this study. First, the sample size was modest, and the sam- ple was almost exclusively Caucasian. Future studies with more diverse nursing home residents would add to

165 the knowledge base in this area. All measures were self-report, and future studies with structured inter- views and behavioral assessments would be stronger. We are also concerned somewhat about the extent to which the WLAS is content valid for older adults. No-

170 tably, a measure of assertive behavior competence has been developed specifically for use with community- dwelling older adults (Northrop & Edelstein, 1998), and this measure appears to be a good choice for future research in the area. A final limitation was that partici-

175 pants were likely the highest functioning of residents because they were required to be able to complete the measures independently and were selected out if there was any overt cognitive impairment (although no for-

mal screening for cognitive impairment was done),
180 thus limiting generalizability to more frail nursing
home residents. Cognitive screening should be done in
future studies. Nonetheless, results of this study suggest a potentially important relationship between assertiveness and depression among nursing home residents.
185    Finally, it is imperative to highlight that there are
many types of interventions to combat depression
among nursing home residents: behavioral interventions to increase exercise, participation in social activities, and other pleasurable activities; cognitive inter-
190 ventions to reduce depressogenic thoughts; and pharmacotherapy, to name a few. (The interested reader is
referred to Molinari, 2000, for a comprehensive description of psychological issues and interventions
unique to long-term care settings.) The present data
195 suggest that training in assertiveness may be yet one
additional option for psychosocial intervention in nursing homes. A controlled outcome study is warranted in
which intensive assertiveness training is compared to a
control group of nursing home residents who do not
200 receive such training. Only with such a study can
cause-and-effect statements be made about the role that
assertiveness skills training may play in the reduction
of depressive symptoms among nursing home residents.

## References

Gambrill, E. B. (1986). Social skills training with the elderly. In C. R. Hollin &
P. Trower (Eds.), *Handbook of social skills training: Applications across the
lifespan* (pp. 211–238). New York: Pergamon.
Hersen, M., Kabacoff, R. L, Van Hasselt, V. B., Null, J. A., Ryan, C. F., Mel-
ton, M. A., et al. (1995). Assertiveness, depression, and social support in
older visually impaired adults. *Journal of Visual Impairment and Blindness,
7,* 524–530.
Kempen, G. I. J. M., & van Eijk, L. M. (1995). The psychometric properties of
the SSL12-I, a short scale for measuring social support in the elderly. *Social
Indicators Research, 35,* 303–312.
Kogan, S. E., Van Hasselt, B. V., Hersen, M., & Kabacoff, I. R. (1995). Relationship of depression, assertiveness, and social support in community-
dwelling older adults. *Journal of Clinical Geropsychology, 1,* 157–163.
Langer, E. J., & Rodin, J. (1976). The effects of choice and enhanced personal
responsibility for the aged: A field experiment in an institutional setting.
*Journal of Personality and Social Psychology, 34,* 191–198.
Molinari, V. (Ed.). (2000). *Professional psychology in long-term care: A
comprehensive guide.* New York: Hatherleigh.
National Center for Health Statistics. (2002). *Health, United States, 2002.*
Hyattsville, MD: Author.
Northrop, L. M. E., & Edelstein, B. A. (1998). An assertive-behavior compe-
tence inventory for older adults. *Journal of Clinical Geropsychology, 4,*
315–331.
Streim, J. E., & Katz, I. R. (1996). Clinical psychiatry in the nursing home. In
E. W. Busse & D. G. Blazer (Eds.), *Textbook of geriatric psychiatry* (2nd
ed., pp. 413–432). Washington, DC: American Psychiatric Press.
Wolpe, J., & Lazarus, A. A. (1966). *Behavior therapy techniques.* New York:
Pergamon.
Yesavage, J. A., Brink, T. L., Rose, T. L., Lum, O., Huang, V., Adey, M., et al.
(1983). Development and validation of a geriatric depression screening
scale: A preliminary report. *Journal of Psychiatric Research, 17,* 314–317.

**Acknowledgment**: The author thanks Jessica Corcoran, M.A., for
assistance with data collection and data entry.

**About the author**: *Daniel L. Segal* received his Ph.D. in clinical
psychology from the University of Miami in 1992. He is an associate
professor in the Department of Psychology at the University of Colorado at Colorado Springs. His research interests include diagnostic
and assessment issues in geropsychology, suicide prevention and
aging, bereavement, and personality disorders across the lifespan.

# Exercise for Article 10

## Factual Questions

1. Were the participants cognitively impaired?

2. Was the mean score for the participants on the GDS near the highest possible score on this instrument? Explain.

3. What is the value of the correlation coefficient for the relationship between the WLAS and the GDS?

4. Was the relationship between SSL12-I and GDS strong?

5. Was the correlation coefficient for the relationship between SSL12-I and GDS statistically significant?

6. Was the relationship between physical health and GDS a direct relationship *or* an inverse relationship?

## Questions for Discussion

7. The researcher obtained participants from "several" nursing homes. Is this better than obtaining them from a single nursing home? Explain. (See lines 56–57.)

8. The researcher characterizes the *r* of −.33 in line 86 as "moderate." Do you agree with this characterization? Explain.

9. In lines 85–107, the researcher reports the values of six correlation coefficients. Which one of these indicates the strongest relationship? Explain the basis for your choice.

10. In lines 85–107, the researcher reports the values of six correlation coefficients. Which one of these indicates the weakest relationship? Explain the basis for your choice.

11. For the *r* of −.50 in line 100, the researcher indicates that "*p* < .01." What is your understanding of the meaning of the symbol "*p*"? What is your understanding of ".01"?

12. Do you agree with the researcher that a different type of study is needed in order to determine the role of assertiveness skills training in the reduction of depressive symptoms? Explain. (See lines 197–204.)

## *Quality Ratings*

Directions: Indicate your level of agreement with each of the following statements by circling a number from 5 for strongly agree (SA) to 1 for strongly disagree (SD). If you believe an item is not applicable to this research article, leave it blank. Be prepared to explain your ratings. When responding to criteria A and B, keep in mind that brief titles and abstracts are conventional in published research.

A. The title of the article is appropriate.

   SA   5   4   3   2   1   SD

B. The abstract provides an effective overview of the research article.

   SA   5   4   3   2   1   SD

C. The introduction establishes the importance of the study.

   SA   5   4   3   2   1   SD

D. The literature review establishes the context for the study.

   SA   5   4   3   2   1   SD

E. The research purpose, question, or hypothesis is clearly stated.

   SA   5   4   3   2   1   SD

F. The method of sampling is sound.

   SA   5   4   3   2   1   SD

G. Relevant demographics (for example, age, gender, and ethnicity) are described.

   SA   5   4   3   2   1   SD

H. Measurement procedures are adequate.

   SA   5   4   3   2   1   SD

I. All procedures have been described in sufficient detail to permit a replication of the study.

   SA   5   4   3   2   1   SD

J. The participants have been adequately protected from potential harm.

   SA   5   4   3   2   1   SD

K. The results are clearly described.

   SA   5   4   3   2   1   SD

L. The discussion/conclusion is appropriate.

   SA   5   4   3   2   1   SD

M. Despite any flaws, the report is worthy of publication.

   SA   5   4   3   2   1   SD

# Article 11

# Correlations Between Humor Styles and Loneliness

WILLIAM P. HAMPES
Black Hawk College

ABSTRACT. In a previous study, a significant negative correlation between shyness with affiliative humor and a significant positive one with self-defeating humor were reported. Since shyness and loneliness share many of the same characteristics, poor social skills and negative affect, for example, significant negative correlations of loneliness with affiliative and self-enhancing humor and a significant positive one with self-defeating humor were hypothesized. 106 community college students (34 men, 72 women) ranging in age from 17 to 52 years ($M = 23.5$, $SD = 7.7$) were tested. The hypotheses were supported. Interrelationships among humor, shyness, and loneliness should be examined within one study.

From *Psychological Reports*, *96*, 747–750. Copyright © 2005 by Psychological Reports. Reprinted with permission.

Various studies, using self-report and rating scales, have yielded correlations of .40 or more between shyness and loneliness (Cheek & Busch, 1981; Jones, Freeman, & Goswick, 1981; Moore & Schultz, 1983; Anderson & Arnoult, 1985). Research studies have shown that those high in both variables tend to have poor social skills (Zahaki & Duran, 1982; Moore & Schultz, 1983; Wittenberg & Reis, 1986; Miller, 1995; Carducci, 2000; Segrin & Flora, 2000), poor interpersonal relationships (Jones, 1981; Jones, Rose, & Russell, 1990; Carducci, 2000), and low self-esteem (Jones et al., 1981; Olmstead, Guy, O'Malley, & Bentler, 1991; Kamath & Kanekar, 1993; Schmidt & Fox, 1995).

Hampes (in press) reported shyness negatively correlated with affiliative humor and positively correlated with self-defeating humor. Affiliative humor is an interpersonal form of humor that involves use of humor (telling jokes, saying funny things, or witty banter, for example), to put others at ease, amuse others, and to improve relationships (Martin, Puhlik-Doris, Larsen, Gray, & Weir, 2003). Since those high on affiliative humor tend to score high on extraversion and intimacy (Martin et al., 2003), and lonely people, like shy people, have poor social skills and relationships, it was hypothesized that loneliness would be negatively correlated with affiliative humor.

Self-defeating humor "involves excessively self-disparaging humor, attempts to amuse others by doing or saying funny things at one's expense as a means of ingratiating oneself or gaining approval, allowing oneself to be the 'butt' of others' humor, and laughing along with others when being ridiculed or disparaged" (Martin et al., 2003, p. 54). Since both lonely and shy people tend to have low self-esteem, and those high in self-defeating humor tend to score low on self-esteem (Martin et al., 2003), it was hypothesized that loneliness and self-defeating humor would be positively correlated.

Hampes (in press) did not find a significant correlation for his total group of 174 subjects between scores on shyness and self-enhancing humor, an adaptive intrapersonal dimension of humor that "involves a generally humorous outlook on life, a tendency to be frequently amused by the incongruities of life, and to maintain a humorous perspective even in the face of stress or of adversity" (Martin et al., 2003, p. 53). However, Martin et al. reported self-enhancing humor scores were positively correlated with those on self-esteem, social intimacy, and social support, just the opposite of the relationships between loneliness and self-esteem, social intimacy, and social support. Therefore, it was hypothesized that loneliness and self-enhancing humor would be negatively correlated.

Hampes (in press) did not find a significant correlation for his total group between scores on shyness and aggressive humor (a maladaptive interpersonal type of humor, involving sarcasm, teasing, ridicule, derision, hostility, or disparagement humor) for the total group. Therefore, it was hypothesized that there would be a nonsignificant correlation between loneliness and aggressive humor.

## Method

The subjects were 106 students (34 men, 72 women) at a community college in the midwestern United States. These students ranged in age from 17 to 52 years ($M = 23.5$, $SD = 7.7$). Students in four psychology classes were asked to participate, and those who volunteered were included in the sample.

The UCLA Loneliness Scale (Version 3) measures loneliness as a unidimensional emotional response to a difference between desired and achieved social contact. It contains 20 items, each of which has four response options in a Likert-type format, anchored by 1 = Never and 4 = Always (e.g., "How often do you feel isolated from others?"). Coefficients alpha for the scale ranged from .89 to .94 (Russell & Cutrona, 1988). Russell, Kao, and Cutrona (1987) reported a 1-yr. test-retest correlation of .73 and estimated discriminant validity through significant negative correlations between scores on loneliness with those on social support and measures of positive mental health status.

In the Humor Styles Questionnaire, each of four scales has eight items. Each item has seven response options in a Likert-type format, anchored by 1 = Totally Disagree and 7 = Totally Agree. The Cronbach alpha for the four scales ranged from .77 to .81. The convergent validity for the Affiliative Humor Scale was indicated by significant correlations with scores on the Miller Social Intimacy Scale and Extraversion on the NEO PI–R. Discriminant validity for the Self-enhancing Humor Scale was estimated by a significant negative correlation with scores on Neuroticism of the NEO PI–R, and convergent validity was estimated with significant positive correlations with the Coping Humor Scale and the Humor Coping subscale of the Coping Orientations to Problems Experienced Scale. Convergent validity for the Aggressive Scale was supported by a significant correlation with scores on the Cook-Medley Hostility Scale. Discriminant validity for the Self-defeating Scale was based on significant negative correlations with ratings on the Rosenberg Self-esteem Scale and on the Index of Self-esteem (Martin et al., 2003).

## Results and Discussion

Four Pearson product-moment correlations were computed for the scores on the UCLA Loneliness Scale-Version 3 ($M = 41.1$, $SD = 10.7$) and those on each of four humor scales: Affiliative ($M = 45.5$, $SD = 7.3$), Self-enhancing ($M = 37.4$, $SD = 8.4$), Aggressive ($M = 25.8$, $SD = 7.4$), and Self-defeating ($M = 26.0$, $SD = 8.9$). In each case, the hypotheses were supported, as correlations were significant for scores in Loneliness with Affiliative Humor ($r = -.47$, $p < .001$, $CI_{95} = -.28$ to $-.66$), Self-enhancing Humor ($r = -.39$, $p < .001$, $CI_{95} = -.20$ to $-.58$), and Self-defeating Humor ($r = .32$, $p < .001$, $CI_{95} = .13$ to .51). The correlation between scores on Loneliness and Aggressive Humor was not significant ($r = -.04$, $p > .05$, $CI_{95} = -.23$ to .15).

Dill and Anderson (1999) posited that shyness precedes loneliness. Given their social anxiety, shy people tend to be unsuccessful in social situations, and so they try to avoid these. Even if they do not avoid social relationships, they tend not to have satisfying personal relationships. As a result, they may report being lonely. The idea that shyness precedes loneliness is supported by the developmental research of Kagan (1994), who stated that shyness has a strong genetic component and

is manifested early in infancy, and Cheek and Busch (1981), who found shyness influenced loneliness reported by students in an introductory psychology course. If shyness does precede loneliness, it could be in part because shy individuals do not use affiliative humor and self-enhancing humor to help them be more successful in social situations and score high in self-defeating humor, which other people might not find appealing. Further studies are needed to evaluate the causal relationships among shyness, loneliness, and styles of humor.

## References

Anderson, C. A., & Arnoult, L. H. (1985). Attributional style and everyday problems in living: Depression, loneliness, and shyness. *Social Cognition, 3*, 16–35.

Carducci, B. (2000). *Shyness: A bold new approach.* New York: Perennial.

Cheek, J. M., & Busch, C. M. (1981). The influence of shyness on loneliness in a new situation. *Personality and Social Psychology Bulletin, 7*, 572–577.

Dill, J. C., & Anderson, C. A. (1999). Loneliness, shyness, and depression: the etiology and interrelationships of everyday problems in living. In T. Joiner & J. C. Coyne (Eds.), *The interactional nature of depression* (pp. 93–125). Washington, DC: American Psychological Association.

Hampes, W. P. (in press). The relation between humor styles and shyness. *Humor: The International Journal of Humor Research.*

Jones, W. H. (1981) Loneliness and social contact. *Journal of Social Psychology, 113*, 295–296.

Jones, W. H., Freeman, J. A., & Goswick, R. A. (1981). The persistence of loneliness: Self and other determinants. *Journal of Personality, 49*, 27–48.

Jones, W. H., Rose, J., & Russell, D. (1990). Loneliness and social anxiety. In H. Leitenberg (Ed.), *Handbook of social evaluation anxiety* (pp. 247–266) New York: Plenum.

Kagan, J. (1994). *Galen's prophecy: Temperament in human nature.* New York: Basic Books.

Kamath, M., & Kanekar, S. (1993). Loneliness, shyness, self-esteem, and extraversion. *The Journal of Social Psychology, 133*, 855–857.

Martin, R. A., Puhlik-Doris, P., Larsen, G., Gray, J., & Weir, K. (2003). Individual differences in uses of humor and their relation to psychological well-being: Development of the Humor Styles Questionnaire. *Journal of Research in Personality, 37*, 48–75.

Miller, R. S. (1995). On the nature of embarassability, shyness, social evaluation, and social skill. *The Journal of Psychology, 63*, 315–339.

Moore, D., & Schultz, N. R. (1983). Loneliness at adolescence: Correlates, attributions and coping. *Journal of Youth and Adolescence, 12*, 95–100.

Olmstead, R. E., Guy, S. M., O'Malley, P. M., & Bentler, P. M. (1991). Longitudinal assessment of the relationship between self-esteem, fatalism, loneliness, and substance abuse. *Journal of Social Behavior and Personality, 6*, 749–770.

Russell, D. W., & Cutrona, C. E. (1988). Development and evolution of the UCLA Loneliness Scale. (Unpublished manuscript, Center for Health Services Research, College of Medicine, University of Iowa.)

Russell, D. W., Kao, C., & Cutrona, C. E. (1987). Loneliness and social support: Same or different constructs? Paper presented at the Iowa Conference on Personal Relationships, Iowa City.

Schmidt, L. A., & Fox, N. A. (1995). Individual differences in young adults' shyness and sociability: Personality and health correlates. *Personality and Individual Differences, 19*, 455–462.

Segrin, C., & Flora, J. (2000). Poor social skills are a vulnerability factor in the development of psychosocial problems. *Human Communication Research, 26*, 489–514.

Wittenberg, M. T., & Reis, H. T. (1986). Loneliness, social skills, and social perception. *Personality and Social Psychology Bulletin, 12*, 121–130.

Zahaki, W. R., & Duran, R. L. (1982). All the lonely people: The relationship among loneliness, communicative competence, and communication anxiety. *Communication Quarterly, 30*, 202–209.

**Address correspondence to**: William Hampes, Department of Social, Behavioral, and Educational Studies, Black Hawk College, 6600 34th Avenue, Moline, IL 61265. E-mail: hampesw@bhc.edu

# Exercise for Article 11

## Factual Questions

1. In the introduction to the research article, the researcher hypothesizes a positive correlation between which two variables?

2. What was the mean age of the students in this study?

3. The correlation coefficient for the relationship between Loneliness with Affiliative Humor was −.47. This indicates that those who had high loneliness scores tended to have

   A. low Affiliative Humor scores.
   B. high Affiliative Humor scores.

4. In lines 111–117, the researcher reports four correlation coefficients. Which correlation coefficient indicates the strongest relationship?

5. Is the correlation coefficient for the relationship between Loneliness and Self-enhancing Humor statistically significant? If yes, at what probability level?

6. Is the correlation coefficient for the relationship between Loneliness and Aggressive Humor statistically significant? If yes, at what probability level?

## Questions for Discussion

7. In your opinion, does the use of volunteers affect the quality of this study? (See lines 63–68.)

8. The correlation coefficient between Loneliness with Affiliative Humor equals −.47. The researcher also reports the 95% confidence interval (CI₉₅) for this correlation coefficient. What is your understanding of the meaning of the confidence interval? (See lines 111–113.)

9. Would you characterize any of the correlation coefficients reported in lines 111–117 as representing a "very strong" relationship? Explain.

10. Would you characterize any of the correlation coefficients reported in lines 111–117 as representing a "very weak" relationship? Explain.

11. The researcher mentions "causal relationships" in line 136. In your opinion, do the results of this study offer evidence regarding causal relationships? Explain.

## Quality Ratings

Directions: Indicate your level of agreement with each of the following statements by circling a number from 5 for strongly agree (SA) to 1 for strongly disagree (SD). If you believe an item is not applicable to this research article, leave it blank. Be prepared to explain your ratings. When responding to criteria A and B, keep in mind that brief titles and abstracts are conventional in published research.

A. The title of the article is appropriate.

   SA   5   4   3   2   1   SD

B. The abstract provides an effective overview of the research article.

   SA   5   4   3   2   1   SD

C. The introduction establishes the importance of the study.

   SA   5   4   3   2   1   SD

D. The literature review establishes the context for the study.

   SA   5   4   3   2   1   SD

E. The research purpose, question, or hypothesis is clearly stated.

   SA   5   4   3   2   1   SD

F. The method of sampling is sound.

   SA   5   4   3   2   1   SD

G. Relevant demographics (for example, age, gender, and ethnicity) are described.

   SA   5   4   3   2   1   SD

H. Measurement procedures are adequate.

   SA   5   4   3   2   1   SD

I. All procedures have been described in sufficient detail to permit a replication of the study.

   SA   5   4   3   2   1   SD

J. The participants have been adequately protected from potential harm.

   SA   5   4   3   2   1   SD

K. The results are clearly described.

   SA   5   4   3   2   1   SD

L. The discussion/conclusion is appropriate.

   SA   5   4   3   2   1   SD

M. Despite any flaws, the report is worthy of publication.

   SA   5   4   3   2   1   SD

# Article 12

# A Night to Remember: A Harm-Reduction Birthday Card Intervention Reduces High-Risk Drinking During 21st Birthday Celebrations

JOSEPH W. LaBRIE
Loyola Marymount University

SAVANNAH MIGLIURI
Loyola Marymount University

JESSICA CAIL
Loyola Marymount University

*Objective.* In collaboration with Residence Life, the Heads UP research team developed a 21st birthday card program to help reduce the risky drinking often associated with these celebrations.

*Participants.* 81 students (28 males, 53 females) completed a post-21st birthday survey. Of these, 74 reported drinking during their 21st birthday and were included in the analyses.

*Methods.* During the 2005–2006 school year, the authors assigned students celebrating 21st birthdays to either receive an alcohol risk-reduction birthday card or to a no-card condition. The students completed a survey after their birthday.

*Results.* Students who received the card consumed fewer drinks and reached lower blood alcohol content (BAC) levels on their birthday than did students who did not receive it. Female students who received the card consumed 40% fewer drinks and reached nearly 50% lower BAC levels than women who did not receive it.

*Conclusion.* This program is easily replicated, inexpensive, and may be used by universities to reduce risk related to celebratory alcohol consumption.

From *Journal of American College Health*, 57, 659–663. Copyright © 2009 by Heldref Publications. Reprinted with permission.

College students frequently report that the celebration of special events is one of the most important reasons to drink alcohol.[1,2] These celebratory occasions, such as sporting events, holidays, graduation, home-coming, spring break, and birthdays often involve hazardous and sometimes fatal levels of alcohol consumption. In particular, the 21st birthday marks a transition to the legal age for drinking, and, as such, alcohol consumption is often considered a rite of passage during these events.[3] In a study investigating the prevalence of acute alcohol intoxication during 21st birthday celebrations, Neighbors and colleagues[4] found that 90.3% of students reported drinking alcohol, and 72.3% engaged in drinking behaviors that could be categorized as heavy episodic drinking (4 [for females] and 5 [for males] or more drinks in a 2-hour period). More alarming, 1 in 4 students had achieved blood alcohol content

(BAC) levels that frequently result in blackouts, coma, and death.

As a result, some colleges have initiated risk-prevention efforts, such as 21st birthday card campaigns in which cards containing alcohol information, social norms, or responsible drinking messages are mailed to students with upcoming birthdays. The most widely used of these campaigns is the Be Responsible About Drinking (BRAD) card, which was inspired by the death of Michigan State student Bradley McCue, who died of alcohol poisoning on his 21st birthday. The BRAD card tells Bradley's story as a cautionary tale that provides information on the symptoms of alcohol poisoning and offers a reminder to celebrate responsibly. Although more than 100 institutions have distributed BRAD cards, research on its effectiveness has shown mixed results.[1,5] Evaluation of other 21st birthday card campaigns has been hindered by methodological limitations, most notably a lack of adequate comparison groups.[5] As a consequence, student health administrators in search of effective and empirically tested 21st birthday card campaigns have been met with limited data. Therefore, the present investigation aims to develop and test the efficacy of a harm-reduction 21st birthday card campaign in order to reduce risky drinking. We hypothesized that students receiving a 21st birthday card will drink at more moderate levels than will those who do not receive the birthday card.

## Methods

The 21st birthday card program was inspired by a student resident advisor (RA) who came to Heads UP with an idea to create a 21st birthday card campaign for fellow students. Heads UP serves as the alcohol prevention and evaluation arm of the university and works campuswide to raise alcohol awareness and prevent risky drinking.[6] The team administers and participates in various campus activities and programs during the academic year, such as social-norms feedback sessions in residence halls, dormitory poster campaigns, and clinical interventions mandated by Judicial Affairs. In addition, Heads UP continues to have a positive pres-

ence on campus by attending campus-community
60 events as well as maintaining an easily approachable
team and readily available resources.

The RA proposed ideas for a 21st birthday card that
would contain an effective harm-reduction message
that would be well received by the students. In an at-
65 tempt to prevent immediate dismissal by students who
planned on drinking during their celebration, the card
did not promote 100% abstinence, but rather it encouraged moderate consumption for those who chose to
drink. Consistent with the Heads UP program's ideals
70 and objectives, it also provided helpful tips and protective behavioral strategies in hopes of reducing risky
drinking during this event.

To evaluate the efficacy of the birthday card program, we piloted this program with students of 4 resi-
75 dence halls on campus. The local Institutional Review
Board (IRB) approved this pilot study, and students in
2 residence halls were randomly chosen to receive the
birthday card ($n = 88$), with students in the other 2
serving as a comparison group that did not receive
80 birthday cards ($n = 104$). One week following their
birthday, all students received an e-mail requesting
their participation in a survey regarding their 21st
birthday celebration. First, the students received an
IRB-approved informed consent form, which they elec-
85 tronically signed. Next, the survey assessed drinking
behaviors during their 21st birthday celebration, such
as the decision to drink or not, the quantity of alcohol
consumed, and the amount of time spent drinking. To
ensure that each student fully understood the opera-
90 tional definition of a standard drink, the survey included a chart detailing the amount in ounces of beer,
wine, and liquor that equal a standard drink. It also
included examples of how many standard drinks compose certain cocktails, such as margaritas or Long Is-
95 land iced teas.

The front of the birthday card read, "Happy 21st
Birthday! Make it a night to remember." The inside of
the card contained 8 location-specific ideas for celebrating a 21st birthday that were unrelated to drinking.
100 Examples included seeing a movie at a nearby theater
or attending a local team's soccer game. The inside of
the card also listed "10 Tips to Party Smart" for those
students who planned to consume alcohol. Examples
included "sip your drink," "skip a drink now and then,"
105 and "accept a drink only when you really want one."
The back of the card contained a campus-specific
drinking norm, "81% of LMU students drink 5 or less
drinks during a typical night of drinking/partying.
Where do you fit in?" (See the Appendix.) As social
110 norms have been found to be among the strongest predictors of alcohol consumption by college students,[7]
social normative information was included in an attempt to reduce misperceptions the students might have
held about college drinking and partying and, thus, to
115 decrease consumption. The card was embossed by
Heads UP and Student Housing. Further, each card

included a personal note from the individual's respective RA.

## Results

Of the 192 students included in the study, 81 (42%;
120 28 males, 53 females) completed the survey. Further,
39 of the 88 (44%) students who received a card (intervention condition) completed the survey, whereas 42 of
the 104 (41%) students who did not receive a card
(control condition) completed the survey. Seventy-four
125 of the respondents (23 males, 51 females) reported
consuming alcohol during their 21st birthday celebration and were included in the subsequent drinking
analyses (see Figure 1).

Average # of Drinks on 21st Birthday

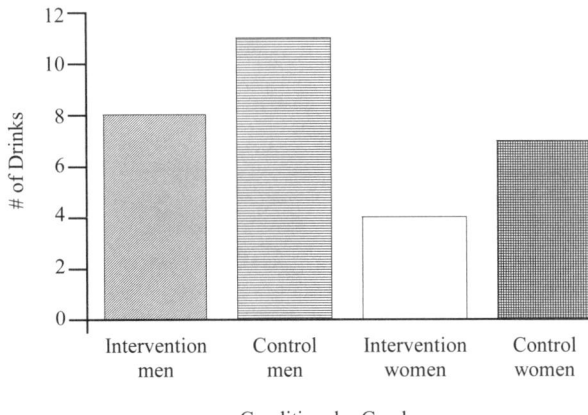

Average BAC on 21st Birthday

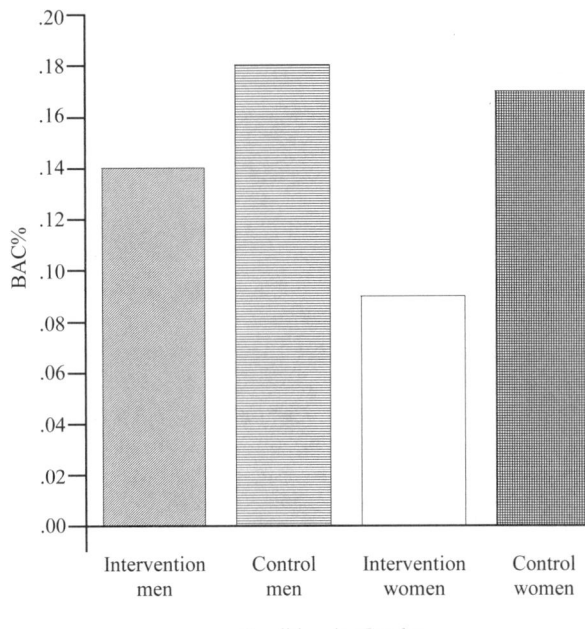

*Figure 1.* Average number of drinks and percentage of blood
alcohol content (BAC) on 21st birthday celebrations.

Overall, there were significant differences between those students who received the card and those who did not regarding number of drinks consumed, $F(1,72) = 4.37$, $p < .05$, and BAC level, $F(1,72) = 6.53$, $p < .05$. Specifically, male students who received the birthday card reported consuming 23.4% fewer drinks (8.58 drinks vs. 11.19 drinks) and had a 22.1% lower BAC level (.14% vs. .18%) than did male students who did not receive the card. Females receiving the card experienced even greater reductions, consuming 40.2% fewer drinks (4.07 drinks vs. 6.80 drinks) and reaching a 46.4% lower BAC level (.08% vs. .17%) than did females who did not receive the card. It is interesting that 6 of the 7 students who chose not to drink on their 21st birthday were in the intervention group. Although this sample is small, it suggests that the intervention may have had some effect on students' decision to drink, and it may warrant further implementation and evaluation.

## Comment

Our 21st birthday card program combined several components to create an innovative and effective card that differentiated it from other interventions. It incorporated a social norms statistic, provided ideas for birthday activities unrelated to alcohol, and suggested protective behavioral strategies for drinking moderately in the event that the student decided to drink.

Overall, students who received the card drank less and reached lower BAC levels than did those who did not receive the card. In all, 61% of students who did not receive the card achieved BACs above .15%, which is often associated with nausea/vomiting, impaired judgment, and blackouts. Furthermore, of those who exceeded that BAC, 23% exceeded a .25% BAC level, at which point severe sensory and motor impairment, comas, and even death by respiratory arrest can occur. In contrast, among students receiving the card, only 27% overall exceeded .15%, and only 8% drank to a BAC of .25%. This 21st birthday card not only reduced alcohol consumption, it most likely contributed to reductions in the alcohol-related negative effects associated with extreme BAC levels. Given that innate physiological differences place women at a greater risk for alcohol-related negative consequences at equivalent BAC levels than men, our finding of greater effectiveness in women is noteworthy. Although it is possible that this result was due to the relatively low number of males who took the follow-up survey, the finding is consistent with Grizzell[8] and suggests the need for future investigations to test whether these birthday card interventions are more effective for women than for men and, if this is the case, to devise ways of engaging men more effectively.

Our findings are tempered by certain limitations. First, although the response rate was consistent with response rates of other online surveys, many students who received cards or were in the control condition did not complete the post-21st birthday survey. The results might be more believable if more students had completed the survey. Additionally, the survey relied on student self-report, which might be prone to underreporting, especially with regard to major celebrations. However, previous research has shown that self-reports[9] are reliable and valid indicators of current alcohol use in college students. Future research might explore whether students can accurately report on their drinking behavior during major celebrations. Further, the card was created collaboratively by an RA and Heads UP staff without student input and included both harm-reduction and social norms information. Future birthday card programs may wish to utilize student focus groups to come up with messaging that is even more salient to students than the present card.

In conclusion, the overall efficacy of the card was most likely strengthened by the fundamental interrelationship among Heads UP, Resident Life, and the student population. Heads UP helped to craft an effective harm-reduction message. The personal note from each student's RA may also have helped to make the students more receptive to the message. The card is also cost-effective; each card costs less than $.50 to create and can be produced in little time. Efficiency may be further improved through the use of electronically delivered e-cards, which could be created quickly, require no postage, and may reach more students than would traditional mail, although future research will need to investigate the efficacy of these cards. In the meantime, we encourage other universities to use this 21st birthday card program because it is easily replicated, inexpensive, requires little effort, and has demonstrated success at reducing alcohol consumption among college students during the high-risk event of 21st birthday celebrations.

## References

1. Hembroff L, Atkin C, Martell, D, McCue C, Greenamyer J T. Evaluation results of a 21st birthday card program targeting high-risk drinking. *J Am Coll Health*. 2007;56:325–333.
2. Institute for Public Policy and Social Research. Executive summary: College students and "celebration drinking." http://www.ippsr.msu.edu/osr/celebrationdrinkingstudy.htm. Published April 11, 2002. Accessed March 17, 2009.
3. Neighbors C, Walters S, Lee C, et al. Event-specific prevention: Addressing college student drinking during known windows of risk. *Addict Behav*. 2007;32:2667–2680.
4. Neighbors C, Spieker CJ, Oster-Aaland L, Lewis M, Bergstrom RL. Celebration intoxication: An evaluation of 21st birthday alcohol consumption. *J Am Coll Health*. 2005;54:76–80.
5. Smith BH, Bogle K, Talbott L, Gant R, Castillo H. A randomized study of four cards designed to prevent problems during college students' 21st birthday celebrations. *J Stud Alcohol*. 2006;67:607–615.
6. LaBrie JW, Pedersen ER, Lamb TF, Bove L. Heads UP! A nested intervention with freshmen male college students and the broader campus community to promote responsible drinking. *J Am Coll Health*. 2006;54:301–304.
7. Neighbors C, Lee CM, Lewis MA, Fossos N, Larimer ME. Are social norms the best predictor of outcomes among heavy-drinking college students? *J Stud Alcohol Drugs*. 2007;68:556–565.
8. Grizzell J, California State University, Pomona. Cal State Pomona 21st birthday card: Drinking social norms and alcohol use safety tips. http://www.csupomona.edu/~jvgrizzell21/card.htm. Published April 2000. Accessed March 17, 2009.

9. O'Hare T. Measuring alcohol consumption: A comparison of the retrospective diary and the quantity-frequency methods in a college drinking
survey. *J Stud Alcohol.* 1991;52:500–502.

**APPENDIX**
**The Birthday Card**

Outside:

81% OF LMU STUDENTS CONSUME FIVE OR LESS
DRINKS DURING A TYPICAL NIGHT OF
PARTYING/DRINKING…
WHERE DO YOU FIT IN?

FROM YOUR FRIENDS AT
STUDENT HOUSING (X82963) AND HEADS UP (X83701)

*(Appendix continues)*

**APPENDIX**
**(continued)**

Inside:

## THINK OF ALL THE WAYS
## YOU CAN CELEBRATE
## YOUR BIRTHDAY

GO TO A FANCY RESTAURANT FOR A GOOD MEAL AND A GLASS OF WINE
TAKE A ROAD TRIP SOMEWHERE YOU HAVE ALWAYS WANTED TO VISIT
HAVE FRIENDS OVER AND PLAY CAPTURE THE FLAG
GO DANCING AT BEACHES IN MANHATTAN BEACH
SEE A PLAY AT THE SKIRBALL THEATRE
GO BOWLING AT EL DORADO LANES
GO TO A GALAXY SOCCER GAME
SEE A MOVIE AT THE BRIDGE

IF YOU CHOOSE TO DRINK, **KEEP IT MODERATE!**

**10 TIPS TO PARTY SMART**

1. KNOW YOUR LIMIT
2. EAT FOOD WHILE YOU DRINK
3. SIP YOUR DRINK
4. NEVER ACCEPT A DRINK FROM SOMEONE YOU DON'T KNOW
5. USE ALCOHOL CAREFULLY WITH OTHER DRUGS
6. DON'T DRINK AND DRIVE — PLAN AHEAD FOR TRANSPORTATION
7. SKIP A DRINK NOW AND THEN
8. STAY WITH PEOPLE YOU KNOW AND TRUST
9. SPACE YOUR DRINKS
10. ACCEPT A DRINK ONLY WHEN YOU REALLY WANT ONE

**REMEMBER** JUST BECAUSE IT'S YOUR 21ST DOESN'T
MEAN YOU HAVE TO DRINK! YOU MAKE THE RULES FOR YOURSELF.

**Acknowledgment**: This research was funded by a Model Award
from the U.S. Department of Education (Grant Q184N050003) and
by Grant Ul8 AA015451-01 from the National Institute of Alcohol
Abuse and Alcoholism.

**About the authors**: *Joseph W. LaBrie, Savannah Migliuri,* and
*Jessica Cail* are with the Department of Psychology at Loyola Marymount University in Los Angeles, California.

**Address correspondence to**: Dr. Joseph LaBrie, Department of
Psychology, Loyola Marymount University, 1 LMU Drive, Los
Angeles, CA 90045. E-mail: jlabrie@lmu.edu

# Exercise for Article 12

## Factual Questions

1. Did the researchers have a hypothesis?

2. Did the participants sign a consent form?

3. Were the participants told the number of ounces in a standard drink?

4. Regarding number of drinks consumed, was there a significant difference between the two groups?

5. Six of the seven students who did not drink were in which group?

6. Do the researchers think that other universities should use their birthday card program?

## Questions for Discussion

7. What is your opinion of the method used to establish the program group and the comparison groups? (See lines 75–80.)

8. Is Figure 1 an important part of this report? Explain.

9. In your opinion, is the overall response rate (42%) adequate? Explain. (See lines 119–120.)

10. What is your opinion of the validity of self-reports of drinking behavior in a study like this one? (See lines 187–194.)

## Quality Ratings

Directions: Indicate your level of agreement with each of the following statements by circling a number from 5 for strongly agree (SA) to 1 for strongly disagree (SD). If you believe an item is not applicable to this research article, leave it blank. Be prepared to explain your ratings. When responding to criteria A and B, keep in mind that brief titles and abstracts are conventional in published research.

A. The title of the article is appropriate.

SA   5   4   3   2   1   SD

B. The abstract provides an effective overview of the research article.

SA   5   4   3   2   1   SD

C. The introduction establishes the importance of the study.

SA   5   4   3   2   1   SD

D. The literature review establishes the context for the study.

SA   5   4   3   2   1   SD

E. The research purpose, question, or hypothesis is clearly stated.

SA   5   4   3   2   1   SD

F. The method of sampling is sound.

SA   5   4   3   2   1   SD

G. Relevant demographics (for example, age, gender, and ethnicity) are described.

SA   5   4   3   2   1   SD

H. Measurement procedures are adequate.

SA   5   4   3   2   1   SD

I. All procedures have been described in sufficient detail to permit a replication of the study.

SA   5   4   3   2   1   SD

J. The participants have been adequately protected from potential harm.

SA   5   4   3   2   1   SD

K. The results are clearly described.

SA   5   4   3   2   1   SD

L. The discussion/conclusion is appropriate.

SA   5   4   3   2   1   SD

M. Despite any flaws, the report is worthy of publication.

SA   5   4   3   2   1   SD

# Article 13

# Foot-in-the-Door Technique Using a Courtship Request: A Field Experiment

NICOLAS GUÉGUEN
Université de Bretagne-Sud

ALEXANDRE PASCUAL
Université de Bordeaux 2

MARIE MARCHAND
Université de Provence

MARCEL LOUREL
Université de Rouen

ABSTRACT. "Foot-in-the-door" is a well-known compliance technique that increases compliance to a request. Many investigations with this paradigm have generally used prosocial requests to test its effect. Evaluation of the effect of foot-in-the-door was carried out with a courtship request. Three hundred and sixty young women were solicited in the street to accept having a drink with a young male confederate. In the foot-in-the-door condition, before being solicited to have a drink, the young woman was asked to give directions to the confederate or to give him a light for his cigarette. Analysis showed foot-in-the-door was associated with greater compliance to the second request. The theoretical implication of such results with this nonprosocial request are discussed.

From *Psychological Reports*, *103*, 529–534. Copyright © 2008 by Psychological Reports. Reprinted with permission.

For many years now, social psychologists have studied several procedures used for gaining compliance to various requests (Pratkanis, 2007); however, the effects of such procedures on courtship requests were
5 rarely examined by scientists.

In 1966, Freedman and Fraser convinced 43% of a group of housewives to allow a team of five or six investigators to stay at their homes for 2 hr. to make an inventory of all products used in cleaning and cooking.
10 Three days before this visit, the women were asked to fill out a questionnaire of eight questions concerning their consumption. Without this preliminary request, only 22% of the persons accepted the visit of the investigators. This technique of presenting the subject with a
15 small request before submitting the request sought has been called the "foot-in-the-door" technique. Various meta-analyses of numerous studies on this technique have shown its effects on compliance (Beaman, Cole, Preston, Klentz, & Mehrkens-Steblay, 1983; Dillard,
20 Hunter, & Burgoon, 1984; Fern, Monroe, & Avila, 1986; Burger, 1999; Pascual & Guéguen, 2005).

It is well-known that this technique is efficient for influencing people to respond positively to various requests. Most requests have been prosocial (e.g., giv-
25 ing someone a dime) (Harris, 1972; Guéguen &

Fischer-Lokou, 1999), answering a questionnaire (Hornik, Zaig, & Shadmon, 1991), and persuading students to take a card designating them as an organ donor (Carducci, Deuser, Bauer, Large, & Ramaekers, 1989).
30 However, the technique's efficiency is not limited to prosocial requests, as Katzev and Johnson (1983) showed in having people decrease their energy consumption at home. Dolin and Booth-Butterfield (1995) found that adult women who were assigned to a foot-
35 in-the-door treatment during a health fair at a shopping mall agreed more favorably to a request to schedule a gynecological examination. Goldman, Creason, and McCall (1981) reported its efficiency in convincing people to call individuals selected from the telephone
40 directory and ask them to take a survey for the profit of a private organization. Guéguen and Jacob (in press) found that foot-in-the-door in a selling context (a footwear store) was associated with greater compliance to the sale suggestion addressed by a seller. Thus, these
45 studies show the foot-in-the-door technique can be applied to requests other than prosocial ones.

In the literature, the foot-in-the-door effect is theoretically explained by self-perception theory (Freedman & Fraser, 1966), in which the preliminary
50 request was assumed to make participants feel they are helping other people or caring for others. Once such a perception is activated, it favors compliance to a second request. The explanation based on self-perception is perhaps readily explained by the prosocial nature of
55 many tested requests.

Yet a few studies show that a positive effect of foot-in-the-door can be obtained with other requests, so use of the self-perception theory could be questioned and other explanations required. The present study was
60 done to explore the range of influence of the foot-in-the-door procedure and its common explanation. The current experiment tested the effect of the foot-in-the-door technique on courtship behavior.

## Method

The participants were 378 young females, ap-
65 proximately 18 to 22 years of age, who were walking

alone in several shopping areas of a medium-sized city (population greater than 60,000) in a very attractive spot of the West Atlantic Coast in France. Participants were assigned to the three experimental conditions using a random distribution. Data of 18 participants in both foot-in-the-door conditions were excluded from analysis because they did not agree with the first initial request. Three young men ages 19 to 21 years acted as confederates. They were neatly dressed in jeans and sneakers like most young people of their age.

In the first experimental condition, a confederate approached a young woman with a cigarette in one hand. In France, the rate of female smokers ages 18 to 24 years is about 38% (Mermet, 2007), and in the town in which the experiment was carried out, 1 young woman out of 11 had a cigarette in hand when walking in the street. Given such a rate, it was easy to obtain sufficient sample size. The confederate approached the target with a smile and said, "Hello, I'm sorry to bother you, but would you have a light for my cigarette?" If the young woman responded, "Yes," then the confederate waited until the young woman gave him a light and then said, "Thank you very much. Are you busy now? If not, we could have a drink together, if you have some time." If the young woman responded that she had no light (6 participants), the confederate said, "It doesn't matter," and then solicited the young woman to have a drink in the same way. In the second experimental condition, a confederate approached a young woman and said, "Hello, I'm sorry to bother you, but I am looking for the Place de Libération." If the young woman responded that she knew where the place was, the confederate waited until she gave him directions and then said, "Thank you very much. Are you busy..." and presented the same request. If the young woman responded that she did not know this place (12 participants), the confederate said, "It doesn't matter," and then addressed his request. In the control condition, a confederate directly addressed the second request to a young woman in this way, "Hello, I'm sorry to bother you, but I was wondering if you were busy now. If not, we could have a drink together if you have some time." In these three experimental conditions, the three confederates were instructed to act in the same way and had practice sessions before the experiment began.

In this experiment, compliance with the proposition to have a drink with the confederate was the only behavioral dependent variable measured. However, confederates were also instructed to take down the possible justification of the participants' refusals. In most cases, the response was only "no" or "no thanks," but some of the women justified their refusal because they were in a committed relationship ("No thanks, I am married," "I am engaged," "I am with someone at the moment") or because they had no time ("I have no time," "I have something else to do," "I am in a hurry"). If the participant accepted the confederate's

solicitation, the confederate debriefed her. She was told that she had participated in an experiment on social behavior in a courtship context. A preprinted information form was then given to the participant who was asked to provide information for the experiment (name, age, address, phone number). Information concerning the role of the experimenter and our laboratory Web site was indicated on the form. The encounter ended with the confederate saying, "Thanks for your participation, and I'm sorry that I've taken up your time. Perhaps we could meet another time. Bye!" If the participant refused, the confederate was instructed to say, "Too bad. It's not my day. Have a nice afternoon!" and to wait for another participant. Each confederate tested 42 participants in the three experimental conditions.

## Results

Differences in frequency of response among the three confederates were not significant; hence, data were collapsed across confederates. In the two foot-in-the-door conditions, the data of participants who did not perform the initial request were excluded from analysis (6 in the first request for a light and 12 in the first request for directions). The numbers of young women who accepted the request of the confederate was 4/120 (3.3%) in the control condition, 18/120 (15.0%) in the first foot-in-the-door condition (request for a light), and 19/120 (15.8%) in the second condition (request for directions). The difference among conditions was statistically significant [$\chi_2^2$ ($N = 360$) = 11.62, $p < .005$; $r = .18$]. Additional comparisons showed that the control condition was significantly different from the first foot-in-the-door condition [$\chi_1^2$ ($N = 240$) = 9.81, $p < .002$; $r = .20$] and the second foot-in-the-door condition [$\chi_1^2$ ($N = 240$) = 10.82, $p < .001$; $r = .21$]. Further, these two conditions were not significantly different [$\chi_1^2$ ($N = 240$) = 0.03, ns; $r = .01$].

Additional analyses were performed using information given by some participants who refused the confederate's request. Indeed, some of the young women who refused the courtship request justified their refusal by telling the confederate that they were married, engaged, or with a man. The rate of young women who justified their refusal in this way was 31/116 (26.7%) in the control condition, 26/102 (25.5%) in the first experimental condition (request for a light) and 24/101 (23.8%) in the second one (request for directions), but the overall difference was not statistically significant [$\chi_2^2$ ($N = 319$) = 0.25, ns]; neither were differences between pairs.

In some other cases, the young women turned down the confederate's proposition by telling him that they did not have enough time. The rate of refusals using this justification was 22/116 (19.0%) in the control condition, 19/102 (18.6%) in the first experimental condition (request for a light) and 20/101 (19.8%) in the second one (request for directions). The overall

180 difference among conditions [$\chi_2^2$ ($N = 319$) = 0.05, ns] or between pairs was not statistically significant. Thus, the reasons addressed by some women to justify their refusal of the confederates' propositions remained the same in the three experimental conditions and sug-
185 gested the samples were similar.

### Discussion

In this experiment, the first request addressed to women by a male confederate predisposed them to accept a second request. Such results are congruent with previous studies that found that the foot-in-the-
190 door technique increased compliance to a request (Beaman et al, 1983; Dillard et al., 1984; Fern et al., 1986; Burger, 1999; Pascual & Guéguen, 2005). However, the present study extends the influence of the technique to another kind of request. In most previous
195 studies of this kind, compliance with prosocial requests was the dependent variable. In some studies, the efficiency of the procedure was not limited to prosocial requests (Goldman et al., 1981; Katzev & Johnson, 1983; Dolin & Booth-Butterfield, 1995; Guéguen &
200 Jacob, in press); however, in the present study, the paradigm used requests in a courtship relation for the first time.

The effect of foot-in-the-door has been explained theoretically using self-perception theory (Freedman &
205 Fraser, 1966): The preliminary request makes the participant feel that she is someone who helps other people or cares for others, which leads to compliance more favorable with a second request of help in a congruent manner. In the present experiment, in the foot-in-the-
210 door condition, the first request was prosocial, but the second request was clearly a courtship request and not congruent with the perception activated with the first request for help. In this experiment, then, the self-perception theory may perhaps not be appropriate.

215 Similarly, consistency is often cited in support of the foot-in-the-door effect (Baer, Goldman, & Juhnke, 1977; DeJong, 1981; Eisenberg, Cialdini, McCreath, & Shell, 1989). This notion posits that people tend to act in ways consistent with their beliefs and values. A par-
220 ticipant who perceives herself to be a nice, helpful person would be predisposed to comply with a request for a cigarette or directions, but this would not explain the greater likelihood of engaging in courtship behavior. Rather, present efficiency of the technique might be
225 accounted for by familiarity. Guéguen (2004) reported that someone introduced through a photograph and a little information (last name, first name, age...) was helped more favorably a few minutes later when the person dropped pamphlets on the floor. This effect of
230 familiarization created by the first request was proposed by Freedman and Fraser (1966), who found that different amounts of familiarization provided during a first request in three foot-in-the-door conditions were associated with differing compliance with a second
235 request. Baer et al. (1977) reported mere interpersonal

contact between two strangers facilitated prosocial behavior. In their experiment, relative to the control condition, compliance with a request was the same in foot-in-the-door paradigm as in a condition in which inter-
240 personal contact was made.

Of course, the explanation in terms of familiarity is clearly speculative given that the present comparisons only focus on participants' behavior. Further studies exploring the perception of familiarity of the solici-
245 tor by the participant are now necessary when the foot-in-the-door technique is employed with a courtship solicitation.

### References

Baer, R., Goldman, M., & Juhnke, R. (1977). Factors affecting prosocial behavior. *Journal of Social Psychology, 103,* 209–216.

Beaman, A. L., Cole, M. C., Preston, M., Klentz, B., & Mehrkens-Steblay, N. (1983). Fifteen years of foot-in-the-door research: A meta-analysis. *Personality and Social Psychology Bulletin, 9,* 181–196.

Burger, J. M. (1999). The foot-in-the-door compliance procedure: A multiple-process analysis and review. *Personality and Social Psychology Review, 3,* 303–325.

Carducci, B. J., Deuser, P. S., Bauer, A., Large, M., & Ramaekers, M. (1989). An application of the foot-in-the-door to organ donation. *Journal of Business and Psychology, 4,* 245–249.

DeJong, W. (1981). Consensus information and the foot-in-the-door effect. *Personality and Social Psychology Bulletin, 7,* 423–430.

Dillard, J. P., Hunter, J. E., & Burgoon, M. (1984). Sequential-request persuasive strategies: Meta-analysis of foot-in-the-door and door-in-the-face. *Human Communication Research, 10,* 461–488.

Dolin, D. J., & Booth-Butterfield, S. (1995). Foot-in-the-door and cancer prevention. *Health Communication, 7,* 55–66.

Eisenberg, N., Cialdini, R. B., McCreath, H., & Shell, R. (1989). Consistency-based compliance in children: When and why do consistency procedures have immediate effects? *International Journal of Behavioural Development, 12,* 351–367.

Fern, E. F., Monroe, K. B., & Avila, R. A. (1986). Effectiveness of multiple request strategies: A synthesis of research results. *Journal of Marketing Research, 23,* 144–152.

Freedman, J. L., & Fraser, S. C. (1966). Compliance without pressure: The foot-in-the-door technique. *Journal of Personality and Social Psychology, 4,* 195–202.

Goldman, M., Creason, C. R., & McCall, C. G. (1981). Compliance employing a two-feet-in-the-door procedure. *Journal of Social Psychology, 114,* 259–265.

Guéguen, N. (2004). *Psychologie de la manipulation et de la soumission.* Paris: Dunod.

Guéguen, N., & Fischer-Lokou, J. (1999) Sequential request strategy: Effect on donor generosity. *Journal of Social Psychology, 139,* 669–671.

Guéguen, N., & Jacob, C. (in press). La chaussure-leurre: Une application de la technique du leurre en situation commerciale. *Décision et Gestion.*

Harris, M. B. (1972). The effects of performing one altruistic act on the likelihood of performing another. *Journal of Social Psychology, 88,* 65–73.

Hornik, J., Zaig, T., & Shadmon, D. (1991). Reducing refusals in telephone surveys on sensitive topics. *Journal of Advertising Research, 31,* 49–56.

Katzev, R. D., & Johnson, T. R. (1983). A social-psychological analysis of residential electricity consumption: The impact of minimal justification techniques. *Journal of Economic Psychology, 3,* 267–284.

Mermet, G. (2007). *Francoscopie 2007.* Paris: Larousse.

Pascual, A., & Guéguen, N. (2005). Foot-in-the-door and door-in-the-face: A comparative meta-analytic study. *Psychological Reports, 96,* 122–128.

Pratkanis, A. R. (2007). *The science of social influence.* New York: Psychological Press.

**Address correspondence to:** Nicolas Guéguen, Université de Bretagne-Sud, UFR LSHS, 4 rue Jean Zay, BP 92116, 56321 Lorient Cedex, France. E-mail: nicolas.gueguen@univ-ubs.fr

# Exercise for Article 13

## Factual Questions

1. In the first experimental condition, each young woman had what in her hand?

2. What was the dependent variable in this experiment?

3. Data for how many women were excluded from the analysis because they did not agree with the first initial request?

4. What percentage of the women in the control condition accepted the request to have a drink?

5. Were the two experimental conditions significantly different?

6. In the control condition, what percentage of the women gave lack of time as the justification for refusal?

## Questions for Discussion

7. Is it important to know that random assignment was used? Explain. (See lines 68–70.)

8. In your opinion, are the three confederates described in sufficient detail? Explain. (See lines 73–75.)

9. Would it be interesting to know more about the practice sessions? Explain. (See lines 108–111.)

10. The researchers refer to their study as an *experiment*. Do you agree with them? Would it be equally accurate to refer to it as a *survey*? Explain.

11. Do the results of this study surprise you? Explain.

12. If you were to conduct a study on the same general topic, what changes, if any, would you make?

## Quality Ratings

Directions: Indicate your level of agreement with each of the following statements by circling a number from 5 for strongly agree (SA) to 1 for strongly disagree (SD). If you believe an item is not applicable to this research article, leave it blank. Be prepared to explain your ratings. When responding to criteria A and B, keep in mind that brief titles and abstracts are conventional in published research.

A. The title of the article is appropriate.

SA    5    4    3    2    1    SD

B. The abstract provides an effective overview of the research article.

SA    5    4    3    2    1    SD

C. The introduction establishes the importance of the study.

SA    5    4    3    2    1    SD

D. The literature review establishes the context for the study.

SA    5    4    3    2    1    SD

E. The research purpose, question, or hypothesis is clearly stated.

SA    5    4    3    2    1    SD

F. The method of sampling is sound.

SA    5    4    3    2    1    SD

G. Relevant demographics (for example, age, gender, and ethnicity) are described.

SA    5    4    3    2    1    SD

H. Measurement procedures are adequate.

SA    5    4    3    2    1    SD

I. All procedures have been described in sufficient detail to permit a replication of the study.

SA    5    4    3    2    1    SD

J. The participants have been adequately protected from potential harm.

SA    5    4    3    2    1    SD

K. The results are clearly described.

SA    5    4    3    2    1    SD

L. The discussion/conclusion is appropriate.

SA    5    4    3    2    1    SD

M. Despite any flaws, the report is worthy of publication.

SA    5    4    3    2    1    SD

# Article 14

# Counting Bones: Environmental Cues
# That Decrease Food Intake

BRIAN WANSINK
Cornell University

COLLIN R. PAYNE
Cornell University

ABSTRACT. At an all-you-can eat buffet in a sports bar, it was tested whether people would eat less if they knew how much they had already eaten. Fifty-two graduate students were seated at 21 tables randomly assigned to be bussed (leftover wings removed) or unbussed (wings left on table). The 31 students at the bussed tables ate more than those at the unbussed tables (7 wings vs. 5.5 wings), with the effect being stronger for men than women. In distracting eating environments, environmental cues may provide an effective means of reducing consumption. Implications for controlling alcohol intake were also noted.

From *Perceptual and Motor Skills*, *104*, 273–276. Copyright © 2007 by Perceptual and Motor Skills. Reprinted with permission.

While a wide range of environmental cues have been identified as contributing to overeating (Wansink, 2004), less attention has been given to the role of environmental cues that contribute to healthful eating. One

5  environmental cue that may lead to healthful eating entails providing evidence of how much food (or of a beverage) has been consumed. For the most part, after food is eaten, there is no environmental cue—no evidence—of how much was consumed. This could be a

10  reason why it is widely reported that people are poor at estimating how much food they have consumed (Polivy, Herman, Hackett, & Kuleshnyk, 1986). Such inaccuracies of estimation could also be further magnified in distracting eating environments, such as when

15  eating with others or when watching television. In combination, the lack of evidence of food eaten and eating in distracting environments may contribute to mindless eating, which has been suggested to account for much of the variance in weight gain (Wansink,

20  2006).

Eating in distracting eating environments may lead people to over-rely on environmental cues to know when to stop eating (Wansink, Painter, & North, 2005). If this is the case, providing an appropriate environ-

25  mental cue could help one monitor and modify intake better. Preliminary evidence for this comes from reports of alcohol consumption. Wait staff who are concerned about customers over-imbibing have been encouraged to leave bottles on the table (environmental

30  cue) to make people more aware of how much they

have drunk (Wansink, Cordua, Blair, Payne, & Geiger, 2006). To examine this idea within the context of food consumption, it was necessary to find a food that could leave a visual reminder after it was consumed (such as

35  bones from meat, seeds or pits from fruit, or wrappers from candy). In addition, it was necessary to find a distracting, low-inhibition environment in which this food was consumed.

## Method

Fifty-two graduate students (17 men, 35 women

40  whose mean age was 24.1 yr.) were invited to a Super Bowl party at a public sports bar in Urbana, Illinois. Super Bowl parties have been successfully used in past research (Wansink & Cheney, 2005) because eating and snacking are commonplace and because such par-

45  ties increase the possibilities of distraction while eating.

A separate dining room was used so regular patrons of the sports bar were not disturbed. Big screen televisions were provided for viewing the football game, and

50  during the party, chicken wings and soft drinks were furnished free-of-charge. At the beginning of the party, tables were randomly assigned to conditions wherein either people's plates would be regularly bussed or to a condition where people's plates would not be bussed.

55  The students were seated at 21 different tables, and they were encouraged to help themselves to three different types of chicken wings centrally available to them in steam trays.

In the bussed condition (11 tables and 31 people),

60  the residual bones from the chicken wings were removed continuously, and participants were encouraged to serve themselves additional wings. The bones were coded by the table, seating position, and sex of the participant, and they were then unobtrusively weighed. In

65  the unbussed condition, bones were allowed to pile up on each plate, and participants were encouraged to serve themselves additional wings at the same frequency as those in the bussed condition. The bones were removed and recorded at half-time after which no

70  more chicken wings were served to any participants. Following the game (approximately 80 minutes later), people were individually asked to report how many

Table 1
*Salience of Chicken Wing Bones on Table*

| Measure | High intake salience unbussed table ($n = 21$) | | Low intake salience bussed table ($n = 31$) | | *df* | *t* | Cohen's *d* |
|---|---|---|---|---|---|---|---|
| | *M* | *SD* | *M* | *SD* | | | |
| Weight of chicken eaten, gm | | | | | | | |
| Total | 192.0 | 85.1 | 244.2 | 82.2 | 50 | 2.2* | .62 |
| Men | 163.3 | 74.0 | 264.8 | 92.4 | 15 | 2.4* | 1.21 |
| Women | 207.3 | 89.0 | 234.3 | 77.3 | 33 | 1.0 | .32 |
| No. of wing pieces eaten | | | | | | | |
| Total | 5.5 | 2.4 | 7.0 | 2.3 | 50 | 2.2* | .64 |
| Men | 4.7 | 1.1 | 7.6 | 1.3 | 15 | 2.4* | 2.40 |
| Women | 5.9 | 1.3 | 6.7 | 2.2 | 33 | 1.0 | .44 |

*$p < .05$.

wing pieces they believed they had eaten. Their estimates were compared with the actual amount they had
75   eaten.

### Results

As expected, people whose leftover chicken wing
bones were not bussed from their respective tables consumed significantly less than those whose chicken
wing bones were bussed (cleared away). As Table 1
80   indicates, those eating from an unbussed table consumed an average of 5.5 wing pieces and those consuming from the bussed table consumed 7.0 pieces
[$t_{pieces}$ (50) = 2.2, $p$ = .02; Cohen's $d$ = .64]. As a percentage difference, those eating from a bussed table
85   consumed 27.3% more pieces than those eating from
an unbussed table.

The influence of this environmental cue was
stronger for the men [$t_{pieces}$ (15) = 2.4, $p$ = .01; Cohen's
$d$ = 2.4] than for the women [$t_{pieces}$ (33) = 1.0, $p$ = .17;
90   Cohen's $d$ = .44]. This is consistent with prior work in
a Super Bowl environment, which showed that women
were less responsive to environmental cues in public
areas (Wansink & Cheney, 2005). While this suggests
higher self-monitoring (Wansink & Kim, 2005),
95   women were generally no more accurate than men
(Wansink, van Ittersum, & Painter, 2006). This might
be explained, instead, by a tendency toward impression
management.

### Discussion

These results suggest that people restrict their con-
100   sumption when an environmental cue (evidence of food
consumed) signaled how much food was eaten. This is
consistent with previous research that suggests people
will report feeling sated not only when they are physio-
logically full, but when they *believe* they are full
105   (Rolls, Bell, & Waugh, 2000). As an environmental
cue, leftover chicken wing bones provided evidence of
how much was eaten. As a consequence, knowing how
much they had eaten might have helped people better
calibrate how many more they cared to eat.

110   There are other possible reasons why such a decrease in consumption might have occurred in this

study. Having the bones in the middle of the table
might have suppressed some people's appetites, leading them to eat less. Or, embarrassment over showing
115   others how much they had eaten might also have
slowed consumption.

Regardless of the explanation, these results show
that environmental cues of how much has been eaten
effectively leads to reduced intake in a distracting so-
120   cial situation such as this. In situations where "counting
bones" is not possible, other proxy environmental cues
might be used to keep track of how much has been
consumed. These might include the empty wrappers of
Halloween candies, the pits or core of fruit, or the bot-
125   tle caps of a beverage.

The use of environmental cues to help curb the
overconsumption of alcohol has also been examined in
field tests. In the distracting environments of college or
fraternity parties, students could be encouraged (or
130   required) to take a fresh plastic glass for each new
drink and to stack these glasses within each other.
Similarly, at a dinner party involving wine, providing
fresh glasses for refills while leaving empty glasses
sitting on the table was an effective curb. Another ver-
135   sion would be to leave the empty bottles on the table.
Efforts to provide an environmental cue of intake can
help people better keep track of how much they have
consumed. In a naturally distracting environment, such
evidence seems an ally in the fight against mindless
140   eating or drinking.

### References

Polivy, J., Herman, C. P., Hackett, R., & Kuleshnyk, I. (1986). The effects of
self-attention and public attention on eating in restrained and unrestrained
subjects. *Journal of Personality and Social Psychology, 50*, 1203–1224.

Rolls, B. J., Bell, E. A., & Waugh, B. A. (2000). Increasing the volume of a
food by incorporating air affects satiety in men. *American Journal of Clinical Nutrition, 72*, 361–368.

Wansink, B. (2004). Environmental factors that increase the food intake and
consumption volume of unknowing consumers. *Annual Review of Nutrition,
24*, 455–479.

Wansink, B. (2006). *Mindless eating: Why we eat more than we think*. New
York: Bantam-Dell.

Wansink, B., & Cheney, M. M. (2005). Super bowls: Serving bowl size and
food consumption. *Journal of the American Medical Association, 293*,
1727–1728.

Wansink, B., Cordua, G., Blair, E., Payne, C., & Geiger, S. (2006). Do promotions for new wines contribute to or cannibalize beverage sales? *Cornell Hotel and Restaurant Administration Quarterly, 47,* 1–10.

Wansink, B., & Kim, J.-Y. (2005). Bad popcorn in big buckets: Portion size can influence intake as much as taste. *Journal of Nutrition Education and Behavior, 37,* 242–245.

Wansink, B., Painter, J. E., & North, J. (2005). Bottomless bowls: Why visual cues of portion size may influence intake. *Obesity Research, 13,* 93–100.

Wansink, B., van Ittersum, K., & Painter, J. E. (2006). Ice cream illusions: Bowl size, spoon size, and self-served portion sizes. *American Journal of Preventive Medicine, 31,* 240–243.

**Address correspondence to**: Brian Wansink, 110 Warren Hall, Cornell University, Ithaca, NY. E-mail: Wansink@Cornell.edu

# Exercise for Article 14

## Factual Questions

1. Were there more men *or* more women participants in this study?

2. Were students *or* tables randomly assigned to the two conditions in this study?

3. What was the average number of wing pieces eaten by men in the bussed condition?

4. Was the difference between the average number of wing pieces eaten by men in the two conditions statistically significant? If yes, at what probability level?

5. In terms of weight of chicken eaten, was the value of *d* higher for men *or* women?

## Questions for Discussion

6. This article is classified as an example of experimental research in the Contents of this book. Do you agree with this classification? Explain.

7. In your opinion, was the sample size adequate for a study of this type? Explain.

8. What is your understanding of the meaning of the statistic named Cohen's *d*? Does it help you understand the results of this study?

9. Do you agree with the authors that there might be more than one explanation for the results of this study? Explain. (See lines 110–116.)

10. Do you think the results of this study are sufficiently important to justify further research on this topic? Explain.

## Quality Ratings

Directions: Indicate your level of agreement with each of the following statements by circling a number from 5 for strongly agree (SA) to 1 for strongly disagree (SD). If you believe an item is not applicable to this research article, leave it blank. Be prepared to explain your ratings. When responding to criteria A and B, keep in mind that brief titles and abstracts are conventional in published research.

A. The title of the article is appropriate.

  SA  5  4  3  2  1  SD

B. The abstract provides an effective overview of the research article.

  SA  5  4  3  2  1  SD

C. The introduction establishes the importance of the study.

  SA  5  4  3  2  1  SD

D. The literature review establishes the context for the study.

  SA  5  4  3  2  1  SD

E. The research purpose, question, or hypothesis is clearly stated.

  SA  5  4  3  2  1  SD

F. The method of sampling is sound.

  SA  5  4  3  2  1  SD

G. Relevant demographics (for example, age, gender, and ethnicity) are described.

  SA  5  4  3  2  1  SD

H. Measurement procedures are adequate.

  SA  5  4  3  2  1  SD

I. All procedures have been described in sufficient detail to permit a replication of the study.

  SA  5  4  3  2  1  SD

J. The participants have been adequately protected from potential harm.

  SA  5  4  3  2  1  SD

K. The results are clearly described.

  SA  5  4  3  2  1  SD

L. The discussion/conclusion is appropriate.

  SA  5  4  3  2  1  SD

M. Despite any flaws, the report is worthy of publication.

  SA  5  4  3  2  1  SD

# Article 15

# The Effects of Wearing a Costume on Charitable Donations

RICHARD OSBALDISTON
Eastern Kentucky University

BRITTANY DE BOER
Eastern Kentucky University

ABSTRACT. Although research has shown a general trend that people dressed in neat or professional clothes elicit more helping behavior from other people than when dressed in casual or sloppy clothes, no research has examined the effects of wearing a costume on helping behavior. In this experiment, confederates dressed either in a Santa suit or in street clothes as they volunteered for the Salvation Army as bell-ringers in front of retail stores. The hypothesis that donations would be greater while wearing the Santa suit was not supported by the data; the Santa suit and the street clothes elicited equal amounts of donations.

From *Psychological Reports*, *108*, 167–168. Copyright © 2011 by Psychological Reports. Reprinted with permission.

Only a small amount of research has examined the effects of clothing on helping behavior. Bushman (1988) tested the effects of clothing on compliance to a small request and found that the confederates wearing a
5  uniform obtained the greatest compliance. Similarly, Levine, Bluni, and Hochman (1998) found that confederates dressed in "preppy" attire received more donations than those dressed in "messy" attire. However, no published research has tested the effects of wearing a
10  costume on participants' helping behaviors.

Building on these studies, the objective of this research was to test the effect of attire on charitable donations. To manipulate attire, research confederates were dressed in either a Santa costume or in regular
15  street clothes while they acted as bell-ringers for the Salvation Army. It was hypothesized that bell-ringers dressed in festive seasonal costume would collect more donations than when dressed in street clothing while controlling for effects due to time of day and location
20  of the retail stores.

Research assistants completed 40 two-hour shifts of bell-ringing for the Salvation Army in front of major retail stores during the last week of November and the first week of December. For each shift, the researchers
25  were randomly assigned to wear a Santa costume for one hour and regular street clothes for the other hour. The money collected during each hour was counted at a later time.

The mean amount of money collected each hour
30  while wearing the Santa suit was $27.41 (*SD* = $13.09)
and while wearing street clothes was $28.33 (*SD* = $15.09). A three-way ANOVA showed no main effect of attire ($F_{1,51} = 0.09$, ns) when controlling for time of day and location effects. None of the two-way or three-
35  way interactions was significant. Thus, the amount of donations did not differ if the research assistants were wearing the Santa costume or street clothes.

There are two explanations for this null result. First, the nature of impulsive donations may minimize the
40  influence of attire: Once a potential donor has recognized the opportunity to donate to the Salvation Army, including the sound of the bell and the sight of the familiar red kettle, then variables beyond that—like the attire of the bell-ringer—may not be important. Sec-
45  ond, the costume consisted only of a jacket and cap, and it may not have been visually different enough from street clothes. Although research has suggested that clothing influences other people's behaviors, this experiment failed to demonstrate that wearing a Santa
50  costume elicited greater charitable donations.

## References

Bushman, B. (1988). The effects of apparel on compliance: A field experiment with a female authority figure. *Personality and Social Psychology Bulletin*, *14*, 459–467. DOI:10.1177/0146167288143004.

Levine, L., Bluni, T., & Hochman, S. (1998). Attire and charitable behavior. *Psychological Reports*, *83*, 15–18. DOI:10.2466/PR0.83.5.15–18.

**Address correspondence to**: Richard Osbaldiston, Department of Psychology, Eastern Kentucky University, 127 Cammack Bldg., 521 Lancaster Ave., Richmond, KY 40475. E-mail: Richard.osbaldiston@eku.edu

# Exercise for Article 15

## Factual Questions

1. Has there been previous published research on this topic?

2. Do the researchers state a hypothesis?

3. What was the mean amount of money collected each hour while wearing the Santa suit?

4. Do the researchers believe that this experiment demonstrated that wearing a Santa suit elicited greater charitable donations?

## Questions for Discussion

5. This study is classified as an example of experimental research in the Contents of this book. Do you agree with the classification? Why? Why not?

6. What is your understanding of the meaning of the term *research confederates*? (See lines 13–16.)

7. Is it important to know that random assignment was used to determine whether the Santa suit or street clothes were worn? Explain. (See lines 24–26.)

8. What is your opinion on the two explanations for the null result? (See lines 38–47.)

9. This article is much shorter than the typical article in this book. In your opinion, does this article make a scientific contribution to social science despite its limited length? Explain.

## Quality Ratings

Directions: Indicate your level of agreement with each of the following statements by circling a number from 5 for strongly agree (SA) to 1 for strongly disagree (SD). If you believe an item is not applicable to this research article, leave it blank. Be prepared to explain your ratings. When responding to criteria A and B, keep in mind that brief titles and abstracts are conventional in published research.

A. The title of the article is appropriate.

SA   5   4   3   2   1   SD

B. The abstract provides an effective overview of the research article.

SA   5   4   3   2   1   SD

C. The introduction establishes the importance of the study.

SA   5   4   3   2   1   SD

D. The literature review establishes the context for the study.

SA   5   4   3   2   1   SD

E. The research purpose, question, or hypothesis is clearly stated.

SA   5   4   3   2   1   SD

F. The method of sampling is sound.

SA   5   4   3   2   1   SD

G. Relevant demographics (for example, age, gender, and ethnicity) are described.

SA   5   4   3   2   1   SD

H. Measurement procedures are adequate.

SA   5   4   3   2   1   SD

I. All procedures have been described in sufficient detail to permit a replication of the study.

SA   5   4   3   2   1   SD

J. The participants have been adequately protected from potential harm.

SA   5   4   3   2   1   SD

K. The results are clearly described.

SA   5   4   3   2   1   SD

L. The discussion/conclusion is appropriate.

SA   5   4   3   2   1   SD

M. Despite any flaws, the report is worthy of publication.

SA   5   4   3   2   1   SD

# Article 16

## Baby Think It Over: Evaluation of an Infant Simulation Intervention for Adolescent Pregnancy Prevention

DIANE de ANDA
University of California

ABSTRACT. In an intervention aimed at showing students the amount of responsibility involved in caring for an infant, 353 predominantly ninth-grade and Latino students carried the Baby Think It Over simulation doll in an intervention and completed matched pre- and posttest measures. Statistically significant gains were found on the total score and the impact of having a baby on academics, social life, and other family members; emotional risks; understanding and handling an infant's crying; and apprehension of the amount of responsibility involved in infant care. On a posttest-only measure, 108 participants reported statistically significant differences before and after carrying the doll with regard to the age at which they wished to have a child, their career and education plans, and the perceived interference of an infant with those education and career plans and their social life.

From *Health & Social Work, 31*, 26–35. Copyright © 2006 by the National Association of Social Workers. Reprinted with permission.

To alter adolescents' perception of the effort involved in caring for a baby and successfully increase their intent to avoid pregnancy in adolescence, students at a Los Angeles County high school participated in an
5 intervention using a life-size infant simulation doll known as "Baby Think It Over" (BTIO). The participating high school is in one of the 10 poorest cities in the nation (United Way of Greater Los Angeles, 1998–1999) and has been designated one of the adolescent
10 pregnancy "hot spots" in California because of its high rates of adolescent pregnancy (California Department of Health Services, 2001). The intervention places the tangible consequences of pregnancy before adolescent participants rather than offering only the abstract mes-
15 sages about pregnancy risks often presented in other programs.

### Adolescent Pregnancy in the United States

The steady rise in adolescent pregnancy rates became a significant concern among social service and health professionals, legislators, and the general public
20 during the 1970s and 1980s. The rates increased from 95.1 per 1,000 for 15- to 19-year-olds and 62.4 per 1,000 for 15- to 17-year-olds in 1972 to an all-time high of 117.1 (in 1990) and 74.4 (in 1989), respectively. Following a variety of intervention efforts, a
25 slow decline in the rates was noted in the first half of the 1990s, followed by a more rapid decrease to below the 1972 rate by 1997: 93.0 for 15- to 19-year-olds and 57.7 for 15- to 17-year-olds (Alan Guttmacher Institute, 1999a). This period included a 20% drop in the
30 pregnancy rate among African American adolescents and a 16% reduction among white adolescents. The pregnancy rate for Latina adolescents, however, increased between 1990 and 1992 and by 1996 decreased by only 6% (Alan Guttmacher Institute, 1999b), result-
35 ing in the birth rate of 149.2 per 1,000 for Latino adolescents—the highest among the total adolescent population (National Center for Health Statistics, 2000). Inasmuch as 54.1% of Latino high school youths report they have had sexual intercourse, and only slightly
40 more than half of those who are sexually active report using protection or birth control, Latino adolescents represent a population at high pregnancy risk (Kann et al., 2000).

As early as 1967, Elkind (1967) posited the impor-
45 tance of cognitive development in understanding adolescent risk-taking behavior, including pregnancy risks. Based on empirical research, the author and colleagues also proposed that adolescent pregnancy resulting from the risk taking of unprotected sexual intercourse might
50 be significantly related to cognitive development. Specifically, this behavior might reflect a lack of full attainment of formal operations and "the sense of invulnerability—described by Elkind as the 'personal fable'" (Becerra, Sabagh, & de Anda, 1986, p.136). For-
55 mal operations refer to the individual's ability to engage in abstract and hypothetical–deductive thinking (Piaget, 1972; Piaget & Inhelder, 1958) and, in this case, project the potential for pregnancy and ultimately becoming a parent. Adolescence typically includes a
60 period of transition from concrete to formal operations, at the beginning of which recognizing oneself as a sexual being is relatively easy because it is in the present and very concrete. By contrast, considering oneself

fertile can be a rather abstract concept for a young adolescent, and the consequences of fertility can be distant and hypothetical. Others have offered similar explanatory frameworks with regard to risk taking and adolescent pregnancy (e.g., Gordon, 1990; Kralewski & Stevens-Simon, 2000; Out & Lefreniere, 2001).

Interventions have been developed to accommodate these cognitive factors by creating simulated parenting experiences to provide a concrete learning situation that will make the hypothetical risks and consequences of adolescent pregnancy more real to the adolescent participants. Some past interventions have involved caregiving situations not directly analogous to caring for an infant, involving, for example, carrying a sack of flour or an egg. More recent interventions have used a simulation more directly analogous to caring for an infant—a computerized infant simulation doll that requires attention to its demands in the form of intermittent periods of crying.

## BTIO: The Intervention

BTIO is an intervention using a computerized infant simulation doll to offer adolescents experiences similar to those involved in attending to an infant. The doll is programmed to cry at random intervals and to stop crying only when the adolescent "attends" to the doll by inserting a key into a slot in the doll's back until it stops crying. An examination of participant logs indicated that most crying periods ranged between 10 and 15 minutes, and the frequency between eight and 12 times in 24 hours (including the early A. M. hours). The key is attached to a hospital-style bracelet, which is worn by the participant 24 hours a day to ensure that the adolescent provides the caregiving responsibilities during an entire two-and-a-half-day study period. The bracelets are designed so that an attempt to remove the bracelet is detectable. "Babysitting" of the doll by another student with a key or by the health class teacher who has extra keys is permitted only in certain situations—to take an examination, for example. The doll records data, including the amount of time the adolescent takes to "attend" to the infant (insert the key) and any form of "rough handling," such as dropping or hitting the doll. The term "rough handling" is used rather than abuse because there is no way to determine intentionality. Students whose records indicate neglect and rough handling receive a private counseling session with the health class teacher and have mandatory participation in a parenting class.

The purpose of carrying the infant simulation doll is to provide the students with an understanding of the amount of time and effort involved in the care of an infant and how an infant's needs might affect their daily lives and the lives of their family and significant others. This experience is augmented by presentations and group discussions led by staff from a local social services agency, covering such topics as the high incidence of adolescent pregnancy in the community, the factors that increase risk of adolescent pregnancy, and the costs of adolescent pregnancy and parenthood, with particular emphasis on the limitation of education and career opportunities and achievement. The health class teacher also offers a pregnancy prevention education program in preparation for carrying the doll and a debriefing discussion period after everyone in the class has carried the doll.

### BTIO in Previous Research

A relatively small amount of research has been conducted on the effectiveness of BTIO. A literature search produced eight published research articles evaluating BTIO interventions aimed at modifying attitudes, perceptions, and behaviors related to pregnancy risk. Six studies examined whether the program affected the adolescents' view of parenthood and child-rearing responsibilities: two found their objectives met in this respect, but four determined no change in perception. In a study conducted by Divine and Cobbs (2001) with 236 eighth-grade students in nine Catholic schools in a midwestern city, a greater number of BTIO students than control group students ($p < .05$) indicated a change on two of seven items: the amount of effort and cost involved in infant care, and the feeling that they have enough knowledge about what taking care of a baby entails. The majority (63% of the male adolescents, 75.5% of female adolescents) felt carrying the doll was effective in "helping me know the challenges of infant care" (p. 599). In Out and Lafreniere's (2001) sample of 114 Canadian students in the 11th grade, BTIO participants reported significantly ($p < .01$) more examples of child-rearing consequences and responsibilities than did control group students.

In contrast to these limited positive findings, Kralewski and Stevens-Simon's (2000) sample of 68 sixth-grade and 41 eighth-grade female Hispanic students from a middle school in a lower socioeconomic status Colorado neighborhood revealed no significant differences between anticipated difficulty and the actual difficulty in caring for the BTIO doll. In addition, BTIO did little to change the girls' desire to have a baby during adolescence, with 13 expressing this intent before BTIO and 16 after carrying the doll. Somers and Fahlman (2001) used a quasi-experimental design with a predominantly white, middle-class sample drawn from three high schools in the Midwest; MANCOVA performed on the posttest scores using the pretest scores as the covariate found no differences between the 151 students in the experiment group and 62 students in the control group on perceptions regarding childcare responsibilities. Somers, Gleason, Johnson, and Fahlman's (2001) study in two Midwest high schools found no change in participants' understanding of the responsibilities involved in child rearing. Strachan and Gorey (1997) did not find a change on their Parenting Attitude Scale measuring "realistic par-

175 enting expectations" (p. 175) in their sample of 48 African American and white youths ages 16 to 18.

Only one of the studies found any significant difference or change in attitudes or behavior related to sexuality. Out and Lafreniere (2001) found that "adolescents in the intervention group…rated themselves as being significantly more susceptible to an unplanned pregnancy compared with adolescents in the comparison group" (p. 577). However, they found no differences between the groups in attitudes toward abstinence and contraceptive use. In studies conducted by Somers and Fahlman (2001) and Somers et al. (2001), no significant change from pretest to posttest in attitudes and behaviors related to sexual behavior, contraception, and pregnancy was detected. Out and Lafreniere found no changes from pretest to posttest in attitudes toward abstinence and contraceptive use. Finally, Divine and Cobbs (2001) found no differences between experimental and control groups in attitudes regarding contraception, abstinence, and sexuality.

195 Although no differences were found between their 245 BTIO participants and 186 control group participants, Tingle (2002) found the majority of parents reported that the intervention had increased both their children's perceptions of the difficulties involved in caring for an infant and parent-child communication regarding sexuality and parenting. Moreover, the great majority (92%) indicated they would recommend the program to a friend; 82% for use in middle schools and 97% for use in high schools. Similarly, the majority of the 89 parents in a rural Ohio sample felt that the program was successful in teaching their children that a baby was a considerable responsibility (85%), time consuming (79%), and a barrier to achieving their life goals (71%), and 90% indicated they would recommend the BTIO program to friends (Price, Robinson, Thompson, & Schmalzried, 2000).

Of the 22 teachers in Tingle's (2002) study, 59% evaluated BTIO as "somewhat effective" in preventing pregnancies and 45% said it was effective in initiating communication between parent and child. In Somers and colleagues' (2001) study, few of the 57 teachers felt that BTIO reduced sexual intercourse (5%) or the number of sexual partners (7%). However, the majority (91%) believed that students learned about the responsibilities of parenthood and recommended that BTIO be continued in the school (86%) and be adopted in other schools (84%).

There were serious methodological limitations and flaws in the preceding studies. Many of the samples were small and not random, thereby limiting generalizability. In addition, volunteers were also used in a number of the studies; for example, Out and Lafreniere's (2001) intervention group consisted of students from elective courses on parenting and the control group from geography and physical education classes at the same schools. Additional research with larger samples, greater control of confounds (especially

235 selection bias), and more rigorous research designs and methodology are needed, preferably with replication, before any conclusions can be drawn regarding the effectiveness of this intervention as a model for reducing the risk of adolescent pregnancy.

## Objectives

The present Baby Think It Over intervention had seven major objectives. The first four posited an increase in the degree to which the adolescent recognized: (1) that caring for a baby affects an adolescent's academic and social life; (2) that other family members are affected by having an adolescent with a baby in the family; (3) that there are emotional risks for each parent in having a baby during adolescence; and (4) that there are family and cultural values related to having a baby during adolescence. The remaining three proposed an increase in the number planning to postpone parenthood: (5) until a later age (for the majority until graduation from high school); (6) until education and career goals were met; or (7) until marriage.

## Research Design and Method

Program objectives and additional constructs were measured with two main instruments: BTIO-1 and BTIO-2. A repeated-measures design was used, with the BTIO-1 measure as the pretest and posttest. To increase validity, participants were used as their own controls through paired pretest-posttest comparisons, with all data entered anonymously. Moreover, confounds related to history and maturation were eliminated because the intervention was conducted sequentially and continuously across the academic year with multiple individuals as their own controls. A posttest-only evaluation measure (BTIO-2) also was used to obtain self-report data on the impact of the program.

*Measures*

265 *BTIO-1.* The four main program objectives were measured using a 25-item, closed-ended instrument with a four-point Likert-type scale, ranging from 4 = strongly agree to 1 = strongly disagree. Total score and scores for each of the first four objectives were created by summing the scores of the relevant items. Two separate scores were also calculated for items pertaining to understanding and dealing with a crying infant and those related to overall infant care. A higher score indicated a higher level of agreement consonant with the program objectives and greater accuracy in their evaluation of the statements. The measure demonstrated good internal consistency ($\alpha = .84$).

In addition, the youths were asked to indicate *when* they would "like to have children": (1) never, (2) right now, (3) when I finish junior high school, (4) when I'm in high school, or (5) after I graduate from high school. Students also checked items they would like to do "before having a baby": (1) have a good paying job, (2) go to college, (3) graduate from a junior college, (4) graduate from a four-year college, (5) go to a trade or technical school, (6) get married, (7) have a career, and (8) "other" write-in responses. Multiple responses were possible.

290 *BTIO-2.* The Baby Think It Over-2 measure is a post hoc, self-report measure indicating whether the experience changed what participants thought it would be like to have a baby; when they thought they would like to have a baby in terms of age and educational and career achievements; beliefs regarding the use of birth 295 control or protection; and how much time and work are involved in taking care of a baby. Perceptions before and after carrying the BTIO doll were indicated along Likert-type scales for use of birth control or protection, amount of effort involved in caring for a baby, and the 300 interference of infant caregiving with education goals, career goals, and social life.

*Data Analysis*

Paired *t* tests were performed on the summated scores for the total number of items on the Likert-type scale, the summated scores for each of the first four 305 objectives, and the scores for crying and overall care. ANCOVAs, using the pretest as the covariate, were also conducted to determine whether there were differences in responses based on gender. Chi-square analyses were performed on the nominal data for the last 310 three objectives on postponing pregnancy and parenthood.

**Findings**

*Demographic Data*

A total of 353 of the students who carried the infant simulation doll completed matched pre- and posttest measures: 140 male participants and 204 female par- 315 ticipants. Nine students did not report gender. The overwhelming majority (94.3%, $n = 333$) of the participants were in the ninth grade, with the remaining five (1.4%) in the 10th and three (.9%) in the 11th grade; 12 students (3.4%) did not indicate grade level. 320 Correspondingly, most of the participants were 14 (48.2%, $n = 170$) to 15 (47.9%, $n = 169$) years old. Reflecting the demographics of the community, 92.9% of the participants in the sample were Latino (70.8% Mexican American, $n = 250$; 5.1% Central American, $n$ 325 $= 18$; 17.0% other Latino, $n = 60$). The remaining participants included one African American, five American Indian, three Asian/Pacific Islander, nine white, and two multiethnic youths; five students did not provide this information.

*BTIO-1*

330 On the BTIO-1 measure, statistically significant gains from pretest to posttest were found on all but one of the paired analyses (Table 1). The statistically significant increase in the means from pretest to posttest indicates that objective 1 was met: a greater recogni- 335 tion of the impact of caring for a baby on academic and social life. The posttest mean approached 20, equivalent to "agree" and edging closer to the "strongly

agree" point on the scale. When items related to the students' academic and social life were summed sepa- 340 rately, the gains were also found to be statistically significant: academics [$t(352) = 7.893$, $p < .001$]; social life [$t(352) = 9.862$, $p < .001$].

The gain from pretest to posttest for objective 2 was also statistically significant, indicating a greater recog- 345 nition of the effect of adolescent parenthood on other family members. However, the gain was modest (from 10.8 to 11.24 in a range of possible scores from four to 16), and the mean at posttest did not quite reach the point of "agree" (12.0) on the scale. An examination of 350 the responses to the various items provides clarification. Most participants "agreed" or "strongly agreed" on items that recognize how adolescent parenthood affects the adolescent's family: 93.8% that an infant's crying or illness might disturb other family members' 355 sleep and 70.8% that a baby's needs would reduce money available for the needs of others in the family. The mean was reduced by the 25% to 30% who disagreed on two items that indicated that other family members would share care and responsibility for the 360 baby.

On objective 3, a statistically significant increase in the recognition of emotional risks accompanying adolescent parenthood was found, with the posttest mean corresponding to "agree."

365 Objective 4—regarding family and cultural values on adolescent parenthood—was not met. The increase was minimal (.14); however, the mean of 8 (in a range of possible scores of 3 to 12) is equivalent to "agree" on the 4-point scale. High pretest scores may have re- 370 sulted in a ceiling effect, and it is likely that cultural and family values are relatively stable.

Responses to items related to understanding why a baby cries and what actions should be taken in response were calculated into a summated score. The 375 gain from pretest ($M = 14.18$) to posttest ($M = 15.98$) achieved statistical significance [$t(352) = 12.266$, $p < .001$], moving the mean beyond a score of 15 (range 5 to 20) or "agree" on the scale. The individual items clearly reflect aspects of the experience of carrying the 380 BTIO doll: 92.6% ($n = 327$) disagreed or strongly disagreed that it was "easy to ignore a fussy, crying baby"; 86.1% ($n = 304$) disagreed or strongly disagreed that babies would not cry if they were loved and loved the parent in return. Moreover, the majority appeared 385 to understand why infants cry and refrained from making inaccurate and judgmental appraisals of both infant and parent behavior: 85.3% ($n = 301$) did not view a baby who "cries a lot" as "spoiled," 65.7% ($n = 232$) did not attribute the crying to insufficient care by par- 390 ents, and 94.6% ($n = 334$) saw crying as a form of communication (trying "to tell you something").

Three questions ascertained the participants' views regarding overall care of an infant. The increase in the mean (from 9.24 to 10.28) was statistically significant 395 [$t(352) = -9.471$, $p < .001$], indicating an increase in

Table 1
*Paired t Test Results on Objectives 1 to 4 of the Baby Think It Over Program (N = 353)*

|  | M | SD | df | t |
|---|---|---|---|---|
| Objective 1: Academic and social |  |  | 252 | −10.633*** |
| Pretest | 18.08 | 3.52 |  |  |
| Posttest | 19.99 | 2.48 |  |  |
| Objective 2: Impact on family members |  |  | 352 | −3.935*** |
| Pretest | 10.80 | 1.65 |  |  |
| Posttest | 11.24 | 1.59 |  |  |
| Objective 3: Emotional risks |  |  | 352 | −6.951*** |
| Pretest | 14.50 | 2.25 |  |  |
| Posttest | 15.46 | 2.11 |  |  |
| Objective 4: Family and cultural values |  |  | 352 | −1.593*** |
| Pretest | 8.44 | 1.40 |  |  |
| Posttest | 8.58 | 1.36 |  |  |

***$p \leq .001$.

the recognition of the substantial time and effort involved in caring for an infant. A high percentage concurred regarding the 24-hour caregiving required for the BTIO doll: 89.8% ($n = 317$) agreed or strongly agreed that, for adolescent parents, taking care of a baby might be "too much for them to handle"; 88.7% ($n = 313$) disagreed or strongly disagreed that taking care of a baby was "fun and easy"; and 96.1% ($n = 339$) agreed or strongly agreed that "taking care of a baby takes a lot of time and hard work."

The difference between the pretest ($M = 72.2$) and posttest ($M = 78.27$) means for the total score on the 25 items was statistically significant [$t(352) = −12.655, p < .001$], demonstrating an increase in agreement with the objectives of the program. With a range of 25 to 100, the posttest mean is equivalent to beyond "agree" (75.0) on the 4-point scale.

To determine whether there were any differences in outcomes based on gender, ANCOVA was conducted using the pretest as the covariate. Female participants demonstrated greater gains on the total score [$F(1, 352) = 6.446, p < .012$]; objective 1 (academic and social life) [$F(1, 352) = 4.411, p < .05$]; objective 3 (emotional risks) [$F(1, 352) = 10.619, p < .001$]; and crying [$F(1, 352) = 9.290, p < .01$]. Male participants showed greater gains on objective 4 (family and cultural values) [$F(1, 352) = 4.679, p < .05$], with gains negligible for both (males: 8.44 to 8.79; females: 8.42 to 8.43).

Objective 5 posited an increase in the length of time the adolescents planned to postpone parenthood. There was only a 1.4% increase (72.5% to 73.9%) in the number of those intending to wait until after graduating from high school to have children. However, the number of those wanting children before graduating from high school decreased dramatically, from 8.7% ($n = 31$) to 1.5% ($n = 5$). Perhaps the BTIO experience was extremely negative for some participants, as the number never wanting children increased from 15.9% ($n = 56$) to 23.8% ($n = 84$).

Objective 6 was met with a statistically significant increase on every item related to postponing pregnancy

to achieve academic and career goals (Table 2). Financial stability was the highest priority, as job and career had the highest frequency at both pretest and posttest. For the majority of the youths, college aspirations took precedence over having a child. Although there was minimal increase in those who desired parenthood within a marital relationship after the BTIO experience—an additional 12 adolescents—the majority of the youths (71%; $n = 251$) had already indicated this preference at pretest.

### BTIO-2

The BTIO-2 measure was completed by 108 participants, 60 female and 48 male, with most ages 14 to 15 (94.4%, $n = 102$), in the ninth grade (99.1%, $n = 107$), and Latino (92.6%, $n = 100$).

To obtain the adolescents' own view of the changes they experienced in perceptions and behavior as a result of carrying the BTIO doll, they were asked to indicate their thoughts, desires, or behavior "before BTIO" and "after BTIO/Now." Paired $t$ test analyses found statistically significant differences in the desired direction on all items (Table 3).

Students reported that carrying the BTIO doll delayed the age at which they desired to have a child, from a mean of 23 to 25 years. A dramatic drop occurred in those indicating an age of 24 years or less (67% to 32.3%). Moreover, the majority (58.3%, $n = 63$) responded "yes," that carrying the BTIO doll had helped them change their mind regarding the age to have a child.

More than three-quarters of the BTIO-2 respondents indicated that they wanted to complete college and have a job or career before becoming parents. The already high "before" rate of 72.2% ($n = 78$) increased to 77.8% ($n = 84$) "after." There was an increase in those indicating that having a baby would interfere with their education (from 65.7%, $n = 71$ to 83.3%, $n = 90$); getting a good job or career (from 54.6%, $n = 59$ to 77.8%, $n = 84$); and their social life (from 58.3%, $n = 63$ to 73.1%, $n = 79$).

Table 2
*Frequency of Response Selected by Participants in the Baby Think It Over Program*

| | Pretest | | Posttest | | |
| Factor | *f* | % | *f* | % | $\chi^2$ (*df* = 1) |
|---|---|---|---|---|---|
| Good-paying job | 298 | 84.4 | 318 | 89.2 | 65.62*** |
| Go to college | 270 | 76.5 | 296 | 83.9 | 71.02*** |
| Graduate from junior college | 108 | 30.6 | 106 | 30.0 | 80.33*** |
| Graduate from four-year college | 173 | 49.0 | 183 | 51.8 | 89.17*** |
| Technical school | 102 | 28.9 | 112 | 31.7 | 59.75*** |
| Career | 288 | 81.6 | 303 | 85.8 | 92.95*** |
| Married | 251 | 71.1 | 263 | 74.5 | 61.02*** |

****p* < .001.

Table 3
*t Test Results BTIO-2: Before and After BTIO*

| | N | M | SD | df | t |
|---|---|---|---|---|---|
| Age want to have first baby | | | | 86 | –7.210*** |
| Before | 87 | 23.16 | 3.55 | | |
| After | 87 | 25.36 | 3.49 | | |
| School/job prior to having baby | | | | 91 | –4.061*** |
| Before | 92 | 5.11 | 1.21 | | |
| After | 92 | 5.51 | 1.08 | | |
| Amount of time it takes to care for baby | | | | 96 | –5.821*** |
| Before | 97 | 3.24 | .998 | | |
| After | 97 | 3.78 | .616 | | |
| How much baby interferes with education | | | | 102 | –3.966*** |
| Before | 103 | 4.43 | .986 | | |
| After | 103 | 4.77 | .675 | | |
| How much baby interferes with job/career | | | | 103 | –4.984*** |
| Before | 104 | 4.16 | 1.18 | | |
| After | 104 | 4.63 | .827 | | |
| How much baby interferes with social life | | | | 100 | –3.287*** |
| Before | 101 | 4.29 | 1.061 | | |
| After | 101 | 4.60 | .873 | | |

*Note.* BTIO = Baby Think It Over
****p* ≤ .001.

More than half of the respondents (55.6%, *n* = 60) answered affirmatively that BTIO changed their perceptions of what having a baby would be like. In the open-ended questions, the most frequently cited reason was that it was much harder work to care for a baby than they had previously thought (39.8%, *n* = 43). Many students chose not to respond to the open-ended questions.

Nearly two-thirds (58.3%) reported that BTIO helped change their minds about using birth control or protection to prevent unwanted pregnancies. Reported use of birth control or protection increased from 22.2% (*n* = 24) to 28.7% (*n* = 31). Few "never" used protection, and the number dropped slightly from 13.9% (*n* = 15) to 11.1% (*n* = 12). The remaining either indicated that they had never had sexual intercourse or left it blank, as the item was supposed to be skipped if not applicable.

Among the varied responses to the open-ended question regarding what they thought of the program in general, a few appeared with greater frequency including comments describing the program as "good" or "effective" (61.1%, *n* = 66), and that BTIO helped them learn how hard taking care of a baby actually was and that they did not want a child at this time (39.9 %, *n* = 43).

**Discussion**

The Baby Think It Over program appears to be a well-designed intervention that has multiple educational components, a well-controlled simulation experience, debriefing procedures, a stable position in the school's curriculum, support from the school faculty and administration, and a working collaboration with the staff from a local social services agency that funds the program through a state grant. Both the results of the data analyses and the adolescents' own evaluation confirm the effectiveness of the Baby Think It Over intervention in changing perceptions regarding the time and effort involved in caring for an infant and in recognizing the significant effect having a baby has on all major aspects of one's life. Participants increased their awareness of how caring for an infant would interfere with future plans and goals with regard to both education and career. The majority aspired to a college education, and the BTIO experience intensified this desire to further their education. Pregnancy prevention was increasingly recognized as important to ensure their future. Furthermore, the adolescents began to have a more realistic understanding of the demands of adolescent parenthood, acknowledging the loss to their social life along with loss of sleep and the freedom to use their time as they desired. The effect on other family members was also noted as well as the emotional stress created by the responsibility for an infant.

Most of the youths were surprised by how labor-intensive taking care of the BTIO doll was, by the frequency with which they had to attend to the doll's needs (crying), and the disruption this caused in their lives. For most, this ended their romanticized view of having a baby—for a few, to the point of never wanting to have a baby. In general, the youths appeared to be more realistic about how much time and work is involved in caring for a baby. The majority responded by adjusting the timeframe within which they desired to have a child, opting for parenthood at a later age and after important educational and career achievements. In summary, the program appears to have been eminently successful in achieving its immediate objectives.

It should be noted, however, that these are all changes in perceptions and intention rather than longitudinal measures of actual behavior. Nevertheless, perceptions and intentions are important antecedents of behavior. From a social learning theory perspective, perception and intention increase or decrease the probability that a behavior will occur. Moreover, the perceived consequences of behavior and one's perceived self-efficacy in determining the outcome of the behavior affect the likelihood that the behavior will occur (Bandura, 1995). In this case, the students appeared to have made a strong connection between unprotected sexual intercourse and what they now evaluate as a negative outcome: having to care for a demanding infant and the subsequent social, emotional, and academic costs. Most of the respondents wished to have financial stability, an established career, and a marital relationship before parenthood.

The quantitative analyses as well as the students' own comments testify to the importance of the "hands on," simulated experience. Given that most of these youths were 14 and 15 years old, still making the transition from concrete to formal operations, the use of a concrete mechanism that offers direct experiential learning appears to be extremely appropriate.

The program appears to be successful in changing perceptions and intentions; however, to increase the likelihood of its effectiveness in preventing adolescent pregnancy in the long term, an intervention that also provides the adolescents with methods for dealing with situations that involve pregnancy risk is needed. A comprehensive program that covers methods from abstinence to birth control methods and access would provide adolescents with the knowledge and skills needed to actualize their intentions and the opportunity for choice in the means to accomplish this.

Finally, a number of strengths in the design of the program should also be noted. First, the intervention was offered to both male and female adolescents. Second, the mechanism (BTIO) ensured that all participants received the same intervention experience. Third, the process was a mandatory part of a required class, so that all students participated, thereby eliminating selection bias within the school sample. Fourth, the intervention was used sequentially throughout the school year with different participants each time used as their own controls so that there was control of confounds, particularly related to history and maturation. Fifth, the program was not simply a two-day intervention, as the simulation is part of a complex educational program that involves both preparation for the experience, group and individual discussion of the experience, and additional intervention for those students who experienced difficulty during the simulation.

It would be ideal to assess the long-term effects of the program by obtaining data on the pregnancy rates of the participants over the subsequent three years. However, an accurate count is questionable as pregnancies are not necessarily reported to the school, and adolescents who become pregnant may drop out of school, transfer, or have a miscarriage or abortion without the school ever knowing they were pregnant. Moreover, because all students in a single grade receive the experience, no long-term control group will be available.

In the short term, students in the educational planning course, which runs parallel with the health course, can be used as controls to improve the validity of the evaluation because assignment to the courses is on a relatively random basis; that is, determined by fit within the student's schedule. Because the students switch classes the second semester, the controls will then also receive the intervention, thus eliminating any ethical questions regarding the withholding of the intervention. Furthermore, to ascertain the effects of the BTIO doll alone, a comparison group who receives all the educational components except the doll could be used.

The findings offer a number of implications for social work practice with adolescents, particularly regarding pregnancy prevention. It appears that an intensive, realistic experience can effect a rapid and significant amount of attitude change about sexual behavior and adolescent parenthood in a relatively short amount of time. Therefore, even if funds are limited, because the

experience is only two-and-a-half days long, a small number of the simulation dolls might suffice to bring
630 about a change. However, it is important to note that the experiential intervention was supported by an educational component that included didactic instruction and peer discussion. It cannot be assumed that merely allowing an adolescent to carry the doll for a couple of
635 days will have the same effect. It is also possible that the memory of the experience may decrease in intensity over time, so that a repeated experience in the later grades might be necessary to reinforce and maintain the long-term effects of the intervention. Moreover, the
640 social worker needs to make sure that the experience is a balanced one, so that infants are not seen primarily as a source of annoyance and frustration. Finally, the findings suggest that an experiential learning component can alter perspectives and behavior, so that simulation,
645 because it makes the situation very concrete, might be a powerful intervention tool in general with youths who are transitioning to formal operations.

## References

Alan Guttmacher Institute. (1999a). *Teenage pregnancy: Overall trends and state-by-state information*. New York: Author.

Alan Guttmacher Institute. (1999b). *U.S. teenage pregnancy statistics: With comparative statistics for women aged 20–24*. New York: Author.

Bandura, A. (Ed.) (1995). *Self-efficacy in changing societies*. New York: Cambridge University Press.

Becerra, R., Sabagh, G., & de Anda, D. (1986). *Sex and pregnancy among Mexican American adolescents: Final report to the Office of Adolescent Pregnancy Programs, Department of Health and Human Services*. Washington, DC: U.S. Department of Health and Human Services.

California Department of Health Services, Maternal and Child Health Branch, Epidemiology and Evaluation Section. (2001). *Teen birth rate hot spots in California, 1999–2000: A resource developed using a geographic information systems approach*. Sacramento: Author.

Divine, J. H., & Cobbs, G. (2001). The effects of infant simulators on early adolescents. *Adolescence, 36*, 593–600.

Elkind, D. (1967). Egocentrism in adolescence. *Child Development, 38*, 1025–1034.

Gordon, D. E. (1990). Formal operational thinking: The role of cognitive-developmental processes in adolescent decision-making about pregnancy and contraception. *American Journal of Orthopsychiatry, 60*, 346–356.

Kann, L., Kinchen, S. A., Williams, B. I., Ross, J. G., Lowry, R., Grunbaum, J., & Kolbe, L. J. (2000). Youth risk behavior surveillance—United States, 1999. *Morbidity and Mortality Weekly Report Surveillance Summaries, 49*, 1–96.

Kralewski, J., & Stevens-Simon, C. (2000). Does mothering a doll change teens' thoughts about pregnancy? [electronic edition], *Pediatrics, 105*, e. 30.

National Center for Health Statistics. (2000). *Health, United States, 2000*. Hyattsville, MD: Author.

Out, J. W., & Lafreniere, K. D. (2001). Baby Think It Over: Using role-play to prevent teen pregnancy. *Adolescence, 36*, 571–582.

Piaget, J. (1972). Intellectual evolution from adolescence to adulthood. *Human Development, 15*, 1–12.

Piaget, J., & Inhelder, B. (1958). *The growth of logical thinking from childhood to adolescence* (A. Parsons & S. Seagrin, Trans.). New York: Basic Books.

Price, J. H., Robinson, L. K., Thompson, C., & Schmalzried, H. (2000). Rural parents' perceptions of the Baby Think It Over Program—A pilot study. *American Journal of Health Studies, 16*, 34–40.

Somers, C. L., & Fahlman, M. M. (2001). Effectiveness of the "Baby Think It Over" teen pregnancy prevention program. *Journal of School Health, 71*, 188–195.

Somers, C. L., Gleason, J. H., Johnson, S.A., Fahlman, M. M. (2001). Adolescents' and teachers' perceptions of a teen pregnancy prevention program. *American Secondary Education, 29*, 51–66.

Strachan, W., & Gorey, K. (1997). Infant simulator lifespan intervention: Pilot investigation of an adolescent pregnancy prevention program. *Child Adolescent Social Work Journal, 14*, 1–5.

Tingle, L. R. (2002). Evaluation of North Carolina "Baby Think It Over" project. *Journal of School Health, 72*, 178–183.

United Way of Greater Los Angeles. (1998–1999). *State of the county report, 1999–1999*. Los Angeles: Author.

**About the author**: *Diane de Anda*, Ph.D., is associate professor, Department of Social Welfare, School of Public Affairs, University of California, 3250 Public Policy Building, Box 951656, Los Angeles, CA 90095. E-mail: ddeanda@ucla.edu

# Exercise for Article 16

## Factual Questions

1. According to the researcher, is the previous research on the effectiveness of the BTIO intervention extensive?

2. According to the researcher, do the previous studies have serious methodological limitations and flaws?

3. Was the BTIO-2 measure administered as both a pretest *and* as a posttest?

4. According to the researcher, was the gain from pretest to posttest for objective 2 very large?

5. For objective 3, was the increase from pretest to posttest statistically significant? If yes, at what probability level?

6. On the pretest, what percentage of the participants desired parenthood within a marital relationship? On the posttest, what percentage desired it?

## Questions for Discussion

7. In your opinion, is the experimental intervention described in sufficient detail? Explain. (See lines 83–127.)

8. Is it important to know that the participants responded anonymously? Explain. (See line 258.)

9. In a future study of the intervention, would you recommend a longitudinal follow-up? Explain. (See lines 543–549 and 597–604.)

10. Is it important to know that participation was a mandatory part of a required class? Explain. (See lines 583–586.)

11. In a future experiment on this topic, would you recommend the use of a control group? Explain. (See lines 605–620.)

12. Based on this experiment, do you regard the intervention as promising? Would you recommend funding to extend the program to additional schools? Explain.

## *Quality Ratings*

Directions: Indicate your level of agreement with each of the following statements by circling a number from 5 for strongly agree (SA) to 1 for strongly disagree (SD). If you believe an item is not applicable to this research article, leave it blank. Be prepared to explain your ratings. When responding to criteria A and B, keep in mind that brief titles and abstracts are conventional in published research.

A.  The title of the article is appropriate.

SA   5   4   3   2   1   SD

B.  The abstract provides an effective overview of the research article.

SA   5   4   3   2   1   SD

C.  The introduction establishes the importance of the study.

SA   5   4   3   2   1   SD

D.  The literature review establishes the context for the study.

SA   5   4   3   2   1   SD

E.  The research purpose, question, or hypothesis is clearly stated.

SA   5   4   3   2   1   SD

F.  The method of sampling is sound.

SA   5   4   3   2   1   SD

G.  Relevant demographics (for example, age, gender, and ethnicity) are described.

SA   5   4   3   2   1   SD

H.  Measurement procedures are adequate.

SA   5   4   3   2   1   SD

I.  All procedures have been described in sufficient detail to permit a replication of the study.

SA   5   4   3   2   1   SD

J.  The participants have been adequately protected from potential harm.

SA   5   4   3   2   1   SD

K.  The results are clearly described.

SA   5   4   3   2   1   SD

L.  The discussion/conclusion is appropriate.

SA   5   4   3   2   1   SD

M.  Despite any flaws, the report is worthy of publication.

SA   5   4   3   2   1   SD

# Article 17

# Benefits to Police Officers of Having a Spouse or Partner in the Profession of Police Officer

RONALD J. BURKE
York University

ASLAUG MIKKELSEN
Stavanger University College

ABSTRACT. This exploratory study of police officers examined potential effects of having a spouse or partner who is also in police work on levels of work-family conflict and spouse or partner concerns. Data were collected from 776 police officers in Norway using anonymously completed questionnaires. Police officers having spouses or partners also in police work reported significantly lower spouse or partner concerns but the same levels of work-family conflict. Possible explanations for these findings are offered.

From *Psychological Reports*, *95*, 514–516. Copyright © 2004 by Psychological Reports. Reprinted with permission.

It has been observed that individuals sometimes follow the same occupation or profession as their parents and that individuals sometimes have a spouse or partner in the same occupation and profession (Hall, 1976).
5 It is not clear, however, how common this is, why this happens, and whether some professions are more likely to have couples working in them. In an earlier study of men and women in policing, it became clear that police officers' children often became police officers and the
10 possible benefits of this association were examined (Burke, 1997). In that research, we found that police officers with family in policing reported fewer job stressors, but the two groups were similar on measures of work outcomes and psychological health.
15 In the present study, the possible benefits are considered of having one's spouse or partner in the same profession: policing. Policing is seen as a demanding, highly stressful occupation, which may have potential negative effects on the psychological well-being and
20 physical health of police officers (Abdollahi, 2002). There is no doubt that police officers sometimes face high-risk, violent, and threatening situations. But police officers most often face the same demands as members of most other occupations, and there is no compelling
25 evidence that policing is in fact more stressful than other occupations (Abdollahi, 2002).

It is likely that having a spouse or partner in the same profession would increase the shared understanding of the experiences and challenges of that profes-
30 sion. The focus of this study is on the effect of the police officer's job on the family and, given the assump-

tion that policing can be dangerous and threatening, on the spouse's or partner's perceived concerns about the officer's safety. It was hypothesized that police officers
35 whose spouse or partner was also in policing would report lower work-family conflict and spouse's or partner's concerns about the respondent officer's safety and security.

Data were collected from a random sample of po-
40 lice officers in Norway ($N = 766$) using anonymous questionnaires that were mailed to respondents by the Police Union and returned to an independent research institute. The response rate was 62%. Most respondents were male (84%), married (82%), had children (88%),
45 held constable positions (62%), worked in urban areas (73%), worked in large departments (100 or more, 36%), worked between 36–39 hours per week (85%), worked 5 or fewer hours of overtime per week (75%), held fairly long police tenure (21 years or more, 39%),
50 and were born in 1960 or before (42%). A total of 623 police officers were married or partnered (538 men and 85 women). Ten percent of male officers and 44% of female officers had a spouse or partner in policing.

The two dependent variables, Work-Family Con-
55 flict and Spousal Concerns, were measured as did Torgen, Stenlund, Ahlberg, and Marklund (2001). Work-Family Conflict was measured by five items ($\alpha = .83$). One item was "My work has a negative impact on my family." Spousal Concerns was also measured by
60 five items ($\alpha = .81$); for example, "My spouse or partner worries about the health effects of my work." Respondents rated how frequently they experienced each item on a 5-point scale (1 = never, 5 = always).

Table 1 shows the comparisons of responses to the
65 Work-Family Conflict and Spouse Concerns scales, separating males' and females' spouses or partners in police work and those whose spouses or partners were not employed in police work. Mean values were compared using one-way analysis of variance. In the latter
70 group, some spouses or partners were employed in other jobs, while others were not employed outside the home for pay.

Both male and female officers reported the same mean values on Work-Family Conflict (nonsignificant
75 difference) whether the spouse or partner was em-

Table 1
*Work-Family Conflict and Spouse Concerns by Sex of Respondent and Whether or Not Spouse or Partner Works in Policing*

| | Spouse/partner in policing | | | Spouse/partner not in policing | | | |
|---|---|---|---|---|---|---|---|
| | *M* | *SD* | *n* | *M* | *SD* | *n* | *p* |
| Male officers | | | | | | | |
| Work-family conflict | 12.7 | 3.90 | 55 | 12.8 | 3.93 | 475 | ns |
| Spouse concerns | 9.6 | 4.07 | 48 | 11.0 | 3.76 | 419 | .01 |
| Female officers | | | | | | | |
| Work-family conflict | 12.6 | 4.36 | 37 | 12.6 | 3.79 | 48 | ns |
| Spouse concerns | 9.2 | 3.62 | 37 | 11.1 | 3.79 | 48 | .05 |

ployed in police work or not. But both male and female police officers reported lower scores on Spousal Concerns if the spouse or partner was also in policing than if they were not.

80   There are several possible reasons why having a spouse or partner in the law enforcement profession may have benefits. Such spouses or partners understand the realities of the job—the challenges, demands, rewards, and frustrations. They may share common 85 experiences and be better able to appreciate the experiences of their spouses or partners. They may also share more common attitudes, values, and aspects of personality. These common factors may diminish unrealistic thoughts on the realities of policing and the nature of 90 their spouse's or partner's job experiences.

It is not clear the extent to which these findings generalize to police officers in other countries or to other occupations. It should also be noted that all data were collected from police officers and not their 95 spouses. It would be informative to collect data from spouses or partners of police officers directly.

### References

Abdollahi, M. K. (2002). Understanding police stress research. *Journal of Forensic Psychology Practice, 2*, 1–24.

Burke, R. J. (1997). On "inheriting" a career. *Psychological Reports, 80*, 1233–1234.

Hall, D. T. (1976). *Careers in organizations.* Pacific Palisades, CA: Goodyear.

Torgen, M., Stenlund, C., Ahlberg, G., & Marklund, S. (2001). *Ett hallbart arbetsliv foralla aldrar.* Stockholm: Arbetslivsinstitutet.

**Acknowledgments**: Preparation of this manuscript was supported in part by the Rogaland Institute, Stavanger, Norway, and the School of Business, York University. We acknowledge the support of the Police Union in conducting the study and collecting the data. Lisa Fiksenbaum assisted with data analysis.

**Address correspondence to**: R. J. Burke, Department of Organizational Behaviour, Schulich School of Business, York University, 4700 Keele Street, North York, ON, Canada M3J IP3. E-mail: rburke@schulich.yorku.ca

# Exercise for Article 17

## Factual Questions

1. What did the researchers hypothesize?

2. What percentage of the respondents were male?

3. For the female officers, was the difference between the means on Work-Family Conflict statistically significant?

4. What was the mean on Spouse Concerns for male officers who had a spouse/partner in policing?

5. What was the mean on Spouse Concerns for male officers who had a spouse/partner *not* in policing?

6. Was the difference between the two means in the answers to Questions 4 and 5 above statistically significant?

## Questions for Discussion

7. Is it important to know that the researchers used a random sample? Explain. (See lines 39–40.)

8. In your opinion, was the response rate satisfactory? Explain. (See line 43.)

9. The researchers indicate that there were two dependent variables. What is your understanding of the meaning of this term? (See lines 54–55.)

10. Speculate on the meaning of "ns" in Table 1.

11. Do you think it would be important in future studies to collect information directly from the spouses (instead of from the police officers)? Why? Why not? (See lines 93–96.)

12. Does this article convince you that being married to a police officer results in less spousal concern? Explain.

13. This research article is shorter than most of the others in this book. Do you think that this article provides valuable information despite its length? Explain.

## *Quality Ratings*

Directions: Indicate your level of agreement with each of the following statements by circling a number from 5 for strongly agree (SA) to 1 for strongly disagree (SD). If you believe an item is not applicable to this research article, leave it blank. Be prepared to explain your ratings. When responding to criteria A and B, keep in mind that brief titles and abstracts are conventional in published research.

A.   The title of the article is appropriate.

SA   5   4   3   2   1   SD

B.   The abstract provides an effective overview of the research article.

SA   5   4   3   2   1   SD

C.   The introduction establishes the importance of the study.

SA   5   4   3   2   1   SD

D.   The literature review establishes the context for the study.

SA   5   4   3   2   1   SD

E.   The research purpose, question, or hypothesis is clearly stated.

SA   5   4   3   2   1   SD

F.   The method of sampling is sound.

SA   5   4   3   2   1   SD

G.   Relevant demographics (for example, age, gender, and ethnicity) are described.

SA   5   4   3   2   1   SD

H.   Measurement procedures are adequate.

SA   5   4   3   2   1   SD

I.   All procedures have been described in sufficient detail to permit a replication of the study.

SA   5   4   3   2   1   SD

J.   The participants have been adequately protected from potential harm.

SA   5   4   3   2   1   SD

K.   The results are clearly described.

SA   5   4   3   2   1   SD

L.   The discussion/conclusion is appropriate.

SA   5   4   3   2   1   SD

M.   Despite any flaws, the report is worthy of publication.

SA   5   4   3   2   1   SD

# Article 18

# Relationship of Personalized Jerseys and Aggression in Women's Ice Hockey

JAMIE BLOME  
University of Northern Iowa

JENNIFER J. WALDRON  
University of Northern Iowa

MICK G. MACK  
University of Northern Iowa

ABSTRACT. The present study examined the relationship between aggression and players' names on uniforms in collegiate women's ice hockey. Aggression was defined as mean penalty minutes per game. Information (i.e., win/loss record, penalties, and names on uniforms) about the 2002–2003 season women's ice hockey team was obtained via e-mail from 53 of 72 (74% return rate) sports information directors (Division I = 23, Division II = 2, Division III = 28). Analysis indicated that teams with personalized jerseys had significantly more penalty minutes per game than teams without personalized jerseys. However, as the majority of the teams with personalized jerseys were Division I teams and the majority of the teams without personalized jerseys were Division III teams, it is unclear whether results were due to personalized jerseys or competition level of play.

From *Perceptual and Motor Skills*, *101*, 499–504. Copyright © 2005 by Perceptual and Motor Skills. Reprinted with permission.

Aggression has become a frequent topic of investigation in sport psychology, and several factors have been examined. For example, researchers have investigated the relationship between aggression and location of games (Lefebvre & Passer, 1974), crowd size (Russell & Drewry, 1976), possible lunar influences (Russell & Dua, 1983), outcome of game (Worrell & Harris, 1986), frequency of competition (Widmeyer & McGuire, 1997), personality (Bushman & Wells, 1998), level of competition (Coulomb & Pfister, 1998), wearing personalized jerseys (Wann & Porcher, 1998), and type of sport (Huang, Cherek, & Lane, 1999). Because ice hockey offers a unique field setting in which aggression is tolerated and often encouraged, many studies have focused on this sport. Not surprisingly, however, they have only examined male hockey teams.

Sex is one potential moderator of aggressive behaviors. For example, women are more likely to use indirect types of aggression (i.e., backbiting, spreading of false rumors, gossiping, etc.), while men are more likely to engage in violence or acts of physical behavior (Bjorkqvist, Osterman, & Kaukiainen, 1992). Most of the previous studies examining sport aggression, however, have been conducted with male athletes so it is not clear whether this relationship would occur in sports with women. With the substantial increase in the number of women participants in contact sports such as soccer, ice hockey, and football (Theberge, 1997), it is now possible to examine physical aggression during women's athletic competitions.

Aggression in sports can be defined as a nonaccidental act that has the potential to cause psychological or physiological harm to another individual (Kirker, Tennebaum, & Mattson, 2000). Because penalty minutes are "acts of interpersonal aggression judged by highly trained and experienced referees to be in violation of the rules of competition" (Russell & Dua, 1983, p. 42), they are often used to measure aggression operationally in men's ice hockey (Russell & Dua, 1983; Widmeyer & Birch, 1984; Widmeyer & McGuire, 1997; Bushman & Wells, 1998; Wann & Porcher, 1998). The use of penalty records has been a valid indicator of aggression in sports (Vokey & Russell, 1992), as more aggressive infractions require longer periods of time of being restricted from participation. The same is true in women's ice hockey. However, it should be noted that there are slight differences in rules between the men's and women's games. The National Collegiate Athletic Association (NCAA) rules for women's ice hockey do not allow body checking but do permit body contact (National Collegiate Athletic Association, 2002[1]). In other words, women's ice hockey has "rules that limit but by no means eliminate body contact" (Theberge, 1997, p. 71). Interestingly, some of the women in Theberge's study believed that not permitting body checking actually caused more illegal contact during competition.

Understanding the triggers for aggression in sports is an important area of investigation and has been studied primarily in relation to men's sporting behaviors. The current study extends Wann and Porcher's study of men's ice hockey (1998) to women's ice hockey teams. Based on 86 Division I, II, and III ice hockey programs, Wann and Porcher found that the teams with personalized jerseys showed more aggression, measured using penalties, than teams without identification

---

[1] Men's and women's ice hockey rules and interpretations. Retrieved November 6, 2003, from http://www.ncaa.org/library/rules/2003/ice_hockey_rules.pdf

on their jerseys and explained the findings using self-presentation theory.

Self-presentation theory predicts that individuals attempt to present themselves in a positive manner to others (Schlenker, 1980). For many male athletes, portraying a positive image to others requires them to be tough. Thus, especially in a sport such as ice hockey, which is known for its aggressive nature, participants may desire to present themselves as being aggressive (Wann & Porcher, 1998). Having one's name appear on the uniform would ensure that personal identity as an aggressor is known and would serve to enhance the "positive" image to their teammates, opponents, and fans.

Because self-presentation is a socially based concept, research examining sport aggression in women may yield different results. For example, researchers have reported that collegiate female athletes from a variety of sports were less violent on the playing field than their male counterparts (Tucker & Parks, 2001). Perhaps, as suggested by Bjorkqvist et al. (1992), women, following traditional norms of femininity, may desire to present themselves in a more socially desirable nonaggressive manner, which suggests that they would be more likely to engage in indirect acts of aggression that "mask" their behavior. This explanation would predict that wearing a jersey with one's name on the back would result in fewer acts of aggression for female athletes than for male athletes. Thus, it was hypothesized that there would be no significant difference between aggression of women's collegiate ice hockey teams, as measured by number of penalty minutes, with and without personalized names on their jerseys.

## Method

A list of all colleges with women's ice hockey in Divisions I, II, and III was obtained from the NCAA Web site. E-mail addresses were obtained, and the sports information directors from each school were then contacted via e-mail. In the two cases where no sport information director was listed, the head coach was contacted. Two weeks following the initial e-mail, a follow-up was sent through e-mail to those who had not yet responded. The sports information directors or coaches of all NCAA women's ice hockey teams ($N = 72$) were contacted and 53 responded (Division I = 23, Division II = 2, Division III = 28). Therefore, the present sample represented approximately 74% of all NCAA women's hockey programs from the 2002–2003 season.

Each e-mail began with an introduction of the researchers' affiliation and an explanation of the research. This was followed by a request for the following information concerning the 2002–2003 women's ice hockey season: (1) What was your win/loss record? (2) What was the total number of penalty minutes? (3) Did your team have personalized names on their jerseys for home games? (4) Did your team have personalized names on their jerseys for away games? One of the sports information directors responded by telephone, while the rest of the directors replied using e-mail.

Aggression was operationally defined as the mean number of penalty minutes per game. This measure was calculated by dividing the total number of penalty minutes for the season by the total number of games. Because penalties for more aggression require more minutes in the penalty box (i.e., 2 min. for a minor penalty versus 5 min. for a major penalty), a larger number indicates more aggression.

## Results

Of the 53 women's hockey teams for which responses were received, 21 had personalized names on both home and away jerseys (Division I = 19, Division II = 1, Division III = 1), 23 teams did not have personalized names on either home or away jerseys (Division I = 2, Division II = 1, Division III = 20), and 9 teams had names on either home or away jerseys, but not both (Division I = 2, Division III = 7). The mean number of penalties per game was 4.5 ($SD = 1.2$), and the mean for penalty minutes per game was 9.5 ($SD = 2.6$).

An independent-samples $t$ test was used to compare penalty minutes per game between teams with and without personalized names on their jerseys. Teams whose jerseys had names for either their home or away games were not included in this analysis. Analysis indicated that the teams with personalized jerseys had significantly more penalty minutes per game ($M = 10.7$, $SD = 2.4$) than teams without personalized jerseys ($M = 8.4$, $SD = 2.2$; $t_{42} = 3.19$, $p < .01$, $d = 1.0$). Because the vast majority of teams having personalized jerseys were Division I ice hockey programs (90.5%), while most teams not having personalized jerseys were Division III programs (87.0%), an additional independent samples $t$ test was performed to examine potential differences between the two divisions. Since data were received from only two Division II ice hockey programs, they were not included in this analysis. The analysis indicated that Division I teams had significantly more penalty minutes per game ($M = 10.7$, $SD = 2.3$) than Division III ($M = 8.2$, $SD = 2.3$; $t_{49} = 3.86$, $p < .01$, $d = 1.1$). For both of the independent samples $t$ tests, the effect size ($d$) was large (Cohen, 1988). In other words, the magnitude or meaningfulness of the difference between the two groups was substantial.

## Discussion

Contrary to what was predicted, results of the present study are similar to Wann and Porcher's findings (1998). The combined results from these two studies indicate that both samples of men's and women's ice hockey teams with personalized jerseys had more penalty minutes and thus more aggression than teams without personalized jerseys. The self-presentation explanation of desiring to be perceived as an aggressive player might be appropriate for both men and women. Both male and female ice hockey players may want an aggressive self-presentation to intimidate opponents, keep their position on the team, or maintain their self-identity (Widmeyer, Bray, Dorsch, & McGuire, 2002).

However, closer scrutiny of the demographic background of the teams involved raises doubts about the potential effectiveness of wearing personalized jerseys. When examining the data in the current study, it was noted that only one team in Division III had personalized jerseys, whereas only two teams in Division I did not have names on their jerseys. Follow-up analyses comparing aggression between the divisions found that Division I teams had significantly higher aggression measured as penalties (min.) than Division III teams. A cursory examination of the demographic data provided by Wann and Porcher (1998) raises similar questions. In their study, 95% of Division I teams had personalized jerseys, while 85% of Division III teams did not have personalized jerseys.

Wann and Porcher's attempt to provide evidence that increased aggression could be attributed to personalized jerseys rather than competition level was also suspect. As noted in their results, small sample sizes precluded statistical analysis at the Division I level. Their analysis at the Division III level could similarly be questioned given the unequal sample sizes (i.e., personalized jerseys = 28 and no personalized jerseys = 5). Unfortunately, the current study's design showed the same limitations, so additional $t$ tests within each division could not be conducted given the small number of teams without personalized jerseys in Division I and teams with personalized jerseys in Division III. Having only nine teams whose names were on jerseys worn during either their home or away games but not both was insufficient data on which to conduct statistical analyses between the groups. Therefore, it is unclear whether differences in aggression were related to wearing personalized jerseys or to competition level.

In summary, research on the possible association of wearing personalized jerseys on aggression in men and women's collegiate ice hockey appears inconclusive given the confounding variable of competition level. Significant differences in penalty minutes may have been a function of the competition level rather than wearing a personalized jersey. Researchers must further delineate the various factors that may be associated with expression of aggression by both male and female participants in ice hockey and other sports.

### References

Bjorkqvist, K., Osterman, K., & Kaukiainen, A. (1992). The development of direct and indirect aggressive strategies in males and females. In K. Bjorkqvist & P. Niemela (Eds.), *Of mice and women: Aspects of female aggression.* San Diego, CA: Academic Press. Pp. 51–64.

Bushman, B. J., & Wells, G. L. (1998). Trait aggressiveness and hockey penalties: Predicting hot tempers on the ice. *Journal of Applied Psychology, 83,* 969–974.

Cohen, J. (1998). *Statistical power analysis for the behavioral sciences.* (2nd ed.) Hillsdale, NJ: Erlbaum.

Coulomb, G., & Pfister, R. (1998). Aggressive behaviors in soccer as a function of competition level and time: A field study. *Journal of Sport Behavior, 21,* 222–231.

Huang, D. B., Cherek, D. R, & Lane, D. (1999). Laboratory measurement of aggression in high school age athletes: Provocation in a nonsporting context. *Psychological Reports, 85,* 1251–1262.

Kirker, B., Tennebaum, G., & Mattson, J. (2000). An investigation of the dynamics of aggression: Direct observations in ice hockey and basketball. *Research Quarterly for Exercise and Sport, 71,* 373–386.

Lefebvre, L., & Passer, M. W. (1974). The effects of game location and importance on aggression in team sport. *International Journal of Sport Psychology, 5,* 102–110.

Russell, G. W., & Drewry, B. R. (1976). Crowd size and competitive aspects of aggression in ice hockey: An archival study. *Human Relations, 29,* 723–735.

Russell, G. W, & Dua, M. (1983). Lunar influences on human aggression. *Social Behavior and Personality, 11,* 41–44.

Schlenker, B. R. (1980). *Impression management: The self-concept, social identity, and interpersonal relations.* Monterey, CA: Brooks/Cole.

Theberge, N. (1997). "It's a part of the game": Physicality and the production of gender in women's hockey. *Gender and Society, 11,* 69–87.

Tucker, L. W., & Parks, J. B. (2001). Effects of gender and sport types on intercollegiate athletes' perceptions of the legitimacy of aggressive behaviors in sport. *Sociology of Sport Journal, 18,* 403–413.

Vokey, J. R., & Russell, G. W. (1992). On penalties in sport as measures of aggression. *Social Behavior and Personality, 20,* 219–225.

Wann, D. L., & Porcher, B. J. (1998). The relationship between players' names on uniforms and athlete aggression. *International Sport Journal, 2,* 28–35.

Widmeyer, W. N., & Birch, J. S. (1984). Aggression in professional ice hockey: A strategy for success or a reaction to failure? *Journal of Psychology, 117,* 77–84.

Widmeyer, W. N., Bray, J. S., Dorsch, K. D., & McGuire, E. J. (2002). Explanations for the occurrence of aggression: Theories and research. In J. M. Silva & D. E. Stevens (Eds.), *Psychological foundations of sport.* Boston, MA: Allyn & Bacon. Pp. 352–379.

Widmeyer, W. N., & McGuire, E. J. (1997). Frequency of competition and aggression in professional ice hockey. *International Journal of Sport Psychology, 28,* 57–66.

Worrell, L. L., & Harris, D. V. (1986). The relationship of perceived and observed aggression of ice hockey players. *International Journal of Sport Psychology, 17,* 34–40.

**Address correspondence to:** Jennifer J. Waldron, Ph.D., School of Health, Physical Education, and Leisure Services, 203 Wellness/Recreation Center, Cedar Falls, IA 50614-0241. E-mail: jennifer.waldron@uni.edu

# Exercise for Article 18

## Factual Questions

1. Near the beginning of the article, the researchers provide a conceptual definition of "aggression." (See lines 31–33.) Later in the article, they provide an operational definition. What is the operational definition?

2. How were the participants contacted for this study?

3. Was there a significant difference between teams with personalized jerseys and teams without personalized jerseys? If yes, at what probability level was it significant?

4. What is the name of the significance test used in this research?

5. According to the researchers, were both effect sizes ($d$) "large"?

6. Are the results of this study consistent with what was predicted (i.e., consistent with the hypothesis)?

## Questions for Discussion

7. Out of the 72 potential participants, 53 responded. In your opinion, does this affect the validity of the study? Explain.

8. If you had planned this study, would you have hypothesized that there would be no significant difference? Explain. (See lines 95–100.)

9. Do you agree with the researchers' statement that "…it is unclear whether differences in aggression were related to wearing personalized jerseys or to competition level."? (See lines 215–217.)

10. In your opinion, would a true experiment in which some women are randomly assigned to wear personalized jerseys while the remaining ones are not provide better information on this potential cause of aggression? Explain.

## Quality Ratings

Directions: Indicate your level of agreement with each of the following statements by circling a number from 5 for strongly agree (SA) to 1 for strongly disagree (SD). If you believe an item is not applicable to this research article, leave it blank. Be prepared to explain your ratings. When responding to criteria A and B, keep in mind that brief titles and abstracts are conventional in published research.

A. The title of the article is appropriate.

    SA  5  4  3  2  1  SD

B. The abstract provides an effective overview of the research article.

    SA  5  4  3  2  1  SD

C. The introduction establishes the importance of the study.

    SA  5  4  3  2  1  SD

D. The literature review establishes the context for the study.

    SA  5  4  3  2  1  SD

E. The research purpose, question, or hypothesis is clearly stated.

    SA  5  4  3  2  1  SD

F. The method of sampling is sound.

    SA  5  4  3  2  1  SD

G. Relevant demographics (for example, age, gender, and ethnicity) are described.

    SA  5  4  3  2  1  SD

H. Measurement procedures are adequate.

    SA  5  4  3  2  1  SD

I. All procedures have been described in sufficient detail to permit a replication of the study.

    SA  5  4  3  2  1  SD

J. The participants have been adequately protected from potential harm.

    SA  5  4  3  2  1  SD

K. The results are clearly described.

    SA  5  4  3  2  1  SD

L. The discussion/conclusion is appropriate.

    SA  5  4  3  2  1  SD

M. Despite any flaws, the report is worthy of publication.

    SA  5  4  3  2  1  SD

# Article 19

# Significance of Gender and Age in African American Children's Response to Parental Victimization

CATHERINE N. DULMUS
University at Buffalo

CAROLYN HILARSKI
Buffalo State College

ABSTRACT. This study examined gender and age differences in children's psychological response to parental victimization in a convenience sample of African American children. Thirty youths, ages 6 to 12, whose parents had been victims of community violence (i.e., gunshot or stabbing), and a control group of 30 children matched on variables of race, age, gender, and neighborhood served as the sample for this study. Parents completed a demographics sheet and the Child Behavior Checklist (CBCL). Data were collected within six weeks of parental victimization. No significant difference was found in male and female youths' internalizing and externalizing behavior at ages 6 to 8. However, beginning at age 9 there was a significant difference in behavior. Youths exposed to parental victimization internalized and externalized to a greater degree than those children who were not exposed. Males externalized more than females, and females internalized more than males. Thus, the perceived trauma response may vary as a function of the child's gender and developmental level or age. These findings suggest that gender-specific response related to trauma exposure may begin as early as age 9.

From *Health & Social Work, 31*, 181–188. Copyright © 2006 by National Association of Social Workers. Reprinted with permission.

The United States is a violent country (Trickett & Schellenbach, 1998), and our children's exposure to this violence is a national public health issue (Glodich, 1998). Violence exposure, as either a witness or victim,
5  is rampant among inner-city youths (Hien & Bukszpan, 1999). Although violence has decreased in recent years, youths in poor urban areas continue to be disproportionately exposed (Gorman-Smith & Tolan, 1998; Gorman-Smith, Tolan, & Henry, 1999). Children
10  exposed to violence (either directly or indirectly) are vulnerable to serious long-term consequences, such as posttraumatic stress (Kilpatrick & Williams, 1997; McCloskey & Walker, 2000), delinquency (Farrell & Bruce, 1997; Gorman-Smith & Tolan, 1998; Miller,
15  Wasserman, Neugebauer, Gorman-Smith, & Kamboukos, 1999), depression (Gorman-Smith et al., 1999;

Kliewer, Lepore, Oskin, & Johnson, 1998), and impaired attention (Ford, Racusin, Ellis, & Daviss, 2000).

Trauma and posttrauma reactions have far-reaching
20  effects beyond the individual victim. Trauma can touch the victim's entire system (e.g., partner, professional helper, family members, and friends) (Figley, 1995a). In fact, the greater the degree of crisis (i.e., type of trauma event and length of stress reaction), the greater
25  the system stress (Peebles-Kleiger & Kleiger, 1994). Concern must be extended beyond the direct victims of violence to include those indirectly affected. Indirect victims include those children who have heard about violence occurring to members of their immediate and
30  extended family or acquaintances. Indirect victims are also those children who fear for their safety and that of their family and friends (Figley, 1995b).

Simply being in the presence of violence is harmful to children (Osofsky, 1995). Safety is an important
35  concept in childhood (Cicchetti & Aber, 1998). Learning to trust others, exploring the environment, developing confidence in oneself, and expanding social contacts outside of the family are important childhood challenges (Cicchetti & Aber, 1998; Dahlberg & Pot
40  ter, 2001). In a predictable, safe, and secure environment, children are more likely to explore their surroundings to learn about themselves, their relationships with others, and the world (Cicchetti & Aber, 1998; Garbarino, 1995a). Violence exposure undermines feel
45  ings of safety and restricts the range of experiences necessary for healthy development (Calvert, 1999).

Exposure to community violence affects children of all ages (Berman, Kurtines, Silverman, & Serafini, 1996; Ensink, Robertson, Zissis, & Leger, 1997;
50  Glodich & Allen, 1998; Gorman-Smith & Tolan, 1998). The response to a perceived violent event may actually overwhelm very young children. For example, they may become obsessed with the details of the event. They may reenact violent themes in play and
55  unconsciously in dreams (Eth, 2001). Younger children are also more likely to engage in bedwetting, thumb sucking, somatic complaints, social withdrawal, and high anxiety during caregiver separation (Eth, 2000).

School-age children exposed to violence display externalizing and internalizing behaviors and show declines in concentration, school performance, and overall functioning (Eth, 2001; Garbarino, 1993; Osofsky, 1999). These children have difficulty regulating their emotions, showing empathy, and integrating cognitions (Cicchetti & Rogosch, 1997). Such behaviors can interfere with the developmental challenges of adapting to the school environment and establishing positive peer relations. For example, traumatized children are often hypervigilant of their environment as a protective mechanism against additional traumatic events. This behavior can lead to environmental misinterpretations of hostile intent by others, thus interfering with constructive social interactions (Dodge, Lochman, Harnish, Bates, & Pettit, 1997).

The effects of exposure to violence may differ from child to child. Following a similar exposure, children who internalize behave differently from those who externalize (Keane & Kaloupek, 1997; Keane, Taylor, & Penk, 1997). Moreover, there is an indication that gender influences traumatic response (Berton & Stabb, 1996; Miller et al., 1999; Singer, Anglin, Song, & Lunghofer, 1995). A study that examined the rates of depression and anxiety among bereaved children found that boys reported fewer depressive symptoms than girls did up to 18 months after the death of a parent (Raveis, Siegel, & Karus, 1999). Leadbeater, Kuperminc, Blatt, and Hertzog (1999) reported gender differences in the internalizing and externalizing of problems relative to stressful life events: Boys were at risk of externalizing their problems, and girls tended to internalize (Dulmus, Ely, & Wodarski, 2003). This study examined the effects of age and gender independently and conjointly on reactions to trauma.

**Theoretical Model**

The adverse effects of trauma on people other than the direct victim have been observed and documented (Terr, 1979, 1981). The actual manner of symptom transfer is not definitively established by empirical research. However, one explanation for externalizing behavior trauma response is the social interactional model of development in which children come to view what they are exposed to as normative and model these behaviors (Lorion & Saltzman, 1993). The cognitive processing theory attempts to explain internalizing response to trauma, suggesting that making sense of community violence can be distressing as it may conflict with the child's beliefs that home and neighborhood are safe (Finkelhor, 1997; Garbarino, 1995a; Marans & Adelman, 1997). The idea that the environment is not safe can challenge the child's basic need to trust and be part of a secure attachment, which is a fundamental developmental process for future health (Cicchetti & Rogosch, 1997; Pynoos et al., 1993). The struggle to cognitively assimilate violent events may lead to unwanted and uncontrolled thoughts resulting in anxiety and depressive symptomatology (Cicchetti & Toth, 1998). Violation of essential developmental processes can lead to internal dissonance and defensive behavioral and cognitive responses that are reminiscent of posttraumatic symptoms (Pynoos et al., 1993; Pynoos, Nader, Frederick, Gonda, & Stuber, 1987). Clinical observations and developmental research indicate that children's distress responses to trauma may manifest as a range of impaired symptomatology (Garbarino, 1995b).

From a developmental perspective, age-relevant achievements in cognition, social relationships, and emotional development provide children with specific vulnerabilities and unique strengths to interpret traumatic events and master violence-related stress and arousal (Apfel, 1996). Internal and external factors, therefore, interact to establish resiliency or risk. Trauma exposure may lead to traumatization or distress when fear, anger, or stress overwhelms the child's internal attributes and protective mechanisms (Finkelhor & Asdigian, 1996). A particular concern is that traumatic stress reactions may prevent young children from resolving stage-salient developmental challenges, which may then present as psychopathology (Cicchetti & Toth, 1998).

In sum, the primary victims of violence are not the only sufferers. Having a personal relationship with someone who has been a victim of violence can have long-term negative consequences. An understanding of the developmental circumstance (i.e., age) and gender-related response of children residing in a family where a parent has been victimized is vital to prevention and treatment efforts. Only by understanding the developmental effects of such exposure can we advance our remedial efforts.

**Current Study**

Internal Review Board (IRB) approval was obtained from the State University of New York at Buffalo before study implementation. Initial analysis of the data set used in this study reported that children in the exposure group were experiencing symptoms in the borderline clinical range (total score of 67–70) as indicated by scores on the Child Behavior Checklist (CBCL) (Achenbach, 1991), and children in the control group fell below this range (Dulmus & Wodarski, 2000). Direct and indirect exposure to community violence can negatively affect children (Dulmus & Wodarski, 2000), often resulting in children showing their distress by engaging in internalizing or externalizing behavior. However, research is unclear regarding the age-related influences of the trauma response, as only a few studies have examined the link between community violence exposure and negative outcomes in children younger than age 10. One study suggested that younger children engage in internalizing behavior more than older children (Schwab-Stone et al., 1999). Fitzpatrick and Boldizar (1993) suggested that younger children indirectly exposed to violence are less likely to engage in internalizing behavior. Hence, there is no real understanding of how age may influence community violence exposure for young children.

175 Another factor that requires consideration is gender. Research has suggested that gender influences the behavioral outcome of violence exposure (Schwab-Stone et al., 1999; Song, Singer, & Anglin, 1998). Our research question thus was: Do children behaviorally 180 respond to perceived trauma differently according to age and gender?

## Method

### Sample and Procedures

A convenience sample of 30 children (exposure group), ages 6 to 12 years, whose parents had been admitted to Erie County Medical Center (ECMC) 185 trauma unit (December 1997 through May 1998) in Buffalo, New York, for treatment of injuries sustained as a result of community violence, were recruited for this study. The principal investigator daily reviewed the surgery list for those individuals who had surgery 190 because of a gunshot or stabbing wound. Such individuals were then approached to determine whether injuries had been sustained as a result of community violence. If so, they were asked whether they had a child between the ages of 6 and 12 who could partici- 195 pate in this study. One hundred percent of parents approached who met the criteria for the study and who had a child between the ages of 6 and 12 provided contact information on how to access their child's primary caregiver for study recruitment purposes. All primary 200 caregivers contacted agreed to allow themselves and their child to participate in this study. Mothers, who were the dominant primary caregivers in the exposure group, offered names of other parents in their neighborhood with a child of the same gender, race, and age as 205 their own child, but who had not had a parent who was a victim of community violence, to compose the control group. An exposure group ($n$ = 30) and control group ($n$ = 30) were matched on age, race, gender, and neighborhood. The sample size was adequate for a 210 large effect size, a .80 level of power, and an alpha of .05 (Cohen, 1992). Inclusion criteria for the exposure group were: (1) The child participant had to be the biological child of the victimized person admitted to the Buffalo trauma unit; (2) The victimized person had to 215 be a victim of community violence (thus, victims of domestic violence and self-inflicted wounds were excluded); (3) The victimized person had to be admitted to a medical floor for at least one night; (4) The child was not a witness to the parent's victimization; (5) The 220 child was not receiving mental health services; (6) The child had no documented history of mental retardation; and (7) Only one child per family could participate.

The exposure and control groups' female caregivers voluntarily provided, through interview and self- 225 administered instruments, demographic and behavioral descriptions of their child during a one-hour appointment with the principal investigator two to eight weeks following the parent's hospitalization. Confidentiality was discussed and ensured. Each parent received $20, 230 and each child $5, in addition to transportation, if needed.

### Measures

A form was developed requesting social and demographic data. In addition, the parent with whom the child resided completed the CBCL. The CBCL can be 235 self-administered or administered by an interviewer and is designed to record in standardized format children's (ages 4 to 18) competencies and problems as reported by their parents or caregiver. The 118-item checklist allows parents to evaluate the behavior of 240 their children and provides a total score, as well as scores for internalizing and externalizing behaviors. It asks questions regarding a wide variety of symptoms and behaviors that children may have experienced in the past six months and asks parents to respond to each 245 question with three possible answers: "not true," "somewhat true or sometimes true," or "very or often true." The CBCL is widely used and accepted with good reliability ($r$ = .87) and validity (Achenbach, 1991).

## Results

### Sample Characteristics

250 All children were African American, with 47% being females, and a mean age of nine years. Half of the sample was age 6 through 8. One child lived with an aunt, and the remaining children lived with their mother. The mean number of siblings in the home was 255 three, and the mean family gross income per month was $985. More than three-quarters of the victimized parents were men. Of those, 77% were shot and 23% had been stabbed. The average hospital stay was nine days, with a range of one to 24 nights. More than half 260 of the youths had visited their parent in the hospital. Sixty-one percent of the youths were in daily contact with their parent before the victimizing event. The remaining youths had a minimum of monthly contact.

### Statistical Analysis of CBCL Internalizing and Externalizing Scores

*Internalizing Scores.* A 2 (gender: male and female) 265 × 2 (group: control or exposure) × 2 (agecode: 1 = 6 to 8 years, and 2 = 9 to 12 years) analysis of variance (ANOVA) was conducted on internalizing CBCL scores. There was a significant main effect for group, $F(1,52) = 9.27$, $p = .004$ and agecode, $F(1,52) = 5.6$, $p = 270$ .022. The control group had lower internalizing CBCL scores ($M = 9.24$, $SE = 1.17$) than the exposure group ($M = 14.24$, $SE = 1.16$). The youths age 9 to 12 had higher internalizing CBCL scores ($M = 13.68$, $SE = 1.16$) than the 6- to 8-year-olds ($M = 9.8$, $SE = 1.16$).

*Externalizing Scores.* A 2 (gender: male and fe- 275 male) × 2 (group: control or exposure) × 2 (agecode)

ANOVA was conducted on externalizing CBCL scores. There was a significant main effect for group, $F(1,52) = 12.73$, $p = .001$ and gender, $F(1,52) = 12.75$, $p = .001$. The control group had lower externalizing CBCL scores ($M – 6.27$, $SE = 1.31$) than the exposure group ($M = 12.86$, $SE = 1.30$). Males had higher externalizing CBCL scores ($M = 12.87$, $SE = 1.31$) than females ($M = 6.27$, $SE = 1.31$).

*Younger Age Group.* Male and female youths ages 6 to 8 years in the exposure group did not differ on their internalizing $t(13) = 1.550$, $p = .145$ and externalizing $t(13) = –0.186$, $p = .855$ CBCL scores according to independent $t$ tests. Similarly, the independent $t$ test was not significant for those 6- to 8-year-old male and female youths not exposed to parental victimization on internalizing $t(13) = .856$, $p = .408$ and externalizing $t(13) = 1.12$, $p = .284$ CBCL scores (see Table 1).

*Older Age Group.* The independent $t$ test was significant for males and females ages 9 to 12 years in the exposure group on externalizing $t(13) = –2.57$, $p = .023$ and internalizing $t(13) = 5.09$, $p = .000$ CBCL scores. Youths ages 9 to 12 years in the control group showed no difference between male and female internalizing $t(13) = –.688$, $p = .503$ and externalizing $t(13) = .012$, $p = .990$ scores (see Table 1).

Table 1
*Mean CBCL Internalizing and Externalizing Scores for Control and Exposure Groups, by Age and Gender*

| | 6–8 year olds' internal/external mean scores | 9–12 year olds' internal/external mean scores |
|---|---|---|
| Control | | |
| Male | 8.25/5.75 | 10.50/7.83 |
| Female | 6.00/3.71 | 12.22/7.78 |
| Exposure | | |
| Male | 12.13/14.88 | 11.13/23.00 |
| Female | 12.86/8.00 | 20.86/5.57 |

*Note.* CBCL = Child Behavior Checklist

## Discussion and Implications for Practice

Initial analysis of these data reported that children in the exposure group were experiencing symptoms in the borderline clinical range, and children in the control group fell below this range (Dulmus & Wodarski, 2000). The current analysis reports additional supportive findings in regard to gender and age-specific differences. No significant difference in male and female youths' internalizing and externalizing behavior at ages 6 to 8 in either the control or the exposure groups was found. In other words, male and female youths in early childhood engage in both internalizing and externalizing behavior. However, youths exposed to parental victimization internalized and externalized to a greater degree, according to caregiver report, than those children who were not exposed. At age 9, there was a significant difference in behavior. In the exposure group, males externalized more than females, and females internalized more than males. In the control group,

there was no significant difference in the internalizing and externalizing behavior of the male and female youths. Thus, the perceived trauma response may vary as a function of the child's gender and developmental level or age.

Research is beginning to suggest that internalizing and externalizing behavior is reciprocal (Hodges & Perry, 1999). For example, youths who engage in externalizing behaviors tend to be socially rejected, which can lead to internalizing behaviors (e.g., withdrawal). Conversely, youths who internalize can be perceived by parents and teachers as passive aggressive and noncooperative (e.g., externalizing) (Shaw et al., 1998). This internalizing and externalizing behavior is the child's defensive coping and is influenced by gender (Carter & Levy, 1991; Dubowitz et al., 2001). Indeed, females can be more reflective or passive, and males more antagonistic (Cramer, 1979; Erikson, 1964; Freud, 1933; Levit, 1991). Support for this premise was found in this study as well. However, the significance here is that both males and females internalize similarly in response to trauma according to age. This is pertinent information regarding assessment of an externalizing male. He may be externalizing because of internalizing a trauma exposure.

Young children respond to trauma by attempting to explain it. The cognitive level or age of the child influences the explanation. For example, a child in the preoperational stage of cognitive development (two to seven years) (Piaget, 1973) is said to view the world egocentrically. Thus, the self is at the root of the explanation for the trauma event. A child in the concrete operations stage of cognitive development (7 to 11 years) is able to produce several explanations for the trauma event, such as blaming others, the self, or both. These distorted or dysfunctional schemas are born from stages of development not equipped to integrate traumatic circumstances. Moreover, the beliefs and attitudes formed during these stages are relatively stable and are the foundations for internalizing and externalizing behavior (Finkelhor, 1995), depending on gender (Levit, 1991). The traumagenic dynamic cites powerlessness as the fundamental dysfunctional cognition stemming from a trauma exposure (Finkelhor, 1997). Helplessness is a core belief for such disorders as anxiety, the need for control, and identification of self as either aggressor or victim, and is linked to depressive and aggressive behavior (Finkelhor, 1997).

Such knowledge has implications for practice as gender-specific assessment and intervention approaches must be used at younger ages than previously presumed. Moreover, feeling unsafe because of trauma exposure can lead to cognitive perceptions of chronic threat and feelings of powerlessness, which is associated with symptoms of psychological distress and maladaptive means of coping, including internalizing or externalizing behavior depending on gender. Failure to identify and intervene with children exposed to violence may result in a lifetime of social, emotional, and vocational difficulties. There is now a beginning understanding that gender and age are important influencing variables regarding a youth's behavioral response to trauma.

*Limitations*

This descriptive study of CBCL scores in a group of children recently exposed to parental trauma versus a similar group of children not recently exposed to parental trauma had a number of limitations. First, the design lacked random assignment and the small sample limits the findings. Second, all participants in the study lived in the same area, which increased the risk of confounding variables and decreased generalizability. Third, all findings were based on self-reported data from primary caregivers (mothers); it is therefore possible that certain events and experiences were overestimated, underestimated, or otherwise distorted through recall or gender influences. Also, the study did not take into account the amount of contact the child had with the parent before the victimization, which may have affected study results. Another limitation is that the sociodemographics of the sample limit the generalizability of the findings because all children in this sample were African American. Finally, there is no historical information regarding the child's primary trauma exposure.

*Future Research*

Additional research needs to be conducted in other locales, with a larger sample size, greater age range, and other racial backgrounds for results to be more conclusive. Studies need to be developed to examine the long-term effects of this type of perceived trauma and children. Although this study did control for the specific trauma of parental victimization, future research may want to focus on children's responses in relation to the gender of the parent who is victimized, as well as the type of the parents' victimizations (i.e., beating, gunshot, stabbing) and circumstances surrounding the incidents as to the impact on children. Last, the development of empirically based gender-sensitive assessment instruments and interventions that respond to individual gender differences in the expression of symptoms related to trauma are essential (Feiring, Taska, & Lewis, 1999).

## References

Achenbach, T. M. (1991). *Manual for the Child Behavior Checklist/4–18 and 1991*. Burlington: University of Vermont.

Apfel, R. J. (1996). "With a little help from my friends I get by": Self-help books and psychotherapy [Essay review]. *Psychiatry, 59*, 309–322.

Berman, S. L., Kurtines, W. M., Silverman, W. K., & Serafini, L. T. (1996). The impact of exposure to crime and violence on urban youth. *American Journal of Orthopsychiatry, 66*, 329–336.

Berton, M. W., & Stabb, S. D. (1996). Exposure to violence and post-traumatic stress disorder in urban adolescents. *Adolescence, 31*, 489–498.

Calvert, W. J. (1999). Integrated literature review on effects of exposure to violence upon adolescents. *ABNF Journal, 10*, 84–96.

Carter, D. B., & Levy, G. D. (1991). Gender schemas and the salience of gender: Individual differences in nonreversal discrimination learning. *Sex Roles, 25*, 555–567.

Cicchetti, D., & Aber, J. L. (1998). Contextualism and developmental psychopathology [Editorial]. *Development and Psychopathology, 10*, 137–141.

Cicchetti, D., & Rogosch, F. A. (1997). The role of self-organization in the promotion of resilience in maltreated children. *Development and Psychopathology, 9*, 797–815.

Cicchetti, D., & Toth, S. L. (1998). The development of depression in children and adolescents. *American Psychologist, 53*, 221–241.

Cohen, J. (1992). A power primer. *Psychological Bulletin, 112*, 155–159.

Cramer, P. (1979). Defense mechanisms in adolescence. *Developmental Psychology, 15*, 477–478.

Dahlberg, L. L., & Potter, L. B. (2001). Youth violence: Developmental pathways and prevention challenges. *American Journal of Preventive Medicine, 20* (Suppl. 1), 3–14.

Dodge, K. A., Lochman, J. E., Harnish, J. D., Bates, J. E., & Pettit, G. S. (1997). Reactive and proactive aggression in school children and psychiatrically impaired chronically assaultive youth. *Journal of Abnormal Psychology, 106*, 37–51.

Dubowitz, H., Black, M. M., Kerr, M. A., Hussey, J. M., Morrel, T. M., Everson, M. D., & Starr, R. H., Jr. (2001). Type and timing of mothers' victimization: Effects on mothers and children. *Pediatrics, 107*, 728–735.

Dulmus, C. N., Ely, G. E., & Wodarski, J. S. (2003). Children's psychological response to parental victimization: How do girls and boys differ? *Journal of Human Behavior in the Social Environment, 7*, 23–36.

Dulmus, C. N., & Wodarski, J. S. (2000). Trauma-related symptomatology among children of parents victimized by urban community violence. *American Journal of Orthopsychiatry, 70*, 272–277.

Ensink, K., Robertson, B. A., Zissis, C., & Leger, P. (1997). Post-traumatic stress disorder in children exposed to violence. *South African Medical Journal, 87*, 1526–1530.

Erikson, E. (Ed.). (1964). *Inner and outer space: Reflections on womanhood.* Boston: Beacon Press.

Eth, S. (2001). *PTSD in children and adolescents: A developmental-interactional model of child abuse.* Washington, DC: American Psychiatric Association.

Farrell, A. D., & Bruce, S. E. (1997). Impact of exposure to community violence on violent behavior and emotional distress among urban adolescents. *Journal of Clinical Child Psychology, 26*, 2–14.

Feiring, C., Taska, L., & Lewis, M. (1999). Age and gender differences in children's and adolescents' adaptation to sexual abuse. *Child Abuse & Neglect, 23*, 115–128.

Figley, C. R. (1995a). Compassion fatigue as secondary traumatic stress disorder: An overview. In R. E. Charles (Ed.), *Compassion fatigue: Coping with secondary traumatic stress disorder in those who treat the traumatized* (pp. 1–20). New York: Brunner/Mazel.

Figley, C. R. (Ed.). (1995b). *Compassion fatigue: Coping with secondary traumatic stress disorder in those who treat the traumatized.* New York: Brunner/Mazel.

Finkelhor, D. (1995). The victimization of children: A developmental perspective. *America Journal of Orthopsychiatry, 65*, 177–193.

Finkelhor, D. (Ed.). (1997). *The victimization of children and youth: Developmental victimology* (Vol. 2). Thousand Oaks, CA: Sage Publications.

Finkelhor, D., & Asdigian, N. L. (1996). Risk factors for youth victimization: Beyond a lifestyles/routine activities theory approach. *Violence Victims, 11*, 3–19.

Fitzpatrick, K. M., & Boldizar, J. P. (1993). The prevalence and consequences of exposure to violence among African-American youth. *Journal of the American Academy of Child & Adolescent Psychiatry, 32*, 424–430.

Ford, J. D., Racusin, R., Ellis, C. G., & Daviss, W. B. (2000). Child maltreatment, other trauma exposure, and posttraumatic symptomatology among children with oppositional defiant and attention deficit hyperactivity disorders. *Child Maltreatment, 5*, 205–217.

Freud, S. (1933). *The psychology of women* (J. Strachey, Trans. Vol. 22). London: Hogarth Press.

Garbarino, J. (1993). Children's response to community violence: What do we know? Irving Harris Symposium on Prevention and Intervention: The effects of violence on infants and young children: International perspectives on prevention (1992, Chicago, Illinois). *Infant Mental Health Journal, 14*, 103–115.

Garbarino, J. (1995a). The American war zone: What children can tell us about living with violence. *Journal of Developmental & Behavioral Pediatrics, 16*, 431–435.

Garbarino, J. (1995b). Growing up in a socially toxic environment: Life for children and families in the 1990s. In B. M. Gary (Ed.), *The individual, the family, and social good: Personal fulfillment in times of change. Nebraska Symposium on Motivation, Vol. 42* (pp. 1–20). Lincoln: University of Nebraska Press.

Glodich, A. (1998). Traumatic exposure to violence: A comprehensive review of the child and adolescent literature. *Smith College Studies in Social Work, 68*, 321–345.

Glodich, A., & Allen, J. G. (1998). Adolescents exposed to violence and abuse: A review of the group therapy literature with an emphasis on preventing trauma reenactment. *Journal of Child & Adolescent Group Therapy, 8*, 135–154.

Gorman-Smith, D., & Tolan, P. (1998). The role of exposure to community violence and development problems among inner-city youth. *Development and Psychopathology, 10*, 101–116.

Gorman-Smith, D., Tolan, P. H., & Henry, D. (1999). The relation of community and family to risk among urban-poor adolescents. In P. Cohen, L. Robins, & C. Slomkowski (Eds.), *Where and when: Influence of historical time and place on aspects of psychopathology* (pp. 349–367). Hillsdale, NJ: Lawrence Erlbaum Associates.

Hien, D., & Bukszpan, C. (1999). Interpersonal violence in a "normal" low-income control group. *Women & Health, 29*, 1–16.

Hodges, E. V., & Perry, D. G. (1999). Personal and interpersonal antecedents and consequences of victimization by peers. *Journal of Personality and Social Psychology, 76*, 677–685.

Keane, T. M., & Kaloupek, D. G. (1997). Comorbid psychiatric disorders in PTSD. Implications for research. *Annals of the New York Academy of Sciences, 821*, 24–34.

Keane, T. M., Taylor, K. L., & Penk, W. E. (1997). Differentiating posttraumatic stress disorder (PTSD) from major depression (MDD) and generalized anxiety disorder (GAD). *Journal of Anxiety Disorders, 11*, 317–328.

Kilpatrick, K. L., & Williams, L. M. (1997). Post-traumatic stress disorder in child witnesses to domestic violence. *American Journal of Orthopsychiatry, 67*, 639–644.

Kliewer, W., Lepore, S. J., Oskin, D., & Johnson, P. D. (1998). The role of social and cognitive processes in children's adjustment to community violence. *Journal of Consulting and Clinical Psychology, 66*, 199–209.

Leadbeater, B. J., Kuperminc, G. P., Blatt, S. J., & Hertzog, C. (1999). A multivariate model of gender differences in adolescents' internalizing and externalizing problems. *Developmental Psychology, 35*, 1268–1282.

Levit, D. B. (1991). Gender differences in ego defenses in adolescence: Sex roles as one way to understand the differences. *Journal of Personality and Social Psychology, 61*, 992–999.

Lorion, R. P., & Saltzman, W. (1993). Children's exposure to community violence: Following a path from concern to research to action. *Psychiatry, 56*, 55–65.

Marans, S., & Adelman, A. (Eds.). (1997). *Experiencing violence in a developmental context*. New York: Guilford Press.

McCloskey, L. A., & Walker, M. (2000). Posttraumatic stress in children exposed to family violence and single-event trauma. *Journal of the American Academy of Child & Adolescent Psychiatry, 39*, 108–115.

Miller, L. S., Wasserman, G. A., Neugebauer, R., Gorman-Smith, D., & Kamboukos, D. (1999). Witnessed community violence and antisocial behavior in high-risk, urban boys. *Journal of Clinical Child Psychology, 28*, 2–11.

Osofsky, J. D. (1995). The effect of exposure to violence on young children. *American Psychologist, 50*, 782–788.

Osofsky, J. D. (1999). The impact of violence on children. *Future of Children, 9*, 33–49.

Peebles-Kleiger, M. J., & Kleiger, J. H. (1994). Reintegration stress for Desert Storm families: Wartime deployments and family trauma. *Journal of Traumatic Stress, 7*, 173–194.

Piaget, J. (1973). The affective unconscious and the cognitive unconscious. *Journal of the American Psychoanalytic Association, 21*, 249–261.

Pynoos, R. S., Goenjian, A., Tashjian, M., Karakashian, M., Manjikian, R., Manoukian, G., Steinberg, A. M., & Fairbanks, L. A. (1993). Post-traumatic stress reactions in children after the 1988 Armenian earthquake. *British Journal of Psychiatry, 163*, 239–247.

Pynoos, R. S., Nader, K., Frederick, C., Gonda, L., & Stuber, M. (1987). Grief reactions in school-age children following a sniper attack at school. *Israel Journal of Psychiatry and Related Sciences, 24*, 53–63.

Raveis, V. H., Siegel, K., & Karus, D. (1999). Children's psychological distress following the death of a parent. *Journal of Youth and Adolescence, 28*, 165–180.

Schwab-Stone, M., Chen, C., Greenberger, E., Silver, D., Lichtman, J., & Voyce, C. (1999). No safe haven II: The effects of violence exposure on urban youth. *Journal of the American Academy of Child & Adolescent Psychiatry, 38*, 359–367.

Shaw, D. S., Winslow, E. B., Owens, E. B., Vondra, J. I., Cohn, J. F., & Bell, R. Q. (1998). The development of early externalizing problems among children from low-income families: A transformational perspective. *Journal of Abnormal Child Psychology, 26*, 95–107.

Singer, M. I., Anglin, T. M., Song, L. Y., & Lunghofer, L. (1995). Adolescents' exposure to violence and associated symptoms of psychological trauma. *JAMA, 273*, 477–482.

Song, L. Y., Singer, M. I., & Anglin, T. M. (1998). Violence exposure and emotional trauma as contributors to adolescents' violent behaviors. *Archive of Pediatric & Adolescent Medicine, 152*, 531–536.

Terr, L. C. (1979). Children of Chowchilla: A study of psychic trauma. *Psychoanalytical Study of Children, 34*, 547–623.

Terr, L. C. (1981). Psychic trauma in children: Observations following the Chowchilla school-bus kidnapping. *American Journal of Psychiatry, 138*, 14–19.

Trickett, P. K., & Schellenbach, C. J. (1998). *Violence against children in the family and the community*. Washington, DC: American Psychological Association.

**About the authors**: *Catherine N. Dulmus*, Ph.D., LCSW, ACSW, is associate professor and director, Buffalo Center for Social Research, University at Buffalo, 221 Parker Hall, Buffalo, NY 14214 (E-mail: cdulmus@buffalo.edu). *Carolyn Hilarski*, Ph.D., LCSW, ACSW, is associate professor, Social Work Department, Buffalo State College, New York.

# Exercise for Article 19

## Factual Questions

1. What is the explicitly stated research question?

2. What percentage of the parents approached who met the criteria provided contact information?

3. Who offered names of children who might serve in the control group?

4. Did the children in the exposure group witness the parents' victimization?

5. Were all the children in daily contact with their parents before the victimizing event?

6. Did the 9- to 12-year olds *or* the 6- to 8-year olds have higher internalizing scores on the CBCL?

## Questions for Discussion

7. Is it important to know that review board approval to conduct this research was obtained? Explain. (See lines 150–152.)

8. The researchers state that they used a "convenience sample." Is it important to know this? Explain. (See lines 182–195.)

9. What is your opinion on the advisability of paying individuals for participation in research? (See lines 229–231.)

10. In your opinion, do the researchers make the meanings of the terms "internalizing" and "externalizing" behavior clear? (See lines 238–241 and 264–284.)

11. In your opinion, does the use of a control group make this study an "experiment"? Explain.

12. The researchers state this limitation: "…the study did not take into account the amount of contact the child had with the parent before the victimization, which may have affected study results." How important is this limitation? (See lines 395–398.)

## Quality Ratings

Directions: Indicate your level of agreement with each of the following statements by circling a number from 5 for strongly agree (SA) to 1 for strongly disagree (SD). If you believe an item is not applicable to this research article, leave it blank. Be prepared to explain your ratings. When responding to criteria A and B, keep in mind that brief titles and abstracts are conventional in published research.

A.   The title of the article is appropriate.

SA   5   4   3   2   1   SD

B.   The abstract provides an effective overview of the research article.

SA   5   4   3   2   1   SD

C.   The introduction establishes the importance of the study.

SA   5   4   3   2   1   SD

D.   The literature review establishes the context for the study.

SA   5   4   3   2   1   SD

E.   The research purpose, question, or hypothesis is clearly stated.

SA   5   4   3   2   1   SD

F.   The method of sampling is sound.

SA   5   4   3   2   1   SD

G.   Relevant demographics (for example, age, gender, and ethnicity) are described.

SA   5   4   3   2   1   SD

H.   Measurement procedures are adequate.

SA   5   4   3   2   1   SD

I.   All procedures have been described in sufficient detail to permit a replication of the study.

SA   5   4   3   2   1   SD

J.   The participants have been adequately protected from potential harm.

SA   5   4   3   2   1   SD

K.   The results are clearly described.

SA   5   4   3   2   1   SD

L.   The discussion/conclusion is appropriate.

SA   5   4   3   2   1   SD

M.   Despite any flaws, the report is worthy of publication.

SA   5   4   3   2   1   SD

# Article 20

# Age Effects in Earwitness Recall of a Novel Conversation

JONATHAN LING
University of Teesside, UK

ALLISON COOMBE
University of Teesside, UK

ABSTRACT. Recall of conversation is an important part of memory for events. Previous studies have focused predominantly on adults. In the present study, 195 participants ages 11 to 63 years listened to a novel audiotaped conversation. They were not informed they would later have to recall elements of this conversation. Recall was a week later. There were no age-related differences in the recall of children ages 11, 13, and 15; however, there was a difference between retention over 7 days of children and adults, with adults recalling more information correctly. No sex differences were observed. These results are evaluated in the context of research on eye and earwitness recall and suggestions for research are given.

From *Perceptual and Motor Skills*, *100*, 774–776. Copyright © 2005 by Perceptual and Motor Skills. Reprinted with permission.

Most investigations of earwitness testimony have focused on identification (Roebuck & Wilding, 1993) rather than recall, although recall of conversation does appear to be a particularly poor aspect of memory (Huss & Weaver, 1996). Researchers have yet to clar-
5   ify whether there is a relationship between age and earwitness performance, as there may be confounds with other variables like knowledge (Chi, 1983). In a study of children ages 8, 11, and 15 yr., Saywitz (1987)
10   found few differences between 11- and 15-year-olds, which may be indicative of a plateau in auditory recall from mid to late childhood. It is unclear whether this plateau persists into adulthood.

The aim of this investigation was to compare the
15   recall of children and adults for a conversation heard as bystanders. No direct comparison has been made, so it is unclear how or whether earwitness recall changes across age groups. To control for knowledge, we presented information to participants about which they
20   would have little knowledge, daily life in rural Angola.

## Method

### Participants

A sample of 195 participants, including 95 females, was recruited. There were 93 children ages 11–16 years. Thirty-five were ages 11–12 ($M = 11.5$), 32 ages from 13–14 ($M = 13.4$), and 26 ages from 15–16 ($M =$
25   15.6). There were 98 adults ages 20–63 years. Adults were divided into four age groups: 20–29 yr. (45 participants; $M = 23.6$), 30–39 yr. (18 participants; $M = 34.5$), 40–49 (17 participants; $M = 44.7$), and 50–59 (18 participants; $M = 54.8$). Children came from one
30   school; adults were recruited from social clubs.

### Materials

A 12-min. audiotape of a conversation between two females was produced. This contained information about one female's experiences in Angola, including information about the weather, the guerilla war, and
35   everyday life in the country.

Recall was assessed by questionnaire, which was checked by teachers from the participating school to ensure comprehension. The questionnaire had 17 questions that related to characteristics of Angola (e.g.,
40   "What was a katanger?").

### Procedure

Children listened to the tape in class; adults listened in quiet areas of the clubs. Participants were not informed they had to recall the conversation; as a cover, adults rated the age-appropriateness of the conversa-
45   tion. A week later, they were read a set of instructions before completion of a questionnaire. There was no time limit. Participants were thanked and fully debriefed.

### Results and Discussion

No age group had a high mean, and no group
50   scored higher than 10 out of a maximum of 17. Analysis of variance ($F_{6,190} = 47.01$, $p < .001$) indicated an age effect. Post hoc tests indicated that children of all ages differed from all age groups of adults (Tukey HSD, all $p < .01$), with children performing more
55   poorly (see Table 1).

There was no sex difference ($F_{1,190} = .330$, $p > .05$) or interaction between sex and age ($F_{6,190} = .665$, $p > .05$).

Overall, recall of conversation after a 1-wk. delay
60   was poor, with no group exceeding 60% correct. Although recall was generally inaccurate, adults showed no age group differences in performance, unlike those in recognition observed by Bull and Clifford (1984). The findings that children did not show good recall for
65   the content of the conversation and the absence of age

Table 1
*Mean Proportion Correct and Raw Scores*

| Age (yr.) | *n* | Proportion correct | *M* | *SD* |
|---|---|---|---|---|
| 11 | 35 | .23 | 3.94 | 2.22 |
| 13 | 32 | .24 | 4.00 | 2.22 |
| 15 | 26 | .22 | 3.68 | 1.74 |
| 20–29 | 45 | .51 | 8.69 | 2.05 |
| 30–39 | 18 | .55 | 9.39 | 1.65 |
| 40–49 | 17 | .51 | 8.59 | 1.87 |
| 50+ | 18 | .53 | 9.06 | 2.04 |
| Overall | 191 | .38 | 6.39 | 3.20 |

differences in recall by children of different ages replicate those of other researchers. Such results indicate children and adults appear to have particular difficulty in remembering conversations.

70    This study highlights that children's recall of conversation may be less reliable than adults', at least when recall occurs some time after the event. However, the reported age differences may be related to the way children were questioned—with a questionnaire—

75 unlike the more supportive methods employed by police and social workers. Although other research using interviews has also shown that children do not have good recall for conversations (Saywitz, 1987), researchers should explore whether such supportive

80 methods may reduce age differences.

### References

Bull, R., & Clifford, B. R. (1984). Earwitness testimony. *Medicine, Science, and the Law, 39,* 120–127.

Chi, M. T. H. (Ed.) (1983). *Trends in memory development.* Basel: Karger.

Huss, M. T., & Weaver, K. A. (1996). Effect of modality in earwitness identification: Memory for verbal and nonverbal auditory stimuli presented in two contexts. *The Journal of General Psychology, 123,* 277–287.

Roebuck, R., & Wilding, J. (1993). Effects of vowel variety and sample length on identification of a speaker in a line-up. *Applied Cognitive Psychology, 7,* 475–481.

Saywitz, K. J. (1987). Children's testimony: Age-related patterns of memory errors. In S. J. Ceci, M. P. Toglia, & D. F. Ross (Eds.), *Children's eyewitness memory.* New York: Springer-Verlag. Pp. 36–52.

**Address correspondence to**: Dr. Jonathan Ling, School of Psychology, Keele University, Keele, Staffs ST5 5BG, UK. E-mail: j.r.ling@psy.keele.ac.uk

# Exercise for Article 20

## Factual Questions

1. The children who participated came from how many schools?

2. The adults were recruited from what?

3. Was the analysis of variance for the age effect statistically significant? Explain.

4. Was there a statistically significant sex difference? Explain.

5. Did the researchers regard the recall of the conversation after one week to be "good"?

6. Table 1 shows the proportion correct for various age groups. Proportions can be converted to percentages by multiplying by 100. What is the correct *percentage* for the 11-year-old group?

## Questions for Discussion

7. The researchers state that to control for knowledge, they presented information to participants about which they would have little knowledge. In your opinion, is this important? Explain. (See lines 18–20.)

8. The questionnaire was checked by teachers to ensure comprehension. Was this a good idea? Explain. (See lines 36–38.)

9. The conversation used in this study concerned daily life in rural Angola. In your opinion, might a conversation on a different topic produce differences in recall? Explain. (See lines 18–20.)

10. Do you think that this study shows that increasing age is related to increased earwitness recall? Explain. (See lines 70–72.)

11. Do you agree with the researchers that measuring recall with a questionnaire might produce different results than more supportive methods (e.g., individual interviews) used by police and social workers? (See lines 72–76.)

## Quality Ratings

Directions: Indicate your level of agreement with each of the following statements by circling a number from 5 for strongly agree (SA) to 1 for strongly disagree (SD). If you believe an item is not applicable to this research article, leave it blank. Be prepared to explain your ratings. When responding to criteria A and B, keep in mind that brief titles and abstracts are conventional in published research.

A.   The title of the article is appropriate.

        SA   5   4   3   2   1   SD

B.   The abstract provides an effective overview of the research article.

        SA   5   4   3   2   1   SD

C.   The introduction establishes the importance of the study.

        SA   5   4   3   2   1   SD

D.   The literature review establishes the context for the study.

        SA   5   4   3   2   1   SD

E.   The research purpose, question, or hypothesis is clearly stated.

        SA   5   4   3   2   1   SD

F.   The method of sampling is sound.

        SA   5   4   3   2   1   SD

G.   Relevant demographics (for example, age, gender, and ethnicity) are described.

        SA   5   4   3   2   1   SD

H.   Measurement procedures are adequate.

        SA   5   4   3   2   1   SD

I.   All procedures have been described in sufficient detail to permit a replication of the study.

        SA   5   4   3   2   1   SD

J.   The participants have been adequately protected from potential harm.

        SA   5   4   3   2   1   SD

K.   The results are clearly described.

        SA   5   4   3   2   1   SD

L.   The discussion/conclusion is appropriate.

        SA   5   4   3   2   1   SD

M.   Despite any flaws, the report is worthy of publication.

        SA   5   4   3   2   1   SD

# Article 21

# Feasibility of an Intergenerational Tai Chi Program: A Community-Based Participatory Research Project

CYNTHIA K. PERRY
University of Washington

KIM WEATHERBY
Fuller Theological Seminary

ABSTRACT. Physical activity programs targeted at only older adults or youth have minimal success. The researchers explore intergenerational programming as an approach to promoting physical activity using community-based participatory research. Study goals are to design and assess the feasibility and efficacy for increasing physical activity and social interaction among older adults and youth through an intergenerational physical activity program. Seven older adults and seven youth completed an eight-week tai chi program. There was interaction between the generations and increased physical activity. Further research is warranted to determine the optimal approach to enhance interaction and physical activity between two generations.

From *Journal of Intergenerational Relationships*, *9*, 69–84. Copyright © 2011 by Taylor & Francis Group, LLC. Reprinted with permission.

Engaging in physical activity on a regular basis is important to the health of both older adults and youth. Despite recognized health benefits from physical activity, fewer than 15% of older adults and 35% of youth
5 report being sufficiently active to achieve health benefits (Trost et al., 2002; United States Department of Health and Human Services, 2000). The percentage of racial and ethnic minority older adults and youth meeting physical activity recommendations is dramatically
10 lower (Eaton et al., 2008; Kruger, Kohl, & Miles, 2007). Compared with other age cohorts, older adult and youth age cohorts both experience a greater decline in physical activity with increasing age. Physical activity programs aimed at only older adults or at youth
15 have had minimal success at best, often not reaching the recommended levels of physical activity (Conn, Minor, Burks, Rantz, & Pomeroy, 2003; Stone, McKenzie, Welk, & Booth, 1998; van der Bij, Laurant, & Wensing, 2002); thus, it is worth considering new
20 approaches such as intergenerational programming. Older adults enjoy interacting with youth, and this interaction might be a source of motivation to engage in physical activity programs. The purpose of this study was to design and implement an enjoyable intergenera-

25 tional physical activity program that encourages intergenerational interaction among a multiethnic population using a community-based participatory research approach.

## Intergenerational Physical Activity Programs

Developing an intergenerational physical activity
30 program that targets older adults and adolescents is an innovative approach to addressing the cohort-related declines in physical activity. There are, however, few published reports of intergenerational programs. One such program was designed to increase physical activ-
35 ity in mothers and daughters through home-based or community-based programs. Using sit-ups to measure muscular endurance, the sit-and-reach test to measure flexibility, and the 1-mile walk test to measure fitness, this study found that both mothers and daughters ex-
40 perienced significant improvement in muscular endurance and mothers experienced significant improvement in fitness and flexibility at the end of the 12-week program (Ransdell et al., 2003). Mothers and daughters exercised together 100% of the time in the community-
45 based program and 59% of the time in the home-based program. These results demonstrate that two related generations are willing to participate in a physical activity program together and can achieve improved physical outcomes. The authors extended this emerging
50 research on intergenerational physical activity and examined whether involving unrelated individuals from two generations in a physical activity program would be enjoyable and challenging for both generations while simultaneously encouraging increased interaction
55 among the generations.

## Youth and Older Adults' Physical Activity Determinants

The recommended amount of physical activity for youth is at least 60 minutes of moderate to vigorous physical activity daily (United States Department of Health and Human Services, 2008) and for older adults
60 30 minutes of moderate intensity activity on most, preferably all, days of the week (Nelson et al., 2007). Factors that influence youth engagement in the recom-

mended level of vigorous physical activity include per-ceived physical competence, prior positive physical activity experiences, body image, fun, and enjoyment (Brooks & Magnusson, 2006; Sallis, Prochaska, & Taylor, 2000); spending time with peers and experiencing positive social interaction and support from them (Sirad, Pfeiffer, & Pate, 2006; Wilson et al. 2005); parental support and physically active siblings (Gordon-Larsen, McMurray, & Popkin, 2000; Sallis et al., 2000). Factors influencing older adults' levels of physical activity include time, energy, self-efficacy, presence of chronic health conditions and disabilities, perceived health benefits from exercise, enjoyment of physical activity, interaction during exercise and social support from family and friends as facilitators (Belza et al., 2004; Dergance et al., 2003).

This community-based participatory research study was conducted in three phases. The goal of the study was to develop and evaluate an intergenerational physical activity program. The specific aims are to assess the feasibility (practicability, acceptability, and perceived benefits/satisfaction) and potential efficacy of increasing physical activity and social interaction among a diverse population of older adults and youth through an intergenerational tai chi program.

## Methods

### Community-Based Participatory Research

We used a community-based participatory research (CBPR) approach, believing that working collaboratively would develop a program that is salient to the community and more likely to be acceptable and effective. In a CBPR project, involvement is commonly achieved by building an equitable academic-community partnership in which each member has equal voice in decisions about data collection and the development and implementation of health promotion programs (Horowitz, Robinson, & Seifer, 2009; Israel, Eng, Schulz, & Parker, 2005). Research endeavors using CBPR are effective and have enhanced data quality and community investment (Horowitz et al., 2009; Viswanathan et al., 2004) and are recommended for advancing chronic disease prevention research (Institute of Medicine, 2001).

### Phase 1: Community Planning

The study was conducted in a multiethnic urban neighborhood in Seattle, Washington, population 80,000, with 38% Asian, 27% African American, 23% white, and 19% other races and ethnicities (United States Census Bureau, 2002). Twelve percent of the population is over 65, and 24% is 18 years of age or less. Median household income is $44,615, with 13% below the federal poverty level (United States Census Bureau, 2002).

Initially, the investigator, who is with the University of Washington School of Nursing, learned about the health issues of a diverse and low-income urban neighborhood by developing relationships with community members and neighborhood stakeholders. Community members reported that they enjoy participating in intergenerational programs. Community leaders expressed interest in developing an intergenerational physical activity program to combine the goals of promoting physical activity and interaction among generations. The investigator and a Christian-based, nonprofit community organization operating in the neighborhood decided to partner and work together on designing and testing an intergenerational physical activity program within the neighborhood because all parties have similar goals and interests. This community organization comprises three main programs: a youth academic program, a community gym, and an economic development program. In concert with a CBPR approach, a community advisory board (CAB) that consisted of four members was established. The CAB met regularly for six months discussing shared concerns and goals and developing a program grant proposal that was subsequently funded.

### Phase II: Program Development

Program objectives include promoting physical activity and promoting interaction among youth and older adults. A CAB member administered a survey and conducted focus groups with the older adults and parents of youth members in the community organization to elicit preferences in programming and interest in participating in an intergenerational physical activity program. Findings reveal an interest in participating in an intergenerational program and a preference for a weekly tai chi class. Since the community expressed an interest in learning tai chi, the researchers chose tai chi for the intergenerational physical activity class. Of note, tai chi has the potential to reduce the risk of falls in the elderly (Low, Ang, Goh, & Chew, 2009).

Over the next two months, the researchers developed the structure of the tai chi class, determining that a weekly 60-minute class held for eight weeks at the community gym was workable, taking into account the available resources for the program. Organizers enlisted a tai chi instructor experienced in working with both older adults and youth to teach the class although she had not previously taught an intergenerational class.

Social cognitive theory guided the use of specific strategies designed to encourage continued and consistent participation in the tai chi classes. Social cognitive theory describes a reciprocal dynamic relationship between intrapersonal, environmental and behavioral factors that influence behavior (Bandura, 1997). The tai chi program focused on increasing confidence, social support, and social interaction among the participants. In order to encourage the development of confidence, the tai chi instructor created an atmosphere that focused on skill building and provided informational messages and positive reinforcement (Bandura, 1997). These methods afford the youth and older adults the

opportunity to learn and practice skills and to acquire a sense of mastery and competence in the skills. Empha-
175 sis is placed on skill building and fun in order to enhance enjoyment and confidence (Bandura, 1997). In order to encourage social support and interaction, the tai chi instructor paired the older adults and youth for interactive exercises or poses. A high school intern
180 who assisted the instructor in the class provided positive reinforcement, encouraged ongoing participation in the classes, and promoted interaction and support between the two generations. These strategies were reviewed with the tai chi instructor and high school
185 intern prior to the start of the classes.

Researchers finalized study methods including recruitment strategies and data collection instruments. In order to foster youth leadership, two high school interns were designated to assist in recruitment and to
190 conduct all data collection. The interns were trained in recruitment, protection of confidentiality, data integrity, and data collection procedures.

*Pilot Test*

Researchers ran a four-week tai chi class during the summer to pilot recruitment strategies, study meas-
195 ures, data collection procedures, and class structure. Older adults were recruited via flyers at the community gym, the community organization center, and local senior center. Researchers used screening forms to ascertain if older adults had medical contraindications to
200 participating in a low- to- moderate-intensity physical activity program. Youth were recruited via flyers at the community organization center. Also, researchers held a focus group with some of the participants to learn about their experiences with the tai chi program. A
205 facilitation guide was developed for the focus group to ensure that key areas were covered. University institutional review board (IRB) approval was obtained prior to the start of the pilot study.

Based on researchers' experiences with this pilot
210 and the findings from the focus group, a few of the study procedures were revised. Only youth enrolled in the pilot. The lack of older adult enrollment is due, in part, to the screening questionnaire excluding interested older adults who have more than one risk factor
215 for heart disease (e.g., hypertension, diabetes). Additionally, researchers had set the upper age limit at 70, which excluded interested older adults who are over 70 years of age. Therefore, organizers replaced use of the screening forms with the requirement of medical re-
220 leases from health care providers and changed the upper age limit to 85. Some participants found one item on one of the questionnaires confusing and, therefore, that item was dropped. Finally, organizers changed the time of the class from 1:00 p.m. to 4:00 p.m. to ac-
225 commodate school hours.

**Phase III: Feasibility Study**

University IRB approval was obtained prior to the start of the feasibility study.

*Design*

A quasi-experimental, one-group prepost test design has been used to assess the feasibility of imple-
230 menting the program and its potential to increase physical activity, enjoyment of physical activity, and intergenerational interaction. Figure 1 delineates the data collection timeframe.

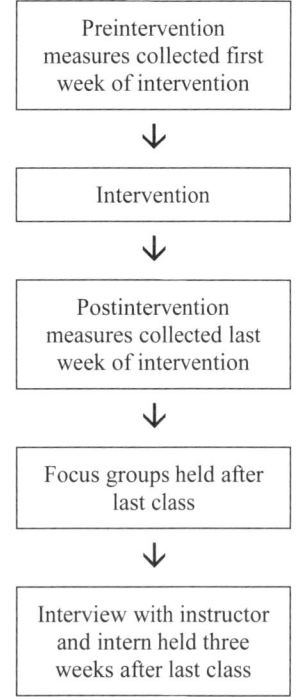

*Figure 1.* Feasibility study design.

*Sample*

Recruitment strategies were the same as in the pi-
235 lot study. Youth were eligible to participate if they were between the ages of 8 and 14. Older adults were eligible to participate if they were between the ages of 60 and 85 and had clearance to participate from their primary health care providers.

*Study Measures*

240 Study measures were collected pre- and postintervention by two high school interns.

*Demographic Data*

Demographic data were collected at the beginning of the study only.

*Physical Activity*

The 7-Day Physical Activity Recall (7DPAR)
245 (Blair et al., 1985; Sallis, 1997; Sallis, Buono, Roby, Micale, & Nelson, 1993) was used to recall physical activity over the past seven days. The 7DPAR measures activity beyond planned exercise sessions, such as active transport or household chores. Participants are
250 asked to estimate the number of hours spent during each day in sleep and moderate, hard, and very hard

activities. It is assumed the rest of the day is spent in light activities that may not be easily recalled. The number of minutes spent in sleep and light, moderate, hard, and very hard activities are totaled for the week. Significant correlations between the 7DPAR and maximum aerobic capability ($VO_2$ max) support concurrent validity (Blair et al., 1985).

*Enjoyment*

The Physical Activity Enjoyment Scale (PACES) was used to measure enjoyment of physical activity (Motl et al., 2001.). The scale consists of 16 statements describing responses associated with physical activity (e.g., exciting, boring). Respondents rate their agreement with the statements on a 5-point Likert scale with 1 being *disagree a lot* and 5 being *agree a lot*. Factor analysis establishes factorial validity and correlation with factors that influence enjoyment in physical activity establishes construct validity (Motl et al., 2001).

*Feasibility Evaluation*

Data were collected to assess intervention feasibility (see Table 1). The program is considered feasible if it is found to be practical and acceptable and attendees report perceived benefits and satisfaction. Practicality is achieved and is defined as if the community organization is capable of carrying out the program and both older adults and youth are able to attend the program. Acceptability is defined as both older adults and youth reporting in the focus groups that they like participating in the exercises and interacting with another generation. The last element of feasibility, perceived benefits and satisfaction, was defined as benefits and satisfaction with the program reported in the focus groups by older adults and youth.

Table 1
*Data Sources to Assess Intervention Feasibility*

| Intervention feasibility components | Data sources |
| --- | --- |
| Practicality | ▪Attendance |
| | ▪Group interview with instructor and high school intern |
| Acceptability | ▪Focus groups with adults and youth |
| Perceived benefits and satisfaction | ▪Focus groups with adults and youth |
| | ▪Group interview with instructor and high school intern |

Attendance was taken at every tai chi class. Focus groups, one with the youth and one with the older adults, were held at the end of the 8-week program. A facilitation guide was developed for the focus group with youth and for the group with older adults to ensure key areas were covered. The purpose of the focus groups was to gain insights regarding the acceptance of the program, concerns with the program, and suggestions for refining the program. A group interview was held with the tai chi instructor and the high school intern to gain insight regarding interaction among the participants, the ease of implementing the program, barriers to implementation, and problems that arose during the course of the eight weeks.

*Data Analysis*

Quantitative data were entered into SPSS (Chicago, IL). Descriptive statistics including the frequencies, distribution, and means were calculated. Wilcoxon signed rank test was used to compare baseline differences by generation for physical activity (total minutes for past seven days). Change in physical activity over time by generation also was analyzed using Wilcoxon signed rank test. Qualitative data were analyzed using qualitative description with the goal of providing a comprehensive descriptive summary of the responses in the focus groups and the group interview. Qualitative description typically stays closer to the data than other interpretive qualitative methods and does not require highly abstract analysis of data (Sandelowski, 2000). Data were coded based on responses and then categorized into themes of practicality, acceptability, and perceived benefits and satisfaction.

## Results

*Outcomes Evaluation*

Eight youth and 10 older adults were recruited, and 7 youth and 7 older adults completed the 8-week program. Table 2 delineates sample characteristics for the 14 participants who completed the intergenerational program.

Youth and older adults experienced an increase in physical activity, although it was not statistically significant (Wilcoxon Signed Rank Test, $p = 0.06$). The pre- and postphysical activity levels based on the 7-day PAR for each participant are depicted in Figure 2. The youth who experienced a dramatic decrease in physical activity pre- and postintervention was involved in a sports team. The team practices and games ended two weeks prior to the end of the intervention, explicating this youth's decline in physical activity pre- to postintervention. Five youth and five older adults rate the program as enjoyable or very enjoyable, and two youth gave the program a neutral rating.

## Feasibility Evaluation

*Practicality*

Five youth and all of the older adults attended at least 50% of the classes. The tai chi instructor and the high school intern commented that the lower youth attendance was, in part, due to lack of transportation to the class. The instructor thought the classes went very well, and she was impressed with the commitment of the older adults. However, the high school intern thought that 60 minutes was too long because some of the youth begin to lose interest toward the latter part of the class. The instructor and the program director thought the program ran smoothly.

Table 2
*Sample Characteristics*

|  | Youth (*n* = 7) | Seniors (*n* = 7) |
|---|---|---|
| Gender: No. (%) |  |  |
| Female | 3 (42.9%) | 6 (85.7%) |
| Male | 4 (57.1%) | 1 (14.3%) |
| Ethnicity: No. (%) |  |  |
| Hispanic | 0 (0%) | 1 (14.3%) |
| Non-Hispanic | 7 (100%) | 6 (85.7%) |
| Racial background: No. (%) |  |  |
| African American | 2 (28.6%) | 2 (28.6%) |
| Asian | 5 (71.4%) |  |
| White | 0 (0%) | 4 (57.1%) |
| Marital status: No. (%) | N/A |  |
| Married |  | 0 (0%) |
| Single |  | 4 (57%) |
| Divorced |  | 2 (28.6%) |
| Widowed |  | 1 (14.3%) |
| Work outside the home: No. (%) | N/A |  |
| Yes |  | 4 (57%) |
| No |  | 3 (42.9%) |
| Age: *M* (*SD*) | 10 (2.0) | 70 (8.0) |
| Years of education: *M* (*SD*) | 4.3 (1.9) | 14.7 (4.1) |

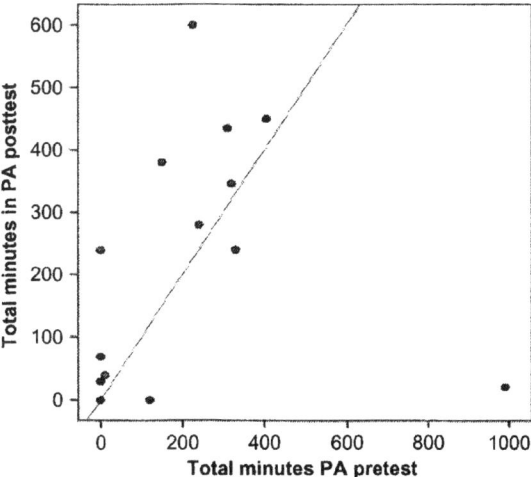

*Figure 2.* Participants' minutes of physical activity in the previous
seven days before and after participation in the tai chi program.

Collecting the pre- and postdata took more time than anticipated; yet both youth and older adults were cooperative with answering the questions.

*Acceptability*

All reported that they enjoyed attending the class. Many of the youth reported that they liked learning the poses. Some of the youth thought the exercises were slow. All stated that they liked spending time and talking with the older adults. One youth stated, "It was fun hanging out with the seniors because some of them have really good stories." Another stated, "They're very nice." All the youth thought that the older adults

worked hard in the class. All the older adults stated that being around the youth was energizing. One of the older adults commented, "I like being around the kids. Kids tend to make you feel a little younger." Many of the older adults commented that they found tai chi mentally challenging because they needed to concentrate on the poses in order to perform them and maintain their balance.

*Perceived Benefits/Satisfaction*

The tai chi instructor observed progress in performing the exercises among all the participants, some more than others. Many of the older adults and some of

365  the youth reported that they felt stronger after the eight-week class. Both the older adults and the youth reported that the exercises involved muscle strength and control and they found that the exercises strengthened their muscles, particularly muscles in the legs and but-
370  tocks. The older adults and youth reported learning new skills. For example, they learned how to focus on using certain muscles in order to perform a pose. A few of the older adults reported that participating in the class makes them more comfortable and likely to be
375  physically active.

The older adults and youth from all backgrounds were comfortable with one another, and interaction increased toward the end of the program. All the older adults reported that, at first, there was little interaction
380  between the generations but, after about a month, they began to interact with one another. One stated that, as time went on, "They got more comfortable with us and likewise with us to them," and the generations interacted more. Because they felt energized, they wanted
385  to do a more active exercise with the youth. Most of the older adults commented that a more active and continually interactive activity might spark more social interaction between the generations, specifically ballroom, line, or square dancing. "I think dancing, we
390  would interact more. You could do it alone or you could do it with a partner and you can do it in circles or squares or every which way. And it could be more vigorous or it could be more calm."

## Discussion

The findings from this feasibility study suggest
395  that older adults and youth enjoy participating in a physical activity class together and that participation in an intergenerational class has the potential to increase overall physical activity. Individuals from differing ethnic and racial backgrounds were comfortable par-
400  ticipating and interacting together in this intergenerational tai chi class. Both generations had the opportunity to learn new skills, be physically active, and interact with one another.

Intergenerational physical activity programs are
405  an innovative approach to addressing physical activity decline in both youth and older adults. Yet there are few published reports of other intergenerational programs, and most have emphasized increasing physical activity in the older adults rather than in both the youth
410  and adults. One program, Free-Wheelers, involved university students and wheelchair bound older adults and found that the participating adults benefitted from the program, which was carried out by the university students (Romack, 2004). As part of a service learning
415  class, students designed and implemented the Free-Wheelers program to 13 nursing home residents for one hour, three times a week for eight weeks. At the end of the eight weeks, the residents showed improved physical performance and diminished hopelessness.
420  However, this program was not designed to promote

physical activity in the university students. In the tai chi program, the researchers were interested in examining whether they could promote physical activity in both generations, simultaneously. This was accom-
425  plished by involving participants in a physical activity that was enjoyable, engaging, and challenging for both generations. The authors undertook the novel approach in our tai chi class in that both generations have the opportunity to learn new skills, be physically active,
430  and interact with one another.

Another intergenerational study examined whether older adults' (ages 60–86) participation in volunteer, yet sedentary, activities at an elementary school could foster an increase in older adults' physical
435  activity and social engagement (Fried et al., 2004). The intergenerational program involved teaching youth for 15 hours a week throughout an academic year. The 69 older adults, randomized to provide voluntary tutoring in elementary schools, increased their level of physical
440  activity and social engagement compared with the 56 older adults in the control group. The volunteer program did not incorporate physical activity within the program; those volunteering increased their physical activity by moving around the school and traveling to
445  and from the school.

In this tai chi study, researchers attempted to foster social engagement and physical activity among the generations, concurrently, in several ways. First, the instructor and high school intern created an atmosphere
450  of acceptance. Second, the tai chi class included exercises that necessitated older adults and youth to work together in pairs. However, the majority of poses were done individually. Third, the tai chi instructor and the high school intern encouraged interaction between the
455  generations before and after class. This time was limited because many came just before class started and left as soon as the class was over. A more effective approach to encouraging interaction might be teaching an inherently interactive form of physical activity, such
460  as line dancing, in which older adults and youth are paired as partners who will need to communicate during the dancing.

The majority of the youth and older adults enjoyed the class and reported learning new skills, and
465  older adults stated that they felt more confident about being physically active. The class provided an opportunity to enjoy and become confident with being physically active. Confidence and enjoyment are essential attributes to developing intrinsic motivation (Ryan &
470  Deci, 2000). The class emphasis on developing confidence and fostering enjoyment might have enhanced the motivation and desire to participate in the class and might have enhanced attendance at the class (Bandura, 1997; Ryan & Deci, 2000). In this study, the youth
475  became less engaged toward the end of the 60 minutes and the older adults stated that they would like to be more active; therefore, for future programs, the authors

recommend trying an activity in which there is more movement, such as dancing.

480    Individuals from differing ethnic and racial backgrounds were comfortable participating and interacting together in this intergenerational physical activity class. Recruitment of participants through an existing community-based program resulted in a greater sense

485 of social connection within the tai chi class from the onset of the study. Several of the enrolled youth were previously acquainted with one another through the community organization's academic program, and several of the enrolled older adults were familiar with one

490 another through the community organization's community gym. The previous connection provided a level of comfort within the group as participants experimented with new elements such as intergenerational interaction and tai chi. The 8-week class was held at

495 the community organization's community gym, a familiar location for many community members within the neighborhood.

The researchers used a CBPR approach in designing and testing the feasibility of the intergenerational

500 physical activity program. Although utilizing a CBPR approach takes additional time and commitment compared to a traditional research approach, these authors recommend using the approach when designing and implementing intergenerational physical activity pro-

505 grams within a diverse community. A CBPR approach facilitates collaborative partnerships between academic researchers and community organizations and builds on the existing strengths within a community to address health concerns (Israel et al., 2005). This approach

510 strengthens the meaning of the project that is undertaken because it takes into account community-specific concerns, resources, and circumstances (Schultz, Krieger, & Galea, 2002). A newly published guide based on best practices outlines the steps involved in

515 creating and implementing a community-based intergenerational physical activity program (Wright, 2008) and is available on the United Generations Web site.

There are limitations to this study. The sample size was small, reducing the power to detect a change

520 in physical activity. The intervention ran for only eight weeks, and the researchers lacked long-term follow-up to ascertain whether increased levels of physical activity were sustained. However, this study is an important first step in assessing the feasibility and potential to

525 increase physical activity of an intergenerational physical activity program prior to embarking on a larger study.

## Conclusion

Intergenerational physical activity programs are a novel approach to the ongoing problem of promoting

530 physical activity in youth and older adults. This approach provides the added benefit of intergenerational involvement. The findings from this feasibility study suggest that an intergenerational program can be im-

535 plemented and that physical activity and social interaction can be encouraged concurrently within the context of an intergenerational program. Further research is warranted to determine the optimal approach to enhance interaction and enjoyment of and amount of physical activity among two generations.

## References

Bandura, A. (1997). *Self-efficacy: The exercise of control*. New York: Freeman.

Belza, B., Walick, J., Shiu-Thornton, S., Schwartz, S., Taylor, M., & LoGerfo, J. (2004). Older adult perspectives on physical activity and exercise: Voices from multiple cultures. *Preventing Chronic Disease, 1*(4), 1–12.

Blair, S., Haskell, W., Ho, P., Paffenbarger, R., Vranizan, K., & Farquhar, J. (1985). Assessment of habitual physical activity by a seven-day recall in a community survey and controlled experiment. *American Journal of Epidemiology, 122*, 794–804.

Brooks, F., & Magnusson, J. (2006). Taking part counts: Adolescents' experience of the transition from inactivity to active participation in school-based physical education. *Health Education Research, 21*(6), 872–883.

Conn, V., Minor, M., Burks, K., Rantz, M., & Pomeroy, S. (2003). Integrative review of physical activity intervention research with aging adults. *Journal of the American Geriatrics Society, 51*, 1159–1168.

Dergance, J., Calmbach, W., Dhanda, R., Miles, T., Hazuda, H., & Mouton, C. (2003). Barriers and benefits of leisure time physical activity in the elderly: Difference across cultures. *Journal of the American Geriatrics Society, 51*, 863–868.

Eaton, D., Kann, L., Kinchen, S., Shanklin, S., Ross, J., Hawkins, J., et al. (2008). Youth risk behavior surveillance—United States, 2007. *Morbidity and Mortality Weekly Report, 57*(SSO4), 1–131.

Fried, L., Carlson, M., Freedman, M., Frick, K., Glass, T., Hill, J., et al. (2004). A social model for health promotion for an aging population: Initial evidence on the experience corps model. *Journal of Urban Health, 81*(1), 64–78.

Gordon-Larsen, P., McMurray, R., & Popkin, B. (2000). Determinants of adolescent physical activity and inactivity patterns. *Pediatrics, 105*(6), 83–89.

Horowitz, C., Robinson, M., & Seifer, S. (2009). Community-based participatory research from the margin to mainstream: Are researchers prepared? *Circulation, 119*, 2633–2642.

Institute of Medicine. (2001). *Health and behavior: The interplay of biological, behavioral, and social influences. Executive Summary*. Washington, DC: National Academy Press.

Israel, B., Eng, E., Schulz, A., & Parker, E. (2005). *Methods in community-based participatory research for health*. San Francisco: Jossey-Bass.

Kruger, J., Kohl, H., & Miles, I. (2007). Prevalence of regular physical activity among adults—United States, 2001 and 2005. *Morbidity and Mortality Weekly Report, 56*(46), 1209–1212.

Low, S., Ang, L., Goh, K., & Chew, S. (2009). A systematic review of the effectiveness of tai chi on fall reduction among the elderly. *Archives of Gerontology and Geriatrics, 48*, 325–331.

Motl, R., Dishman, R., Saunders, R., Dowda, M., Felton, G., & Pate, R. (2001). Measuring enjoyment of physical activity in adolescent girls. *American Journal of Preventive Medicine, 21*(2), 110–117.

Nelson, M., Rejeski, W., Blair, S., Duncan, P., Judge, J., King, A., et al. (2007). Physical activity and public health in older adults. Recommendation from the American College of Sports Medicine and the American Heart Association. *Circulation, 116*(9), 1094–1105.

Ransdell, L., Taylor, A., Oakland, D., Schmidt, J., Moyer-Mileur, L., & Shultz, B. (2003). Daughters and mothers exercising together: Effects of home-and community-based programs. *Medicine & Science in Sports & Exercise, 35*(2), 286–296.

Romack, J. (2004). Increasing physical activity in nursing home residents using student power, not dollars. *Educational Gerontology, 30*(1), 21.

Ryan, R., & Deci, E. (2000). Self-determination theory and the facilitation of intrinsic motivation, social development, and well-being. *American Psychologist, 55*(1), 68–78.

Sallis, J. (1997). Seven-day physical activity recall. *Medicine and Science in Sports and Exercise, 29*, (S89–103).

Sallis, J., Buono, M., Roby, J., Micale, F., & Nelson, J. (1993). Seven-day recall and other physical activity self-reports in children and adolescents. *Medicine and Science in Sports and Exercise, 25*, 99–108.

Sallis, J., Prochaska, J., & Taylor, W. (2000). A review of correlates of physical activity of children and adolescents. *Medicine and Science in Sports and Exercise, 32*(5), 963–975.

Sandelowski, M. (2000). Whatever happened to qualitative description? *Research in Nursing & Health, 23*, 334–340.

Schultz, A., Krieger, J., & Galea, S. (2002). Addressing social determinants of health: Community-based participatory approaches to research and practice. *Health Education and Behavior, 29*, 287–295.

Sirad, J., Pfeiffer, K., & Pate, R. (2006). Motivational factors associated with sports program participation in middle school students. *Journal of Adolescent Health, 38*, 696–703.

Stone, E., McKenzie, T., Welk, G., & Booth, M. (1998). Effects of physical activity interventions in youth: Review and synthesis. *American Journal of Preventive Medicine, 15*(4), 298–315.

Trost, S., Russell, P., Sallis, J., Freedson, P., Taylor, W., Dowda, M., et al. (2002). Age and gender differences in objectively measured physical activity in youth. *Medicine and Science in Sports & Exercise, 34*(2), 350–355.

United States Census Bureau. (2002). *Census 2000.* Washington, DC: Author.

United States Department of Health and Human Services. (2000). *Health people 2010: Understanding and improving health,* 2nd ed. Washington, DC: Government Printing Office.

United States Department of Health and Human Services. (2008). *2008 physical activity guidelines for Americans.* Washington, DC: U.S. Department of Health and Human Services.

van der Bij, A., Laurant, M., & Wensing, M. (2002). Effectiveness of physical activity interventions for older adults: A review. *American Journal of Preventive Medicine, 22*(2), 120–133.

Viswanathan, M., Ammerman, A., Eng, E., Gartlehner, G., Lohr, K., Griffith, D., et al. (2004). *Community-based participatory research: Assessing the evidence.* Evidence Report/Technology Assessment No. 99 (Prepared by RTI–University of North Carolina Evidence-based Practice Center under Contract No. 290-02-0016). AHRQ Publication 04-E022-2.

Wilson, D., Evans, A., Williams, J., Mixon, G., Sirad, J., & Pate, R. (2005). A preliminary test of a student centered intervention on increasing physical activity in underserved adolescents. *Annals of Behavioral Medicine, 30*(2), 119–124.

Wright, S. (2008). *A guide to intergenerational physical activity. A practical guide to implementing IGPA programs.* Ontario: Lifestyle Information Network.

**Address correspondence to**: Cynthia K. Perry, Ph.D., ARNP, Assistant Professor, Family and Child Nursing, University of Washington, Box 357262, Seattle, WA 98195-7262. E-mail: perryc@u.washington.edu

# Exercise for Article 21

## Factual Questions

1. Are there many published reports of intergenerational programs?

2. *CBPR* stands for what words?

3. Did older adults participate in the pilot test?

4. How many of the youth attended at least 50% of the classes?

5. Did the older adults indicate that being around the youth was energizing?

6. What was the mean age of the seniors?

## Questions for Discussion

7. What is your understanding of the meaning of the term *focus group*? (See lines 139–144 and 202–206.)

8. Is the pilot test an important part of this program evaluation? Explain. (See lines 193–225.)

9. In future studies on this topic, would you recommend the inclusion of a control group? Explain.

10. Are the limitations described in lines 519–528 important? Explain.

11. Do you agree that further research is warranted? (See lines 537–540.)

12. Has this study convinced you that an intergenerational program is superior to a single-generation program? Explain.

## Quality Ratings

Directions: Indicate your level of agreement with each of the following statements by circling a number from 5 for strongly agree (SA) to 1 for strongly disagree (SD). If you believe an item is not applicable to this research article, leave it blank. Be prepared to explain your ratings. When responding to criteria A and B, keep in mind that brief titles and abstracts are conventional in published research.

A. The title of the article is appropriate.

SA 5 4 3 2 1 SD

B. The abstract provides an effective overview of the research article.

SA 5 4 3 2 1 SD

C. The introduction establishes the importance of the study.

SA 5 4 3 2 1 SD

D. The literature review establishes the context for the study.

SA 5 4 3 2 1 SD

E. The research purpose, question, or hypothesis is clearly stated.

SA 5 4 3 2 1 SD

F. The method of sampling is sound.

SA 5 4 3 2 1 SD

G. Relevant demographics (for example, age, gender, and ethnicity) are described.

SA 5 4 3 2 1 SD

H. Measurement procedures are adequate.

SA 5 4 3 2 1 SD

I. All procedures have been described in sufficient detail to permit a replication of the study.

SA 5 4 3 2 1 SD

J. The participants have been adequately protected from potential harm.

SA 5 4 3 2 1 SD

K. The results are clearly described.

SA   5   4   3   2   1   SD

L. The discussion/conclusion is appropriate.

SA   5   4   3   2   1   SD

M. Despite any flaws, the report is worthy of publication.

SA   5   4   3   2   1   SD

# Article 22

# Using the Internet to Facilitate
# Positive Attitudes of College Students
# Toward Aging and Working With Older Adults

FRIEDA R. BUTLER
George Mason University

HEIBATOLLAH BAGHI
George Mason University

ABSTRACT. Published data suggest that a preponderance of negative attitudes toward the elderly and insufficient knowledge of aging may be the primary reasons that geriatrics is not the primary choice of employment for nurses. This study measured attitude changes toward the elderly as a result of participation by nursing, gerontology, and health science students in an intergenerational reciprocal service-learning program. Using a pre- and posttest design, results revealed a significant improvement ($p < .001$) for the total group, with undergraduates showing a significantly greater mean increase in positive attitudes toward the elderly ($p < .001$). This study suggests that pairing students with well elderly and engaging in ongoing exposure, meaningful intergenerational exchanges, and using Internet-based activities to communicate are effective strategies to improve attitudes of students toward the elderly.

From *Journal of Intergenerational Relationships*, 6, 175–189. Copyright © 2008 by The Haworth Press. Reprinted with permission.

Selection of geriatrics as a career specialization is a low priority among nursing students and other students in the health professions in the United States (Fusner & Staib, 2004; Happell & Brooker, 2001; Kotzabassaki, 2002). Of the total registered nurse population employed in the United States, only 6.3% currently work in nursing homes or extended care facilities—down from 6.9% in 2000 (U.S. Department of Health and Human Services, 2004). With a growing workforce shortage, this lack of geriatric education will have a profound impact on health care delivery to the older population, particularly with the aging of the baby boomers (Mion, 2003). According to Wells et al. (2004), improving gerontological education most likely would increase positive attitudes of nursing students and practitioners toward aging and would help to lessen the nursing shortage in long-term care.

The purpose of this study was to measure students' attitude changes toward the elderly and toward working with the elderly as a result of their participation in an intergenerational service-learning project over a three-month period. It was hypothesized that student partici-pation in a reciprocal service learning project would facilitate more positive attitudes toward aging. Specific objectives were to explore the effectiveness of the Internet as a means of engagement between seniors and student partners and determine the effects of journaling and class reflections on student attitude change.

Angeles (2000) defines service-learning as structured activities that blend community service with academic learning. This reciprocal intergenerational service learning project was developed to provide gerontological education to nursing and other students in the health disciplines, while at the same time, meeting health education needs of the well elderly. Mintz and Goodwin (1999) indicated that redesigning the gerontology curriculum by integrating innovative service-learning components increases learning opportunities for students and provides high-quality service to communities.

Service learning has been utilized by various educational programs as a strategy to enhance learning and stimulate interest in working with the elderly. For example, Fusner and Staib (2004) provided service-learning experiences for their nursing students and reported positive outcomes for seniors and students with additional exposure.

It is apparent from the existing literature that, with a few exceptions, prevailing perceptions of aging by nursing students mirror those held by the general public and have shown little change over the past decade. While there is a preponderance of evidence that older adults in the U.S. are healthy and are valued, contributing members of society, much of the public still perceive the elderly as weak, sickly, slow, immobile and senile. Unfortunately, the research literature indicates that undergraduate nursing students continue to believe these myths, which may significantly influence career choices (Moyle, 2003; Gething et al., 2004; Wells et al., 2004).

In many instances, the first and only contact students have are with the institutionalized elderly, a setting which many students found heavily work intensive, routine, physical and nonstimulating. As a result,

65 this is their least-preferred career choice (Bergland & Laerum, 2002; Fusner & Staib, 2004; Happell, 2002; Tovin, Nelms, & Taylor, 2002; McLafferty & Morrison, 2004). Employing focus groups, McLafferty and Morrison (2004) found that nurses employed in these
70 facilities tended to focus on the negative, thus doing little to improve the image of gerontological nursing.

Further, McKinlay and Cowan (2003) identified specific areas of curriculum improvement that focus on factors underlying the views of the nursing students.
75 Participants were asked about their beliefs concerning behavioral outcomes of working with the elderly. Examples of such beliefs or views were: *Making older people feel valued; viewing older persons as blocking beds; finding working with older people intellectually*
80 *stimulating; working with older people as uninteresting; and viewing older people as hard to please* (p. 302).

The dimensions and style of gerontological education are significant factors in selecting work with the
85 elderly (Avorti, 2004; Kotzabassaki, Vardaki, Andrea, & Parissopoulos, 2000). Avorti (2004) found a significant relationship between professional status, level of education, and attitude in a study conducted in Ghana; however, a large number of students lacked adequate
90 gerontological knowledge, which may account for their lack of interest in the field. To support the belief that feelings of nursing students and registered nurses toward older people may change when given more experience in caring for older adults, Soderhamn et al.
95 (2001) collected data on a convenience sample which included 151 undergraduate nursing students in Sweden using Kogan's Old People Scale (KOP). Results showed that limited experience of students who were less than 25 years of age was a significant factor in
100 holding less favorable attitudes toward the elderly.

Interestingly, findings of a study conducted with baccalaureate students in Hong Kong revealed no clear connection between attitudes toward care of the elderly and work with the elderly (Herdman, 2002). Perhaps
105 this distinction can be attributed to the Asian culture, since filial piety and respect toward elders are accepted cultural elements in many Asian countries. For example, Japan, whose aging population at this time is growing faster than any other country, implemented a suc-
110 cessful after-school program where frail elders and young children competed together in *Intergenerational Olympics* (Kaplan & Larkin, 2007). Although these studies are limited in geographical scope and lacking in representative samples, it is highly likely that career
115 choices by gerontology students are influenced by the care setting regarding initial exposure and type and extent of experiences with the elderly. Moreover, while many studies determined students' attitudes and reasons for not working with the elderly, only a few stud-
120 ies examined changes in attitudes following an intergenerational gerontological educational program that included early exposure to well elderly. With a few exceptions, the literature focuses on student learning, companionship and meeting elder needs rather than
125 attitude change, positive student-elder interactions and *reciprocal* learning activities. Intergenerational reciprocity or shared learning is a concept which utilizes the theory that exchanges between older and younger generations help to dispel aging myths and stereotypes,
130 promote mutually beneficial experiences and foster positive attitudes toward the elderly (Butler, 2000).

Prior studies that were evaluated for attitude change as a result of service-learning, student-elder interactions, and/or nurse education presented both positive
135 and negative results (Achalu, 1999; Happell, 1999; Health Advisory Service, 1999; Johnson & Atkin, 2002; Lookinland & Anson, 1995; Roberts, Hearn, & Holman, 2003). On the plus side, several studies specifically provided evidence of positive attitude changes
140 in both old and young as a result of service-learning and satisfying intergenerational exchanges (Brosky, Deprey, Hopp, & Mayer, 2006; Doll, 2006; Jones, Herrick, & York, 2004). According to study participants, there is an overreliance on teaching the negative as-
145 pects of aging, rather than emphasizing the positive.

## Method

An intergenerational service learning program was incorporated into two elective aging courses, "*Health Aspects of Aging*," an undergraduate introductory course, and "*Health Care of Aging Persons with*
150 *Chronic Illness*," a graduate introductory course. These courses were among the few health-related electives offered to students at convenient hours during the day; hence, the scheduled time of offering appeared to have been a strong selection factor for the undergraduate
155 students. Graduate students were enrolled in the gerontology major and had few elective aging courses from which to choose.

*Health Aspects of Aging* focused on the physiological, psychological, social, and cultural factors that in-
160 fluence the health status of older adults. It identified assessment strategies and their corresponding interventions and techniques, which promote health and prevent deterioration in old age. *Health Care of Aging Persons With Chronic Illness* focused on the biologi-
165 cal, psychological, and sociocultural factors in aging that influence the development, treatment, and management of chronic illnesses. Emphasis was on examining the functional capacity of persons and the capacity for self-care. The courses were modified to incorpo-
170 rate effective intergenerational exchange and careful reflection in journal entries. It was hoped that this would facilitate more positive attitudes toward aging persons and increased understanding of aging health issues for both students and older adults.
175 Increasingly, older adults are using the computer and expanding their Internet skills. Because of this trend, we added a technology component to the traditional service-learning model and created a new model,

which we called George Mason University (GMU) AgeNet. Partnering with older adults and incorporating a technology component, we created an enthusiastic environment for both students and seniors. This model provided an effective reciprocal learning environment, in which seniors and students learned from each other in group sessions, email, social gatherings, face-to-face with one-on-one dialogue, and Web postings on health and wellness issues. An additional feature was that students and seniors learned new Internet skills in class together at the Learning in Retirement Institute (LRI).

This study examined changes in attitudes toward the elderly by college students enrolled in the two elective gerontology courses. Primarily, the investigators were interested in knowing if students exhibited any change in attitudes toward the aged and working with older adults as a result of participating in a reciprocal learning intergenerational project, GMU AgeNet. The program embraces the philosophy of intergenerational learning through regular intergenerational exchanges. GMU AgeNet addresses issues most relevant to successful aging through a reciprocal learning relationship.

The senior partners in this project used computers but had varying skill levels; therefore, the investigators seized this opportunity to present a joint class to students and their senior partners to improve their Internet communication skills. This technology was utilized in order for students to provide current health information to older adults. These seniors were in relative good health, sophisticated and well educated; therefore, students were challenged to present timely, in-depth, and interesting health promotion and disease prevention information. In turn, older adults were encouraged to share their experiences, life stories, life events, and knowledge concerning healthy living and/or their perspectives on aging with students through regular ongoing communication.

The specific aim of this paper is to present the effects of the GMU AgeNet project on the attitudes of students who participated in the project. This was indeed a challenge, since educators throughout the U.S. are struggling with the lack of student engagement with the elderly (Angeles, 2000) and are looking for ways to influence their decisions to choose gerontology as a career.

### Student Participants

Eighteen undergraduate and 10 graduate students from nursing, social work, and other programs, who were enrolled in the two introductory gerontology courses, partnered with 26 older adults in the LIR Center. Ages of the students ranged from 23 to 60, with a mean age of 34.5. Two students were over 50, one of which was specifically requested as a partner by a senior participant. Seventy-five percent were female and 64.3 percent were undergraduate students. Student population consisted of 7 males and 21 females, which included 20 Caucasians, 2 African Americans, 1 non-white Hispanic, and 1 Asian. This was the first gerontology class for 18 undergraduate students and the second gerontology class for the remaining 10 graduate students. In both courses, students were provided opportunities to examine current aging theories in relation to reality-based situations.

### Older Adult Participants

Twenty-six older adults were recruited from the program's agency partner, a senior center for well elderly, which promotes learning in retirement. Recruitment strategies included distribution of flyers, announcements in meetings, and word of mouth. Criteria for inclusion were age 65 and over and membership and attendance at the center.

An initial welcoming event was held and included refreshments, a brief PowerPoint presentation, introductions, and orientation by the investigators and faculty. Following a *get acquainted* session, students and seniors paired up based upon mutual interests and other personal characteristics.

### Instruments

The investigators administered a simple 20-item Aging IQ Quiz, designed by the National Institute on Aging, to the students at the beginning of the project to determine students' basic knowledge of aging. The *Geriatric Attitude Scale* developed by Reuben et al. (1998) was also administered to student participants at the beginning of the project and again at the conclusion of the project to measure any changes in attitudes as a result of participation in the project. This 14-item Likert scale, originally developed for primary care residents, was easy to administer and needed little modification for use with nursing and health science students. The internal consistency reliability of the scale measured by Cronbach's alpha has been reported to be .76 (Reuben et al., 1998). The instrument included questions such as "*Most old people are pleasant to be with,*" and, "*If I have the choice, I would rather see younger patients than elderly ones,*" which were for the students to answer.

### Communication Strategies

Subsequent to the initial get acquainted meeting, interaction between students and their partners was primarily electronic, consisting of Town Hall Forums, personal emails, and telephone calls between partners. Partners, on average, spent approximately 20 minutes per week in various electronic communication. Students were required to keep a journal of all contacts and interactions with their partners and record their reflections, indicating their impressions, knowledge gained and questions or concerns raised. With faculty as facilitators, students shared their reflections during class time each week. In addition to shared communications in class, there were several joint classroom sessions with senior partners, replete with an open discussion of aging, socializing, and refreshments.

## Results

Quantitative data were analyzed using descriptive and inferential statistical methods. Tests of significance, including paired t-tests and Pearson Correlation, were used to determine differences in knowledge level between the undergraduate and graduate students, and changes in attitude at the conclusion of the project. Since the attitude scale was originally designed for primary care residents, tests for internal consistency reliability using Cronbach's alpha (Cronbach, 1990) yielded a reliability coefficient of .66 on pretest and a coefficient of .84 on posttest for the total group.

Summary statistics (mean and standard deviation of the scores) for pretest and posttest administration of the Aging IQ test and Attitude measures are presented in Table 1. Pretest and posttest assessments were compared using paired t tests to find evidence of statistically significant improvement in the scores. Scores for each item within the Aging IQ scores ($k = 20$) and attitude measures ($k = 14$) were added across participants' responses to derive summary statistics for the dependent variables, knowledge and attitude. Means and standard deviations were computed using these scores for the two test administrations for the entire group as well as the undergraduate and graduate students. The paired t-test results indicated that there was a statistically significant change ($p < .001$) from pretest to posttest administration of the Aging IQ test in the total group, and for each individual group of undergraduate and graduate students. The paired t-test results indicated that there was a statistically significant change ($p < .001$) from pretest to posttest administration of attitude measure in the total group, with the significance being attributed primarily to undergraduate students. However, the changes in attitude measures were not statistically significant ($p > .05$) for graduate students alone.

Knowledge of aging posttest scores correlated significantly with scores on the Attitudes Toward Aging Posttest. The correlation coefficient for scores on post aging IQ and scores on the Attitudes Toward Aging Posttest for the total group was moderately high and statistically significant ($r = .75, p < 001$).

### Qualitative Analyses

Qualitative data were analyzed using thematic processes and contextual examination of student journals, using rigorous review procedures. Three nursing faculty members facilitated class discussions, reviewed student journals, and identified themes and categories that emerged.

Six major themes emerged from review of student journals. These were: (1) immediate application of theory to real life situations, (2) a stronger connection to seniors, (3) a more positive image of aging, (4) increased sensitivity to the feelings, beliefs, and values of the elderly, (5) increased knowledge of the elderly, and (6) working with the elderly as a possible career choice.

Table 1

*Score Changes in Pretest and Posttest Administration of the Aging IQ and Attitude Scales*

| Variables | Pretest | | Posttest | | Paired |
|---|---|---|---|---|---|
| | Mean | SD | Mean | SD | t test |
| **Total group** | | | | | |
| Aging IQ scores | 12.18 | 1.98 | 19.82 | .47 | 20.37*** |
| Attitude scores | 45.50 | 6.76 | 49.03 | 5.60 | 2.50** |
| **Undergraduates** | | | | | |
| Aging IQ scores | 11.11 | 1.60 | 19.78 | .55 | 21.44*** |
| Attitude scores | 42.89 | 4.17 | 47.28 | 6.08 | 2.87** |
| **Graduates** | | | | | |
| Aging IQ scores | 14.10 | .74 | 19.9 | .32 | 29.00*** |
| Attitude scores | 50.00 | .20 | 52.2 | 2.62 | N.S. |

***Significant at $p < .001$
**Significant at $p < .01$

Through interviews, analyses of journals, and faculty discussions, it was found that in general, significantly more students and seniors were pleased with the interactions than were not. Seniors who were not pleased indicated that they expected to do more teaching of the students. A subsequent article will focus on senior outcomes. The following quotes illustrate student responses to the project:

### Examples of Student Written Reflections

Although most students provided positive comments, several comments indicated areas for improvement and refinement of the project.

*Undergraduate Students:*

Older adults increased my awareness about the phenomenon of aging as an opportunity for empowerment and the creation of positive images of aging. I feel that working with older individuals is the flame that heats my spirit and kindles my desire for inner growth and self-expression. It was difficult setting up a discussion time with my partner. She seems to be very busy and communication between us was sporadic.

Challenging/successful approaches included involving senior adults in planning the project and carefully planning for face-to-face group activities for maximum attendance.

My partner wanted to come back to the classroom for discussion and sharing and wanted to know when we were going to do this.

He was more interested in teaching us than in receiving information from us.

*Graduate Students:*

My service learning experience has been a very successful combination of academics and community service. Service learning provides a way of applying what is learned in class and through texts to the real world. It allows active student participation, the creation of connections and the opportunity for reflection. Our project—AgeNet—in conjunction with the Learning in Retirement Institute, became a gift to both senior and student. In so doing, it created a benefit, an outcome, a product and a connection of which to be proud.

Communicating with older persons has heightened the creative perspective in my mind and resulted in my developing a new attitude and understanding of the way older people approach life experiences, relationships, and activities.

Unfortunately, my partner had symptoms which troubled her and it was difficult to get her to talk at times. She has to push herself to stay involved with whatever is going on.

Sometimes I did not know what to say to her when she refused to believe what her physician has told her. What do you do for someone who has been told that tests show deterioration in the part of the brain that governs balance and she has to live with it for the rest of her life?

AgeNet couldn't be anything but a success. Generations need to come together and share. In these interactions, we finally were able to begin breaking down the stereotypes and misconceptions of ageism. Certainly, differences exist between generations. Yet we start to realize that there are also many similarities. Age does not take away the interest to learn, socialize, or attain future goals. It does not eradicate ambition or desire, the need for love and affection. Possibly, greater understanding and communication through intergenerational interaction will make transitions into late adulthood easier, more rewarding. AgeNet may be one of the first steps toward this end.

## Discussion

As expected, the study showed that the knowledge level of undergraduate nursing and gerontology students improved significantly ($p < .01$) when an innovative Intergenerational Reciprocal Service Learning Project using the Internet as a primary means of communication was added to the gerontology curriculum. The students, as a group, had a positive change in their attitudes toward aging at the completion of the project; however, more non-nursing students than nursing students showed a positive change.

Not surprisingly, scores were higher for graduate students than for undergraduates on pretesting; however, scores for both groups increased significantly on posttesting for both knowledge and attitude changes, with most of the changes being attributed to the undergraduate students. Attitude scores for graduate students remained more or less the same. It was not surprising that the greatest variance was attributed to the undergraduate students, since graduate students most likely had a predetermined preference for work with older patients. Since many of the graduate students enrolled in the course had chosen gerontology as a career, and had extensive work experience already, they were more likely to maintain a positive attitude toward working with the older population, resulting in little change in attitudes toward aging measurements. Whereas younger students, who enrolled with preconceived stereotypical notions of the elderly, learned a great deal and appeared to have changed their attitudes toward working with the elderly.

Further, many of the undergraduates expressed enjoyment regarding working with the elderly on this project and would reconsider a career working with older adults. Most likely the setting (residential community) combined with the higher health status of the senior partners had a positive influence on the attitudes of the students. This is consistent with the findings of Wells et al. (2004) and Avorti (2004) who reported that work setting is a strong influence on attitudes toward older adults and can influence the delivery of care.

As with Robinson and Cubit (2005), these investigators believed individual reflection and group discussions were critical in increasing knowledge and improving attitudes toward aging. It was observed that all students expressed a greater appreciation of the vast knowledge this group of seniors possessed and expressed a new respect and understanding of aging.

In general, journal reflections and classroom discussions indicated that undergraduates as well as graduate students who are exposed to well older adults and who engage in intergenerational reciprocal learning strategies appear to develop more positive attitudes toward aging and are more likely to consider working with older adults as a career choice.

### Limitations

*This study is not without limitations.* The small sample size and the fact that all elderly participants were Caucasian may limit the generalizability of these results. Also, it was not possible in this study to compare various components of the courses in order to ascertain the relative value of each component, including the reciprocal intergenerational activities. In addition, two of the students were over 50 years of age, possibly introducing a slight bias to the study. All of the graduate students had taken a previous gerontology class, whereas this was the first gerontology class for the undergraduate students. Most likely this had a significant influence on the outcomes of the Aging IQ pretest. However, during the course of the project, the instructors taught all of the material related to the aging IQ test to both groups, resulting in insignificant differences between the two groups on Aging IQ posttest. Self-selection was a limitation since all enrolled students participated as a class requirement.

The authors recognize that students' personal experiences, work experiences, and academic experiences are intervening variables and most likely influenced knowledge and attitude scores. Further, the interaction of undergraduate and graduate students may have been a factor in the increase in knowledge and attitude scores of the undergraduates. Finally, the graduate students, who were older, had specifically chosen gerontology as a career path and this may have influenced posttest scores on the attitude toward aging. Evidence of personal and intellectual growth and development was discerned from student journals and class discussions. Rethinking career goals by students was an additional outcome of this unique project. However, it would be naive to assume that interesting and innovative educational strategies are the only means for changing attitudes toward working with the elderly.

## Conclusions and Recommendations

500     Based on this research and other observations, it is possible to make several recommendations regarding gerontological and geriatric education programs at the undergraduate and graduate level. These recommendations include the need to: (1) improve gerontology cur-

505 ricula with meaningful service-learning components, (2) provide continuing education in various settings to change public perceptions, (3) encourage changes in media portrayals of the elderly, (4) improve work environments in facilities for the elderly, and (5) provide

510 adequate compensation to individuals working with older persons. These are real-world challenges to increase a much-needed workforce for a growing population of culturally diverse aging clients.

    Although findings cannot necessarily be general-

515 ized to students working with a more impaired population of elders, this study suggests that first exposure to well elderly in a reciprocal intergenerational service-learning project may influence decision-making regarding working with older adults. The investigators rec-

520 ommend further exploration with a larger and more culturally diverse sample, as well as the use of more in-depth measures of outcomes among the older adult participants.

## References

Achalu, O. (1999). Attitudes of student nurses to older patients in Nigeria. *Elderly Care, 11*(2), 5–8.

Administration on Aging. (2002). *Profile of Older Americans: 2002.* Retrieved February 5, 2003, at www.aoa.gov/stats/profile/2002/default.htm

Angeles, J. (2000). Service Learning is the great connector. *Generations United, 5*(1), 1–26.

Avorti, G. S. (2004). Attitude of nurses towards the care of the elderly in Ghana. *West African Journal of Nursing, 15*(2), 81–86.

Bergland, A., & Laerum, H. (2002). Norwegian student nurses' attitudes towards pursuing a career in geriatric nursing after graduation. *Nursing Science and Research in the Nordic Countries, 22*(2), 21–26.

Brosky, J., Deprey, S., Hopp, J., & Mayer, E. (2006). Physical therapist student and community partner perspectives and attitudes regarding service-learning experiences. *Journal of Physical Therapy Education, 20*(3), 38–41.

Butler, F. R. (2000). Computer technology and intergenerational service learning. *Intergenerational Service Learning in Gerontology: A Compendium, 111*, 12–16.

Cooper, S. A., & Coleman, P. G. (2001). Caring for the older person: An exploration of perceptions using personal construct theory. *Age and Ageing, 30*(5), 399–402.

Cronbach, L. J. (1990). *Essentials of Psychological Testing* (5th Ed.). New York: Harper & Row.

Fusner, S. & Staib, S. (2004). Students and senior citizens learning from each other. *Journal of Gerontological Nursing, 30*(3), 40–45.

Gething, L., Fethy, J., McKee, K., Goff, M., Churchward, M., & Mathews, L. (2004). Knowledge, stereotyping and attitudes towards self-ageing. *Australian Journal of Ageing, 21*(20), 74–79.

Happell, B. (1999). When I grow up I want to be a.... Where undergraduate student nurses want to work after graduation. *Journal of Advanced Nursing, 29*(2), 499–505.

Happell, B. (2002). Nursing home employment for nursing students: Valuable experience or harsh deterrent? *Journal of Advanced Nursing, 39*(6), 529–536.

Happell, B., & Brooker, J. (2001). Global aging. Who will look after my grandmother? Attitudes of student nurses toward the care of older adults. *Journal of Gerontological Nursing, 27*(12), 12–17.

Health Advisory Service (1999). *Not because they are old: An independent inquiry into the care of older people on acute wards in general hospitals.* London, HAS.

Herdman, E. (2002). Challenging the discourses of nursing ageism. *International Journal of Nursing Studies, 39*(1), 105–114.

Hill, H. (2007). Research indicates: Intergenerational interactions enhance creating relationships through dance and movements. *Together: The Generations United Magazine, 12*(1), 6.

Jones, E., Herrick, C., & York, R. (2004). An intergenerational group benefits from emotionally disturbed youth and older adults. *Issues in Mental Health Nursing, 25*(8), 753–757.

Kaplan, M., & Larkin, E. (2007). Japan and international partners host intergenerational conference. *Together: The Generations United Magazine, 12*(1), 7.

Kotzabasaaki, Vardaki, Z., Andrea, S., & Parissopoulos, S. (2002). Student nurses' attitudes towards the care of elderly persons: A pilot study. *ICU's & Nursing Web Journal, 12.* Retrieved March 27, 2006 from http://cinahl.com/cgi_bin/refscv?jid=837& accno=2003030388

Lohman, H., & Aitken, M. (2002). Occupational therapy students' attitudes toward service-learning. *Physical Occupational Therapy in Geriatrics, 20*(3/4), 155–164.

Lookinland, S., & Anson, K. (1995). Perpetuation of ageist attitudes among present and future health care personnel: Implications for elder care. *Journal of Advanced Nursing, 1*(1), 47–56.

McKinlay, A., & Cowan, S. (2003). Student nurses' attitudes towards working with older patients. *Journal of Advanced Nursing, 43*(3), 298–309.

McLafferty, I., & Morrison, F. (2004). Attitudes towards hospitalized older adults. *Journal of Advanced Nursing, 47*(4), 446–453.

Mintz, S., & Liu, G. (1999). Service learning: An overview. *Corporation for National and Community Resource Guide. The Corporation for Service Learning, 9–16.*

Mion, L. C. (2003). Care provision for older adults: Who will provide? *Online Journal of Issues in Nursing, 8*(2). Retrieved March 27, 2006 from http://www.cinahl.com/ cgi_bin/refsvc?jid= 1331&accno=2004010891

Moyle, W. (2003). Nursing students' perceptions of older people: Continuing society's myths. *Australian Journal of Advanced Nursing, 20*(4), 15–21.

Roberts, S., Hearn, J., & Holman, C. (2003). Picture this: Using drawing to explore student nurses' perceptions of older age. *Nursing Older People, 15*(5), 14–18.

Ruben, D. (1998). Development and validation of geriatric attitude scale for primary care physicians. *The Journal of the American Geriatrics Society, 46*(11), 1425–1430.

Soderhamn, O., Lindencrona, C., & Gustavsson, S.M. (2001). *Nurse Education Today, 21*(3), 225–229.

Tovin, M. M., Nelms, T., & Taylor, L. F. (2002). The experience of nursing home care: A strong influence on physical therapists students' work intentions. *Journal of Physical Therapy Education, 16*(1), 11–19.

U.S. Department of Health and Human Services. (2004). *Preliminary findings: 2004 National Sample Survey of Registers.* Retrieved March 27, 2006, from http://www.bhpr.hrsa.gov/healthworkforce/reports/rnpopulation/preliminaryfindings.htm

Wells, Y., Foreman, P., Gething, L., & Petralia, W. (2004). Multicultural Aging. Nurses' attitudes toward aging and older adults. Examining attitudes and practices among health services providers in Australia. *Journal of Gerontological Nursing, 30*(9), 5–13.

**About the authors:** *Frieda R. Butler* is a professor and coordinator of the George Mason University Gerontology Programs, housed in the College of Health and Human Services, 4400 University Drive MS5B7, Fairfax, VA 22030-4444 (e-mail: fbutler@gmu.edu). *Heibatollah Baghi* is an associate professor and coordinator of the Master of Science in Epidemiology and Statistics Programs, George Mason University, College of Health and Human Services, 4400 University Drive MS5B7, Fairfax, VA 22030-4444 (e-mail: hbaghi@gmu.edu).

**Address correspondence to:** Frieda R. Butler, Ph.D., George Mason University, 4400 University Drive, MS5B7, Fairfax, VA 22030-4444.

# Exercise for Article 22

## *Factual Questions*

1. What was the hypothesis for this study?

2. What were the criteria for the inclusion of older adult participants?

3. For the total group, was the pretest-posttest difference on the Aging IQ test statistically significant?

4. What was the value of the correlation coefficient (*r*) for the relationship between Aging IQ posttest scores and Attitudes Toward Aging posttest scores?

5. Do the researchers believe that the results can clearly be generalized to students working with a more impaired population of elders?

## Questions for Discussion

6. In your opinion, is the program that was evaluated in this study described in sufficient detail? Explain. (See lines 146–223 and 273–287.)

7. Is the initial welcoming event described in sufficient detail? Explain. (See lines 248–253.)

8. Are the quantitative results (lines 288–328) *or* the qualitative results (lines 329–409) more interesting? More informative? Explain.

9. If you were to evaluate the same program, would you use a control group? Why? Why not?

10. Overall, does this evaluation convince you that the program is effective? Explain.

## Quality Ratings

Directions: Indicate your level of agreement with each of the following statements by circling a number from 5 for strongly agree (SA) to 1 for strongly disagree (SD). If you believe an item is not applicable to this research article, leave it blank. Be prepared to explain your ratings. When responding to criteria A and B, keep in mind that brief titles and abstracts are conventional in published research.

A. The title of the article is appropriate.

SA 5 4 3 2 1 SD

B. The abstract provides an effective overview of the research article.

SA 5 4 3 2 1 SD

C. The introduction establishes the importance of the study.

SA 5 4 3 2 1 SD

D. The literature review establishes the context for the study.

SA 5 4 3 2 1 SD

E. The research purpose, question, or hypothesis is clearly stated.

SA 5 4 3 2 1 SD

F. The method of sampling is sound.

SA 5 4 3 2 1 SD

G. Relevant demographics (for example, age, gender, and ethnicity) are described.

SA 5 4 3 2 1 SD

H. Measurement procedures are adequate.

SA 5 4 3 2 1 SD

I. All procedures have been described in sufficient detail to permit a replication of the study.

SA 5 4 3 2 1 SD

J. The participants have been adequately protected from potential harm.

SA 5 4 3 2 1 SD

K. The results are clearly described.

SA 5 4 3 2 1 SD

L. The discussion/conclusion is appropriate.

SA 5 4 3 2 1 SD

M. Despite any flaws, the report is worthy of publication.

SA 5 4 3 2 1 SD

# Article 23

# Reducing Adolescent Substance Abuse and Delinquency: Pilot Research of a Family Oriented Psychoeducation Curriculum

THOMAS EDWARD SMITH
Florida State University

JEFFREY RODMAN
Here-4-You Consulting

SCOTT P. SELLS
Savannah Family Institute

LISA RENE REYNOLDS
Nova Southeastern University

ABSTRACT. Ninety-three parents and 102 adolescents were referred by juvenile court and treated for substance abuse and a co-morbid diagnosis of either oppositional defiant or conduct disorder using a parent education program over a six-week period. The goals of this study were to assess whether or not active parent involvement and the concurrent treatment of severe behavior problems would reduce teen substance abuse as measured by the adolescent SASSI scale. In addition, if the SASSI scale indicated a significant reduction in substance abuse, would these changes be maintained after a 12-month follow-up period as measured by re-arrest rates through juvenile court records? The results indicated that parents' participation in their teen's treatment of substance abuse and other severe behavioral problems did have a major positive impact. Even though the adolescents' attitudes and defensiveness toward drugs or alcohol did not significantly change, their substance abuse did. This was demonstrated by both the statistically significant changes on the adolescents' SASSI scores and the fact that 85% did not relapse over the course of an entire year after treatment was completed.

From *Journal of Child & Adolescent Substance Abuse*, *15*, 105–115. Copyright © 2006 by The Haworth Press, Inc. Reprinted with permission.

## Introduction

There is a growing concern in our society about the dramatic increase of adolescent drug and alcohol abuse and dependence. There is no shortage of reports describing these alarming trends (e.g., Muck, Zempolich,
5   Titus, Fishman, Godley et al., 2001; Rowe & Liddle, 2003). Overall, drug abuse by teenagers has risen dramatically since 1996 while the overall use among adults has stayed the same or dropped (Department of Health and Human Services, 2002).
10   Increases in teen substance use have led to a greater need for theoretically based and empirically supported treatments (*The Brown University Digest*, 1999). Indeed the number of studies devoted to substance abuse and treatment in youth is continually growing (e.g.,
15   Coatsworth, Santisteran, McBride, & Szapocznik,

2001; Latimer & Newcomb, 2000; Liddle, Dakof, Parker, Diamond, Barrett et al., 2001). However, many agree that a gap still exists between research on adolescent substance abuse and the treatments currently being
20   provided (Liddle, Rowe, Quille, Mills et al., 2002; Robbins, Bachrach, & Szapocznik, 2002; Rowe & Liddle, 2003).

Recent studies have pointed to three critical gaps in adolescent substance-abuse research and treatment.
25   First, there is a growing body of evidence that links adolescent substance abuse to dysfunctional family dynamics (e.g., Carr, 1998; Friedman, Terras, & Glassman, 2000; Liddle & Schwartz, 2002; McGillicuddy, Rychtarik, Duquette, & Morsheimer, 2001; Public
30   Health Reports, 1997; Tuttle, 1995). Brown, Monti, Myers, Waldron, and Wagner (1999) reported that "family support" was often cited by teens as being most helpful in quitting drugs and maintaining sobriety. Despite the growing support for the incorporation
35   of family therapy into adolescent substance abuse treatment (e.g., Berlin, 2002; Lambie & Rokutani, 2002; Rowe, Parker-Sloat, Schwartz, & Liddle, 2003; Wallace & Estroff, 2001), many programs still do not involve the family as an intricate part of their approaches. Instead, the primary emphasis is still on the
40   proaches. Instead, the primary emphasis is still on the individual teen through traditional treatment approaches (e.g., Alcoholics Anonymous [AA] or Narcotics Anonymous [NA]), which are often designed for adults without taking into consideration the unique
45   needs of adolescents (Berlin, 2002). Deas and Thomas (2001) agree that many tenets of twelve-step programs may be overly abstract and distasteful for developing adolescents (p. 187).

Second, the majority of substance-abusing teens in
50   treatment also exhibit other problems such as truancy, fighting, and defiance (Fisher & Harrison, 2000), running away (Slesnick, Myers, Meade, & Segelken, 2000), or other problem behaviors (Schmidt, Liddle, & Dakof, 1996). In these cases, family-based treatments
55   were found to be highly effective not only in reducing

substance use, but also in alleviating associated symptomatic behaviors. In 1999, the National Assembly on Drug and Alcohol Abuse and the Criminal Offenders concluded that addressing "adolescent drug addiction

60  or substance abuse without also treating, for example, behavioral problems such as truancy, running away, or threats of violence reduced the likelihood of success" (p. 2). Yet researchers at the National Assembly cited the failure of most treatment programs to address both

65  substance abuse and severe behavioral problems concurrently.

Finally, researchers have found the psychoeducational component of family substance-abuse treatment to be successful in reducing the teen's drug use as well

70  as heightening parents' functioning. Studies have highlighted the utility of psychoeducation in adolescent substance abuse treatment, including parent training (Bamberg et al., 2001; Schmidt et al., 1996) and skills training (McGillicuddy et al., 2001; Wagner, Brown,

75  Monty, & Waldron, 1999). One problem with traditional parenting groups, however, is the significant dropout rate of parents and teens. Parents are often resistant to acceptability for their children's substance abuse. Not surprisingly, they state that adolescents are

80  responsible for their own difficulties. Thus, they resent coming to a parent education group to learn new skills because their teen "got caught" abusing drugs or alcohol. As a result, parents are resistant to helping their teen overcome their substance abuse. However, a sys-

85  temic approach to teen substance abuse treatment has been shown to result in a higher level of engagement in treatment and to lower dropout rates than other routine procedures (Cormack & Carr, 2000).

To address these deficits, a parent education pro-

90  gram was used to treat teens who were diagnosed with substance abuse as well as oppositional defiant or conduct disorders (*DSM-IV*; American Psychiatric Association [APA], 1994) and the teens' parents. Ninety-three parents and 102 adolescents were referred by

95  juvenile court and treated using the parent education program over a six-week period. Research studies have shown that teen substance abuse and conduct disorder relapse rates are typically extremely high, with some as high as 75% (Long, 1999; Sholevar & Schwoeri,

100  2003).

The goals of this study were to assess whether or not active parent involvement and the concurrent treatment of severe behavior problems would reduce teen substance abuse as measured by the adolescent

105  SASSI scale and if these changes would be maintained over a 12-month period after treatment ended.

### Research Questions

Three questions were examined in this study. First, would active parent involvement and the concurrent treatment of severe behavior problems reduce teen sub-

110  stance abuse as measured by the adolescent SASSI subscales? Second, would reductions in substance

abuse behavior as measured by the SASSI subscales be maintained at the 12-month follow-up? Third, would adolescents relapse within a 12-month period as meas-

115  ured by re-arrest rates through juvenile court records?

### Methods

The sample consisted of 102 adolescents and 93 parents who together attended a six-week *Parenting with Love and Limits*™ substance-abuse prevention program. The adolescents ranged in age from 9 to 18,

120  with the average participant being 15 years old. Each participant was diagnosed with substance abuse and a co-morbid diagnosis of either oppositional defiant or conduct disorder. The study was conducted within an opportunistic window of opportunity. This required

125  that the study be nonreactive in terms of measurement. As a result, we were unable to track demographic variables such as socioeconomic data and severity of offense.

The majority of the adolescents were white

130  (82.4%). The remaining participants were African American (11.8%) and Mexican American (1.0%). Both males and females were present in the sample, with males accounting for the majority of the participants (56.9%). These adolescents committed a wide

135  variety of offenses, with the most commonly occurring offense being shoplifting (22.5%). The next most frequent offense was possession of marijuana (14.7%). Each participant was court-ordered into treatment by the judge at juvenile court. Once those cases that were

140  missing data related to the SASSI subscales were deleted, 93 adolescents remained in the sample.

### Parenting with Love and Limits™

The six-week *Parenting with Love and Limits*™ psychoeducational program was developed from a three-year process-outcome research study (Sells,

145  1998; Sells, 2000; Sells, Smith, & Sprenkle, 1995) and integrated the best principles of a structural family therapy approach. Structural Family Therapy was rated a Model Program in the United States Department of Education's *Applying Effective Strategies to Prevent or*

150  *Reduce Substance Abuse, Violence, and Disruptive Behavior Among Youth* (Scattergood, Dash, Epstein, & Adler, 1998). Programs using the framework of structural family therapy have consistently demonstrated success in reducing or eliminating substance abuse in

155  adolescents (Lambie & Rokutani, 2002; Springer & Orsbon, 2002; Rowe, Parker-Sloat, Schwartz, & Liddle, 2003).

Two group facilitators led a small group of parents, caregivers, and their teenagers (no more than 4–6 fami-

160  lies with no more than 15 people total in the group) in six classes, each two hours long. Two co-facilitators were needed because breakout groups were an essential piece of the program. Parents and teens met together collectively as a group but there were times in which

165  each group met separately in breakout groups. The rationale for these breakouts was that oftentimes both

parents and teens need to meet separately to address issues that collectively they cannot.

The *Parenting with Love and Limits*™ program provides parents with a detailed six-module treatment manual on curtailing their teenagers' substance abuse and other behavior problems. To assist in intervention delivery, workbooks were available for parents, their children, and group facilitators. In addition, a final workbook was available on how to train group facilitators to implement the program.

In the first module, parents learned reasons why teens engage in substance abuse, disrespect, running away, or violence as a form of "parent abuse." Presumably, parents are faced with adolescents whose normal rebellious stance is compounded by self-injurious behaviors such as substance abuse, extreme disrespectful behaviors, and so on. At the end of this module, parents and teens form respective breakout groups to vent their feelings and frustrations.

In the second module, presentations are made on how adolescents engage in provocative behavior (e.g., swearing, argumentative discussions). Presentations are also made on how parents engage in activities that are ineffective (e.g., lecturing, criticizing, acrimonious comments about past conflict).

In the third module, effective behavioral contracting methods are presented. Parents arc taught to critique their contingency management contracts to ensure that adolescents will be apprised on the consequences of violating provisions of a behavioral contract. Parents and adolescents retire into separate breakout groups to critique and write new contracts.

In the fourth module, presentations are made on how adolescents creatively circumvent seemingly well-designed behavioral contracts.

In the fifth module, parents choose from a recipe menu of creative consequences to respond to adolescents' provocative behaviors. Such behaviors include skipping school, drug/alcohol abuse, sexual promiscuity, violence, and threats of suicide.

In the sixth module, parents and children are taught about the necessity to recreate a positive climate within a household and specific methods of doing so.

The rationale behind the use of this program is twofold. First, *Parenting with Love and Limits*™ is one of the first parent education programs of its kind to specifically address both substance abuse and oppositional and conduct disorder behaviors concurrently. Traditional psychoeducation group programs are not based on a lengthy period of process and qualitative research with adolescents and their families. Further, they are not designed to address a range of extreme behavior problems in adolescents. Finally, teens are not typically active participants in the parenting group process. Traditional groups are either for the parents only or the teens as passive observers and not active participants.

The high completion rate (i.e., an 85% completion rate by adolescents and a 94% completion rate by parents of all six weeks of the *Parenting with Love and Limits*™ program) ensured that the study was a credible investigation into the programmatic effects.

*Measures*

The Adolescent SASSI questionnaire was administered to the 93 adolescents before they began the first *Parenting with Love and Limits*™ class and again after the last parenting class was completed. It has five subscales: The FVA subscale measured self-perception of alcohol abuse. The FVOD subscale measured self-perception of other drug abuse (e.g., marijuana). The OAT (overt measure of attitudes toward drug use) and SAT (subtle measure of attitudes toward drug use) together measured adolescents' overt and covert willingness to admit that they have personality characteristics that are commonly and stereotypically associated with substance abusers (e.g., impatience, low frustration tolerance, grandiosity, etc). The fifth subscale was the DEF, which measured defensiveness toward drug use.

The Adolescent SASSI has a high reliability coefficient of .91 and high face validity for each of its five subscales (SASSI Manual, 2000). To assess for change following program participation, paired sample *t* tests were conducted for each subscale of the SASSI.

Recidivism or relapse rates for all 93 adolescents who completed the program were measured through juvenile court records for each adolescent. Re-arrest records for substance abuse or conduct-related problems, such as shoplifting, were obtained for all 93 adolescents six months after the completion of the parenting program, and then again after twelve months of completing the program.

## Results

Table 1 indicates both the FVA and FVOD subscale scores were significantly lower following their participation in the *Parenting with Love and Limits*™ six-week program. The pretest mean for the FVA was 2.06, whereas the posttest mean was .73. The pretest mean for the FVOD was 2.83, whereas the posttest mean was .95.

The adolescents' attitudes about their drug or alcohol use were measured through the OAT and SAT. On the OAT subscale, the average respondent changed only slightly. The pretest mean for the OAT subscale was 6.19, whereas the posttest mean was 5.85. A similar pattern is seen in the SAT subscale, with the exception of direction. The average respondent had a pretest SAT score of 1.90 and a posttest SAT score of 2.08. The difference between these scores was not statistically significant.

The last subscale (DEF) measured defensiveness concerning substance use. The primary purpose of the DEF scale is to identify defensive clients who are trying to conceal evidence of personal problems and limitations. Whether it is due to life events or to personality characteristics, excessive defensiveness can be prob-

Table 1
*Paired Sample t-Test Results for the SASSI Subscales*

| Subscale | Pretest mean (standard deviation) | Posttest mean (standard deviation) | $t$-score | $p$-value |
|---|---|---|---|---|
| FVA | 2.06 (2.79) | .73 (1.41) | 4.532 | < .001 |
| FVOD | 2.83 (4.94) | .95 (2.05) | 3.732 | < .001 |
| OAT | 6.19 (3.23) | 5.85 (3.65) | 1.176 | .243 |
| SAT | 1.90 (1.76) | 2.08 (1.80) | −1.038 | .302 |
| DEF | 6.60 (2.46) | 7.05 (2.90) | −1.830 | .070 |

lematic and it must be taken into account in treatment
planning.

On this subscale, the average respondent's score increased slightly (6.60–7.05). This indicates that the average program participant increased slightly in defensiveness. However, this change was very small and did not reach statistical significance. In addition, the average respondent was in the normal range at the time of pretest, so high levels of change were not expected on this subscale.

Only six (15%) of the 93 adolescents who completed the *Parenting with Love and Limits*[TM] program relapsed or re-offended over a 12-month period as indicated by juvenile court arrest records that tracked each of the 93 adolescents. Re-offenses included both substance abuse behaviors (e.g., illegal possession of alcohol or drugs like marijuana) and conduct disorder behaviors (e.g., shoplifting, violence, running away, etc.).

## Discussion

The results indicate that parents' participation in adolescents' treatment of substance abuse and severe behavioral problems can have a major positive impact on program effectiveness. One key indicator was adolescents' self-reported substance use dropped significantly. This finding was juxtaposed by the finding that adolescents' attitudes and defensiveness toward drugs or alcohol did not significantly change. The significant change in subscales on perceived alcohol and drug use showed that adolescents believed that they misused these substances. This was demonstrated by both the statistically significant changes on the adolescents' SASSI scores and the fact that 85% did not relapse over the course of an entire year after treatment ended.

The low OAT and SAT scores among adolescents were not unexpected because while they may judge themselves as misusing or using drugs or alcohol, they do not see themselves as having a drug or alcohol problem. That is, adolescents often do not see themselves as chemically dependent or having personality characteristics that are associated with society's stereotypical alcoholic or drug abuser on skid row (SASSI Manual, 2000). Thus, a high score and level of change on these subscales was not wholly unexpected.

This evidence suggests that a group-oriented, family therapy informed psychoeducation is effective in helping parents reassert their authority and reduce, if not curtail, their teen's severe behavior problems and substance abuse. Additionally, attitudes toward alcohol and drug abuse may well change following behavioral changes. Notwithstanding this optimistic viewpoint, there are potential problems with the lack of congruence between attitudes and behavior. Without understanding why adolescents changed their behavior, the possibility of recidivism is elevated. The lack of recidivism in this study suggests that this process needs to be further studied.

One key ingredient in the current study may be parental involvement and providing them with the proper skills to address their adolescents' behavioral problems. The parental involvement may explain the 94% completion rate by parents and the 84% completion rate by adolescents of all six two-hour parenting classes. One intuitive explanation for adolescents' high rate of attendance was that they were ordered into treatment. However, that does not explain why parents' involvement was so elevated. High parent attendance in this six-week course contradicts research findings that this population of parents is resistant to treatment and shows a lack of participation in the overall therapeutic process. Therefore, the 94% completion rate shows promise that programs with the right curriculum can engage a population of parents who are traditionally highly resistant to participation.

Future studies that use qualitative research methods are needed to discover what particular concepts or techniques within the *Parenting with Love and Limits*[TM] program are reducing parental resistance and increasing their readiness to change. The identified key concepts can then be refined and modified to increase both parent and teen participation and readiness to change.

## References

Bamberg, J., Toumbourou, J. W., Blyth, A., & Forer, D. (2001). Change for the BEST: Family changes for parents coping with youth substance abuse. *Australian and New Zealand Journal of Family Therapy, 22,* 189–198.

Berlin, M. (2002). Adolescent substance abuse treatment: A unified model. *Dissertation Abstracts International: Section B: The Sciences & Engineering, 63,* 2999.

Brown, S.A., Monti, P. M., Myers, M. G., Waldron, H. B., & Wagner, E. F. (1999). More resources, treatment needed for adolescent substance abuse. *The Brown University Digest of Addiction Theory and Application, 18,* 6–7.

Carr, A. (1998). The inclusion of fathers in family therapy: A research based perspective. *Contemporary Family Therapy, 20,* 371–383.

Coatsworth, J. D., Dsanisteban, D. A., McBride, C. K., & Szapocznik, J. (2001). Brief strategic family therapy versus community control: Engagement, retention, and an exploration of the moderating role of adolescent symptom severity. *Family Process, 40,* 313–333.

Cormack, C., & Carr, A. (2000). Drug abuse. In A. Carr (Ed.), *What works with children and adolescents? A critical review of psychological interventions with children, adolescents, and their families.*

Deas, D., & Thomas, S. E. (2001). An overview of controlled studies of adolescent substance abuse treatment. *The American Journal on Addictions, 10,* 178–189.

Fisher, G. L., & Harrison, T. C. (2000). *Substance abuse: Information for school counselors, social workers, therapists, and counselors.* Needham Heights, MA: Allyn & Bacon.

Friedman, A. S., Terras, A., & Glassman, K. (2000). Family structure versus family relationships for predicting substance use/abuse and illegal behavior. *Journal of Child & Adolescent Substance Abuse, 10,* 1–16.

Lambie, G. W., & Rokutani, J. (2002). A systems approach to substance abuse identification and intervention for school counselors. *Professional School Counseling, 5,* 353–360.

Latimer, W. W., & Newcomb, M. (2000). Adolescent substance abuse treatment outcome: The role of substance abuse problem severity. *Journal of Consulting and Clinical Psychology, 68,* 684–697.

Liddle, H. A., Dakof, G. A., Parker, K., Diamond, G. S., Barrett, K., & Tejeda, M. (2001). Multidimensional family therapy for adolescent drug abuse: Results of a randomized clinical trial. *American Journal of Drug and Alcohol Abuse, 27,* 651–688.

Liddle, H. A., Rowe, C. L., Quille, T. J., Dakof, G. A., Mills, D. S., Sakran, E., & Biaggi, H. (2002). Transporting a research-based adolescent drug treatment into practice. *Journal of Substance Abuse Treatment, 22,* 231–243.

Liddle, H. A., & Schwartz, S. J. (2002). Attachment and family therapy: The clinical utility of adolescent-family attachment research. *Family Process, 41,* 455–476.

Long, W. C. (1999). The dilemma of addiction and recovery during adolescence. *Dissertation Abstracts International Section A: Humanities and Social Sciences, 59,* 2440.

McGilliuddy, N. B., Rychtarik, R. G., Duquette, J. A., & Morsheimer, E. T. (2001). Development of a skill training program for parents of substance-abusing adolescents. *Journal of Substance Abuse Treatment, 20,* 59–68.

Muck, R., Zempolich, K. A., Titus, J. A., Fishman, M., Godley, M. D., & Schwebel, R. (2001). An overview of the effectiveness of adolescent substance abuse treatment models. *Youth and Society, 33,* 143–168.

Public Health Reports. (1997). Adolescent substance abuse tied to family structure. *Public Health Reports, 112,* 4–6.

Robbins, M. S., Bachrach, K., & Szapocznik, J. (2002). Bridging the research-practice gap in adolescent substance abuse treatment: The case of brief strategic family therapy. *Journal of Substance Abuse Treatment, 23,* 123–132.

Rowe, C. L., & Liddle, H. A. (2003). Substance abuse. *Journal of Marital and Family Therapy, 29,* 97–120.

Rowe, C. L., Parker-Sloat, E., Schwartz, S., & Liddle, H. (2003). Family therapy for early adolescent substance abuse. In S. J. Stevens & A. R. Morral (Eds.), *Adolescent substance abuse treatment in the United States: Exemplary models from a national evaluation study* (pp. 105–132). New York: The Haworth Press, Inc.

Schmidt, S. E., Liddle, H. A., & Dakof, G. A. (1996). Changes in parenting practices and adolescent drug abuse during multidimensional family therapy. *Journal of Family Psychology, 10,* 12–27.

Sholevar, G. P., & Schwoeri, L. D. (2003). Alcoholic and substance-abusing families. In G.P. Sholevar (Ed.), *Textbook of family and couples therapy: Clinical applications* (pp. 671–694). Washington, DC: American Psychiatric Publishing, Inc.

Slesnick, N., Meyers, R. J., Meade, M., & Segelken, D. H. (2000). Bleak and hopeless no more: Engagement of reluctant substance-abusing runaway youth and their families. *Journal of Substance Abuse Treatment, 19,* 215–222.

Springer, D. W., & Orsbon, S. H. (2002). Families helping families: Implementing a multifamily therapy group with substance-abusing adolescents. *Health and Social Work, 27,* 204–208.

Tuttle, J. (1995). Family support, adolescent individuation, and drug and alcohol involvement. *Journal of Family Nursing, 1,* 303–327.

Wagner, E. F., & Waldron, H. B. (1999). Innovations in adolescent substance abuse intervention. *Alcoholism: Clinical and Experimental Research, 23,* 236–249.

Wallace, S., & Estroff, T. W. (2001). Family treatment. In T. W. Estroff (Ed.), *Manual of adolescent substance abuse treatment* (pp. 235–252). Washington, DC: American Psychiatric Publishing, Inc.

**About the authors**: *Thomas Edward Smith*, PhD, is professor, Florida State University, School of Social Work, Tallahassee, FL (E-mail: tsmith@mailer.fsu.edu). *Scott P. Sells*, PhD, is director of the Savannah Family Institute, Savannah, GA (E-mail: spsells@difficult.net). *Jeffrey Rodman*, MA, is executive director, Here-4-You Consulting, LLC (E-mail: Jeffter46@hotmail.com). *Lisa Rene Reynolds*, PhD, is affiliated with the Nova Southeastern University (E-mail: lreynolds@norwalkreds.com).

**Address correspondence to**: Thomas Edward Smith, PhD, Florida State University, School of Social Work. Tallahassee, FL 32306. E-mail: tsmith@mailer.fsu.edu

# Exercise for Article 23

## Factual Questions

1. According to the researchers, there are how many "critical gaps" in adolescent substance abuse research and treatment?

2. The adolescents in this study committed a wide variety of offenses. What was the most commonly occurring offense?

3. The initial sample consisted of 102 adolescents. The researchers had complete data for how many?

4. What did the FVA subscale measure?

5. Was the pretest mean *or* the posttest mean on the FVA subscale higher?

6. Using .05 as the cutoff level for statistical significance, was the difference between the pretest and posttest means on the FVA subscale statistically significant? Explain.

## Questions for Discussion

7. In your opinion, how important is the fact that a follow-up was conducted? Is 12 months an appropriate amount of follow-up for an evaluation of this type? (See the research questions in lines 107–115.)

8. How important is it to know that each participant was court-ordered into treatment by a judge? Would you be willing to generalize the results of this study to adolescents who volunteered to participate? (See lines 138–139 and 341–343.)

9. In your opinion, is the program that was evaluated in this study described in sufficient detail, keeping in mind that journal articles tend to be relatively short? Explain. (See lines 142–227.)

10. The researchers report a 15% relapse rate. Would it have been informative to have determined the relapse rate for a control group that did not receive the program? Explain. (See lines 289–297.)

11. In your opinion, might it be informative to ask the parents for their personal reactions to the program in a future evaluation of the program? Explain. Note that the completion rate for parents was 94%. (See lines 223–227 and 338–341.)

12. Do the data in this research article convince you that the *Parenting with Love and Limits*™ program is effective? Explain.

## *Quality Ratings*

Directions: Indicate your level of agreement with each of the following statements by circling a number from 5 for strongly agree (SA) to 1 for strongly disagree (SD). If you believe an item is not applicable to this research article, leave it blank. Be prepared to explain your ratings. When responding to criteria A and B, keep in mind that brief titles and abstracts are conventional in published research.

A. The title of the article is appropriate.

    SA   5   4   3   2   1   SD

B. The abstract provides an effective overview of the research article.

    SA   5   4   3   2   1   SD

C. The introduction establishes the importance of the study.

    SA   5   4   3   2   1   SD

D. The literature review establishes the context for the study.

    SA   5   4   3   2   1   SD

E. The research purpose, question, or hypothesis is clearly stated.

    SA   5   4   3   2   1   SD

F. The method of sampling is sound.

    SA   5   4   3   2   1   SD

G. Relevant demographics (for example, age, gender, and ethnicity) are described.

    SA   5   4   3   2   1   SD

H. Measurement procedures are adequate.

    SA   5   4   3   2   1   SD

I. All procedures have been described in sufficient detail to permit a replication of the study.

    SA   5   4   3   2   1   SD

J. The participants have been adequately protected from potential harm.

    SA   5   4   3   2   1   SD

K. The results are clearly described.

    SA   5   4   3   2   1   SD

L. The discussion/conclusion is appropriate.

    SA   5   4   3   2   1   SD

M. Despite any flaws, the report is worthy of publication.

    SA   5   4   3   2   1   SD

# Article 24

# Evaluation of a Program Designed to Reduce Relational Aggression in Middle School Girls

CHERYL DELLASEGA
Penn State College of Medicine

PAMELA ADAMSHICK
Moravian College

ABSTRACT. Physical and verbal aggression is an increasing problem in both middle and high schools across the United States. While physical forms of aggression are targeted in traditional "bullying" programs, relational aggression (RA), or the use of relationships to hurt another, is often not detected or addressed. For girls in the stage of identity formation, RA can impact negatively on self-concept, peer relationships, school performance, and mental and physical health. An innovative program designed specifically to help middle school girls confront and cope with issues related to RA was developed, implemented, and evaluated in two school systems. Attitudes and self-reported behaviors were measured before and after the program. Results show an improvement in relationship skills after participation in the program. Most noticeable improvements were in a girl's stated willingness to become involved when witnessing another girl being hurt and girls benefiting from the mentoring they received from high school juniors and seniors.

From *Journal of School Violence*, 4, 63–76. Copyright © 2005 by The Haworth Press, Inc. Reprinted with permission.

## Introduction

### Aggression in Youth

Since Columbine, the issue of aggression in youth has been at the forefront of the nation's consciousness. Across the country, administrators, guidance counselors, school nurses, and teachers witness violence be-
5   tween young people in the classroom, often on a daily basis. In a recent survey of high school students, more than one-third of respondents reported being in a physical fight in the past twelve months (CDC, 2002). A report commissioned by former President Clinton
10  showed that 30 to 40 percent of male youths and 15 to 30 percent of female youths admit to having committed a serious violent offense by age 17. The violent offenses included in this group are homicides, robberies, aggravated assaults, and forcible rapes (U.S. Depart-
15  ment of Health and Human Services, 2001).

Statistics on adolescent female violence show that the self-reported rate of violent acts by female adolescents is closing the gender gap. In 1998, the prevalence rates for male and female violence were similar to
20  1993, but the incidence rate for violent acts by females

rose (U.S. Department of Health and Human Services, 2001). In addition, the arrest of girls for assault and weapons charges has increased and exceeds that for boys (Smith & Thomas, 2000). According to U.S. De-
25  partment of Justice statistics from 1991, 54% of reported violent crimes against 12–15-year-old girls were committed by other girls or women (Whitaker & Bastian, 1991). In response to these troubling data, one of the national goals designated in *Healthy People 2010* is
30  to decrease physical fighting among adolescents (U.S. Department of Health and Human Services, 2000).

### Bullying and School Violence

Bullying is a form of violence that may include behaviors that are verbally and/or physically aggressive. While many different definitions of bullying are used,
35  consensus has been reached on these characteristics: the bully's intent to inflict harm, his or her perceived or real power over the victim, repeated nature of the aggression, nonprovoking behavior by the victim, and the occurrence of the bullying within familiar social groups
40  (Griffin & Gross, in press; Olweus, 1994; Greene, 2000).

The bullying dynamic is a complex interrelational process that relies on and is fueled by behaviors and responses of more than one participant. Typical roles
45  are the aggressor, the victim, and bystanders (also referred to as "witnesses" or "in-betweeners"). Victims may or may not provoke their aggressors, and many victims become retaliatory aggressors. As observers or passive participants, bystanders can deliberately or
50  inadvertently facilitate bullying (Hazler, 1996).

### Relational Aggression

In studies on styles of aggression, interesting gender-specific findings have emerged. Researchers Lagerspetz, Bjorkqvist, and Peltonen (1988) studied 167 children aged 11–12 years and found that girls
55  engaged in more indirect aggression, a circuitous type of attack on another that amounted to social manipulation. Boys tended to use direct means of aggression. The term "social aggression" is sometimes applied to these behaviors because they occur within the context
60  of groups and because the participants have some de-

gree of relationship with one another (Underwood, Galen, & Paquette, 2001).

Some behaviors that can be involved in this type of nonphysical aggression can be found in Figure 1.

---

Gossip
Manipulation
Intimidation
Exclusion
Gestures
Ridicule
Saying something mean then pretending you were "joking"
Name calling
Teasing
Cliques
Campaigns
"On again–off again" friendships
Betrayal of confidence
Sending hurtful messages via cell phone or computer
Other subtle or not-so-subtle forms of harassment

---

*Figure 1.* Examples of Relational Aggression.

65   Crick and Grotpeter (1995) also found that girls were significantly more relationally aggressive than boys. They chose the term "relational aggression" rather than "indirect aggression" to describe the type of aggression displayed by females because the behaviors
70  they found were aimed at harming others through purposeful manipulation and damage of peer relationships. Their research, done with 491 third- through sixth-grade children in a Midwestern town in the United States, included children of varying ethnic backgrounds
75  (60% European American), thus supporting cross-cultural validity of gender differences in style of aggression. Their study added greater refinement to terms by using an instrument that did not confound relational aggression with nonverbal aggression.

80   The notion that girls can be bullies too is a phenomenon of great interest, as demonstrated by the recent movie *Mean Girls*. While physical aggression is an obvious cause for concern and intervention, the types of social aggression portrayed in the movie and
85  played out in classrooms, sports, and online every day are harder to detect and measure. These behaviors are sometimes dismissed as a female rite of passage, perhaps because RA seems to be most problematic in adolescent girls in middle and secondary school (Ahmad &
90  Smith, 1994).

RA may be more threatening to girls than physical forms of violence. In an online survey of over 2,000 girls ages 8–17, 41% of preteen girls and 22% of teen girls listed being teased or made fun of as their top
95  safety concern, remarkable when choices such as "terrorism" and "kidnapping" were other alternatives offered (Girl Scout Research Institute, 2003).

The developmental needs of adolescent girls who are struggling with identity formation through forging
100 connections with others may explain many RA behaviors (Gilligan, 1982). For example, exclusionary tactics

whereby a girl distances herself from peers she identifies as being "not like me," allows her to perceive a sense of status and being part of a select group (Hazler,
105 1996). There is also evidence that RA occurs within a girl's friendship circle, whereas males tend to aggress outside their circle of friends (Dellasega & Nixon, 2003). Relational aggression can impair normal development in that girls who consistently use RA behaviors
110 to interact with others begin to believe that their indirect bullying is not only acceptable, but also normal (Dellasega & Nixon, 2003).

Research by Galen and Underwood (1997) added another dimension to understanding nonphysical ag-
115 gression in youth. They defined social aggression to include not only verbal rejection or social exclusion, but also negative facial expressions or body movements. Their use of vignette measures that included nonverbal examples of social aggression had high in-
120 ternal consistency. The importance of nonverbals in aggression was further supported in a study by Paquette and Underwood (1999) with pre-adolescents. Findings showed that nonverbal forms of social aggression are experienced most frequently in that age group.

125   Cillessen and Mayeux (2004) followed a group of 905 students from fifth to ninth grade and examined the interplay between popularity and aggression during this developmental period. They found that as participants moved from middle childhood into early adolescence
130 relational aggression increasingly predicted high popularity, but low levels of liking. However, the concept of popularity itself changed during this span of time. "Popular" evolved from being well liked as a fifth grader to being influential and powerful in the ninth
135 grade. The researchers conclude that adolescents use relational aggression to maintain their dominant, influential position in the peer group. The results suggest that intervention studies to reduce bullying should take into account the status enhancing and rewarding quali-
140 ties of relationally aggressive behaviors for this developmental period.

While the old adage of "names will never hurt you" (as opposed to sticks and stones, which will break bones) is often cited, the reality is that RA can have
145 serious outcomes for both aggressors and victims (Crick & Grotpeter, 1995; Dellasega & Nixon, 2003; Nansel et al. 2001; Paquette & Underwood, 1999). These include risk for substance abuse, bulimic behaviors, delinquency, and development of low self-esteem
150 and adjustment problems in victims (Crick, Casas, & Nelson, 2002). In one tragic case, repeated RA led a Canadian girl to suicide, and others have observed that in girls, RA often precedes physical forms of violence (Dellasega, in preparation). Some negative impacts
155 specifically reported by aggressors include a sense of loneliness and depression (Tomada & Schneider, 1997). Crick and Grotpeter (1995) found that relationally aggressive youth were significantly more rejected than their nonrelationally aggressive peers and reported

160 higher levels of isolation, depression, and loneliness. Young women often replicate these roles into adulthood, adopting a "victim" or "bully" stance in their relationships with men (Dellasega, in press).

165 Risk for relationally victimized females is supported by the research of Crick and Grotpeter (1995), which showed females had a stronger relationship between relational aggression and social-psychological maladjustment than males. Paquette and Underwood's (1999) study of gender differences in the experience of 170 peer victimization found that girls were more distressed by social aggression than boys were. Their findings showed that frequency of social aggression was more strongly related to girls' self-concepts than to boys'.

Studies on factors that motivate young females to 175 use relational aggression in their relationships have also been conducted. One qualitative study using focus groups was completed with adolescent females in Australia to determine their perspectives on the causes of relational aggression. Some explanations for the behav- 180 ior included boredom and desire for excitement (Owens, Shute, & Slee, 2000). Further studies are needed to determine factors that underlie relational aggression in girls of nonwhite cultures and disadvantaged economic groups. By illuminating the experience 185 of peer-to-peer aggression in diverse groups of adolescent females, a more comprehensive view of etiological factors in relational aggression will emerge.

*Interventions*

Empirical studies of antibullying interventions in general suggest that school-based interventions 190 (Olweus, 1994), strategies aimed at peer involvement ("befriending") (Menesini, Codecasa, Benelli, & Cowie, 2003) and peer support processes (Stevens, De Bourdeaudhuij, & van Oost, 2000) may be effective. The most efficacious treatments for bullying appear to 195 be those that utilize the peer group in a supportive way to assist the bully or victims.

Few interventions to specifically address RA have been developed, and often teachers admit they feel illprepared to handle these behaviors (Smith, personal 200 communication, 2003). While empirical studies are lacking, innovative approaches to mediate relational aggression seem to be achieving success. Camp Ophelia$^{TM}$ and Club Ophelia$^{TM}$ are two initiatives that function in a preventive mode for middle school girls. 205 These programs are designed to create safe environments for middle school girls to learn positive relational skills. The programs use an arts-based curriculum and mentoring by high school girls in an ERI model: educate, relate, and integrate. Girls first are 210 taught about RA and how it hurts others. They then relate RA to their everyday lives and develop alternative behaviors. Finally, they integrate the new healthy relationship behaviors they have identified as feasible for them into their everyday life. For example, not 215 every girl who is a bystander or witness of RA is brave

enough to speak out. One realistic alternative some girls felt they could use was to move away from the aggressor and stand next to the victim.

**The Study**

This study involved a program evaluation of Club 220 Ophelia$^{TM}$, which was offered at two middle schools serving a diverse population of girls during the 2003–2004 academic year. Each program lasted throughout a semester (twelve weeks) and utilized the same ERI model.

*Methods*

225 In both locations, the director of Club Ophelia (CD) implemented the program with a school faculty as co-director. Middle school girls could self-select or be referred into the program. Junior and senior girls from the same school system served as mentors for the mid- 230 dle school girls with a 1:5 ratio. Each session of the program was supervised by the director and at least one other adult director with counseling skills.

*Evaluation*

A basic demographic sheet, which also measured relationship-oriented behaviors, was the first part of the 235 evaluation. These questions asked girls what they thought their "RA role" was and how often they suffered from the consequences of RA in a week's time.

To assess the impact of the program on relationship skills of the participants, The Girls Relationship Scale 240 (GRS) was administered. This scale was developed using a previous evaluation tool from camp and club as well as input from participants. It contains 20 items in a four-point Likert-type format that measures Knowledge About Relationships (4 items), Beliefs About Self (4 245 items) and Beliefs About Relationships with Others (10 items). A higher score represents better relational skills. To prevent response-set bias, some items are reverse coded. After establishing content validity, to assess the reliability of the scale, a test-retest Pearson's 250 correlation coefficient was calculated and revealed a coefficient of .74.

*Procedures*

Forty-two girls (*M* age 13.2 yrs.) participated in the program. In addition to a face sheet that collected demographic and relationship information, the GRS 255 was given before beginning and upon completion of the program. Girls responded anonymously by using birth date rather than name, so confidentiality was preserved. In the closing session, girls were also given the opportunity to share what, if anything, they had learned 260 during the program in small and large group discussions.

*Analysis*

Data were coded and entered using Minitab, Release 14 (2003). Summary statistics on demographic data at baseline were performed first. Although re- 265 sponses were matched from pre- to post-program for those girls who completed two evaluation forms, only 26 girls (62%) did so. The data here, therefore, use group averages to estimate changes in behavior.

270   Characteristics of participants are presented in Table 1. Due to the preliminary nature of the program evaluation, details such as self-referral vs. referral by others, history of delinquency, and other variables which would be relevant in an empirical study were not collected.

Table 1
*Demographic Characteristics of Participants*

| Variable | N | (%) |
|---|---|---|
| Ethnicity | | |
| Caucasian | 16 | (66) |
| Black | 3 | (3) |
| Bi- or Multiracial | 5 | (20) |
| No response | 18 | |
| Your role in RA in the last week | | |
| Bully | 1 | (2) |
| Bystander | 10 | (23) |
| Victim | 9 | (21) |
| All three | 12 | (28) |
| None | 10 | (23) |
| Difficulty concentrating in school because of RA | | |
| Very often | 4 | (10) |
| Often | 5 | (12) |
| Not sure | 19 | (45) |
| Not often | 3 | (7) |
| Never | 11 | (26) |
| Think of staying home from school due to RA | | |
| Very often | 4 | (10) |
| Often | 5 | (12) |
| Not sure | 19 | (45) |
| Not often | 6 | (23) |
| Never | 3 | (12) |

275   The next series of analyses focused on RA behaviors. First, girls were asked to identify how many times in the previous week relationships with other girls had influenced their behavior. A separate series of *t*-tests were used to compare before and after program re-
280   sponses. These results are in Table 2.

Table 2
*RA Behaviors*

| Variable | Pre | Post |
|---|---|---|
| # of times hurt by RA | 5.2 | 3.04 |
| # of times seen others hurt by RA | 6.3 | 4.8 |
| # of times girl used RA | 2.4 | 2.4 |
| # of times RA message sent via computer | 1.1 | .76 |
| # of times felt physically sick or depressed because of RA | .90 | .88 |

*Note.* All questions within context of week immediately before.

Next, the subscales and total scores of the GRS were compared using *t*-test and ANOVA to check for significant differences (Table 3).

Table 3
*Means for Responses on the Girls Relationship Scale*

| Item | Time one | Time two | Change | p |
|---|---|---|---|---|
| Feelings about self | 2.8 | 2.9 | +.1 | NS |
| Believe girls are nice | 2.1 | 2.4 | +.3 | NS |
| Trust other girls | 1.2 | 1.5 | +.3 | NS |
| Want more friends | 2.0 | 2.0 | | NS |
| Okay to be mean back | 1.5 | 1.4 | −.1 | NS |
| Enjoy being with girls | 2.2 | 2.1 | −.1 | NS |
| Girls in my school are nicer | 1.2 | 1.2 | | NS |
| I know what RA is | 1.4 | 1.6 | +.2 | NS |
| Okay to defend physically | 2.3 | 2.0 | −.3 | NS |
| Want to change behavior | 1.7 | 1.9 | +.2 | NS |
| Relationships make me afraid to come to school | 3.1 | 3.0 | −.1 | NS |
| I know where to get help | 2.8 | 2.8 | | NS |
| I know what to do when hurt | 2.7 | 2.8 | +.1 | NS |
| Feel confident of friend-ability | 2.7 | 2.9 | +.2 | NS |
| Mentoring helps | 2.2 | 2.7 | +.5 | NS |
| Feeling safe is important | 2.4 | 2.3 | −.1 | NS |
| Ability to communicate | 2.4 | 2.5 | +.1 | NS |
| Okay to hurt back | 1.8 | 1.9 | −.1 | NS |
| Don't get involved when other girl hurt | 1.8 | 2.4 | +.6 | NS |
| Total score | 45.2 | 47.1 | +1.9 | NS |

## Results

Nearly a quarter of this diverse group of middle
285   school girls experienced an impact of RA on their behavior, either in thinking of staying home from school, being unable to concentrate, or actually feeling physically sick or depressed because of relationship issues with girls. Girls recognized that they could play all
290   three RA roles at some time or another in an average week.

Actual behaviors were reported to change in a favorable direction, although, again, not statistically significant. Girls were hurt less by RA, did not see others
295   hurt by RA as much (perhaps because they intervened), and sent fewer hurtful messages on the computer. Although none of the change scores on the GRS or the total score reached significance, relationship skills improved in the expected dimension for all items except
300   "Feeling safe with other girls is important to me," which girls indicated was slightly less important. The most noticeable improvement (but still nonsignificant) in relationship skills was demonstrated for two items that related to getting involved when you saw another
305   girl being hurt and benefiting from mentoring.

## Limitations of the Study

Obviously, this was a very preliminary study with a small sample and new evaluation tool. Since the two middle schools used were very different in demographic and ethnic composition, specific comparisons
310   across sites with a larger sample would enhance the findings of the study. Since the evaluation was focused on the program, more sophisticated data collection that

could assess variables connected with RA did not occur.

## Discussion

315 This study shows that the everyday life of many middle school girls is profoundly influenced by the negative consequences of RA, whether it arrives face-to-face or online. The degree to which girls could not concentrate in school or thought of staying home from 320 school because of relationship issues with other girls suggests that verbal aggression is as intimidating and distressing as physical forms of violence. However, after completing a program specifically targeted at RA, girls developed a sense of confidence about them- 325 selves, their friend-ability, and what to do when hurt and where to go for help.

## Implications for Practice

Although many excellent programs exist for addressing overt physical bullying, this study suggests that strategies for overcoming relational aggression are 330 equally important. Perhaps more significant than the statistics contained here is the observation of a guidance counselor in one of the participating schools that the frequency of certain girls' visits to her office decreased during the program. One administrator calcu- 335 lated (roughly) that delinquent episodes decreased 33% in girls participating in the program.

Girls in middle school need to feel safe in relationships. Initiatives such as Club Ophelia™ address the core safety issues in girls' relationships through a plat- 340 form of mentoring that allows girls to experience a positive and safe relationship with an older peer. Research on bullying has confirmed that processes using befriending and peer support are the most efficacious (Menesini, Codecasa, Benelli, & Cowie, 2003; Stevens, 345 De Bourdeaudhuij, & van Oost, 2000).

Teachers, school nurses, administrators, guidance counselors, and school social workers are in a front line position to facilitate use of the ERI model to educate, relate, and integrate principles of RA for girls. The 350 addition of the arts-based curriculum and mentoring from senior girls as occurs in Club Ophelia™ can enhance effectiveness of this intervention.

Girls in this study responded that they have awareness of where and how to get help when hurt in their 355 relationships, which is another important strategy that can be promoted by school personnel. Asking each girl to identify a "safe place, safe person" empowers her to have a response ready when RA occurs.

School personnel need to be alert to aggressive sub- 360 tleties that are the hallmark of relational aggression. Early and appropriate recognition of these behaviors as well as an understanding of the damage they can inflict is a key first step in combating RA. Ground rules for classroom RA behaviors and student-generated conse- 365 quences for infringement can be a powerful experiential activity that accomplishes both of these purposes. To address RA on a school-wide basis, one middle

school administrator chose to have all girls participate in a brief intervention that used the ERI model.

370 Middle school is the learning laboratory for relationship skills that can last a lifetime. In this study, an intervention with concrete skills for "helping rather than hurting" demonstrated that girls really do want to be kind.

## References

Centers for Disease Control. (2002). Youth risk behavior surveillance—United States, 2001. *MMWR, 51* (SS-04) 1–64.

Cillessen, A. H. N., & Mayeux, L. (2004). From censure to reinforcement: Developmental changes in the association between aggression and social status. *Child Development, 75.*

Club Ophelia a safe place for girls. (n.d.). *What's Club Ophelia? You are!* Retrieved March 8, 2004, from http://www.clubophelia.com/index.htm

Crick, N. R., Casas, J. F., & Nelson, D. A. (2002). Toward a more comprehensive understanding of peer maltreatment: Studies of relational victimization. *Current Directions in Psychological Science, 11,* 98–101.

Crick, N. R., & Grotpeter, J. (1995). Relational aggression, gender, and social–psychological adjustment. *Child Development, 66,* 710–722.

Dellasega, C. (in preparation). *The impact of mentoring.*

Dellasega, C. (in press). *Two faced: Adult women who aggress.* John Wiley: 2005.

Dellasega, C., & Nixon, C. (2003). *Girl wars: Twelve strategies that will end female bullying.* New York: Fireside.

Galen, B. R., & Underwood, M. K. (1997). A developmental investigation of social aggression among children. *Developmental Psychology, 33,* 589–600.

Gilligan, C. (1982). *In a different voice: Psychological theory and women's development.* Cambridge, MA: Harvard University Press.

Girl Scout Research Institute. (2003). *Feeling safe: What girls say.* New York: Girl Scouts of the USA.

Greene, M. B. (2000). Bullying and harassment in schools. In R. S. Moser, & C. E. Franz (Eds.), *Shocking violence: Youth perpetrators and victims—A multi-disciplinary perspective* (pp. 72–101). Springfield, IL: Charles C. Thomas.

Griffin, R. S. & Gross, A. M. (in press). Childhood bullying: Current empirical findings and future directions for research. *Aggression and Violent Behavior.*

Hazler, R. J. (1996). *Breaking the cycle of violence: Interventions for bullying and victimization.* Washington, DC: Taylor & Francis.

Lagerspetz, K. M., Bjorkqvist, K., & Peltonen, T. (1988). Is indirect aggression typical of females? Gender differences in aggressiveness in 11 to 12 year old children. *Aggressive Behavior, 14,* 403–414.

Menesini, E., Codecasa, E., Benelli, B., & Cowie, H. (2003). Enhancing children's responsibility to take action against bullying: Evaluation of a befriending intervention in Italian middle schools. *Aggressive Behavior, 29,* 1–14.

Nansel, T. R., Overpeck, M., Ramani, S. P., Pilla, R. S., Ruan, W. J., Simons-Morton, B. et al. (2001). Bullying behaviors among U.S. youth: Prevalence and association with psychosocial adjustment. *Journal of the American Medical Association, 285,* 2094–2100.

Olweus, D. (1994). Annotation: Bullying at school: Basic facts and effects of a school-based intervention program. *Journal of Child Psychology and Psychiatry, 35,* 1171–1190.

Owens, L., Shute, R., & Slee, P. (2000). "I'm in and you're out...." Explanations for teenage girls' indirect aggression. *Psychology, Revolution, and Gender, 2.1,* 19–46.

Paquette, J. A., & Underwood, M. K. (1999). Gender differences in young adolescents' experiences of peer victimization: Social and physical aggression. *Merrill-Palmer Quarterly, 45,* 242–266.

Smith, H., & Thomas, S. P. (2000). Violent and nonviolent girls: Contrasting perceptions of anger experiences, school, and relationships. *Issues in Mental Health Nursing, 21,* 547–575.

Stevens, V., De Bourdeaudhuij, I., & van Oost, P. (2000). Bullying in Flemish schools: An evaluation of anti-bullying intervention in primary and secondary schools. *British Journal of Educational Psychology, 70,* 195–210.

Tomada, G., & Schneider, B. H. (1997). Relational aggression, gender, and peer acceptance: Invariance across culture, stability over time, and concordance among informants. *Developmental Psychology, 33,* 601–609.

Underwood, M. K., Galen, B. R., & Paquette, J. A. (2001). Top ten challenges for understanding gender and aggression in children: Why can't we all just get along? *Social Development, 10,* 248–266.

U.S. Department of Health and Human Services. (2000). *Healthy people 2010.* (Conference Edition, in Two Volumes). Washington, DC: U.S. Government Printing Office.

U.S. Department of Health and Human Services. (2001). *Youth violence: A report of the surgeon general.* Washington, DC: U.S. Government Printing Office.

Whitaker, C., & Bastian, L. (1991). *Teenage victims: A national crime survey report.* Washington, DC: U.S. Department of Justice, Bureau of Justice Statistics.

**About the authors**: *Cheryl Dellasega* is professor, Penn State College of Medicine, Hershey, PA. *Pamela Adamshick* is assistant professor of nursing, Moravian College, 1200 Main Street, Bethlehem, PA 18018.

**Address correspondence to**: Dr. Dellasega, Department of Humanities, H134, 500 University Drive, P.O. Box 850, Hershey, PA 17033-0850. E-mail: cdellasega@psu.edu

# Exercise for Article 24

## Factual Questions

1. For the GRS, what is the value of the test-retest Pearson correlation coefficient?

2. Did the girls respond anonymously?

3. What percentage of the girls completed two evaluation forms (pre and post)?

4. What was the mean total score at time one on the GRS?

5. Was the difference between the time one and time two means on the GRS statistically significant?

## Questions for Discussion

6. In your opinion, is the program described in sufficient detail? (See lines 197–232.)

7. This evaluation used a one-group, pretest-posttest design. In future studies, would you recommend using a control group? Explain.

8. The researchers describe the limitations of the evaluation in lines 306–314. In your opinion, are there any additional limitations that are not mentioned here?

9. Do you agree with the statement in the last sentence of the article? (See lines 371–374.)

10. Based on this evaluation, would you recommend funding for widespread implementation of this program? Would you want to see the results of additional evaluations before making such a recommendation? Explain.

## Quality Ratings

Directions: Indicate your level of agreement with each of the following statements by circling a number from 5 for strongly agree (SA) to 1 for strongly disagree (SD). If you believe an item is not applicable to this research article, leave it blank. Be prepared to explain your ratings. When responding to criteria A and B, keep in mind that brief titles and abstracts are conventional in published research.

A. The title of the article is appropriate.

   SA   5   4   3   2   1   SD

B. The abstract provides an effective overview of the research article.

   SA   5   4   3   2   1   SD

C. The introduction establishes the importance of the study.

   SA   5   4   3   2   1   SD

D. The literature review establishes the context for the study.

   SA   5   4   3   2   1   SD

E. The research purpose, question, or hypothesis is clearly stated.

   SA   5   4   3   2   1   SD

F. The method of sampling is sound.

   SA   5   4   3   2   1   SD

G. Relevant demographics (for example, age, gender, and ethnicity) are described.

   SA   5   4   3   2   1   SD

H. Measurement procedures are adequate.

   SA   5   4   3   2   1   SD

I. All procedures have been described in sufficient detail to permit a replication of the study.

   SA   5   4   3   2   1   SD

J. The participants have been adequately protected from potential harm.

   SA   5   4   3   2   1   SD

K. The results are clearly described.

   SA   5   4   3   2   1   SD

L. The discussion/conclusion is appropriate.

   SA   5   4   3   2   1   SD

M. Despite any flaws, the report is worthy of publication.

   SA   5   4   3   2   1   SD

# Article 25

# An Application of Fear Appeal Messages to Enhance the Benefits of a Jail Encounter Program for Youthful Offenders

JAMES O. WINDELL
Oakland County Circuit Court
Family Division Psychological Clinic

J. SCOTT ALLEN, JR.
Oakland County Circuit Court
Family Division Psychological Clinic

ABSTRACT. Research has consistently shown that so-called Scared Straight types of jail encounter programs do not have positive benefits for youthful offenders. However, few, if any, inmate-youth encounter programs have utilized the results of fear appeals message research. Results of the present study suggest that an inmate-youth encounter program may lead to attitude change in youthful offenders if components of successful fear appeals are incorporated into the program.

From *Youth Violence and Juvenile Justice*, 3, 388–394. Copyright © 2005 by Sage Publications, Inc. Reprinted with permission.

After almost 20 years of researching and studying aversion programs for juveniles, Finckenauer and other criminologists have concluded that Scared Straight and similar programs are failures (Finckenauer, Gavin, Hovland, & Storvoll, 1999; Sherman et al., 1998). Nonetheless, such programs persist, usually with public and governmental approval. The underlying theory of all such programs is criminal deterrence. Program advocates believe that the realistic depiction of adult prison will deter juvenile delinquents or children at risk from becoming delinquent and from further involvement with crime (Finckenauer, 1982; Szymanski & Fleming, 1971).

However, no matter how often researchers review programs that provide juveniles with scary messages about crime and delinquency, the results are at best disheartening. Most recently, Petrosino, Turpin-Petrosino, and Finckenauer (2000) reviewed nine randomized evaluations of Scared Straight prison programs conducted between 1967 and 1992. Data from this review indicate that such programs likely have harmful effects leading to increased crime and delinquency. The authors concluded that given the harmful effects of these kinds of interventions, governments have an ethical responsibility to rigorously evaluate the policies, practices, and programs they implement (Petrosino et al., 2000).

Although Scared Straight types of programs have a dubious theoretical and research history, there is a considerable body of research related to persuasive messages that arouse fears. The psychology of using fear to influence people has been studied during the past 50 years, but this research has not been applied to Scared Straight types of programs. Because the purpose of jail tours and youth-inmate confrontations is to evoke fear of consequences, the psychology of fear appeals is particularly relevant. Witte and Allen (2000) indicate that the nearly 5 decades of research on fear appeals show that certain fear appeals are successful. Recent research (Witte & Allen, 2000) suggests that the stronger the fear appeal, the greater the potential influence over attitudes toward relevant behaviors, intentions to change, and actual behavior changes.

Witte (1992) proposed a model known as the extended parallel process model (EPPM) that postulates that threat and corresponding fear motivates a response, and that the efficacy of the threat determines the nature of that response. The possible responses to the perceived threat include either danger-control or fear-control actions. In this model, if the perceived threat is low, then the individual does no further cognitive processing of the fear because of a lack of motivation. If the perceived threat is high and there is also a high perception of one's ability (efficacy) to perform the recommended action (for instance, avoid further criminal behavior), the individual will be more inclined to follow the danger control recommendations. On the other hand, if the threat is high but the individual's perceived ability to deal with the danger is low or the individual believes the recommended action might not work (e.g., an individual might believe that he or she has no power to avoid criminal behavior), then the individual will be more likely to take some action to control his or her fear. A possible way of dealing with the fear is to become defensive or deny that the threat is real or that it applies to him or her.

Pratkanis and Aronson (1991) claim that a fear appeal is most effective when (a) it genuinely scares people, (b) it offers a specific recommendation for overcoming the fear-aroused threat, (c) the recommended

75 action is perceived as effective for reducing the threat, and (d) the message recipient believes he or she can perform the recommended action.  These four criteria for an effective fear appeal may help explain why previous research on Scared Straight types of programs shows negative results.

It is suggested that the EPPM theoretical model is useful for understanding adolescent juvenile offenders who participate in any fear-arousing jail tour program 80 or any modified Scared Straight type of program. The Jail Tour Program (JTP) in the present study involved scheduling a group of adolescent offenders to go to an adult jail, view the facilities, hear lectures from police officers, and have a series of face-to-face confronta- 85 tions and encounters with inmates. Inaugurated in 1992 and run continuously since then, the program has had several hundred adolescent participants. To date, there has been no evaluation or assessment of its effectiveness, even though it continues to be included as a stan- 90 dard part of the probation requirements for many young people in the juvenile court selected for this study.

Most fear-inducing inmate-youth encounter programs do not couple the induced fear with either an 95 underlying theoretical approach or specific components that have been found to bring about effective results in the fear appeals literature. In comparing the JTP of the present study to previous Scared Straight types of programs, it was the addition of a segment incorporating 100 support for positive choices and recommendations to avoid future delinquency that differentiated it from others. The authors recognized that this fit with a fear appeals model and suggested the approach may hold greater potential for success than those previously stud- 105 ied. The program herein studied was unique in that it does use components that lead to more efficacious fear appeals.

The jail exposure program in the present study incorporated fear, followed by useful recommendations 110 and efforts to heighten participants' efficacy—all components outlined by the EPPM model. Therefore, it was hypothesized that adolescent offenders participating in the program would report less favorable attitudes toward jail following the jail tour. Second, research has 115 shown that fear appeals do not affect males and females in a differential manner. Therefore, it was hypothesized that adolescent offenders in the present study would develop less favorable attitudes toward jail regardless of their gender.

**Method**

*JTP Description*

120 The data collection for the present study took place in the county jail of a suburb of a large Midwestern city. Corrections officers in the county jail developed a program for juvenile offenders, referred to as the JTP. The 2-hour JTP, in brief, utilizes a fear appeal coupled 125 with encouragement and recommendations for avoid-

ing future criminal activity. The evening JTP begins shortly after juveniles, who were court-ordered to participate, arrive with their parents. Three deputies (often three males but sometimes two males and one female) 130 experienced in running this program start by treating the adolescents as if they are new inmates of the jail. They are asked to store coats, hats, and belts in a locker and to stand in a line. They are led into the jail (without their parents, as parents are discouraged from going on 135 the tour) and in the succeeding hour and a half are introduced to how adult inmates are expected to adhere to a concrete, limited behavioral repertoire. In addition, the juveniles are given harsh messages about the magnitude of reduced individuality and restrictions on free- 140 dom in jails and the likelihood of experiencing unpleasantness or harm. Vivid and personal language is used by the officers to emphasize the similarities between the participants and the adult inmates. Messages, commands, and remarks that heighten the seriousness 145 of incarceration and even the likelihood that the juveniles are highly susceptible to being incarcerated are repeated. The juveniles are allowed to see various sections of the jail and to get a firsthand view of how inmates are housed. Along the way, they are given in- 150 formation about recidivism, jailhouse management, and typical treatment of prisoners. When they reach group cells housing several prisoners, they are told to stand outside of these cells and ask any questions of the inmates they choose. There is a give-and-take with in- 155 mates, with some inmates trying to intimidate the juveniles. Some inmates reiterate the themes that were delivered by the corrections officers, whereas others offer useful and well-intentioned advice.

In the last half hour of the JTP, the tone of the tour 160 changes, and the corrections officers soften their approach. They ask more questions and try to relate more with the juveniles. The officers focus more on efficacy messages (e.g., "You can make the choice to avoid high-risk situations") and offer recommendations. 165 Based on Witte and Allen (2000), how individuals think about the threat and their assessment of their own power in dealing with that threat leads to adaptive or maladaptive attitudes and behaviors. The juveniles are finally taken to a cafeteria where they are encouraged 170 to talk about their goals and aspirations along with how they can avoid becoming jail inmates in the future. The officers give encouragement about how the juveniles will be able to implement their goals, stay in school, and avoid troublesome peers. The officers provide rein- 175 forcing statements that suggest they believe the juveniles have it within their abilities to avoid further criminal behavior.

*Participants*

Juvenile Court hearing officers routinely order adolescents between the ages of 16 and 17 who have been 180 adjudicated for a criminal offense to go through the JTP. Overall, 327 adolescents participated in this study.

Table 1

*Means and Standard Deviations for Scores on a Measure of Impressions of Jail for Juvenile Offenders*

| Group | Pretest | | Posttest | |
|---|---|---|---|---|
| | *M* | *SD* | *M* | *SD* |
| Male | 25.7 | 6.17 | 20.1 | 3.03 |
| Female | 25.6 | 5.69 | 19.9 | 6.19 |
| Violent | 27.8 | 5.32 | 22.3 | 5.07 |
| Nonviolent | 25.2 | 5.90 | 20.0 | 6.61 |

*Note.* The maximum possible score was 65, and the minimum possible score was 13.

Of these, 282 were males and 45 were females. A planned exploratory analysis necessitated identifying the nature of the offenses committed by the females in the sample. Of the females, 32 had committed nonviolent crimes, whereas 13 had been convicted of violent offenses.

*Instrument*

An instrument, termed the Jail Tour Adolescent Questionnaire (JTAQ), was developed for use in the present study. The JTAQ was constructed with the assistance of psychologists who work with adolescent offenders, and it was reviewed by juvenile probation officers and corrections officers. The JTAQ has 13 self-report items with a 5-point Likert-type scale (the points include strongly disagree, disagree, not sure, agree, and strongly agree). Each question asks the respondent to evaluate certain behaviors that occur in jail. The JTAQ items address favorable or unfavorable attitudes toward incarceration held by the respondent. Examples of items include, "Prisoners these days are treated very nicely by prison staff," "While in prison, prisoners get along and support each other," and "I think living in jail would be fun sometimes." The instrument was completed just prior to the program and again following the JTP.

**Results**

This study looked at the overall effect of the JTP on participants' responses on a self-report questionnaire. A one-way analysis of variance was used to assess the degree to which there were changes in adolescent offenders' scores on a questionnaire designed to reflect favorable and unfavorable evaluations of certain behaviors in jail. It was anticipated that participants would report a less favorable impression of jail after the JTP relative to their reported attitude before the JTP. A significant time effect was found, $F(1, 327) = 139.9$, $p < .001$, indicating that significant changes on the measure of attitude were associated with the JTP. Means for the pre-JTP versus post-JTP groups were 25.7 ($SD = 6.11$) and 20.1 ($SD = 6.06$), respectively.

This study also examined if significant differences existed between male and female participants on the instrument before and after the program. Previous research found no differential effect of fear appeals on boys and girls. No studies have examined the differential effect of a Scared Straight type of program on boys' and girls' evaluations of jail. Therefore, a subse-quent focus of the current project was to identify if the sex of the participant mattered in whether or not they responded to the JTP as measured by changes in their attitudes as measured by the JTAQ. It was expected that male and female participants would develop a more critical attitude toward incarceration.

Based on these predictions, the data were analyzed using two-tailed paired samples *t* tests with a 95% confidence interval computed for the true differences between each pair of group means. All assumptions were met to allow for a parametric test. First, boys' pre-JTP and post-JTP mean standard scores on the JTAQ were compared. The boys' perspectives decreased significantly from pre-JTP to post-JTP: $t(281) = 14.6$, $p < .001$. Second, girls' mean pre-JTP and post-JTP standard scores on the JTAQ were compared using a paired *t* test. The girls' perspectives also decreased significantly from pre-JTP to post-JTP: $t(44) = 14.6$, $p < .001$. Both boys and girls were influenced by the JTP as reflected in the changes on the JTAQ (see Table 1 for means and standard deviations).

**Discussion**

The present study integrated fear appeal theory (the EPPM in particular) with a naturalistic inmate-juvenile encounter program. It was hypothesized that participants would report differences in their attitudes and impressions of jail after the JTP and that there would be no difference between the attitude of boys and the attitude of girls.

Consistent with the first hypothesis, it was found that participants did report a less favorable impression of jail after experiencing the JTP. Boys and girls were analyzed separately, and it was found that both groups had less favorable impressions of jail.

Although other studies found no difference or a negative influence from Scared Straight and juvenile-inmate encounter programs, this study found, on a questionnaire administered both before and after the encounter, that there was a significant and positive difference. One reason for this finding may be that this study used a pre-JTP and post-JTP self-report survey that was designed to measure attitudes toward jail and incarceration. Other research projects have used recidivism and various other indicators of attitude change as a measurement (Finckenauer, 1982; Petrosino, Turpin-Petrosino, & Buehler, 2003). The JTAQ was developed for this research project to gauge adolescent respon-

dents' attitudes toward jail. However, no psychometric properties were established for the JTAQ. Neverthe-
275 less, the results from the use of the JTAQ suggest that going through the JTP may have had a significant effect on the participants' impressions of jail. In particular, their attitudes toward being incarcerated became less favorable following the JTP.

280 Although the theory underlying the JTP is criminal deterrence, the mechanism for change in this type of intervention is through fear appeal. Because the purpose of jail tours and youth-inmate confrontations is to invoke fear, the psychology of fear appeals is particu-
285 larly relevant. That is, the JTP offers solutions that may be viewed by the juveniles as within their ability. In the EPPM explanation of fear appeals, messages that fail to offer solutions that the participants believe they can implement are less likely to lead to attitude and behav-
290 ior change. This theory suggests that for any jail tour program to be effective, it should incorporate the elements necessary for a fear appeals program to be successful. It should not only deliver a strong and scary message, but it should also tell adolescents very clearly
295 how they can avoid the scary outcome (going to jail). Then, participants need to come away convinced that they can apply the strategy successfully in their own life. The JTP may satisfy the conditions of a successful fear appeal.

300 A strength of this study is that it was conducted in a naturalistic setting. Most previous research into the effectiveness of fear appeals has studied participants in artificial settings (Witte & Allen, 2000). However, a limitation of this study is that multiple independent $t$
305 tests were conducted with no correction for chance significant findings. At least one significant finding may be because of chance. Furthermore, the questionnaire used in this study may not be a measurement of attitude but a measure of fear or some other construct.
310 Therefore, normed and standardized instruments need to be employed to better understand the effectiveness of the JTP. Also, this study did not have a follow-up phase, nor did it take into account recidivism or post-JTP behavior.

315 Finally, this research needs to be extended with the addition of other measures (such as recidivism) to determine effectiveness. A future direction for research could include development of an instrument that is based on the EPPM model to determine more precisely
320 if this model does explain positive changes. Determining this can help in the development of a paradigm for Scared Straight types of programs with a greater potential for bringing about the expected results.

### References

Finckenauer, J. O. (1982). *Scared straight! And the panacea phenomenon.* Englewood Cliffs, NJ: Prentice Hall.

Finckenauer, J. O., Gavin, P. W., Hovland, A., & Storvoll, E. (1999). *Scared straight: The panacea phenomenon revisited.* Prospect Heights, IL: Waveland Press.

Petrosino, A., Turpin-Petrosino, C., & Buehler, J. (2003). Scared straight and other juvenile awareness programs for preventing juvenile delinquency: A systematic review of the randomized experimental evidence. *The Annals of the American Academy of Political and Social Science, 589,* 41–62.

Petrosino, A., Turpin-Petrosino, C., & Finckenauer, J. O. (2000). Well-meaning programs can have harmful effects! Lessons from experiments of such programs as scared straight. *Crime & Delinquency, 46,* 354–379.

Pratkanis, A., & Aronson, E. (1991). *Age of propaganda.* New York: Freeman.

Sherman, L. W., Gottfredson, D. C., MacKenzie, D. L., Eck, J., Reuter, P., & Bushway, S. D. (1998). *Preventing crime: What works, what doesn't, what's promising* (NCJ 171676). Rockville, MD: National Institute of Justice, U.S. Department of Justice.

Szymanski, L., & Fleming, A. (1971). Juvenile delinquency and an adult prisoner—A therapeutic encounter? *Journal of the American Academy of Child Psychiatry, 10,* 308–320.

Witte, K. (1992). Putting the fear back into fear appeals: The extended parallel process model. *Communication Monographs, 59,* 329–349.

Witte, K., & Allen, M. (2000). A meta-analysis of fear appeals: Implications for effective public health campaigns. *Health Education & Behavior, 27,* 591–615.

**About the authors**: *James O. Windell*, M.A., is a court psychologist at the Oakland County Court Clinic, where he runs adolescent treatment groups and conducts high-conflict, postdivorce treatment groups. He is also an instructor in the Criminal Justice Department of Wayne State University. His major interests include parenting, juvenile delinquency, social skills training of adolescents, and treatment of high-conflict divorces. *J. Scott Allen, Jr.*, Ph.D., works as a senior psychologist at the Oakland County Court Clinic, where he primarily conducts court-ordered psychological evaluations for children, adolescents, and adults and supervises doctoral candidate students. His private practice focuses on family issues (e.g., child behavior management, challenges of adolescence) and mood and anxiety disorders.

# Exercise for Article 25

## Factual Questions

1. The letters "JTP" stand for what three words?

2. The researchers state two hypotheses. What is the first one that they state?

3. How many of the females had committed nonviolent crimes?

4. What was the mean pretest score for the females? What was the mean posttest score for the females?

5. Was the difference between the two means in your answer to Question 4 above statistically significant? If yes, at what probability level?

6. According to the researchers, what is cited as a "strength" of this study?

## Questions for Discussion

7. In your opinion, is the program described in sufficient detail? Explain. (See lines 120–177.)

8. The researchers provide examples of the JTAQ self-report items in lines 200–203. To what extent do these examples help you understand what the instrument measures?

9. In this evaluation, the researchers used a self-report instrument. An alternative is to use recidivism as an outcome measure for judging the effectiveness of such a program. In your opinion, is self-report or recidivism a better measure? Are they equal? (See lines 265–270 and 312–314.)

10. For a future study on the effectiveness of this program, would you recommend using a control group? Why? Why not?

11. If you were on a panel considering the possibility of major funding to permit widespread use of the JTP, what recommendation would you make? Would you recommend major funding? Limited funding until additional evaluations are made? No funding? Explain.

## Quality Ratings

Directions: Indicate your level of agreement with each of the following statements by circling a number from 5 for strongly agree (SA) to 1 for strongly disagree (SD). If you believe an item is not applicable to this research article, leave it blank. Be prepared to explain your ratings. When responding to criteria A and B, keep in mind that brief titles and abstracts are conventional in published research.

A. The title of the article is appropriate.

SA 5 4 3 2 1 SD

B. The abstract provides an effective overview of the research article.

SA 5 4 3 2 1 SD

C. The introduction establishes the importance of the study.

SA 5 4 3 2 1 SD

D. The literature review establishes the context for the study.

SA 5 4 3 2 1 SD

E. The research purpose, question, or hypothesis is clearly stated.

SA 5 4 3 2 1 SD

F. The method of sampling is sound.

SA 5 4 3 2 1 SD

G. Relevant demographics (for example, age, gender, and ethnicity) are described.

SA 5 4 3 2 1 SD

H. Measurement procedures are adequate.

SA 5 4 3 2 1 SD

I. All procedures have been described in sufficient detail to permit a replication of the study.

SA 5 4 3 2 1 SD

J. The participants have been adequately protected from potential harm.

SA 5 4 3 2 1 SD

K. The results are clearly described.

SA 5 4 3 2 1 SD

L. The discussion/conclusion is appropriate.

SA 5 4 3 2 1 SD

M. Despite any flaws, the report is worthy of publication.

SA 5 4 3 2 1 SD

# Article 26

# A Review of Online Social Networking Profiles By Adolescents: Implications for Future Research and Intervention

AMANDA L. WILLIAMS
Oklahoma State University

MICHAEL J. MERTEN
Oklahoma State University

ABSTRACT. This study explored content posted and interactions taking place on adolescent online social networking profiles. Although "blogging" continues to soar in popularity, with over half of teenagers online participating in some form, little research has comprehensively explored blog communication within the context of adolescent development. Content was qualitatively coded from 100 randomly selected profiles authored by adolescents between the ages of 16 and 18. Rich thematic elements were identified, including family and social issues, risk behaviors, disclosure of personally identifiable information, and frequent peer interaction. Results indicate adolescent blogs frequently contain appropriate images, positive comments about parents and peers, athletics, a variety of risk behaviors, and sexual and profane language. In addition, school type was examined (public versus private, religious) as a potential factor in understanding the differences in content posted by adolescents; however, no significant differences were found. Implications for parental monitoring and intervention are discussed as well as direction for future research. Adolescents' online profiles contain a wealth of intimate, candid, and publicly available information on a wide range of social issues pertinent to adolescence that contribute to the understanding of adolescent development and well-being.

The Internet has earned its own niche in social research (Greenfield & Yan, 2006) and the newest phenomena of online social networking is rapidly developing its own field of inquiry in the social sciences (Herring, Scheidt, Wright, & Bonus, 2005; Mee, 2006). In
5  fact, researchers are scrambling to understand the phenomenon almost as quickly as the technology advances. Mazur (2005) defined blogs as updateable public records of private thoughts. As our knowledge of
10  this new social forum advances, research is beginning to differentiate between social networking sites and blogs. However, for the purposes of this study, blogs, Web journals, and social networking profiles are considered synonymous as they all involve individuals
15  creating and maintaining personal Internet sites allowing authors and other users to post content, thus creating a personal network.

Lenhart and Madden (2007), senior researchers for the Pew Internet and American Life Project, said that
20  in the past five years social networking has "rocketed from a niche activity into a phenomenon that engages tens of millions of Internet users" (p. 3). Previous studies have examined surface content found in various Web journal forums, such as demographic information,
25  communication styles, thematic content, purposes for blogging, and disclosure of personally identifiable information—also referred to by Huffaker (2006) as identity vulnerability (Lenhart & Fox, 2006; Fox & Madden, 2005; Subrahmanyam, Smahel, & Greenfield,
30  2006; Huffaker & Calvert, 2005; Mazur, 2005; Herring et al., 2005; Mee, 2006). However, to date there has been very little research on dynamic social and emotional content provided in blogs and how such content relates to adolescent development, peer relationships,
35  and indicators of emotional well-being. The present study proposes that online social networking profiles posted by adolescents contain intimate, candid, and observable self-disclosure and peer interaction that can be analyzed, creating an overall picture of adolescent
40  behavior, highlighting specific areas needing additional research and addressing implications for parental monitoring and intervention.

## Adolescent Social Networking

Fifty-five percent of teenagers online use and create online social networking profiles (Lenhart & Madden,
45  2007). With more than half of teenage Internet users interacting online, the concept of blogging is a salient research topic investigating what adolescents are blogging about, how they are socially interacting, and what potential effects this phenomena may have on other
50  dimensions of their lives.

Social networking profiles present a unique research opportunity as the process of blogging involves individuals voluntarily posting information about themselves—personal thoughts, feelings, beliefs, activities—in a public arena with unlimited access for
55  anyone with an Internet connection. The amount of

personal information contained in a blog is completely dependent on the author's judgment. This situation is ideal for social scientists as it allows unobtrusive observations of authentic human behaviors and interactions with no "real" contact or interference. Adolescent blogs are full of information about their daily lives (Mazur, 2005) documenting whatever they choose to disclose about themselves and any subsequent written interaction by individuals posting comments to the blog. A recent study involving adolescents and the Internet sums up the communication medium's impact and potential:

> The Internet is more exciting and challenging as a research environment than earlier media because it is a complex, virtual, social, and physical world that children and adolescents participate in and co-construct, rather than something that is merely watched or used such as television or personal computers. It becomes a complex virtual universe behind a small screen on which developmental issues play out...offering new views into the thoughts, feelings, and behaviors of children and adolescents (Greenfield & Yan, 2006, p. 393).

Themes often permeating adolescent blogs include romantic relationships, friends, parents, substance use, sexuality, popular culture, eating disorders, school, depression, conflicts, self-expression, and self-harm (Mazur, 2005; Whitlock, Powers, & Eckenrode, 2006). Blogs have become a standard form of teenage communication comparable to cell phones, email, or instant messaging (Mee, 2006). The differences between blogging and other forms of communication are: (1) they are accessible at any time, from any location, (2) they leave a trail of observable dialogue that can be printed or stored, and (3) they incorporate advanced multimedia components. Adolescents have the ability to construct a personal profile or online environment, depicting how they view themselves or how they want others to view them.

It is unwise to write off Internet communication as superficial or unconnected to real life. Symbolic interactionists would argue that blogging is as meaningful to adolescents as they believe it to be and plays as large a role in their life as they allow. White and Klein (2002) proposed that "the more individuals put into something, the more they get out of it *[sic]*" (p. 68). The more adolescents participate in blogging activities, the more importance they are likely to associate with it. The words on the screen have as much power as they are assigned by both the author and the reader—thus developing co-constructed meanings. An ecological perspective makes this method of communication even more complex by appreciating that while teens are unique individuals sitting at a computer typing their thoughts, they are also students, children, employees, and citizens, with various rules, regulations, codes of ethics, and standards of behavior attached to each identity. Online communication has the potential to interact with, affect, or be influenced by all other spheres of life.

According to Lenhart and Fox (2006), as reported in the Pew Internet and American Life Project, the top two reasons individuals create blogs are for creative self-expression and to document and share personal experiences. These reasons are even more significant for adolescents as they actively explore new forms of self-expression, identity development, and social interaction (Kidwell, Dunham, Bacho, & Pastorino, 1995). Some researchers attribute the popularity of reality television shows with adolescents' comfort in sharing intimate details of their lives with a global audience in real time (Mee, 2006). Perhaps online social networking tempers the Eriksonian concept of antagonism between adolescents and their environment. Nearly two decades ago, he acknowledged that new forums for growth and formation would arise, thus necessitating adaptable and progressive traditions to maintain a normative, expectable developmental environment. In 1968, he said, "Today, when rapid technological changes have taken the lead the world over, the matter of establishing and preserving...an 'average expectable' continuity for child rearing and education everywhere has, in fact, become a matter of human survival" (p. 222). In order to develop and maintain the ego, adolescents seek "conflict-free energy in a mutually supportive psychosocial equilibrium" (Erikson, 1968, p. 223)—a desire online social interaction has great potential to fulfill.

The Internet provides an unrestricted laboratory setting for adolescent identity experimentation as they seek to understand how they fit into the world around them. Concurrently, the Internet is a functioning community involving personal morals and regulatory processes. However, these processes are stunted if adolescents do not see their online activities as subject to any ethical code. In day-to-day "real-life" interactions, adolescents are in a constant state of checks and balances with parents, teachers and school administrators, peers, and societal norms. Their actions generate perceivable reactions that they use to gauge future decisions and behaviors. The Internet, specifically blogging, does not provide this type of "real" reinforcement or punishment. Internet standards for behavior are established via text communication normalizing or encouraging various activities or attitudes. These "invisible cyberfriendships" (Mee, 2006, p. 1) allow adolescents to co-construct the environments that will shape their psychosocial development (Greenfield & Yan, 2006).

Identity formation is a primary task in adolescence (Erikson, 1968) and young people who actively explore their identities are more likely to experience mood swings, self-doubt, confusion, disturbed thinking, impulsivity, conflict with parents, reduced ego strength, and increased physical symptoms (Kidwell et al., 1995). These indicators of identity exploration are generally observable in adolescent self-disclosure and peer

relationships. As adolescents explore their identity, they will go through behavioral patterns that on the surface may appear to be cause for concern, but are
175 actually developmentally appropriate and healthy. This may explain why certain risky behaviors and discussions observed online look like "an adult's worst nightmare" (Mazur, 2005, p. 9), but may be a positive and safe outlet for self-expression and experimentation.
180 Adolescents who feel they have lost their voice or are unheard by authority figures in their personal lives can channel their energy and need for attention into their online journal, versus feeling confused, worried, negative, misunderstood, or physically acting out (Kidwell
185 et al., 1995).

Prior research has identified specific behaviors associated with adolescence and identity exploration, and researchers have observed such behaviors in various Internet forums. For example, adolescents use blogs to
190 communicate information via Web text that would be obvious in face-to-face interaction, such as gender, ethnicity, and physical appearance. Adolescents also use Internet communication to explore their sexuality. Subrahmanyam, Smahel, and Greenfield (2006) ob-
195 served teenagers' chat rooms and recorded one sexual comment per minute and one obscenity every two minutes, elevating sexual content and adult language high in the ranks of what teens talk about online. Through systematic review of adolescents' online profile con-
200 tent, researchers hope to achieve a comprehensive understanding of how adolescents use online social networking sites and what role such sites play in teenagers' ontogenetic and social development.

### Method

*Sample*

Social network profiles were randomly collected
205 from a major hosting site with more than one-fourth of users registered as teenagers (Anonymous, 2006). Utilizing random multistage cluster sampling, 100 adolescent blog authors were selected between the ages of 16 and 18 years who maintained active networks. "Ac-
210 tive" status was determined by frequency of profile updates and/or comment posts that had to have occurred within the 60 days prior to date of analysis. Though the term "participants" is used to refer to profile authors, there was no contact, interaction, interven-
215 tion, or interference between researcher and subjects as all content studied was publicly available without any special knowledge, fee-based subscription or membership, or authorization. Per regulations outlined in the host site's terms of use and privacy agreement, all Web
220 site participants were required to acknowledge and consent to unlimited public access of any information posted to their profile by themselves or by anyone else.

The participants were selected based on region, school affiliation, gender, and age. Five nationally rep-
225 resentative locations were selected, equally distributed throughout the country, representing each coast as well

as central, north-, and south-central regions of the U.S. Two schools were randomly selected from each state—one public and one parochial. From each school, five
230 male- and five female-authored profiles were randomly selected for review. The age distribution within the sample was purposively organized as follows: two 16-year-olds, one 17-year-old, and two 18-year-olds. Participants were also equally distributed between public
235 and parochial high schools to determine if any content or online behaviors differed based on type of school attended. As parochial schools are founded in religious doctrine, it is reasonable to speculate that behaviors and peer relationships would differ based on school
240 environment.

Content posted by participants was systematically coded based on various demographic, behavioral, and thematic elements. Themes were assigned based on content alone, without applying any intent or inference
245 to the text or imagery. For example, if a comment said, "I think I would really kill myself without you," it was coded as violent—regardless of the spirit in which it was intended by the author. Similarly, sexual comments were coded based on text alone and categorized
250 by their reference to sexual activity versus sexual language. Precodes were created prior to data collection for anticipated content such as gender, last log-on date (to ensure recent activity), and presence of personally identifiable information. While reviewing each profile,
255 open codes were created to record unexpected, exploratory data such as differentiation between types of risk behaviors discussed and other unanticipated behaviors requiring unique coding strategies. Scales were in the form of questions "asked" of the profile. For example,
260 "Is there an image of the author posted to the blog?" (0 = no; 1 = yes). The majority of categories were dichotomous based on presence of any specific variables (0 = not present, 1 = present); several categories implemented multiple nominal response options.

*Measures*

265 *Demographic content.* The demographic characteristics of participants were classified into five categories: gender, school affiliation, relationship status, religious affiliation, and sexual orientation. Location was also coded but was omitted from results to preserve
270 participant anonymity. Once demographic information was obtained, each profile was reviewed for additional precoded content pertaining to preselected categories and unexpected themes encompassing an array of attitudes and behaviors.

275 *Social content.* Each unique profile was reviewed for text-based and pictorial content and captions. The 50 most recent comments posted to the authors' profiles within the preceding 60 days were reviewed for the same qualifying variables. Social variables included
280 image (did the author post an image and was it appropriate?), family issues (positive/negative comments about parents/siblings), school issues (skipping school,

collegiate aspirations, and athletics), social issues (positive/negative comments about peers), discussion of special interests such as reading, music, movies, and sports, and discussions of "parties," which were indicated by comments about prior social gatherings or specifically referenced attended "parties."

*Image appropriateness.* This was assessed based on a number of factors. Images labeled "appropriate" would generally include photos of an individual (assumed to be the owner of the blog) fully clothed, and not participating in any risky or suggestive behaviors. Inappropriate images generally included photos in which an individual was not wearing a shirt, pants, or was wearing provocative swimwear, underwear, or other suggestive attire. Swimsuit photos were not deemed inappropriate unless they were accompanied by sexual body position, explicit captions, or swimwear that was generally inappropriate for the age of the sample. Inappropriate activities included sexual body language or positioning usually accompanied by suggestive captions or risk behaviors, such as holding weapons, fighting, or using substances. Overtly conservative images were deemed inappropriate if they were accompanied by suggestive, profane, or otherwise inappropriate captions.

*Family issues* encompassed comments about parents and/or siblings. Positive parent/sibling comments: make positive statements about one or both parents or any sibling. Negative comments: make negative or derogatory statements about one or both parents or any sibling. Coded "issues" ranged from simple statements such as "I love my dad," to detailed stories retelling positive, negative, or neutral experiences with family. Again, no comments were coded based on assumed intent, perceptions, or feelings of the author. Positive, negative, or neutral attitudes were scaled based on descriptive content alone and any obvious relationship with family cohesion or conflict.

*School issues* dealt with attendance, school participation, and future academic goals. A comment was coded if it referenced skipping school or a desire to skip school. College attendance was coded if a comment or survey was posted that specifically addressed wanting to attend college (generally with a "yes" or "no" response). If a comment was posted about wanting to be a lawyer, for example, it was assumed they also wanted to attend college. Discussion of athletics, including participation in sports, was also coded.

*Social issues* consisted of comments relating to peers' interactions, special interests, and socialization. Peer comments were evaluated based on text provided. Positive comments: made a friendly or positive statement about a peer. Negative comments were overtly negative, derogatory, or confrontational. Each category, positive and negative, was coded based on presence, which often resulted in each blog having multiple responses because both types of comments were made. Special interests included references to hobbies or enjoyable activities such as reading books, listening to or playing music, and watching movies. Discussions of social gatherings, or "parties," were coded if a comment directly referenced a previously attended "party" or other social gathering such as homecoming dance, birthday event, and club or bar attendance. The type of gathering was not discerned in coding, only the presence of the discussion.

*Risk behaviors* were addressed in regard to substance use, criminal activity, sexual content, profanity, and physical violence. Substance use was recorded if the profile or comment section included discussion or images of alcohol and/or drugs. Most blogs contained a survey-type question asking if participants smoked and their response was coded as either "smokes" or "doesn't smoke." Profiles that did not contain a "do you smoke?" survey question were listed as "no response." Criminal activity was merely assessed as present or not present and qualitative details pertaining to type of crime was attached to the coded data.

*Sexual content* is a rather abstract umbrella for adolescent behavior, so responses were split into two categories: explicit/graphic language and comments referencing sexual activity. Responses that were sexual in nature but did not fit into one of these categories were coded as general sexual content. Profanity includes standard curse words as well as slang and sexual profanity. Because of the tendency for profane language and sexual language to overlap, certain terms and phrases were coded under both headings. Physical harm was recorded regardless of victim/perpetrator status. Violence was noted as present or not present if physical harm was discussed toward self or others, by self or others.

*Identity vulnerability* (Huffaker, 2006) is the term developed to reference personally identifiable information posted on the Internet. Such data include adolescent's full name (first, last), phone number, business name, online contact information (e-mail, instant message user name), or other type of identifiable data. An "other" category was necessary as some personally identifiable data were not easily categorized, such as school schedule with room numbers, general directions to home, scanned image of driver's license, etc. As blogs frequently included at least one image of the author, any information providing location or contact information could make the teenager an easy target for Internet predators. "Many (students) don't grasp that not only their friends and classmates are reading their sites, but also complete strangers who may have the worst intentions" (Anonymous, 2006, p. 25).

*Peer interaction* included size of personal network, frequency of interaction among "friends" within the network, and prior/past or proposed/future "real-life" encounters. The networks consisted of anyone the participant registered as a "friend"—whether they knew that person in their day-to-day lives or exclusively online. Frequency of comments was determined based

400 on the first 50 available comments that display in chronological order, summing the time distance between posts, and then dividing by number of entries. This information is important to determine how frequently adolescents use their online social network to communicate. Finally, prior or proposed meetings ref-

405 erence comments that specifically state whether the participant and "friend" had met in person, a.k.a. "real-life," or whether they had made specific plans to meet. This information can be positive, indicating that online socialization includes and/or facilitates live interaction

410 between adolescents who are physically involved in each other's lives. However, it can also be negative if data infers adolescents are meeting people they have known only online or people who are not appropriate to interact with (i.e., older adults, unknown adults from

415 out of town, proponents of risk behaviors).

*Procedure*

Once a sample of 100 profiles had been accumulated, each profile was reviewed following the same "script" of variables and presence of specific content recorded in an Excel database. The original HTML

420 profiles were saved on a separate electronic storage device and numerically coded so that any identifiable information was detached from the profile data. After reviewing all profiles and posting all variable responses to the database, information was transferred to SPSS

425 statistical software for further evaluation and analysis.

Based on thematically coded categories of adolescent blog data, a systematic review was conducted to account for behaviors, identify any patterns between observed behaviors, and infer any possible association

430 with type of school attended. Such data were also explored for indicators of potential dysfunction or questionable emotional states. As no significant variations were found between adolescents attending public vs. parochial school, results were consolidated to present

435 an overview of online social networking content based on the total sample size and organized by gender. Based on the overall picture of adolescent Web content, implications for future research are discussed as well as potential intervention needs/strategies for par-

440 ents and educators.

**Results**

Available demographics contained in the sample blogs indicate that the majority of adolescent profile authors reported being single (61%) or in a serious relationship (32%). The majority of these authors did

445 not reference their religious affiliation (39%); 26% stated a Catholic affiliation; 22% stated other Christian affiliations. A substantial 75% of blog authors reported being heterosexual, 3% declared homosexuality, another 3% claimed to be bisexual, and 2% said they

450 were unsure about their sexual orientation. Of the entire sample, 17% did not include any information pertaining to their sexual preferences (see Table 1).

Table 1

*Profile Demographic Content Posted by Adolescents Listed by Gender*

| | Males (n = 50) | Females (n = 50) | Total (n = 100) |
|---|---|---|---|
| Relationship status | | | |
| Single | 33% | 28% | 61% |
| Married | 2% | 2% | 4% |
| Divorced | 1% | 1% | 2% |
| In relationship | 14% | 18% | 32% |
| No response | - - - | 1% | 1% |
| Religious affiliation | | | |
| Catholic | 13% | 13% | 26% |
| Christian-other | 11% | 11% | 22% |
| Other | 8% | 5% | 13% |
| No response | 18% | 21% | 39% |
| Sexual orientation | | | |
| Heterosexual | 41% | 34% | 75% |
| Homosexual | 2% | 1% | 3% |
| Bisexual | 1% | 2% | 3% |
| Unsure | 1% | 1% | 2% |
| No response | 5% | 12% | 17% |

All profiles contained images posted by the author (n = 100), 83% of which were deemed appropriate

455 while 17% were inappropriate. Examples of inappropriate images included an individual urinating, shirtless females dancing on tables with shirtless males, photos of a homemade device captioned as a "working bomb," individuals drinking alcohol as well as pictures of al-

460 cohol bottles/cans. There were also photos taken from mirror reflections of nude males with the image stopping just above the genitals, often referred to by authors and friends as their "V" because of the V-shaped abdominal muscles just above male genitalia. These

465 "V" images typically excluded part or all of the face of the individual photographed. Some pictures were conservative in content, but were accompanied by inappropriate captions containing references to alcohol or substance use and intoxication, profanity, obscene ges-

470 tures, or suggestive/sexual body postures.

Of comments made about family, 37% were positive about parents and 22% were positive about siblings; 16% of participants made negative comments about parents with negative sibling comments accounting

475 ing for 2% of responses. Regarding school issues, male profiles did not contain content related to skipping school while 4% of female profiles contained the topic. Fourteen percent of males' and 13% of females' profiles referenced a plan or desire to attend college. Of all

480 blogs reviewed, 58% referenced athletics in some capacity—either making participatory comments or discussing a general interest (males 34%; females 24%).

Social issues included comments about peers with 97% of the entire sample making positive statements

485 about or to their friends; 100% of female profiles contained positive peer comments compared to 94% of male profiles. Most blogs included special interest topics such as movies, music, books, and hobbies (71%), and 40% of all blogs reviewed referenced prior social

490 gatherings or attended "parties"—some with revealing

details of participants' activities, such as this comment posted about a new club in town: "Very loose 18 ID to enter; You know how the rest goes…" (see Table 2).

Table 2
*Social Content Observed in Adolescent Profiles Listed by Gender*

|  | Males ($n = 50$) | Females ($n = 50$) | Total ($n = 100$) |
|---|---|---|---|
| Image |  |  |  |
| Appropriate | 40% | 43% | 83% |
| Inappropriate | 10% | 7% | 17% |
| Family issues |  |  |  |
| Positive parental comment | 16% | 21%[1] | 37% |
| Negative parental comment | 5% | 11%[1] | 16% |
| Positive sibling comment | 11% | 11% | 22% |
| Negative sibling comment | 1% | 1% | 2% |
| School issues |  |  |  |
| Skipping school | - - - | 4% | 4% |
| Aspires to attend college | 14% | 13% | 27% |
| Athletics | 34%[1] | 24% | 58% |
| Social issues |  |  |  |
| Positive peer comments | 47% | 50% | 97% |
| Negative peer comments | 19% | 17% | 36% |
| Special interests | 33% | 38% | 71% |
| Discussion of "parties" | 18% | 22% | 40% |

[1]Indicates significant difference at .05 between males and females

Risk behaviors made up a significant portion of content observed from the sample, with 84% of profiles and blog discussions containing some type of risk-taking behaviors; 83% of profiles included discussion or referencing of substances, 81% referenced alcohol, and 27% discussed illegal drugs. Fifty-six percent of authors stated that they did not smoke. Across-sample rates of criminal activity content were near-equal with 15% of blogs discussing some type of crime; 9% of blogs referenced shoplifting or stealing, while others referenced rape, selling drugs, gambling, vandalism, and automobile infractions.

Nearly half of all blogs contained some form of sexual content, with 44% using explicit or graphic language and 16% referencing sexual activity. Some of the sexual content was extremely explicit in nature, as represented in text and imagery. Certain references were also made about specific types of sexual activity, including individuals' virginity statuses. Naturally, profanity is intimately intermingled with sexual content, and the overall frequency of any type of profane language among all profiles was 81%, almost evenly distributed within the sample. Twenty-seven percent of profiles include statements relating to physical harm of self or others such as gang references, suicidal ideation, discussion of fights, or images of weapons implying violence.

Regarding personally identifiable information disclosed by adolescents, 43% listed their full name; 10% listed their phone number; 11% disclosed their place of employment, and 20% revealed their online contact information (i.e., e-mail address). Overall, nearly half the sites analyzed contained information that could

potentially jeopardize the identity security of the adolescent participants (see Table 3).

Table 3
*Risk Behaviors Observed in Adolescent Online Social Networking Profiles Listed by Gender*

|  | Males ($n = 50$) | Females ($n = 50$) | Total ($n = 100$) |
|---|---|---|---|
| Risk behaviors | 44% | 40% | 84% |
| Substance use | 44%[1] | 39% | 83% |
| Alcohol discussion/ comments | 42% | 39% | 81% |
| Author smokes | 9% | 9% | 18% |
| Author doesn't smoke | 31% | 25% | 56% |
| Illegal drugs discussion/ comments | 15% | 12% | 27% |
| Criminal activity | 8% | 7% | 15% |
| Stealing/shoplifting | 5% | 4% | 9% |
| Sexual content | 29% | 20% | 49% |
| Explicit/graphic language | 25% | 19% | 44% |
| Sexual activity comment | 10% | 6% | 16% |
| Profanity | 42% | 39% | 81% |
| Physical harm–self/others | 18% | 9% | 27% |
| Included full name (first, last) | 23% | 20% | 43% |
| Included phone number | 2% | 8% | 10% |
| Included employer name | 2% | 9% | 11% |
| Provided online contact information | 10% | 10% | 20% |

[1]Indicates significant difference at .05 between males and females

In an effort to tie the virtual world of adolescent bloggers to their "real" day-to-day lives, their frequency of interaction with other users was collected. Comments about physical meetings and frequency of comment postings were indicative of "real" relationships; 83% of the sample referenced previous in-person contact as well as proposed future in-person encounters and such "real" contact was evenly distributed across the sample. Profiles had an average network size of 194 "friends" with a standard deviation of 162.28. This figure not only represents the number of contacts made and maintained online but also highlights the diversity in network sizes. The average frequency of interaction was 2.79 days, with a standard deviation of 3.10 days. Such a short time lapse between postings indicates that adolescents frequently use online social networks to communicate and maintain relationships on a regular basis. With a standard deviation of less than a week, it is safe to assume that adolescents use these networks as a major method of interpersonal communication (see Table 4).

## Discussion

### Process

This study brought to light two aspects of online social networking research: process and content. The process function of the analysis was to determine if content from adolescent social networking profiles could be systematically and scientifically studied. Though broad and randomly led with diverse content, social networking profiles successfully fit into a coding scheme that allowed for exploratory collection of qualitative themes relating to adolescent thought, behavior, and socialization. The proposition that such content could be successfully researched was strongly supported. The information adolescents post online does contain intimate and candid personal information as well as peer interaction that can be randomized, sorted, and systematically coded, creating a comprehensive overview of online social behavior. The process of reviewing profiles was time-consuming and detail-oriented, thus requiring intense focus on accuracy and unbiased recording. With that said, and considering the variety and amount of data collected in this study, it is concluded that adolescent blogs are an ideal research opportunity with many diverse avenues for analysis.

Table 4
*Peer Interaction: Frequencies and Means of Adolescents By Gender*

| | Males ($n = 50$) | Females ($n = 50$) | Total ($n = 100$) |
|---|---|---|---|
| In-person contact (not online) | | | |
| Prior | 42% | 41% | 83% |
| Future/proposed | 40% | 43% | 83% |
| Length of "friend" list (number of users) | | | |
| Mean | 218.00 | 170.00 | 194.00 |
| Standard deviation | 196.30 | 133.36 | 168.73 |
| Frequency of comment posts (in days) | | | |
| Mean | 2.97 | 2.61 | 2.79 |
| Standard deviation | 4.17 | 2.23 | 3.33 |

*Content*

The second aspect of the study relating to blog content resulted in concurrent findings with prior literature as profiles included personal demographic details, comments relating to family well-being and functioning, peer interactions, substance use, sexual activity, body-image issues, identity vulnerability, and frequency of contact among bloggers. Findings of sexual and profane content strongly supported prior research by Subrahmanyam, Smahel, and Greenfield (2006) in that adolescents use online forums to explore their sexuality. Because of the vastness and richness of content available, it is recommended and strongly encouraged that future studies focus on specific aspects of adolescence (e.g., body image), and collect only data pertinent to such focus. It is not feasible to address a broad array of variables with extreme depth or comprehension. However, unlike prior research, this study thoroughly assessed for thematic, overarching variables adolescents frequently include in their online discussions providing direction for future, more contemplative analyses. During the course of this investigation, many salient research topics presented themselves (adolescent alcohol use, parent-child relationships, gender differences in body image, adolescent sexual

expression) as ideal future research themes related to adolescent development. This study was successful in demonstrating the diverse information that is literally at the research world's fingertips and freely available for analysis.

Future studies must address the concept of "freely available" information, and clear lines must be drawn regarding how ethical it is to observe controversial and disturbing material posted by minors. Prior to embarking on a study of this kind, researchers must outline what information they will collect, and what they will report to site administrators or authorities as inappropriate or dangerous. Though social network participants must waive any rights to the content, one cannot assume users—specifically adolescents—thoroughly review hosting sites' terms of use, privacy policies, or register with sites using accurate demographic information.

*Identity Exploration*

Through observation of adolescents' online interactions and behaviors, it is evident that identity exploration is facilitated by online social networking. Topics that have been associated with adolescence and individuation were present in online profiles—especially in the areas of self-disclosure, peer relations, risk behaviors, and sexual exploration. The content posted to adolescent blogs followed expected paths of identity and role experimentation as originally understood by Erikson's developmental stages (1968). It is an advantage to understand that adolescents use social networking sites to quasi-publicly experiment with their identity, trying out different roles. However, it is much more beneficial for researchers, parents, and educators to have firsthand knowledge of the specific ways adolescents communicate with their peers and social networks and to view blogging as a relatively safe method of role exploration. Understanding *how* teenagers communicate with one another potentially facilitates better communication between authority figures and adolescents and enables adults to be more aware of adolescent emotional health and well-being.

*School Environment*

Through the lens of school environment, results did not highlight any demonstrative trends associated with attendance at any type of school but provided enough interesting data to warrant additional research. Faith, or attendance at a faith-based school, was not observed either as a risk or protective factor. However, in light of the expectations that accompany parochial school attendance, it is possible that a lack of difference between public and private-religious school is, in itself, a significant finding—especially considering the provocative topics that were equally present among all students.

**Intervention**

Findings from this review highlight several areas

where adolescent social networking profiles could be useful in educating parents about adolescents' attitudes and behaviors, as well as indicate several areas where intervention may be needed, primarily in the areas of risk-taking behavior and personal identity disclosure. Based on results from this study, adolescents are blogging about a considerable amount of risk behaviors such as substance use, crime, and promiscuity. The infinite and unguarded nature of the Internet may require parents to revisit their philosophy on adolescent privacy expectations and parent-child communication about such behaviors. Not only can parents benefit from observing their child's uncensored disclosure and behavior by gaining a greater understanding of their attitudes and motivations, they can also learn more about the Internet world, their child's level of participation within it, and how their parental role as monitor fits into the scheme of virtual reality.

If parents are able to observe their adolescents' peer communications, they may be able to embrace a more realistic perspective of their attitudes, values, and motivations and be able to adapt their parenting styles appropriately. In other words, parents will be able to know their children better. Adolescents view their parents as more permissive or more authoritarian than parents often see themselves, which significantly affects emotional autonomy and parent-child conflict (Smetana, 1995). Instead of perceiving online content as a form of personal diary that adolescents are entitled to keep private, parents should view the medium as an invaluable tool for helping them understand their teenagers better—their hopes, challenges, opinions, communication styles, activities, and social networks.

"The explosive growth in the popularity of (social networking sites) has generated concerns among some parents, school officials, and government leaders about the potential risks posed to young people when personal information is made available in such a public setting" (Lenhart & Madden, 2007, 3). Parents and educators could take an appreciation of online social networking, and its role in adolescent life, a step further by incorporating it into routine discussion and curriculum. By transforming computer-mediated communication (CMC) from a contemporary phenomenon, where parents have no presence and limited understanding, to common knowledge incorporated into everyday language, CMC loses its power and stigma as a technology that only adolescents use or comprehend. Alienating the Internet from the academic environment would only succeed in creating a greater divide between young people and authority figures. It is also essential that school administrators stay abreast of online networking within their institution to monitor the social climate of their school community. It is imperative that teachers, school administrators, and most certainly parents familiarize themselves with the Internet well enough to at least monitor who students are talking to and about what.

By addressing online activities with teens, in relation to ethics, propriety, safety, and language, all parties involved learn more about one another and create a safer environment in which this modern method of communication will continue to grow. As demonstrated in the current study, online social networks can be a positive form of communication within the school system. Several sites were created to maintain friendships after students had relocated to another state or, in one instance, when a foreign-exchange student returned to his home country. A series of comments were found on a male's profile welcoming him to his new school and initiating new friendships. Within parameters guided by parents, schools, and other invested authorities, online social networking could be a positive outlet for peer interaction and appropriate self-disclosure.

## Limitations

The findings of this study should be understood solely as indicators of the need for more focused research. The most obvious limiting factor of the analysis is the inability to verify any of the information collected or understand it from the participants' perspectives. Everything included in online social networking profiles, or on the Internet for that matter, is completely subjective and limited by what the authors choose to disclose or their subjective depiction of themselves. However, these limitations are not so different from the challenges encountered with any type of self-report data collection that is dependent on honest disclosure of participants.

A second limitation affecting generalizability is the small sample size. But each of the 100 profiles reviewed contained extensive detail that provides insight into adolescents' online social networking. The amount of detail in this analysis mandated a smaller, more manageable sample size with limited scope, but resulted in more complex and salient recordings. Social networking sites are, as Mazur (2005, p. 180) noted, "mines of adolescent data." The information is out there and is rich in substance and meaning; it just needs to be systematically collected and coded for generalizable analysis.

## Conclusion

This study certainly begs more questions than it answers; however, that was the purpose. The intention of reviewing adolescent blogs was not to learn more about the Internet, but to learn how online social networking sites could benefit and give direction for future research on adolescent behavior and development. The question of what topics teenagers discuss online was answered and content ranged from families and friends, hobbies and athletics, to drug use, profanity, and promiscuity. Observing adolescent behavior within an online network supported the notion that profiles are rich in behavioral data as related to development and individuation. Researchers continually strive to understand the teenage mind better, especially as society advances and new modes of communication and exploration develop. Blogging could be viewed as more authentic behavior compared to cross-sectional methods asking

765 adolescents how often they participate in or feel about certain aspects of life. The inconsistencies found within the 100 blogs observed in this analysis demonstrate that what a teenager marks on a survey form may be very different from how they actually feel or behave

770 with their peers.

In this sample, few patterns were evident, though some phenomena appeared promising, such as communication style, self-image, sexual behavior, or violence. More research that explores readily available informa-

775 tion to create a more comprehensive analysis from which stronger inferences and generalizations can be made is needed. Even though no patterns were established based on school environment, that does not mean no associations are to be found. This review

780 highlighted a dire need for more data collection addressing adolescent behaviors—both positive and risky—to see if and how they are affected by the school environment. The content analyzed from the profiles in this study indicate the importance of adoles-

785 cent behavior and peer interaction as it relates to social relationships, risk behaviors, special interests, extracurricular activities, and family dynamics. The overall goal of this study was achieved—an overview has been developed outlining what adolescents are communicat-

790 ing online. Future studies should take this research further by investigating the specific behaviors observed in order to understand what they mean within the context of the adolescent's "real life."

### References

Erikson, E. (1968). *Identity: Youth and crisis*. New York: Norton.

Fox, S., & Madden, M. (2005, December). Generations online (Memo). *Pew Internet and American Life Project*. Retrieved October 22, 2006, from: www.pewInternet.org

Greenfield, P., & Yan, Z. (2006). Children, adolescents, and the Internet: A new field of inquiry in developmental psychology. *Developmental Psychology, 42*(3), 391–394.

Herring, S., Scheidt, L., Wright, E., & Bonus, S. (2005). Weblogs as a bridging genre. *Information Technology and People, 18*(2), 142–171.

Huffaker, D. (2006). *Teen blogs exposed: The private lives of teens made public*. Presented at the American Association for the Advancement of Science in St. Louis, MO., February 16–19.

Huffaker, D., & Calvert, S. (2005). Gender, identity, and language use in teenage blogs. *Journal of Computer-Mediated Communication, 10*(2), article 1. http://jcmc.indiana.edu/vol10/issue2/huffaker.html

Kidwell, J., Dunham, R., Bacho, R., & Pastorino, E. (1995). Adolescent identity exploration: A test of Erikson's theory of transitional crisis. *Adolescence, 30*(120), 785–794.

Lenhart, A., & Fox, S. (2006, July 19). A portrait of the Internet's new storytellers. *Pew Internet and American Life Project*. Retrieved October 22, 2006, from: www.pewInternet.org

Lenhart, A., & Madden, M. (2007, January 7). Social networking websites and terms: An overview (Memo). *Pew Internet and American Life Project*. Retrieved January 26, 2007, from: www.pewInternet.org

Mazur, E. (2005). Teen blogs as mines of adolescent data. *Teaching of Psychology, 32*(3), 180–182.

Mee, C. (2006). To blog or not to blog. *On Target, 2*(1), 30–31.

"MySpace" cadets are up for sudden death. (2006, September). *The Education Digest, 72*(1), 25.

Smetana, J. (1995). Parenting styles and conceptions of parental authority during adolescence. *Child Development, 66*, 299–316.

Subrahmanyam, K., Smahel, D., & Greenfield, P. (2006). Connecting developmental constructs to the Internet: Identity presentation and sexual exploration in online teen chatrooms. *Developmental Psychology, 42*(3), 395–406.

White, J., & Klein, D. (2002). *Family Theories* (2nd ed.). Thousand Oaks, London, New Delhi: Sage Publications.

Whitlock, J., Powers, J., & Eckenrode, J. (2006). The virtual cutting edge: The Internet and adolescent self-injury. *Developmental Psychology, 42*(3), 1–11.

**About the authors**: *Amanda L. Williams* and *Michael J. Merten*, Department of Human Development and Family Science, Oklahoma State University.

**Address correspondence to**: Michael J. Merten, Department of Human Development and Family Science, Oklahoma State University, 1111 Main Hall, Tulsa, Oklahoma 74106. E-mail: michael.merten@okstate.edu

# Exercise for Article 26

## Factual Questions

1. Was random selection used in this study?

2. In addition to substance abuse and criminal activity, what other "risk behaviors" were addressed?

3. Were significant differences (i.e., variations) found between adolescents attending public versus parochial schools?

4. Was there a statistically significant difference between the percentage of males and females mentioning athletics in their profiles?

5. According to the researchers, what is the "most obvious limiting factor" of the analysis?

6. According to the researchers, what is the "second limitation" of this study?

## Questions for Discussion

7. The researchers examined profiles on "a major hosting site," but did not name the site. Speculate on why they did not name it. (See lines 204–206.)

8. The researchers identified themes based on "content alone." If you had conducted this study, would you also have done this *or* would you have made inferences about the intent of the participants? (See lines 243–248.)

9. In your opinion, would it be difficult to make judgments on image appropriateness? Explain. (See lines 289–307.)

10. What is your opinion on the researchers' suggestion that future studies should address the concept of "freely available" information? Is this an important issue? Explain. (See lines 601–613.)

11. Do you agree that the researchers achieved their "overall goal"? Explain. (See lines 787–790.)

12. If you were to conduct a study on this topic, what changes in research methodology, if any, would you make?

## Quality Ratings

Directions: Indicate your level of agreement with each of the following statements by circling a number from 5 for strongly agree (SA) to 1 for strongly disagree (SD). If you believe an item is not applicable to this research article, leave it blank. Be prepared to explain your ratings. When responding to criteria A and B, keep in mind that brief titles and abstracts are conventional in published research.

A. The title of the article is appropriate.

SA    5    4    3    2    1    SD

B. The abstract provides an effective overview of the research article.

SA    5    4    3    2    1    SD

C. The introduction establishes the importance of the study.

SA    5    4    3    2    1    SD

D. The literature review establishes the context for the study.

SA    5    4    3    2    1    SD

E. The research purpose, question, or hypothesis is clearly stated.

SA    5    4    3    2    1    SD

F. The method of sampling is sound.

SA    5    4    3    2    1    SD

G. Relevant demographics (for example, age, gender, and ethnicity) are described.

SA    5    4    3    2    1    SD

H. Measurement procedures are adequate.

SA    5    4    3    2    1    SD

I. All procedures have been described in sufficient detail to permit a replication of the study.

SA    5    4    3    2    1    SD

J. The participants have been adequately protected from potential harm.

SA    5    4    3    2    1    SD

K. The results are clearly described.

SA    5    4    3    2    1    SD

L. The discussion/conclusion is appropriate.

SA    5    4    3    2    1    SD

M. Despite any flaws, the report is worthy of publication.

SA    5    4    3    2    1    SD

# Article 27

# Professional Human Service Occupation Biases Represented in General Psychology Textbooks

MICHAEL W. FIRMIN
Cedarville University

ERICA J. JOHNSON
Cedarville University

JEREMIAH WIKLER
Cedarville University

ABSTRACT. We examined the coverage given by general psychology textbooks, representing eight major commercial publishers, regarding the professions of psychology, counseling, marriage and family therapy, and social workers. Of the 24 textbooks assessed, we found substantial bias favoring the coverage of psychology. While 25% of the texts mentioned social workers, there was relatively little attention given to professional counselors or marriage and family therapists. A case is made for more parity to be shown for a larger cross-section of professions in these texts—since general psychology courses tend to hold some measure of gate-keeping exposure for the human service professions.

From *Journal of Instructional Psychology*, 36, 194–202. Copyright © 2009 by the Journal of Instructional Psychology. Reprinted with permission.

The human service professions have a sordid history relative to collaboration (Schmitt, 2001). This partly relates to their history, with psychology deriving itself first from philosophy and then the hard sciences 5 (Hunt, 1993), whereas counseling emerged from the American guidance movement, following World War II (Capuzzi & Gross, 1997; Nowlin, 2006). Social work sketches a separate family tree, tracing its roots to caring for the poor, indigent, and immigrants at the turn of 10 the century who were mistreated or needed advocacy in society (Barker, 1998). Marriage and family therapy largely was derived eclectically from behavioral and cognitive psychology, with many of the original founders being psychoanalytically trained (Gurman & 15 Fraenkel, 2002).

Although all the professions share much in common, they also possess differences that bear unique emphases for training, supervision, and practice. Traditional clinical psychologists have advocated a historic 20 scientist-practitioner model of the profession (Albee, 2000), whereas counselors, marriage and family therapists, and social workers, comparatively, are more practice oriented (Booth & Cottone, 2000; Houston, 2005). Psychologists often are considered the leading 25 professionals, since they require the doctoral degree as the entry-level credential for state licensure. The other helping professions require only a master's degree for independent practice.

Interprofessional collaborative efforts have not 30 generally been strong between the main human service professions (Goldin, 1997). Weigle (1977) notes that the 1970s became a period when increased conflicts among the professions arose, mostly due to licensure laws being passed by the states for the respective pro- 35 fessions. Randolph (1988) labeled the mental health community organizations as their own worst enemies in this regard. This largely is because of the interprofessional squabbles and sometimes outright hostility that exists between the groups, often expressed in the 40 open media.

Goodyear (2000) indicates that the Community Mental Health Centers Act of 1963 began the modern tension and that the professions had relatively little conflict prior to that time, compared to present quar- 45 rels. This act provided federal funds for reimbursing the fees of particular mental health professionals. As this act has been updated over time, and insurance companies heavily have weighed in on the matter, the contention has grown worse—not better. Irvine, Ker- 50 ridge, McPhee, and Freeman (2002) concluded, "Conflicts over authority, power, control, and jurisdiction pose an undeniable barrier to effective collaboration and teamwork, particularly when occupational groups attempt to defend activities that are thought to be stra- 55 tegic to the maintenance of their professional identity" (p. 204).

Cummings (1990) notes further evidence of battles between these professional organizations vis-à-vis the Joint Commission on Interprofessional Affairs (JCIA) 60 in the late 1980s and early 1990s. Although the organization was initiated to encourage cooperation among various mental health organizations, they chose to include only four major professions: psychiatry, psychology, social work, and psychiatric nursing. Marriage 65 and family therapists, professional mental health counselors, and rehabilitation counselors were markedly excluded. Brooks and Gerstein (1990a & 1990b), Van Heteren and Ivey (1990), and Bloom et al. (1990) noted that, at the time, the other professionals, such as coun- 70 selors, were, fairly or unfairly, considered by various other professions to be inadequately trained to function independently as mental health experts. Although psychologists and counselors may share some personality qualities (Swanson & O'Saben, 1993), they often have been worlds apart in defending turf and professional advancement.

Freeth (2001), Irvine, Kerridge, McPhee, and Freeman (2002), and many others have called for the human service professions to lay aside their differences and focus on the overall good of client care. Myers, Sweeney, and White (2002) further call for recognition of a general parity among the spectrum of mental health professionals. However, much is at stake, including significant financial incentives for the respective professions not to experience this idealistic harmony. The pool of available monies from governmental sources and insurance companies is finite. By boxing out some groups, there are more resources available for those who persuade the public of their own professional superiority (Katzar, 2007).

Firmin (2004), Pistole and Roberts (2002), and others have provided a fairly comprehensive treatment of how some of the mental health professions differ from each other, showing that the disparities are more than mere semantics. While the organizations have some shared cultures and aims (Gulliver, Peck, & Towell, 2002), they also possess varying philosophical assumptions, protocols, and ethical guidelines that separate them from one another. The likelihood of obtaining unity among the various mental health professional organizations is not great—at least not for the foreseeable future—and past collaborative efforts largely have not been successful (Freeth, 2001).

Given the above dynamics as a backdrop, human service professions are left with power struggles (Schmitt, 2001). That is, some organizations will achieve greater measures of stature, financial reward, and professional privileges due to their perceived status among the ranked professions. Generally, with status comes tangible reward. And these largely will come at the cost of the other mental health professions since, to some degree, the available power is a zero-sum game. That is, given the limited austerity afforded the human services professions in contemporary culture, what exists will be shared among the psychologists, counselors, marriage and family therapists, and social workers. Power given to one group will be, in effect, taken by another.

In this paradigm, psychologists enjoy a significant advantage. This is because the course general psychology is a staple requirement in many general education (liberal arts) components across university curricula (Firmin & Firebaugh, in press), offered at almost every university (Perlman & McCann, 1999), enrolling over a million students annually (Griggs & Proctor, 2002). That is, for various universities, the course tends either to be required of all students or a class that is approved within a list of general education courses, any of which students may complete in order to fulfill a general education requirement. In contrast, courses such as introduction to counseling, marriage and family counseling, or social work are not generally considered liberal arts classes.

Assuming that general psychology is taught by psychologists, it follows that the psychological profession possesses a significant advantage over the other mental health professions in what exposure university students across the nation have regarding the respective human service professions. Obviously, all general psychology students will be exposed to the nature and work of professional psychologists as core concepts (Nairn, Ellard, Schialfa, & Miller, 2003), including potential career paths. However, it is unknown to what degree they also have apt exposure to the other mental health professions. Assuming general psychology is the only human service-related course that most students take in college (Griggs & Proctor, 2002), and they have no, or extremely limited, exposure to the professions of counseling, marriage and family therapy, or social work, then how will these professions draw the best and brightest into their professional ranks? Social psychology has long documented the potency of the primacy effect: First exposures to any construct are extremely powerful to the formation of later constructs and perceptions (Asch, 1946).

The task of surveying every general psychology course across the nation is daunting, although obviously it would be a very worthy study for a future project. As a present precursor, we began with a preliminary investigation of general psychology textbooks. Via primacy effects, the exposure that students have to the spectrum of mental health professions early in their collegiate experience through these texts will impact their eventual perceptions of the respective groups and, to some degree, taint their outlooks toward future involvement with them. Consequently, the present study will provide important foundational data on which future research in this area of professional comparative studies can build.

## Method

All 13,752 pages of text were examined from 21 general psychology textbooks. We obtained the names of the books by asking our university bookstore for the texts that were the national best-sellers at the time of data collection. The sample represents around one third of the total number of general psychology textbooks sold by major companies annually (Griggs & Koenig, 2001; Griggs, Proctor, & Cook, 2004). Each of the books enjoyed a relatively popular cross-section among national public and private universities. The publishers represented in the sample included Atomic Dog, Houghton-Mifflin, McGraw-Hill, Norton, Prentice-Hall, Wadsworth, Wiley, and Worth. The textbooks largely were selected based on the publishers' willingness to provide complimentary copies of the texts for

185 the express purpose of the present research study, although the publishers did not know the specific construct under investigation. W. W. Norton publishing 190 was asked to participate but did not provide complimentary texts. Table 1 lists the textbooks and identifying information used in the present study.

Table 1
*Textbooks, Publishers, and Descriptive Data*

| Text | Psychologists | | Counseling | | Marriage and family therapist | | Social work | | APA | ACA/ AAMFT/ NASW |
|---|---|---|---|---|---|---|---|---|---|---|
| | # of ¶s | Charts or Tables | # of ¶s | Charts or Tables | # of ¶s | Charts or Tables | # of ¶s | Charts or Tables | | |
| *Psychology: Journey of Discovery,* by Franzoi, Atomic Dog Publishing | 15 | 1 | 0 | 0 | 0 | 0 | 1 | 1 | Yes | No |
| *Essentials of Psychology*, 2nd ed., by Nash, Houghton-Mifflin | 9 | 0 | 0 | 0 | 0 | 0 | 0 | 0 | Yes | No |
| *Psychology*, 6th ed., by Bernstein, Penner, Clarke-Stewart, and Roy, Houghton-Mifflin | 12 | 0 | 0 | 0 | 1 | 0 | 0 | 0 | Yes | No |
| *Psychology*, by Kowalski & Westen, John Wiley & Sons | 0 | 1 | 0 | 0 | 0 | 0 | 0 | 0 | Yes | No |
| *Psychology in Action*, by Huffman, John Wiley & Sons | 5 | 2 | 0 | 0 | 0 | 0 | 0 | 1 | Yes | No |
| *Essentials of Understanding Psychology*, 5th ed., by Feldman, McGraw-Hill | 22 | 2 | 0 | 0 | 0 | 0 | 0 | 1 | Yes | No |
| *Psychology*, 5th ed., by Sdorow and Rickbaugh, McGraw-Hill | 17 | 1 | 0 | 0 | 0 | 0 | 0 | 0 | Yes | No |
| *Psychology*, 7th ed., by Santrock, McGraw-Hill | 38 | 2 | 0 | 0 | 0 | 0 | 0 | 0 | Yes | No |
| *Psychology: An Introduction*, 8th ed., by Lahey, McGraw-Hill | 18 | 1 | 0 | 0 | 0 | 0 | 0 | 0 | Yes | No |
| *Psychology: The Science of Mind and Behavior*, 2nd ed., by Passer and Smith, McGraw-Hill | 7 | 2 | 0 | 0 | 0 | 0 | 0 | 0 | Yes | No |
| *Psychology*, 4th ed., by Kassin, Pearson/Prentice Hall | 13 | 1 | 0 | 0 | 0 | 0 | 1 | 0 | Yes | No |
| *Psychology: An Introduction*, 12th ed., by Morris and Maisto, Pearson/Prentice Hall | 9 | 1 | 0 | 0 | 0 | 0 | 0 | 0 | Yes | No |
| *Introduction to Psychology*, by Coon, Thomson Wadsworth | 6 | 4 | 1 | 1 | 0 | 0 | 1 | 1 | Yes | No |
| *Introduction to Psychology*, by Kalat, Thomson Wadsworth | 25 | 2 | 0 | 0 | 0 | 0 | 0 | 1 | Yes | No |
| *Psychology*, by Sternberg, Thomson Wadsworth | 24 | 1 | 0 | 0 | 0 | 0 | 0 | 0 | Yes | No |
| *Psychology: The Adaptive Mind*, by Nairne, Thomson Wadsworth | 6 | 0 | 0 | 0 | 0 | 0 | 0 | 0 | Yes | No |
| *Psychology: Themes & Variations*, by Weiten, Thomson Wadsworth | 6 | 1 | 0 | 0 | 0 | 0 | 0 | 0 | Yes | No |
| *Introduction to Psychology*, 6th ed., by Plotnik, Thomson Wadsworth | 29 | 0 | 0 | 0 | 0 | 0 | 1 | 0 | Yes | No |
| *Discovering Psychology*, by Hockenbury & Hockenbury, Worth Publishers | 12 | 1 | 0 | 1 | 0 | 1 | 0 | 1 | Yes | No |
| *Exploring Psychology*, by Myers, Worth Publishers | 6 | 1 | 0 | 1 | 0 | 1 | 0 | 1 | Yes | No |
| *Psychology*, by Gray, Worth Publishers | 9 | 0 | 1 | 0 | 0 | 0 | 1 | 0 | Yes | No |
| *Psychology*, by Hockenbury & Hockenbury, Worth Publishers | 12 | 1 | 0 | 1 | 0 | 1 | 0 | 1 | Yes | No |
| *Psychology*, 7th ed., by Myers, Worth Publishers | 6 | 1 | 0 | 0 | 0 | 1 | 0 | 1 | Yes | No |

Any page that mentioned a human service profession was photocopied, catalogued, and analyzed for content. The authors of the present article examined the data independently in order to ensure congruence and comprehensiveness of content coverage. Data were utilized in the study when all authors agreed that the content met the criteria of referencing a human service profession. We did not use the book's index or table of contents. Rather, the data was collected at the micro-level, reading each word of each page, making notes whenever a single reference to a human service profession appeared and the number of paragraphs that contained these references. We believe that the level of rigor applied was better following this approach than potentially would have occurred if we had been influenced by editors' or publishers' indexes.

Frequency was the sole statistic of interest in this particular study. That is, we desired to discover the pure number of references that the authors made in the textbooks, since that addressed most directly the research question being asked in the study. Consequently, descriptive statistics were generated based on the individual and aggregate data generated, relative to the number of references made by authors to the respective human service professions. We also recorded when texts used charts that included references to the respective human service professions, although they were not in the actual text proper. Additionally, we recorded all text references to the professional organizations of the American Psychological Association (APA), the American Counseling Association (ACA), the American Association for Marriage and Family Therapy (AAMFT), and the National Association of Social Workers (NASW).

In sum, a coding system was unnecessary for the data collection of this study. The criteria were clear, and the most difficult element of data collection was the length of time needed to accrue the information and the tedious nature of the work. We operationalized a definition of human services professionals being any reference to a counselor, social worker, marriage and family therapist, and psychologist. As previously stated, any derivations of these professionals also were noted (e.g., the professional organizations of these professions).

## Results

Regarding coverage of psychologists within their texts, 96% of the textbooks included at least 1 paragraph referring to psychologists, and 76% of the textbooks included at least 1 table or chart regarding the vocation of professional psychology. Social workers faired second best, with 24% making references to their profession and 36% having at least one reference chart. Professional counselors had the third most references, with 12% including mention in a paragraph and 20% being in a chart. Marriage and family therapists fared the worst, having only 4% of the texts making refer-

ences to them and 20% including them in a chart. Figures 1 and 2 summarize the reference frequencies. Regarding the coverage of the APA, ACA, AAMFT, and NASW within the texts, 100% included the APA and 0% of the textbooks included coverage of the others. There were no clear themes apparent from inspecting the data regarding how individual textbook authors covered these professions. That is, using typical qualitative research methodology (e.g., Liamputtong & Ezzy, 2006; Silverman & Marvasti, 2008), we did not discern any pattern as to how any of the individual authors included references to human service professions. If patterns existed, then they were not readily evident and, despite considerable time spent assessing the data, there simply did not seem to be thematic evidences.

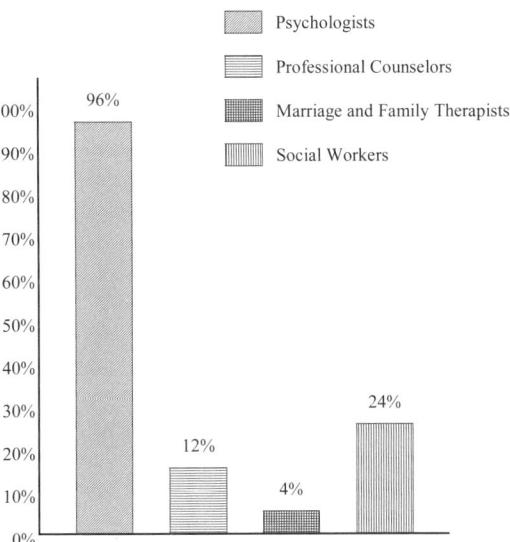

*Figure 1.* Paragraphs in text regarding various professions.

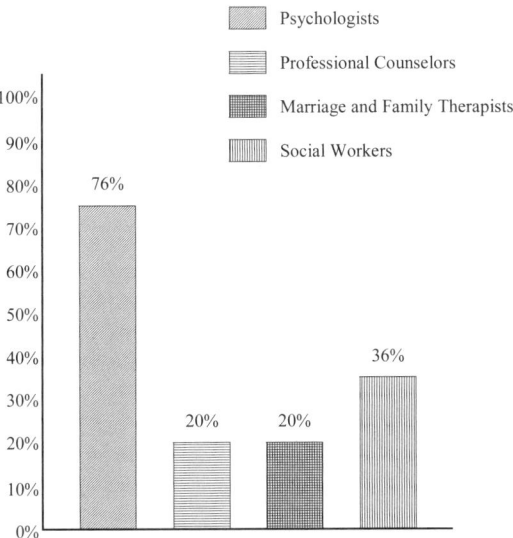

*Figure 2.* Charts/tables in text regarding various professions.

## Discussion

As expected from the article's literature review, results from our study show that psychology clearly dominates the coverage given to mental health professions in the general psychology textbooks sampled in this study. Of particular note is the fact that none of the textbooks provided any respectable coverage of professional counselors, social workers, or marriage and family therapists. Also, having no mention of the other human service professional organizations (i.e., ACA, AAMFT, and NASW) shows that the APA possesses sole prominence in how students are exposed to mental health professions. As previously noted, general psychology plays somewhat of a gate-keeping role (McClenon, Roig, Smith, & Ferrrer, 2003) for college students' exposure and knowledge regarding these professional fields of study, and psychology seems to have a relatively firm control over the gate's swing.

Although the results from the present study could be approached from a variety of perspectives, we advocate an aggressive response. Particularly, we believe that the results of the present study should be an alarm to the ACA, AAMFT, and NASW professions. Leaders from each should contact the major textbook publishers, aggressively advocating parity with the APA for coverage of their respective professions. They should offer to review future editions of all the company's general psychology textbooks, making suggestions—as needed—regarding how the respective professions are portrayed to freshman general psychology students. It is somewhat remarkable that no leaders have done so to date, or if they have, then little results have come from the efforts.

MacDonald (2007) indicates that college students are a significant consumer of psychotherapeutic services in America. Particularly, an estimated 9% or so of all university students nationwide use university counseling services, and 92% of counseling center directors believe that cases with severe psychological issues are rising (Gallagher, 2006). Thus, students needing current or future mental health services likely are unaware regarding the broad range of therapeutic options available to them other than psychological, at least relative to the exposure provided by their general psychology course.

Although the present authors have discussed among ourselves various reasons for why the textbooks would fail to mention the respective human service professionals, we always have returned to the matter of turf issues. With 800+ pages typically dedicated to psychology texts, there is little merit for an argument that space is unavailable for a single paragraph. None of the textbook authors self-identified with the counseling, marriage and family therapy, or social work professions. There is an obvious, natural tendency to give an edged advantage to one's own profession. However, we argue that it is in the students' (the consumers who pay money for the texts) best interests to have a broader exposure to the mental health spectrum. Covering only—or predominantly—psychologists supplies students with too narrow of an academic view. In sum, although the results of the present study, obviously, are bad news for the nonpsychology human service professions, the study also should serve as a wake-up call for immediate action relative to professional advocacy.

### Limitations and Future Research

The most obvious limitation of the present study is that it did not assess all general psychology textbooks. We believe that such a comprehensive study is the next step in the evolution of where researchers should proceed in this research vein. Either grant funding or cooperation from all major textbook publishers would enable access to all introductory textbooks—not just ones provided for a sample, as in the present study.

Researchers should use the present study as baseline data for a follow-up study, subsequent to aggressive intervention by administrators from the ACA, AAMFT, and NASW. That is, researchers should secure active advocating by the presidents (or their delegates) from the respective human service organizations not presently represented in general psychology textbooks. Assuming some level of receptivity by the administrations of the textbook publishers, periodic follow-up studies should be conducted in order to see if changes—either in terms of particular publishers, authors, or both—are effectual. If change does occur in time, then obviously representatives from the respective professional organizations should assess and monitor the adequacy and appropriateness of the future coverage provided. That is, while no coverage of a profession is bad, poor coverage in general psychology textbooks might, in the long run, be even worse.

## References

Albee, G. W. (2000). The Boulder model's fatal flaw. *American Psychologist, 55*, 247–248.

Asch, S. (1946). Forming impressions of personality. *Journal of Social Psychology, 41*, 258–290.

Barker, R. L. (1998). *Milestones in the development of social work and social welfare*. Washington, DC: NASW Press.

Booth, T. J., & Cottone, R. R. (2000). Measurement, classification, and prediction of paradigm adherence of marriage and family therapists. *American Journal of Family Therapy, 28*, 329–346.

Brooks, D. K. Jr., & Gerstein, L. H. (1990a). Counselor credentialing and interprofessional collaboration. *Journal of Counseling and Development, 68*, 477–484.

Brooks, D. K. Jr., & Gerstein, L. H. (1990b). Interprofessional collaboration: Or shooting yourself in the foot only feels good when you stop. *Journal of Counseling and Development, 68*, 509–510.

Capuzzi, D., & Gross, D. R. (1997). *Introduction to the counseling profession*. Boston: Allyn & Bacon.

Cummings, N. A. (1990). The credentialing of professional psychologists and its implication for the other mental health disciplines. *Journal of Counseling and Development, 68*, 485–490.

Firmin, M. (2004). A critical analysis of counselors' identification as a profession. *American Association of Behavioral and Social Sciences Journal, 7*, 53–65.

Firmin, M., & Firebaugh, S. (in press). The discussion of politics in general psychology textbooks. *American Association of Behavioral and Social Sciences Journal*.

Freeth, D. (2001). Sustaining interprofessional collaboration. *Journal of Interprofessional Care, 15*, 37–46.

Gallagher, R. P. (2006). *National survey of counseling center directors*. Alexandria, VA: International Association of Counseling Services, Inc.

Goldin, E. C. (1997). Interprofessional cooperation concerning counselor licensure: A survey of American mental health counselor association branch presidents. *Journal of Mental Health Counseling, 19,* 199–205.

Goodyear, R. K. (2000). An unwarranted escalation of counselor-counseling psychologist professional conflict: Comments on Weinrach, Lustig, Chan, and Thomas. *Journal of Counseling and Development, 78,* 103–106.

Griggs, R.A., & Koenig, C. S. (2001). Brief introductory psychology text-books: A current analysis. *Teaching of Psychology, 28,* 36–40.

Griggs, R. A., & Proctor, D. L. (2002). A citation analysis of who's who in introductory textbooks. *Teaching of Psychology, 29,* 203–206.

Griggs, R. A., Proctor, D. L., & Cook, S. M. (2004). The most frequently cited books in introductory texts. *Teaching of Psychology, 31,* 113–116.

Gulliver, P., Peck, E., & Towell, D. (2002). Balancing professional and team boundaries in mental health services: Pursuing the holy grail in Somerset. *Journal of Interprofessional Care, 16,* 359–370.

Gurman, A. S., & Fraenkel, P. (2002). The history of couple therapy: A millennial review. *Family Process, 41,* 199–260.

Houston, S. (2005). Philosophy, theory and method in social work. *Journal of Social Work, 5,* 7–20.

Hunt, M. (1993). *The story of psychology.* New York: Double Day.

Irvine, R., Kerridge, I., McPhee, J., & Freeman, S. (2002). Interprofessionalism and ethics: Consensus or clash of cultures? *Journal of Interprofessional Care, 16,* 199–210.

Kazar, (2007, November). Psychologists must protect tests and terminology. *National Psychologist, 61*(6), 18.

MacDonald, G. J. (2007). Where to turn for counseling? *USA Today,* September 20, 7D.

McClenon, J., Roig, M., Smith, M. D., & Ferrier, G. (2003). The coverage of parapsychology in introductory psychology textbooks: 1990–2002. *The Journal of Parapsychology, 67,* 167–179.

Myers, J. E., Sweeney, T. J., & White, V. E. (2002). Advocacy for counseling and counselors: A professional imperative. *Journal of Counseling and Development, 80,* 394–402.

Nairn, S. L., Ellard, J. H., Scialfa, C. T., & Miller, C. D. (2003). At the core of introductory psychology: A content analysis. *Canadian Psychology, 44,* 93–99.

Nowlin, J. E. (2006). The death of a profession: School counseling in the twenty-first century. *National Social Science Journal, 26,* 66–72.

Perlman, B., & McCann, L. I. (1999). The most frequently listed courses in the undergraduate psychology curriculum. *Teaching of Psychology, 26,* 177–182.

Pistole, M. C., & Roberts, A. (2002). Mental health counseling: Toward resolving identity confusions. *Journal of Mental Health Counseling, 24,* 1–19.

Randolph, D. L. (1988). The enemy is us. *Counselor Education and Supervision, 27,* 301–307.

Schmitt, M. H. (2001). Collaboration improves the quality of care: Methodological challenges and evidence from US health care research. *Journal of Interprofessional Care, 15,* 47–66.

Swanson, J. L., & O'Saben, C. L. (1993). Differences in supervisory needs and expectations by trainee experience, cognitive style, and program membership. *Journal of Counseling and Development, 74,* 601–608.

Van Hesteren, F., & Ivey, A. (1990). Counseling and development: Toward a new identity for a profession in transition. *Journal of Counseling and Development, 68,* 524–528.

Weigel, R. G. (1977). I have seen the enemy and they is us—And everyone else. *The Counseling Psychologist, 7,* 50–53.

Zimpfer, D. G., & Mohdzain, A. Z. (1992). Professional identification of counselor preparation programs. *Counselor Education and Supervision, 32,* 91–107.

**About the authors**: *Michael W. Firmin,* Ph.D., professor of psychology; *Erica J. Johnson,* B.A; *Jeremiah S. Wikler,* J.D., Cedarville University.

**Address correspondence to**: Dr. Michael W. Firmin at firmin@cedarville.edu

# Exercise for Article 27

## Factual Questions

1. The researchers obtained the names of best-sellers from what source?

2. Why were texts by W. W. Norton not included in this study?

3. What percentage had at least one paragraph referring to social workers?

4. Which text had the smallest number of paragraphs mentioning psychologists?

5. How many of the texts mention NASW?

6. What percentage of the texts mention APA?

## Questions for Discussion

7. What is your opinion on the decision to base selection on the provision of complimentary texts? (See lines 182–187.)

8. Was it a good idea to examine data independently? (See lines 193–198.)

9. The researchers examined only frequencies (e.g., number of paragraphs)—not other factors such as the accuracy of the texts. Was this a limitation? (See lines 207–211.)

10. Do you agree with the limitation mentioned in lines 326–327?

11. In general, do you think that examining textbooks is a good way to determine what is covered in class in college-level courses?

## Quality Ratings

Directions: Indicate your level of agreement with each of the following statements by circling a number from 5 for strongly agree (SA) to 1 for strongly disagree (SD). If you believe an item is not applicable to this research article, leave it blank. Be prepared to explain your ratings. When responding to criteria A and B, keep in mind that brief titles and abstracts are conventional in published research.

A. The title of the article is appropriate.

SA 5 4 3 2 1 SD

B. The abstract provides an effective overview of the research article.

SA 5 4 3 2 1 SD

C. The introduction establishes the importance of the study.

SA 5 4 3 2 1 SD

D. The literature review establishes the context for the study.

SA 5 4 3 2 1 SD

E.  The research purpose, question, or hypothesis is clearly stated.

    SA   5   4   3   2   1   SD

F.  The method of sampling is sound.

    SA   5   4   3   2   1   SD

G.  Relevant demographics (for example, age, gender, and ethnicity) are described.

    SA   5   4   3   2   1   SD

H.  Measurement procedures are adequate.

    SA   5   4   3   2   1   SD

I.  All procedures have been described in sufficient detail to permit a replication of the study.

    SA   5   4   3   2   1   SD

J.  The participants have been adequately protected from potential harm.

    SA   5   4   3   2   1   SD

K.  The results are clearly described.

    SA   5   4   3   2   1   SD

L.  The discussion/conclusion is appropriate.

    SA   5   4   3   2   1   SD

M.  Despite any flaws, the report is worthy of publication.

    SA   5   4   3   2   1   SD

# Article 28

# Perceptions and Beliefs About Body Size, Weight, and Weight Loss Among Obese African American Women: A Qualitative Inquiry

CHRISTIE A. BEFORT
University of Kansas Medical Center

JANET L. THOMAS
University of Kansas Medical Center

CHRISTINE M. DALEY
University of Kansas Medical Center

PAULA C. RHODE
University of Kansas Medical Center

JASJIT S. AHLUWALIA
University of Minnesota

ABSTRACT. The purpose of this qualitative study was to explore perceptions and beliefs about body size, weight, and weight loss among obese African American women in order to form a design of weight loss intervention with this target population. Six focus groups were conducted at a community health clinic. Participants were predominantly middle-aged with a mean Body Mass Index of $40.3 \pm 9.2$ kg/m$^2$. Findings suggest that participants (a) believe that people can be attractive and healthy at larger sizes; (b) still feel dissatisfied with their weight and self-conscious about their bodies; (c) emphasize eating behavior as the primary cause for weight gain; (d) view pregnancy, motherhood, and caregiving as major precursors to weight gain; (e) view health as the most important reason to lose weight; (f) have mixed experiences and expectations for social support for weight loss; and (g) prefer treatments that incorporate long-term lifestyle modification rather than fad diets or medication.

From *Health Education & Behavior*, 35, 410–426. Copyright © 2008 by Sage Publications, Inc. Reprinted with permission.

African American (AA) women are 60% more likely to become obese (Lewis et al., 1997) and 50% more likely to be moderately to severely obese than Caucasian women in the United States (Flegal, Carroll, Ogden, & Johnson, 2002). Congruent with their higher rates of obesity, AA women are less likely to engage in regular physical activity (Centers for Disease Control, 2004) or to consume healthy diets (Arab, Carriquiry, Steck-Scott, & Gaudet, 2003). Likewise, obesity among AA women has been linked to their higher mortality and incidence rates of coronary heart disease, hypertension, diabetes mellitus, cerebral vascular disease, and certain cancers (American Cancer Society, 2005; Harris, 1998; Must et al., 1999).

Although nearly two-thirds of obese AA women report that they want to lose weight and are attempting to do so (Clark et al., 2001), their weight loss efforts tend to be shorter in duration (Tyler, Allan, & Alcozer, 1997) and less successful compared to Caucasian women (Kumanyika, Obarzanek, Stevens, Hebert, & Whelton, 1991; Wing & Anglin, 1996; Wing et al., 2004). In a number of controlled clinical trials, AA participants lost on average only half as much weight as Caucasian participants (Kumanyika et al., 1991; Wing & Anglin, 1996). As Kumanyika, Morssink, and Agurs (1992) have articulated, mainstream weight loss programs may not be effective for AA women because they are based on assumptions and values of the dominant culture, for example, personal autonomy and self-management, whereas AA culture is more oriented toward interconnectedness and group support. In response to this, several lifestyle intervention trials have been culturally tailored to promote weight loss among AA women; however, the results of these trials have been mixed, with many reporting only minimal weight loss and high attrition among participants (Agurs-Collins, Kumanyika, Ten Have, & Adams-Campbell, 1997; Kanders et al., 1994; Karanja, Stevens, Hollis, & Kumanyika, 2002; Kennedy et al., 2005; Kumanyika & Charleston, 1992; Kumanyika et al., 2005; McNabb, Quinn, Kerver, Cook, & Karrison, 1997; Walcott-McQuigg et al., 2002; Yanek, Becker, Moy, Gittelsohn, & Koffman, 2001). More work is needed to better understand how to maximize the potential for AA women to be successful in weight loss interventions.

Several researchers have suggested that greater acceptance of larger body sizes among AA women contributes to their higher risk for obesity (Flynn & Fitzgibbon, 1998; Wolfe, 2000). Body image studies comparing African Americans and Caucasians have used questionnaires and figure drawings of graduated sizes to quantify preferences for, and satisfaction with, body sizes. Many studies have found that AA women have a larger ideal body size, are less likely to perceive themselves as overweight, are more satisfied with their bodies at heavier weights, and are more likely to report feeling attractive even when they are dissatisfied with their weight (DiLillo, Gore, Jones, Balentine, & West, 2004; Fitzgibbon, Blackman, & Avellone, 2000; Flynn

60 & Fitzgibbon, 1998; Stevens, Kumanyika, & Keil, 1994). However, this research has been limited by a lack of culturally relevant and racially neutral figure rating scales, which only recently have been developed (Pulvers et al., 2004). Furthermore, some research has
65 found that after controlling for age, education, and body weight, racial/ethnic differences in body image perceptions are diminished (Cachelin, Rebeck, Chung, & Pelayo, 2002). Indeed, data show that many overweight and obese AA women are largely dissatisfied
70 with their weight and experience fluctuating levels of negative body image (Baturka, Hornsby, & Schorling, 2000; Davis, Clark, Carrese, Gary, & Cooper, 2005).

Qualitative research is well suited to provide in-depth answers to complex questions and to suggest
75 ways of developing successful interventions with specific target groups (Bernard, 2002). In recent years, focus groups have been used to gain a better understanding of how AA culture may contribute to dietary patterns, physical activity, and weight loss behavior.
80 Barriers to physical activity viewed as central to AA culture include the perception that occupational and daily activities provide sufficient exercise and the high value placed on rest and relaxation after work. Other barriers commonly reported by AAs include lack of
85 motivation, time constraints because of family responsibilities (especially for AA women), child care and monetary costs, and concerns about neighborhood safety (Airhihenbuwa, Kumanyika, Agurs, & Lowe, 1995; Richter, Wilcox, Greaney, Henderson, & Ains-
90 worth, 2002; Wilcox, Richter, Henderson, Greaney, & Ainsworth, 2002). Young, Gittelsohn, Charleston, Felix-Aaron, and Appel (2001) conducted focus groups with AA women older than 40 to assess motivation for exercise and found that women who were already exer-
95 cising were more likely to report being motivated by health, weight control, and stress reduction, whereas sedentary women reported they would be motivated by social support and enjoyment of physical activities (Young et al., 2001).
100 Focus group studies have also provided insight into various cultural aspects of eating and food patterns among AAs. For example, AAs from differing socioeconomic groups have associated healthy eating with giving up their traditions of large family meals, fried or
105 roasted meats as the centerpiece of the meal, and preferences for high-fat foods and sweets (Hargreaves, Schlundt, & Buchowski, 2002; James, 2004). AA food traditions have often been passed down across generations from mothers to daughters (Wilson, Musham, &
110 McLellan, 2004), and efforts to change eating patterns may therefore be hindered by sociocultural influences, such as family tradition and church socials (Hargreaves et al., 2002). These sociocultural influences may vary depending on level of acculturation to mainstream val-
115 ues (Beech et al., 2004).

Although each of these previous qualitative studies offers important insights, none of the studies included

solely obese AA women; none classified participants according to measured height and weight; and none
120 specifically addressed perceptions and beliefs about body size, weight, and weight loss per se. Within the context of AA culture, obese women may have unique perceptions regarding body image and weight loss that influence their weight-related behaviors. Given that
125 weight loss interventions are typically targeted for obese participants, it is important to have an in-depth understanding of the relevant perceptions and beliefs of this subgroup of AA women. Therefore, the purpose of this study was to explore perceptions and beliefs re-
130 lated to body size, weight, and weight loss among this target group in order to inform the design of appropriate interventions with an obese AA female population.

## Method

### Participants

Participants were recruited with flyers posted throughout an urban, predominantly low-income, AA
135 community in a Midwestern state. Flyers were posted in churches, shopping centers, work sites, gyms, health centers, and neighborhoods. In addition, a research assistant sat at a booth and handed out flyers to interested participants in the lobby of a community health
140 clinic that serves under- and uninsured, predominantly AA patients. This health clinic was also the site where the focus groups were held. The one-page recruitment flyer was designed to recruit AA women who "thought [they] might be overweight" and were "interested in
145 participating in a discussion about weight and weight loss." Eligible participants were 18 years or older, AA, female, and had self-reported height and weight that classified them as obese according to the National Institutes of Health clinical guidelines (calculated as
150 body mass index [BMI] = 30 kg/m$^2$). Exclusion criteria included obvious intoxication or current inpatient substance abuse treatment, marked inappropriate affect or behavior, acute illness, or impaired cognition that would hinder participation in a group discussion.
155 Of 93 women who responded to the study flyers, 83 were eligible. Reasons for exclusion were BMI < 30 ($n$ = 7), impaired cognition ($n$ = 1), acute illness ($n$ = 1), and younger than 18 years ($n$ = 1). Of those eligible, 10 were unable to attend a focus group because of sched-
160 uling conflicts, and another 11 did not show up for their scheduled appointment. Thus, the final sample included 62 women.

### Procedure

Women who responded to the flyer were screened for eligibility by phone or in the health clinic lobby.
165 Eligible participants provided contact information and available times and were contacted by phone within 2 weeks to be scheduled for a group. We had anticipated a 50% attendance rate based on our previous experience conducting focus groups in the same setting using
170 a similar recruitment strategy. Therefore, we scheduled 12 to 16 participants per group, expecting to have at

Table 1
*Outline of Focus Group Topics and Questions*

| Topic | Questions |
| --- | --- |
| Beliefs about body size and attractiveness | How do you feel about your current body shape? |
| | How does your body size affect how attractive you feel? |
| | What does it mean to have a healthy body size? |
| Attributions for weight | What do you think caused you to become overweight? |
| Reasons to lose weight | Why might you want to lose weight? |
| | Of all the reasons to lose weight, which one is most important? |
| Social support for weight loss | How do you think your family and friends feel about your weight? |
| | How do you feel about discussing your weight concerns with your family or friends? |
| | What kind of support would you like from your family and friends? |
| Experiences with weight loss | What have you done to try to lose weight? |
| | What has been most helpful? |
| | What has been least helpful? |
| Treatment preferences | What would you like to see in a weight loss program? |

least six to eight women attend each group. The actual attendance rate was 85% and ranged from 62% to 100% per group. In response to the high attendance, we
175 recruited two additional research staff during the study and divided the last group into two smaller groups. The group sizes ranged from 6 to 16 participants.

Six focus groups were conducted in a 2-week period. Two clinical psychologists with training in group
180 facilitation moderated the focus groups, alternating between serving as the moderator and assistant moderator. In addition, two research assistants with training in the study protocol, focus group facilitation, and protection of human subjects helped by welcoming par-
185 ticipants, offering them healthy snacks, completing forms, video- and audiorecording, and distributing incentives. One research assistant was an AA woman from the local community who was employed by the research team for more than 1 year and whose primary
190 task was to assist with focus group studies. Prior to data collection, all participants provided informed consent and permission to audio- and videorecord. Participants then completed a 15- to 20-minute pre-focus group survey on demographic information, medical
195 diagnoses, and weight history. The assistant moderator read all questions aloud while a research assistant circulated to assist individual participants as needed.

The focus groups followed a semistructured format with a standard guide of open-ended questions to
200 stimulate discussion about perceptions and experiences with body size and weight. Researchers with experience in weight loss treatment and focus group methodology developed the guide according to published methodological suggestions (Fern, 2001). Table 1 dis-
205 plays questions from the focus group guide.

During each focus group meeting, the moderator probed participants' responses and encouraged all

members to participate. The assistant moderator took detailed notes and provided a summary at the end of
210 the meeting. The group discussions lasted approximately 90 to 100 minutes. After the meetings ended, the research assistants measured each participant's height and weight behind a privacy partition to corroborate their self-reported data. Measurements were
215 taken without shoes and heavy clothing using a balance beam scale and height rod and were rounded to the nearest 0.1 inch and 0.1 pound. After being weighed, participants received a $40 Wal-Mart gift card as compensation for their travel cost, time, and effort. We
220 stopped data collection after we felt that data saturation had occurred for the majority of our topic areas (i.e., no new data would be found by conducting further focus groups [Bernard, 2002]). The research protocol was approved by the University of Kansas Medical Center's
225 Human Subjects Committee prior to implementation.

### Data Analysis

Survey data were double-data entered into a database, and descriptive statistics were computed using SPSS Version 13.0. Audiorecordings of the focus groups were transcribed verbatim by a contracted pro-
230 fessional transcription service. The focus group moderators proofread each transcript and compared them to the videorecordings to check for completeness and accuracy. A medical anthropologist with 10 years of experience using qualitative methodology led the
235 analysis and trained the additional coders. Three independent coders first deductively categorized verbatim transcripts by hand into six major topic areas using initial codes developed by the research team based on the focus group moderator's guide. Coders then induc-
240 tively open-coded by hand within each major topic area using a grounded theory approach whereby categories

Table 2
*Participant Demographics, Weight History, and Comorbid Conditions*

| Characteristic | % |
|---|---|
| Age, years | |
| $\leq 35$ | 17.7 |
| 36–45 | 22.6 |
| 45–55 | 35.5 |
| $\geq 56$ | 24.2 |
| Education | |
| Some high school | 14.5 |
| High school graduate | 21.0 |
| Some college | 62.9 |
| College graduate | 1.6 |
| Partner status | |
| Married/living with partner | 25.8 |
| Divorced | 37.1 |
| Single | 35.5 |
| Caretaker/parent status | |
| One or more children living in home | 52.6 |
| Employment | |
| Employed full-time | 50.0 |
| Employed part-time | 8.1 |
| Unemployed | 41.9 |
| Body mass index (BMI), kg/m$^2$ | |
| Class 1 obesity, BMI = 30–34.9 | 38.7 |
| Class 2 obesity, BMI = 35–39.9 | 16.1 |
| Class 3 obesity, BMI $\geq$ 40 | 45.2 |
| Weight perceptions and history | |
| Classify self as overweight | 88.6 |
| Currently trying to lose weight | 83.6 |
| No. lifetime weight loss attempts | 5.0 (median) |
| No. times lost $\geq$ 10 lbs. | 3.0 (median) |
| Comorbid conditions | |
| Smoker | 19.6 |
| Diabetes | 25.8 |
| Hypertension | 48.4 |
| Heart disease | 11.3 |
| Asthma or emphysema | 36.1 |
| No. of comorbid diseases | |
| 0 | 24.2 |
| 1 | 30.6 |
| 2 | 16.1 |
| $\geq$ 3 | 29.1 |

and concepts emerge from the text and are then linked together (Bernard, 2002). This approach allows the data to speak for themselves. A fourth independent
245 researcher cross-checked inductive codes and identified minor discrepancies in the coding and different terminology used by each coder to describe the same content. Cross-checking codes provides a measure of how well the data are indexed and, thus, gives a qualitative
250 measure of intercoder reliability (Stewart, 1998). Overall, the independent researcher found high intercoder reliability and identified major themes within the codes. The research team then met as a group to discuss the major themes and reach a consensus. Specifi-
255 cally, the fourth investigator presented her interpretation of each coder's inductive work and the coder clari-

fied as necessary. The seven major saturated themes were identical across coders. An additional six unsaturated themes were identified and will be used for the
260 development of further research.

**Results**

*Participant Characteristics*

Table 2 displays participant characteristics. The women were on average middle-aged ($M = 46.6 \pm 10.9$ years), had a high school level education plus some college ($M = 12.7 \pm 1.4$ years of education), and were
265 divorced or single. Participants' mean BMI was 40.3 kg/m$^2$, with 49% of the women being classified as having Class 3 extreme obesity (BMI $\geq$ 40 kg/m$^2$). Nearly 20% were current smokers, and 75.8% had at least one

Table 3
*Focus Group Themes*

1. Belief that people can be attractive and healthy at larger sizes

2. Dissatisfaction with weight and self-consciousness about body

3. Recognition of eating behavior as the primary cause for weight gain

4. Pregnancy, motherhood, and family caregiving as precursors to weight gain

5. Health and functional status as motivators to lose weight

6. Mixed social support for weight loss

7. Preference for lifestyle modification and distrust of medication for weight loss

comorbid chronic disease, including 25.8% with diabetes and 48.4% with hypertension. Most participants classified themselves as either a little overweight (23.0%) or very overweight (65.6%), and the vast majority was interested in losing weight.

## Thematic Analysis

Seven themes emerged across focus groups and reached saturation (see Table 3).

### Belief That People Can Be Attractive and Healthy at Larger Sizes

Participants expressed a sense of acceptance of larger body sizes, both in terms of attractiveness and perceived health. They stated that attractiveness does not depend on being a particular size and that people of many sizes can look good. "The [size] 10 is in your mind," one 40-year-old woman said, "it doesn't have to be a 10. You could be a 20 and look good." Rather than associating attractiveness with body size, attractiveness was described as having self-esteem and feeling beautiful as a person, and to a lesser extent with dress, makeup, and hair. Many women reported that even though they knew they were overweight, they could still feel attractive and positive about themselves. A 27-year-old woman stated,

> I think I look good even though I'm overweight. I feel like I'm not the ugliest person in the world. To myself, I'm an attractive black female. That's the way I feel about myself. Might feel even better about myself if I did lose an extra 100 pounds or so.

Often, their feelings of attractiveness were amplified by nice clothing. "As long as I'm happy about myself inside, it will show on the outside," a 34-year-old woman said, "but I have always tried to wear great clothes...I feel good about myself inside, so I feel I'm just beautiful."

Participants also expressed the view that being healthy does not depend on being a certain size and that a person can be just as unhealthy if they are underweight, as one 35-year-old woman stated, "You can be too small and be unhealthy as well as being too big." Some women expressed the belief that height and weight charts are unrealistic and AA women naturally have larger body frames. "I think a healthy body size could be almost any size," a 41-year-old woman said, "as long as it's not too much weight for that person.

Because, you know, there's all sizes and shapes of people."

### Dissatisfaction with Weight and Self-Consciousness About Body

Although participants expressed tolerance of larger body sizes, most also acknowledged that they were overweight and were largely dissatisfied with their weight. In fact, most women reported that losing weight was the number one thing they wanted to change about themselves. Many reported feeling self-conscious about their bodies, and they described a sense of discomfort when unclothed or when seeing themselves in a mirror. "When I'm dressed up and got my hair together and makeup, you can't touch me," one 57-year-old woman said, "but when these clothes come off, that's when I have a problem." Another 53-year-old woman stated,

> I've got a mirror by the side of [my bed] on my closet...and I sit there by accident if I'm watching something on TV and then I look around at the mirror and see myself, I look and I just can't believe it. I am, my body is so ugly.

Several women expressed a sense of surprise when seeing a picture or reflection of their bodies. "I didn't know that I looked like I did until someone took a picture of me and I said, 'Oh, is that me?'" They noted specific likes and dislikes about body parts, with many women describing a specific dislike of their waist. As one 46-year-old woman stated,

> I feel conscious about my size because around my waistline, my belt don't fit in my pants. I have a hard time trying to get my belt to buckle, and most of my pants I have to get Spandex...my stomach is my most, well that's my guilt...I change in my closet and hide from my fiancé because my stomach is so big.

Again, the extent to which participants felt uncomfortable with their bodies was often related to how they felt in their clothes. They spoke about coping with feeling self-conscious by covering up the body parts that they disliked or avoiding looking at themselves, especially when unclothed. "I just don't show my arms," a 49-year-old woman said, "but I feel good. I just don't show my arms. I cover them up." Other women indicated that they do not dwell on their weight dissatisfaction or let it affect their mood. "I'm not content [with my body size], but I don't dwell on it. When you dwell

355 on things, everything seems to go backwards." Another 41-year-old woman stated, "I want to wear a bikini once in my life and look good in it, but overall, I'm not unhappy with myself because if I did, I would be in a depression. I'd be a sad person."

*Recognition of Eating Behavior as the Primary Cause for Weight Gain*

360    When asked what led them to become overweight, participants were much more likely to name behavioral reasons as opposed to medical and genetic causes. The most common attribution was related to eating behavior. They spoke about their love for cooking and eating,
365 as one 54-year-old women stated, "Oh goodness, I'm a good cook and I love my food. I do. I love my food. I really do." They also spoke about how taste preferences are woven into their culture. "I love to eat, and for my ethnic group, you know, we like to eat those
370 Southern stuff. I enjoy cooking that, and I enjoy eating that, so it's very difficult for me to stop it." Another 33-year-old woman echoed this sentiment, stating that "once you already tasted fried foods, you get a taste for it…you want the neck bones and all the good soul
375 food." Participants also spoke about their childhood experiences with family meals, as a 57-year-old woman stated,

> All of my aunts were heavy, you know, they stayed in the kitchen. They would feel offended if when we came to
380 > their house, we didn't sit down to macaroni and cheese, potatoes and gravy, fried chicken, homemade rolls, and Kool-Aid.

Many of these women themselves prepared meals for large family gatherings and enjoyed bringing family
385 together with food.

> The whole family comes over to our house on Sundays to eat, and I'm the one that cooks, and all the nephews and sisters and brothers and nieces, they all come over and eat, and I love to see them eat, but I'll lose those 5
390 > pounds, and on Sunday I'll gain them all back.

For many women, enjoyment of eating with family and friends often took precedence over eating healthy. As one 57-year-old woman from another group stated, "We have family gatherings, and they all come over to
395 my house eating, and then they talk about me losing weight…but they like for me to cook so I can't have it both ways."

    Many participants named specific eating behaviors as contributors to their weight gain, including eating
400 late, eating excessive portions, consuming too much soda and junk food, and eating at fast food and all-you-can-eat restaurants. Lack of physical activity was also named as a cause of weight gain, although less frequently and typically in the context of eating behavior.
405 For example, one woman stated, "I was at a job where I sat all day, and I would have the nerve to go to an all-you-can-eat for lunch."

*Pregnancy, Motherhood, and Family Caregiving as Precursors to Weight Gain*

    Motherhood was commonly reported as a precursor to weight gain. Many women reported that they never
410 lost the weight they gained during pregnancy, and then they gained even more because of lifestyle changes associated with motherhood, for example, snacking more often, cooking larger meals, and being less active outside the house. Although participants recognized
415 changes in their behavior as contributing to their post-pregnancy weight gain, pregnancy was named as a primary antecedent. Many women across groups echoed the following statement from a 57-year-old woman:

420 > I was never overweight until I had my first child. When I got pregnant with her, I weighed 110, and I never, she's 34, and I never went back. It's overeating during [pregnancy]…and then after I had them, I was home with them until they were all in school, so they ate breakfast, I ate
425 > breakfast. They ate lunch, I ate lunch. They had snacks, I had snacks. So you just ate with them, and when they slept, I slept. So it's just the way your lifestyle changes.

    In addition, several women either had been or were currently caretakers for older family members. Similar
430 to motherhood, they reported that caretaking responsibilities and the added stress they caused resulted in weight gain. One 40-year-old woman recalled,

> My aunt passed, it will be a year…and I was her caretaker for about 2-1/2 years. During that time your activity, your lifestyle, your everything just tends to change.
435 > You know, so stress has a lot to do with it.

*Health and Functional Status as Motivators to Lose Weight*

    Participants unanimously reported that health was their number one reason for wanting to lose weight. Many participants had chronic medical conditions (e.g.,
440 diabetes, hypertension, heart disease, pain) and had received advice from their physicians to lose weight. They wanted to avoid further medical complications, as one 62-year-old women indicated: "For me, it's just health because they told me my cholesterol will go
445 down, definitely the high blood pressure, and I'll get my diabetes within normal range."

    Participants who did not have chronic conditions often spoke about their families' medical histories and acknowledged the association of health problems with
450 excess weight. Many had a strong desire to prevent the weight-related diseases that they had witnessed in their family members.

> I'm getting fairly close to 60, so I'm trying to improve my health to, you know, keep my blood pressure down,
455 > because there are a lot of health problems that run in my family, and I'm trying to keep, I'm going to try to keep from developing those problems myself.

    Participants also spoke about wanting to lose weight to improve their daily functioning. They com-
460 plained about low energy, feeling tired, and having

difficulty breathing with only minimal exertion. Many wanted to lose weight so they would have more energy to play with their children or grandchildren, whereas others were functionally limited because of their
465 weight (e.g., not fitting in seats, not being able to bend over easily, or having difficulty walking up several flights of stairs).

> I think a healthy size for me would mean, it wouldn't really be a size as much as it would be a freedom to just
470 do whatever I want to do. Just anything because so much, so many things I just don't do because I'm tired.

### Mixed Social Support for Weight Loss

Participants reported very mixed experiences regarding social support for weight loss. About half of the women indicated that their families were suppor-
475 tive, either of their weight status or their efforts to lose weight. The most common forms of perceived support were acceptance regardless of body size, assistance with weight loss through tangible tools such as diet books and exercise videos, and simply not saying any-
480 thing about their weight. One 30-year-old woman stated,

> I've never felt judged and probably because most of the women in my family are overweight…I think their acceptance of me for all that I am and not just for how much I
485 weigh has always been just sort of something I could count on.

A 54-year-old woman in another group stated,

> I have a bunch of sisters, and I guess you could say we're real supportive of one another in that we don't say any-
490 thing to each other. We've all been fat, and we all understand. When one is thin, they visit more. And when one's fat, they don't visit as much. They don't talk about it.

Many women also reported a lack of support for weight loss and negative social experiences, such as
495 teasing from family members, criticism regarding food choices (e.g., "Are you going to eat that?"), disapproval of their weight loss efforts, and sabotaging their weight loss by bringing home unhealthy food. "I wish my family would support me a lot more on my weight
500 as far as compliments or something like that," one 66-year-old woman said. "They were kind of harsh when I was younger." Likewise, some women reported experiences in which partners or family members discouraged them from losing weight.

505 > I have people tell me, what are you trying to lose weight for?…I said, "Well, I'm trying to lose weight for me and my health," and I leave it at that. I don't discuss it with people because I don't feel like I have to answer to anybody to lose weight.

510 When asked what kind of support they wanted, participants again responded in mixed ways. On one hand, they indicated that the only support they need is to not be "nagged." "I wouldn't mind being supported but just don't get to the nagging point." Some women indicated
515 they wanted to lose weight on their own.

> I'd rather not have no support. I'd rather be able to do it on my own. Because without that support, I don't have to worry about, oh, if I don't do it, will they be mad, or if I do it, will they be mad or something…doing it on my
520 own, it's just better for me.

On the other hand, participants said they wanted more constructive support, typically in the form of a partner or buddy who is also attempting to lose weight and who would hold them accountable and help motivate
525 them. Typically, they indicated that this person would ideally be outside their common social network.

> I think [you have to] go outside to get support through other ways. So it's not necessarily going to be coming from your family or your friends, but say, if you join
530 Weight Watchers or some other weight loss [program] or if you had another friend and you did a buddy system, get support that way.

### Preference for Lifestyle Modification and Distrust of Medication for Weight Loss

Participants expressed a strong interest in group-based weight loss programs, where they could meet
535 with "like-minded" women and learn skills for healthy cooking and eating, increasing regular physical activity, and changing their lifestyle. They also spoke about a need for tailored exercise plans that were appropriate for their level of fitness. They were generally opposed
540 to fad diets and understood that weight loss takes a great deal of time and effort. Thus, their preference was for a long-term (i.e., 1 year) weight loss program. Again, they frequently mentioned a need for ongoing social support, both during the structured components
545 of the program and afterwards.

The vast majority of participants held negative views about weight loss medications. They spoke about medication as being "unnatural" or "putting a band-aid on the real problem." They were distrustful about po-
550 tential side effects and unforeseen interactions with other medications. Many women were also concerned about becoming dependent on medications.

> I'm leaning more toward wanting to do it naturally without pills. Anything that would make you psychologically
555 dependent upon it, because if you lose the weight on it, then you kind of become dependent, if you start gaining weight back then you go, oh, I need to get those pills again.

### Discussion

This study examined the perceptions and beliefs
560 about body size, weight, and weight loss among a community sample of obese AA women, and the findings offer insights for understanding and treating obesity in this target population. Consistent with prior research, the women in this study expressed an accep-
565 tance of larger body sizes and believed that body size should not influence a person's feelings of attractiveness, self-esteem, or happiness. At the same time, they were concerned about their weight and largely self-conscious of their bodies. They described various

570 strategies to cope with these self-conscious feelings and perhaps reconcile them with a culturally embedded acceptance of larger body sizes. For example, clothing was emphasized as a way to feel attractive despite feeling self-conscious about body size, and many partici-
575 pants avoided thinking about their weight or looking at themselves in the mirror as a way to ward off negative feelings. These strategies provide insight into how AA women are able to preserve feelings of attractiveness even when they are dissatisfied with their weight (Ku-
580 manyika, 1998).

Although participants expressed body image concerns, their interest in weight loss was largely driven by a desire to improve their health, a finding that is underscored by the fact that more than three-fourths of
585 the participants reported having at least one comorbid chronic disease. This comorbidity rate is similar to the report of Hope, Kumanyika, Whitt, and Shults (2005), where 76% of obese AAs in a weight loss program had at least one obesity-related chronic disease. Women in
590 the current study were knowledgeable about the health benefits of weight loss and the behavioral causes of weight gain; however, they spoke about poor dietary behavior much more than lack of physical activity, suggesting less awareness or importance placed on
595 physical activity. Further research is needed to understand how cultural differences may influence the use of physical activity specifically for controlling weight. For example, the "rest ethic" of AA culture, or the belief that rest is important after a "busy" day (Airhihen-
600 buwa et al., 1995; Wilcox et al., 2002), may conflict with recommendations to decrease leisure-time activity to manage weight.

Participants spoke frequently and in-depth about sociocultural influences on food choices, such as their
605 preference for traditional AA foods, including high-fat meats and sweets (Kumanyika & Odoms, 2003), and the strong connection between food and social affiliation (Airhihenbuwa et al., 1996). The family centeredness of their culture was evident as they spoke about
610 food as a way to bring family members together, and many women enjoyed cooking large meals for this reason. They also revealed a connection between family responsibility and weight gain; many seemed to prioritize family caretaking over their own health behavior
615 change. This observation is consistent with the work of Kumanyika et al. (1992) and others suggesting that AA women have a limited inclination to assume the self-centered posture that is typically the focus of health behavior programs. AA women may be reluctant to
620 focus on themselves, often considering their own health as secondary to that of their children, or prioritizing caretaking responsibilities over self-care (Ahye, Devine, & Odoms-Young, 2006; Samuel-Hodge et al., 2000). Consistent with this, the women in the current
625 study described pregnancy as a critical time when they gained weight and after which they struggled to lose weight, largely because of lifestyle changes associated

with caretaking responsibilities of motherhood. Several longitudinal studies indicate that AA women struggle
630 with childbearing-associated weight gain more so than Caucasian women (Rosenberg et al., 2003).

Our findings and those of others are consistent with the extant literature examining *collectivism* as an important cultural construct that distinguishes AAs from
635 dominant culture, most markedly for AA women (Baldwin & Hopkins, 1990). Collectivism is the belief that the central unit of society is social groups, most commonly the extended family, and not the individual. Collectivism prioritizes group goals over individual
640 goals and thus emphasizes cooperation, responsibility for others, loyalty, helpfulness, forgiveness, family security, and respect for traditions (Nobles, 1991). The women in the current study conveyed a collectivist orientation toward mutual support among family and
645 peers, but they reported a need for more social support specific to weight loss.

Indeed, one of the most challenging findings was the mixed responses to questions about social support for weight loss. Participants were uncertain about how
650 to obtain and integrate social support for weight loss from their existing social networks, perhaps because of lack of guidance from common individualistically oriented weight loss treatments. They largely perceived weight-related feedback as critical and an absence of
655 feedback as accepting, and they preferred support from overweight peers who were also attempting to lose weight over support from family. One interpretation of these findings may be that within a collectivistic value system, mutual support (i.e., two or more women sup-
660 porting one another toward the same goal) is value congruent more so than individual support (e.g., one spouse supporting the other spouse toward her individual goal). In addition, other interactions surrounding weight issues may be perceived as more supportive if
665 they are congruent with deep-rooted values. For example, the participants derived social support from large family gatherings centered on cooking and eating and from their family members' acceptance of their body sizes, and both of these sources of social support may
670 be rooted in collectivistic values such as loyalty and respect for traditions. Although this interpretation is speculative, further research along these lines is warranted given the accumulating evidence indicating that social support is a crucial factor affecting obese AA
675 women's weight loss (Wolfe, 2004).

The results of this study should be viewed in the context of the methodology and the characteristics of the sample. Because qualitative research is designed to provide in-depth understanding of a specific group or
680 topic, the results from this study may not generalize across groups but rather may be transferred to similar groups and settings (Fern, 2001). However, as noted above, the findings of this study are consistent with other focus group results with AA women from other
685 regions of the United States and provide useful infor-

mation for generating testable hypotheses. As this area of scientific inquiry progresses, the emerging themes should be validated with larger and more representative samples.

690   In the context of focus group methodology, the current study was limited in that it was not designed as a nested sampling frame that would help to parcel out differences between subgroups of AA women (e.g., age group, educational level, or obesity class) or subcultures within the larger AA group. In addition, the large number of participants (greater than 10 participants) in three of the six focus groups may have limited the depth of response among some participants. However, we did not detect any systematic differences in responses across groups, and we observed that the participants quickly developed rapport with one another and all women participated, even in the larger groups. Strengths of this study are that the community recruitment attracted women who were candid in discussing weight-related issues, had a long history of weight loss attempts, and desired to lose weight. In addition, the objective measurement of height and weight established that on average, participants were morbidly obese. Thus, the findings reflect the perspectives and experiences of obese AA women who could not only greatly benefit from weight loss but who would likely agree to participate in a weight loss intervention. The rapid response to recruitment flyers and the high attendance rate further indicate a need for weight loss programs in the community.

### Implications

This study indicates that among a community sample of obese AA women, many will be interested in weight loss, experienced in weight loss attempts, knowledgeable regarding dietary causes of weight gain, and motivated to lose weight for health reasons. The findings corroborate existing recommendations for tailoring weight loss programs for AA women, such as the importance of involving social networks and adapting materials and recipes to be culturally relevant (Bronner & Boyington, 2002). The findings also provide several new suggestions for future programs. First, results indicate that obese AA women in a weight loss program may feel self-conscious about their bodies and actively engage in behaviors to maintain feelings of attractiveness. Although appearance concerns are not as important as health concerns for motivating weight loss in this population, negative body image may still play a role in weight-control behaviors and should therefore not be overlooked. For example, some evidence suggests that women with negative body image are more likely to be chronic dieters (Gingras, Fitzpatrick, & McCargar, 2004) and are less successful in losing weight (Teixeira et al., 2002). Second, obese AA women may be less knowledgeable and/or ready to increase energy expenditure compared to decreasing caloric intake, thus interventions may need to pay spe-

745   cial attention to knowledge, perceived barriers, and benefits related to physical activity. Third, pharmacotherapy for weight loss may not be well received with this population. Finally, given that participants may have varying levels, experiences, and preferences for social support for weight loss, the provision of support should be rooted in a clear understanding of the perceived needs and values of each participant. As others have suggested (Kreuter et al., 2002), by building on existing values and practices, such as mutual responsibility and caretaking, AA women may become more involved in weight loss and other health-related programs.

### References

Agurs-Collins, T. D., Kumanyika, S. K., Ten Have, T. R., & Adams-Campbell, L. L. (1997). A randomized controlled trial of weight reduction and exercise for diabetes management in older African-American subjects. *Diabetes Care, 20*(10), 1503–1511.

Ahye, B. A., Devine, C. M., & Odoms-Young, A. M. (2006). Values expressed through intergenerational family food and nutrition management systems among African American women. *Family & Community Health, 29*(1), 5–16.

Airhihenbuwa, C. O., Kumanyika, S., Agurs, T. D., & Lowe, A., (1995). Perceptions and beliefs about exercise, rest, and health among African-Americans. *American Journal of Health Promotion, 9*(6), 426–429.

Airhihenbuwa, C. O., Kumanyika, S., Agurs, T. D., Lowe, A., Saunders, D., & Morssink, C. B. (1996). Cultural aspects of African American eating patterns. *Ethnicity & Health, 1*(3), 245–260.

American Cancer Society. (2005). *Cancer facts and figures for African Americans 2005–2006.* Atlanta: Author.

Arab, L., Carriquiry, A., Steck-Scott, S., & Gaudet, M. M. (2003). Ethnic differences in the nutrient intake adequacy of premenopausal US women: Results from the Third National Health Examination Survey. *Journal of the American Dietetic Association, 103*(8), 1008–1014.

Baldwin, J. A., & Hopkins, R. (1990). African-American and European-American cultural differences as assessed by the worldviews paradigm: An empirical analysis. *Western Journal of Black Studies, 14*, 38–52.

Baturka, N., Hornsby, P. P., & Schorling, J. B. (2000). Clinical implications of body image among rural African-American women. *Journal of General Internal Medicine, 15*(4), 235–241.

Beech, B. M., Kumanyika, S. K., Baranowski, T., Davis, M., Robinson, T. N., Sherwood, N. E., et al. (2004). Parental cultural perspectives in relation to weight-related behaviors and concerns of African-American girls. *Obesity Research, 12*(Suppl.), 7S–19S.

Bernard, H. R. (2002). *Research methods in anthropology: Qualitative and quantitative approaches* (3rd ed.). Walnut Creek, CA: AltaMira Press.

Bronner, Y., & Boyington, J. E. (2002). Developing weight loss interventions for African-American women: Elements of successful models. *Journal of the National Medical Association, 94*(4), 224–235.

Cachelin, F. M., Rebeck, R. M., Chung, G. H., & Pelayo, E. (2002). Does ethnicity influence body-size preference? A comparison of body image and body size. *Obesity Research, 10*(3), 158–166.

Centers for Disease Control. (2004). Prevalence of no leisure-time physical activity—35 states and the District of Columbia, 1988–2002. *Morbidity and Mortality Weekly Report, 53*(4), 82–86.

Clark, J. M., Bone, L. R., Stallings, R., Gelber, A. C., Barker, A., Zeger, S., et al. (2001). Obesity and approaches to weight in an urban African-American community. *Ethnicity & Disease, 11*(4), 676–686.

Davis, E. M., Clark, J. M., Carrese, J. A., Gary, T. L., & Cooper, L. A. (2005). Racial and socioeconomic differences in the weight-loss experiences of obese women. *American Journal of Public Health, 95*(9), 1539–1543.

DiLillo, V., Gore, S., Jones, J., Balentine, C., & West, D. S. (2004). Body image dissatisfaction among Black and White women enrolled in a weight loss program. *Annals of Behavioral Medicine, 27*(Suppl.), S83.

Fern, E. (2001). *Advanced focus group research.* Thousand Oaks, CA: Sage.

Fitzgibbon, M. L., Blackman, L. R., & Avellone, M. E. (2000). The relationship between body image discrepancy and body mass index across ethnic groups. *Obesity Research, 8*(8), 582–589.

Flegal, K. M., Carroll, M. D., Ogden, C. L., & Johnson, C. L. (2002). Prevalence and trends in obesity among US adults, 1999–2000. *Journal of the American Medical Association, 288*(14), 1723–1727.

Flynn, K. J., & Fitzgibbon, M. (1998). Body images and obesity risk among Black females: A review of the literature. *Annals of Behavioral Medicine, 20*(1), 13–24.

Gingras, J., Fitzpatrick, J., & McCargar, L. (2004). Body image of chronic dieters: Lowered appearance evaluation and body satisfaction. *Journal of the American Dietetic Association, 104*(10), 1589–1592.

Hargreaves, M. K., Schlundt, D. G., & Buchowski, M. S. (2002). Contextual factors influencing the eating behaviours of African American women: A focus group investigation. *Ethnicity & Health, 7*(3), 133–147.

Harris, M. I. (1998). Diabetes in America: Epidemiology and scope of the problem. *Diabetes Care, 21*(Suppl. 3), C11–C14.

Hope, A. A., Kumanyika, S. K., Whitt, M. C., & Shults, J. (2005), Obesity-related comorbidities in obese African Americans in an outpatient weight loss program. *Obesity Research, 13*(4), 772–779.

James, D. C. (2004). Factors influencing food choices, dietary intake, and nutrition-related attitudes among African Americans: Application of a culturally sensitive model. *Ethnicity & Health, 9*(4), 349–367.

Kanders, B. S., Ullmann-Joy, P., Foreyt, J. P., Heymsfield, S. B., Heber, D., Elashoff, R. M., et al. (1994). The Black American Lifestyle Intervention (BALI): The design of a weight loss program for working-class African-American women. *Journal of the American Dietetic Association, 94*(3), 310–312.

Karanja, N., Stevens, V. J., Hollis, J. F., & Kumanyika, S. K. (2002). Steps to Soulful Living (STEPS): A weight loss program for African-American women. *Ethnicity & Disease, 12*(3), 363–371.

Kennedy, B. M., Paeratakul, S., Champagne, C. M., Ryan, D. H., Harsha, D. W., McGee, B., et al. (2005). A pilot church-based weight loss program for African-American adults using church members as health educators: A comparison of individual and group intervention. *Ethnicity & Disease, 15*(3), 373–378.

Kreuter, M. W., Lukwago, S. N., Buchholtz, D. C., Clark, E. M., & Sanders-Thompson, V. (2002). Achieving cultural appropriateness in health promotion programs: Targeted and tailored approaches. *Health Education & Behavior, 30*(2), 133–146.

Kumanyika, S. K. (1998). Obesity in African Americans: Biobehavioral consequences of culture. *Ethnicity & Disease, 8*(1), 93–96.

Kumanyika, S. K., & Charleston, J. B. (1992). Lose weight and win: A church-based weight loss program for blood pressure control among Black women. *Patient Education and Counseling, 19*(1), 19–32.

Kumanyika, S. K., Morssink, C., & Agurs, T. (1992). Models for dietary and weight change in African-American women: Identifying cultural components. *Ethnicity & Disease, 2*(2), 166–175.

Kumanyika, S. K., Obarzanek, E., Stevens, V. J., Hebert, P. R., & Whelton, P. K. (1991). Weight-loss experience of Black and White participants in NHLBI-sponsored clinical trials. *American Journal of Clinical Nutrition, 53*(6 Suppl.), 1631S-1638S.

Kumanyika, S. K., & Odoms, A. (2003). Nutrition. In R. L. Braithwaite & A. J. Taylor (Eds.), *Health issues in the Black community* (pp. 419–447). San Francisco: Jossey-Bass.

Kumanyika, S. K., Shults, J., Fassbender, J., Whitt, M. C., Brake, Y., Kallan, M. J., et al. (2005). Outpatient weight management in African-Americans: The Healthy Eating and Lifestyle Program (HELP) study. *Preventive Medicine, 41*(2), 488–502.

Lewis, C. E., Smith, D. E., Wallace, D. D., Williams, O. D., Bild, D. E., & Jacobs, D. R., Jr. (1997). Seven-year trends in body weight and associations with lifestyle and behavioral characteristics in Black and White young adults: The CARDIA study. *American Journal of Public Health, 87*(4), 635–642.

McNabb, W., Quinn, M., Kerver, J., Cook, S., & Karrison, T. (1997). The pathways church-based weight loss program for urban African-American women at risk for diabetes. *Diabetes Care, 20*(10), 1518–1523.

Must, A., Spadano, J., Coakley, E. H., Field, A. E., Colditz, G., & Dietz, W. H. (1999). The disease burden associated with overweight and obesity. *Journal of the American Medical Association, 282*(16), 1523–1529.

Nobles, W. (1991). African philosophy: Foundations for Black psychology. In R. Jones (Ed.), *Black psychology* (3rd ed.). Berkeley, CA: Cobb & Henry.

Pulvers, K. M., Lee, R., E., Kaur, H., Mayo, M. S., Fitzgibbon, M. L., Jeffries, S. K., et al. (2004). Development of a culturally relevant body image instrument among urban African Americans. *Obesity Research, 12*(10), 1641–1651.

Richter, D. L., Wilcox, S., Greaney, M. L., Henderson, K. A., & Ainsworth, B. E. (2002). Environmental, policy, and cultural factors related to physical activity in African American women. *Women & Health, 36*(2), 91–109.

Rosenberg, L., Palmer, J. R., Wise, L. A., Horton, N. J., Kumanyika, S. K., & Adams-Campbell, L. L. (2003). A prospective study of the effect of childbearing on weight gain in African-American women. *Obesity Research, 11*(12), 1526–1535.

Samuel-Hodge, C. D., Headen, S. W., Skelly, A. H., Ingram, A. F., Keyserling, T. C., Jackson, E. J., et al. (2000). Influences on day-to-day self-management of Type 2 diabetes among African-American women: Spirituality, the multi-caregiver role, and other social context factors. *Diabetes Care, 23*(7), 928–933.

Stevens, J., Kumanyika, S. K., & Keil, J. E. (1994). Attitudes toward body size and dieting: Differences between elderly Black and White women. *American Journal of Public Health, 84*(8), 1322–1325.

Stewart, A. (1998). *The ethnographer's method.* Thousand Oaks, CA: Sage.

Teixeira, P. J., Going, S. B., Houtkooper, L. B., Cussler, E. C., Martin, C. J., Metcalfe, L. L., et al. (2002). Weight loss readiness in middle-aged women: Psychosocial predictors of success for behavioral weight reduction. *Journal of Behavioral Medicine, 25*(6), 499–523.

Tyler, D. O., Allan, J. D., & Alcozer, F. R. (1997). Weight loss methods used by African American and Euro-American women. *Research in Nursing & Health, 20*(5), 413–423.

Walcott-McQuigg, J. A., Chen, S. P., Davis, K., Stevenson, E., Choi, A., & Wangsrikhun, S. (2002). Weight loss and weight loss maintenance in African-American women. *Journal of the National Medical Association, 94*(8), 686–694.

Wilcox, S., Richter, D. L., Henderson, K. A., Greaney, M. L., & Ainsworth, B. E. (2002). Perceptions of physical activity and personal barriers and enablers in African-American women. *Ethnicity & Disease, 12*(3), 353–362.

Wilson, D., Musham, C., & McLellan, M. S. (2004). From mothers to daughters: Transgenerational food and diet communication in an underserved group. *Journal of Cultural Diversity, 11*(1), 12–17.

Wing, R. R., & Anglin, K. (1996). Effectiveness of a behavioral weight control program for Blacks and Whites with NIDDM. *Diabetes Care, 19*(5), 409–413.

Wing, R. R., Hamman, R. F., Bray, G. A., Delahanty, L., Edelstein, S. L., Hill, J. O., et al. (2004). Achieving weight and activity goals among diabetes prevention program lifestyle participants. *Obesity Research, 12*(9), 1426–1434.

Wolfe, W. A. (2000). Obesity and the African-American woman: A cultural tolerance of fatness or other neglected factors. *Ethnicity & Disease, 10*(3), 446–453.

Wolfe, W. A. (2004). A review: Maximizing social support—A neglected strategy for improving weight management with African-American women. *Ethnicity & Disease, 14*(2), 212–218.

Yanek, L. R., Becker, D. M., Moy, T. F., Gittelsohn, J., & Koffman, D. M. (2001). Project joy: Faith based cardiovascular health promotion for African American women. *Public Health Reports, 116*(Suppl. 1), 68–81.

Young, D. R., Gittelsohn, J., Charleston, J., Felix-Aaron, K., & Appel, L. J. (2001). Motivations for exercise and weight loss among African-American women: Focus group results and their contribution towards program development. *Ethnicity & Health, 6*(3–4), 227–245.

**About the authors**: *Christie A. Befort, Janet L. Thomas, Christine M. Daley,* and *Paula C. Rhode,* University of Kansas Medical Center, Kansas City. *Jasjit S. Ahluwalia,* Office of Clinical Research, University of Minnesota, Minneapolis.

**Address correspondence to**: Christie A. Befort, University of Kansas Medical Center, 3901 Rainbow Blvd., MS 1008, Kansas City, KS 66160. E-mail: cbefort@mc.edu

# Exercise for Article 28

## *Factual Questions*

1. Was the setting for this study urban, suburban, *or* rural?

2. How many women were in the final sample?

3. What question was asked about attributions for weight?

4. What did the participants receive as compensation?

5. What percentage of the participants were between 45 and 55 years of age?

6. Are the results of this study consistent with previous focus group results?

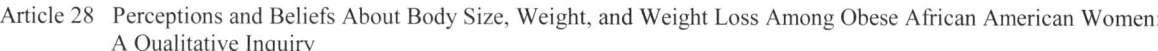

## Questions for Discussion

7. Eleven of the potential participants did not show up for their appointments for the focus groups. Could this have affected the results of this study? (See lines 155–161.)

8. Is the fact that six focus groups were conducted (instead of only one) an important strength of this study? Explain. (See lines 178–179.)

9. Is the method of data analysis described in sufficient detail? Explain. (See lines 226–260.)

10. What is your understanding of the meaning of the term "independent coders"? (See lines 235–239.)

11. To what extent do the quotations in the Thematic Analysis section of this report help you understand the results? (See lines 274–558.)

12. If you were to conduct a study on a similar topic in the future, would you use qualitative *or* quantitative methodology? Why?

## Quality Ratings

Directions: Indicate your level of agreement with each of the following statements by circling a number from 5 for strongly agree (SA) to 1 for strongly disagree (SD). If you believe an item is not applicable to this research article, leave it blank. Be prepared to explain your ratings. When responding to criteria A and B, keep in mind that brief titles and abstracts are conventional in published research.

A. The title of the article is appropriate.

SA   5   4   3   2   1   SD

B. The abstract provides an effective overview of the research article.

SA   5   4   3   2   1   SD

C. The introduction establishes the importance of the study.

SA   5   4   3   2   1   SD

D. The literature review establishes the context for the study.

SA   5   4   3   2   1   SD

E. The research purpose, question, or hypothesis is clearly stated.

SA   5   4   3   2   1   SD

F. The method of sampling is sound.

SA   5   4   3   2   1   SD

G. Relevant demographics (for example, age, gender, and ethnicity) are described.

SA   5   4   3   2   1   SD

H. Measurement procedures are adequate.

SA   5   4   3   2   1   SD

I. All procedures have been described in sufficient detail to permit a replication of the study.

SA   5   4   3   2   1   SD

J. The participants have been adequately protected from potential harm.

SA   5   4   3   2   1   SD

K. The results are clearly described.

SA   5   4   3   2   1   SD

L. The discussion/conclusion is appropriate.

SA   5   4   3   2   1   SD

M. Despite any flaws, the report is worthy of publication.

SA   5   4   3   2   1   SD

# Article 29

# Newlyweds' Unexpected Adjustments to Marriage

SCOTT S. HALL
Ball State University

REBECCA ADAMS
Ball State University

ABSTRACT. The purpose of this study was to investigate the unexpected adjustments to marriage of contemporary couples. Twenty-one couples were interviewed. The criteria were as follows: All of the couples were childless, in their first marriage, and the couples had been married less than a year. Qualitative analysis based on a phenomenological approach was used in the investigation. Six themes emerged regarding unexpected adjustments. The themes were as follows: The little things, competing loyalties, letdowns, serious responsibility, relationship roles, and sex. In some cases, gender of the spouse and premarital cohabitation appeared to be relevant to distinct types of adjustments. Implications for conceptualizing the transition to marriage and for further research and application toward premarital education are discussed.

From *Family & Consumer Sciences Research Journal*, *39*, 375–387. Copyright © 2011 by the American Association of Family and Consumer Sciences. Reprinted with permission.

People enter marriage with expectations about spousal behavior and the nature of the marital relationship (Baucom, Epstein, Rankin, & Burnett, 1996). Once married, these expectancies become comparisons with the realities of marriage, and couples' adjustment to marriage is influenced by the level of consistency between what they expected and what they experience in the actual marriage relationship (McNulty & Karney, 2002; Pretzer, Epstein, & Flemming, 1991). Unrealistic expectations especially can lead to dissatisfaction and poorer quality interaction (Baucom et al., 1996; Bradbury & Fincham, 1993; McNulty & Karney, 2002). Newlywed couples may be vulnerable to experiencing relational challenges as they transition into marriage because of inaccurate expectations, particularly if such expectations are unrealistic.

Because the institution of marriage has been undergoing significant transformations in recent decades, contemporary expectations about marriage may differ from past generations. For example, there have been general shifts toward gender role similarity and egalitarianism (Smock, 2004), romanticism (Cooper, 1999), and a lack of expected permanence (Johnston, Bachman, & O'Malley, 1997). The general destigmatization of nonmarital cohabitation and childbearing may influence the assumptions people bring into their marital or other adult relationships (Cherlin, 2004). People likely enter marriage with unprecedented diversity of expectations and ranges of premarital experiences. What it means to get married and how it transforms a relationship have become increasingly subjective and complex, possibly adding greater variation and challenge to the transition to marriage.

Previous research that has addressed early adjustments during the transition to marriage typically consisted of samples from at least 25 years ago (i.e., Arond & Pauker, 1987; Huston, McHale, & Crouter, 1986). More recent research exists that analyzed topics over which newlyweds argue (e.g., Oggins, 2003; Risch, Riley, & Lawler, 2003), but the research does not focus on the expectations people bring into marriage and the extent to which these expectations are consistent with the realities of marriage. The purpose of this study was to investigate unforeseen adjustments experienced early in marriage—including unmet premarital expectations—by contemporary (the current era) newly married couples. Qualitative methodology was used to examine contemporary expectations to better understand what newlyweds experience that is unexpected about being married.

The findings could have important implications for understanding how the transition to marriage and early marital relationships contribute to challenges faced by contemporary couples. These challenges may propel couples on a trajectory toward a high- or low-quality marriage or perhaps divorce. Learning from newlywed couples about unexpected aspects of marriage may yield information that can be incorporated into premarital and early marital intervention efforts designed to bolster newly established marriages. Because some couples decline in satisfaction more rapidly than others (McNulty & Karney, 2004), newlyweds might learn to manage their distress in ways that maintain a higher level of satisfaction for a longer period of time.

## The Transition to Marriage

Family Development Theory provides a framework for analyzing the transition to marriage. Specifically, getting married triggers a transition to a new and unique stage of life that includes a variety of norms and roles that influence the behavior of new spouses (Rodgers & White, 1993). With the accompanying title of "husband" or "wife," new spouses begin to function according to the social norms and structures attached to those new roles and to integrate them with other cross-institutional norms in their lives, such as those dealing with employment. Despite the complexities of this adjustment period, couples typically report being most satisfied very early in their marriages before a subsequent dropping off of satisfaction (Huston, Niehuis, & Smith, 2001; Vaillant & Vaillant, 1993). Huston and colleagues remarked that an "information vacuum" existed regarding the roots of marital distress and divorce within the first years of marriage (Huston, Caughlin, Houts, Smith, & George, 2001). What people expect from modern marriage may contribute to contemporary marital problems.

Newlyweds may be prone to having idealized notions of marriage and of each other, which may put newlyweds at risk for disillusionment with marriage (Huston et al., 2001). Even couples who live together prior to marriage may have idealized expectations because marriage is typically thought of as a distinct type of relationship with some unique meanings (Hall, 2006). Because beliefs about marriage have become more pluralistic and subjective (Cherlin, 2004), it may be more difficult for couples to know what to expect by getting married. Conversely, couples may have few set expectancies because marriage is more open to personal interpretation. This study was an effort to investigate how contemporary couples view and approach marriage, with an emphasis on what they expect marriage to be like and the accuracy of their expectations.

## Methodology

### Sample and Procedures

The sample consisted of 21 couples who were childless, in their first marriage, and who had been married from 3 to 12 months. The goal was to find couples whose premarital expectancies were relatively fresh in their memories although they had been married long enough to experience some of the adjustments in early marriage. These criteria helped avoid diverse issues related to remarriage and/or children that might contribute uniquely to marital adjustment for certain couples. Couples were recruited through local newspaper advertisements in the largest local paper of a mid-sized Midwestern city (approximately 60,000 residents). The advertisement and an initial screening phone call informed couples that the researchers were interested in hearing about their "ups and downs of getting and being married" and (during the phone call only) that they would receive $25 for their participation.

The 21 men ranged from ages 20 to 35 ($M = 24.62$, $SD = 3.98$). The men were Caucasian except for one Latino American. All of the men had at least graduated from high school. Thirteen of the men were current undergraduate students or had experienced some college; six men had completed a 4-year degree or more education. The 21 women ranged from ages 19 to 29 ($M = 22.62$, $SD = 2.67$). All of the women were

Caucasian, and all had at least graduated from high school. Fourteen of the women were current undergraduate students or had some college experience; six women had completed a 4-year degree or more education.

The couples had been married between 3 and 12 months ($M = 6.9$, $SD = 3.11$). Eight couples had lived together before they married, ranging from 1 to 48 months ($M = 15.50$, $SD = 15.32$). Eight couples had received extensive, structured premarital counseling (typically 4–6 organized sessions); none of the cohabiting couples were part of this group. Nine other couples reported having met with their pastors a couple of times before the wedding, typically discussing basic marriage and wedding preparation. Twelve couples reported weekly church attendance (only one of which cohabited—and for only 1 month). In comparison, the community from which the sample was drawn was 85% Caucasian, and 76% of adults over age 24 had graduated from high school, and 19% had at least a bachelor's degree (U.S. Census Bureau, 2000).

A semi-structured interview guide was used while interviewing participants in their homes (with the exception of one couple who were interviewed in the researchers' campus offices) for approximately 60 min. Husbands and wives were interviewed separately (though concurrently in different rooms). The male interviewer (first author) interviewed each husband and the female interviewer (second author) interviewed each wife, using the same interview guide. Separate interviews increased the potential for spouses to express feelings and concerns about their early marital relationship. After gathering personal and relationship histories, several questions focused on their general recollection of their premarital expectations for themselves, their eventual spouse, and for their marriage (see Appendix). The questions also focused on whether marriage matched the couples' expectations and whether anything about marriage had surprised them.

### Analytic Approach

The qualitative analysis was based on a phenomenological approach. This approach is useful in examining everyday lived experiences and the meanings people create out of interaction with the objective world (Giorgi & Giorgi, 2003). A key element of phenomenology is *problematics*—new experiences that do not fit with an individual's predictions that were based on previous experiences and observations (Daly, 2007). Thus, this approach is helpful in analyzing processes involved in adjustments to marriage that were not foreseen.

Initially, the researchers read the transcripts from the first 10 couples together, frequently reflecting on and discussing how the participants perceived their own experiences (Daly, 2007). Then, the researchers separated the experiences into smaller parts that were most pertinent to the research questions. As the re-

185 searchers read through targeted portions of the transcripts, they shared their interpretation of data and worked to achieve consensus on a categorical label or code to assign to each portion of data (Hill, Thompson, & Williams, 1997). The researchers used constant
190 comparison of previously coded transcripts and codes as they read and coded subsequent transcripts to ensure consistency in the use of codes, or the creation of new codes for domains that had not yet been identified. Together they created and assigned these codes to repre-
195 sent the essence of the participants' expectancies, and they maintained a list of the codes to assist with distinguishing different categories of codes.

As codes from different cases were analyzed, the researchers attempted to identify possible clusters of
200 codes that represented broader conceptual themes. To facilitate this process, they created a tree of concepts that incorporated microconcepts into larger constructs (e.g., type of unexpected adjustment, negative or positive). The researchers discussed possible clusters of
205 codes—as the main constructs—seeking distinctions between the codes. Once they achieved consensus of the initial coding scheme, they coded the remaining transcripts independently. Then, they shared how their transcripts were coded and worked to build consensus
210 on their coding. They reevaluated the clusters and overall coding scheme and developed consensus on the final clusters of codes that would represent the resulting themes of the analysis.

For additional analysis, the researchers recorded
215 which people offered a given code into a spreadsheet and made note of the background characteristics in each case. Specifically, they looked for patterns regarding gender, premarital cohabitation, and extent of premarital counseling that might have contributed to the
220 individual's unexpected adjustments. These tendencies may only be coincidental but they might create an impetus for further and broader investigation through additional research. The researchers reapplied the overall thematic framework to see how consistently it in-
225 corporated the individual codes and themes as a means to validate the framework (Strauss & Corbin, 1998).

## Findings

Initially, some participants were slow to recall some of their premarital expectancies as a means to describe unexpected adjustments to marriage. How-
230 ever, when probed with specific questions about a given expectation they might have had before marriage (e.g., how affection would be shown, what roles they would have) and how accurate that expectation proved to be, they typically offered multiple examples of un-
235 expected adjustments. Six major themes emerged regarding unexpected adjustments to marriage. See Table 1. In the next sections, the themes are defined and illustrated by statements made by the participants. Variation based on gender, cohabitation, and premarital edu-
240 cation will be described if they were observed by the researchers.

### The Little Things

It was common for newlyweds to experience adjustments having to do with getting used to what they referred to as "small" or "little things" associated with
245 the day-to-day elements of being married. There were quirks about a spouse that had not been appreciated until marriage, often over seemingly petty issues regarding toilet paper or shampoo usage, biting fingernails, and other "real things" that dating couples who
250 usually just "think about having fun" may have failed to appreciate before marriage. Part of the day-to-day adjustment of marriage was how routine the days had become, when couples found themselves "always doing the same thing." One husband considered these
255 types of daily issues especially challenging.

> So when we were dating, because we weren't together 24-7, we weren't always staying with each other at night, getting up together, it was kind of natural for me—this is what I do after I brush my teeth, and she doesn't neces-
260 sarily understand. So we have to meet in the middle. So sometimes those are the toughest things. It just causes us frustration because we never thought about that stuff. The big stuff, we planned out, how are we going to do our budget, what are we going to do about a car, and where
265 are we going to live, haven't been big issues. It's been little things that come up day to day when you're living with someone and are that close.

Table 1
*Summary of Themes and Subthemes*

| Theme | Description | Subthemes |
|---|---|---|
| The little things | Day-to-day elements of marriage | Routines<br>Interdependence/identity |
| Competing loyalties | Competition of loyalty between relationship with spouse and others | Parents/in-laws<br>Friends |
| Letdowns | Disappointment with realities of marriage | Affection/time<br>Not better than before |
| Serious responsibility | Pressures of responsibility | |
| Relationship roles | Who does what, when, and how | Gender |
| Sex | Issues with the sexual relationship | Let down<br>Frequency |

Some of the *little things* newlyweds faced had to do with managing day-to-day issues of interdependence. Although such issues may not be "little" as in being superficial or inconsequential, they were often reflected in the daily routines and occurrences. For example, new spouses had to get used to considering the perspective of another person instead of acting unilaterally all the time. As one participant explained, it was no longer a matter of doing "what I want, when I want. I'm used to just being able to go, but I have to check with [spouse] now." Sometimes issues of daily independence and identity ran deep, as described by one wife:

> For a while I thought I lost my identity because it was like, everything that I did by myself before, like I used to have a bank account, and my own credit cards, and now it's different, because now it's in both of our names, and I felt like I didn't really have anything that made me feel independent. But that's sometimes hard to adjust to, and I don't want to have everything separate, like bank accounts and that, but I still want to be able to take a role in some of the things.

With one exception, the newlyweds that mentioned these daily types of adjustments had not lived together before marriage. The one previous cohabiter was a wife who noted how even after 18 months of cohabitation that once the honeymoon was over, her husband felt more comfortable to let his guard down around her and become more irritating. In contrast, most of the examples from those who had not cohabited were in regard to the tasks of sharing a household or challenges to their conceptions of individuality.

*Competing Loyalties*

Getting married created situations in which loyalties to a new spouse competed at times with loyalties to other intimate relationships. Parents and in-laws were frequently sources of unexpected adjustments. It may have been a matter of how much time to spend with each spouse's parents, especially regarding holidays and vacations, or how the two sets of in-laws differed in ways that created stress for the newlyweds when the two sets of families interacted with each other. Choosing to spend time with one's parents instead of with one's spouse was also a new dilemma for some spouses, as suggested by this wife's description below. Spouses may struggle to appreciate the reasons behind such choices.

> ...we live 4 miles from his parents' house, we live 2 hours away from my parents' house, and sometimes when I tell [husband] I'm going to ask off work so I can go up and see my family, "Why do you need to do that?" "You just saw them last month?" I'm like, "Because I saw them last month."... He doesn't really have that much interaction with his family but I love interaction with my family. Sometimes he doesn't really understand why I need the comfort and support I do up there, but I do.

Examples about conflicting loyalties between one's spouse and one's parents came from about twice as many wives as husbands. The examples from both husbands and wives typically focused on the wife's parents (except for those that referred generally to appeasing both sets of parents regarding how to spend the holidays). It appeared that wives especially may have been deeply affected by tension between loyalties to a husband and to parents, or they were more often the target of complaining by dissatisfied husbands and parents.

Loyalty issues with friendships were also apparent. Some spouses, especially husbands (by their own report or by the observations of wives), felt friction between their desires to spend time with their spouse and to pursue or maintain friendships outside of the marriage. One husband described how this friction played out in his marriage:

> The first couple months have been great, and it's kind of getting to where, oh, it'd be nice to see other people to get a breath. Like once a night hang out with the guys or something like that. Or once a week, not once a night. But um, she'd have a problem with that. Or even just doing things that couples do, so we can actually do stuff together, but do it with other people.

*Letdowns*

The newlyweds often held very positive expectancies regarding how marriage would improve their relationship and fulfill their needs. Although they felt that some of these expectations had been realized, there were some elements of their relationships that did not improve with marriage and some that unexpectedly changed in dissatisfying ways. Some newlyweds were surprised and disappointed that they argued more once married (even some of those who had cohabited). Some letdowns had to do with being busy and "just figuring out how to spend time with each other and still getting things done." When couples were together, sometimes the level of affection was not as high as desired or they did not feel as strong a sense of togetherness as previously hoped. Husbands were just as likely as wives to bemoan the lack of time to be with the other, but wives were especially likely to express dissatisfaction with levels of affection. The sentiments below were expressed similarly by several women:

> I guess I just thought that we would be a lot closer than we are...like emotionally and especially physically. That we'd be having a lot more emotional closeness based on shared experiences, and time spent talking to each other and things like that. Like our lives would be more like unified, and working together, as opposed to just being together.

Another type of letdown focused on the fact that marriage did not create a specific positive change they had hoped for, like a spouse changing an undesirable attitude or behavior, that arguments would be easier to resolve or, as in the example below, the feelings one felt for a partner would be stronger after marriage:

380 I thought maybe there'd be some different feelings once we got married and it honestly wasn't, I didn't love her any more or any less. Just kind of the same feeling. Now I say my wife instead of girlfriend. Kind of a letdown, but not enough to cause me any grief.

385 Even newlyweds who had lived together for a significant amount of time before marriage mentioned letdowns regarding togetherness and affection. However, those who had expected positive changes or transformations with marriage were predominantly newly-
390 weds who did not cohabit with their eventual spouse before marriage.

*Serious Responsibility*

New pressures and "the stress of the future" weighed heavily on some of the newlyweds. Marriage consisted of "much stuff you had to do by yourself"
395 that parents had taken care of in the past. Marriage also required "big decisions"—often financial—that had serious implications for the future. Some individuals commented on personal growth and development that marriage had promoted in them because of the weight-
400 ier responsibilities of marriage. Husbands especially were prone to focus on the pressures of responsibility, and wives were prone to mention feeling the need to be saving money for the future. The seriousness of these realities felt overwhelming at times:

405 Once the planning was over and everything, the day you get back from the honeymoon, it's like 'wow' you don't have to keep figuring everything out. Now what? ...Is my job good enough to sustain us and our kids, and is the place we are living in where I want to raise a kid? Stuff
410 like that. You start doubting whether you're good enough, I think. That stuff's what scares me.... After we got married it was more like, well there's so much more stuff that happens now, how am I going to deal with it? Because it's real after you get married, it's not like you're
415 playing house, it's actually real.

*Relationship Roles*

Who does what, when, and how were common issues faced by couples. Often, gender was a part of the expectancies regarding specific roles or responsibilities. Common frustrations included chores and money.
420 Some individuals were surprised how uneven the roles were (especially wives, who tended to complain that the roles were not as balanced as they had anticipated), while others were surprised how even they became (especially husbands, who thought they would have
425 more control over relationship decisions than they did). A few participants were frustrated with the lack of mutuality that they had hoped for regarding financial management. Sometimes there were assumptions about gender roles that were manifested in disagreements
430 about household cleanliness:

He's thinking about his school...about his music. I can't interrupt his life with the stupid little petty things that I

worry about, you because it's just not equal. So some-
435 times he'll put that back in my face, 'I've got school to worry about, I can't worry about cleaning up after myself.' [laughing] I'm just like, 'I work, I clean up after myself, how hard is it?'

*Sex*

None of those who mentioned unexpected adjustments about sex had lived together before marriage.
440 Several newlyweds reported having been virgins when they married, so marriage itself represented a major change in their sexual relationship. Some of these individuals were prone to having romanticized or stereotyped expectations about sex that ended up being inac-
445 curate. Sex was not always "what [they] believed it was built up to be before [they] were married." One wife even felt "misled" by the media. Another wife was surprised that she wanted to have sex more often than did her husband. The researchers did not ask about
450 the reactions of those who had had premarital sexual relations; thus, there is no point of comparison for the couples described earlier.

It was also surprising to some (even those who had a previous sexual relationship with one another)
455 that the frequency of sexual encounters was less than expected (or less than they had been before). As one wife explained, sometimes the other pressures and commitments of life got in the way: "We had more sex before we were married. I guess I figured we'd have
460 more, but it's not bad. It's not as often as I figured it would be. But that's because we're busy and tired."

**Discussion**

The study investigated the unexpected adjustments to marriage of newlywed couples. The researchers asked the 21 newlywed couples to reflect (in sepa-
465 rate interviews) on their premarital expectations of what marriage would be like. In the cognitive-behavioral literature, what people expect or anticipate the future to be like is termed an *expectancy*, which acts as points of comparison for perceived realities of a
470 situation (McNulty & Karney, 2002). Unrealistic or dysfunctional expectancies correlate with marital dissatisfaction marriage-harming behavior (Baucom et al., 1996; Bradbury & Fincham, 1993). Contradiction between the expectancies and the realities of marriage
475 and one's spouse becomes more apparent within the intimate confines of marriage and leads to distress (Huston et al., 2001). The newlyweds in the sample were able to identify examples of how their marital realities did not match up with their premarital expec-
480 tancies, resulting in unanticipated marital adjustments. Six themes emerged among these adjustments.

The themes were generally consistent with past research on the transition to marriage. For example, experiencing *competing loyalties* among friends, fam-
485 ily, and spouse is consistent with prior observations of the effort required by newlyweds to negotiate and establish "boundaries" among these relationships (Carter

& McGoldrick, 1989). Eventually, the social networks of each spouse typically become more intertwined ("structural interdependence") and some of these divided loyalties may smooth out as networks mesh together (Kearns & Leonard, 2004). Struggles with determining, manipulating, and incorporating *relationship roles* is a predicable part of transitioning to marriage (Rodgers & White, 1993) and has been coined as "identity bargaining" (Blumstein, 1975). For decades, experiencing *letdowns* after marriage has been noted as predictable disillusionment, a natural result of the romanticization of marriage and of one's choice of mate (Huston et al., 2001; Waller, 1938). Generally, the specific issues mentioned within the themes coincided with the variety of noted emotional, cognitive, social, legal, and economic changes associated with the institution of marriage (Bohannan, 1970; Schramm, Marshall, Harris, & Lee, 2005).

It appears that for this sample, the transition to marriage had not been completely transformed in light of recent social relationship and marital trends. The focus of the study was on *unanticipated* adjustments and *unmet* expectancies, and the findings revealed that couples were still caught off guard by challenges that were typical and abundant as identified in previous research. The identified issues may be difficult for engaged couples to conceptualize or prepare for, even with premarital counseling and cohabitation.

Although there was much similarity regarding unexpected adjustments for husbands and wives, some differences stood out. For example, with conflicting loyalties between spouse and parents, it was more commonly the wife's parents who were the source of unexpected controversy. This pattern is consistent with other research that has found the wife's family to play a greater role in the marital adjustment of couples (Sabatelli & Bartle-Haring, 2003; Timmer & Veroff, 2000). Because the wife–mother-in-law relationship can be particularly challenging (Turner, Young, & Black, 2006), some of these wives may have felt torn between their own parents' influences and those of the husband's parents. However, the husbands may have felt less invested in the cross-family relationships and thus experienced fewer divided loyalties.

Husbands were also more prone to be the ones seeking connections with friends outside of marriage, and wives were prone to complain about them doing so. Other research has found the integration of spouses' friendship networks to be more salient to a wife's than a husband's early marital quality (Kearns & Leonard, 2004). Perhaps some of these wives viewed their husbands' attempts at apparent social independence as a threat to this integration even though it seemed that the husbands' motives were to maintain a part of their own individuality or sense of the familiar. Husbands more than wives tend to keep the nature of their friendships separate from their marital work (Helms, Crouter, & McHale, 2003).

Husbands were also especially likely to mention the weighty responsibilities that come with marriage, which would be consistent with a pervasive provider gender role orientation for men. The sharing of domestic responsibilities was often not the anticipated balance—be it less traditional than some husbands expected and more traditional than some wives expected. Newlywed couples commonly struggle with this type of a negotiation, particularly in terms of how traditional the gender roles become as the couple transitions to marriage (Schramm et al., 2005). Newlywed couples may struggle with competing expectations about marital roles given the more pluralistic nature of what it means to be married (Cherlin, 2004). Overall, husbands and wives may have some distinct expectancies about issues of togetherness, loyalty, and roles that become hurdles in early marriage, especially if they assume that their eventual spouse's (and in-laws') expectancies are compatible with their own.

The researchers investigated the themes for any differences that appeared to exist based on the incidence of premarital cohabitation. With cohabitation becoming more common as a predecessor to marriage, the transition to marriage has become more diverse and complex (Cohan & Kleinbaum, 2002). Furthermore, the timing of cohabitation relative to engagement also appears to be relevant to the marital experience. Research has shown that marriages often differ for couples who only cohabited once they intended to marry (more positive interaction, less divorce proneness) from those who decide to marry after having already lived together (Stanley, Rhoades, Amato, Markman, & Johnson, 2010). This distinction might imply that the transition to marriage differs for couples who cohabited for different reasons. In the sample, half of those couples who cohabited got engaged after they started living together (these were the couples who cohabited the longest—at least 18 months before marriage). However, they appeared to mention the same adjustments as often as the couples who were engaged before (or as) they began cohabiting. However, the numbers are too small to form any substantive conclusions. Although it was not evident that such a distinction influenced the adjustment experiences of the couples in this sample, it is an important consideration to keep in mind when investigating variation in adjustments during the transition to marriage.

Many people believe that the cohabitation experience would shape premarital expectancies of marriage to be more realistic as the couple have already experienced coresidency and have a greater familiarity with each other (Rhoades, Stanley, & Markman, 2009). In terms of the daily adjustments to living with another person, there was a lack of examples offered by those who cohabited. These couples might have become more used to the *little things* that tend to appear when sharing a residence with a committed partner. However, couples who had cohabited were not immune to

605 unexpected adjustments. As noted, some experienced the typical letdowns after marriage, including an increase in conflict and a decrease in togetherness and affection, as well as loyalty issues (especially regarding in-laws) and challenges with new roles (especially regarding chores). Cohabitation may offer some preparation for certain aspects of marriage—especially those associated with sharing a living space—but may fall short of helping couples anticipate other more relationship-oriented adjustments in marriage.

## Limitations and Implications

615 Overall, the participants were very enthusiastic about their recent marriages, although they had experienced unexpected frustrations with the transition to marriage. Other types of couples—particularly those who may experience the most negative or challenging transition to marriage—might have different sets or types of expectancies and unexpected adjustments. They should be included in similar, future research. The researchers found that requesting volunteers to talk about their recent marriage generally attracted people who were eager to share their successes. Other recruitment methods might attract couples who were happier or had more frustration that could lead to greater insight. Also, a longitudinal study might yield different results when participants do not rely as much on memory of prior hopes and anticipations.

630 The researchers did not explicitly measure the outcomes of experiencing unexpected adjustments. Research that includes measures of discouragement or

enhancement may be able to predict the effects of certain types of mismatches between expectancies and
635 realities. It is also possible that newlyweds (or maybe only some) do not overly focus on such mismatches—even though mismatches are typically cited to explain dissatisfaction in relationships (McNulty & Karney, 2004). An unsure spouse may purposefully let go of or
640 explain away unmet expectations as a means to cope with or curb potential disappointment.

Future research on the coping strategies of newlyweds could add to the understanding of processes related to adjusting to marriage. The categories and
645 examples that were identified in this data collection might assist in developing extensive, quantifiable measures that could be used to explore the intricacies of getting married in a period where marriage is becoming less clearly defined.

650 Premarital counselors and educators might glean from the themes of unexpected adjustments the types of preparation engaged couples may find beneficial—some of which may include sensitivities to expectations that differ by gender. Efforts to educate couples in
655 ways that make marital adjustments predictable might lessen some anxieties and help couples prepare for adjustments, but there may also be value in experiencing the unpredictable elements of the transition to marriage. Perhaps equipping soon-to-be-spouses with an
660 attitude that embraces the unforeseen nature of marital challenges might be a helpful strategy for practitioners.

## Appendix

### Abbreviated Interview Guide

Thinking back before you got married, what did you think marriage would be like? What type of expectations did you have for your marriage?

(Probes)
How chores would get done—How has it actually been?
How decisions are made—How has it actually been?
How conflict would be handled—How has it actually been?
How finances would be handled—How has it actually been?
How (nonerotic) affection would be shown—How has it actually been?
How leisure time would be handled—How has it actually been?
How your relation to in-laws would be—How has it actually been?

How did you expect marriage would, if at all, change your relationship (how you would interact with one another/treat each other/feel about each other)?
How has it actually changed?
When did those changes begin to occur?
How do you feel about the changes?

How did you expect marriage would, if at all, change your individual identity?
How has it actually changed?

How did you expect marriage would, if at all, change your spouse?
How has your spouse actually changed?

Looking back at your expectations of marriage, has anything (else) surprised you about marriage?

## References

Arond, M., & Pauker, S. L. (1987). *The first year of marriage: What to expect, accept, and what you can change for a lasting relationship*. New York: Warner Books.

Baucom, D. H., Epstein, N., Rankin, L. A., & Burnett, C. K. (1996). Assessing relationship standards: The inventory of specific relationship standards. *Journal of Family Psychology, 10*, 72–88.

Blumstein, P. (1975). Identity bargaining and self-conception. *Social Forces, 53*, 476–485.

Bohannan, P. (1970). *Divorce and after*. New York: Doubleday.

Bradbury, T. N., & Fincham, F. D. (1993). Assessing dysfunctional cognition in marriage: A reconsideration of the relationship belief inventory. *Psychological Assessment, 5*, 92–101.

Carter, B., & McGoldrick, M. (1989). *The changing family life cycle*. Boston: Allyn and Bacon.

Cherlin, A. J. (2004). The deinstitutionalization of American marriage. *Journal of Marriage and Family, 66*, 848–861.

Cohan, C. L., & Kleinbaum, S. (2002). Toward a greater understanding of the cohabitation effect: Premarital cohabitation and marital communication. *Journal of Marriage and Family, 64*, 180–192.

Cooper, S. M. (1999). Historical analysis of the family. In M. B. Sussman, S. K. Steinmetz, & G. W. Peterson (Eds.), *Handbook of marriage and the family* (pp. 13–38). New York: Plenum Press.

Daly, K. J. (2007). *Qualitative methods for family studies and human development*. Los Angeles: Sage.

Giorgi, A., & Giorgi, B. (2003). Phenomenology. In J. A. Smith (Ed.), *Quantitative psychology: A practical guide to research methods* (pp. 25–50). London: Sage.

Hall, S. S. (2006). Marital meaning: Exploring young adults' belief systems about marriage. *Journal of Family Issues, 27*, 1437–1458.

Helms, H. M., Crouter, A. C., & McHale, S. M. (2003). Marital quality and spouses' marriage work with close friends and each other. *Journal of Marriage and Family, 65*(4), 963–977.

Hill, C. E., Thompson, B. J., & Williams, E. N. (1997). A guide to conducting consensual qualitative research. *Counseling Psychologist, 25*, 517–572.

Huston, T. L., Caughlin, J. P., Houts, R. M., Smith, S. E., & George, L. J. (2001). The connubial crucible: Newlywed years as predictors of marital delight, distress, and divorce. *Journal of Personality and Social Psychology, 80*, 237–252.

Huston, T. L., McHale, S. M., & Crouter, A. C. (1986). When the honeymoon is over: Changes in the marriage relationship over the first year. In R. Gilmore & S. Duck (Eds.), *The emerging field of personal relationships* (pp. 109–132). Hillsdale, NJ: Lawrence Erlbaum.

Huston, T. L., Niehuis, S., & Smith, S. E. (2001). The early marital roots of conjugal distress and divorce. *Current Directions in Psychological Science, 10*, 116–119.

Johnston, L. D., Bachman, J. G., & O'Malley, P. M. (1997). *Monitoring the future: Questionnaire responses from the nation's high school seniors, 1995*. Ann Arbor, MI: Institute for Social Research.

Kearns, J. N., & Leonard, K. E. (2004). Social networks, structural interdependence, and marital quality over the transition to marriage: A prospective analysis. *Journal of Family Psychology, 18*(2), 383–395.

McNulty, J. K., & Karney, B. R. (2002). Expectancy confirmation in appraisals of marital interactions. *Personality and Social Psychology Bulletin, 28*, 764–775.

McNulty, J. K., & Karney, B. R. (2004). Positive expectations in the early years of marriage: Should couples expect the best or brace for the worst? *Journal of Personality and Social Psychology, 86*, 729–743.

Oggins, J. (2003). Topics of marital disagreement among African-American and Euro-American newlyweds. *Psychological Reports, 92*, 419–425.

Pretzer, J., Epstein, N., & Flemming, B. (1991). The Marital Attitude Survey: A measure of dysfunctional attributions and expectancies. *The Journal of Cognitive Psychotherapy: An International Quarterly, 5*, 131–148.

Rhoades, G. K., Stanley, S. M., & Markman, H. J. (2009). Couples' reasons for cohabitation: Associations with individual well-being and relationship quality. *Journal of Family Issues, 30*(2), 233–258.

Risch, G. S., Riley, L. A., & Lawler, M. G. (2003). Problematic issues in the early years of marriage: Content for premarital education. *Journal of Psychology and Theology, 31*, 253–269.

Rodgers, R. H., & White, J. M. (1993). Family development theory. In P. G. Boss, W. J. Doherty, R. LaRossa, W. R. Schumm, & S. K. Steinmetz (Eds.), *Sourcebook of family theories and methods: A contextual approach* (pp. 225–254). New York: Plenum Press.

Sabatelli, R., & Bartle-Haring, S. (2003). Family-of-origin experiences and adjustment in married couples. *Journal of Marriage and Family, 65*, 159–169.

Schramm, D. G., Marshall, J. P., Harris, V. W., & Lee, T. R. (2005). After 'I do': The newlywed transition. *Marriage & Family Review, 38*(1), 45–67.

Smock, P. J. (2004). The wax and wane of marriage: Prospects for marriage in the 21st century. *Journal of Marriage and Family, 66*, 966–973.

Stanley, S. M., Rhoades, G. K., Amato, P. R., Markman, H. J, & Johnson, C. A. (2010). The timing of cohabitation and engagement: Impact on first and second marriages. *Journal of Marriage and Family, 72*(4), 906–918.

Strauss, A., & Corbin, J. (1998). *Basics of qualitative research: Techniques and procedures for developing grounded theory*. Thousand Oaks, CA: Sage.

Timmer, S. G., & Veroff, J. (2000). Family ties and the discontinuity of divorce in black and white newlywed couples. *Journal of Marriage and Family, 62*, 349–361.

Turner, M. J., Young, C. R., & Black, K. I. (2006). Daughters-in-law and mothers-in-law seeking their place within the family: A qualitative study of differing viewpoints. *Family Relations, 55*, 588–600.

U.S. Census Bureau. (2000). Retrieved June 1, 2009, from http://quickfacts.census.gov/qfd/states/18/1851876.html

Vaillant, C. O., & Vaillant, G. E. (1993). Is the U-curve of marital satisfaction an illusion? A 40-year study of marriage. *Journal of Marriage and the Family, 55*, 230–239.

Waller, W. (1938). *The family: A dynamic interpretation*. New York: Cordon.

**About the authors**: *Scott S. Hall*, Ph.D. and *Rebecca Adams*, Ph.D. are associate professors in the Department of Family and Consumer Sciences at Ball State University.

**Address correspondence to**: Scott S. Hall, Department of Family and Consumer Sciences, Ball State University, AT 150, Muncie, IN 47306. E-mail: sshall@bsu.edu

# Exercise for Article 29

## Factual Questions

1. How many of the couples were in their first marriage?

2. What was the average age of the men?

3. Did the researchers code all the transcripts independently?

4. Did the researchers reach a consensus on the final cluster of codes?

5. Did the researchers conclude that, overall, the participants were very enthusiastic about their recent marriages?

6. Do the researchers suggest using other types of couples in future research?

## Questions for Discussion

7. What is your opinion on including in the sample couples who had lived together before they were married? (See lines 135–137.)

8. What is your opinion on interviewing the husbands and wives in separate rooms? (See lines 154–155 and 158–161.)

9. In your opinion, is the analytic approach described in sufficient detail? (See lines 168–226.)

10. In their Findings section, the researchers provide quotations from the participants. How useful are these quotes in helping you understand the results of this study? Explain. (See lines 227–461.)

11. Do you think that in future research on this topic, quantifiable measures should be used? (See lines 642–649.)

12. How helpful was the Abbreviated Interview Guide in the Appendix at the end of this article in helping you understand the results of this study?

## Quality Ratings

Directions: Indicate your level of agreement with each of the following statements by circling a number from 5 for strongly agree (SA) to 1 for strongly disagree (SD). If you believe an item is not applicable to this research article, leave it blank. Be prepared to explain your ratings. When responding to criteria A and B, keep in mind that brief titles and abstracts are conventional in published research.

A.  The title of the article is appropriate.

SA   5   4   3   2   1   SD

B.  The abstract provides an effective overview of the research article.

SA   5   4   3   2   1   SD

C.  The introduction establishes the importance of the study.

SA   5   4   3   2   1   SD

D.  The literature review establishes the context for the study.

SA   5   4   3   2   1   SD

E.  The research purpose, question, or hypothesis is clearly stated.

SA   5   4   3   2   1   SD

F.  The method of sampling is sound.

SA   5   4   3   2   1   SD

G.  Relevant demographics (for example, age, gender, and ethnicity) are described.

SA   5   4   3   2   1   SD

H.  Measurement procedures are adequate.

SA   5   4   3   2   1   SD

I.  All procedures have been described in sufficient detail to permit a replication of the study.

SA   5   4   3   2   1   SD

J.  The participants have been adequately protected from potential harm.

SA   5   4   3   2   1   SD

K.  The results are clearly described.

SA   5   4   3   2   1   SD

L.  The discussion/conclusion is appropriate.

SA   5   4   3   2   1   SD

M.  Despite any flaws, the report is worthy of publication.

SA   5   4   3   2   1   SD

# Article 30

# "More Than a Liver": Social Work's Contribution to the Well-Being of People Undergoing Treatment for Hepatitis C

MARLIZE MOUTON

Liverpool Hospital

ABSTRACT. Hepatitis C is a rapidly growing infectious disease in Australia. People with hepatitis C face challenges and need help managing the psychosocial impact of the disease and treatment on their daily lives. A qualitative study design was used to explore social workers' understanding of the psychosocial consequences of the hepatitis C treatment experience and to clarify the roles and suggested practices for social workers dealing with this population. The study findings contribute to the knowledge base about how social workers, on multidisciplinary teams, contribute to meeting the psychosocial needs of people who receive treatment for hepatitis C.

From *Journal of Social Work Practice in the Addictions*, *11*, 40–59. Copyright © 2011 by Taylor & Francis Group, LLC. Reprinted with permission.

Hepatitis C is regarded as a significant and fast-growing public health problem in Australia. At the end of 2008, there were an estimated 284,000 people who had been exposed to hepatitis C, of whom 212,000 were estimated to have chronic hepatitis C. Injection drug use (IDU) is the primary cause of hepatitis C, accounting for 80% of all cases (National Centre in HIV Epidemiology and Clinical Research, 2009). Hepatitis C is a stigmatized disease that is difficult to live with and is often associated with drug and alcohol problems, mental health problems, poor general health, unstable lifestyles, and other problems of a psychosocial nature (Anti-Discrimination Board of New South Wales, 2001; Dore, Law, MacDonald, & Kaldor, 2003; Hopwood & Treloar, 2003; Zigmund, Ho, Masuda, Ippolito, & LaBrecque, 2003). Projections of the future burden of chronic hepatitis C, advanced liver disease, and cirrhosis on the health care system of Australia indicate that the number of people accessing treatment for their hepatitis C will triple (Ministerial Advisory Committee on AIDS Sexual Health and Hepatitis C Sub-Committee, 2006). In consideration of these projections, it seemed relevant to investigate how the presence of a social worker on a treatment team could aid the treatment process for people with hepatitis C. The lack of guidelines and shortage of literature on the role of the social worker in hepatitis C treatment became apparent during the literature search for this study. Although there are similarities with other areas of social work in chronic and stigmatized diseases, such as HIV, it is important to consider the intricacies of the hepatitis C disease specifically and the psychosocial factors associated with the disease and treatment thereof, to tailor social work services to suit the needs of the clients and the rest of the multidisciplinary treatment team.

The conventional treatment process for hepatitis C is challenging for the client and his or her family members due to the strict treatment regime, the duration of the treatment, the side effects, and the uncertainty of the treatment outcome (Anti-Discrimination Board of New South Wales, 2001; Dore et al., 2003; Hopwood & Treloar, 2003; Zigmund et al., 2003). Conventional treatment causes a range of side effects that affect people's lives on a physical, an emotional, and a mental level (Dolan, 1997; Hopwood & Treloar, 2004; Sievert, 2003). In the hepatitis C treatment center, the notion of "the person in the situation" needs to be kept in mind together with a holistic approach that treats individuals and connected social systems as whole entities (Ell & Northern, 1990; Gregorian, 2005; Stein, 2004; Teeters, 2005). This viewpoint supports the argument that social workers are valuable members of hepatitis C treatment teams. Their knowledge and skills base, together with the roles they fulfill, can aid the treatment process to the benefit of the client, his or her family, and the multidisciplinary team (Clare, 2001; Ehsani, Vu, & Karvelas, 2006; Fook, 2002; Giles, Gould, Hart, & Swancott, 2007; Gregorian, 2005; Mellor & Lindeman, 1998).

In the context of the related field of HIV treatment, Rier and Indyk (2006) reported the factors that hindered compliance to treatment. These included unpleasant side effects, the high cost of treatment, psychological factors, and problems that the client might have with the way that the treatment is delivered within the medical structure. The importance of having health care professionals devote the necessary time to explain the treatment regimen and its implications was emphasized. For social workers to help their clients overcome the psychosocial obstacles that could prevent them from complying with hepatitis C treatment regimes and completing the treatment program, it is important to understand what interventions clients find helpful.

People who are affected by hepatitis C are a multicultural group who have multifaceted needs that have to be taken into consideration in providing services. Moreover, hepatitis C is a highly stigmatized disease, and there is a great deal of discrimination (Anti-Discrimination Board of New South Wales, 2001; Conrad et al., 2006; Hopwood & Treloar, 2003; Zigmund et al., 2003). Several authors, including Conrad et al. (2006) and Hopwood, Treloar, and Bryant (2006), suggest that people often avoid disclosing they have hepatitis C infection out of fear that they might be discriminated against.

The aims of this study were to explore the psychosocial consequences of the hepatitis C treatment experience; to clarify the roles of social workers in hepatitis C treatment clinics and social workers' views of their abilities to fulfill these roles; to discuss the merits of the social work role in hepatitis C treatment clinics; and to suggest changes. To achieve the aims of the study, and guided by the relevant literature, the following research questions were posed:

1. What do social workers perceive to be the most prominent psychosocial needs of hepatitis-C-positive clients during the various stages of their pretreatment, on-treatment, and posttreatment journey with hepatitis C?

2. How do social workers respond to those needs and ensure the needs are met?
3. What value does a social worker on the treatment team add to the treatment process and outcome?
4. To render an effective social work service, is there any special knowledge, experience, or attributes that the social worker needs to have in the context of work in the hepatitis C treatment center?

## Method

This qualitative research study consisted of semi-structured, in-depth interviews with a sample of 10 social workers in public hepatitis C treatment centers in New South Wales, Australia. Ethics approval for the research project was obtained from the ethics committees of the university and the area health services where the research took place. Through a purposeful sampling strategy, a sample of 10 out of an estimated possible 15 social workers in public hepatitis C treatment centers in New South Wales was recruited. With the exception of one male, all the participants were female. All were experienced social workers with a wealth of social work and counseling experience in a variety of fields. Most participants had over 3 years of experience in the field of hepatitis C. Except for one social worker who had qualified in England, all participants had obtained their social work qualifications from universities in Australia. Participants were informed about relevant aspects of the research, and written consent was obtained from each. Table 1 lists the training and experience of the 10 social workers who participated in the study.

Table 1
*Profiles of Social Work Participants*

| Participant number | Gender | Years and details of social work experience | Country where qualified as a social worker |
|---|---|---|---|
| 1 | F | 7 years: HCV services and community health services | Australia |
| 2 | M | 33 years: HCV services, general hospital social work, community health and mental health services, probation and parole, juvenile justice | Australia |
| 3 | F | 10 years: HCV services, HIV services, child protection and community services | U.K. |
| 4 | F | 6 years: HCV services, HIV services, drug and alcohol services, child protection services | Australia |
| 5 | F | 10 years: HCV services, community health and community mental health services | Australia |
| 6 | F | 7 years: HCV services, sexual assault and sexual health services, adoption services | Australia |
| 7 | F | 9 years: HCV services, sexual health services, general hospital social work, domestic violence services | Australia |
| 9 | F | 4 years: HCV services, aged care services, sexual health services | Australia |
| 9 | F | 7 years: HCV services, HIV services, general hospital social work | Australia |
| 10 | F | 9 years: HCV services, rehabilitation services, chronic disease services, child protection services | Australia |

*Note.* HCV = hepatitis C virus.

Semistructured interview topics were related to the research questions, which covered aspects of the social workers' experiences in their daily work in the clinics. Interviews with research participants were audiotaped, transcribed, and checked for accuracy by the researcher and the two study supervisors at the university. The coding and data analysis process consisted of the identification of key themes and patterns, first from a small sample of interview transcripts. Codes were applied to these transcripts by the researcher and reviewed by the supervisors. After revision, the codes were applied to all data. Coded sections were gathered together by manual manipulation of word-processed documents. Coded sections of the interview transcripts were read closely to address the research questions and to engage in theory building through identification and elaboration of emergent themes.

## Results

The results of the research interviews with the social workers who participated illustrate their perceptions of the main needs of their clients and how to meet those needs in the context of their clinics and on a wider health promotion level. The data gathered also identify the knowledge, skills, experience, and values that a social worker should have to be able to work effectively in a hepatitis C treatment center. Table 2 summarizes these findings.

Table 2

*Clients' Needs; Strategies Employed; and Social Work Knowledge, Skills, Experience, and Values*

| Main needs of clients | Strategies to meet needs | Social work knowledge, skills, experience, and values |
|---|---|---|
| Need for information and identifying misconceptions about diagnosis and treatment | Pretreatment psychosocial assessment | Wide range of general and specific knowledge and experience |
| Acceptance of diagnosis | Individualized interventions according to client's needs | Disease and treatment |
| Disclosure issues and overcoming stigma and discrimination | Counseling of client and partner and family members | Drugs and alcohol and harm minimization |
| Identify strengths and resources | Emotional support | Mental health |
| Stability in client's circumstances of living, finances; relationships; drug and alcohol matters; and mental health | Therapeutic, motivational, supportive counseling; validation; normalizing of symptoms; reassurance; encouragement; attribution | Domestic violence |
| Balancing employment with treatment | Practical support | Grief and loss |
| Compliance and motivation to stay on treatment despite side effects | Referral for external services | Relationship dynamics |
| Managing side effects | Appropriate facilities and setting and contextually combined work of social work and rest of team | Knowledge about effects of chronic disease and stigmatized illness |
| Psychiatric and spiritual support | | Knowledge of legal system |
| Posttreatment support | | Nonjudgmental attitude |
| | | Interviewing and counseling techniques and skills |
| | | Knowledge regarding support services |
| | | Workload management |
| | | Multidisciplinary teamwork |
| | | Cultural awareness |
| | | Self-awareness |
| | | Sensitive, compassionate approach |
| | | Open-mindedness |
| | | Social justice |
| | | Balance between open and firm boundaries |
| | | Empathy, acceptance, respect |
| | | Practical approach |
| | | Empowerment |
| | | Flexibility |
| | | Continued learning, including from clients |

*Social Workers' Perceptions of Psychosocial Needs of Hepatitis C Positive Clients*

The five main themes pertaining to the psychosocial needs of their clients identified by the social workers were the need for information, the need for acceptance of the diagnosis together with disclosure issues, the need to help the client identify strengths and resources, the need to attend to drug and alcohol issues, and the need to assist clients to understand the implications of treatment and stay motivated to complete treatment by providing psychiatric support to clients during the treatment journey.

*Need for information.* Social workers saw the most prominent need of clients throughout all the stages of the treatment journey as the need for information and support from a variety of sources. They felt clients needed to obtain accurate information about the implications of the disease and its treatment before they began treatment. Such knowledge helped clients to make an informed decision about whether they wanted to have treatment at a certain point in time and helped prepare them for treatment on a practical and emotional level by, for example, establishing support networks and coping strategies. This is exemplified in the following comments:

At all stages, the most prominent need is information…. Good quality, reliable information is the key to develop support networks and coping strategies for themselves. (SW 10)

Clients need to have information and resources and we need to provide them with appropriate referrals, literature, information and give them an understanding about what treatment can be like; the impact on their lives; and we need to answer their questions. Some people feel wonderful about the opportunity to get well and others are terrified and worried and apprehensive about side effects and the impact on family, friends, and relationships. The people around them also need to have an idea about what potentially could happen. (SW 4)

*Acceptance of diagnosis and disclosure.* In accordance with Conrad et al. (2006), social workers reported that another aspect of the pretreatment needs of clients was their reaction to the diagnosis. Due to the many ways in which people have become infected, reactions to the diagnosis can be variable, and social workers need to be able to respond to and work with this range of reactions.

We get a range of people who have hepatitis C—from women who have contracted it through blood transfusions prior to 1989, possibly in childbirth; people from endemic backgrounds who have probably contracted it in their countries and people who are actively using drugs and people who have used drugs in their youth and now live pretty "normal" lives but who have held hepatitis C over from their experimentation with drugs in their youth. (SW 8)

The social workers remarked that decisions about disclosing hepatitis C status were closely related to acceptance of the diagnosis and the shame and fear that often accompany people's feelings about their diagnosis. Social workers recognized the importance of addressing the matter of disclosure with their clients by helping them to prepare what they were going to say to different people, as well as considering the level of disclosure they preferred. Social support for clients, avoidance of social isolation, and support at work were described as being important.

*Identifying strengths and resources.* Results indicated that social workers typically do a thorough client-focused pretreatment assessment to identify with the client strengths and resources that might be helpful during treatment as well as potential difficulties that could hinder treatment. This approach is in accordance with social work roles in the related field of HIV care as described by Stein (2004) and Teeters (2005) and general social work literature that emphasizes the importance of the family's social situation, family dynamics, and capacity to cope with the illness and treatment of the client (Gregorian, 2005). The social workers believed that a psychosocial assessment was of vital importance because it gave information about the person's life circumstances and support systems. It also provided an idea of the clients' understanding and acceptance of their diagnosis, what the impending treatment would mean to them, and their motivation to pursue treatment. Furthermore, the assessment revealed details about past and present mental health, together with drug and alcohol use, and brought these into perspective with treatment requirements.

Covering these topics opened up the opportunity for social workers to begin working therapeutically with unresolved issues in the client's history. Social workers felt that this approach helped to uncover misconceptions that the client might have regarding routes of hepatitis C transmission and provided opportunities for education on several aspects of the disease. In the process of discussing these topics, any psychological, emotional, or social barriers that might interfere with treatment and positive outcomes could be identified.

The pretreatment assessment was also regarded as helpful in identifying a person's ability to adjust to the anticipated difficulties of treatment. Hopwood et al. (Hopwood & Treloar, 2008; Hopwood, Treloar, & Redsull, 2006) suggested incorporating elements of the resilience theory, which acknowledges the client's skill and resourcefulness in solving his or her own problems during pretreatment assessments. Resilience theory (Van Breda, 2001) indicates that people use the same adaptive techniques and resources from past experiences to cope with any current challenges, such as hepatitis C treatment. These resources include the client's personal skills, spiritual beliefs, family support, community resources, welfare organizations, support groups, and professional assistance from counselors and psychologists who have helped them cope during difficult times in the past. Results indicated that the social workers used principles of resilience theory to some extent; however, a structured focus on strengths-based assessments (Epstein & Sharma, 1998) to effectively utilize the principles of resilience theory appeared to be lacking.

General stability in clients' lives with regard to living arrangements, employment or source of income, relationships, support systems, and emotional stability was regarded as especially important, so that they are "able to withstand rigors [of treatment]" (SW 2).

> They need to have social support. Treatment may affect relationships, so relationships need to be strong and stable. We need to look at disclosure, support systems [like] family, friends, and work. (SW 1)

The literature acknowledges the effect of clients' symptoms on relationships and highlights the need for support to partners and family members (Australian Government Department of Health and Aging, 2005; Dolan, 1997; Hopwood & Treloar, 2004; Hopwood, Treloar, & Redsull, 2006). The social workers in this study confirmed that relationships are often challenged by treatment and its side effects. Therefore, interventions that include couple and family work were typically undertaken to prevent relationships from disintegrating during treatment.

> I find it is very important to consult partners, family members, friends, because often these people pull back because they are not used to seeing their loved one like this. They are not used to seeing this angry person around and nothing they can do is quite right. It is about letting them know, normalizing all this stuff. (SW 6)

The timing of the treatment has been emphasized by participants as an important factor to consider and is in accordance with the opinion of Crofts, Dore, and Locarnini (2001), who proposed that along with the medical considerations, the psychosocial situation of a person with hepatitis C will influence the decision whether to commence antiviral therapy.

> It has to be the best opportunity for treatment…. We evaluate the appropriateness of treatment at this time and follow a team approach. (SW 4)

*Drug and alcohol issues.* In working with clients in the pretreatment phase, participants indicated that an important medical requirement was that the clients' alcohol intake was controlled and the client understood the importance of adhering to the alcohol limits while on treatment. Where injecting drug use was an issue, participants recommended that harm minimization principles be followed. The literature on hepatitis C treatment for injecting drug users suggests that people who inject drugs should not be automatically excluded from the opportunity to go on treatment, but encourages counseling for those clients about the risk of reinfection in ongoing injecting drug use (Crofts et al., 2001; Paylor & Orgel, 2004; Sylvestre & Zweben, 2007).

We do lots of harm minimization—harm minimization is a big thing that we use here, particularly if it is related to drug and alcohol. With regard to hep C, it is really important that their liver is kept healthy, so you are really just providing them with as much information that they need. We are not telling them to stop partying and having fun, we are just telling them how to manage it a bit better and how to reduce the risks and keep themselves healthier; how to do it safely. (SW 6)

*Understanding implications of treatment and maintaining motivation to complete treatment.* A phenomenon called *unrealistic optimism* (UO)—believing that they are less likely than others to experience treatment side effects—sometimes affects clients while preparing for treatment. Treloar and Hopwood (2008) reported examples of UO in clients' approach to preparing for and coping with hepatitis C treatment side effects. Examples include clients having a dismissive attitude about pretreatment information and regarding information about side effects as being irrelevant to them, being blasé about possibilities of side effects, and making judgments on future vulnerability based on past experience. These findings of Treloar and Hopwood are congruent with the remarks of the social workers who commented on how difficult it was to prepare clients for what to expect of treatment side effects, and clients perceived that they would be able to easily cope with them.

> People have a psychological need to understand what treatment would do and the side effects to be expected; and what we find is it is really difficult to convey side effects that people may expect to some people, and they misjudge what that might be. (SW 9)

The social workers described an extensive range of needs experienced by clients while on treatment. They also conveyed their commitment and enthusiasm to do "whatever it takes" to help meet the needs of their clients, including the need to help them stay motivated to complete treatment.

> Oh whatever it takes! Support, encouragement…. While on treatment, they [clients] need constant support. Clients experience a huge range of problems while on treatment. (SW 2)

> Dealing with the tiredness, the fatigue and the mood changes—all the side effects. Depending on how they react to the treatment, side effects can be quite prominent. Partners and support people often don't realize what effect it would have on them and implications it would have for them. Also [attending to] more practical things, [for example] looking at how structured their day is, whether they can cut back from certain activities, especially when they find it difficult to cope. It doesn't mean necessarily giving up work, but fitting it in a better way. (SW 9)

Therapeutic, motivational, and supportive counseling, as well as cognitive behavioral therapy techniques, were described by participants as helpful in keeping the client motivated to stay on treatment. Furthermore, a

385 task-centered, strengths-based, solution-focused therapy approach was reported to be useful in the challenging task of helping clients to complete treatment. In accordance with resilience theory, it is valuable to acknowledge the clients' skills and resourcefulness in
390 solving their own problems and to view each person as the master of his or her life (Hopwood & Treloar, 2008). Conveying respect for the person and a belief that he or she can get through whatever difficulty he or she is facing at the moment can also empower the cli-
395 ent to feel more capable of handling the situation than he or she did before. This concept ties in with the technique of appraisal support, which includes affirmation as described by Allen (1998).

Validation and normalizing of symptoms were de-
400 scribed by social workers as being helpful to clients. Reinforcing the fact that it was the medication that was causing the side effect symptoms, thus separating the person from the medication, was deemed appropriate. Moreover, reminding clients that side effects are tem-
405 porary, part of the treatment, and will pass were outlined as helpful because these actions reinforced the time-limited nature of the treatment experience. Finally, reassuring clients that they were in good medical hands was regarded as beneficial to helping clients
410 develop confidence in the treatment team.

> [The client needs] one or more individuals that they can lean on when they feel physically or emotionally unwell…emotional support and practical…they need to feel comfortable with the team…they need to feel able to talk
> 415 about anything of concern to them and they need to know that if anything goes wrong with them, they are in good medical hands. (SW 5)

Engaging the client as a partner in the planning process within a supportive framework was described
420 by social workers as being an effective approach. When the client was engaged as a partner in the process, the focus changed from dictating to the client what to do and placing responsibility on the client to comply (Compton & Galaway, 1979; Ehsani et al., 2006;
425 Moore, 2004).

> Side effects can have a big effect on their home life and work life, and they may need counseling around that. Clients may tell me they don't have any patience any more—then I need to normalize it and work out some
> 430 strategies with them about things like anger management, sleep management. (SW 8)

Acknowledging the value of spiritual support was regarded as an important aspect to include in discussions where the client regards spirituality as important.
435 Spiritual beliefs and practices are increasingly being recognized as relevant to treatment and care of clients (Benson, 1998; Dossey, 1993; Furman, Benson, Grimwood, & Canda, 2004).

> There is another level of client discussion that sometimes
> 440 goes into spiritual, or what is God—more existentialist issues—so that is important to include that sort of discus-

sion if that is the client's need. I sometimes ask them what helps them through difficult times as a support, for some it [spiritual support] is a core part of their being. I
445 think it is quite fundamental and important to bring that in. (SW 1)

*Psychiatric support.* Psychiatric side effects to treatment are well documented and confirmed by social worker participants in this study. According to Raw-
450 storne, Treloar, and Richters (2005), the occurrence of mood disorders during treatment was the most common reason given for discontinuation of interferon-based treatment and emphasized the importance of professional support. The most common psychiatric side ef-
455 fects reported are symptoms of depression, anxiety, irritability, anger, and emotional sensitivity (Ehsani et al., 2006; Monji, Yoshida, Tashiro, Hayashi, & Tashiro, 1998).

> Coping with depression; coping with mental health stuff.
> 460 Mental health problems are huge while people are on treatment, I find. Again, the stigma and shame [factors] are huge and weigh down on them very much, you know, their self-worth and self-esteem are deeply affected, but also the side effects of the treatment [are] quite horren-
> 465 dous, so that again can contribute to depression—for instance, when they have lack of sleep, or lack of appetite, not being able to eat, their hair starts falling out; I mean it is quite a serious form of medication that they are taking. (SW 6)

470 Participants indicated that some treatment centers were well supplied with psychiatric support and some were undersupplied. Where a dedicated psychiatric support service was in place for the hepatitis C clients, it ensured continuation of care for the clients and the
475 possibility of being seen quickly by a psychiatrist when needed. It was clear from the responses of the participants that where there was a lack of clear pathways to psychiatric consultation, it hampered the service to the clients and caused frustration for the social workers
480 and other team members as well as for the clients on treatment.

The findings suggest that clients often gained wider benefits of treatment, regardless of whether they cleared the virus or not. The significance of having
485 completed the program was broached by participants, together with the acknowledgment that having done the program was "a big effort" and achievement for the patient (SW 9). It seemed that for some patients the end of treatment also signified a closure of their past ex-
490 periences, which might include a history of drug use. The end of treatment signified a "new beginning" for these patients (SW 9). However, when clients had not cleared the virus, a great deal of debriefing and support was needed from social workers to help clients to come
495 to terms with the disappointment and remind them of the other benefits of treatment, like strengthening their liver and lowering the viral load, so that they did not feel they went through it "for nothing." (SW 8)

500 They need ongoing contact with the team, follow-up support—especially if they did not clear the virus, they need to know this is not the end of the world. Support from the hepatitis C team is imperative. (SW 5)

*Social Work Strategies*

505 Results indicated that social workers used a variety of strategies to respond to the identified needs of their patients and ensure their needs were being met. The social workers indicated that interventions were individualized according to the needs of the client. Coun-
510 seling of clients and their partners and family members seemed to be a core function of the social worker in hepatitis C treatment centers. The literature (Clare, 2001; Fook, 2002) and the results of this study indicated that the setting of the treatment clinic influences the parameters of the service. The therapeutic value of appropriate space in the hepatitis C setting (e.g., coun-
515 seling rooms for interview purposes) was remarked on by the social workers. They regarded the facilities available to them as an important determinant that could, if favorable, enhance the therapeutic engagement enjoyment of their work.

520 I see my clients in a room in the medical outpatients department of the hospital. It is not adequate. The room is designed for medical consultation. It is small, with medical paraphernalia, a bed, and looks clinical…does not allow for needs of families with children…designed for
525 medical consultations, not for psychosocial consultations. I don't like it, but I have no choice. (SW 5)

I see my clients here, in my own office. I love my office. It is comfortable, and private, and adequate for my needs. There is a great reception facility, and it is close to other
530 [staff] offices. (SW 8)

Beyond being influenced by the setting, Fook (2002) emphasized that social workers have to strive to influence their environments by challenging and resisting different aspects of the contexts within which they
535 work. In this study, the ways the social workers influenced the contexts within which they worked were not examined, but the fact that they typically expressed the importance of concepts such as social justice, empowerment, and ensuring access to services for minority
540 groups indicates that they saw the importance of getting involved in influencing the settings where they work. However, further research would be needed to articulate the strategies used to bring these concepts into a treatment service where the biomedical and "pa-
545 thology" (Jones, 2003, p. 5) are the focus for service users, like hepatitis C clients, who often have a history of illegal and marginalized activity.

[The previous social worker was] a strong advocate, and she did a lot to ensure that people have access to treat-
550 ment. It is about access and not setting people up to fail, ensuring that people with mental health issues or drug and alcohol issues have access to treatment. The focus is on not turning people away, but on access; not setting people up for failure, but explaining to them and asking
555 "Would you like to come back in 6 months?" But it is

that stuff that once a client is on; we are all a team here and need to get the client through. (SW 7)

*Multidisciplinary Teamwork*

All the social workers strongly expressed the im-
560 portance of a multidisciplinary team approach to ensure a holistic approach to client care. Words and phrases like *imperative, vital, best possible way, paramount, essential, absolutely necessary, can't have hepatitis C treatment without a multidisciplinary team,* and *it*
565 *would be a disservice to the clients on treatment not to have a multidisciplinary team approach* were used to describe how strongly the participants felt about its importance. The point was made that the social worker assists the client to get through treatment and it is an important part of the care process to introduce the ser-
570 vice of the social worker early in the treatment process.

The value of synergy among team members was highlighted when the issue of availability and time of staff members to see the clients was explored. It be-came clear from the social workers' responses that the
575 doctors did not have the time to address the psychosocial needs of clients on treatment and, therefore, it was important to have other team members who were more flexible in their availability see people on a regular and irregular basis and ensure that the client was supported
580 in a range of ways:

You can't have hepatitis C treatment without a multidisciplinary team. A client usually has multiple issues that verge on hepatitis C, and even if it is just the hepatitis C, there are a lot of side effects that can take place that can't
585 be solely attended to by the doctor, and the doctor is not available all the time. Therefore, it is important to have social workers and nurses and other team members who are more flexible in their times and can see people on a regular basis. (SW 9)

590 It is the best possible way of supporting patients through treatment if you have a professional range where everyone respects each other's professional value base and knowledge. Then you bring together the widest range of services available to the client. (SW 5)

595 The importance of maintaining a psychosocial focus, in the midst of the biomedical model, was broached by the social workers.

It impacts on how we deliver our services; acknowledging that social issues are just as important as medical is-
600 sues. It impacts greatly on the process by assessing people initially and planning their progression through treatment and follow up. Outcome is influenced by how we interact with our clients and come out with support networks, so that they come out with work and relationships
605 still intact. You don't want them to be healthy but with no work left, no family left, etc. They would be worse off then. (SW 9)

Clare (2001) and Fook (2002) emphasized the contextual and combined nature of the work of social
610 workers as part of teams in organizations. Participants noted that by attending to the psychosocial aspects of their clients' lives, the rest of the team valued the input

615 of the social worker, was supported, and felt reassured that those aspects had been dealt with. It was also indicated that the role of the social worker contributes in terms of ensuring continuation of client care and assisting clients through the treatment process so that clients do not give up and terminate treatment prematurely.

620 However, in spite of the acknowledgment of the importance of the social work role on the team, this was not always demonstrated in terms of funding for social work positions. Lack of sufficient funding was reported to be a barrier to expanding the services of the social worker or to appointing more social workers.

625 Greater funding to increase social work involvement in the hepatitis C field is necessary for expanding services to the hepatitis C client group.

*Knowledge, Experience, and Value Basis of Social Workers*

The social work participants expressed the belief that social workers in hepatitis C treatment centers

630 need a wide range of general and specific knowledge and experience to be effective in the role due to the complex needs of the client group and the issues they face. In accordance with Fook's (2002) views on transferability of knowledge and experience for application

635 in different situations or contexts, social work participants regarded previous social work experience as valuable. The comments of SW 5 about whether a hepatitis C social work position is suitable for a new graduate summed up the various issues raised:

640 Not a position for a new graduate, they would struggle. Even as a mature graduate to have come straight from university in a job like this, you would not be able to bring with you the richness of social work experience that you get from working in social work. The client group

645 can be quite demanding at times, they have special needs. Their needs can be complex in psychosocial ways, and because of their life experience, they obviously have often been high risk takers in their lives and they have an expectation to setting themselves up for failure and you

650 have to change their outlook, and a new graduate is in no way able to deal with that…to establish rapport with clients straight away, you have to know what you do, not learning to do that. This position would not accommodate that. I think a new graduate would struggle to accommo-

655 date the needs of this client group, but also to manage the workload that comes with a client load in this setting. The social worker works as part of the multidisciplinary team…having the self-confidence to be part of a professional team and you need to give a professional opinion

660 and weight is placed upon that opinion and you need to be able to give and substantiate your opinion. I don't think a new graduate would have the self-confidence to do that. (SW 5)

There was one contradictory point of view where

665 the right person with the appropriate values, receiving the appropriate support, was regarded as more important than professional experience.

The social workers repeatedly raised the importance of having an appropriate professional attitude and value

670 base for the position. As demonstrated by a large body of research on the subject (Anti-Discrimination Board of New South Wales, 2001; Conrad et al., 2006; Fraser & Treloar, 2006; Hopwood & Treloar, 2003; Zigmund et al., 2003), hepatitis C is a highly stigmatized disease

675 with discrimination seen in both the general public and health care workers. This makes self-awareness and a nonjudgmental attitude important qualities for all those who work with people who have hepatitis C. Furthermore, a sensitive, compassionate approach combined

680 with empathy, acceptance, and respect, including respect of life path and learning pace, were regarded as important qualities for social workers.

Being able to be respectful of clients' background from cultural, racial, and ethnic perspectives and their outlook

685 on life and you need to make a clear decision to not judge them on their lifestyle choices. The choices they make about what they do with their lives lie with them. They still have the right to treatment. Clients make the decision whether they continue to damage their liver by drinking

690 and doing drugs. You can only inform them. You cannot impose your will on them. By doing it, you reinforce the medical approach. (SW 5)

The social workers raised the value of the importance of continued learning, including from their cli-

695 ents, and building up a good knowledge base "in order to feel comfortable in one's own professional knowledge." (SW 5) The social workers in this study generally regarded supervision as helpful, but not always available. Sometimes informal peer support and team

700 review meetings aided in providing professional support in addition to formal supervision.

**Discussion**

This study on the professional activities and roles of social workers in hepatitis C treatment has high-

705 lighted a number of specific findings and recommendations for the field. First, in spite of the acknowledgment of the importance of the social work role on the multidisciplinary treatment team, it was clear that the significance of the role was not confirmed in terms of funding for social work positions. The lack of sufficient fund-

710 ing resulted in limited service delivery to the hepatitis C client group. Additional funding would increase the availability of social work services in the clinics and make time available for other health promotion activities to increase knowledge and combat stigma around

715 the disease. It is recommended that social workers keep statistics of their activities and document their work to advocate for increased resources for social work positions. It is also recommended that social workers raise the profile of hepatitis C, related psychosocial issues,

720 and the input of the social worker in this context.

The results indicated the importance of ongoing learning and professional development for social workers in hepatitis C treatment clinics. The social work participants recommended that training to improve

725 social workers' readiness for a hepatitis C treatment

position could also be used as supervision topics and as the basis for in-service training or professional staff development programs for social workers. A general understanding of the psychosocial issues of disease,
730 particularly because it is a stigmatized disease, and the issues that clients face was considered an important foundation for effective social work. Similarly, the development of advanced counseling skills to help clients in resolving their health-related issues and their
735 personal and interpersonal issues was pointed out. The value of teamwork to provide a holistic service to the client was highlighted.

### Limitations of the Study

The major limitation of the study was the small sample size drawn from an urban geographical area in
740 Australia. Despite this limitation, the sample represented two thirds of social workers employed in hepatitis C treatment clinics in New South Wales. The findings appear to be applicable to other hepatitis C treatment centers because the data approached theoretical
745 saturation and the main themes aligned with the literature on the experience of social work practice in other settings as well as those who treat hepatitis C.

### Conclusion

More research into effective strategies to assist in maintaining clients on treatment might help to inform
750 effective services in this challenging aspect of social workers' roles. Research to identify the benefits and less positive outcomes of treatment for nonresponders to treatment might guide social workers in helping clients with their posttreatment needs. A more focused
755 study on the psychiatric services that are available, referral pathways, and barriers to utilization of existing psychiatric services is recommended to ascertain whether more services are, in fact, needed or whether existing services can be used more effectively.
760 Although it is anticipated that the findings of this study could be applied in other treatment settings (e.g., drug and alcohol centers, needle syringe programs, prisons, and general practitioner practices), this possibility has not been specifically researched. Given the
765 direct relationship between hepatitis C and these areas of service, this study also highlights the need for further research about the nature and impact of social work intervention on hepatitis C positive clients who are served by these services. Central to these areas of
770 research is exploration of effective interventions that ensure professional practice based on the principles of inclusion, social justice, equitability of access, and empowerment for marginalized groups.

### References

Allen, F. (1998). *Health psychology: Theory and practice.* St. Leonards, Australia: Allen & Unwin.

Anti-Discrimination Board of New South Wales. (2001). *C change: Report of the enquiry into hepatitis C-related discrimination.* Sydney, Australia: Author.

Australian Government Department of Health and Aging. (2005). *National hepatitis C strategy 2005–2008* (Pub. Approval No. 3642[JN9005]). Sydney: Author.

Benson, H. (1998, July). The faith factor: The health benefits of spirituality. *The Shambhala Sun.* Retrieved from http://www.imagery4relaxation.com/articles-benson.htm

Clare, B. (2001). One practitioner's reflections on the reconstruction and reconceptualisation of social work: A response to McDonald and Jones and colleagues. *Australian Social Work, 54*(1), 103–107.

Compton, B. R., & Galaway, B. (1979). *Social work processes.* Homewood, IL: Dorsey.

Conrad, S., Garrett, L. E., Cooksley, W., Graham, E., Dunne, M. M. P., & MacDonald, G. A. (2006). Living with chronic hepatitis C means "You just haven't got a normal life any more." *Chronic Illness, 2*, 121–131.

Crofts, N., Dore, G., & Locarnini, S. (Eds.). (2001). *Hepatitis C: An Australian perspective.* Melbourne, Australia: IP Communications.

Dolan, M. (1997). *The hepatitis C handbook.* London, UK: Catalyst Press.

Dore, G., Law, N. G., MacDonald, M., & Kaldor, J. (2003). Epidemiology of hepatitis C virus infection in Australia. *Journal of Clinical Virology, 26,* 171–184.

Dossey, L. (1993). *Healing words: The power of prayer and the practice of medicine.* San Francisco, CA: Harper. Retrieved from http://www.spiritualityandpractice.com/teachers/

Ehsani, J. P., Vu, T., & Karvelas, M. (2006). Exploring the need for hepatology nurses and allied health professionals in Victorian liver clinics. *Australian Health Review, 30,* 211–218.

Ell, K., & Northern, H. (1990). *Family social work and health care.* Hawthorne, NY: Aldine de Gruyter.

Epstein, M. H., & Sharma, J. M. (1998). *Behavioural and Emotional Rating Scale: A strength-based approach to assessment.* Austin, TX: PRO-ED. Retrieved from http://cecp.ait.org/interact/expertonline/strength/transition8.asp

Fook, J. (2002). *Social work—Critical theory and practice.* London, UK: Sage.

Fraser, S., & Treloar, C. (2006, June). "Spoiled identity" in hepatitis C infection: The binary logic of despair. *Critical Public Health, 16,* 99–110.

Furman, L. D., Benson, P. W., Grimwood, C., & Canda, E. (2004). Religion and spirituality in social work education and direct practice at the millennium: A survey of UK social workers. *British Journal of Social Work, 34,* 767–792.

Giles, R., Gould, S., Hart, C., & Swancott, J. (2007). Clinical priorities: Strengthening social work practice in health. *Australian Social Work, 60,* 147–165.

Gregorian, C. (2005). A career in hospital social work: Do you have what it takes? *Social Work in Health Care, 40*(3), 1–14.

Hopwood, M., & Treloar, C. (2003). *The 3D project, diagnosis disclosure, discrimination and living with hepatitis C.* Sydney, Australia: National centre in HIV Social Research, The University of New South Wales.

Hopwood, M., & Treloar, C. (2004). Receiving a hepatitis C positive diagnosis. *Internal Medicine Journal, 34,* 526–532.

Hopwood, M., & Treloar, C. (2008). Resilient coping: Applying adaptive responses to prior adversity during treatment for hepatitis C infection. *Journal of Health Psychology, 13*(1), 17–27.

Hopwood, M., Treloar, C., & Bryant, J. (2006). Hepatitis C and injecting-related discrimination within health care in New South Wales, Australia. *Drugs: Education, Prevention & Policy, 13,* 61–75.

Hopwood, M., Treloar, C., & Redsull, L. (2006). Experiences of hepatitis C treatment and its management—What some patients and health professionals say (Monograph No. 4/2006). Sydney, Australia: National Centre in HIV Social Research.

Jones, K. (2003). *Health and human behaviour.* Melbourne, Australia: Oxford University Press.

Mellor, M. J., & Lindeman, D. (1998). The role of the social worker in interdisciplinary geriatric teams. *Journal of Gerontological Social Work, 30*(3–4), 3–7.

Ministerial Advisory Committee on AIDS Sexual Health and Hepatitis C Sub-Committee. (2006). *Annual report.* Canberra, Australia: Commonwealth Department of Health & Ageing Ministerial Advisory Committee on AIDS, Sexual Health and Hepatitis, and the Australian Population Health Development Principal Committee. Retrieved from http://www.health.gov.au

Monji, A. K., Yoshida, I., Tashiro, K., Hayashi, Y., & Tashiro, N. (1998). A case of persistent manic-depressive illness induced by interferon-alpha in the treatment of chronic hepatitis C [Letter]. *Psychosomatics, 39,* 562–564.

Moore, D. (2004). Governing street-based injecting drug users: A critique of heroin overdose prevention in Australia. *Social Science and Medicine, 59,* 1547–1557.

National Centre in HIV Epidemiology and Clinical Research. (2009). *National surveillance report.* Sydney, Australia: The University of New South Wales.

Paylor, I., & Orgel, M. (2004). Sleepwalking through an epidemic—Why social work should wake up to the threat of hepatitis C. *British Journal of Social Work, 34,* 907–914.

Rawstorne, P., Treloar, C., & Richters, J. (Eds.). (2005). Annual report of behaviour 2005: HIV/AIDS, hepatitis and sexually transmissible infections in Australia. Sydney, Australia: National Centre in HIV Social Research, University of New South Wales.

Rier, D., & Indyk, D. (2006). Flexible rigidity: Supporting HIV treatment adherence in a rapidly changing treatment environment. *Social Work in Health Care, 42,* 133–150.

Sievert, W. (2003). Antiviral therapy for chronic hepatitis. *Australian Family Physician, 32*, 826–832.

Stein, G. L. (2004, February). *Social worker roles in HIV care*. Paper presented at OSI Public Health Seminars, Kiev, Ukraine.

Sylvestre, D. L., & Zweben, J. E. (2007). Integrating HCV services for drug users: A model to improve engagement and outcomes (Special issue). *The International Journal of Drug Policy, 18*(5).

Teeters, C. (2005). *HIV/AIDS–How social workers help*. New York, NY: Healthology, Inc. Retrieved from http://www.helpstartshere.org/health_and_wellness/hiv/aids/how_social-workers-help

Treloar, C., & Hopwood, M. (2008). "Look, I'm fit, I'm positive and I'll be all right, thank you very much": Coping with hepatitis C treatment and unrealistic optimism. *Psychology, Health & Medicine, 13*, 360–366.

Van Breda, A. D. (2001). *Resilience theory: A literature review*. Pretoria, South Africa: South African Military Health Service. Retrieved from http://www.vanbreda.org/adrian/resilience.htm

Zigmund, S., Ho, E. Y., Masuda, M., Ippolito, L., & LaBrecque, D. R. (2003). "They treated me like a leper": Stigmatization and the quality of life of patients with hepatitis C. *Journal of General Internal Medicine, 18*, 835–844.

**Acknowledgments**: The author would like to acknowledge the Consortium for Social and Policy Research on HIV, Hepatitis C and Related Diseases and the National Centre in HIV Social Research for the scholarship awarded to me; the Hepatitis C council of New South Wales, Australia; my supervisor, Professor Carla Treloar at the National Centre for HIV Social Research, University of New South Wales; and my co-supervisor, Dr. Elizabeth Fernandez from the School of Social Work, University of New South Wales.

**Address correspondence to**: Marlize Mouton, Department of Gastroenterology, Liverpool Hospital, Liverpool, NSW 1871, Australia. E-mail: marlize.mouton@sswahs.nsw.gov.au

# Exercise for Article 30

## Factual Questions

1. Did the researcher find an abundance of literature on the role of the social worker in hepatitis treatment?

2. Were the interviews semistructured?

3. How many participants were male?

4. Was written consent obtained from each participant?

5. Were the transcriptions checked for accuracy?

## Questions for Discussion

6. Is it important to know that ethics approval was obtained? Explain. (See lines 112–115.)

7. Speculate on the meaning of the term *purposeful sampling*. (See lines 115–118.)

8. In your opinion, how important is the information in Table 1? Explain.

9. In your opinion, is the method of data analysis described in sufficient detail? Explain. (See lines 136–147.)

10. Do the quotations in the Results section help you understand the results? Explain. (See lines 148–702.)

11. Are any of the results especially surprising? Explain. (See lines 148–702.)

12. Do you agree with the researcher's statement of limitations? Explain. (See lines 739–748.)

## Quality Ratings

Directions: Indicate your level of agreement with each of the following statements by circling a number from 5 for strongly agree (SA) to 1 for strongly disagree (SD). If you believe an item is not applicable to this research article, leave it blank. Be prepared to explain your ratings. When responding to criteria A and B, keep in mind that brief titles and abstracts are conventional in published research.

A. The title of the article is appropriate.

SA    5    4    3    2    1    SD

B. The abstract provides an effective overview of the research article.

SA    5    4    3    2    1    SD

C. The introduction establishes the importance of the study.

SA    5    4    3    2    1    SD

D. The literature review establishes the context for the study.

SA    5    4    3    2    1    SD

E. The research purpose, question, or hypothesis is clearly stated.

SA    5    4    3    2    1    SD

F. The method of sampling is sound.

SA    5    4    3    2    1    SD

G. Relevant demographics (for example, age, gender, and ethnicity) are described.

SA    5    4    3    2    1    SD

H. Measurement procedures are adequate.

SA    5    4    3    2    1    SD

I. All procedures have been described in sufficient detail to permit a replication of the study.

SA    5    4    3    2    1    SD

J. The participants have been adequately protected from potential harm.

SA    5    4    3    2    1    SD

K. The results are clearly described.

SA    5    4    3    2    1    SD

L.   The discussion/conclusion is appropriate.

SA   5   4   3   2   1   SD

M.   Despite any flaws, the report is worthy of publication.

SA   5   4   3   2   1   SD

# Article 31

# Exploring Young Adults' Perspectives on Communication With Aunts

LAURA L. ELLINGSON
Santa Clara University

PATRICIA J. SOTIRIN
Michigan Technological University

ABSTRACT. Women are typically studied as daughters, sisters, mothers, or grandmothers. However, many, if not most, women are also aunts. In this study, we offer a preliminary exploration of the meaning of aunts as familial figures. We collected 70 nieces' and nephews' written accounts of their aunts. Thematic analysis of these accounts revealed nine themes, which were divided into two categories. The first category represented the role of the aunt as a teacher, role model, confidante, savvy peer, and second mother. The second category represented the practices of aunting: gifts/treats, maintaining family connections, encouragement, and nonengagement. Our analysis illuminates important aspects of aunts in family schema and kin keeping.

From *Journal of Social and Personal Relationships*, 23, 483–501.

Despite the tremendous proliferation in family forms, the popular image associated with "the family" is still overwhelmingly a heterosexual nuclear family with a husband, wife, and children (Garey & Hansen,
5  1998). Many family communication researchers, particularly feminists, are committed to honoring a plurality of family forms and relationships, for both ideological and pragmatic reasons because families that deviate from the idealized nuclear norm outnumber supposedly
10 normative families (Coontz, 2000). Kinship resources are important to many families, yet these resources have been understudied by family researchers (Johnson, 2000). Anecdotal evidence of the significance of kin exists, but modern studies demonstrate a decline
15 both in families' involvement with, and scholarly interest in, kinship ties (Johnson, 2000). We know little about the relationship between aunts and their nieces/nephews. Aunts are not nuclear family members, but neither are they obscure, distant relations.
20 They are typically a sibling from a parent's immediate family of origin. Traeder and Bennett (1998), in their popular tribute, claim that aunts are a crucial resource for maintaining and enriching family and community life, and provide anecdotal evidence of the importance
25 of aunts in family relations in family stories and everyday conversation.

Women are typically studied by family communication researchers as daughters, sisters, mothers, or grandmothers. Yet many, if not most, women in these
30 roles are also aunts. In this study, we explore the meaning of aunts as extended kin. We contend that the meanings of aunting have been ignored in favor of framing motherhood as women's essential role (e.g., O'Reilly & Abbey, 2000; Peington, 2004). As feminist
35 researchers, we seek not to idealize aunts or to essentialize them within a single, fixed identity. Instead, we intend to recognize the complexities of the roles aunts may play in their nieces' and nephews' lives. Our goal is to uncover patterns among nieces' and nephews'
40 experiences of relating to their aunts. We frame our thematic analysis by first offering a theoretical perspective on family communication and reviewing literature on kinship and kin keeping.

### Theoretical Perspective

The traditional nuclear family model of family
45 communication is "losing its ecological validity" due to the proliferation of alternative family forms in modern society (Koerner & Fitzpatrick, 2002, p. 71). Koerner and Fitzpatrick suggest that theories of family communication "increasingly define family as a group of inti-
50 mates who generate a sense of home and group identity and who experience a shared history and a shared future" (p. 71). Transactional definitions are useful because they expand the boundaries of the family and therefore better reflect the tremendous variation in how
55 families define themselves (Noller & Fitzpatrick, 1993). Jorgenson (1989) positions the family "as a system of relations that comes about as individuals define those relations in their everyday communication with another" (p. 28). Boundaries between households in
60 extended kin networks are porous and negotiable, rather than fixed or rule bound (Wellman, 1998). Hence, extended families may be understood as constituted through their communication as they mutually negotiate relationship norms. Our intention in this
65 study was to delineate the organized knowledge structures, or schemas, that nieces and nephews have for aunts. Koerner and Fitzpatrick (2002) proposed a theory of family communication that identified a hierarchy of relational schemas used by family members to inter-

70 pret their communication with other family members. Relational schemas consist of declarative and procedural knowledge and interpersonal scripts. Such schemas include information and beliefs concerning: "Intimacy, individuality, affection, external factors, conver-
75 sation orientation, and conformity orientation" (p. 88). Individuals cognitively process interactions with other family members by drawing upon relationship-specific schemas first (e.g., a sister's relationship to her younger brother). If a schema does not provide the in-
80 formation or insights necessary to interpret or address the family member's behavior or to form an appropriate response, the person then draws upon more general family relationship schemas. If family relationship schemas also prove insufficient, then an individual
85 family member draws upon general social schemas regarding relationships for information. It follows, then, that when nieces and nephews communicate with aunts and with others about aunts, they both rely on and construct schemas for who aunts are and how they
90 behave. These schemas develop through communication and, in turn, influence subsequent communication. Because knowledge contained in family relationship schemas influences family communication, it is imperative to understand such knowledge (Koerner &
95 Fitzpatrick, 2002).

Researchers suggested that the concept of family scripts also is helpful in exploring understanding of kinship roles and relationships. Family scripts "are mental representations that guide the role performance
100 of family members within and across contexts" (Stack & Burton, 1998, p. 408). In extended kin relationships, "kin-scripts" designate who is obligated or entitled within a particular network to perform types of kin-work tasks, when such tasks should be performed (kin-
105 time), and how the process of assigning kin-work should be handled (kin-scription) (Stack & Burton, 1998). We posit that underlying their extended family's kin-scripts, people have relationship schemas regarding the norms and expectations of aunts, as well as
110 relationship-specific schema for particular aunts. Moreover, there are social level messages in the dominant U.S. culture about what it means to be or have an aunt (Sotirin & Ellingson, in press). Hence, perceived cultural norms will influence aunts' and
115 nieces'/nephews' schema for family communication (Koerner & Fitzpatrick, 2002).

## Aunts and Kinship

### Kinship and Kin Keeping

Garey and Hansen (1998) define kinship as a "system of rights and responsibilities between particular categories of people...'kinship' refers not only to bio-
120 logical or legal connections between people but also to particular positions in a network of relationships" (p. xviii). Cultures vary in the norms for determining who counts as kin, in the rights and responsibilities accorded to various types of kin, and in the degree to

125 which kinship association is voluntary (Wellman, 1998). Kinship networks may also change over time (Garey & Hansen, 1998). Aunts are part of the extended kinship network. Aunts can be either "consanguineal" kin (related biologically) or "affinal" (related
130 through marriage). In some families "fictive" kin are created by inducting people not biologically related into a network of kinship, such as calling one's mother's best friend "aunt" (Stack, 1974).

Researchers have demonstrated that women are the
135 primary "kin keepers" in extended families (Dill, 1998). This suggests the importance of aunts in establishing and maintaining relational bonds with nieces and nephews (Arliss, 1994) and implies that kin keeping is likely part of relationship-type schemas for aunts.
140 Kin keeping has been traditionally associated with feminine roles and remains largely the province of women, despite changing gender roles (Garey & Hansen, 1998). Feminist scholars rendered visible the unpaid work of women—including kin keeping—and
145 acknowledged its importance within a capitalist society that values only paid labor (di Leonardo, 1998). Moreover, feminists have reclaimed women's focus on kin networks as potential sources of personal satisfaction, empowerment, and, at times, vital material and emo-
150 tional resources (Gerstel & Gallagher, 1993). Juggled beside paid employment, housework, and child care, *kin work* involves "the collective labor expected of family centered networks across households and within them" (Stack & Burton, 1998, p. 408). Kin work in-
155 cludes such activities as child and dependent care, wage and nonwage labor, relationship-maintaining communication, and tasks such as "visits, letters, telephone calls, presents, and cards to kin; the organization of holiday gatherings; the creation and maintenance of
160 quasi-kin relations" (di Leonardo, 1998, p. 420). Leach and Braithwaite (1996) found that kin keeping communication has five primary outcomes: providing information, facilitating rituals, providing assistance, maintaining family relationships, and continuing a previous kin
165 keeper's work.

Kin keepers are most likely to be mothers, aunts, or grandmothers (Leach & Braithwaite, 1996); and of course, mothers and grandmothers are also likely to be aunts within kinship networks. Many kinship studies
170 discuss mothers, grandmothers, and sisters without considering aunting. Rather, kin work is framed in terms of sisterhood or motherhood (e.g., di Leonardo, 1998). Thus the experience and meaning of an aunt's role is implied more than specified in research. Re-
175 search on communication among adult siblings and their spouses implicitly addresses communication with aunts when they focus on women's roles and sister relations (e.g., Cicirelli & Nussbaum, 1989). Given that sibling relationships among parents affect children's
180 perceptions of their relatives, aunts who are emotionally close to a child's parents are likely to be perceived as more integral in the child's experiences of family

185 life. At the same time, Troll (1985, as cited in Arliss, 1994) points out that conflicts among adult siblings obligate husbands and wives to distance themselves from their siblings, and such "family feuds" negatively impact relationships within the extended family including aunts, nieces, and nephews. Further, adult sisters who may have gone separate ways often become closer

190 as they begin to follow parallel paths in life (marriage, children), providing material and emotional support for each other and renewing familial bonds (Arliss, 1994). Cicirelli and Nussbaum (1989) suggest that the association of women with feminine nurturing and expressive-

195 ness leads family members to turn to their sisters for support and aid as adults. This observation implies both the likelihood that aunts will be closer to their nieces and nephews if aunts and mothers find themselves on parallel life paths and that aunts may provide emotional

200 and material support not only for their sisters and other adult family members but for their nieces and nephews as well. Sisters may work to make their respective children close to each other as cousins (di Leonardo, 1998).

205 Moreover, aunting schemas are likely to reflect other culturally significant female figures. The significance of "othermothers" (Collins, 2000) and "godmothers" in Black, Latino, and Native American childrearing practices has been recognized and even cele-

210 brated and promoted as a model for White, mainstream American culture (see Clinton, 1996). Godmothers also are particularly important in Catholic communities (e.g., Italian-Americans, see di Leonardo, 1984; Mexican-Americans, see Falicov & Karrer, 1980), whose

215 members choose godparents for their child as a crucial aspect of religious and cultural practice (Sault, 2001). Of course, "othermothers" and "godmothers" may or may not overlap the aunt, so despite the increased, often feminist-inspired, attention to such practices, there

220 is not an explicit focus on aunts and aunting per se in this research. So although we may know where aunts are and that they are important within extended family configurations, we do not know much about how they communicatively enact those locations.

225 One topic in family communication where aunts are explicitly identified are studies of extended family configurations. Studies of extended family roles and practices generally focus on the following three themes: the extended family as a historically, racially, or ethnically

230 identified familial form (the African American urban family, the traditional Latino family, or the immigrant Asian family; e.g., Stack, 1974); mapping extended family configurations (e.g., Galvin, Bylund, & Brommel, 2003) or family histories (e.g., Halsted, 1993); and

235 the extended family as threatened by contemporary patterns of mobility, divorce, and nonfamilial commitments and identifications (Stone, 2000). These themes overshadow the particular communication characteristics and functions (as they constitute relationship-type

240 schemas) of aunt-niece/nephew relationships.

Other types of kinship studies in which aunts appear are kinship foster care, kinship networks for immigrants, and family histories, all of which constitute kin keeping and thus are likely to be reflected in stu-

245 dents' relationship schema for aunts. Studies of kinship foster care show that aunts are second only to grandmothers in numbers of kin who function voluntarily (although increasingly regulated and, in some states, compensated) as foster caregivers for children removed

250 from their parents' custody (Davidson, 1997; Thorton, 1991). Research also explores the importance of kinship networks for new immigrants needing financial and social support. For instance, aunts featured prominently in the accounts of Mexican migrant women as

255 they relocated, found work, and established households (Bastida, 2001). Finally, aunts often figure prominently in family stories (Wilmot, 1995), perhaps because family culture and lore are preserved and promulgated primarily by women (Stone, 2000). Stone holds that

260 family stories define the family, providing rules for its enactment, identities for its members, and a shared memory and view of family and the world. For example, women report learning "commonplace" wisdom about relating to men from older women relatives, in-

265 cluding aunts (Romberger, 1986).

Our goal in this project is to follow up on the allusions to the aunt in family scholarship by describing nieces' and nephews' family relational schemas for aunts. If kinship is constituted through communication

270 rather than through biological and legal ties (Koerner & Fitzpatrick, 2002), then exploring how aunts are constructed in nieces' and nephews' communication is a good starting point for understanding the meaning of aunts in families. Further, this inquiry may shed light

275 on the issue of choice and voluntary association with extended kin of various types: "Because the American kinship networks are flexible in their expectations, personal preferences can play a key role" in how the meaning of kin ties is negotiated (Johnson, 2000, p.

280 626). To these ends, we posed our research question: How do nieces and nephews describe communication with their aunts?

## Method

*Participants*

Participants in this study were 70 undergraduate students enrolled in communication courses in a private

285 university in the western U.S., a public university in the northern U.S., Midwest, and a public university in the southeast U.S. Our sample ranged in age from 18 to 27, with the vast majority being between 20 and 22 years of age (median age = 21, $M$ = 21.07). Most par-

290 ticipants self-identified as European American or White ($n$ = 51), 4 as Latino/a, 4 as African American, 7 as Asian American, and 1 each as: from Kurdistan, biracial African American and White, Guyanese East Indian, and Ecuadorian Romanian. Most participants

295 ($n$ = 52) were female and 18 were male.

*Data Collection and Analysis*

Students in four courses were offered extra credit points to write a brief (typed) narrative in response to the statement, "Please describe communicating with one or more of your aunts." We consciously left the parameters of the response open by phrasing the prompt broadly. Participants were also asked to provide their age, sex, and ethnic/racial group. Responses were written outside of class over a 1- to 2-week span and returned to the course instructor.

We collected 70 responses that ranged in length from less than one double-spaced page to four pages, with an average of about two pages (154 pages of data). We used Owen's (1984) criteria for inductively deriving themes in our qualitative data: repetition, recurrence, and forcefulness. Repetition exists when the precise word or phrase is present across the data. Recurrence is present when different wording is used to express similar ideas. The third criterion, forcefulness, includes nonverbal cues that stress words or phrases (e.g., underlining, bolding, or italicizing text, one or more exclamation points, or all-caps for a word or phrase).

Thematic analysis began with the two authors independently reading the narrative data. We noted key words that repeated, recurrent ideas, and forceful words and phrases. We then independently inductively grouped repeated, recurrent, and forceful phrases into a set of preliminary themes. At that point, we discussed our themes and continually refined our inductive categorization until we were confident that our themes were coherent, inclusive, and saturated in data (Fitch, 1994). Finally, because our sample was predominantly female and European American, the first author inspected the responses from males and people of color and reviewed them to determine whether all themes were present and whether other critical ideas emerged within this subset of the data. After careful consideration, we judged that the male responses and person of color responses did not vary collectively from the larger sample, and there were no differences that could be attributed to gender or race. There was as much variation within these groups as there was between groups.

## Results

We derived nine content themes from the data and divided them into two groups. The first group of themes focused on aunting roles, such as teacher, role model, confidante, savvy peer, and second mother. The second group focused on aunting practices, such as gifts/treats, maintaining family connections, encouragement, and nonengagement. We contend that these roles and practices collectively reflect nieces' and nephews' relationship-type schema for aunts.

*Aunting Roles*

*Teacher.* Participants indicated that their aunts taught them many skills. Aunts taught their niece/nephew everything from how to ride a bike, knit, and cook special meals, to running a successful business and the meaning of religion. Nieces/nephews depicted learning from an aunt as fun, particularly in comparison to school and to learning from parents. An Asian American woman wrote: "The reason why [my aunt] and I became more communicative was because she'd show me how to bake cakes and cookies. And I loved cooking, so this was a fun and good thing for us both." At times, an aunt may teach an appreciation or understanding of something rather than a specific skill or technique, for example, a European American male student reported, "[My aunt] got me started being a fan of Duke basketball, which I still am today." Or it may be appreciation of a serious topic, such as religious faith. As one European American woman student explained: "When I was confused about the Lord and my beliefs, [my aunt] took the time to explain things to me, and why faith is important." Other nieces/nephews described their aunts as preparing them for life by guiding them to become competent adults. One European American woman noted that her aunts "have helped me with a million lessons.... They have taken me college hunting, apartment searching, as well as [on] trips across the country so I could learn and live and see what this big world was made of." We understand teaching as conscious efforts by aunts to instill skills or attitudes in a niece/nephew. The next theme, role model, places more emphasis on nieces'/nephews' agency.

*Role model.* Aunts function as role models to their nieces/nephews when they serve as examples of how to be in the world. Participants reported that they looked to their aunts as models of proper behavior, religious devotion, wives, mothers, and successful career women. Aunts may embody appropriate or ideal actions, roles, and identities for their nieces and nephews. One European American woman wrote:

> She has been one of my greatest role models. Her work has taken her to many exciting places, and she is now the CEO of a nonprofit charity that offers services to families and children. She has accomplished so much in her life...and she has set a great example for women.

Clearly, this niece will benefit from her aunt's example when she begins her career. Aunts also provide role models for how to be aunts, of course. A European American woman explains how her aunt inspired her to be a good aunt to her niece. In this case, her sister "asked me to be [niece's] godmother...I am going to be the best aunt to that little girl. I hope that I can be as good an aunt to her as [my aunt] was to me." This niece considers her aunt to embody the standard for aunting that the niece wants to reach. The participant's sister's designation of her as a godmother adds a sense of formality and responsibility to the aunt role.

Several participants also noted that aunts can serve as negative role models, reinforcing to nieces/nephews what they do not want to be. One European American woman poignantly explained that she did not want to be like one of her aunts in whom there was

> just always something missing—like she lacked a spirit, or vitality, that I seek in others. My uncle is hilarious—we get along great…but I think he kind of pushes her around. Not literally, but it is very clear who wears the pants in that relationship. I guess I always knew that, even when young, and I have always preferred strong, independent women.

This niece perceives her aunt's submissiveness to a dominating husband as a barrier to her connection with her aunt. The niece does not indicate disapproval of her uncle's behavior, and instead frames her lack of closeness with her aunt as due to her aunt's personality. While we found her placement of blame problematic, clearly the niece believes her aunt has nonetheless served a vital role in her life. That is, watching her aunt's life inspired the niece to think about the kind of woman she wants to be and the type of relationships she wants to have. Another European American woman explains how her aunt went from being a positive to a negative role model: "My aunt was my idol. As a young girl…she represented everything I thought a woman should: Beauty and femininity. In my eyes—she was perfect…[Now] I truly have lost all respect for [her]…." As an adult, this niece understood that feminine behavior she found charming in her aunt as a small child—obsessive attention to hairstyling, makeup, and other beauty regimes at the expense of being fiscally responsible, holding down a job, or maintaining healthy relationships—was irresponsible and reflected consistently poor judgment by her aunt. Clearly, aunts were powerful figures—both positive and negative—to nieces and nephews.

*Confidante/advisor.* Many participants reported that the aunts with whom they were closest were those to whom they could talk easily, who listened carefully and sympathetically, and were trustworthy. One European American man was confident of his aunt's willingness to listen: "I know that if I ever need advice or financial help or just wanted someone to talk to for fun, my aunt would be absolutely thrilled that I chose her to call." These aunts functioned as important confidantes and sources of good advice. The terms "nonjudgmental" and "open minded" were repeated. The aunt functioned as a safe person to turn to when a mistake had been made or a tough decision needed to be faced, and advice was needed.

A key component of this theme is that nieces/nephews discussed with their aunts topics that they felt they could not approach with their parents. Participants reported that aunts were not as closely tied to them as were their parents, and that this differing relational dynamic enabled aunts to help the niece/nephew without the emotional upheaval expected from their parents. In this sense, the aunt's third-party perspective enabled them to become ideal confidantes. The aunt knew both the niece/nephew and the parent, and hence was in a good position to understand the nature of the problem, the personalities involved, and what steps would best address the problem. This "third-party" perspective was articulated by a European American man who offered an analysis of why he could confide in his aunt:

> I have one small theory on why I'm so close to my aunt. She wasn't immediate family, so when I was introduced to her when I was 11 or so…I got to choose just how much I wanted to accept my aunt. It sort of took the family part out of the equation…I don't trust a lot of people, and I don't really have that many close friends…I mention this because what I share with my aunt is really special.

Likewise, another European American man explained that with his aunt, "Its [sic] almost like talking to a long-distance friend, your [sic] not afraid to really tell them anything because they are not present in your life, yet you still feel comfortable with them when they are around."

Sometimes the problem actually involved one or more parents. "When there is a huge family fight between my mother and I, I would call [my aunt]," explained one Asian American man. Other times, the issues involved sensitive topics. One European American woman explained: "If I need someone to talk to about taboo issues that my mom would slip into cardiac arrest over, I call [my aunt]." Confidante aunts can also be trusted to have integrity. A Latina described her aunt: "I can trust her with my problems— that she'll be empathetic, loving, kind, nonjudgmental…not only will she be wonderful at providing wisdom…she'll also call it like she sees it, whether she thinks I'll like hearing it or not." For this niece, her aunt's willingness to express an unpopular opinion was taken as a sign of her aunt's love and respect for her. While not all aunts fulfilled the role of confidante and advisor, aunts considered by nieces/nephews to be "favorite," "the best," or "the aunt I am closest to" shared this role.

*Savvy peer.* This theme involves references to an aunt who is closer in age to the respondent than other relatives. This youngest aunt is often the "coolest." That is, the aunt who is closest in age to her nieces/nephews is most often the one who was described as being able to identify with the niece/nephew, being the most fun, giving the best gifts, and being the most able to understand the experiences of the niece/nephew. Age was frequently mentioned as the primary reason why the aunt shared many common interests. A European American man described the nature of his conversations with his young aunt: "[My aunt] is quite a bit younger than my mother is and it seems like our conversations are more about the 'cooler' stuff in my life…she understands the vernacular of kids in their early 20s." For this nephew, his aunt speaks a language that his mother is unable or unwilling to speak. He perceived that he was comprehensible to his aunt because of her biological age. For a Guyanese/East Indian niece, her favorite aunt is much like herself:

> The reason why I think my aunt is the coolest, is because she is not old fashion[ed] at all: she is outgoing, loves shopping, likes to be in style with the young girls and she fits in well. I also like that she has a lot of energy to keep up with me, we would often go out on Friday and Saturday night every week, and we don't get home until 5 a.m.

The ability to share common activities brings nieces/nephews closer to younger aunts. Of course, commonalities could also bring nieces and nephews together with older aunts, but participants' descriptions strongly associated age similarity of an aunt with shared views and interests. An Asian American woman contrasted aunts who "are very old and very traditional and so they do not understand some of the things I do" to the youngest of her mother's sisters who "dresses very fashionably and loves to party...I refer to her as my cool aunt who loves to have fun." Such aunts are seen as more like slightly older peers than like parents, and that perception appears to be critical to nieces'/nephews' views of their aunts. Aunts who were kind and nurturing but who did not understand youth culture fit into the next theme, second mother.

*Second mother.* Participants described their nurturing aunts as a "second mother" and "like another mother to me," and described themselves as like an aunt's child: "I'm her other daughter." A Kurdistan man stated that he often stayed at his aunts' homes where his aunts "were parents to me." An African American male said of one aunt, "I believe she looks at me as another son of her own," and of another aunt, "We spent so much time together that she developed a 'mother's sense' (the sense that a mom 'just knows') and helped me through those tough times." Sometimes the second mother title was literal: the aunt had been instrumental in raising the niece/nephew. For example, one European American woman related that her mother had been an unwed mother and was expected to give up her baby. A week before giving birth, her mother went to her sister's home to stay with her. She says of her mother's sisters: "My mom's sisters are my closest aunts. They had a hand in raising me. They were my second mothers." Other aunts provided childcare for young nieces/nephews. A European American woman recalled that her aunt regularly provided childcare: "[My aunt] is my Godmother, and in a lot of ways, my mother. She took very good care of me when I was a little girl and my mom was at work."

For other nieces/nephews, aunts provided a temporary home in times of trouble during their teen years. A Latina described her aunt's kindness in inviting her niece to live with her "for a short period in high school when I wasn't getting along with my parents.... This was an important time in our relationship...a whole lot of bonding went on." This aunt allowed breathing room for her niece and the niece's parents until their differ-ences could be resolved. For those months, she served as a mother to her niece. An Asian American niece has lived with her aunt throughout high school and college: "She acts on behalf of my mother who lives overseas; she is my guardian.... Basically, I treat her like another mother." One European American male reported that he turned to his aunt for comfort during college:

> I am closest to her because she was there for me when I first went away to college. I was homesick and she would pick me up and I would stay weekends at her house.... *Every* time I go to her house she makes a gourmet meal.... Whenever I go over to her house that room is "my room," and I love it, I feel like I have a home away from home.

In some ways, the second mother has an easier role than the mother. As one European American woman succinctly put it: "To me, an aunt is like a mom, only they don't have to enforce the rules. They just give you guidance and direction but never have to punish you, so they always stay on your good side." Like the confidante, the second mother has the benefit of a third-party perspective. From her position outside the parent-child relationship, she is able to nurture without having to be responsible for many parents' duties, particularly discipline.

*Aunting Practices*

Having explored the roles aunts play in their nieces'/nephews' lives, we now turn to specific practices that emerged in our data as central to participants' perceptions of aunts.

*Gifts/treats.* Nieces/nephews reported that gifts offered tangible evidence of the quality of their relationships with aunts. Participants considered the receiving of holiday and birthday gifts that were appropriate to their age and interests to be signs of a caring aunt. Spontaneous gift giving and/or taking them for special meals, trips, movies, or other activities that parents did not provide often were especially valued. Sometimes, the treat involves special foods; a Latina enthusiastically stated: "Every time I go to visit, she cooks for me—anything I want. She spoils me rotten!" An Asian American male shared this memory of his aunt: "My greatest memory of [my aunt] was when I was still a little boy was when we went to [a local] park.... We would all bike around the park and then go to the museum." Other aunts allowed indulgences that parents presumably did not. One European American female stated that her favorite aunt "often took us out to the movies or out to dinner...and shopping for toys. We went to Lake Tahoe every summer together. She would cook for us every night and let us eat junk food on the beach."

Allowing such tame but "naughty" behavior was seen as a sign of affection and indulgence. Other aunts were prized because they indicated their understanding of a child's point of view, as in this example from a European American man: "I remember going to a family Christmas party and [aunt] was so cool, she was the only relative that got my brother and I completely separate gifts." As a little boy, having his own gift was meaningful, and the aunt who provided separate gifts was "cool" because she understood her nephews' desires. Conversely, receiving no gifts or gifts that reflected a lack of understanding of the niece's or nephew's personality (e.g., a doll given to a 16-year-old) were seen as signs of an aunt not caring enough to find out what the child likes.

*Maintaining family connections.* Aunts were key hubs in the networks of extended family kin. We were intrigued by the fact that virtually all participants—with no prompting—volunteered explanations of how their aunts were related to them through their mother's or father's family and the aunt's position in that family (e.g., younger or older than the participant's parent). For example, one European American man explained that he would discuss "my mother's sister…[my aunt] is the second oldest child in a family of seven. [My aunt] has two female children." Locating the aunt within the constellation of relationships was critical to understanding the relationship to the aunt. That is, as a nonnuclear family member, the aunt had to be accounted for. This is in contrast to participants' mentioning of their parents or siblings, who evidently needed no such kinship contextualization before they could be described.

Family gatherings also helped to maintain relationships. Nieces/nephews described family celebrations (e.g., Christmas, birthdays, Thanksgiving) as primary times for seeing aunts, particularly those who did not live nearby. The sharing of family rituals influenced the relationships of some nieces/nephews to their aunts. A Latina explained: "Tia [Spanish for 'aunt'] is the aunt that I know the best. Our family spent numerous holidays with her family." For others, family gatherings were the only occasions in which they interacted with aunts. Another Latina said of her mother's sister, "While all the other siblings moved on…[my aunt] stayed behind to take care of my grandparents…. I get to see her most because…when I go [to] visit my grandparents, [my aunt] is there." An Asian American woman explained how a family gathering provided her with an opportunity to converse with an aunt: "I went to a family gathering for my grandma's birthday. This was the first one I had gone to in a few years…. I got to talk to my aunt again and amazingly, we had a great conversation." Aunts were often strongly associated with family gatherings, whether as primary organizers of such events or as key participants. One Asian American woman explained that in Hawaii, women in the community, such as neighbors and parents' friends, are addressed as "aunty." She describes one aunty who has been her neighbor "since the day I was brought home from the hospital" as instrumental to organizing gatherings:

[My aunty] maintains very close relationships with all the kids in the cul-de-sac and is known as the "Party Coordinator." Ever since I can remember, Aunty has planned the neighborhood parties for Christmas, Easter, and summer…. So, if someone asked me how many people were in my family, I would not be able to give them an exact number because my family extends beyond my Mom and Dad, it consists of other special people…and aunties like my Aunty [name].

Finally, an African American woman told of attending her great-grandmother's 90th birthday party in a distant state and assumed she was invited to stay with her aunt. Upon her arrival, "I realized that my grandmother and uncle were staying with my great-grandparents, and I had just invited myself to [my aunt's] home…. She just laughed and said it was ok because I'm young and I'm family." Thus, family connections are facilitated by aunts whose presence, cooperation, and (often) hospitality fosters interaction and ritual celebrations among extended kin.

*Encouragement.* Participants described the aunts they liked as those who were very encouraging to them in school, sports, work, and other activities. Aunts' verbal encouragement appeared to significantly and positively influence nieces'/nephews' self-esteem. Sometimes this encouragement was a sense of being cherished. A Latina participant described her affectionate aunt: "My aunt is also demonstrative with her love for me. Not only does she make herself available when I need her but she lets me know how much she cares with her tender hugs and kisses." An African American nephew characterized aunts as increasing his self-worth: "I think that is the great thing about aunts: They make you feel good about yourself." A European American woman reported how much her aunt increased her self-confidence. She explained: "[My aunt] made me feel like queen of the world. I remember when she gave birth to my cousin Katie. I was only 8 and she let me hold her." By trusting in her niece to behave competently, this aunt demonstrated her faith in her young niece and made her feel special.

At the same time as making nieces/nephews feel good about themselves, aunts provide encouragement to do and be more. An African American man explained that: "My aunts love to 'push' all of their nephews and nieces toward success by any means necessary…. They are also big advocates of higher education. They have pushed my whole life." This participant attributed his educational success in part to his aunts' "pushing," and he valued their role in his success. Likewise, an African American woman explained that "when no one [in] the family thought I should leave home and got [sic] to college, [my aunt] supported the idea of me leaving and recommended it…. She [talked] with the rest of [my] family," and eventually the aunt persuaded her niece's parents to support her plan to attend college. Participants felt inspired by

750 their aunts' belief in them and appreciated their efforts to encourage them in their goals.

*Nonengagement.* Perhaps one of the most intriguing findings was the unapologetic way in which nieces/nephews expressed a lack of closeness with 755 some aunts. While examples of nonengagement were numerous, participants rarely stated that they perceived the lack of closeness as regrettable or problematic. We propose that this is an important difference between aunting and mothering: in the dominant U.S. culture, 760 reporting that one is not close to one's mother would seem to require some explanation, and perhaps be accompanied by an expression of regret, sadness, or anger. No such feelings are needed for lack of closeness to an aunt. For example, a European American woman 765 stated: "I'm not as close to [my aunts] as I am with my friends or cousins. They just kind of exist as relatives." A Latina described her communication with an aunt as fairly impersonal: "We tend to discuss more general, 'safe' topics rather than anything deeply per- 770 sonal…because I don't feel all that close to her." An Asian American woman reported that "I am not particularly close to any of my aunts, and do not look forward to talking to them. When I do, it is mostly for practical reasons or to be sociable…. This is not be- 775 cause I have a bad relationship with them, but that tends to be how [it is]."

The lack of closeness is just something to be accepted and not worried over. The matter-of-fact attitude toward lack of closeness with some aunts was 780 explained as due to lack of proximity that precluded frequent interaction. A European American man's explanation is representative: "As I was growing up I did not get many opportunities to see her, as I [was]…raised in [another state]. So as a result of this 785 distance, my relationship with [aunt] is not a very close one." Living close to an aunt did not necessarily entail great emotional attachment. However, more frequent interactions with their aunts did seem to relate to perceptions of them as meaningful figures in participants' 790 lives. While geographic distance recurred, no other consistent or cohesive reason was given for not being close to an aunt. Nieces and nephews listed personality traits they disliked, unfortunate events, and family patterns that led to or perpetuated nonengagement, but 795 such justifications were diverse, and we found no pattern among them.

## Discussion

The themes reported here illustrate the roles (teacher, role model, confidante, savvy peer, and second mother) and practices (gifts/treats, family gather- 800 ings, encouragement, and nonengagement) of aunts as perceived by their nieces and nephews. Participants described how communication (or the lack thereof) with aunts is integral to their self-development and has significant impacts on their relationships and their 805 lives. While the relationship-specific schemas (Koerner

& Fitzpatrick's first level of cognitive processing) necessarily varied among the nieces and nephews and the relationships with each of their aunts, central characteristics of a relationship-type schema (second level of 810 Koerner & Fitzpatrick's model) emerged. Taken together, the themes in our data point to four core aspects of a relational schema for aunts.

First, aunts are defined within the kin network but outside of the nuclear family. The biological, marital, 815 and/or fictive relationships that create both connection and "third-party" perspectives for aunts and their nieces/nephews are part of what made aunts powerful in their lives. That is, whether an aunt was wonderful, weird, dull, absent, or unpleasant, her position as non- 820 parent and nonsibling is an integral part of her identity *as an aunt*. Occupying a niche outside the nuclear family enables the aunt to avoid the deep identification, responsibility, and vulnerability of the parent-child bond that (ideally) leads both to closeness and to chil- 825 dren's need to rebel to establish their own identity. Perceived vulnerability is a critical factor in an individual's decisions over what information to disclose to others (Petronio, 2002). Thus, it follows that nieces and nephews are likely to feel less vulnerable with aunts 830 than with parents.

Aunts usually are free from the burden of imposing everyday rules, and nieces and nephews need not separate themselves from their aunt in order to establish their independence. Hence, aunts may make ideal con- 835 fidantes for nieces and nephews who do not wish to discuss sensitive issues with their parents, and fun and indulgent time spent with aunts does not threaten a child's sense of having a stable and secure home. Likewise, lack of attention from an aunt generally is 840 unlikely to wound a child, certainly not to the degree that rejection by a parent would, and a niece's or nephew's choice to not engage with a particular aunt was generally not problematic. Thus to be structurally apart from the nuclear family was to enjoy a greater 845 degree of flexibility in determining the relationship-specific schema for each aunt-niece/nephew relationship. Multiple ways of enacting roles and practices fit within the boundaries of aunt schemas. Unlike motherhood, the successful performance of which generally is 850 circumscribed within the boundaries of a full-time nurturer of children (e.g., Rich, 1977; Trebilcot, 1984), the aunt can be successful as an aunt in a multiplicity of ways. Enacting the role of nurturer (second mother) is acceptable, but so is visiting just once a year, mailing 855 cards or gifts without regular visits, briefly interacting at family gatherings, or engaging in a fun, peer relationship.

Second, the benefits of the relationship are almost entirely unidirectional, focusing on the aunt as fulfill- 860 ing the needs and desires of the niece or nephew, with no implicit or explicit reciprocity. Nieces and nephews told of learning skills from their aunts but not teaching their aunts, confiding in their aunts but not of being confidantes for them, receiving gifts and encourage-ment from aunts, but not of giving to them, and so on. From college-age nieces' and nephews' perspective, the role of aunt is that of a giver rather than a receiver of care and support. This phenomenon is likely related to the age difference between nieces and nephews who participated in this study and their aunts; reciprocity may increase over time as nieces and nephews leave college, assume adult responsibilities (e.g., full-time work), and grow older.

Third, the aunt relationship-type schema included passing on of a wide range of knowledge from aunts to nieces and nephews. This knowledge included specific skills, religious beliefs, family lore and traditions, and broader knowledge of the world. Knowledge was transmitted through direct instruction and interpersonal conversations, but also more diffusely through role modeling, such as when nieces/nephews sought to emulate aunts' career paths.

Fourth, when the previous two conditions were met (i.e., aunts focused on the nieces'/nephews' needs, knowledge was passed on), the communication in-volved in the aunt-niece/nephew relationship fostered (and in turn was fostered by) a sense of closeness to the aunt. The word "close" was invoked again and again to describe participants' feelings toward their aunts. Many emphasized that a close relationship was maintained despite geographical distance, busy schedules, and other obstacles. Aunts with whom the niece or nephew was not engaged (whether by conscious choice or cir-cumstances) were labeled "not close" relationships and accepted as such. The nonengagement of (some) aunts in their nieces' and nephews' lives should not be dis-missed as a failure or an unacknowledged kinship tie. Limited, infrequent, or even no contact between aunts, nieces, and nephews is not necessarily negative or a violation of the aunt schema. Nieces and nephews stated their lack of involvement matter of factly, ex-pressing no discomfort about revealing the lack of a close tie with a given aunt.

We posit that these four aspects constitute an ex-ploratory relationship-type schema that may be useful in understanding how nieces and nephews engage in cognitive processing regarding interactions with (and about) their aunts (Koerner & Fitzpatrick, 2002). While there is variation among our participants, there were also several prominent themes that suggest that U.S. culture reflects some shared commonalities in the un-derstandings of and enactment of aunting.

*Limitations*

This study was limited in several ways. Our partici-pants included a convenience sample of undergraduate students. Families whose members are enrolled in col-lege may have different expectations for aunts than those whose members have not attended college, par-ticularly poor and immigrant communities. Also, the age range of participants reflects one life stage: young adulthood. In some ways, this is an ideal group to study, for whom childhood was recent enough to be easily recalled and for whom going to college made shifts in familial relationships and roles more immedi-ate and evident. However, future research should ex-plore niece/nephew perspectives on aunts across the lifespan. Our findings also reflect predominantly Euro-pean Americans and females. Clearly, more research is required to locate potential gender and ethnic/racial group understandings of aunts. Finally, the study fo-cused on communication with aunts solely from the perspective of nieces and nephews. Of course, aunts' perspectives must be incorporated into our understand-ing of aunting in order to construct a more complex rendering of these roles and relationships. Ideally, matched pairs of aunts and nieces or nephews could shed light on how the perceptions of aunts reflect and/or vary from those of their nieces/nephews.

## Implications and Conclusion

Several implications of our findings are relevant to research on communication within family and kin net-works. First, aunts embody a great deal of flexibility in their enactment of acceptable roles and practices, and we recognize and celebrate flexibility within this gen-dered construct. Despite changing social gender roles, women's roles in the home and family too often are circumscribed within narrow parameters of appropriate (feminine) behavior (e.g., Coontz, 2000; Wood, 2002). Aunts, nieces, and nephews are making choices of how to communicate together, and we suggest that the range of behavior reported here reflects openness to privileg-ing the needs and desires of each niece/nephew and aunt dyad over those of a perceived social standard. While most of the communication and behavior re-ported here is hardly radical or unusual, the ability for nieces and aunts to choose a variety of ways of inter-acting with a variety of aunts reflects a truly transac-tional definition of a family relationship constituted in interaction rather than dictated by legal or biological ties (Noller & Fitzpatrick, 1993). Such a pseudo-aunt model of flexibility could be instructive or even inspi-rational to those adapting to new family forms, such as blended families (e.g., Braithwaite, Olson, Golish, Soukup, & Turman, 2001).

Our study also contributes to studies of extended families and kinship. Aunts' kin-keeping work reported here is consistent with previous studies' findings that many women put significant effort into kin keeping (e.g., Dill, 1998). It also suggests that while the recent trend away from studying extended kin may reflect declining interest in maintaining kinship relationships, that also may not be the case. Johnson (2000) proposed that studies that find declining instances of kin keeping may suffer from methodological flaws that focus on sustained interaction and thus fail to consider contem-porary means of maintaining close ties over large geo-graphical distances and within increased nuclear family mobility. Our findings support that critique, as our participants clearly recognized and valued aunts' kin-keeping work and participation in rituals, gatherings, and long-distance communication.

980    Our third implication concerns the lack of reciprocity of nieces/nephews toward meeting aunts' needs or desires. We believe that the almost complete lack of reciprocity reported is a function of the age of our participants. As college students, they appear to have not

985    yet assumed the role expectations of adults, and remain self-focused, as is characteristic of children. Preliminary data analysis of interviews with aunts, nieces, and nephews indicates that at least some adult nieces and nephews feel an obligation and/or take pleasure in ma-

990    terially and emotionally giving to their aunts (Sotirin & Ellingson, 2006). Some research has shown cultural differences in this area of kinship; in African American families, for example, nieces and nephews were considered by their elderly aunts and uncles to be impor-

995    tant family members and the latter reported receiving assistance from them, while elderly Whites reported no expectations of assistance from siblings' children (Johnson & Barer, 1995). Clearly, more research is needed on how aunt-niece/nephew relationships change

1000   over time.

Finally, we note that none of the participants mentioned popular culture images of aunts. Given Koerner and Fitzpatrick's (2002) position that cultural messages about relationships influence the formation and main-

1005   tenance of family relationship schemas, we anticipated that nieces and nephews might compare their aunts to popular figures, perhaps claiming that an aunt was cruel like *Harry Potter*'s Aunt Petunia or very kind and maternal, like *Andy Griffith*'s Aunt Bea. Such was not

1010   the case, indicating that at least in this exploratory study nieces and nephews made no conscious associations between their own experiences with aunts and those in the media. Future research should seek to determine what, if any, relationships exist between

1015   relationship-type schemas for aunts and cultural messages about aunts.

Our findings support the value of inquiry into aunts, family relationship schemas, and kin keeping. While the practices and functions of family communication

1020   and kinship may be changing, extended family such as aunts remain vital aspects of many people's lives. As Gerstel and Gallagher (1993) suggest, "contemporary extended family does not simply persist. Someone expends a great deal of time and energy to maintain it"

1025   (p. 598). That many aunts, nieces, and nephews are expending time and energy with each other is significant to our scholarly understanding of contemporary extended family networks and certainly warrants further study.

## References

Arliss, L. P. (1994). *Contemporary family communication: Meanings and messages*. New York: St. Martin's Press.

Bastida, E. (2001). Kinship ties of Mexican migrant women on the United States/Mexico border. *Journal of Comparative Family Studies, 32*, 549–569.

Braithwaite, D. O., Olson, L. N., Golish, T. D., Soukup, C., & Turman, P. (2001). "Becoming a family": Developmental processes represented in blended family discourse. *Journal of Applied Communication Research, 29*, 221–247.

Cicirelli, V., & Nussbaum, J. (1989). Relationships with siblings in later life. In J. Nussbaum (Ed.), *Life-span communication: Normative processes* (pp. 283–299). Hillsdale, NJ: Lawrence Erlbaum.

Clinton, H. (1996). *It takes a village: And other lessons children teach us*. New York: Simon & Schuster.

Collins, P. H. (2000). *Black feminist thought: Knowledge, consciousness and the politics of empowerment*. New York: Routledge.

Coontz, S. (2000). *The way we never were: American families and the nostalgia trap* (revised ed.). New York: Basic Books.

Davidson, B. (1997). Service needs of relative caregivers: A qualitative analysis. *Families in Society, 78*, 502–510.

di Leonardo, M. (1984). *The varieties of ethnic experience: Kinship, class, and gender among California Italian-Americans*. Ithaca, NY: Cornell University Press.

di Leonardo, M. (1998). The female world of cards and holidays: Women, families, and the work of kinship. In K. V. Hansen & A. I. Garey (Eds.), *Families in the U.S.: Kinship and domestic politics*. Philadelphia: Temple University Press.

Dill, B. T. (1998). Fictive kin, paper sons, compadrazgo: Women of color and the struggle for family survival. In K. V. Hansen & A. I. Garey, (Eds.), *Families in the U.S.: Kinship and domestic politics* (pp. 431–445). Philadelphia, PA: Temple University Press.

Falicov, C. J., & Karrer, B. M. (1980). Cultural variations in the family life cycle: The Mexican-American family. In E. A. Carter & M. McGoldrick (Eds.), *The family life cycle: A framework for family therapy* (pp. 383–425). New York: Gardner Press.

Fitch, K. L. (1994). Criteria for evidence in qualitative research. *Western Journal of Communication, 58*, 32–38.

Fitzpatrick, M. A., & Vangelisti, A. L. (Eds.). (1995). *Explaining family interactions*. Thousand Oaks, CA: Sage Publications.

Galvin, K. M., Bylund, C. L., & Brommel, B. J. (2003). *Family communication: Cohesion and change*. Boston, MA: Allyn & Bacon.

Galvin, P. J., & Cooper, P. J. (2000). *Making connections: Readings in relational communication*. Los Angeles: Roxbury.

Garey, A. I., & Hansen, K. V. (1998). Introduction: Analyzing families with a feminist sociological imagination. In K. V. Hansen & A. I. Garey (Eds.), *Families in the U.S.: Kinship and domestic politics* (pp. xv–xxi). Philadelphia, PA: Temple University Press.

Gerstel, N., & Gallagher, S. K. (1993). Kin keeping and distress: Gender, recipients of care, and work–family conflict. *Journal of Marriage and the Family, 55*, 598–607.

Halsted, I. (1993). *The aunts*. Boston, MA: Sharksmouth Press.

Hansen, K. V., & Garey, A. I. (1998). *Families in the U. S.: Kinship and domestic politics*. Philadelphia, PA: Temple University Press.

Johnson, C. L. (2000). Perspectives on American kinship in the later 1990s. *Journal of Marriage and the Family, 62*, 623–639.

Johnson, C. L., & Barer, B. M. (1995). Childlessness in late life: Comparisons by race. *Journal of Cross Cultural Gerontology, 9*, 289–306.

Jorgenson, J. (1989). Where is the "family" in family communication?: Exploring families' self-definitions. *Journal of Applied Communication Research, 17*, 27–41.

Koerner, A. F., & Fitzpatrick, M. A. (2002). Toward a theory of family communication. *Communication Theory, 12*, 70–91.

Leach, M. S., & Braithwaite, D. O. (1996). A binding tie: Supportive communication of family kin keepers. *Journal of Applied Communication Research, 24*, 200–216.

Noller, P., & Fitzpatrick, M. A. (1993). *Communication in family relationships*. Englewood Cliffs, NJ: Prentice Hall.

O'Reilly, A., & Abbey, S. (Eds.). (2000). *Mothers and daughters*. Lanham, MD: Rowman & Littlefield.

Owen, W. F. (1984). Interpretive themes in relational communication. *Quarterly Journal of Speech, 70*, 274–287.

Peington, B. A. (2004). The communicative management of connection and autonomy in African American and European American mother-daughter relationships. *Journal of Family Communication, 4*, 3–34.

Petronio, S. (2002). *The boundaries of privacy: Dialectics of disclosure*. New York: SUNY Press.

Rich, A. (1977). *Of woman born: Motherhood as experience and institution*. New York: Bantam Books.

Romberger, B. V. (1986). "Aunt Sophie always said....": Oral histories of the commonplaces women learned about relating to men. *American Behavioral Scientist, 29*, 342–367.

Rosenthal, C. S. (1985). Kin keeping in the familial division of labor. *Journal of Marriage and the Family, 47*, 965–974.

Sault, N. L. (2001). Godparenthood ties among Zapotec women and the effects of Protestant conversion. In J. W. Dow & A. R. Sandstrom (Eds.), *Holy saints and fiery preachers: The anthropology of Protestantism in Mexico and Central America* (pp. 117–146). Westport, CT: Praeger.

Sotirin, P., & Ellingson, L. L. (2006). The "other" woman in family life: Aunt/niece/nephew communication. In K. Floyd & M. Morman (Eds.), *Under-studied family relationships* (pp. 81–99). Thousand Oaks, CA: Sage Publications.

Sotirin, P., & Ellingson, L. L. (in press). Rearticulating the aunt in popular culture. *Cultural Studies*.

Stack, C. (1974). *All our kin*. New York: BasicBooks.

Stack, C. B., & Burton, L. M. (1998). Kinscripts. In K. V. Hansen & A. I. Garey (Eds.), *Families in the U.S.: Kinship and domestic politics* (pp. 405–415). Philadelphia, PA: Temple University Press.

Stone, L. (2000). *Kinship and gender: An introduction*. Boulder, CO: Westview Press.

Thorton, J. (1991). Permanency planning for children in kinship foster homes. *Child Welfare, 5*, 593–601.

Traeder, T., & Bennett, J. (1998). *Aunties: Our older, cooler, wiser friends*. Berkeley, CA: Wildcat Canyon Press.

Trebilcot, J. (Ed.). (1984). *Mothering: Essays in feminist theory*. Lanham, MD: Rowman & Littlefield.

Troll, L. E. (1985). *Early and middle adulthood*. Pacific Grove, CA: Brooks/Cole.

Wellman, B. (1998). The place of kinfolk in personal community networks. In K. V. Hansen & A. I. Garey (Eds.), *Families in the U.S.: Kinship and domestic politics* (pp. 231–239). Philadelphia, PA: Temple University Press.

Wilmot, W. (1995). The relational perspective. In *The relational communication reader* (pp.1–12). New York: McGraw-Hill.

Wood, J. T. (2002). "What's a family, anyway?" In J. Stewart (Ed.), *Bridges not walls: A book about interpersonal communication* (pp. 375–383). New York: McGraw-Hill.

**Address correspondence to**: Laura L. Ellingson, Communication Department, Santa Clara University, Santa Clara, CA 95053. E-mail: lellingson@scu.edu

# Exercise for Article 31

## Factual Questions

1. According to the literature review, how is the term *kinship* defined?

2. What is the research question posed by the researchers?

3. What was the median age of the participants?

4. Of the 70 participants, how many were female?

5. In analyzing the data, the researchers used Owen's (1984) criteria. What were the criteria?

6. What is a key component of the theme of "confidante/advisor"?

## Questions for Discussion

7. The researchers refer to themselves as "feminist researchers." Speculate on the meaning of this term. (See lines 34–35.)

8. The sample was heterogeneous in terms of racial and ethnic background. If you had conducted this study, would you have used a heterogeneous sample or a homogeneous one (e.g., only European

Americans)? (See lines 289–294, 327–337, and 926–929.)

9. Is it important to know that the researchers *independently* read and *independently* grouped responses into themes? Explain. (See lines 318–323.)

10. The researchers used a "convenience sample." What is your understanding of the meaning of this term? Could the fact that it was a convenience sample affect the validity of the results? Explain. (See lines 913–915.)

11. What is your opinion on the researchers' suggestion for using matched pairs of aunts and nieces or nephews in future research on this topic? (See lines 934–937.)

12. If you had planned this study, would you have opted to use qualitative *or* quantitative methodology (*or* both)? Explain.

## Quality Ratings

Directions: Indicate your level of agreement with each of the following statements by circling a number from 5 for strongly agree (SA) to 1 for strongly disagree (SD). If you believe an item is not applicable to this research article, leave it blank. Be prepared to explain your ratings. When responding to criteria A and B, keep in mind that brief titles and abstracts are conventional in published research.

A. The title of the article is appropriate.

    SA    5    4    3    2    1    SD

B. The abstract provides an effective overview of the research article.

    SA    5    4    3    2    1    SD

C. The introduction establishes the importance of the study.

    SA    5    4    3    2    1    SD

D. The literature review establishes the context for the study.

    SA    5    4    3    2    1    SD

E. The research purpose, question, or hypothesis is clearly stated.

    SA    5    4    3    2    1    SD

F. The method of sampling is sound.

    SA    5    4    3    2    1    SD

G. Relevant demographics (for example, age, gender, and ethnicity) are described.

    SA    5    4    3    2    1    SD

H.  Measurement procedures are adequate.

SA   5   4   3   2   1   SD

I.  All procedures have been described in sufficient detail to permit a replication of the study.

SA   5   4   3   2   1   SD

J.  The participants have been adequately protected from potential harm.

SA   5   4   3   2   1   SD

K.  The results are clearly described.

SA   5   4   3   2   1   SD

L.  The discussion/conclusion is appropriate.

SA   5   4   3   2   1   SD

M.  Despite any flaws, the report is worthy of publication.

SA   5   4   3   2   1   SD

# Article 32

# The Multiple Roles That Youth Development Program Leaders Adopt With Youth

KATHRIN C. WALKER
University of Minnesota, Minneapolis

ABSTRACT. The roles that program leaders establish in their relationships with youth structure how leaders are able to foster youth development. This article examines the complex roles program leaders create in youth programs and investigates how they balanced multiple roles to most effectively respond to the youth they serve. Analyses of qualitative data from 12 high-quality programs for high-school-aged youth suggest that program leaders take on different roles. In some cases, youth experienced their program leader as a trusted friend, caring parent figure, or influential mentor. In other instances they described him or her as having the knowledge and authority of a teacher or boss. Analyses further suggest that moving across multiple roles appeared to make the program leaders more effective.

From *Youth & Society*, *43*, 635–655. Copyright © 2011 by Sage Publications. Reprinted with permission.

The nature of the role a professional constructs with the people he or she serves influences that professional's effectiveness. In their interactions with young people, youth development program leaders assume

5  diverse and complex social roles. They may adopt the role of friend (Young, 1999), parent (Hirsch, 2005), mentor (Rhodes, 2004), or teacher (Halpern, 2005). These different types of roles position program leaders to serve distinct functions, from offering guidance and

10  emotional support to providing authority and expertise. It is important to understand the different roles youth professionals adopt and how these roles function.

This article examines the various roles program leaders[1] create in youth development programs and

15  investigates how they balance multiple roles to most effectively respond to given youth in particular instances. The research studied program leaders in 12 high-quality programs for high-school-aged youth. Given limited prior research, qualitative methods of

20  discovery research were employed to gain preliminary understanding of the topic from the point of view of the people involved (Strauss & Corbin, 1998).

The theoretical approach of the study draws from social role theory that posits that nearly all roles in-

25  volve reciprocal relationships (Bronfenbrenner, 1979; Newman & Newman, 2007). Thus, each role is typi-

cally functionally connected to a related role, such as parent to the role of daughter or son and teacher to the role of student. The roles that leaders establish in their

30  relationships with youth structure how leaders are able to support youth and foster their development. Developmental role theory suggests that different types of role partners may help youth develop in different ways; each also helps youth learn because they have to enact

35  the demands of different positions (Bronfenbrenner, 1979; Newman & Newman, 2007).

Program leaders often position themselves in more than one role; they have a portfolio of role relationships with youth. Zeldin, Larson, Camino, and O'Conner

40  (2005) suggest that the ability to balance the different roles they create is the most important skill in the art of sustaining relationships with youth. Yet because they involve adopting different postures, practitioners' role relationships with the youth they serve are often chal-

45  lenging to negotiate (Seligson & MacPhee, 2004; Walker & Larson, 2006).

Youth development programs are a unique arena where youth and adults come together to form role relationships on different terms than typically occur in

50  others settings and institutions. In youth programs, there is often less hierarchy and more room for negotiation of status among youth and adults. Youth programs serve as "intermediate spaces" that bridge the worlds of adults and youth (Noam & Tillinger, 2004). Youth

55  programs have been characterized as providing a "bridging function" (Rhodes, 2004) or serving as a "border zone" (Heath, 1994) that links youth and mainstream culture. In fact, it's been suggested that these contexts often serve as a transition to professional

60  worlds and adult life (Larson & Walker, 2006). This border zone may allow program leaders to have role portfolios that are distinct from those of other adults in youth's lives and that bridge peerlike and hierarchical relationships. It is important to understand how pro-

65  gram leaders negotiate, balance, and blend multiple role relationships.

This qualitative study examined the nature of the roles of program leaders with the youth in 12 programs. First, it identifies the range of roles and the

70  character and function of these different dimensions of

the program leader role. For each role, literature on that type of role is described, analysis of how that role relationship was enacted in the programs studied is presented, and the distinct character and function of the given role is discussed. It then looks at how program leaders balanced multiple roles to most effectively respond to the youth they serve.

## Method

### Data Collection

This study followed 12 high-quality programs for high-school-aged youth over a 2- to 9-month period of participation in 2003–2005. The 12 programs included arts and leadership programs, ranging from visual, media, and performance arts to programs focused on leadership development and community change. Seven were urban and 5 were in small cites or rural areas; 6 were in community-based organizations, 4 were in schools, and 2 were in faith-based organizations (Larson, Pearce, Sullivan, & Jarrett, 2007). In three of the programs, youth were paid for their participation, and in two others some youth had paid positions. The programs were selected through a process similar to that used by McLaughlin, Irby, and Langman (1994) for selecting high-quality programs. A program was first identified by its strong reputation and recommendations by local youth development experts and practitioners, and then program staff were interviewed and the program was observed to verify that youth were engaged, features of effective programs were evident, and the program leaders had been in their position for at least 2 years.

A representative sample of 5 to 12 (mean = 9.5) youth in each program and their 18 primary program leaders were interviewed and observed over a several-month cycle of program activity. The primary data source for this investigation was the 659 interviews conducted with 113 youth (Table 1). Secondary data sources included 111 interviews with the 18 primary program leaders, 14 interviews with 7 secondary program leaders, and 167 program observations. Interviews at the beginning, middle, and end of the research period were longer and conducted in person; briefer phone interviews were conducted at regular intervals in between (every 2 weeks in most programs). As the larger study's objective was to observe the occurrence of developmental processes, the interview protocols sought ongoing accounts of the program experience and developmental areas. In interviews with both the youth and their program leaders, we asked specifically about the relationships between youth and program leaders and the roles that program leaders played with the youth.[2] The majority of data for this study come from these questions, although in a few instances interviewees used the language of roles in response to other interview questions.

Table 1
*Programs and Youth in the Research*

| Program | Program description | Number of youth in program | Number of youth in study | Number of youth interviews |
|---|---|---|---|---|
| Clarkston FFA | School-based FFA chapter in a rural town; provides leadership development through agricultural education | 77 | 11 | 74 |
| Art First | Community-based nonprofit; provides high-quality art education to Chicago's underserved youth | 16 | 12 | 76 |
| Youth Action | Community-based youth activist program in Chicago; youth develop action campaigns to address problems that affect their lives | 20 | 10 | 62 |
| Les Miserables | School-based musical production in a rural town | 110 | 10 | 73 |
| Youth Builders | Faith-based program in a rural city; provides safe alternative activities to youth during the summer | 20 | 5 | 13 |
| Faith in Motion | Faith-based dance troupe in a midsized city | 25 | 9 | 53 |
| Prairie County 4-H | Community-based chapter of 4-H Federation; provides leadership opportunities across the rural county | 15 | 8 | 58 |
| Media Masters | School-based media arts program in Chicago; instructors from a community-based organization provide a 10-week training | 22 | 8 | 35 |
| The Studio | Community-based career development program in Chicago; provides training in multimedia arts | 22 | 10 | 44 |
| Harambee | School-based summer program in Chicago; targets community building and leadership | 37 | 10 | 52 |
| El Concilio | Community-based youth council in Chicago; involves youth in community leadership and service | 21 | 10 | 56 |
| SisterHood | Community-based all-female youth group in Chicago; focuses on identity and leadership development | 10 | 10 | 63 |

*Youth.* Youth were selected to be representative of 125 active program participants in terms of age, gender, ethnicity, and years in the program. The sample included 62 females and 51 males (average age = 16.2). The sample of 113 youth included approximately equal numbers of African American ($N$ = 37), European 130 American ($N$ = 36), and Latino ($N$ = 32) youth. Some of these participants were new to the program, but many had been involved in it (or other offerings sponsored by the same parent organization) prior to our study (for a median of 1.8 years; range 0 to 6 years).

135   *Program leaders.* The 18 primary program leaders included 11 women and 7 men (ages 22–55). Eight of these leaders were European American, 7 were African American, 1 was Latino, 1 was Arab American, and 1 was East Indian. They had been in their current posi-140 tions for 2 to 19 years (median 4 years), and some had worked with youth for much longer. One exception was Janet,[3] who joined the program mid-study to replace a SisterHood leader who had left. Working with youth was their primary, full-time responsibility in 145 seven cases, supplemented the leaders' regular jobs in six cases, and was one aspect of a full-time position that included other administrative responsibilities in five cases.

*Data Analysis*

To analyze the roles adopted by the program lead-150 ers, I employed procedures of grounded theory and related analytic techniques designed to identify underlying themes in narrative data and find meaningful theoretical categories that capture these themes (Auerbach & Silverstein, 2003; Patton, 2002; Strauss & Cor-155 bin, 1998). First, because the objective was to understand how the youth experienced their program leaders, all the youth interview data were read to identify passages that bore on the program leaders' roles and relationships with youth. A preliminary review identified 160 five types of roles (friend, parent, mentor, teacher, and boss). To evaluate the fidelity of these categories, an independent rater utilized my coding system to analyze a randomly selected set of 50 passages from the data, and our rate of agreement was satisfactory (Cohen's 165 Kappa = .83). I then developed a working definition for each role to code interview passages. Sometimes interviewees named a role, and in other instances they described features that embodied a role. The youths' own language and assessments of the roles were used to 170 identify the core characteristics and function associated with each role type. For instance, when youth described a leader as a "friend," they explained that "he can come down to my age and relate," "we joke around, we tell each other stories," or "when things 175 were hard for me, friends that I thought I had, they were never there, but she was." I then analyzed the data from the program leader interviews, which echoed the themes identified in the youth interviews. In fact, the descriptions of these roles provided by the leaders did 180 not diverge in any clear way from those provided by the youth. The working definitions were then further refined by a review of the literature discussing each role. These analyses led to the development of a description of each type of role relationships, including a 185 definition from the literature and data to illustrate the character and functions associated with each. These descriptions are presented in the section that follows.

A similar process was used to review and analyze the data to determine which program leaders played 190 multiple roles and how and why they blended and balanced these various roles in different instances and with different youth. Because youth accounts are the best guide for how a program leader is perceived, transcripts from the youth interviews were analyzed to de-195 termine the range of roles each leader played. I first used the working definitions to code each passage and determine how many different roles were identified for a given leader. Then I went through the passages to examine how program leaders balanced multiple roles 200 to most effectively respond to the youth they serve. These analyses and case examples are presented in the section on playing multiple roles.

*Descriptions of Roles' Relationships and Functions*

Analyses confirmed that the program leaders took on different roles. Some roles were more personal, 205 where the leader related as a friend, cared as a parent, and offered guidance as a mentor. In other instances, the leader acted as a teacher or a boss, roles that necessitated more formal or professional interactions.

*Friend.* Conditions marking friendship among ado-210 lescents include enjoying mutual regard, desiring to spend time together, and having fun (Bukowski, Newcomb, & Hartup, 1996). But beyond having fun, friendships are an important source of social support, intimacy, a place to explore new identities, and a 215 means for facilitating autonomy from parents (Brown, 1990; Lempers & Clark-Lempers, 1992; Youniss & Smollar, 1985). Adolescent friendships are characterized by "mutual reciprocity" (Youniss & Smollar, 1985), a concept that describes relationships in which 220 individuals perceive each other as relative equals, respect each other's point of view, and are involved in ongoing and open communication. Young people describe their friends as people with whom they have fun, share similar interests, and trust.

225   Across all the programs we studied, youth described at least one of their program leaders in terms of friendship. The leaders shared enjoyable and egalitarian interactions with the youth they served. As a young woman in SisterHood put it, "Even though her official 230 title is Coordinator, she's more than a Coordinator. Not just to me, like with everybody. She is like a friend, and we could talk to her about anything." A young man in Clarkston FFA described how he developed a friendship with his FFA advisor over 4 years, "We've 235 gotten to be close friends. It's become more and more

personal. It's not on a student-teacher basis; it's more of an adult-young adult basis. It's more personal. You get to know them a lot better." A young man in Youth Action described the fun side of his relationship with the adult organizer this way, "We're like really kind of like buddies. Like after we're done with work, we just talk a lot, make a bunch of dumb jokes. You get to have fun." Many young people described their program leaders as friends; adults whom they regarded as equals and whose company they enjoyed. This friendly rapport allowed the program leaders to build trust and sustained relationships with the youth.

Yet the youth-adult relationships formed were more nuanced than terms of friendship suggest, reflecting the adult's obligation to maintain a professional stance. One Media Masters youth referred to the limits between having fun and getting down to business: "You can socialize with them. You can joke with them, but then there's a period where you have to be serious." Although youth and their program leaders shared in jokes, activities, and interests, their relationships were primarily for and about the youth—their lives, their concerns—as opposed to those of the adults. This is incongruent with friendship in the traditional sense, which suggests greater reciprocity. The youth reported recognizing this distinction, noting that although elements of friendship developed between youth and their program leaders, the relationships did not cross the line into conventional friendship.

*Parent.* Parent-adolescent relationships are typically characterized by both emotional closeness and benevolent authority. Research indicates that parent-child relationships remain important social and emotional resources well beyond the childhood years (Collins & Laursen, 2004; Lempers & Clark-Lempers, 1992). Yet unlike the mutuality of friendships, parents remain authority figures for their children. Youniss and Smollar (1985) examined adolescents' perceptions of their relations with their parents and found that parents are perceived as authorities who assert opinions and use standards that they expect their sons and daughters to accept (Youniss & Smollar, 1985). Yet while adolescents perceive their parents as authorities, they perceive parental authority as rightful and benevolent (Youniss & Smollar, 1985). Parents remain close to their teens while maintaining their authority.

In most of the programs studied, the program leaders were described by the youth as parental figures. For example, we observed many members of the cast and crew of Les Miserables referring to the director as "Mom." A student actor in Les Miserables characterized the support offered by the director this way: "It's literally almost like a second mother. I can come and sob to her, or I can tell her, 'Hey, I got an A in Spanish.' Definitely a mother figure with her." A youth in Faith in Motion described her program leader this way, "Susan is like my second mother. I would be adopted by her if my parents would put me up for adoption."

The kind of intimacy and communication typically provided by parents was a hallmark of these relationships.

In addition to the closeness reflective of parent-child relations, the relationships adult leaders created with youth also evoked the authority and disciplinary roles of parents. For example, a young man in Clarkston FFA described how the adult advisors intervened when he was caught misbehaving:

> I got in trouble one day for doing something on the computer I wasn't supposed to be doing. And they came to me that next morning and talked to me about it and told me how they felt about it and why I shouldn't do it again and just basically were almost parental.

According to a youth in Youth Builders, "He's on me about everything, I tell you. Sometimes he thinks he's my dad." When admonishing youth for poor behavior or grades, for example, these program leaders took on authoritative roles that are more emblematic of parents. By building parental-like relations with the youth, the program leaders cultivated an emotional closeness that afforded them the ability to discipline when needed.

While the youth sometimes described their program leaders as a "second mom" or a "father figure," they also recognized a distinction between the program leader's role and that of a parent. Both the intimacy and the authority that youth reported experiencing with the program leaders were not as strong as what the youth experienced with their own parents. For example, when asked to describe the kind of role that her program leader plays, a young woman in Prairie County 4-H replied,

> It's not really a parent because they don't boss you around and tell you to be home in the middle of this...it's more that they have their set of control, I guess, pushing in the right direction that we should be going in; that they're there.

The program leaders possessed influence that was grounded in intimacy and authority, but it was perceived as distinct from that of parents.

*Mentor.* A mentor is an older, more experienced person who provides ongoing guidance, instruction, and encouragement aimed at developing the competence and character of an unrelated, younger protégé (Rhodes, 2002). Although parents have authority in terms of legal and normative power and control, mentors' influence rests more solely on wisdom and experience. So while the parent role is more about authority and being directive, the mentor role is more about influence freely taken. Mentoring relationships are still strongly affective in nature, but they are more instrumental. Hirsh and Wong (2005) examined research relevant to mentoring within after-school programs and identified emotional support, guidance or teaching, and sponsorship and advocacy as three mentoring behaviors of adult staff. Furthermore, as Rhodes (2002) points out, a mentor-protégé relationship is not necessarily mutually empathic; mentors are there to listen, support, and offer advice to the protégés. Equal reciprocity is less likely to characterize relations between adolescents and unrelated adults than relations between adolescents and friends (Darling, Hamilton, & Niego, 1994). In sum, mentoring relationships are characterized by their combination of influence and asymmetry.

Young people in all 12 programs likened their program leaders to a mentor, an older sibling, or a role model. Youth described these adults as a valued additional resource—an adult whom they could confide in or seek advice from. Of the program leaders, a young man in Harambee said, "They'll, like, help you out since they are older than you and give you tips on what not to do or how you should do certain things when you are in certain places." And a young man from The Studio described the program leader this way: "She knows all the right things to say, all the time. No matter where you are or what situation you're in, she will help you out. She is the greatest big sister I've had in a while." Youth described their program leaders as people they looked up to and as valuable resources they could rely on for wise counsel and support.

While youth drew parallels between these adults and other adult figures in their lives, they often said that these program leaders were in fact more effective; they could tell them more than they'd tell their sibling, and they were more available than their school counselor. "He's like an older brother you could say. Like a real cool older brother though because I trust him with shit that I don't even trust my brother with." The youth reported valuing their program leader's presence—their availability, their nonjudgmentalness, and their ability to listen. Many described trusting the program leaders and seeking their advice about matters beyond the program, from parents and romantic partners to college and careers. As a young woman in Art First put it,

> Through the bad times, like when I came to consult her about family and stuff, she would try to give me all these methods that I should try…. She is always there for you. I mean, she is there for everybody. You could always consult her, any problem or any task; she always has some idea that you could work with or do.

In sum, as trusted and respected adults, the program leaders influenced the youth they served by offering wise judgment and emotional support.

*Teacher.* Teachers are perhaps the most common nonparental adults in the lives of youth, spending a considerable amount of time in almost daily contact with youth. However, research has indicated that teachers are not generally perceived as very personally important by adolescents, and these relationships tend to be less affectively charged than relationships with other adults (Clark-Lempers, Lempers, & Ho, 1991; Galbo, 1986, 1989; Lempers & Clark-Lempers, 1992). Unlike the more effective roles of parents and mentors,

a teacher's role is more instrumental with the purpose being to facilitate learning in students (Darling, Hamilton, & Shaver, 2003). Although some teachers are able to successfully transform traditional teacher-student relationships (Bernstein-Yamashiro, 2004), most teachers maintain professional boundaries, and most students perceived teachers as providing more instructional than emotional support.

Youth in most of the programs described their program leaders as teachers, and this role was implicit in the day-to-day activities and objectives of all the programs. Whether teaching acting, activism, or studio engineering, the program leaders had an intentional learning objective. For example, a young actor described how the director taught him technical singing skills:

> Her advice on singing and how to do it—some mechanical things about how you sing—have really helped me. The first time I sang that [line] it was horrible, but after some coaching, she tells you to put your hand on your stomach and then press in as hard as you can. The first time you do it you just kind of go, "Eh?" But she says, "No, press," and then she like shoves her hand in your gut and you're like, "Ah!" So that helped me.

At The Studio, Neisha possessed the engineering expertise that the youth sought to obtain. According to observation notes, she would instruct the youth in the equipment and offer guidance like "It's peaking on the master fader" or "Tell her to do the first verse, and if we need to split up her verse, we can do that." She would also quiz the youth on what needed to be done and lecture them on the ethics of music pirating. When asked to describe Neisha's role, one young man offered, "Making sure that she teaches us the responsibilities from the program and what we have to do, and she's been doing a great job of it. She's been living up to her role as teacher." Like teachers, the program leaders possessed authority in terms of knowledge and expertise, and they offered instrumental support to enhance learning.

Nevertheless, a number of youth reported that the teacher dimension of their relationships was distinct from traditional teacher-student relations in that their relationships encompassed a more effective nature. For example, a young woman in Prairie County 4-H made this distinction when describing Lisa as a teacher: "Not a mean teacher, a very nice teacher. A favorite class teacher." A young woman from Art First compared Rebecca to her teachers at school, "Rebecca is kind of like a teacher a little bit, but she's a lot more, I guess you could say, maternal than the teachers at school. But that's because you know her better and everything like that." In general, many of the youth recognized a teacher aspect to the program leader role but felt that it was less formal and more intimate than a traditional teacher role. The program leaders we studied taught important skills and ideas, yet the role they played

465 seemed to transcend traditional teacher-student relations.

*Boss.* A boss is someone who supervises others. In this model, the employee is expected to perform productive work and is paid for doing so, whereas the boss
470 is expected to teach knowledge and skills that will enable the young person to become progressively more productive and ultimately qualified (Hamilton & Hamilton, 2004). Furthermore, a boss provides critical oversight and management. Distinct from the other roles,
475 boss-employee relations are more regulated or official, and there is the additional layer of accountability linked to situations when an employee is being paid. A boss provides direction, supervision, and accountability.

480 In most cases where youth were paid for their participation in the program, they identified their program leader as a boss who assumed a different sort of authority in terms of power and offered instrumental support to enhance performance. According to a young woman
485 at Harambee,

> He's sort of like a supervisor. They give us a specific job, and we have to do it. If we get stuck, he would help us with something but really he's just like a supervisor. He makes sure that we're doing the right [thing], that we're
490 staying focused, and that we're on time.

Even in one nonemployment program, El Concilio, a youth identified the program leader as a boss: "He's like the boss of everything, where he tells us something and we have to have it done by a certain date." When
495 adopting a boss-like stance, the program leaders had to hold youth accountable to expectations, whether it was attendance, deadlines, or job performance.

The youth interviewed seemed able to reconcile this added dimension and understand why it was necessary.
500 One Art First youth described the new power dynamic this way:

> It's kind of like, "I'm your boss," but kind of joking about it, like, "So now remember now, I'm now your boss" [in sweet, mock condescending voice] kind of like,
505 reminding you that if she tells you something about being late, or something, she really means it, whereas if she's a teacher, then she can take it a couple times. Now that she's your employer and she's paying you, she has a little bit more power.

510 A Youth Action intern reflected on how being a boss didn't diminish how she felt about the adult leader: "I consider him to be a friend, even though he's considered to be my boss during the summer." When program leaders assumed an additional supervisory
515 role, this dimension of their relationships tended to be downplayed by the youth.

### Playing Multiple Roles

Analysis revealed that across the 12 programs studied, program leaders adopted multiple roles in their relationships with the youth in their programs. In some
520 cases, a young person likened their program leader to a trusted friend, caring parent figure, or influential mentor. In other instances, they described him or her as having the knowledge and authority of a teacher or boss. Although the program leaders embodied elements
525 of these archetypal roles, the relationships they cultivated with the youth they serve appeared to be more nuanced than these standard labels suggest. In this section, I describe the range of roles program leaders played and discuss how they balanced these multiple
530 roles to effectively respond to the youth they served.

*Range of roles.* Youth accounts were used to determine the range of roles each program leader played. A leader was identified as playing a given role if the youth specifically used that role to describe that leader
535 (Table 2). Sometimes in programs with more than one leader, the youth referred to the leaders collectively, in which case that role was attributed to both leaders. However, to be coded as playing a given role in Table 2, a program leader was referred to as such directly by
540 at least one youth or collectively by more than one youth.

All 18 of the program leaders in our study played multiple roles in their relationships with the youth in their programs. As Table 2 illustrates, all were described as mentors, most were described as friends
545 (83%), parents (78%), and teachers (67%), and about one third were described as bosses (28%). All five roles were attributed to four of the leaders, and just two roles were attributed to three of the leaders.

550 In a few programs, the coleaders had somewhat different role portfolios that combined in ways that appeared to facilitate their work. Tanya, The Studio's employment specialist, developed more focused adult relationships with youth, while her counterpart, Neisha,
555 took up the full range of roles in her interactions with the youth. The Clarkston FFA coleaders were often described collectively and both were identified as playing the same four types of roles. We observed, however, that they did not always adopt the same role in a
560 given situation. Mr. Jensen described how they intentionally took on different but complementary roles:

> One person has to be the bad guy and try to get some things out, and then the other person has to help smooth things over. It's kind of like parents. You know, one per-
565 son has to initiate the discipline, and sometimes the other parent tries to say, "Hey, you know, you're still a good kid."

By bringing together and moving across different role types, the coleaders were able to jointly serve
570 more functions.

The division of role functions between coleaders was illustrated in a program in which the program leaders changed midway through the study. At the start of the year, SisterHood was a tight-knit group run by
575 two young coleaders, Linda and Kim, who had a high threshold for the youths' antics and informal behavior within the group. The youth had to adjust when Kim—

Table 2
*Roles the Youth Describe Their Program Leader as Playing*

| Program | Program leaders | Friend | Parent | Mentor | Teacher | Boss |
|---|---|---|---|---|---|---|
| Clarkston FFA | Mr. Baker | X | X | X | X | |
| | Mr. Jensen | X | X | X | X | |
| Art First | Rebecca | X | X | X | X | X |
| Youth Action | Jason | X | X | X | X | X |
| Les Miserables | Ann | X | X | X | X | |
| Youth Builders | Charles | | X | X | | |
| | Karen | X | X | X | | |
| Faith in Motion | Susan | X | X | X | | |
| Prairie County 4-H | Lisa | X | X | X | X | |
| Media Masters | Janna | X | | X | X | |
| | Gary | X | | X | X | |
| The Studio | Neisha | X | X | X | X | X |
| | Tanya | | X | X | X | |
| Harambee | Mike | X | | X | X | X |
| El Concilio | Pablo | X | X | X | X | X |
| SisterHood | Linda | X | X | X | | |
| | Kim | X | | X | | |
| | Janet | | X | X | | |

whom the youth saw as a friend—was replaced mid-year by Janet, whom the youth described as more ma-
580 ternal. Janet positioned herself as more of a community elder, and she was less tolerant of their cursing, for example. One young woman described how "a lot of the members in the group didn't appreciate her just coming in and trying to change things." However, she
585 told how Linda—who played both a friendly and a maternal role for the youth—"recognized how a lot of us were taken [a]back by how [Janet] entered the group." She went on to describe how Linda was able to diffuse these tensions by reaching out to listen to the
590 girls' concerns. She appeared to do this without under-cutting Janet's position. In the flow of daily life and across different occasions, individual program leaders adopted multiple roles that allowed them to create or restore conditions for positive youth development.
595 *Function of multiple roles.* Analysis suggested that playing multiple roles allowed the program leaders to effectively respond to the needs of a given youth or the group in a particular instance. In some instances, the youth needed the influence of a wise mentor; in other
600 cases, youth needed the benevolent authority of a parent figure. In this section, I use several cases to illustrate how moving across multiple roles seemed to make the program leaders more effective.

This interplay was illustrated in The Studio, where
605 the primary program leader, Neisha, was effective at striking a balance between friend and parent figure. The Studio targets high-risk urban youth, many of whom have dropped out of high school and are focused on immediate concerns of money, work, and survival.
610 Program leaders assist these youth in securing jobs, taking the GED, applying for school, and avoiding negative influences. Neisha earned the trust and respect of the youth she worked with, but she also provided these young people a necessary degree of authority and
615 accountability when they weren't doing what was in

their own best interest. One young woman described Neisha this way: "Either she's buddy-buddy with you, or the next minute she's like your mom. It's like she switches on you, but it's like for a good thing; she
620 makes sure it's a good cause." Another male youth reiterated of Neisha,

> She could be a mother, she could be a friend, but no matter what, she's just there. So one day she'll be your friend and everything, but then one day she'll just start acting
625 > like a mother and flip out on you if you're doing something wrong. So, it's like everything that a person really needs.

She was able to move from being perceived as a casual friend, who shares jokes and music interests
630 with the youth, to a stern mother who nags them to take the GED or calls them on drug use depending on the circumstances and the needs of the youth at hand. Observation suggests that because she was effective at building trusted rapport, Neisha was able to shift to
635 hold youth accountable when needed.

Another case illustrates how a foundation of personal connection allowed the program leader to provide instructional support. Gary, one of the leaders for Media Masters, shared many interests and hobbies with
640 the participating youth. His friendly demeanor and mutual regard helped differentiate the program, which was housed within the school's computer lab, from the regular school day and dynamics. Before the program start time, Gary was often found hanging out with the
645 youth talking about the latest video game or animation film. This rapport facilitated his ability to effectively play an instrumental role in helping youth master the computer programs and technology that were the basis for the program. When it was time to get down to busi-
650 ness, Gary was able to establish his authority, provide instruction, and redirect off-task behavior. A youth described how Gary's affable manner helped him keep

the program on track and be a more effective leader: "He does it in a cool way, where you don't have to even keep [youth] in line because they respect you already." This same youth went on to explain that trusting relationships between youth and instructors helped the program run more smoothly: "Not just leadership is needed, but a certain kind of trust where you won't just take them as an instructor, but as a friend, too. And therefore everybody's working better." As this quote illustrates, building a connection of friendship with youth allowed the program leaders the latitude to have authority as a teacher in ways that did not alienate the youth.

Data for these and other leaders suggest that playing multiple roles served the function of meeting the diverse needs of the youth. For nearly all leaders, there was a personal peerlike dimension to their relationships, where program leaders grew close and offered emotional support to youth. Another layer of their work constituted a professional dimension where program leaders played the adult and provided vital structure, standards, and knowledge. Most of the primary program leaders we studied were able to bridge the role of friend and parent or teacher in an effort to best support the youth in differing situations.

A few of the secondary program leaders, however, failed to build personal trust, which risked violating youths' sense of fairness, turning them off, and crossing over into murky professional terrain. For example, at Harambee there were several new, inexperienced interns who changed roles in ways that were disconcerting to the youth. Youth expressed disgruntlement at how a male intern "switches up and wants to be [their] friend one minute and the next he is reprimanding [them]." Youth described that it was hard to know how to take him because he was never the same. It is a delicate and dynamic balance of personal feelings and comfort zones with professional obligations and objectives.

The more experienced program leaders were able to effectively take up different roles with individual youth in varying situations in an effort to best meet the needs and interests of the youth they served. In examining how the program leaders moved across these various roles, I identified several techniques they employed for navigating these complicated relationships[4] (Walker, 2005). First, as stated, they described the foundational importance of building trust and sustained, caring relationships with youth over time. This gave them the latitude to switch roles, including taking authority when needed in ways that did not alienate youth. Second, they recognized the importance of being aware of and responsive to youths' needs. They were responsive to youth and context and able to anticipate situations and intercept challenges and setbacks by switching roles accordingly. Third, they emphasized the importance of being clear and consistent with regard to their interactions with youth. In this way, youth understood

and trusted the program leaders and did not feel undermined by their switching roles. The findings suggest that by building trust, being responsive, and being consistent, the program leaders were able to successfully balance multiple roles in ways that increased their effectiveness at achieving their intentions.

### Conclusions

The importance of youth-adult relationships to youth work has been established in the literature. This article extends our understanding by examining the complex role relationships program leaders create in youth programs as well as how these roles function, for social role theory suggests that the role relationships that program leaders forge with youth structure how leaders are able to foster youth development in different ways. This article proposes that within the unique context of youth programs, program leaders assume a broad role portfolio that allows them to effectively meet a range of youth development needs.

Program leaders share features of roles such as parents and teachers, yet they are distinct from, and in some respects less confined than, these other adults in youth's lives. Faced with fewer curricular demands than teachers, for example, program leaders are afforded unique opportunities to engage in informal conversations and enjoyable activities that can give rise to close bonds with youth (Rhodes, 2004). Moreover, because of the voluntarily nature of youth programs, the meaningful relationships forged can be a reason for youth to choose to participate. To be sure, parents, teachers, and employers play multiple roles in the lives of youth as well. But they are often constrained by the nature of their roles as authorities, evaluators, and supervisors or, in the case of schools and workplaces, by the nature of their more formal, less intimate settings. By standing outside of these roles and constraints, program leaders appear to have an advantage and an opportunity to provide a kind of guidance that other adults are not always trusted to give.

In addition, program leaders were able to effectively respond to the youth they served because they had a broad role portfolio. Their role as friend allowed them to build trust and sustain personal relationships with the youth. In a parent role, they cultivated an emotional closeness that afforded them the ability to set limits and exert authority when needed. As respected adults in the role of mentor, they influenced youth by offering wise judgment and emotional support. As teacher and boss, they possessed authoritative knowledge and expertise, and they offered instrumental support to enhance both learning and performance.

These program leaders embodied elements of archetypal reciprocal roles, yet the role relationships they cultivated with the youth appeared to be more nuanced. Although they possessed authority likened to a parent, teacher, or boss, the youth tended to perceive their role relationship as less hierarchical and more intimate in

770 nature. In the intermediate zone of youth programs, program leaders appeared to be able to transcend traditional reciprocal roles, straddle the adult and youth worlds, and position themselves in a range of ways that allowed them to meet the varied needs of the youth.

775 There are both methodological and conceptual limitations to this study. First, the scope of this inquiry and its sample size are limited. Furthermore, the program leaders were selected for being in high-quality programs and thus are not necessarily representative. My goal was not to describe the typical youth development program leader but rather to develop theoretical understanding about the roles program leaders play. Future 780 research should attend to the roles of program leaders serving younger youth and youth from different cultural and programmatic contexts. Moreover, further inquiry is needed to understand how leaders switch roles, under what circumstances, and how this corre-785 lates with meeting the needs of youth. Undoubtedly, other roles and techniques are employed by program leaders, and those discussed are not intended as a prescription for practice. Rather, by outlining some of these dimensions and strategies, I hoped to help practi-790 tioners become more intentional, both in the relationships they forge with youth and in the strategies they employ to balance their multiple roles in youth's lives.

### Notes

1. For consistency, I refer to these adults as *program leaders*, but other terms like *youth worker*, *advisor*, *director*, *lead organizer*, and *teacher* were used in the specific settings.
2. Copies of the interview protocol are available from the author on request.
3. The names of people and programs have been changed to preserve their anonymity.
4. The techniques used are discussed at length elsewhere (Walker, 2005).

### References

Auerbach, C. F., & Silverstein, L. B. (2003). *Qualitative data: An introduction to coding and analysis.* New York: New York University Press.

Bernstein-Yamashiro, B. (2004). Learning relationships: Teacher-student connections, learning, and identity in high school. In G. G. Noam (Ed.), *New directions for youth development: After school worlds: Creating space for development and learning* (pp. 55–70). San Francisco, CA: Jossey-Bass.

Bronfenbrenner, U. (1979). *The ecology of human development: Experiments by nature and design.* Cambridge, MA: Harvard University Press.

Brown, B. (1990). Peer groups and peer cultures. In S. Feldman & G. R. Elliot (Eds.), *At the threshold* (pp. 171–196). Cambridge, MA: Harvard University Press.

Bukowski, W. M., Newcomb, A. F., & Hartup, W. W. (1996). Friendship and its significance in childhood and adolescence: Introduction and comment. In W. M. Bukowski, A. F. Newcomb, & W. W. Hartup (Eds.), *The company they keep: Friendship in childhood and adolescence* (pp. 1–15). New York: Cambridge University Press.

Clark-Lempers, D. S., Lempers, J. D., & Ho, C. (1991). Early, middle, and late adolescents' perceptions of their relationships with significant others. *Journal of Adolescent Research, 6,* 296–315.

Collins, W. A., & Laursen, B. (2004). Parent-adolescent relationships and influences. In R. M. Lerner & L. Steinberg (Eds.), *Handbook of adolescent psychology* (2nd ed., pp. 331–361). Hoboken, NJ: Wiley.

Darling, N., Hamilton, S. F., & Niego, S. (1994). Adolescents' relations with adults outside the family. In R. Montemayor, G. R. Adams, & T. P. Gulotta (Eds.), *Advances in adolescent development, Vol. 6: Personal relationships during adolescence* (pp. 216–235). Thousand Oaks, CA: Sage.

Darling, N., Hamilton, S. F., & Shaver, K. H. (2003). Relationships outside the family: Unrelated adults. In G. Adams & M. Berzonsky (Eds.), *Blackwell handbook of adolescence* (pp. 349–370). Malden, MA: Blackwell.

Galbo, J. J. (1986). Adolescents' perceptions of significant adults: Implications for the family, the school and youth serving agencies. *Children and Youth Services Review, 8,* 35–51.

Galbo, J. J. (1989). The teacher as significant adult: A review of the literature. *Adolescence, 24,* 549–556.

Halpern, R. (2005). Instrumental relationships: A potential relational model for inner-city youth programs. *Journal of Community Psychology, 33*(1), 11–20.

Hamilton, M. A., & Hamilton, S. F. (2004). Contexts for mentoring: Adolescent-adult relationships in workplaces and communities. In R. M. Lerner & L. Steinberg (Eds.), *Handbook of adolescent psychology* (2nd ed., pp. 395–428). Hoboken, NJ: Wiley.

Heath, S. B. (1994). The project of learning from the inner-city youth perspective. In F. A. Villarruel & R. M. Lerner (Eds.), *New directions for child development: Promoting community-based programs for socialization and learning* (pp. 25–34). San Francisco, CA: Jossey-Bass.

Hirsch, B. (2005). *A place to call home: After-school programs for urban youth.* Washington, DC: American Psychological Association.

Hirsh, B., & Wong, V. (2005). After-school programs. In D. Dubois & M. Karcher (Eds.). *The handbook of youth mentoring* (pp. 364–375). Thousand Oaks, CA: Sage.

Larson, R., Pearce, N., Sullivan, P., & Jarrett, R. L. (2007). Participation in youth programs as a catalyst for negotiation of family autonomy with connection. *Journal of Youth and Adolescence, 36,* 31–45.

Larson, R., & Walker, K. (2006). Learning about the "real world" in an urban arts program. *Journal of Adolescent Research, 21,* 244–268.

Lempers, J. D., & Clark-Lempers, D. S. (1992). Young, middle, and late adolescents' comparison of the functional importance of five significant relationships. *Journal of Youth and Adolescence, 21*(1), 53–96.

McLaughlin, M. W., Irby, M. A., & Langman, J. (1994). *Urban sanctuaries: Neighborhood organizations in the lives and futures of inner-city youth.* San Francisco, CA: Jossey-Bass.

Newman, B. A., & Newman, P. R. (2007). Social role theory. In B. M. Newman & P. R. Newman (Eds.), *Theories of human development* (pp. 160–172). Mahwah, NJ: Lawrence Erlbaum.

Noam, G. G., & Tillinger, J. R. (2004). After-school as intermediary space: Theory and typology of partnerships. In G. G. Noam (Ed.), *New directions for youth development: After school worlds: Creating space for development and learning* (pp. 75–113). San Francisco, CA: Jossey-Bass.

Patton, M. Q. (2002). *Qualitative research and evaluative methods* (3rd ed.). Thousand Oaks, CA: Sage.

Rhodes, J. (2002). *Stand by me: The risks and rewards of mentoring today's youth.* Cambridge, MA: Harvard University Press.

Rhodes, J. E. (2004). The critical ingredient: Caring youth-staff relationships in after-school settings. In G. G. Noam (Ed.), *New directions for youth development: After school worlds: Creating space for development and learning* (pp. 145–161). San Francisco, CA: Jossey-Bass.

Seligson, M., & MacPhee, M. (2004). Emotional intelligence and staff training in after-school environments. In G. G. Noam (Ed.), *New directions for youth development: After school worlds: Creating space for development and learning* (pp. 71–83). San Francisco, CA: Jossey-Bass.

Strauss, A., & Corbin, J. (1998). *Basics of qualitative research: Techniques and procedures for developing grounded theory* (2nd ed.). Thousand Oaks, CA: Sage.

Walker, K. C. (2005). *Understanding youth worker-young person relationships: How youth workers position themselves to support youth.* Unpublished doctoral dissertation, University of Illinois at Urbana-Champaign.

Walker, K. C., & Larson, R. W. (2006). Balancing the professional and the personal. In D. A. Blyth & J. A. Walker (Eds.), *New directions for youth development: Exceptional learning experiences for the middle years: Where high quality programs meet basic youth needs.* No. 112 (pp. 109–118). San Francisco, CA: Jossey-Bass.

Young, K. (1999). *The art of youth work.* Lyme Regis, UK: Russell House.

Youniss, J., & Smollar, J. (1985). *Adolescent relations with mothers, fathers, and friends.* Chicago, IL: University of Chicago Press.

Zeldin, S., Larson, R., Camino, L., & O'Conner, C. (2005). Intergenerational relationships and partnerships in community programs: Purpose, practice and directions for research. *Journal of Community Psychology, 33*(1), 1–10.

**Acknowledgments**: The author would like to thank the program leaders and youth who shared their experiences as well as Reed Larson for his valuable guidance and support. This study was supported by a grant from the William T. Grant Foundation.

**About the author**: *Kathrin C. Walker,* Ph.D., is a research associate at the University of Minnesota Extension Center for Youth Development, where she conducts applied research and evaluation on youth development practice and programs. Her current research focuses on the dilemmas that practitioners face in their everyday work with youth and their strategies for addressing these challenges.

**Address correspondence to**: Kathrin C. Walker, University of Minnesota Extension Center for Youth Development, 200 Oak Street SE, Minneapolis, MN 55455. E-mail: kcwalker@umn.edu

# Exercise for Article 32

## Factual Questions

1. What are the names of the two theories that the researcher mentions in the Introduction to the research report?

2. Does the researcher state that the sample is representative?

3. Of the 10 youths in the SisterHood program, how many were included in the study?

4. What was the program leaders' age range?

5. Did the researcher employ the procedure of grounded theory?

6. How many of the program leaders were perceived by the youth as being a boss?

## Questions for Discussion

7. The 12 programs were diverse in their purposes. Do you think it was a good idea to use such a diverse set of programs for this study? Explain. (See lines 80–83.)

8. Would you like to know more about the identification of the programs for this study? (See lines 92–99.)

9. Would it be helpful to see the interview protocol? Explain. (See line 120 for the footnote, which appears at the end of the article.)

10. What is your opinion of the researcher's definition of the role of friend? (See lines 165–187.)

11. Are any of the results especially interesting or surprising to you? (See lines 203–716.)

12. If you were to conduct a study on the same topic, would you use a qualitative research approach as was used in this study, or would you use a quantitative research approach? Explain.

## Quality Ratings

Directions: Indicate your level of agreement with each of the following statements by circling a number from 5 for strongly agree (SA) to 1 for strongly disagree (SD). If you believe an item is not applicable to this research article, leave it blank. Be prepared to explain your ratings. When responding to criteria A and B, keep in mind that brief titles and abstracts are conventional in published research.

A. The title of the article is appropriate.
SA   5   4   3   2   1   SD

B. The abstract provides an effective overview of the research article.
SA   5   4   3   2   1   SD

C. The introduction establishes the importance of the study.
SA   5   4   3   2   1   SD

D. The literature review establishes the context for the study.
SA   5   4   3   2   1   SD

E. The research purpose, question, or hypothesis is clearly stated.
SA   5   4   3   2   1   SD

F. The method of sampling is sound.
SA   5   4   3   2   1   SD

G. Relevant demographics (for example, age, gender, and ethnicity) are described.
SA   5   4   3   2   1   SD

H. Measurement procedures are adequate.
SA   5   4   3   2   1   SD

I. All procedures have been described in sufficient detail to permit a replication of the study.
SA   5   4   3   2   1   SD

J. The participants have been adequately protected from potential harm.
SA   5   4   3   2   1   SD

K. The results are clearly described.
SA   5   4   3   2   1   SD

L. The discussion/conclusion is appropriate.
SA   5   4   3   2   1   SD

M. Despite any flaws, the report is worthy of publication.
SA   5   4   3   2   1   SD

# Article 33

# Adventure Therapy: A Supplementary Group Therapy Approach for Men

DAVID E. SCHEINFELD
University of Texas, Austin

AARON B. ROCHLEN
University of Texas, Austin

SAM J. BUSER
Houston, Texas

ABSTRACT. This exploratory study investigated the use of adventure therapy (AT) as a supplementary group therapy approach to enrich the therapeutic experience for 11 middle-aged men seeking therapy in an office setting. Results from a semistructured group interview suggested participants found AT encouraged deeper therapeutic processing compared with their accounts of traditional group therapy. Participants noted the wilderness context, retreat length, and shared adventure activities as critical factors for reflection and therapeutic processing. Involvement in AT provided opportunities for gaining new perspectives, developing trust rapidly, and sharing personal issues more readily. The single-gendered nature of the group seemed to enhance a sense of camaraderie and empathy. Clinical implications are discussed within the context of AT and therapeutic interventions for men.

From *Psychology of Men & Masculinity, 12*, 188–194. Copyright © 2011 by the American Psychological Association. Reprinted with permission.

Nontraditional therapeutic approaches for men have received increased interest in the help-seeking literature (Brooks, 2010). Examples include life/executive coaching (McKelley & Rochlen, 2010), men's move-
5  ment events (Brooks, 2010), mythopoetic and weekend retreats (Andronico, 2001), online counseling (Rochlen, Land, & Wong, 2004), activity-oriented approaches (Rabinowitz, 2002; Rabinowitz & Cochran, 2002), support groups (Blazina & Marks, 2001), and
10  psychoeducational workshops (Levant, 1990). Within this area of research, authors have increasingly recognized the utility of out-of-office therapeutic experiences (Brooks, 2010).

One out-of-office approach that has received lim-
15  ited attention is adventure therapy (AT), which combines the benefits of adventure-based experiences with aspects of traditional therapy (Bandoroff & Newes, 2004). Adventure activities range from short-term initiatives and trust-building activities lasting several
20  hours to wilderness-based adventure experiences (e.g., camping, backpacking, rock climbing) lasting days, weeks, or months. These experiential activities are opportunities for intra- and interpersonal development (Itin, 2001). Processing the adventure-based activities
25  through group or individual counseling during the AT

experience is considered critical in facilitating insight and promoting change (Nadler & Luckner, 1992).

While research on AT with adult men is sparse, anecdotal evidence supports its potential (Buser, 2009;
30  Northern California Men's Center, 2010; Men's Vision Quests, n.d.). Furthermore, AT has shown to be effective with adolescents (Clark, Marmol, Cooley, & Gathercoal, 2004; Davis-Berman & Berman, 2008; Norton, 2009, 2011; Russell, 2001, 2003). For example, ado-
35  lescents participating in AT showed positive changes regarding their depressive symptoms (Norton, 2008, 2009), substance abuse/dependence (Russell, 2008) self-awareness (Bandoroff & Scherer, 1994; Hattie, Marsh, Neill, & Richards, 1997), self-esteem (Cason &
40  Gillis, 1994; White & Hendee, 2000), interpersonal skills (Bedard, Rosen, & Vacha-Haase, 2003), and internal locus of control (Cason & Gillis, 1994). Because of the challenge of living in the wilderness, participants have also shown progress in teamwork, communica-
45  tion, physical fitness, and creative problem-solving (Itin, 2001; Phillips-Miller & Russell, 2002).

Research indicates AT can provide an experientially based outlet for men to open up with other group members. Marsh and Richards (1989) found that older
50  adolescent males enrolled in an adventure-based therapeutic program became increasingly comfortable sharing personal information. Results suggested the experience created a noncompetitive bonding environment that helped participants focus on personal development.
55  Commonly, this group support is established through emphasizing teamwork and compassion.

Central to the adventure therapy process is the establishment of a supportive group culture (Hoyer, 2004; Russell, 2000). In general, there is growing evi-
60  dence affirming the benefits of group therapy for men (Andronico, 1996; Brooks, 1998; Nahon & Lander, 2008; Rabinowitz, 1991, 2005). Group therapy has been described as helpful for men in allowing for the reexperiencing of difficult affect, while simultaneously
65  creating a supportive net for bonding and expressing vulnerabilities (Brooks, 1996). Furthermore, men's groups help normalize men's concerns. Through creating a therapeutic space where men can find a sense of commonality and camaraderie, the need to compete

70 and perform male displays may be reduced (McPhee, 1996).

Considering the dearth of research on adventure therapy with adult males, the goal of this exploratory study was to investigate the ways in which an all-male 75 AT experience can be used as a supplementary approach to enrich the therapeutic experience for men seeking therapy in an office setting. Our research questions included (a) What were the helpful or unhelpful aspects of AT? (b) How did being in the wilderness 80 and engaging in adventure activities influence their therapeutic experience? (c) In what ways did being male and being with only men impact their therapeutic experience?

**Method**

*Participants*

Nine Caucasian and two Latino men of middle- to 85 upper-socioeconomic status from urban/suburban backgrounds served as participants. The lead therapist of the retreat e-mailed current and former clients informing them of an opportunity to attend an annual wilderness-based therapeutic retreat. Participants vol-90 untarily attended and paid $400.00. Participants ranged in age from 32 to 58 (median = 49, *SD* = 8.99) and were all college educated. All had a history of individual therapy ranging from 2 to 240 months (median = 24, *SD* = 91.55). Ten participants were currently seeing 95 the lead therapist for individual therapy. Eight had been involved with men's therapy groups for 1 to 60 months (median = 18, *SD* = 18.74). Four of those eight were currently involved in a weekly men's group led by the lead therapist. Five participants attended the retreat for 100 the first time, whereas the remaining six had attended previously. At least 50% of the clients' presenting issues pertained to marriage, family of-origin history, loss/grief, self-esteem, depression, and anger.

*Procedures*

The retreat lasted four days in a remote wilderness 105 area. The lead therapist and one other licensed psychologist, both specializing in therapy with men, led the retreat. The group established a base camp and spent all four days hiking (4–6 miles daily) and cooking together. Several group therapy sessions (2–3 110 hours) took place intermittently during hikes or in the evening. While hiking and cooking, the men informally conversed about personal issues brought up in group therapy or otherwise on their minds.

The principal investigator (PI) acted as a partici-115 pant-observer. He notified participants on the first evening he would be observing all activities, engaging in moderate interpersonal relations, and conducting an optional 2-hr group interview immediately following the retreat. All participants provided consent on the 120 first evening. The choice of a semistructured group interview was offered to meet the time constraints of the retreat. Sample interview questions included (a) How did the experience of being in the wilderness and

engaging in outdoor activities affect the group therapy 125 experience? (b) What was the most impactful experience or activity during the retreat? The complete interview protocol is available upon request.

*Data Analysis*

Because of the small sample size and exploratory nature of this study, qualitative analysis adapting mul-130 tiple methodologies was used to illustrate the impact of AT on the participants' therapeutic experience. First, the PI transcribed the audiorecording verbatim and reviewed it for errors. Second, the PI and two graduate students independently employed an open coding proc-135 ess of all the participants' responses (Strauss, 1987), with an emphasis on inductively identifying emic themes (Maxwell, 1996). The remainder of analysis was drawn from aspects of Consensual Qualitative Research (Hill et al., 2005). A theme was defined as a 140 pattern of ideas, observations, or experiences expressed in at least three participants' responses. Third, the reviewers sorted themes by research questions. Fourth, the research team engaged in cross-analysis by deliberating until reaching consensus on the final set of 145 themes. Finally, qualitative validity was established by having a professor with expertise in men's studies audit the themes and associated responses. Based on this audit, minor changes were made to the themes and representative responses.

**Results and Discussion**

150 Table 1 provides an overview of the themes, descriptions, and frequency of responses sorted by research question. The first research question addressed the ways in which the AT experience was helpful or unhelpful. Many participants noted that a beneficial 155 aspect was the separation from typical home distractions (work, family, etc.). This separation seemed to provide substantial space for members to reflect upon and address personal issues. One participant stated,

> The wilderness is the best because you can detach from 160 the rest of the world, and clear your mind…. It is a deliberate act, sure you can turn your cell phones off [in the city], but when you go to bed you switch it on and connect with the world, whereas here you have no choice.

Furthermore, participants reported the retreat's 4-165 day duration created additional time to address personal issues during the group therapy sessions and informally during the day's events. A participant noted, "The experience is more intense than group [back home] because you are not confined to 90 minutes, 170 there's more time to work out issues and see things carried forward." This finding is corroborated by findings from Ewert (1982), suggesting AT experiences create more opportunities to discover and apply insight within the group setting. In fact, Ewert suggests groups 175 experience the most therapeutic benefit when in the wilderness for several weeks.

Table 1
*Summary of Themes, Descriptions, and Percentages by Research Question*

| Theme and description[a] | $n$[b] (%) |
| --- | --- |
| **Q1: What were the helpful or unhelpful aspects of AT?** | |
| Home separation | 8 (73) |
| Being away from home enhanced the therapeutic experience by providing a space to distance themselves from distractions at home and clear their minds. | |
| Duration | 5 (45) |
| The 4-day duration of the therapy experience provided more time to work through issues. | |
| Appeal of AT | 5 (45) |
| Participants found the wilderness setting and shared activities increased their desire to be there and engage in therapeutic work. | |
| **Q2: How did being in the wilderness and engaging in adventure activities influence their therapeutic experience?** | |
| Perspective-gaining | 10 (91) |
| Being in the wilderness and engaging in hiking helped participants clear their minds and gain new perspectives on their lives. | |
| Interdependence/trust | 5 (45) |
| The collaborative nature of shared adventure and camp activities established interdependence, which fostered feelings of trust among group members. | |
| Accessing vulnerability and openness | 5 (45) |
| Adventure activities provided more opportunity and motivation for participants to share their thoughts and feelings. | |
| Spontaneous connection | 3 (27) |
| During hiking, cooking, or down time, participants engaged in additional and spontaneous therapeutic processing among dyads or small groups. | |
| **Q3: In what ways did being male and being with only men impact their therapeutic experience?** | |
| Shared insight | 7 (63) |
| Participants gained insight and experienced empathy when group members shared similar problems and provided nonjudgmental feedback. | |
| Male vulnerability | 6 (54) |
| Men being nonjudgmental and vulnerable with other men increased participants' ability to share and be vulnerable. | |
| Male camaraderie | 6 (54) |
| Participants experienced a unique male connection because men formed relationships around emotional sharing. | |

*Note. N* = 11.
[a]Themes with three or fewer responses were not included.
[b]$n$ = number of participants responding to each theme.

Some participants found the wilderness setting and shared activities increased their desire to attend and engage in therapeutic work.

180 One man reflected, "I don't think I might have participated in [group therapy] with strangers at someone's house. However I think the camping and hiking [with other men] was intriguing." This affinity toward adventure activity mirrors the general finding that men

185 tend to value coming together through shared physical activity (Kiselica, Englar-Carlson, Horne, & Fisher, 2008; Mortola, Hiton, & Grant, 2008). In fact, some participants commented their motivation to attend the retreat was partially because of the group activity for-

190 mat.

The second research question addressed the impact of being in the wilderness and engaging in adventure activities on the participants' therapeutic experience. The majority of participants experienced the wilderness

195 and hiking as an opportunity to gain new perspectives. One participant commented, "Hiking in nature, it gives you a chance to look at things and reassess, reset the button and come back with new information and interesting thoughts about how to approach life." Kaplan

200 and Talbot (1983) found the tranquility of the wilderness often leads to deep contemplation. The wilderness encouraged one participant on the retreat to, "[strip] things down to the bare essentials," which helped him focus on what's most important to him. This finding is

205 consistent with literature that suggests the novel and unknown quality of the wilderness context encourages clients to form fresh intrapersonal and interpersonal perspectives (Gass, 1993).

The teamwork and a sense of group challenge inherent

210 in the shared adventure activities appeared to encourage interdependence. One participant noted that because of the physicality and teamwork required during hikes, it became a "legendary challenge" that helped the group grow closer. Experiencing challeng-

215 ing events in conjunction with emotional sharing often quickly strengthens trust among group members (Hill,

2007) because they have to rely on each other to live in the wilderness while engaging one another on an emotional level (Gillis, 1995). For example, a participant commented, "The shared cooking, shared trekking, and isolation. We are dependent on each other…that fosters a trust relationship." Similar to this finding, Jolliff and Horne (1996) discovered trust-building activities within men's groups can help teach men to trust, protect, support, and nurture one another.

Adventure activities appeared to create alternative avenues for participants to engage in therapeutic processing. One participant reflected, "The long trekking allows you to open up verbally whenever you are ready. Doing something to communicate and connect would not have worked as well if there hadn't been physical activity." This finding parallels literature that suggests creating varying outlets for emotional expression and processing are important (Englar-Carlson, 2006) because men may fear emotional expression because of feelings of shame associated with being vulnerable (Good & Fischer, 1997; Wong, Pituch, & Rochlen, 2006). In fact, Wong and Rochlen (2005) suggest sharing emotions without assistive activities can be unproductive for some men. Furthermore, exercise studies suggest physical exercise can facilitate heightened short-term cognitive differentiation (Tompprowski & Ellis, 1986) and improve self-perceptions and mood states (Fox, 1999).

The shared activities outside of group therapy seemed to provide participants flexibility and opportunity to address personal issues in small, spontaneously formed groups. One participant noted,

> On hikes small groups form, break up, and change. You can meet more closely with individuals…. You learn a lot about the people on the way up or down, which you don't when you're sitting around in a larger group discussion.

Flexibility and space for participants to freely share provides greater opportunity to self-disclose and process emotions. Hoyer (2004) posited clients benefit from this unstructured time because the therapist and group members can observe and informally process with each other outside of structured group therapy. Thus, the overall AT process involves an interplay where information from group therapy is processed during shared activities and vice versa.

Finally, the third research question addressed the impact of attending a male-only retreat. Many participants noted the commonality of their shared issues helped them feel closer and identify with one another. One participant commented he felt "enlightened" after discovering other group members faced similar problems, and he would not be negatively judged. Furthermore, participants noted greater comfort in sharing personal information after witnessing other men open up. A participant commented, "The fact I see other men being vulnerable, it allowed me to feel more comfort-

able opening up." These findings are consistent with literature on men's groups (Andronico, 1996).

Participants seemed to experience this openness among group members as a unique opportunity to develop camaraderie through becoming emotional and sharing personal issues. In fact, several responses suggested participants would be less candid and uninterested in a mixed-gendered retreat. One participant reflected, "I think having male friends where one can speak about [personal issues] is unusual for most men in our society, and that is one of the advantages of why this is such a powerful experience." Historically men have formed camaraderie in groups (Berstein, 1987). However, they tend toward competitive interactions (Farr, 1986; Meth & Pasick, 1990). Adventure therapy discourages competition and provides space for collaborative activities, while creating a supportive environment to become vulnerable and address personal issues (Hill, 2007).

The results of our study may provide clinical insight into the use of AT as a supplementary group therapy approach to enrich the therapeutic experience for adult males seeking therapy in the office setting. Four unique clinical aspects of the AT format are highlighted. First, the physical separation from home for at least four days seems to help male clients gain clarity and focus on personal issues. Separation can be further achieved by holding the retreat in a remote wilderness setting absent of cell phone reception or media sources that may serve as distractions. Second, incorporating adventure activities appears to appeal to male clients and may increase their interest in therapeutic experiences. Third, the interdependence and teamwork required to live in the wilderness and engage in adventure activities seems to facilitate trust among group members in an expedited fashion. Practitioners may want to consider shared physical activities to build trust. Fourth, the time spent in shared adventure-activities can provide an alternative outlet for male clients to express themselves emotionally and interpersonally, which provides more opportunity to process personal issues. Finally, AT training opportunities are available through universities and private institutions providing intensive workshops, continuing education credits, and master's degrees. Additional information on these training opportunities is available from the first author upon request.

The above findings and clinical implications are speculative and need to be considered in light of the study's multiple limitations. First, because of the small sample size and large variation in participants' previous therapy experience and presenting issues, there is limited generalizability. Second, external validity is limited because the group interview data were collected on one occasion in one context. Third, the announcement of the group interview after the participants arrived may have influenced their experience, biasing their responses. Fourth, a demand characteristic may have been present: participants could have presented biased responses because of the relationship formed with the principal investigator as a participant observer during the retreat. Considering the exploratory nature 335 of this study, it is recommended further research focus on longitudinal data collection, using a larger and more diverse sample size, and controls for participants' previous therapy experience.

## References

Andronico, M. P. (Ed.). (1996). *Men in groups: Insights, interventions, and psychoeducational work.* Washington, DC: American Psychological Association.

Andronico, M. P. (2001). Mythopoetic and weekend retreats to facilitate men's growth. In G. R. Brooks & G. E. Good (Eds.), *The new handbook of counseling and psychotherapy with men.* (pp. 464–480). San Francisco, CA: Jossey Bass.

Bandoroff, S., & Newes, S. (Eds.). (2004). *Coming of age: The evolving field of adventure therapy.* Boulder, CO: Association for Experiential Education.

Bandoroff, S., & Scherer, D. G. (1994). Wilderness family therapy: An innovative treatment approach for problem youth. *Journal of Child and Family Studies, 3,* 175–191.

Bedard, R. M., Rosen, L. A., & Vacha-Haase, T. (2003). Wilderness therapy programs for juvenile delinquents: A meta-analysis. *Journal of Therapeutic Wilderness Camping, 3,* 7–13.

Berstein, J. (1987). The male group. In L. Mahdi, S. Foster, & M. Little (Eds.), *Betwixt and between* (pp. 135–145). LaSalle, IL: Open Court Press.

Blazina, C., & Marks, L. I. (2001). College men's affective reactions to individual therapy, psychoeducational workshops, and men's support group brochures: The influence of gender-role conflict and power dynamics upon help-seeking attitudes. *Psychotherapy: Theory, Research, Practice, Training, 38,* 297–305.

Brooks, G. R. (1996). Treatment for therapy resistant men. In M. P. Andronico (Ed.), *Men in groups: Insights, interventions, and psychoeducational work* (pp. 7–20). Washington, DC: American Psychological Association.

Brooks, G. R. (1998). *A new psychotherapy for traditional men.* San Francisco, CA: Jossey Bass.

Brooks, G. R. (2010). *Beyond the crisis of masculinity: A transtheoretical model for male-friendly therapy.* Washington, DC: American Psychological Association.

Buser, S. (2009, December). *Big Bend Men's Retreat.* Retrieved from http://drsamjbuser.com/care_services_bigbend.html

Cason, D. R., & Gillis, H. L. (1994). A meta analysis of adventure programming with adolescents. *Journal of Experiential Education, 17,* 40–47.

Clark, J. P., Marmol, L. M., Cooley, R., & Gathercoal, K. (2004). The effects of wilderness therapy on the clinical concerns (on axis I, II, and IV) of troubled adolescents. *Journal of Experiential Education, 27,* 213–232.

Davis-Berman, J., & Berman, D. (2008). *The promise of wilderness therapy.* Boulder, CO: The Association for Experiential Education.

Englar-Carlson, M. (2006). Masculine norms and the therapy process. In M. Englar-Carlson & M. A. Stevens (Eds.), *In the room with men: A casebook of therapeutic change* (pp. 13–47). Washington, DC: American Psychological Association.

Ewert, A. (1982). The effect of course length on the reported self-concepts of selected Outward Bound participants (Doctoral dissertation, University of Oregon, 1982). *Dissertation Abstracts International, 43,* 3111 A.

Farr, K. A. (1986). Dominance bonding through the good old boys socializing group. *Sex Roles, 18,* 259–277.

Fox, K. R. (1999). The influence of physical activity on mental well-being. *Public Health Nutrition, 2,* 411–418.

Gass, M. (1993). *Adventure therapy: Therapeutic applications of adventure programming.* Dubuque, IA: Kendall/Hunt.

Gillis, H. L. (1995). If I conduct outdoor pursuits with clinical populations, am I an adventure therapist? *Journal of Leisurability, 22,* 5–15.

Good, G. E., & Fischer, A. R. (1997). Men and psychotherapy: An investigation of alexithymia, intimacy, and masculine gender roles. *Psychotherapy: Theory, Research, Practice, Training, 34,* 160–170.

Hattie, J., Marsh, H. W., Neill, J. T., & Richards, G. E. (1997). Adventure education and Outward Bound: Out-of-class experiences that make a lasting difference. *Review of Educational Research, 67,* 43–87.

Hill, C. E., Thompson, B. J., Hess, S. A., Knox, S., Williams, E. N., & Ladany, N. (2005). Consensual qualitative research: An update. *Journal of Counseling Psychology, 52,* 196–205.

Hill, N. R. (2007). Wilderness therapy as a treatment modality for at-risk youth: A primer for mental health counselors. *Journal of Mental Health Counseling, 29,* 338–349.

Hoyer, S. M. (2004). Effective wilderness therapy: Theory-informed practice. In S. Bandoroff & S. Newes (Eds.), *Coming of age: The evolving field of adventure therapy* (pp. 56–73). Boulder, CO: Association for Experiential Education.

Itin, C. M. (2001). Adventure therapy: Critical questions. *The Journal of Experiential Education, 24,* 80–84.

Jolliff, D. L., & Horne, A. M. (1996). Group counseling for middle-class men. In M. P. Andronico (Ed.), *Men in groups: Insights, interventions, and psychoeducational work* (pp. 51–68). Washington, DC: American Psychological Association.

Kaplan, S., & Talbot, J. F. (1983). Psychological benefits of wilderness experience. In I. Altman & J. F. Wohwill (Eds.), *Behavior and the environment* (pp. 166–203). New York: Plenum Press.

Kiselica, M. S., Englar-Carlson, M., Horne, A. M., & Fisher, M. (2008). A positive psychology perspective on helping boys. In M. S. Kiselica, M. Englar-Carlson, & A. Horne (Eds.), *Counseling troubled boys* (pp. 31–48). New York: Routledge.

Levant, R. F. (1990). Psychological services designed for men: A psychoeducational approach. *Psychotherapy: Theory, Research, Practice, Training, 27,* 309–315.

Marsh, H. W., & Richards, G. E. (1989). A test of bipolar and androgyny perspectives of masculinity and femininity: The effect of participation in an Outward Bound program. *Journal of Personality, 57,* 115–120.

Maxwell, J. A. (1996). *Qualitative research design.* Thousand Oaks, CA: Sage.

McKelley, R. A., & Rochlen, A. B. (2010). Conformity to masculine role norms and preferences for therapy or executive coaching. *Psychology of Men & Masculinity, 11,* 1–14.

McPhee, D. M. (1996). Techniques in group psychotherapy with men. In M. P. Andronico (Ed.), *Men in groups: Insights, interventions, and psychoeducational work* (pp. 7–20). Washington, DC: American Psychological Association.

Meth, R. L., & Pasick, R. S. (1990). *Men in therapy: The challenge of change.* New York: The Guilford Press.

Mortola, P., Hiton, H., & Grant, S. (2008). *Bam! Boys advocacy and mentoring.* New York: Routledge.

Nadler, R. S., & Luckner, J. L. (1992). *Processing the adventure experience: Theory and practice.* Dubuque, IA: Kendall/Hunt.

Nahon, D., & Lander, N. R. (2008). Recruitment and engagement in men's psychotherapy groups: An integrity model, value-based perspective. *International Journal of Men's Health, 7,* 218–236.

Northern California Men's Center 2010, Men's Vision Quests. (n.d.). *A Transformational wilderness experience.* Retrieved January 4, 2010, from http://www.mensgroups.com/_p_quests.htm

Norton, C. (2008). Understanding the impact of wilderness therapy on adolescent depression and psychosocial development. *Illinois Child Welfare, 4*(1), 166–178.

Norton, C. L. (2009). Into the wilderness—A case study: The psychodynamics of adolescent depression and the need for a holistic intervention. *Clinical Social Work Journal, 38,* 226–235.

Norton, C. L. (2011). *Innovative interventions in child and adolescent mental health.* New York, NY: Routledge.

Phillips-Miller, D., & Russell, K. C. (2002). Perspectives on the wilderness therapy process and its relation to outcome. *Child and Youth Care Forum, 31,* 415–437.

Rabinowitz, F. E. (2002). Utilizing the body in therapy with men. *Society for the Psychological Study of Men and Masculinity Bulletin, 8,* 12–13.

Rabinowitz, F. R. (2005). Group therapy for men. In G. Good & G. Brooks (Eds.), *New handbook of psychotherapy and counseling with men: A comprehensive guide to settings, problems, and treatment approaches* (pp. 264–277). San Francisco, CA: Jossey Bass.

Rabinowitz, F. (1991). The male-to-male embrace: Breaking the touch taboo in a men's therapy group. *Journal of Counseling and Development, 69,* 574–576.

Rabinowitz, F., & Cochran, S. V. (2002). *Deepening psychotherapy with men.* Washington, DC: American Psychological Association.

Rochlen, A. B., Land, L. N., & Wong, Y. J. (2004). Male restrictive emotionality and evaluations of online versus face-to-face counseling. *Psychology of Men & Masculinity, 5,* 190–200.

Russell, K. C. (2000). Exploring how the wilderness therapy process relates to outcomes. *Journal of Experiential Education, 23,* 170–176.

Russell, K. C. (2001). What is wilderness therapy? *Journal of Experiential Education, 24,* 70–84.

Russell, K. C. (2003). An assessment of outcomes in outdoor behavioral healthcare treatment. *Child and Youth Care Forum, 32,* 355–381.

Russell, K. C. (2008). Adolescence substance use treatment: Service delivery, research on effectiveness, and emerging treatment alternatives. *Journal of Groups in Addiction and Recovery, 2*(2–4), 68–96.

Strauss, A. (1987). *Qualitative analysis for social scientists.* New York, NY: Cambridge University Press.

Tompprowski, P. D., & Ellis, N. R. (1986). Effects of exercise on cognitive processes: A review. *Psychological Bulletin, 99,* 338–346.

White, D. D., & Hendee, J. C. (2000). Primal hypotheses: The relationship between naturalness, solitude, and the wilderness experience benefits of development of self, development of community, and spiritual development.

*Proceedings of the USDA Forest Service Proceedings RMRS-P-15, USA, 3*, 223–227.

Wong, Y. J., Pituch, A. P., & Rochlen, A. B. (2006). Men's restrictive emotionality: An investigation of associations with other emotion-related constructs, anxiety, and underlying dimensions. *Psychology of Men & Masculinity, 7*, 113–126.

Wong, Y. J., & Rochlen, A. B. (2005). Demystifying men's emotional behavior: New directions and implications for counseling and research. *Psychology of Men & Masculinity, 6*, 62–72.

**Acknowledgments:** We thank Erin Reilly and Kathryn Piazza for their time coding data. We are also greatly appreciative of Drs. Dan and Sandra Scheinfeld for their insight and thoughtful feedback.

**Address correspondence to:** David E. Scheinfeld, Department of Educational Psychology, Counseling Psychology Program, University of Texas at Austin, 1 University Station D5800, Austin, TX 78712. E-mail: dscheinfeld@mail.utexas.edu

# Exercise for Article 33

## Factual Questions

1. According to the researchers, is there an abundance of research on AT?

2. To whom did the therapist e-mail information about the retreat?

3. How many of the participants have been involved with men's therapy groups?

4. In the data analysis, how was the theme defined?

5. Did all the participants provide consent?

6. How many of the participants responded to the theme of male vulnerability?

## Questions for Discussion

7. In your opinion, are the adventure therapy activities described in sufficient detail? Explain. (See lines 18–22.)

8. How important is it to know the clients' presenting issues? (See lines 101–103)

9. What is your understanding of the meaning of the term *semi-structured interview*? (See lines 120–127.)

10. Is it important to know that a professor audited the results? Explain. (See lines 145–149.)

11. How useful is Table 1 in helping you understand the results of this study? Would the results be as understandable without the table? Explain.

12. Do you agree with the researchers that the study has multiple limitations? Explain. (See lines 320–338.)

## Quality Ratings

Directions: Indicate your level of agreement with each of the following statements by circling a number from 5 for strongly agree (SA) to 1 for strongly disagree (SD). If you believe an item is not applicable to this research article, leave it blank. Be prepared to explain your ratings. When responding to criteria A and B, keep in mind that brief titles and abstracts are conventional in published research.

A. The title of the article is appropriate.

SA   5   4   3   2   1   SD

B. The abstract provides an effective overview of the research article.

SA   5   4   3   2   1   SD

C. The introduction establishes the importance of the study.

SA   5   4   3   2   1   SD

D. The literature review establishes the context for the study.

SA   5   4   3   2   1   SD

E. The research purpose, question, or hypothesis is clearly stated.

SA   5   4   3   2   1   SD

F. The method of sampling is sound.

SA   5   4   3   2   1   SD

G. Relevant demographics (for example, age, gender, and ethnicity) are described.

SA   5   4   3   2   1   SD

H. Measurement procedures are adequate.

SA   5   4   3   2   1   SD

I. All procedures have been described in sufficient detail to permit a replication of the study.

SA   5   4   3   2   1   SD

J. The participants have been adequately protected from potential harm.

SA   5   4   3   2   1   SD

K. The results are clearly described.

SA   5   4   3   2   1   SD

L. The discussion/conclusion is appropriate.

SA   5   4   3   2   1   SD

M. Despite any flaws, the report is worthy of publication.

SA   5   4   3   2   1   SD

# Article 34

# Help-Seeking Behaviors and Depression Among African American Adolescent Boys

MICHAEL A. LINDSEY
University of Maryland

WYNNE S. KORR
University of Illinois

MARINA BROITMAN
National Institute of Mental Health

LEE BONE
Johns Hopkins University

ALAN GREEN
Johns Hopkins University

PHILIP J. LEAF
Johns Hopkins University

ABSTRACT. This study examined the help-seeking behaviors of depressed, African American adolescents. Qualitative interviews were conducted with 18 urban, African American boys, ages 14 to 18, who were recruited from community-based mental health centers and after-school programs for youths. Interviews covered sociodemographic information, questions regarding depressive symptomatology, and open-ended questions derived from the Network-Episode Model—including knowledge, attitudes and behaviors related to problem recognition, help seeking, and perceptions of mental health services. Most often adolescents discussed their problems with their family and often received divergent messages about problem resolution; absent informal network resolution of their problems, professional help would be sought, and those receiving treatment were more likely to get support from friends but were less likely to tell friends that they were actually receiving care. Implications for social work research and practice are discussed.

From *Social Work*, *51*, 49–58. Copyright © 2006 by the National Association of Social Workers. Reprinted with permission.

Childhood depression is a serious public health concern for families, schools, social workers, and other mental health practitioners. Annual estimates in the general population indicate that 8.3% of adolescents
5 suffer from depression (Birmaher et al., 1996). Although research indicates that depression is highly amenable to treatment (Petersen et al., 1993), the *Surgeon General's Report on Mental Health* (U.S. Department of Health and Human Services [HHS], 2001)
10 indicated that few children and adolescents with a depressive disorder receive care.

African American adolescents who reside in urban, high-risk communities may be among the most underserved populations. African American adolescents ex-
15 perience depression more than adolescents from other racial and ethnic groups (Garrison, Jackson, Marsteller, McKeown, & Addy, 1990; Roberts, Roberts, & Chen, 1997; Wu et al., 1999). Because African American adolescents are more likely than other groups to live in
20 low-income households, they may be at particularly

high risk of depression. Depression among African American adolescent boys, in particular, has been linked to having fewer perceived future opportunities (Hawkins, Hawkins, Sabatino, & Ley, 1998); low
25 neighborhood social capital and kinship social support (Stevenson, 1998); and violent behavior in African American adolescent boys living in an urban, high-risk setting (DuRant, Getts, Cadenhead, Emans, & Woods, 1995). Furthermore, African American adolescents
30 may experience barriers to identifying and using effective treatments.

Although African American adolescent boys have been recognized as a group having multiple needs, few of these discussions address their mental health needs.
35 High rates of substance abuse, academic failure (i.e., dropout rates), and high arrest and incarceration rates are problems disproportionately experienced by urban African American adolescent boys (Gibbs, 1990; Hutchinson, 1996; Majors & Billson, 1992). Unrecognized
40 and untreated mental illness may underlie these problems. Although researchers have recognized that few African American children and adolescents in need of mental health services receive them (Angold et al., 2002; HHS, 2001), there has been little discussion of
45 the attitudes and beliefs of the youths, their families, and their peers that might contribute to their underutilization of mental health services.

It is unlikely that access to services will increase unless we achieve a better understanding of how these
50 youths view their symptoms and service options and how their networks influence these views. For example, studies indicate African American adolescents and adults are less likely than white adolescents and adults to acknowledge the need for mental health services and
55 to be skeptical of using mental health services, especially when they believe they may be stigmatized by their social networks because of their service use (McKay, Nudelman, McCadam, & Gonzales, 1996; Richardson, 2001). African American adolescents and
60 their families are therefore likely to have many negative perceptions (and experiences) of mental health

care that reduce the likelihood of their seeking care even when it is available.

Social networks (peers and families) play an impor-
65   tant role regarding help-seeking behaviors and re-
sponses to ill health (Pescosolido & Boyer, 1999; Pescosolido, Wright, Alegria, & Vera, 1998; Rogler & Cortes, 1993). Studies regarding access to care indicate that pathways to care are shaped by the type of prob-
70   lem experienced, as well as the social support provided by network members (Bussing et al., 2003; Pescosolido, Gardner, & Lubell, 1998). Social net-
works may attempt to provide care or are used as a resource for identifying pathways to formal help,
75   sometimes coercing the affected individual into care (Pescosolido, Gardner, & Lubell; Pescosolido & Boyer). Social networks also monitor the care received and provide assistance with maintenance of care (i.e., offer transportation to care, give appointment remind-
80   ers), or network members may perpetuate stigma re-
garding formal service use.

Earlier studies examining the use of mental health services have tended to ignore the social processes related to seeking care and advice (Pescosolido, 1991),
85   but these processes may be particularly cogent in considering service seeking among African American ado-
lescent boys. A majority of African American adults use informal help sources exclusively or in combination with professional help in response to psychological
90   distress (Chatters, Taylor, & Neighbors, 1989). These processes are particularly important to consider when discussing adolescents because adolescents turn first to family members and friends when experiencing a mental health problem (Boldero & Fallon, 1995; Offer,
95   Howard, Schonert, & Ostrov, 1991; Saunders, Resnick, Hobermann, & Blum, 1994).

It is important to improve access to care for African American adolescent boys in mental health treatment. Therefore, the purpose of this study was to explore the
100   help-seeking behaviors and mental health attitudes of depressed African American adolescent boys. To better control for variability in disorder type, the study focused on depression in youths. To better understand the factors that facilitate or hinder entrée into treatment,
105   participants included both youths receiving mental health services and youths not in treatment. Findings from this study can inform social work practitioners and other mental health providers in their efforts to facilitate this group's use of services through better
110   understanding of the role that network members play in facilitating or inhibiting service use and increase the number of services perceived as acceptable and effec-
tive to this underserved group through the design of more culturally appropriate interventions and engage-
115   ment strategies.

## Method

*Participants and Data Collection*

Eighteen respondents ages 14 to 18 who were al-
ready participating in a broader study titled "Social Network Influences on African American Adolescents'
120   Mental Health Service Use" (Lindsey, 2002) were re-
cruited for this study. Participants ($n = 10$) were re-
cruited from community-based mental health treatment centers and a mental health practitioner in private practice and from community-based, nonclinical programs
125   for high-risk youths (i.e., a violence prevention pro-
gram, truancy abatement center, and homeless shelter) ($n = 8$). In each setting, all potential participants were individually approached by a therapist or program staff member who explained the study and assessed their
130   participation interest. Flyers were posted in each re-
cruitment site describing the study. Informed consent for participation was obtained from parents or guardians, and informed assent was obtained from partici-
pants.

Participants in this study were selected on the basis
135   of elevated depressive symptoms as assessed by the Center for Epidemiologic Studies Depression Scale (CES-D) (Radloff, 1977). Of the 69 who participated in the original study, 18 met this criterion and agreed to participate. This study received Institutional Review
140   Board (IRB) approval at the University of Pittsburgh (IRB Approval: #001132).

Data were collected through a semi-structured in-
terview schedule. Questions were derived from the Network-Episode Model (NEM) (Pescosolido, 1991);
145   in particular, the NEM concept *network content* (i.e., degree of support, attitudes, and beliefs toward mental illness and mental health care). In addition to network content, questions were derived from the literature on help-seeking behaviors among adolescents (i.e., help-
150   seeking pathways engaged in by youths), as well as the literature on mental health service utilization among African Americans. (See Table 1 for examples of the questions and follow-up probes used in the protocol.) Most of the interviews were conducted in the respon-
155   dents' homes and a few in community sites: mental health centers or community-based organizations. All interviews were conducted in private areas and lasted between 45 min and 1 hr and 45 min.

The interview covered processes and help-seeking
160   patterns, network influences, and attitudes toward men-
tal health care and race or ethnicity of the provider. The first author and a trained research assistant conducted the interviews. Participants were encouraged to talk at length about their help-seeking behaviors in relation to
165   their depressive symptoms, with detailed accounts re-
garding the ways their network influenced their behav-
iors. They were also asked how they conceptualized and defined mental health and associated emotional and psychological struggles (described in the protocol
170   as "feeling sad or hurt inside").

Interviews were tape-recorded, transcribed, and analyzed using inductive coding techniques (Miles & Huberman, 1994). Three readers, including the first author and two research assistants, independently re-

Table 1

*Sample Interview Questions and Follow-Up Probes Regarding the Help-Seeking Behaviors Among African American Adolescent Boys*

| Question | Probe |
|---|---|
| When you start feeling like something makes you feel sad or hurt inside, what do you do? | How did you know that you needed to talk with somebody? |
| | Was there anyone who helped you to recognize or identify the feelings that you were having? |
| | Whom did you turn to first for help? |
| | Are there other things you tried to do to help you feel better beyond talking with other people? |
| | How did these other things work? |
| If you felt you just couldn't handle things going on in your life, where would you prefer to go for help? Why? | (If therapist/counselor not mentioned) Why wouldn't you go to a therapist/counselor? |
| | What would your friends think if you went to a therapist/counselor? |
| | What about your family? |

175 viewed and coded transcripts to identify patterns and themes emerging from the data. After the review and designation of codes, the readers convened consensus sessions to determine the categories and subcategories of themes. A final coding matrix was developed by the
180 first author to indicate the category and subcategory of themes, a definition clarifying the meaning for each category and subcategory, and corresponding sample quotes that best captured the theme.

### Findings

Themes emerged in the following areas: type of
185 problems experienced, descriptions of help-seeking behaviors, dealing with emotional pain, influence of the social network on help seeking, and perceptions of mental illness and mental health care. Within these themes, differences emerged between respondents in
190 treatment for their depressive symptoms and those not in treatment (see Table 2).

*Influences of Social Network on Experiences of Depression*

Family members played an important role as sources for help and support as the respondents discussed how they actively sought out family members
195 for help when dealing with depressive symptoms—that is, feeling sad or hurt inside. In many cases, respondents from both groups reported that their mother was the family member they talked to most frequently:

When problems are too bad where I just can't, I can't like
200 stop them, I can't do nothing, can't control it or nothing. I try to go out and play, but for some reason it pops back up in my head, and I can't get it out so I go to her [referring to his mother]. (*Participant not in treatment.*)

(*Referring to what prompts him to talk to his mother.*)
205 Like, I mean if something happened like with me or my friends that we couldn't handle as friends, we couldn't handle as minors, but something that my mother should know…. I mean I'm thankful that I have an understanding mom and all that. (*Participant in treatment.*)

210 Family members were equally important for both groups regarding advice or counsel received when feeling sad or hurt inside. However, those in treatment typically received advice and counsel from friends as well, whereas those not in treatment typically sought
215 the advice and counsel of only their family members.

As a way to deal with feeling sad or hurt inside, some respondents talked about how they would spend time alone or isolate themselves before or in place of talking with someone in their network:

220 Just deal with it. There's nothing—I mean it's just life. I go through. I mean, I don't know. I don't seek no help. I don't talk to nobody or nothing. I just go on with whatever I'm doing. (*Participant in treatment.*)

I try to go within myself, so I pretty much get the an-
225 swers. It's like a self-conscious. (*Participant in treatment.*)

Adolescent boys in treatment typically identified their emotional and psychological struggles on their own, first, with eventual assistance from family mem-
230 bers:

I just feel it…. It's a certain, it's a certain rush that you get sometimes. Nothing like on a football field or anything, but just your heart's racing, and I think that's the best sign of you knowing when to talk to someone. Even
235 if you say you don't have the courage or you say you don't want to, but deep down you really do because the only way to really solve anything is to talk to someone. (*Participant in treatment.*)

Engagement in religious or spiritual activities was
240 not a common response to feeling sad or hurt inside among this sample. This finding was striking given the historical role of spirituality and religion as a source for coping, support, and healing among African Americans. Only two of the 18 respondents, one from each
245 group, reported that they currently engaged in activities such as praying or going to church.

Table 2

*Emerging Themes Regarding Help Seeking and Depression Among African American Adolescent Boys, by Treatment Status*

| Area | In treatment (*n* = 10) | Not in treatment (*n* = 8) |
|---|---|---|
| Problems experienced | Interpersonal conflict among peers | Family strain |
| | Problems at school (behavioral or academic) | |
| Behaviors when dealing with a problem | Talks to family and friends | Talks to family only |
| | Isolation | |
| People helping to identify the problem (other than family) | Self | No one |
| | Teacher or other school personnel | |
| Preference for help | Family first, then professionals | Family only |

### Influences of Social Network on Help Seeking and Service Use

*Network's Influence on Receipt of Formal Services.* The respondents who were in treatment (*n* = 10) were asked to address questions regarding the process by which they were initially referred to formal mental health treatment. Five of the 10 respondents reported that they were referred to treatment by their school when teachers noted a decrease in functioning (academically and behaviorally) and parents or guardians agreed that professional help should be sought for these problems:

> They [teachers and school officials] were like, maybe what you should do is and they were feeding her [mother]—and it's like more than one teacher saying it…. And they're like maybe you should do this. And then she put me in the program up at [outpatient treatment facility].

> It was a recommendation…. It was a recommendation, yeah, from a lady at school…to my mother. And they had said, you know, try this out. They thought I had ADHD, they thought I was bipolar and all this stuff, but they couldn't put their finger on it. There was nothing that they could do to figure out exactly what was wrong with me.

Four of the 10 reported that a parent suggested or referred them for treatment:

> My mom, yeah. Because she thought I had, you know, problems, issues or whatever. She just got me a counselor.

A parent's suggestion, however, should be distinguished here from a parental mandate. Several respondents (3 of 10) reported that a parent mandated formal mental health treatment, and they disagreed with this mandate:

> She's making me [go to a MH professional]. If I had a choice or my say so, all this wouldn't be going on because I'm cool. I don't feel there's nothing wrong. I don't need no help. She asked me if I did. I laughed at her like, "What? Yeah, right."

*Network Members' Thoughts about Respondent's Use of Formal Services.* When asked whether family or friends would be supportive of their use of mental health services, respondents from both groups said that their family would support their use of formal mental health treatment:

> They've [family] always been very supportive…. Even though a lot of them aren't really around me, aren't really that close to me. There's still enough love to go around. And with that, it makes it easier to come here [to treatment] instead of just being alone and coming here…. That [if family was not supportive] would definitely affect my mood at least. Maybe not necessarily coming here, but confidence-wise, it would definitely be a lot lower than what it is right now. (*Participant in treatment.*)

In contrast to those respondents not in treatment who reported that their family would support their use of mental health services, some from this group said that their family would not support their use of formal services. This finding should be further viewed in light of the problem the not-in-treatment group typically reported experiencing: family strain (problems related to family relations). Two respondents not in treatment reported that their family would want to handle problems regarding family relations among themselves without seeking professional help:

> Because they feel as though why [should I] go to a counselor when I could come to them?

> I think my mom would probably ask me why I didn't come to her first or something like that. "What's wrong with you?" She'd probably get mad. I don't know. But it's like, why didn't I come to her first and talk to her about it instead of me going to a therapist.

Respondents not in treatment also said that they would not talk to friends about their problems typically because their friends would not be supportive of their receipt of formal mental health services. In contrast, many respondents in treatment would talk to their friends when dealing with depressive symptoms. However, they would not tell their friends they were receiving mental health treatment—fearing that friends would laugh, joke, or tease them:

> They'd probably think—they might joke around and say like, it's bad for me, you know, like I'm crazy or some-

330 thing, so I would like keep it to my family and myself. (*Respondent in treatment.*)

*Attitudes toward Mental Health Care and Professionals*

Respondents from both groups were asked to share their thoughts and perceptions regarding why it is diffi-cult for mental health treatment providers to engage
335 African American adolescent boys in mental health services. The respondents talked about the issue of stigma as a barrier associated with mental health ser-vice use. In particular, shame, embarrassment, and ex-clusion emerged from the interviews as themes regard-
340 ing the influences of the network on mental health ser-vice use:

Because their friends might sometimes think like they're crazy and stuff like that. Wouldn't want to hang around them. And they'll just sit there and make up more ex-
345 cuses to stay away from them. It [mental health treat-ment] would draw all that person's friends away from him too. Then that person would just be, like, down in the dumps. (*Respondent in treatment.*)

Respondents from both groups said that many Afri-
350 can American adolescent boys sought to handle their problems on their own or had too much pride to go to formal mental health treatment:

And I guess a lot of them would think, well, I don't need it. I'm this. I'm from here. I can do this. I can do that. So
355 they would…they have a certain feeling where they think they could get through it alone when they really couldn't. (*Respondent in treatment.*)

(*Referring to pride.*) Like I'm not, you know, I'm too good to go to a counselor. Like I don't think I'm very
360 sick or I don't think nothing's wrong with me. I act nor-mal. I'm normal. You know, different things like that. False sense of themselves. (*Respondent not in treatment.*)

Furthermore, respondents shared their perceptions that talking to a mental health professional, for some
365 African American adolescent boys, meant that they would have to express their emotions associated with feeling sad or hurt inside, and that the expression of emotions was viewed as a sign of weakness among this population:

370 Like they weren't manly enough. Like little girls. (*Re-spondent in treatment.*)

(*Asking for help.*) …means that you're gay. That's what it means. That's how they [African American adolescent boys] interpret it. It means—well, I mean you go down
375 the line. If you ask for help, or if you cry, or if you look emotional, if you feel depressed, that means you're soft. If you're soft, then you're gay and you're not hard and not tough…. You can't let anybody know that you're soft. I swear it's like being in jail. (*Respondent in treat-*
380 *ment.*)

These comments reflect a certain machismo related to what may be defined among this population as a lack of strength when expressing emotions (i.e., crying) or asking for help. Similarly, use of the vernacular "gay"

385 among this group is part of a machismo culture that ascribed being weak or lacking strength to being femi-nine and further serves as an impediment to acknowl-edging the need for help and engaging in healthy forms of emotional expression.

390 When asked whether race of the provider affected mental health service utilization among African American adolescent boys, respondents said:

They [African American adolescent boys] don't think that they [white professionals] can understand what
395 they're coming from. (*Respondent in treatment.*)

And I mean it might be one of the…it might be a race is-sue because some—I think that there are some black peo-ple who close themselves off from white people. And, you know, in the mental health field, there is a majority
400 of white people, I think. (*Respondent in treatment.*)

Although the majority of the respondents said that race mattered, a few indicated that race of the provider was not as important; rather, what was important was how the provider treated them and how well the pro-
405 vider engaged them. One respondent said:

I can't say it [race of the provider] would make a differ-ence at all because it's about getting help. It's about hav-ing someone that's there for you to understand what you're going through and to give you advice, to give you
410 encouragement, to help you sort out things that you're going through. So with me, white or black doesn't really make a difference. What matters is that we're trustworthy of each other. (*Respondent in treatment.*)

## Discussion

The adolescent boys in this study were generally
415 similar to those in broader studies of nonclinical popu-lations (see Boldero & Fallon, 1995; Snell, 2002) in terms of seeking help first from family and at other times from friends and peers. In particular, peers ap-pear to have a powerful influence on this group regard-
420 ing the admission of emotional or psychological prob-lems, as well as the acknowledgment of the receipt of formal mental health services. Those who were in treatment said that they received emotional support from their friends, and that they were able to talk to
425 friends about their problems. However, additional analyses of this group revealed that most were reluctant to tell their friends that they were going to formal men-tal health services, fearing that friends would poke fun at them.

430 These contrasting findings reflect the importance of distinguishing between individually felt stigma (i.e., negative beliefs or perceptions of service use emanat-ing from within the individual) and network-induced stigma (i.e., negative beliefs or perceptions articulated
435 by friends regarding the affected individual's service use) when developing interventions and strategies to combat stigma related to service use for this group. Findings regarding the influence of peer networks also reflect the seemingly reasoned calculation about
440 friends by respondents in this study, such as when to

talk to them, what to share with them, and how supportive friends would be regarding the problem they are facing.

445 This study gives a detailed description of the pathways to help seeking for African American adolescent boys with depressive symptoms, in particular, the roles of family, schools, and social agencies. For respondents receiving mental health care, identification of their mental health problems was more likely to come

450 from family members and school personnel. Although respondents in mental health treatment reported that they initially tried to solve their problems on their own, family members and school personnel still played an active role in confirming their depressive symptoms

455 and facilitating their access to mental health services. It is worth noting that the majority of the respondents who were receiving mental health services reported that the types of problems they experienced concerned issues associated with the school environment (that is,

460 academic achievement or behavioral problems). This finding highlights the important role teachers and other school personnel (such as school social workers) play in the assessment of mental health problems and making referrals to treatment.

*Challenges for Social Work*

465 Adolescent boys with high levels of depressive symptoms who are not in treatment, however, may pose a special challenge. Respondents who were not in treatment in this study reported that the problems they most often experienced concerned strained family rela-

470 tions. However, family members often counseled them against going to a professional for help regarding these emotional problems.

The predicament of the subgroup of respondents in this study who were experiencing high levels of de-

475 pressive symptoms but were not in mental health treatment raises concern. At the time of the interview, each respondent was involved in community-based programs targeting high-risk youths, including a youth employment program, a violence prevention program,

480 a truancy abatement program, and a homeless shelter. However, no one in these settings engaged them about their emotional and psychological struggles by attending to their needs or referring them to care. Although it is important that social work practitioners and other

485 mental health professionals target the development of strategies to address the attitudes of youths toward mental illness and treatment, the situation for this subgroup of youths also reveals that those involved with serving them need to be more sensitive to their mental

490 health needs. These professionals could provide assistance to youths by being referral agents and sources of personal support.

For this high-risk group, religious congregations and affiliated organizations that address contemporary

495 youth problems from a spiritual perspective may serve as an alternative to seeking formal professional help

when dealing with mental health problems. However, unlike earlier literature (e.g., Varon & Riley, 1999) that documented the importance of spirituality and the

500 church in the lives of African Americans, problem solving through prayer or seeking support from the church did not play a significant role in the lives of respondents in this study. This finding could be misleading and illustrates the need for more empirical re-

505 search to examine the extent to which the general population of African American adolescent boys seeks help from lay and ministry counselors and other adult spiritual figures.

Functional impairment as a result of experiencing

510 depressive symptoms may clarify the issue of why two subgroups of youths with similar depressive symptom scores have disparate treatment trajectories. Based on the self-report of problems experienced between the two subgroups, respondents in treatment said that their

515 problems related to interpersonal conflict and problems at school—behavioral or academic—whereas respondents not in treatment said that their problems related to family strain. Depressive symptoms and associated problems seemed to be recognized or identified by

520 network members when there was an accompanying issue related to functionality. Thus, the perceptions of network members regarding what constitutes impairment needs to be understood as a potential facilitator or barrier to formal mental health treatment.

*Limitations of the Study*

525 Because this study focused on depressive symptoms as an indicator of mental health need, we cannot determine how other mental health problems, for example, behavioral disorders (such as conduct disorder and ADHD), in addition to depressive disorders might

530 differentially or concomitantly affect service referral or service use.

Confirmatory and comparative analyses from the perspective of actual network members would have been desirable, but limitations of time and funding dic-

535 tated that this study be restricted to the adolescents' perceptions of their social network's influences on mental health services use or nonuse. Although the findings are based on the perspectives of a subgroup of African American adolescent boys, this study laid the

540 groundwork for a more extensive investigation of these issues in follow-up studies and for the design of an outreach and an engagement strategy for depressed African American adolescents.

**Implications for Practice**

Findings from this study have important implica-

545 tions regarding the recognition and identification of depressive symptoms among African American adolescent boys. Strategies to improve the identification and recognition of depressive symptoms among members of this group are needed, especially in schools and

550 other community-based organizations. Social workers and mental health services providers might be looking

for depressive symptom expression that fits the *Diagnostic and Statistical Manual of Mental Disorders* (DSM-IV-TR) criteria (American Psychiatric Association, 2000) and may miss the more subtle forms of expression unique to this group. Social workers and mental health service providers need to work collaboratively with community-based organizations serving this group. For example, social workers may provide training and education to staff regarding the signs and symptoms of depression, target strategies that attempt to ameliorate the perceived stigma among this group and those in their network, and develop intervention models that better engage families by incorporating them into the treatment process throughout the course of care. Better identification of mental health problems (i.e., depression) by social network members and those who provide treatment needs to become a targeted education strategy.

Quite often, professional help is a source of mental health care of last resort. There are multiple barriers regarding the help-seeking behaviors among adolescents enrolled in community-based programs, including stigma associated with mental illness, machismo and pride, and families and adolescents who believe that depression can be resolved without professional help. Therefore, it is necessary to reframe help-seeking as a positive, proactive behavior among African American adolescent boys and their families.

**Implications for Research**

Future research needs to address the role of family and peers in the help-seeking process. Interventions that are effective for African American youths are particularly needed because social and family networks are not likely to be active users of mental health services, except when these are initiated through school. Survey research is needed to determine the extent to which the attitudes shown by youths in the single community studied are consistent across the country and the extent to which these attitudes are similar to or different from those of youths from other racial and ethnic groups. Particular attention should be given to determining the extent to which parents, especially mothers, and peers may inhibit help-seeking among this group. Once a better understanding of the network members' role in inhibiting the help-seeking process is ascertained, strategies for removing these barriers can be developed.

Studies examining the impact of referral type (mandated versus choice) on perceptions and use of mental health services have been done with adults (Pescosolido, Gardner, & Lubell, 1998). However, future research needs to examine this issue among adolescents of color, as well as the extent to which parent and child disagreement regarding problem identification and definition negatively affect the engagement process and utilization of mental health services.

Finally, findings from this study indicate that race of the provider was seen as an important issue among some respondents, particularly the belief that providers who were not African American would be unable to effectively treat this population. Thus, future research regarding the mental health treatment experiences of this group is necessary to determine how provider characteristics (i.e., race and gender) affect engagement and mental health treatment.

**References**

American Psychiatric Association. (2000). *Diagnostic and statistical manual of mental disorders (text revision)* (DSM-IV-TR). Washington, DC: American Psychiatric Press.

Angold, A., Erkanli, A., Farmer, E. M. Z., Fairbank, J. A., Burns, B. J., Keeler, G., & Costello, E. J. (2002). Psychiatric disorder, impairment, and service use in rural African American and white youth. *Archives of General Psychiatry*, 59, 893–901.

Birmaher, B., Ryan, N. D., Williamson, D. E., Brent, D. A., Kaufman, J., Dahl, R. E., Perel, J., & Nelson, B. (1996). Childhood and adolescent depression: A review of the past 10 years. Part I. *Journal of the American Academy of Child & Adolescent Psychiatry*, 35, 1427–1439.

Boldero, J., & Fallon, B. (1995). Adolescent help-seeking: What do they get help for and from whom? *Journal of Adolescence*, 18, 193–209.

Bussing, R., Zima, B. T., Gary, F. A., Mason, D. M., Leon, C. E., Sinha, K., & Garvan, C. W. (2003). Social networks, caregiver strain, and utilization of mental health services among elementary school students at high risk for ADHD. *Journal of the American Academy of Child & Adolescent Psychiatry*, 42, 842–850.

Chatters, L., Taylor, R., & Neighbors, H. (1989). Size of informal helper network mobilized during a serious personal problem among black Americans. *Journal of Marriage and the Family*, 51, 667–676.

DuRant, R. H., Getts, A., Cadenhead, C., Emans, S. J., & Woods, E. R. (1995). Exposure to violence and victimization and depression, hopelessness, and purpose in life among adolescents living in and around public housing. *Developmental and Behavioral Pediatrics*, 16, 233–237.

Garrison, C., Jackson, K., Marsteller, F., McKeown, R., & Addy, C. (1990). A longitudinal study of depressive symptomotology in young adolescents. *Journal of the American Academy of Child & Adolescent Psychiatry*, 29, 581–585.

Gibbs, J. (1990). Mental health issues of black adolescents: Implications for policy and practice. In A. Stiffman & L. Davis (Eds.), *Ethnic issues in adolescent mental health* (pp. 21–52). Newbury Park, CA: Sage Publications.

Hawkins, W., Hawkins, M., Sabatino, C., & Ley, S. (1998). Relationship of perceived future opportunity to depressive symptomotology of inner-city African-American adolescents. *Children and Adolescent Services*, 20, 757–764.

Hutchinson, E. (1996). *The assassination of the black male image*. Los Angeles: Middle Passage Press.

Lindsey, M. (2002). *Social network influences on African-American adolescents' mental health service use*. Unpublished doctoral dissertation, University of Pittsburgh.

Majors, R., & Billson, J. (1992). *Cool pose—The dilemmas of black manhood in America*. New York: Lexington Books.

McKay, M., Nudelman, R., McCadam, K., & Gonzales, J. (1996). Involving inner-city families in mental health services: First interview engagement skills. *Research on Social Work Practice*, 6, 462–472.

Miles, M., & Huberman, A. (1994). *Qualitative data analysis: An expanded source book* (2nd ed.). Thousand Oaks, CA: Sage Publications.

Offer, D., Howard, K., Schonert, K., & Ostrov, E. (1991). To whom do adolescents turn for help? Differences between disturbed and nondisturbed adolescents. *Journal of the American Academy of Child & Adolescent Psychiatry*, 30, 623–630.

Pescosolido, B. (1991). Illness careers and network ties: A conceptual model of utilization and compliance. *Advances in Medical Sociology*, 2, 161–184.

Pescosolido, B., & Boyer, C. (1999). How do people come to use mental health services? Current knowledge and changing perspectives. In A. Horwitz & T. Scheid (Eds.), *A handbook for the study of mental health: Social contexts, theories, and systems* (pp. 392–411). New York: Cambridge University Press.

Pescosolido, B., Gardner, C., & Lubell, K. (1998). How people get into mental health services: Stories of choice, coercion, and "muddling through" from "first timers." *Social Science and Medicine*, 46, 275–286.

Pescosolido, B., Wright, E., Alegria, M., & Vera, M. (1998). Social networks and patterns of use among the poor with mental health problems in Puerto Rico. *Medical Care*, 36, 1057–1072.

Petersen, A. C., Compas, B. E., Brooks-Gunn, J., Stemmler, M., Ey, S., & Grant, K. (1993). Depression in adolescence. *American Psychologist*, 48, 155–168.

Radloff, L. S. (1977). The CES-D Scale: A self-report depression scale for research in the general population. *Applied Psychological Measurement, 1*, 385–401.

Richardson, L. (2001). Seeking and obtaining mental health services: What do parents expect? *Archives of Psychiatric Nursing, 15*, 223–231.

Roberts, R., Roberts, C., & Chen, R. (1997). Ethnocultural differences in prevalence of adolescent depression. *American Journal of Community Psychology, 25*, 95–110.

Rogler, L., & Cortes, D. (1993). Help-seeking pathways: A unifying concept in mental health care. *American Journal of Psychiatry, 150*, 554–561.

Saunders, S., Resnick, M., Hobermann, H., & Blum, R. (1994). Formal help-seeking behavior of adolescents identifying themselves as having mental health problems. *Journal of the American Academy of Child and Adolescent Psychiatry, 33*, 718–728.

Snell, C. (2002). Help-seeking and risk-taking behavior among black street youth: Implications for HIV/AIDS prevention and social policy. *Journal of Health and Social Policy, 16*, 21–32.

Stevenson, H. (1998). Raising safe villages: Cultural–ecological factors that influence the emotional adjustment of adolescents. *Journal of Black Psychology, 24*, 44–59.

U.S. Department of Health and Human Services. (2001). *Mental health: Culture, race, and ethnicity—A supplement to mental health: A report of the surgeon general*. Rockville, MD: Author.

Varon, S., & Riley, A. (1999). Relationship between maternal church attendance and adolescent mental health and social functioning. *Psychiatric Services, 50*, 799–805.

Wu, P., Hoven, C., Bird, H., Moore, R., Cohen, P., Alegria, M., Dulcan, M., Goodman, S., Horwitz, S., Lichtman, J., Narrow, W., Rae, D., Regier, D., & Roper, M. (1999). Depressive and disruptive disorders and mental health service utilization in children and adolescents. *Journal of the American Academy of Child & Adolescent Psychiatry, 38*, 1081–1090.

**Acknowledgments**: This study was funded by the National Institute of Mental Health through a dissertation grant (1 RO3 MH63593-01), the W. K. Kellogg Foundation (Community Health Scholars Program), Michael A. Lindsey, Ph.D., principal investigator; as well as the Grants for National Academic Centers of Excellence on Youth Violence Prevention (R49/CCR318627-01), Philip J. Leaf, Ph.D., principal investigator. An earlier version of this article was presented at the meeting of the Society for Social Work and Research, January 2004, New Orleans.

**About the authors**: *Michael A. Lindsey*, Ph.D., MSW, MPH, is assistant professor, School of Social Work, University of Maryland, 525 West Redwood Street, Baltimore, MD 21201 (e-mail: mlindsey@ssw.umaryland.edu). *Wynne S. Korr*, Ph.D., is dean and professor, School of Social Work, University of Illinois, Urbana-Champaign. *Marina Broitman*, Ph.D., is scientific review administrator, Division of Extramural Affairs, National Institute of Mental Health, Bethesda, MD. *Lee Bone*, MPH, RN, is associate public health professor, Bloomberg School of Public Health, Johns Hopkins University; *Alan Green*, Ph.D., is assistant professor, School of Counseling and Professional Services, Johns Hopkins University; and *Philip J. Leaf*, Ph.D., is professor; Bloomberg School of Public Health, Johns Hopkins University.

# Exercise for Article 34

## Factual Questions

1. What is the explicitly stated purpose of this research?

2. What is the total number of participants in this study?

3. What is the name of the scale used to assess depressive symptoms?

4. In determining the categories and subcategories of themes, did the researchers convene to arrive at a consensus?

5. Which group (those in treatment *or* those not in treatment) typically sought the advice and counsel of only their family members?

6. Do the researchers explicitly discuss the limitations of their study?

## Questions for Discussion

7. Is it important to know that the researchers obtained informed consent? Explain. (See lines 130–133.)

8. Is it important to know where the interviews were conducted? Explain. (See lines 154–158.)

9. In your opinion, are there advantages to tape-recording the interviews? Are there disadvantages? Explain. (See lines 171–173.)

10. The researchers state that three readers independently reviewed and coded transcripts. Is it important to know that this was done independently? Explain. (See lines 173–176.)

11. To what extent did the sample questions in Table 1 help you understand this research?

12. In your opinion, are the suggestions for future research important? Explain. (See lines 580–615.)

13. If you had planned a study on this topic, would you have planned a qualitative study (as the authors of this article did) *or* a quantitative study (e.g., a survey with closed-ended questions)? Explain.

## Quality Ratings

Directions: Indicate your level of agreement with each of the following statements by circling a number from 5 for strongly agree (SA) to 1 for strongly disagree (SD). If you believe an item is not applicable to this research article, leave it blank. Be prepared to explain your ratings. When responding to criteria A and B, keep in mind that brief titles and abstracts are conventional in published research.

A. The title of the article is appropriate.

SA   5   4   3   2   1   SD

B.  The abstract provides an effective overview of the research article.

SA   5   4   3   2   1   SD

C.  The introduction establishes the importance of the study.

SA   5   4   3   2   1   SD

D.  The literature review establishes the context for the study.

SA   5   4   3   2   1   SD

E.  The research purpose, question, or hypothesis is clearly stated.

SA   5   4   3   2   1   SD

F.  The method of sampling is sound.

SA   5   4   3   2   1   SD

G.  Relevant demographics (for example, age, gender, and ethnicity) are described.

SA   5   4   3   2   1   SD

H.  Measurement procedures are adequate.

SA   5   4   3   2   1   SD

I.  All procedures have been described in sufficient detail to permit a replication of the study.

SA   5   4   3   2   1   SD

J.  The participants have been adequately protected from potential harm.

SA   5   4   3   2   1   SD

K.  The results are clearly described.

SA   5   4   3   2   1   SD

L.  The discussion/conclusion is appropriate.

SA   5   4   3   2   1   SD

M.  Despite any flaws, the report is worthy of publication.

SA   5   4   3   2   1   SD

# Article 35

# Evaluating the Use of
# Reflective Counseling Group Supervision
# for Military Counselors in Taiwan

PETER JEN DER PAN
Chung Yuan Christian University,
Chung-Li, Taiwan

LIANG-YU F. DENG
Chung Yuan Christian University,
Chung-Li, Taiwan

SHIOU-LING TSAI
Chung Yuan Christian University,
Chung-Li, Taiwan

ABSTRACT. The purpose of this study is to examine the effects of reflective counseling group supervision (RCGS) for military counselors. A convenience sampling method is adopted. Twenty-two military counselors participated in this study. Both qualitative and quantitative research methods were used for collecting and analyzing data. The results support our hypothesis that participants who received the RCGS would show a significant increase in their counseling competences. Four primary categories related to supervisory style, supervisory alliance, self-assessment, and supervising outcomes emerge as prominent and consistent from participants' learning experiences. RCGS can be an effective supervision model for participants. Implications of the findings for group supervision and further research are discussed.

From *Research on Social Work Practice*, *18*, 346–355. Copyright © 2008 by Sage Publications, Inc. Reprinted with permission.

Counseling supervision is central to both counselor education and the ongoing professional development of counselors. Although considerable attention has been paid to counseling supervision in a variety of counsel-
5 ing professions, counseling supervision by military counselors has not been extensively studied. Military counselors work in the Military Mental Hygiene Center and have been working with troops in Taiwan since 1991. They are responsible for assisting officers, non-
10 commissioned officers, and soldiers with adjustment issues, prevention of self-destruction, and enhancement of mental health (Ministry of National Defense, 2006). However, because of the frequent incidence of mental disorders, accidents, and self-injury that have occurred
15 in the military, the nature of the military mental hygiene work has been recently challenged by public discussions on the proper educational role of soldiers in the military system. Such discussions also led to a call for enhancing military counselors' competences.
20 In response to new needs in military mental hygiene work, the military system has had to alter their traditional strategies and actions in training counselors (Hu, 2006). Hu demonstrated an index system of mili-

tary counselor competence that includes professional
25 knowledge, professional commitment, and professional techniques. Only one study has explored the impact of solution-focused supervision related to military counselors (Chen, 2004). Chen's findings indicated that the experiences of developing group projects and strate-
30 gies, learning from supervisors' characteristics and aptitudes, enhancement of counseling skills and intervention, self-awareness of personal issues, and feelings with regard to the supervisory method and process influenced a military counselor's role and professional
35 development (Chen, 2004). Undoubtedly, the need to be supervised exists to enhance professional development of military counselors and ensure the client's welfare.

Previous literature has demonstrated (Bernard &
40 Goodyear, 2004; Holloway, 1999) that supervision, in addition to helping counselors offer professional services, can also assist them in achieving maximum personal and professional growth. The goal of effective supervision is to develop a facilitative supervisory rela-
45 tionship characterized by empathy, warmth, trust, mutual respect, and flexibility (Worthen & McNeill, 2001). The tasks of supervision include teaching counseling skills, case conceptualization, professional role and practice, emotional awareness, and self-evaluation
50 (Holloway, 1999). Supervisors can teach supervisees professional knowledge in their roles as instructors, supporters, trainers, and consultants (Holloway, 1999). Watkins (1997) pointed out that supervision provides the supervisees with vital feedback about their per-
55 formance in the counseling session, offers guidance during periods of confusion, allows for alternative views, and offers a secure base for the supervisees. Supervisors were perceived as more trustworthy when they helped to establish clear goals for supervision,
60 gave direct feedback about the trainee's work, helped the supervisee develop his or her own style, suggested alternative ways of conceptualizing cases, and called the supervisee by name (Heppner & Handley, 1981). There was general agreement with regard to the top six

65　interpersonal skills that appeared most salient: providing direction, providing constructive feedback, building supervisee confidence, helping supervisees assess own strengths and growth areas, confronting when appropriate, and responding to supervisee concerns
70　(Wetchler & Vaughn, 1991). Tsui (2005) further indicated that social work supervision has been identified as one of the most important factors in determining the job satisfaction levels of social workers and the quality of service to clients.

75　　　Ward and House (1998) developed specific procedures regarding how to conduct a model of counseling supervision that integrates reflective learning theory with the concurrent development of counselor-in-training and supervisory relationship. Reflective learn-
80　ing is contingent on the quality of the supervisory relationship (Sexton & Whiston, 1994). It is through this "constructed interaction" that active learning occurs and knowledge of how to change behavior develops (Shih, 1995; Shou & Shih, 1995). This implies a cycli-
85　cal supervisory interaction that aids a counselor-in-counseling context with a meaningful change in perception and practice. The supervisory relationship becomes a container to review a counselor's intentionality, belief, and base assumptions surrounding disorient-
90　ing professional events (Ward & House, 1998). In this relationship, a reexamination of professional assumptions assists the supervisee in developing a metaperspective of the counseling process. Therefore, a counseling supervisor is challenged to create a learning con-
95　text that enhances supervisees' skills as they construct relevant frames from which to devise effective strategies in working with clients (Holloway, 1999). The learning alliance of reflective counseling group supervision (RCGS) is illustrated as a series of four phases
100　representing the developmental process of counseling supervision: contextual orientation, trust establishment, conceptual development, and clinical independence (Ward & House, 1998). Each phase of the supervisory relationship illustrates the learning experiences of the
105　participants and the central focus for the reflective learning experiences of the supervisees. The model represents a dynamic interchange that demonstrates the concurrent development of supervisory relationships, which in turn leads to the clinical independence of the
110　counselor trainees. Griffith and Frieden (2000) provided support for the notion that counselor educators can facilitate reflective thinking in students through the practices of Socratic questioning, journal writing, interpersonal process recall, and reflecting teams. Cor-
115　coran (2001) asserted that structural, process, and individual factors within the supervision environment were identified as intervening conditions to reflective process. Moreover, the consequences of reflective process included changes in condition, skills and behaviors,
120　and the personhood of trainee (Corcoran, 2002).
　　　The group supervision model is the most popular model of supervision in a variety of professions, in-

cluding psychotherapy (Holloway, 1999), counseling (Christensen & Kline, 2001), and social work
125　(Kadushin & Harkness, 2002). Group supervision is often used as a supplement to, rather than a substitute for, individual supervision. As defined by Kadushin and Harkness (2002), group supervision uses a group setting to fulfill the responsibilities of social work su-
130　pervision. In addition, there are more teaching and learning experiences available in a group context because the participants share their difficulties and experiences. Support for using group supervision is based on the belief that it offers opportunities for vicarious
135　learning in a supportive group environment (Christensen & Kline, 2001). It is stressed that, once established, this environment contributes to decreased supervisee anxiety, increased self-efficacy and confidence, and enhanced learning opportunities (Brown & Bourne,
140　1996; Starling, 1996). In addition, group supervision is seen as having the potential to reduce the issues of hierarchy and dependency found in individual supervision (Bernard & Goodyear, 2004). This has a particular meaning to military counselors because the first prior-
145　ity obligation of soldiers is obedience to orders and conformity to rules. In most cases, military counselors are not only soldiers who assume multiple obligations of military policy and superintendent's expectancy but also counselors who serve clients, clients' families, and
150　society at large. These multiple obligations can, and often do, come into conflict, and a major task of group supervision is to help military counselors address such conflicts. Finally, group supervision is advocated because it is an efficient use of supervisory time and ex-
155　pertise (Christensen & Kline, 2001; Hawkins & Shohet, 1989; Holloway & Johnston, 1985).
　　　Despite a proliferation of research on the supervision and its related issues, little attention has been given to RCGS. Although procedures for conducting
160　RCGS appeared in the literature (Griffith & Frieden, 2000; Shih, 1995; Shou & Shih, 1995; Ward & House, 1998), there has been no reported evaluation of this model. There are a number of reasons why RCGS for military counselors is needed in the field of supervi-
165　sion. First, little group supervision is available to military counselors in any setting (Chen, 2004). Second, military counselors, as officers, have, more or less, their professional hierarchical ethics in the process of administration supervision. Therefore, they may not be
170　able to report directly to their counseling supervisors in their offices or comment freely to their officers because of rank. Third, military counselors already spend a significant portion of their time working with the military troops. Acting within the military counselor's role
175　function in the troops, they are used to teaching, asking, admonishing, and advising clients to change. The RCGS, however, by providing a context for the critical analysis of base assumptions and beliefs about clients, change, and one's practice may be able to offer a new
180　conceptualization of supervisory working alliance for

military counselors. The provision of a context that encourages supervisees to willingly explore the dissonant counseling experiences and move to the center of the learning situation is the essence of a reflective supervisory relationship. This is necessary to enable counselors to shift to a higher order of conceptual processing (Ward & House, 1998).

Because of the lack of basic research in the effects of RCGS, Shih (1995) suggested that future qualitative and quantitative research is necessary. In response to such requests and suggestions, the effects of RCGS are examined by both qualitative exploration and quantitative method in this study. However, the entire study was categorized as exploratory, as the quantitative research design is preexperimental. The purposes of this study were to examine quantitatively the effects of group supervision based on RCGS for military counselors and also to highlight findings from a qualitative exploration. Our hypothesis was that military counselors who received RCGS would show significant increase in their counseling competences between pretest and posttest.

## Method

### Participants and Procedures

A convenience sample was used in this study. Twenty-two military counselors, based on the availability of their time, participated in RCGS as part of an in-service counseling training program. One young counselor dropped out of this program because of a new task assignment. Twenty-one military counselors completed this training program. Thirty-three percent of the participants were female ($n = 7$), and 67% were male ($n = 14$). Ages ranged from 28 to 49, with a mean and modal age of 35. Eighty-one percent of the participants graduated from counseling-related majors ($n = 17$), and 19% of participants had received noncounseling-related majors ($n = 4$). Twenty-four percent of the participants have master's degrees ($n = 5$), 62% of the participants have bachelor's degrees ($n = 13$), and 14% graduated from junior colleges ($n = 3$). During the 2-year period, a monthly 2-hour group supervision session based on the RCGS model was conducted for the participants. Twenty-four sessions were completed.

### Measures

*Demographic questionnaire.* The demographic form asked for the participants' gender, major, and educational background.

*The Counseling Competence Inventory (CCI).* The CCI (S. H. Liu & Wang, 1995) was used to measure the level of counseling competences for supervisee participants. The CCI is a 49-item, 7-point Likert-type measure ($1 = strongly\ disagree$, $7 = strongly\ agree$). The CCI comprises eight subscales, including Professional Behavior, Depth Interaction, Message Interaction, Basic Communication, Conceptualization Skill, Personalization Skill, Personal Traits, and Methodological Foundation. Each subscale ranges from five to seven items. High scores on the CCI indicate good counseling competences in the specific subscales mentioned above. The Cronbach alpha is reported at .89 for the total score and .81 to .90 for the subscales. The test-retest reliability is reported at .91 over a period of 4 weeks. The concurrent validity, based largely on its correspondence with the Self-Rating Measures, has a correlation coefficient of .92 (Liu, 1999).

*Counseling Group Supervision Feedback (CGSF).* The CGSF was developed from open-ended descriptions of significant learning experiences from counseling group supervision for this study. Chou (1997) found that becoming an effective counselor is a complicated process for novice counselors. Based on his findings, a key factor that affects counselors' professional development is probably related to the quality of the counseling training they received (Lee, 2000). Therefore, in addition to the CCI, it was considered necessary to add open-ended questions to collect more precise information. This was accomplished by conducting a focus group interview 2 weeks after the program was completed. The current investigation is a preliminary effort to understand supervisees' perceived experiences by employing a qualitative research method. In reviewing previous research findings (C. J. Liu, 1997; Shih, 1995), the first question was to ask what they feel about the supervision program. The second question was to examine the supervisees' own experiences in the supervision program that benefited their professional development. Finally, the supervisees were asked to "list three important things learned from the process of supervision."

### The RCGS Format

In this framework, military counselors are encouraged to reflect on the moment of action when situations do not present themselves as given, and clinical direction must be constructed from events that are puzzling, troubling, and uncertain. During the first meeting, the supervisor directs supervisees to formulate and share learning goals and facilitates an exploration of the roles and procedures supervisees would enact during the supervision group meeting. This discussion facilitates the development of supervision norms and is also the first step in the supervisors' ongoing efforts to establish a supportive learning environment in the supervision group. It is crucial to build up a supportive environment because learning is assumed to rely on effective feedback exchanges of the supervisees (Ward & House, 1998).

In each supervision session, one or two military counselors take turns presenting a case report. The presenting supervisee, group members, and the supervisor participate in a series of interactive activities according to a reflection on the civilian and military counselors' supervisory framework. This model implies that military counselors learn from observing and discussing clinical issues with the supervisor, offering and soliciting feedback, and addressing emotional and cognitive reactions to the here-and-now process of group supervision.

A primary characteristic of a reflective supervisory dialogue is a focus on themes rather than content patterns of the supervisees' report of the counseling session (Ward & House, 1998). Open-ended thematic observations can prompt a shift from content review to process-oriented supervisory conversation. To promote self-assessment, supervisors address the following questions:

1. What hypotheses are possible for explaining the client needs?
2. Do you have the skills to address these effectively and ethically?
3. If not, what do you need to do to fill in this gap?

*Data Collection and Analysis*

Participants were asked to complete the CCI before the first session and immediately after the final session. A series of one-way repeated measures ANOVA were used to determine the differences between the timing variables (see Table 1). Significance of difference between means was tested at the .01 level. In addition, the CGSF was collected shortly after the final session.

The participants' responses to these open-ended questions were analyzed with a qualitative research method developed by Strauss and Corbin (1990) and Christensen and Kline (2001). We first read all of the participants' responses to provide us with a general sense of their contents ($N = 296$). Subsequently, each of the participants' responses was written on an index card based on different questions. Two research team members then read these cards, clustered responses, and put them into meaningful domains and categories through careful discussion. At this point, the assessment of interrater reliability was conducted. After the first test and retest, the interrater reliabilities were .89 and .92, respectively. Open coding was completed by separating, identifying, labeling, and categorizing data in terms of general themes. In open coding, based on participants' responses, a theme surrounding "outcome" was developed by researchers. Subsequently, we grouped all data that seemed to relate to "outcome" into one large group named "supervising outcomes." Then, we further used participants' responses to build properties and provide characteristics within the domain to help describe it. For example, as participants responded to interview questions and shared their perceptions, we identified affect, cognition, behavior, and attitude as four interrelated properties characterizing "supervising outcomes" in group supervision. Thus, initial categories emerged from significant learning experiences generated by the participants.

Next, axial coding was used to reconnect data and highlight relations between categories and subcategories (Christensen & Kline, 2001). In axial coding, we explored those aspects that seemed to contribute to participants' "outcome," such as awareness of self and interactions, increased clarification of personal assumptions about the counseling process, mastering counseling skills, and military counselor's limits and strengths.

In selective coding, all information attained through previous data analysis was integrated and employed to develop a clearer, more abstract explanation and description of themes and relations emerged in the research. For this purpose, data were examined for changes in conditions that influenced actions, interactions, and participants' responses over time (Christensen & Kline, 2001; Strauss & Corbin, 1990). To do this, each of the domains and categories were then reviewed, and data were coded or deleted as appropriate. For example, we explored data by means of explicating a story line that consisted of relations between all categories, identification of a core category and validation of existing concepts, and refinement of properties and domains was used to define categories and concepts. Finally, four primary categories related to supervisory style, supervisory alliance, self-assessment, and supervising outcomes were constructed.

Maxwell (1996) indicated that each type of the qualitative research has its potential validity threat in the process of data description, interpretation, and theoretical selection. In this study, throughout the process of data collection and analysis, prolonged engagement as well as researcher and method triangulation were used to ensure the credibility of findings (Christensen & Kline, 2001). For triangulation, this study involved peer researchers' interpretation of the data at different times. The prolonged engagement consisted of a 30-minute group interview that was conducted by the researchers, which served as a final form of clarification and verification.

## Results

*Differences Between Pretests and Posttests on the CCI*

A series of one-way repeated measures ANOVA was used to determine if military counselors' perceived counseling competence could be explained by selected timing variables. The timing variables examined in this study were the pretest and posttest. The dependent variables were the CCI. The independent variables were the timing variables.

Means and standard deviations on participants' perceptions of the CCI during the pretest and posttest were calculated for Professional Behavior, $F(1, 20) = 11.64$, $p < .01$; Depth Interaction, $F(1, 20) = 51.26$, $p < .01$; Message Interaction, $F(1, 20) = 34.73$, $p < .01$; Basic Communication, $F(1, 20) = 31.97$, $p < .01$; Conceptualization Skill, $F(1, 20) = 55.17$, $p < .01$; Personalization Skill, $F(1, 20) = 19.61$, $p < .01$; Personal Traits, $F(1, 20) = 36.53$, $p < .01$; and Methodological Foundation ($p < .01$). The results indicate that after conducting 24 sessions of GCGS, military counselors' perceived counseling competences have significantly increased in

Table 1
*Summary of One-Way Repeated Measures ANOVA of the CCI*

| Subscale | $M$ | $SD$ | $F$ | $p$ | Effect size |
|---|---|---|---|---|---|
| Professional behavior | | | | | |
|   Pretest | 28.19 | 5.77 | 11.64 | .003* | .368 |
|   Posttest | 32.62 | 4.86 | | | |
| Process skill | | | | | |
|  Depth interaction | | | | | |
|   Pretest | 26.10 | 6.81 | 51.26 | .000* | .719 |
|   Posttest | 36.00 | 7.04 | | | |
|  Message interaction | | | | | |
|   Pretest | 24.33 | 6.98 | 34.73 | .000* | .635 |
|   Posttest | 31.19 | 6.60 | | | |
|  Basic communication | | | | | |
|   Pretest | 17.76 | 4.33 | 31.97 | .000* | .615 |
|   Posttest | 22.10 | 4.04 | | | |
| Conceptualization skill | | | | | |
|   Pretest | 28.05 | 5.26 | 55.17 | .000* | .734 |
|   Posttest | 36.38 | 7.17 | | | |
| Personalization skill | | | | | |
|   Pretest | 25.81 | 6.02 | 19.61 | .000* | .495 |
|   Posttest | 30.62 | 7.03 | | | |
| Personal traits | | | | | |
|   Pretest | 37.33 | 6.74 | 36.53 | .000* | .646 |
|   Posttest | 44.05 | 5.47 | | | |

*Note.* CCI = Counseling Competence Inventory. $N = 21$. Effect sizes are reported for statistically significant differences ($p < .01$).
*$p < .01$.

all subscales of the CCI. Finally, the eta-squared was used to calculate effect size. Large effect sizes for all subscales found from the current study reveal significant practical meaning of the results.

*Responses to the CGSF*

Final data collection and analyses yield four primary categories related to supervisory style, supervisory alliance, self-assessment, and supervising outcomes, which emerged as prominent and consistent in the RCGS. Supervisory style referred to the supervisor's leader style. It was defined as supervisor-generated directions, feedback, information, and a unique approach to facilitate a reflective learning process. Supervisory alliance was characterized as the supervisor's developing and maintaining a positive supervisory alliance, which was crucial for enhancing the supervisee's willingness to reflect on the dissonant counseling experiences as well as on conceptual and clinical demands. Self-assessment was defined as the supervisees' development of insight regarding sense of contextual urgency in counseling relationships, ambiguity associated with the application of overall principles to crisis intervention, and ability to self-supervise. Supervising outcomes referred to what supervisees perceived in the group supervision. These outcomes included awareness of self and interactions, increased clarification of personal assumptions about the counseling process, mastering counseling skills, and military counselor's limits and strengths.

*Supervisory style.* Participants found the supervisory style to be highly facilitative. The supervisor was frequently described as positive, safe, nonjudgmental, and a thoughtful person with whom they could take risks and learn to develop their own style of being a helper and counselor. One participant talked about being comfortable in supervision for the first time, making statements such as, "I have no idea what to do with this person.... This is a whole new ball game for me." She attributed her increased openness and lack of defensiveness to the supervisor's statement: "This is a learning environment, and let me go with each one of you." Participants described the supervisor's involvement on a continuum that ranged from the facilitator (e.g., observing and encouraging interaction) to the director (e.g., providing directions, offering unsolicited conceptual input, and giving feedback). Participants perceived the facilitative roles of the supervisor more positively than directive participation: "I really enjoy this approach because it allows us as students to observe the process and give our own feedback, rather than hear from an instructor to tell us what we need to improve"; "Through interactions in the group, I gained a lot of insight about how I relate to my clients"; and "I've realized that a supervisory group is a place where I can go to express myself and receive others' feedback." At this point, the supervisor is most effective when he or she assumes less directive and more facilitative roles. The supervisor is, however, also imparting knowledge and integrating information in the supervi-

460 sory process. One participant indicated, "I really enjoy the amount of information we are getting." Specifically, supervisors' provision of information regarding the counseling strategies, mental disorders, and clinical situations increased awareness of themselves, their

465 roles, and role behaviors. Another stated, "Information dissemination by the supervisor was especially helpful."

*Supervisory alliance.* In the beginning of the supervision, clarification of the supervisory relationship was

470 the major issue, and quality supervision was discriminated by perceived trustworthiness and expertise of the supervisor. The supervisor supplied initial structure and highlighted the collaborative relationships between interactions, feedback, positive atmosphere, and skill

475 development. When supervisees began group supervision, they were anxious about how they would be judged by other supervisees and by the supervisor. As a result, they became observers and avoided giving feedback. Over time, supervisees became more interested in

480 their relationships with other participants and the supervisor because they increasingly valued, trusted, and respected the feedback they received. "I began to trust others' feedback. That trust helps me take more risks, share my comments in the supervision process, ask

485 questions, and basically stay engaged in the process," said one supervisee. "Interactions with members and the supervisor are the most valuable part of group supervision," said another one. Another supervisee said, "I realize that my tension was reduced once I pushed

490 myself to interact more in group supervision. Consequently, I learned more, trusted others, and enhanced my relationships with everyone in group supervision." Others had this to say: "I think, by encouraging us to take responsibility for learning from one another, the

495 supervisor has allowed me to grow as a counselor. We have a wonderful environment to learn, as all have learned from one another"; "This is a positive atmosphere for me to grow and step out to do things differently in role play"; "It is a special experience to know

500 no matter how badly we acted in role-playing situations, we all know that a supervisor is always there with us." Participants indicated engagement and group support as the two beneficial components: "I could not believe how quickly I've felt like doing teamwork with

505 my group members and supervisors; they are very supportive—yet challenging, which makes me feel comfortable to share and to be myself." Participants pointed out that it was helpful to receive feedback during the supervisory process.

510 *Self-assessment.* Supervisees realized that learning was minimized when they were not actively involved in the feedback exchange process in group supervision. This was a process of participants' self-assessment. One supervisee indicated, "I got frustrated because I

515 wasn't learning anything. When I was confronted I realized I interacted minimally and refrained from giving and soliciting feedback. I finally got it: I wasn't

involved in feedback and I was not learning." There was a growing awareness that participants examined

520 the reflection in different ways. One participant mentioned,

> For me, the most important part of reflection in a general way, is to reflect: how is my work with clients, how is my personal life, how are these factors influencing my
525 psychological status…for me, I evaluate my stress level. How is that balance going? Now I see professional and personal identity as part of one thing. They are just different parts, but inseparable.

As supervisees attained awareness during supervision,

530 they gained a better understanding of counseling work concepts. By learning about themes, theories, and philosophical assumptions and by paying attention to the learning experiences, supervisees began to understand the counseling process in both supervision and the cli-

535 ent's contexts, "I've realized that the struggle of dealing with personal issues is what group supervision and individual counseling are all about," said one supervisee.

*Supervising outcomes.* Three domains emerged

540 from supervisees' perspectives: cognitive changes, skill developments, and personal growth. The cognitive domain included awareness of the military counselor's limits and strengths, moving away from dichotomous thinking, awareness of counselor's development as a

545 lengthy process, and those related to one's knowledge base. Knowing the military counselors' limits and strengths are essential for all mental hygiene workers in military systems. Many participants stated, "I accept feeling frustrated and disappointed with my superin-

550 tendent, but it's okay to have a 'bad working environment' as long as I am learning from it." Another participant expressed,

> Each superintendent has different leader style and therefore has a variety of expectations. Following his rules or
555 creating good relationships with clients under the professional ethics was really tough to me. The most important thing is to learn how to adjust yourself. As long as I'm learning or getting better, I don't have to be perfect.

Many supervisees expressed,

560 > What came out for me at this period of time is that there isn't one answer. All things have two sides and it depends on where the client is and how you present it. So there is not just one intervention. It is more complex.

For some supervisees, a more complex understanding

565 of clients naturally led them to the recognition of the need for more creative decision making with regard to interventions. A supervisee shared his opinion: "Looking at the supervisory sessions, one thing I've learned is that each case is unique and what works with one is

570 not necessarily going to work with another." The skill domain included listening skills, goal-setting skills, and basic counseling skills. Supervisees also learned about specific skills to be employed in supervision and in their groups. As supervisees used techniques to interact

575 more effectively in supervision, they learned how to conduct their individual counseling more effectively. Similarly, as they gained awareness of themselves and used themes, theories, and philosophical assumptions throughout their learning process, they came to under-

580 stand counseling theories, counseling processes, and counseling skills more clearly. One supervisee indicated, "Fortunately, I learned about skills I can use in counseling, in RCGS, or in my real life." Another supervisee said, "I was suffering from being confronted

585 and I got frustrated because I felt I wasn't learning new things. I finally got it: I wasn't involved in interactions and I was not learning." The personal domain included openness to feedback, empathetic understanding to clients, and increased awareness of the need for self-

590 reflection. Many participants clearly expressed confidence in themselves as growing to become counselors. For example, one of the participants stated, "I am confident that I will become more skilled in my counseling encounters and I will be able to benefit others." When

595 participants were actively involved in group supervision, they gained increased awareness of themselves, conceptual development, relationships with others, and understanding of client issues.

## Discussion and Applications to Social Work

According to the results of this study, significant

600 differences were found on the CCI between pretests to posttests, and the responses to open-ended questions also revealed meaningful supervisory experiences. Because the CCI is designed to assess a diverse range of competences including Professional Behavior, Depth

605 Interaction, Message Interaction, Basic Communication, Conceptualization Skills, Personalization Skill, Personal Traits, and Methodological Foundation, the results seem to fully support the hypothesis that military counselors who received RCGS would show a

610 significant increase in their counseling competences from pretests to posttests. Although previous research on group supervision (Christensen & Kline, 2001; S. H. Liu, 1999; McMahon & Simons, 2004) indicated that group supervision has effects on the training of super-

615 visees during their supervisory experience, the results in this study need to be examined more carefully. The use of pretest and posttest test design may have provided some spurious effects because of some uncontrollable threats to internal validity.

620 A number of explanations can be provided with regard to the changes reported after RCGS experiences. First, the model outlines the sequence of supervisee development as well as the interactive reflective learning cycle between the supervisor and supervisee.

625 Hence, developing and maintaining a positive learning alliance is crucial for enhancing the supervisee's willingness to reflect on the dissonant counseling experiences as well as on the conceptual and clinical demands that are essential for further counselor develop-

630 ment. Second, as trust is experienced within the super-

visory dyad, the dissonant experiences of supervisees are transformed into meaningful schemas and corresponding counseling skills. The supervisee develops in concert with the progression of the on-site supervision

635 relationship (Shih, 1995; Ward & House, 1998). Third, the supervisory relationship provides a context in which supervisees become more confident in professional risk-taking behaviors and strategies related to counseling relationships. Fourth, observing how fellow

640 members conduct an individual counseling may aid in learning counseling skills. As a person watches peers learn a skill, he or she feels more empowered to practice that skill. Observing a peer completing a task instills confidence in the person's ability to perform the

645 same task (Christensen & Kline, 2001).

Based on the data collected from the open-ended questions, results were congruent with previous findings regarding supervisory experiences, which include the following: (a) RCGS provides an opportunity to

650 learn through both participation and observation (Brown & Bourne, 1996; Ward & House, 1998), (b) supervisors must assume a facilitative role as an information integrator in the supervision process (Corcoran, 2001), (c) supervisors can also promote self-awareness

655 in supervisees (Chen, 2004; Christensen & Kline, 2001), (d) developing a positive learning alliance is crucial for the quality of the supervisory relationship (Holloway & Johnston, 1985), and (e) the more supervisees perceived supervisors as supportive, the more

660 both perceived level of trust and the supervisee's learning and growth (Shih, 1995; Wark, 1995; Worthen & McNeill, 1996).

In addition, theoretical constructs derived from this investigation highlight new perspectives directed at the

665 understanding of self-assessment. Self-assessment was related to supervisees' development of insight regarding the sense of contextual urgency in counseling relationships and ability to self-supervise. Based on RCGS, an emphasis on constructing professional experiences

670 is to believe that meaningful learning occurs only through self-examination of assumptions, patterns of interactions, and the operating premises of an action. Thus, providing a systematic and detailed account of the important experiences throughout the group super-

675 vision can evolve supervisees' experiences and knowledge. Learning from the supervisory process was consistently valued as the most important benefit, which is congruent with earlier findings (Chen, 2004; Liu, 1997; Shih, 1995; Tsui, 2005). This may be indicative of a

680 reflective supervisory dialogue, which is the primary nature of RCGS. One of the characteristics of reflective dialogue is an emphasis on self-assessment. Central to reflective learning theory, this internal process is characterized by the trainee's ability to reflect objectively

685 on the counseling process in relation to the needs of clients. The supervisees observed and learned from supervisory interactions directly and continually. Hence, participants' dissonant experiences can be

690 transformed into meaningful schemas. From this perspective, supervisors can promote self-assessment in supervisees by encouraging (a) an identification of goals regarding client issues and the counseling process, and (b) an increased self-direction in identifying professional gaps and strategies for development of the 695 skills. The result provides insight into the developmental process of RCGS from this point of view. It is meaningful and valuable for military counselors when situations do not present themselves as given, and clinical direction must be constructed from events that 700 are puzzling, troubling, and uncertain in the troops.

Information about ethical practice and legal challenges is not included in this study. Krushinski (2005) and McGlothlin, Rainey, and Kindsvatter (2005) reported that supervisors should know how to make their 705 supervisees aware of professional and ethical standards and legal responsibilities of the counseling profession. This may reflect a controversial issue of military counselors' tasks. The role function of military counselors is to promote military officers' mental hygiene, and if 710 necessary, to protect client welfare. It appears that military counselors were suffering from role conflicts and role confusion in Taiwan. Though conflicts of obligation are unavoidable for most members in complex societies, it seems clear that we ought to avoid assum-715 ing obligations we know will put us in frequent or irreconcilable conflict. Therefore, in advanced supervision, we can begin to analyze the moral situation of military counselors by reviewing some of their fundamental obligations and considering whether these obli-720 gations create special difficulties or irreconcilable conflicts. Bernard and Goodyear (2004) saw this as the supervisor's paramount responsibility. Because the purpose of supervision is to foster the supervisees' professional development, to ensure clients' welfare, and 725 to improve the clinical outcome of the supervisee (Bernard & Goodyear, 2004), some risks have existed for military counselors in the supervisory process. Thus, future studies should include role conflict as a factor in the investigation of professional development. Fur-730 thermore, there is an enormous need for effective, qualified military counselors to deal with family and individual issues occurring in military families, especially during times of war. An ethical guideline may provide a framework for supervision of military coun-735 selors working with troubled clients. As a result, a qualified military counselor can provide services of good quality.

Of course, group supervision has advantages and disadvantages. Based on the findings of current qualita-740 tive research, group supervision provides a wide variety of learning experiences, including supervisory style, supervisory alliance, self-assessment, and supervising outcomes perceived by the participants in the group supervision sessions. However, as Brown and 745 Bourne (1996) cautioned, group supervision focuses on issues that have relevance to the largest number of group members in social work. Specific and urgent needs cannot be handled immediately. In many cases, it may seem easier to opt out of responsibility to engage 750 in exploration, problem solving, and decision making. Finally, conformity to group norms may be harmful to the creativity and productivity of the work team (Tsui, 2005).

Although supervision has been identified as one of 755 the most important factors in determining the quality of service to clients in a variety of professions, it is surprising that supervision has not received as much attention as other components in social work practice, such as social work research or administration (Tsui, 2005). 760 This is the first study that provides a comprehensive and in-depth exploration of the use of an important supervision model, RCGS, for military counselors. As it appears that RCGS can be an effective supervision tool for supervisees and supervisors, it is important that 765 future research expands, confirms, and/or negates these initial conceptualizations. In particular, future researchers are encouraged to explore (a) supervisors' perceptions of this modality of supervision, (b) the difference of the supervisory working alliance between 770 RCGS and a variety of supervisory models, (c) RCGS experiences with diverse populations of supervisees, and (d) clients' perceptions of the military counselor's role function of following the supervisory development.

775 Although these findings have generated several research questions for future research, this study is not without its limitations, and results should be interpreted with caution. First, a single-subject (one-group) design was chosen to examine the changes of operation in 780 RCGS. Although this design provided the clearest means to describe the group, specify changes in the behavior or actions of the group over time, and link one or more selected process variables to outcome (Heppner, Kivlighan, & Wampold, 1992), the repeated use of 785 measures without a comparative group might cause some methodological problems. Second, the use of pretest and posttest design has its weaknesses and limitations because threats to internal validity cannot be easily controlled. Finally, based on the findings of 790 McMahon and Simons's (2004) study, a 3- to 6-month follow-up evaluation is recommended to test the ongoing progress and enduring changes. With these limitations in mind, the generalizability of the findings and the replication of this study should be undertaken with 795 care. These limitations, however, provide opportunities for further exploration of RCGS.

## References

Bernard, J. M., & Goodyear, R. K. (2004). *Fundamentals of clinical supervision* (3rd ed.). New York: Allyn & Bacon.

Brown, A., & Bourne, I. (1996). *The social work supervisor*. Buckingham, UK: Open University Press.

Chen, S. Z. (2004.). *An exploratory study on solution-focusing group supervision impacts of the counselor: An example of counselors in military*. Unpublished master's thesis, Fu Hsing Kang Political College, Taiwan.

Chou, Y. C. (1997). *A study of influential factors of counseling training process: An example of the practice of the brief counseling training.* Unpublished doctoral dissertation, National Changhua University, Taiwan.

Christensen, T. M., & Kline, W. B. (2001). The qualitative exploration of process-sensitive peer group supervision. *Journal for Specialists in Group Work, 26,* 81–99.

Corcoran, K. B. (2001). *An ethnographic study of therapist development and reflective within the context of postmodern supervision and training.* Unpublished doctoral dissertation, University of Akron.

Griffith, B. A., & Frieden, G. (2000). Facilitating reflective thinking in counselor education. *Counselor Education and Supervision, 40,* 82–93.

Hawkins, P., & Shohet, R. (1989). *Supervision in the helping professions.* Buckingham, UK: Open University Press.

Heppner P. P., & Handley, P. G. (1981). A study of the interpersonal influence process in supervision. *Journal of Counseling Psychology, 28,* 437–444.

Heppner, P. P., Kivlighan, D. M., Jr., & Wampold, B, E. (1992). *Research design in counseling.* Pacific Grove, CA: Brooks/Cole.

Holloway, E. L. (1999). *The strategic approach to supervision.* London, Sage.

Holloway, E. L., & Johnston, R. (1985). Group supervision: Widely practiced but poorly understood. *Counselor Education and Supervision, 24,* 332–340.

Hu, Z. S. (2006). Building an index system of military counselor's professional competence. *Military Science Journal, 38,* 318–439.

Kadushin, A., & Harkness, D. (2002). *Supervision in social work.* New York: Columbia University Press.

Krushinski, M. (2005). A comparison of the perceptions of the importance of formal supervision training between formally trained counselor supervisors and nonformally trained counselor supervisors. *Dissertation Abstracts International: Section B: The Sciences and Engineering, 65*(10-B), 5408.

Lee, H. H. (2000). *A qualitative research of the process of counselors' development.* Unpublished doctoral thesis, National Changhua University of Education, Taiwan.

Liu, C. J. (1997). *The verbal behaviors of supervisors and supervisees in the supervision process of the cyclical developmental model.* Unpublished doctoral thesis, National Changhua University of Education, Taiwan.

Liu, S. H. (1999). The verification of the self-rating version of Counseling Competence Inventory and the analyses of self-rated change pattern. *Chinese Annual Report of Guidance and Counseling, 7,* 201–244.

Liu, S. H., & Wang, S. T., (1995). An evaluation of individual counseling competence and analysis of category. *Chinese Annual Report, 3,* 1–40.

Maxwell, J. A. (1996). *Qualitative research design: An interactive approach.* Thousand Oaks, CA: Sage.

McGlothlin, J. M., Rainey, S., & Kindsvatter, A. (2005). Suicidal clients and supervisees: A model for considering supervisor roles. *Counselor Education and Supervision, 45,* 135–146.

McMahon, M., & Simons, R. (2004), Supervision training for professional counselors: An exploratory study. *Counselor Education and Supervision, 43,* 301–320.

Ministry of National Defense. (2006). Retrieved February 20, 2006, from http://www.mnd.gov.tw/eng/ROC/gpwb/pcp/index.htm

Sexton, T. L., & Whiston, S. C. (1994). The status of the counseling relationship: An empirical review, theoretical implications, and research directions. *Counseling Psychologist, 22,* 6–78.

Shih, S. J. (1995). *The construct of counseling supervision process: Analysis of the cyclical developmental model.* Unpublished doctoral thesis, National Changhua University, Taiwan.

Shou, W., & Shih, S. J. (1995). Comments and suggestions for establishing the cyclical developmental counseling supervision model. *Journal of Guidance and Counseling, 31,* 34–40.

Starling, P. V. (1996). The impact of peer supervision in a structured group on first-time practicum supervisees. *Dissertation Abstracts International Section A: Humanities and Social Sciences, 57*(1-A), 118.

Strauss, A., & Corbin, J. (1990). *Basics of qualitative research: Grounded theory procedures and techniques.* Newbury Park, CA; Sage.

Tsui, M. S. (2005). *Social work supervision: Contexts and concepts.* Thousand Oaks, CA: Sage.

Ward, C. C., & House, R. M. (1998). Counseling supervision: A reflective model. *Counselor Education and Supervision, 38,* 23–33.

Wark, L. (1995). Live supervision in family therapy: Qualitative interviews of supervision events as perceived by supervisors and supervisees. *American Journal of Family Therapy, 23,* 25–37.

Watkins, C. E., Jr. (1997). Defining psychotherapy supervision and understanding supervisor functioning. In C. E. Watkins, Jr. (Ed.), *Handbook of psychotherapy supervision* (pp. 3–10). New York: John Wiley & Sons.

Wetchler, J. L., & Vaughn, K. A. (1991). Perceptions of primary supervisor interpersonal skills: A critical incident analysis. *Contemporary Family Therapy, 13,* 61–69.

Worthen, V. E., & McNeill, B. W. (1996). A phenomenological investigation of "good" supervision events. *Journal of Counseling Psychology, 43,* 25–34.

Worthen, V. E., & McNeill, B. W. (2001). *What is effective supervision? A national survey of supervision experts.* Retrieved January 13, 2008, from http://0-search.epnet.com.cylis.lib.cycu.edu.tw:80/1ogin.aspx?direct=true&db=eric&an=ED455466& lang=zh-t

**Acknowledgments**: The authors wish to express their deepest appreciation to Y. J. Wang, Jenny S. S. Yuan, and Wendy H. Y. Yu, research assistants, for their contributions to this study.

**Address correspondence to**: Peter Jen Der Pan, College of Humanities and Education, Chung Yuan Christian University, Chung-Li, Taiwan. E-mail: jender@cycu.edu.tw

# Exercise for Article 35

## Factual Questions

1. What was the researchers' explicitly stated hypothesis?

2. When was the CGSF used?

3. What was the pretest mean for Personal Traits on the pretest? What was the pretest mean for Personal Traits on the posttest?

4. Was the difference between the two means in your answer to Question 3 above statistically significant? If yes, at what probability level?

5. Do the researchers consider the lack of a control group to be a limitation of their study?

## Questions for Discussion

6. What is your understanding of the meaning of the term "preexperimental"? (See lines 193–195.)

7. The researchers state that they used a "convenience sample." In your opinion, is this a desirable form of sampling? Explain. (See lines 203–206.)

8. In this study, counseling competencies were measured with a structured questionnaire and open-ended questions. In your opinion, is one type of measure better than the other? Explain. (See lines 225–266.)

9. In your opinion, is the analysis of the qualitative data described in sufficient detail? Explain. (See lines 314–382.)

10. Do you regard the quantitative results (lines 383–405) *or* the qualitative results (lines 406–598) to be more informative? Explain.

## *Quality Ratings*

Directions: Indicate your level of agreement with each of the following statements by circling a number from 5 for strongly agree (SA) to 1 for strongly disagree (SD). If you believe an item is not applicable to this research article, leave it blank. Be prepared to explain your ratings. When responding to criteria A and B, keep in mind that brief titles and abstracts are conventional in published research.

A. The title of the article is appropriate.

SA 5 4 3 2 1 SD

B. The abstract provides an effective overview of the research article.

SA 5 4 3 2 1 SD

C. The introduction establishes the importance of the study.

SA 5 4 3 2 1 SD

D. The literature review establishes the context for the study.

SA 5 4 3 2 1 SD

E. The research purpose, question, or hypothesis is clearly stated.

SA 5 4 3 2 1 SD

F. The method of sampling is sound.

SA 5 4 3 2 1 SD

G. Relevant demographics (for example, age, gender, and ethnicity) are described.

SA 5 4 3 2 1 SD

H. Measurement procedures are adequate.

SA 5 4 3 2 1 SD

I. All procedures have been described in sufficient detail to permit a replication of the study.

SA 5 4 3 2 1 SD

J. The participants have been adequately protected from potential harm.

SA 5 4 3 2 1 SD

K. The results are clearly described.

SA 5 4 3 2 1 SD

L. The discussion/conclusion is appropriate.

SA 5 4 3 2 1 SD

M. Despite any flaws, the report is worthy of publication.

SA 5 4 3 2 1 SD

# Article 36

# Prevalence and Pedagogy: Understanding Substance Abuse in Schools

TWYLA SALM
University of Regina, Saskatchewan, Canada

VAL MULHOLLAND
University of Regina, Saskatchewan, Canada

PHIL SEVIGNY
University of Regina, Saskatchewan, Canada

HIRSCH GREENBERG
University of Regina, Saskatchewan, Canada

ABSTRACT. This case study examines not only the prevalence of substance abuse in one rural Canadian high school but also how teachers understand teaching and learning in relation to substance abuse. Over one third of students reported that they had used marijuana (37%) and alcohol (38%) in the last seven days, a rate considerably higher than typical Canadian averages. Pedagogical implications were informed by three main themes that emerged from staff interviews. Several teachers normalized substance abuse in adolescence, others coped silently "under the radar," and a few called for specialized support from other human services. Further, in-school approaches require that the entire staff be involved to enhance awareness of substance abuse, interprofessional collaboration, and a sense of interdependence.

## Background to the Research

While excessive alcohol consumption and the use of illicit drugs by youth is problematic across North America (Healthy People, 2000; Health Canada, 2008), international comparisons of alcohol and cannabis use by young people indicate that Canada ranks among the leading countries for rates of prevalence and frequency (CCSA, 2007). It is well known that prevalence and patterns of substance abuse vary among regions and even within communities, however, evidence suggests that adolescents are the most likely to use substances, engage in risky behaviors, and experience harm as a result (CCSA, 2007). Additionally, not all youth are subject to equal risk, as some minority populations that experience greater poverty, trauma, and cultural alienation account for a disproportional number of individuals who abuse alcohol and other substances (Sharma, 2008; CCSA, 2007). Further, assessing risk is a problem; "most adolescent instruments are still in the development stages, and their effectiveness for problem identification diagnosis and treatment planning is largely unknown" (Heister & Miller, 1995, p. 65).

The vast majority of schools use various classroom-based drug abuse prevention strategies and curricula as an approach to curb drug abuse and its adverse consequences and to deter early-stage drug use (Birkeland, Murphy-Graham, & Weiss, 2005; Hecht, Graham, & Elek, 2006); however, much less is known about how teachers understand substance abuse issues within their schools. Moreover, since there is widespread support for the effects of social context on adolescent substance abuse, understanding the role of the school as one organization within the community network influencing young people is paramount.

Davis (2007) reports that schools do not have the time or the resources to adequately address issues related to substance abuse; consequently, the impact of school curricula and other efforts to prevent adolescent alcohol abuse have been less successful than desired (Bauman, Foshee, Ennett, Hicks, & Pemberton, 2001). While popular programs such as D.A.R.E (Drug Abuse Resistance Education) appear to have no lasting influence on adolescent use of substances (Vincus, Ringwalt, Harris, & Shamblen, 2010; Pan & Bai, 2009; West & O'Neal, 2004), there is evidence that there are other psychosocial benefits to D.A.R.E., including building relationships with community members (Birkeland, Murphy-Graham, & Weiss, 2005), enhancing self-esteem, and institutional bonding (Lucas, 2008). Additionally, many scholars believe that the school context provides a unique environment for not only prevention curricula (Sloboda, Pyakuryal, Stephens, Teasdale, Forrest, Stephens, & Grey, 2008) but also for acting as a crucial partner in successful addiction treatment and rehabilitation (CCSA, 2007).

Although there is some evidence that teachers perceive substance abuse as increasingly common, having an impact on academic performance, and causing behaviors such as withdrawal, truancy, reduced ability to concentrate, and absenteeism (Van Hout & Connor, 2008), few studies have specifically examined addictive behaviors in a school context and have asked teachers about substance abuse in school (Finn & Willert, 2006). Van Hout and Connor (2008) concluded that "teachers needed timely information and teacher-specific training in order to recognize the varying signs of adolescent problematic substance abuse" (p. 89), but little is known about how teachers' pedagogical decisions are affected by students with these issues.

This case study examines not only the prevalence of substance abuse in one rural Canadian school with a high minority population, but also how teachers understand teaching and learning in relation to substance abuse. With a view to develop a comprehensive school-community drug prevention and intervention strategy, an interprofessional support services team including an educational psychologist, principal, addictions counselor, and a superintendent of student services initiated the study to provide background information and evidence to guide policy and decisions for this school community as well as for other schools in the school district. Prompted by concerns from other local stakeholders, including the chiefs of two First Nation Bands, the local Royal Canadian Mounted Police (RCMP) and a mental health care worker, the interprofessional support services team hypothesized that the prevalence and frequency of substance abuse in their rural high school was higher than the national average. Their concerns stemmed from anecdotal experiences of working with students who exhibited common social indicators of substance abuse including delayed education, high nonattendance, school suspensions, as well as heavy demand for therapeutic interventions for addiction.

The school that is the focus of this case study services Kindergarten to Grade 12 students and is located in a small rural community in a remote area. Assessing the prevalence of adolescent substance abuse through a survey was considered appropriate, but for many stakeholders, it was somewhat redundant since there was already widespread consensus within the group that substance abuse in youth in this school community was highly problematic. In spite of their skepticism, a list of questions was developed, which surveyed student's experience with substances as well as a number of items assessing protective factors. The primary purpose of the study, however, was to explore how teachers' pedagogical decisions are affected by student substance abuse.

## Method

Coupled with the paucity of research of how pedagogical decisions are influenced by student substance abuse, and the fact that there were no local data reflecting prevalence and frequency of substance abuse in this school-community, both quantitative and qualitative data were collected to address the research questions. Students in Grades 6–12 ($n = 175$) were asked to voluntarily complete a confidential, nonstandardized survey. Although other standardized surveys were reviewed (Martz & Wagner, 2008; Addiction Research Institute, 2010), none of the surveys fully provided the information specifically requested by the support services team in a way succinct enough to accommodate feasible concentration levels for youth.

From the demographic information collected, a majority (70%) of the students identified themselves as First Nation or Métis, 17% of students identified as Caucasian, 3% as Asian, and 11% did not select an option. The survey consisted of 43 multiple choice questions and seven open-ended questions aimed at assessing not only risky behavior related to substance abuse, but also assets that serve as protective factors.

There was a 94% student participation rate in the survey, and although it was conducted on a school day in late spring 2010, one fourth of students were absent. This rate of absenteeism was not atypical since numerous students had, by that point of the school year, become nonattenders. Given these facts, it is possible that students who were the most likely to struggle with substance abuse and its related effects were simply not part of the survey population. Moreover, staff members commented that they had worked very hard to make the school a safe place for students to attend. In creating this safe environment, it is possible that students who engage in negative behavior such as abusing substances had been "disinvited" to attend school. In that way, it is possible that the survey actually under-reports the prevalence of substance abuse in this school.

In addition to the student survey, semi-structured individual interviews were conducted with 20 out of 37 staff members, including administrators, school counselors, teachers, and educational assistants. Prior to the collection of data, researchers made a presentation to the entire staff, outlining the general purpose and parameters of the intended research. Draft survey and interview questions were shared through school e-mail to incorporate teacher feedback into the process. E-mail was also used to apprise staff of the interview date and invite interested volunteers to attend an individual interview.

Because the interviews were scheduled during the school day and took place in offices within the school, the researchers tried to preserve some participant confidentiality by creating an interview schedule and providing out-of-school substitute teachers. Interviews were confidentially scheduled throughout the school day, often when teachers were normally in class. The substitute teachers moved from classroom to classroom throughout the day facilitating the lessons while the teacher slipped out of class to attend an interview in a private meeting room without the knowledge of their school colleagues.

Three research questions guided the interview: (a) How does student substance abuse affect the decisions you make in your role related to such things as instruction, evaluation, and relationships? (b) In relation to teaching and learning, provide examples of the ways you problem solve in response to "substance abuse" situations? (c) What, if any, supports and resources might you need to assist students with addiction issues?

The analysis of the interviews was guided by a Basic Interpretative Qualitative research design that illuminates a deeper understanding of the participants' lived experiences (Merriam, 2002). To ensure systematic and rigorous data analysis, a grounded theory approach was used to code and identify emerging themes. All data were manually aggregated, coded, and themed using two complementary strategies, constant comparison method (Strauss & Corbin, 1998) and initial and focused coding (Charmaz, 2006). It was through these grounded theory analysis strategies that the broader categorical themes emerged from the data.

This case study was collectively designed by researchers and stakeholders to provide specific information for a particular geographical location. Using a single small-scale study served the purpose of the local audience, but it also exemplified the limitations in case study research (Yin, 2009). While the collection of both qualitative and quantitative data enabled the researchers to construct a vivid picture of the local situation, the researchers are also aware of case study limitations. It is impossible to make any claims of representativeness or generalizability of the data; however, the researchers are hopeful that both the analysis of the data and the process of a mix-method case study will provide insight for others.

## Student Questionnaires

Descriptive statistics for each of the 43 items on the survey were explored. The survey contained questions related to school attendance, academic achievement, frequency, and severity of drug usage among respondents and their peers. The full survey is available from the first author. The data presented in this section represent a summary of the survey, highlighting the results that are most notable in comparison to national averages.

While the majority of students reported that they were not involved with alcohol or other substances, some students reported occasional substance use, and a few indicated that they were frequently using substances. According to student responses, in the previous 4 months, 35% of youth reported being high or drunk at least once at school, of which 12% reported being high or drunk over 9 or more days. When asked to report how many of their four best friends smoked cannabis in the last month, 72% believed at least one of their friends had done so, and 30% reported that all four of their best friends smoked pot. By comparison, less than 2% of students reported that any of their friends had used the fictitious drug *derbisol*, suggesting a minimum of intentional deception in responding. Over one third of students (37%) indicated that they had used drugs at least once in the last seven days. Similarly, 38% of students indicated that they had at least one alcoholic drink in the previous seven days, and 21% had 5 or more drinks. Even though the majority of students had not experienced a "blackout" after

drinking, 25% of students reported that they had. Accessibility to drugs (69%) and alcohol (72%) was considered by students to be "really easy" or "sort of easy." The majority of students (52%) had tried at least once to get a friend to cut down on drinking, with 6% of the students reporting that they had tried 5 or more times. Some students believed that drugs "sometimes or always" builds confidence (42%) and relieves stress (43%). Risky behaviors such as fighting while drunk were likely in 21% of the population, and 53% of students reported that they sometimes ride with a drunk driver.

Substantial differences were not found in comparing results of Aboriginal versus non-Aboriginal students. The only statistically significant difference found between the ethnic groups was for recent drug usage, with Aboriginal students reporting more frequent drug usage in the past seven days, $t(121.9) = 2.65$, $p < .01$. In terms of sex differences, females were more likely than males to use drugs to handle angry feelings, $\chi^2 (2, N = 152) = 8.97$, $p < .05$; deal with stress, $\chi^2 (2, N = 153) = 8.43$, $p < .05$; and forget about their problems, $\chi^2 (2, N = 154) = 8.08$, $p < .05$. Females were also more likely than males to have spoken to a counselor or social worker about a drug or alcohol problem, $\chi^2 (1, N = 169) = 8.15$, $p < .01$.

To examine age effects, responses of younger students (Grades 6–8) were compared to those of older students (Grades 9–12). In terms of frequency of abuse, older students reported going to school under the influence of drugs or alcohol more often, $t(163.8) = 2.26$, $p < .05$, as well as more frequent drug usage in the preceding week, $t(161.4) = 2.70$, $p < .01$. Compared to the younger group, older students reported that it was easier to access both alcohol, $t(160) = 7.85$, $p < .001$, and drugs, $t(162) = 6.44$, $p < .001$. In terms of high-risk behaviors, older students were significantly more likely than younger students to ride in a car driven by someone who was under the influence of drugs or alcohol, $\chi^2 (1, N = 166) = 4.55$, $p < .05$.

To examine the relationships between drug and alcohol abuse, school attendance, and achievement, we used bivariate correlations (see Table 1). As expected, positive correlations were found between alcohol and drug usage as well as the frequency of skipping school. Significant negative correlations were found between alcohol and drug use and report card grades, indicating that higher levels of substance use was associated with lower levels of academic achievement.

A number of items on the student questionnaires were included to assess the presence of protective factors. Also referred to as prosocial factors, protective factors are those individual, family, and community variables that protect youth from substance use (Taylor, 2010). The National Institute on Drug Abuse (2011) suggests that strong bonds with family, clear rules, and success in school are examples of protective factors. Examining the item frequencies, we found that

Table 1
*Correlations Among Drug and Alcohol Abuse, School Attendance, and Achievement*

|  | 1 | 2 | 3 | 4 |
|---|---|---|---|---|
| 1. Past week alcohol use |  |  |  |  |
| 2. Past week drug use | .44*** |  |  |  |
| 3. Under the influence at school | .42*** | .67*** |  |  |
| 4. Report card grades | −.16* | −.27*** | −.25** |  |
| 5. Skipping school | .29*** | .29*** | .27*** | −.30*** |

*Note.* $*p < .05$, $**p < .01$, $***p < .001$.

over 85% of students endorsed each of the following protective factors as being present in their lives: liking their community, having consistent adult encouragement, having an adult to talk to, participating in extracurricular activities, receiving teacher praise often, being perceived as a helpful person, being perceived as caring, honest, and responsible.

To simplify the analysis, a protective factors index was created by summing individual scores for the above items. While scores could have potentially ranged from 8–40, the actual observed range was 13–35 ($M = 25.77$, $SD = 3.99$). To explore possible group differences on the protective factor index, $t$ tests were conducted. No statistically significant differences were found comparing Aboriginal with non-Aboriginal students and comparing younger (Grades 6–8) versus older (Grades 9–12) students. Females, however, scored significantly higher on this index than males, $t(172) = 4.12$, $p < .001$ (girls range 18–35, $M = 26.86$, $SD = 3.37$; boys range 13–33, $M = 24.46$, $SD = 4.31$). Bivariate correlations were also calculated to examine the association between the protective factor index, alcohol and drug abuse, school attendance, and school achievement. As expected, the protective factor index was significantly associated with academic grades, $r(166) = .19$, $p < .05$, and skipping school, $r(173) = −.26$, $p < .001$. Surprisingly though, the protective factor index was not associated with frequency of drug or alcohol use or with attending school under the influence of a substance. To help clarify the associations, correlations between each putative protective factor of alcohol use and drug use were examined individually. As expected, receiving encouragement from a number of adults was negatively associated with drug and alcohol abuse. Greater frequency of teacher praise was also associated with less alcohol use. Interestingly, the number of extracurricular activities the youth participated in was positively associated with their drug use. Thus, being involved in more activities was associated with higher drug usage.

The survey findings were presented to the entire school staff, with an opportunity for researchers to engage in discussion with this group, which was also useful in understanding how teachers interpreted the results.

**Interviews With School Staff**

In order to preserve some measure of anonymity and confidentiality, the term *staff* was selected to represent the composite of individuals interviewed. Most of the participants were teachers, but some of the teachers also had additional roles such as principal, vice principal, or counselor, and a few were not teachers, but rather, educational assistants. When the term *teacher* is used, it includes all staff who are certified teachers but it does not exclude those individuals who may also serve in other administrative roles. The term *educational assistant* is used only when referring to this subgroup within the staff.

*Our School is Normal*

Although there were some exceptions, many staff suggested that there was a "normal amount" of student substance abuse, and there was minimal concern for classroom issues related to drugs and alcohol. Not surprisingly then, most of the staff did not perceive substance abuse as a factor that influenced their pedagogical decisions. The general sentiment is captured by this teacher, who said, "I suppose some of the students use drugs, but I have never seen it, so I can't say anything about what they do or don't do." Thus, it was difficult to discuss pedagogical issues related to substance abuse with participants when they did not perceive substance abuse as a problem. Although some teachers talked about differentiated instruction for students with "various learning needs," there were few examples of specific ways instruction, evaluation, or relationships were modified to support students who might be vulnerable to substance abuse or who were experiencing side effects such as mood swings, violent outbursts, and declining grades (Lasser & Schmidt, 2009).

Most staff members reported that some students were occasionally high in school, but most said they had never seen a student intoxicated, even though 35% of students stated they had been high or drunk at school in the last four months. The interviews were consistent with many comments made in the staff meetings conducted pre- and postsurvey, where several comments were made that suggested, regardless of the amount of substance abuse that occurred, it was within a normal range. Not surprisingly, many teachers echoed this comment, "I'm sure some of the students use drugs and drink, but it is not different here than any other school; most of the kids here are not into that." In an emphatic tone, another teacher highlighted the majority of students who do not participate in substance abuse and

385 questioned the need to "study the few that always will." Even though some staff members thought substance abuse was normal, they did not associate it with recent teen suicides and a suspension rate 5 times higher than comparable schools of its size and demographics. Many staff reported they could only recall 390 one or two students in recent history who had attended school drunk or high, whereas the interprofessional support team reported that in the last two years, there had been several substance abuse incidences every month referred to them from the school.

395 Although many participants resisted naming substance abuse as a significant concern, and to do so seemed problematic for the participants, there was less reluctance to dismiss issues of chronic absenteeism, lethargy, and intergenerational trauma. One teacher 400 said, "It is their home life. Substance abuse is just part of the picture. Kids are just coping with parents fighting or not having enough food." Many teachers described negative student behaviors in relation to wider community and social issues and emphasized they were 405 not blaming students for their conduct. One staff member described it this way:

> They [students] say things very matter of fact, "mom's boyfriend left—he's gone." They tend to have people in and out of their life, and this is normal. When they are
> 410 tired, I let them sleep if they are that tired; they need to sleep. No kid can control if there is a party in their home.

This teacher identified that she addressed sleepy students by letting them sleep and not judging or punishing them, but most participants could not provide 415 substantial examples of ways they problem solved in their classroom in response to a "substance abuse" situation.

Participant responses often indicated that safety and behavioral issues were primarily an administrative 420 issue and not within the purview of a teacher's responsibility or role. One teacher lamented that the "expanding mandate of the teacher was overwhelming and teachers couldn't do it all." There were varying opinions regarding the degree to which school policies were 425 effective in supporting students who had breached policies. One teacher described her students as generally being disrespectful and "accountable to no one"; she called for harsher punishment. Other teachers questioned policies particularly related to the ineffective-430 ness of out-of-school suspensions. One teacher believed that in addition to the cumulative negative effects of too much unstructured time out of school, suspended students also became a magnet for other students to neglect or to abandon school. She explained,

> 435 If one [student] gets suspended [for substance use], they all want to be with their friends, so they all try to get into trouble. I say, "I don't care what you do or say—I'm not sending you to the office." And then eventually they just get back to [school] business.

440 In this way, this teacher tried to curtail substance abuse and other harmful behaviors by ensuring that the students stay in her classroom rather than being suspended and exposed to out-of-school often unstructured and unsupervised time. Creating a supportive and 445 meaningful place to be while the students were in school sometimes meant overlooking deviant behavior that might have otherwise warranted a suspension had school policies been strictly adhered to or enforced.

The administrative team followed school division 450 policies related to substance abuse and school safety, often suspending students when it was required or, more often, seeking appropriate agency or professional services for students experiencing difficulties. When asked to "guesstimate" the number of students that 455 regularly abuse substances, many teachers guessed between 5%–10%. A few staff members, particularly those in administration, estimated 40%–50% of students were using substances at least occasionally. The contradiction between the perception of teachers, 460 school administrators, the results of the survey, and national and provincial averages is notable.

*Under the Radar*

Not all participants reported limited knowledge of student substance abuse. A few staff members reported that they knew about substance abuse in the school, but 465 as long as the students kept it under the radar and it did not affect the daily routine of the classroom, they did not report what they either knew or suspected was going on. These participants reported being aware of who was dealing, how the drugs were moved in and out of 470 the school, and were sold between students. Through careful observation and sustained interaction with at-risk students, they had deciphered student gestures and signals that served as codes to make deals in bathrooms and other key locations. One staff member said,

> 475 They have code names for teachers like "perv," and I can tell what is going on by the way they wear their hoods. In class, if they want to tell someone to meet them, they put their hood in a particular position to say where they are going. Then the other student knows they have the stuff
> 480 and how to get it.

Another staff member who was deeply concerned about the level of student substance abuse and articulated a myriad of other concerns including poverty, lack of parenting skills, residential school trauma, 485 gangs, and lack of student participation in nonacademic programs stated, "The school as a social institution has limited responsibility, and the reality is that the problem is shuffled around until the student is in crisis."

In response to questions related to supports and 490 resources, the staff focused on generic suggestions that would help youth with all types of needs, not just students who abuse. Ostensibly, they often spoke of the aberrant adult influences in the students' lives not only related to substance abuse but to gangs and pimping as 495 well. The call for more services and outside agency support was a common request among participants, and this appeal prompted the second theme: "just fix it."

*"Just Fix It"*

For a variety of reasons, most staff members did not position themselves in the circle of care to partici-

500 pate in the prevention, intervention, or rehabilitation of students involved with substances. Even though they expressed compassion and acknowledged serious social issues that contribute to substance abuse, the classroom was often described as sacred space for learning. From

505 this perspective, students who were not able to fully participate in the learning opportunities, regardless of the reason, needed to be provided with external supports. Sometimes this meant a student was assigned an educational assistant; in others, it meant a student was

510 removed from the regular classroom; and less frequently, human service professions provided support. One educational assistant stated, "The teachers here are very good; they never turn [students] away"; but at the same time, there was a clear call by participants for

515 human service providers or school administrators to "fix the students" and then return them "repaired" to the classroom (Lawson, 1999). There was a sense of helplessness and hopelessness represented by this staff member:

520   I look at them and think "I know you are doomed." No
matter what we do here. They are doomed. There is lots
more support than 10 years ago, but we need support both
on and off the reserve. We need more agencies to help.

While staff members reported being concerned

525 about issues such as poor attendance, sleepiness, and unengaged students, they did not talk about these issues within the context of substance abuse but rather reacted to these behaviors by enlisting the support of the addiction counselor who is on-site one half day per week.

530 Although seemingly contradictory, many staff members did not articulate substance abuse as a significant problem, despite there being a collective call for the addiction counselor to have more time at the school. One staff member stated,

535   Our addiction worker is really good but he needs to be
here more than half a day a week. A lot of the program
focuses on awareness, making better choices and getting
the message out about abstinence and harm-reduction,
but there is a disconnect with a lot of the teachers when
540   they refer kids to the program. You can't rely on him to
fix them in a half a day per week.

There was also confusion about the responsibilities associated with various professional roles. Educational assistants, teachers, administrators, and counsel-

545 ors all expressed sentiments that suggested that they do not understand each others' jobs, nor do they have a consistent method of working together. For example, the lack of communication among some staff regarding student intervention plans for those abusing substances

550 was described as fragmented. One staff member said,

Usually students are referred to either an internal or external resource, but follow-up within the school and between the school and outside agencies is limited or non-existent...we can't share personal information of students with outside organizations...the structure of school systems just doesn't meet the needs of kids using substances.

Lack of effective communication extended beyond the school community. The line delineating the school from "the external community" was most marked by race. Many of the staff members talked

555 about inviting students and parents into the school, but they had not traveled out to the reserves or to the communities of their students. One teacher explains,

I would be very apprehensive to go into their homes, even if I had someone with me. They wouldn't want me.
560   If they are not willing to come to the school, then I would be apprehensive. We get invited to ceremonies, events like powwows and feasts. We are invited. Everyone is invited on the announcements. I have not attended, but we try to meet them half way. I know teachers have gone to
565   certain funerals.

The notion that someone should "fix it" extended beyond the confines of the school and individual students who had been identified as having a substance abuse problem. The interviews revealed a general de-

570 sire for service providers to fix families outside the school.

**Discussion**

The purpose of this case study was not only to determine the prevalence of substance abuse but also to explore how teacher's pedagogical decisions are af-

575 fected by student substance abuse. In the analysis of the data, the notion of pedagogical decisions evolved into more fully exploring the staff's understanding of student substance abuse rather than how their teaching was influenced by it. Serendipitously, the mixed meth-

580 ods were more complementary than originally anticipated. The survey provided a useful starting point to compare student responses to national and provincial averages but became even more poignant coupled with the findings from the interviews.

585   Overall, most of the student reports of substance abuse were higher than national averages, particularly given the age range (11–18 years), as compared to other studies that typically use a narrower range of older students. In this study, students reported that

590 within the last 7 days, they had used marijuana (37%) and alcohol (38%), which is higher than a Canadian average for marijuana use in youth 15–24 (11%) and alcohol use (16%) within a year (Health Canada, 2008). These Canadian statistics are comparable to American

595 statistics,[1] which suggest rates closer to 13% for this age range for marijuana and 29% for alcohol (Center for Disease Control, 2009). Similarly, in another American report, 12–17 year olds reported using marijuana (5.8%) and alcohol (16%) in the last year (Na-

600 tional Survey on Drug Use and Health, 2007), which is

considerably lower than this study's findings. Also, a British Columbia study, one with a comparable population and age range, found that 25% of youth consumed alcohol and 12% used marijuana in the last 7 days (McCreary Centre Society, 2008). Martz and Wagner (2008) report that in Saskatchewan, 15% of 12–17 year olds had consumed alcohol and 8% had tried marijuana in the last month. Almost 17% had tried marijuana in their lifetime.

Even though it is difficult to precisely compare this case study population to national and provincial statistics, it is reasonable to say that alcohol consumption is above average, and marijuana usage is considerably higher than in other jurisdictions, including the province of origin. Since this study was conducted in Saskatchewan, it would be expected that marijuana usage would be closer to the provincial average, rather than over 3 times higher. Alcohol consumption was double that of both national and provincial averages, which is notable given the provincial rate is already higher than many other provinces. The Saskatchewan Ministry of Health (2009) reports that 75% of youth (Grades 7–12) have consumed alcohol in the past year and 70% of 17 year olds report drinking 5 or more drinks in a 2-hour period at least once in the past month. Given that alcohol is the most frequently used drug in Saskatchewan, it is helpful to understand the findings from this study in relation to the provincial context.

Furthermore, it is also important to note that all of the aforementioned statistics report on youth substance abuse, but they do not reflect whether students are under the influence or using at school. This case study also asked students to report whether they were high or intoxicated at school, and almost the same number of students that abused drugs and alcohol also reported being high and intoxicated at school in the last four months.

Unlike the McCreary Study (2008) from British Columbia, this study did not find that protective factors such as school connectedness guarded against drug and alcohol abuse. While academic grades increased and skipping school decreased with higher levels of protective factors, the typical positive influences, such as having encouragement and an adult to talk to, did not deter substance abuse. While further research is warranted, this finding suggests that strategies to decrease substance abuse extend beyond fostering individual strength-based relationships and mentoring and include wraparound approaches using the entire resources of the community in collaborative ways. Individual intervention strategies may be limiting in this context, as the social conditions in the lives of students may be a far more powerful influence than generally recognized. In addition, Bennett and Holloway (2005) suggest that individual substance abuse must go beyond user activities by considering the source of the illegal use.

The survey responses provide a rich context in which to understand and interpret the qualitative interviews. Initially, it was perplexing to the research team to hear how many teachers accepted and how many teachers vehemently argued that substance abuse was a normal activity in adolescence. These findings stand in stark contrast to the views of the local interprofessional team that expressed serious concerns about local student substance abuse. Since some staff members estimated that only 5% of the students were using, it is possible that lack of awareness or knowledge of the signs and symptoms of substance abuse identifies a serious deficit in teacher in-service and training. It also may be advisable to provide professional development opportunities for teachers to learn not only how to recognize substance abuse symptoms but also to learn how to become part of the network of professionals that can support efforts to prevent, intervene, and rehabilitate substance abusers. It is also possible that some staff members have normalized alcohol and marijuana as part of contemporary society or have theorized that intervening is beyond the scope of practice of teachers and schools. Since 52% of their students have tried to help a friend cut down on drinking or smoking marijuana, knowledge of this statistic may be a catalyst for adults to build capacity to change social conditions that foster, if not normalize, substance abuse.

Staff members who expressed concerns and knowledge of student substance abuse were sometimes the participants most worried about their anonymity being preserved. In other words, the burden of knowledge bore unanticipated consequences. These staff members ranged from feeling helpless and hopeless to make change to others who felt they were addressing substance issues by their own initiative. As the interprofessional team moves forward, it will be important to find ways to provide opportunities for all voices to be heard, for power differentials to be revealed, and for support to be given for those who feel they cannot make a difference. Given the divisions created by the largely White, middle-class staff and the predominantly First Nation student population, it might also be useful for staff to engage in more than culturally competent practices but to engage in anti-oppressive pedagogy.

Current substance abuse literature stresses the need for comprehensive community-based efforts that acknowledge the diversity within and among communities (Gliksman, Rylett, & Douglas, 2007). These strategies are developed locally and recognize the interrelatedness of substance abuse with other social factors. According to Hawkins and Catalano (1992), community-based approaches include all aspects of the community, including the school, in creating a broad base of support for behavioral change. Efforts to engage in this complex process may be thwarted by expectations that others' will fix the problem. Interprofessional literature calls for professionals to change their discourse from "fix it" to "build it," as collaborative communities must not only work together, but they must do so in new and innovative ways. Entering into genuine interdependent relationships with other organizations and professionals often calls for the develop-720 ment of interprofessional competencies. These skills are not only about tolerance and working together but are about understanding scopes of practice, managing confidentiality, and being innovative (Barr, Koppel, Reeves, Hammick, & Freeth, 2005). If professionals 725 and organizations continue to work in familiar ways, the changes that are required are unlikely to occur.

No matter what we visualize or desire in our future, if we keep thinking and acting in the same old ways, we will always get the same old results. If we are to create a new 730 kind of future for ourselves (or within our families, organizations or community), we will need to learn new ways of thinking and acting that will lead to the new outcomes we desire. (Bopp & Bopp, 2006, p. 36)

## Conclusion

This case study confirmed the anecdotal predic-735 tions that the rate of substance abuse is considerably higher in this rural community than the national and provincial averages. Given that over one third of students reported that they had used marijuana (37%) and alcohol (38%) in the last seven days or had come to 740 school being high or drunk at least once at school in the previous four months, collective community action to prevent and address substance abuse issues is warranted. Pedagogical implications were informed by three main themes that emerged from staff interviews. 745 Several teachers normalized substance abuse in adolescence, others coped silently under the radar, and a few called for specialized support from other human services. Further, in-school approaches require that the entire staff be involved to enhance awareness of sub-750 stance abuse, interprofessional collaboration, and a sense of interdependence must occur at the community level to have any sustained effect.

## End Note

1. Centers for Disease Control reports: Marijuana usage for seniors −19.4%, Grade 10 −13.8%, Grade 8 −5.8%. Alcohol by seniors −43%, Grade 10 −28.8% and Grade 8 − 15.9%.

## References

Addictions Research Institute. (2010). Alcohol and Substance Abuse Measurement Instrument Collection. Retrieved January 24, 2010 from http://www.utexas.edu/research/cswr/nida/instrumentListing.html

Barr, H., Koppel, I., Reeves, S., Hammick, M., & Freeth, D. (2005). Effective interprofessional education: Argument, assumption & evidence. Oxford: Blackwell.

Bauman, K., Foshee, V., Ennett, S., Hicks, K., & Pemberton, M. (2001). Family matters: A family directed program designed to prevent adolescent tobacco and alcohol use. Health Promotion Practice, 2(1), 81–96.

Bennett, T., & Holloway, K. (2005). Understanding, drugs, alcohol and crime. Open University Press, Berkshire, England.

Birkeland, S., Murphy-Graham, E., & Weiss, C. (2005). Good reasons for ignoring good evaluation: The case of the drug abuse resistance education (D.A.R.E.) program. Journal of Evaluation and Program Planning, 28(3), 247–256.

Bopp, M., & Bopp, J. (2006). Recreating the world: A practical guide to building sustainable communities. Calgary, Alberta: Four Worlds Press.

CCSA [Canadian Centre on Substance Abuse]. (2007). Substance abuse in Canada: Youth in focus. Ottawa, ON: Canadian Centre on Substance Abuse.

Centers for Disease Control and Prevention. (2010). Health, United States, 2009: A special feature on medical technology. US Department of Health and Human Services. Retrieved March 1, 2010 from http://www.cdc.gov/nchs/data/hus/hus09.pdf#064

Charmaz, K. (2006). Constructing grounded theory: A practical guide through qualitative analysis. Beverly Hills, CA: Sage.

Davis, M. (2007). Schools not up to task of anti-drug education. Education Week, 27(7), 4–8.

Ennett, S., Tobler, N., Ringwalt, C., & Flewelling, R. (1994). How effective is drug abuse resistance education? A meta-analysis of project DARE outcome evaluations. American Journal of Public Health, 84(9), 1394–1401.

Finn, K., & Willert, J. (2006). Alcohol and drugs in schools: Teachers' reactions to the problem. Phi Delta Kappan, 88(1), 33–40.

Gliksman, L., Rylett, M., & Douglas, R. (2007). Aboriginal community alcohol harm reduction policy project: A vision for the future. Substance Use and Misuse, 42, 1851–1866.

Hawkins, J., & Cantalano, R. (1992). Reducing the risk and promoting positive social development. In J. E. Hawkins and R. R. Catalano, (Eds.), Communities that care: Action for drug abuse prevention. San Francisco, CA: Jossey Bass.

Health Canada. (2008). Major Findings: Canadian Alcohol Drug Use and Monitoring Survey. Retrieved from http://www.hc-sc.gc.ca/hc-ps/drugs-drogues/stat/index-eng.php

Healthy People 2010. (2000). Understanding and Improving Health (2nd Ed.). United States Department of Health and Human Services. Retrieved March 21, 2010 from http://www.healthypeople.gov/Document/html/uih/uih_4.htm#subsabuse

Hecht, M., Graham, J., & Elek, E. (2006). The drug resistance strategies intervention: Program effects on substance use. Health Communication, 20(3), 267–276.

Hester, K., & Miller, W. (1995). Handbook of alcoholism treatment approaches: Effective alternatives. Massachusetts. A Simon and Schuster Company, Needham Heights.

Lasser, J., & Schmidt, E. (2009). Substance use, abuse and dependency in adolescence. Principal Leadership, 9(5), 12–15.

Lawson, H. (1999). Two mental models for schools and their implications for principals' roles, responsibilities and preparation. NASSP Bulletin, 83(611), 8–27.

Lucas, W. (2008). Parents' perceptions of the drug abuse resistance education program (DARE). Journal of Child & Adolescent Substance Abuse, 14(4), 99–114.

Martz, D., & Wagner, A. (2008). Saskatchewan rural youth healthy lifestyles and risk behavior needs assessment. Saskatchewan Population Health and Evaluation Research Unit (SPHERU). Retrieved March 25, 2010 from http://www.spheru.ca/research-projects/rural-youth-risk-behaviours-and-healthy-lifestyles-project/saskatchewan-rural-youth-healthy-lifestyles-and-risk-behaviour-needs-assessment

McCreary Centre Society. (2009). A picture of health: Highlights from the adolescent health survey. Retrieved March 1, 2010 from http://www.mcs.bc.ca/pdf/AHS%20IV%20March%2030%20Final.pdf

Merriam, S. (2002). Qualitative research in practice. Examples for discussion and analysis. San Francisco, CA: Jossey Bass.

National Survey on Drug Use and Health. (2007). Department of Health and Human Services. Retrieved March 1, 2010 from http://www.oas.samhsa.gov/NSDUH/2k7NSDUH/2k7results.cfm#Ch2

National Institute on Drug Abuse. (2011). Preventing drug abuse for children and youth: Risk and protective factors. Retrieved on January 3, 2011 from http://www.drugabuse.gov/Prevention/risk.html

NNADAP [National Native Alcohol and Drug Abuse Program]. (1998). Health service workers questionnaire. Retrieved from http://www.hc-sc.gc.ca/fniah-spnia/pubs/substan/_ads/1998_rpt-nnadap-pnlaada

Page, R., Hammermeister, M., & Roland, M. (2002). Are high school students accurate or clueless in estimating substance use among peers? Adolescence, 37(147), 567–575.

Pan, W., & Bai, H. (2009). A multivariate approach to meta-analytic review of the effectiveness of the DARE program. International Journal of Environmental Research and Public Health, 6(1), 267–277.

Saskatchewan Ministry of Health. (2009). Youth trends and patterns of alcohol abuse. Retrieved on March 25, 2010 from http://www.health.gov.sk.ca/Default.aspx?DN=2ffb9694-40aa-4c59-8561-c9c30c294889&l=English

Sharma, M. (2008). Substance abuse in minorities. Journal of Alcohol and Drug Education, 52(3), 3–9.

Slobada, Z., Pyakuryal, A., Stephens, P., Teasdale, B., Forrest, D., Stephens, R., & Grey, S. (2008). Reports of substance abuse prevention programming available in schools. Prevention Science, 9, 276–287.

Strauss, A., & Corbin, J. (1998). Basics of qualitative research and procedures for developing grounded theory (2nd Ed.). London: Sage.

Taylor, O. (2010). Predictors and protective factors in the prevention and treatment of adolescent substance use disorders. Journal of Human Behavior in the Social Environment, 20(5), 601–617.

Van Hout, M., & Connor, S. (2008). A qualitative study of Irish teacher's perspective of student substance use. Journal of Alcohol and Drug Education, 52(1), 80–91.

Vincus, A., Ringwalt, C., Harris, M., & Shamblen, S. (2010). A short-term quasi-experimental evaluation of DARE's revised elementary school curriculum. *Journal of Drug Education, 40*(1), 37–49.

West, S., & O'Neal, K. (2004). Project DARE outcome effectiveness revisited. *American Journal of Public Health, 94*, 1027–1029.

Yin, R. (2009). *Case study research: Design and methods (4th ed.).* Thousand Oaks CA: Sage.

**Address correspondence to**: *Twyla Salm*, Ph.D., University of Regina, Saskatchewan, Canada. Phone: 306-585-4604, E-mail: twyla. salm@uregina.ca

# Exercise for Article 36

## Factual Questions

1. What was the researchers' hypothesis?

2. What was the primary purpose of this study?

3. Were administrators included as "staff members"?

4. Do the researchers claim the data are generalizable?

5. What was the only statistically significant difference found between the ethnic groups?

6. Did most staff members say that they had never seen an intoxicated student?

## Questions for Discussion

7. In your opinion, are the quantitative and qualitative data equally important? Explain. (See lines 112–114.)

8. Is it important to know that one fourth of the students were absent on the day the study was conducted? Explain. (See lines 130–145.)

9. Do you think the researchers' effort to preserve some participant confidentiality is important? Explain. (See lines 158–169.)

10. Is the procedure used to analyze the interview data described in sufficient detail? Explain. (See lines 178–189.)

11. The researchers provide quotations in their description of the results of the interviews. Were any of the quotes surprising to you? Were any of them especially important to understanding the results of this study? (See lines 337–571.)

12. Would you recommend a follow-up study in which students are interviewed? Explain.

## Quality Ratings

Directions: Indicate your level of agreement with each of the following statements by circling a number from 5 for strongly agree (SA) to 1 for strongly disagree (SD). If you believe an item is not applicable to this research article, leave it blank. Be prepared to explain your ratings. When responding to criteria A and B, keep in mind that brief titles and abstracts are conventional in published research.

A. The title of the article is appropriate.

   SA   5   4   3   2   1   SD

B. The abstract provides an effective overview of the research article.

   SA   5   4   3   2   1   SD

C. The introduction establishes the importance of the study.

   SA   5   4   3   2   1   SD

D. The literature review establishes the context for the study.

   SA   5   4   3   2   1   SD

E. The research purpose, question, or hypothesis is clearly stated.

   SA   5   4   3   2   1   SD

F. The method of sampling is sound.

   SA   5   4   3   2   1   SD

G. Relevant demographics (for example, age, gender, and ethnicity) are described.

   SA   5   4   3   2   1   SD

H. Measurement procedures are adequate.

   SA   5   4   3   2   1   SD

I. All procedures have been described in sufficient detail to permit a replication of the study.

   SA   5   4   3   2   1   SD

J. The participants have been adequately protected from potential harm.

   SA   5   4   3   2   1   SD

K. The results are clearly described.

   SA   5   4   3   2   1   SD

L. The discussion/conclusion is appropriate.

   SA   5   4   3   2   1   SD

M. Despite any flaws, the report is worthy of publication.

   SA   5   4   3   2   1   SD

# Article 37

# Unretired and Better Than Ever:
# Older Adults As Foster Parents for Children

DONALD H. GOUGHLER
Family Services of Western Pennsylvania

ANNETTE C. TRUNZO
Family Services of Western Pennsylvania

ABSTRACT. The authors explore issues concerning employing older adults as foster parents for children. A survey of agencies in the United States suggests that agencies that utilize older adults as foster parents experience benefits, including elders' abilities to impart life experience and to offer a high degree of tolerance and time flexibility. Older foster parents, when surveyed, reported that fostering benefited them, citing pleasures they derived and defining contributions gained to their own welfare. The authors recommend strategies for agencies to recruit older adults as foster parents as well as public consciousness-raising efforts that promote the value gained by society and the older adults when they choose second careers in child care.

From *Families in Society: The Journal of Contemporary Social Services*, *86*, 393–400. Copyright © 2005 by Children and Families. Reprinted with permission.

Foster parents are a vital part of the child welfare system and are asked to fulfill all the role responsibilities of natural parents. Each year, family foster care is being provided to an estimated 542,000 children who
5 have been abused or neglected (Adoption and Foster Care Analysis and Reporting System [AFCARS], 2003). Two significant factors contribute to the challenge of foster care placement for social service agencies. On one hand, continuing high numbers of children
10 are entering the child welfare system, whereas, on the other hand, the number of available foster care homes is declining. Although the total number of licensed family foster homes in the United States is not known, 38 states reported a total of 133,503 homes on the last
15 day of 1998 (Child Welfare League of America [CWLA], 2000). When compared with the number of children in out-of-home placement, it becomes clear that the number of foster homes has been insufficient to accommodate the demand. Of the children in out-of-
20 home care, 19% were cared for in a group home or institutional placement, with the remaining children primarily being cared for in a nonrelative foster home or relative placement (AFCARS, 2003). Unfortunately, the lack of foster homes sometimes leads child welfare
25 agencies to place the child in a more restrictive level of care than needed.

## Foster Care: The Literature
### Changes in Foster Care Service Arena

Shifts arose in the foster care system with the passage of the Adoption Assistance and Child Welfare Act of 1980, an amendment to the Social Security Act of
30 1935. This law emphasized family reunification and permanency planning for children who are in out-of-home placement (Pecora, Whittaker, Maluccio, & Barth, 2000), and with the inception of this law, the population of children in foster care was reduced by
35 nearly one-half (CWLA, 2002). However, with the rate of co-occurring mental health disorders and substance abuse in the adult population estimated to have ranged from 29% to 59% in 1978 (Regier et al., 1990), alcohol and drug abuse issues in the birth parents were factors
40 for out-of-home placement in nearly 75% of all children entering care (Child Welfare Partnership, 1999). In spite of the decrease of the number of children in out-of-home care as a result of this legislation, the number of children who are not living with their parents
45 has grown, requiring more foster home families. Between 1986 and 1995, there was a 44% increase in children in out-of-home placements in the United States (Child Welfare Partnership, 1999). In addition to the number of children involved in the child welfare
50 system, there were, and continue to be, many children who are being cared for by grandparents or other relatives not placed through formal mechanisms. There are approximately 6 million children living in the United States who are being cared for in a household headed
55 by a grandparent or other relative who is not a birth parent (Brown, 2003).

Adoption was renewed as a viable option for a child to achieve permanency with the passage of the Adoption and Safe Families Act of 1997. The foster parents
60 who were already caring for the child in their home were often looked upon as the first option to achieving permanency. When they adopted children, these foster parents typically left the resource pool of foster care providers, leaving a shortage of experienced and capa-
65 ble foster families for many agencies. In addition, changes in economics and social customs over the past several decades have exacerbated the shortage. Throughout earlier generations in American history

240

when there was a different economic climate, two-parent households could afford one wage earner and a parent at home. On the contrary, most modern households need two wage earners. In addition, with the rise of single-parent-headed households over recent years, the pool of families with time to assume the role of foster parent has decreased.

### The Role of Older Adults in Foster Care

Traditionally, older adults have served a vital role in the lives of children, whether as grandparents or community members. In the field of foster care, older adults could become a major resource in providing the necessary stable homes for the child who is in need of a temporary home. Older adults bring with them a perspective on life and life experiences that makes them uniquely suitable for the task of foster parents. They have been recognized in a volunteer capacity as being more flexible and spontaneous in their interactions with others and for their ability to contribute to a program's services (Strom & Strom, 1999). At the voluntary level, they have demonstrated notable capacities to provide care for children in such national programs as the Foster Grandparent Program. Older foster parents may also be more committed to providing foster care services once involved with an agency. In a study of predictors of foster parents' satisfaction, older foster mothers tended to be more satisfied in their role as foster parents and more content in continuing to be foster parents than younger foster mothers (Denby, Rindfleisch, & Bean, 1999).

Benefits derived from continued work or volunteer experience for the older adult have been demonstrated in the literature. In Dulin and Hill (2003), altruistic activity in older adults was predictive of positive affect. The older adult worker who engaged in providing services to others reported better psychological functioning than their nonaltruistic cohorts. In a large sample of members of a church, those who engaged in altruistic social behaviors experienced higher levels of mental health functioning than those who did not engage in these activities (Schwartz, Meisenhelder, Ma, & Reed, 2003). Other findings suggest that older adults who participated in community service work derived benefits of positive social integration and the activity served as a buffer against stress (Piliavin, 2003). Older adults who participated in The Foster Grandparent Program reported less depression, more social support, and enhanced life satisfaction than did adults who were not foster grandparents (Sweeney, 2000).

### Older Americans

#### Changes in the Older Population

In 1965, the United States Congress passed the Older Americans Act, which established a strong policy of support for 10 important social objectives that addressed concerns of older people. Among those objectives was the declaration that "older people should have the opportunity for employment with no discrimi-natory practices because of age" (Older Americans Act of 1965). At the time when the act was passed, a relatively small proportion (9.2%) of the United States population was 65 years of age or older (U.S. Department of Commerce, Bureau of the Census, 1960, Table 45). At the same time, an unusually high proportion of Americans (39%) were younger than 20 and were filling schools and colleges at unprecedented rates (U.S. Department of Commerce, Bureau of the Census, 1960, Table 45). American society built new structures and developed new resources based on the ascendancy of that group of young people, the so-called baby boom generation.

Today, 40 years after the passage of the Older Americans Act, the first born of the baby boom generation are nearly 60 years old, now number 77 million people, and soon will become the subjects of this legislation. In some ways, these new elders will represent importantly different demographic characteristics from their grandparents of the mid-1960s. For one, they constitute a larger proportion of the total population than the earlier older generation (12.4% as compared with 9.2%), and by 2040, this group will peak at 19.5% of the population (Hobbs & Damon, 2004). They also differ from their grandparents because they can expect to live longer, experience better health, are better educated, and have more retirement income.

Panek (1997) notes that the current aging generation will be expected to remain in the workforce longer for a variety of reasons, including increased longevity. This group has experienced improvements in health and life expectancy, which could allow them to remain active in the work force until older ages (Johnson, 2004). In the area of education, the American population as a whole, as well as older adults specifically, has a higher level of educational achievement than was the case 40 years ago. Only 6.5% of the older adults of 1965 had graduated from college (U.S. Department of Commerce, Bureau of the Census, 1960, Table 173), as compared with 10.0% of persons who were 65 in 2002 (U.S. Department of Commerce, Bureau of the Census, 2002). Although economic security is still an important concern for older adults, they are better off than their cohorts of the past. In contrast to the older adults of the 1960s, today's elders have benefited from the development of Medicare and the increases in Social Security and enjoy a stronger base of retirement income than their predecessors had. The Social Security program has been key to bringing the poverty rate among the elderly down from 28% in 1967 to about 12% today (Zimmerman, 2000).

#### Potential for Future Worker Shortages

In fact, economic advances represented by Social Security and pension advances have significantly improved the retirement prospective, and some believe that employer and government pensions and health plans will prompt them to leave the labor force and stay out, causing shortages in the labor force (Penner, Perun, & Steuerle, 2003). This trend has already been recognized in Europe and is the subject of major employment policy research and planning (Employment Task Force of the European Union, 2003). Dychtwald, Erickson, and Morison (2004) observed,

While the ranks of the youngest workers (16–24) are growing at 15% this decade, the 25- to 34-year-old segment is growing at just half that, and the workforce population between ages 35 and 44, which are the prime executive development years, is actually declining. (p. 1)

Much has been written about the impact this retired generation will impose on the economy. Some draw the conclusion that as the income provided by this retired generation recedes, some level of continued work by them is needed to contribute to the support of American society (Ekerdt, 2004; Kleyman, 2003; Penner et al., 2003; Steuerle & Carasso, 2001). The Older Americans Act of 1965 recognized that work might continue to retain a role in the lives of older adults. Although the Act focused on community service employment, administration of this employment program over the years has featured an effort to develop unsubsidized employment across all sectors of the economy.

*Self-Actualization Through Work*

Another reason to encourage able and willing elders to continue to work is that work is a positive lifestyle option for many. Gradual retirement via part-time jobs or new careers can be compatible with better health and self-actualization (Dahlherg, 2004; Dychtwald et al., 2004). Older adults in the 21st century are now and will continue to be more educated and physically and mentally active; these factors will have significant implications for both the quality and quantity of older adults as a labor force in the coming years (Besl & Kale, 1996; McManus, 2004). Many of these individuals will seek to continue working in endeavors that provide self-actualization as a primary benefit even if financial rewards are more limited. In recent research by the American Association for Retired Persons, 2,000 preretirees confirmed that for them, retirement work will need to "keep you mentally active" (80%), "make you feel useful" (74%), and "provide fun and enjoyment" (73%) (Brown, 2003).

*Resource for Social Services*

Social service agencies are among those employers that need to consider the attractive characteristics of these new elders in terms of future staffing needs. Agencies should evaluate the potential of older workers to be employed in those categories of jobs that currently present agencies with a recruitment challenge, as well as those categories expected to challenge recruitment in the future. The focus should be on retaining people beyond normal retirement or proactively developing strategies to recruit older adults into some of these jobs. Agencies need to examine myths about the capacity of older adults to perform effectively in specific social service job categories.

The field of child foster care is an example of a social service area in which older adults in the 21st century may seek and find a rewarding experience that offers them a direct opportunity to contribute to the social good. This field is also being challenged to recruit a workforce in the 21st century.

**Method**

*Participants and Procedures*

In gathering background information for this article, we were interested in the experiences of foster care agencies and older adults who are foster parents, so we drew a stratified random sample of foster care agencies from the Alliance for Children and Families and the Foster Family Treatment Association membership lists. The original sample size contained 132 agencies, with 66 agencies coming from states with the highest percentage of older adult residents (13.8% to 17.6% of older adults in the population) and the remaining 66 agencies dispersed across the United States. Of the 132 agencies surveyed, 44 returned the questionnaire (33%). In these agencies, there were a total of 2,387 foster families with 261 individuals who were identified as being aged 60 or older. The agency foster care programs varied in size from two foster families to 443 families, with the average agency having 55 foster families.

We also distributed 261 surveys to older foster parents who were identified by the agencies, and from these, we received 67 (26%) responses. The average age of these respondents was 64, with 22% being male and 78% female; 68% were married, and the responding foster parents had provided an average of 23 years of foster care services. The minimum time of providing services in this population was 6 months and the maximum time was 36 years.

All potential participants were sent a letter explaining the purpose of the study to encourage their participation. Respondents were asked to complete a one-page questionnaire and return the completed questionnaire in a self-addressed, stamped envelope. In addition to the agency surveys, a foster parent questionnaire was supplied for the older adults serving as foster parents. Agencies that were sent the agency surveys were asked to distribute the foster parent surveys to their foster parents who were 60 and older. Overall, the questionnaires were mailed and collected over a period of 8 weeks.

*Measures*

The agency questionnaire contained 10 questions relating to the foster care program. Specifically, we were interested in the number of older adults who were employed as foster parents, any recruitment efforts they utilized to enroll older adults, and their perception of challenges and benefits in utilizing older adults as foster parents. The foster parent questionnaire had 4 questions about providing foster care services that were rated on a 5-point scale, with 5 being the highest positive response. In addition, there was an open-ended question regarding the foster parents' "favorite thing" about being a foster parent; there were also two satisfaction questions and demographic information questions.

## Findings

Of the agencies responding, 32% acknowledged a concern or challenge related to the prospect of using older adults as foster parents. The identified challenges tended to be centered on concerns over the foster parent's health or physical capabilities (43%) and negative personality characteristics such as "being set in own ways" (35%). The agencies reported 58% positive responses in the question of benefits associated in having an older adult as a foster parent. Many of the respondents (48%) identified the older adult's experience and wisdom as a benefit for the children and program. Other responses cited the older adult's time and flexibility afforded by being retired as a positive aspect (13%); others noted favorable characteristics such as patience, understanding, and tolerance (15%); and others felt that the older foster parents provided more stability and dependability (10%). Another beneficial element that was noted was the tendency of birth families to relate differently to older foster parents, feeling less challenged by a foster parent who is in the age range of a grandparent (8%; see Table 1). Only two of the agencies had age requirements not allowing people older than 65 to serve as foster parents, whereas most of the agencies had requirements that a foster parent had to be at least 21 years of age. Only three agencies specifically focused on recruiting older adults as foster parents.

Table 1
*Challenges and Benefits of Older Adults as Foster Parents*

|  |  | N | % |
|---|---|---|---|
| Challenges (*N* = 23) | Health/lifespan issues | 10 | 43 |
|  | Negative characteristics | 8 | 35 |
|  | Technology use/ documentation | 2 | 9 |
|  | Need for more support/ training | 2 | 9 |
|  | Other | 1 | 4 |
| Benefits (*N* = 52) | Experience/wisdom | 25 | 48 |
|  | Patience/tolerance | 8 | 15 |
|  | Flexibility with time schedules | 7 | 13 |
|  | Stability/dependability | 5 | 10 |
|  | Decreased role confusion | 4 | 8 |
|  | Other | 3 | 6 |

The foster parents responded quite positively concerning their feelings about providing foster care services. Such questions as, "How much do you like providing foster care?" yielded a 4.71 rating, and "How often are your main interests and pleasures in life con-

nected with doing foster care?" yielded a rating of 4.08. Foster parents felt very strongly that providing foster care was valuable (4.82), and they were very satisfied with doing foster care (4.37; see Table 2).

Table 2
*Mean Score for Foster Parent Survey*

|  | N | M | SD |
|---|---|---|---|
| 1. How much do you like providing foster care? | 65 | 4.71 | .46 |
| 2. How often do you feel satisfied with doing foster care? | 65 | 4.37 | .57 |
| 3. How often are your main interests and pleasures in life connected with doing foster care? | 63 | 4.08 | .75 |
| 4. How often do you feel it is valuable to provide foster care? | 65 | 4.82 | .39 |

In determining a foster parent's perceptions about being a foster parent, respondents indicated several categories of responses. Many identified an altruistic desire or pleasure in seeing changes or growth in the child (44%), and the pursuit of providing care and love to a child emerged as being almost equally important (33%; see Table 3).

Table 3
*Foster Parents' Favorite Things About Providing Foster Care (N = 57)*

|  | N | % |
|---|---|---|
| Changes/growth in child | 25 | 44 |
| Providing/caring for child | 19 | 33 |
| Companionship | 7 | 12 |
| Challenge | 3 | 5 |
| Other | 3 | 5 |

## Qualitative Research: Foster Parent Interviews

Survey data were augmented by qualitative interviews of 12 foster parents. The interviews were conducted in person with older foster parents from the foster care program at Family Services of Western Pennsylvania. All foster parents 55 years of age or older from the agency were telephoned by an agency researcher who asked whether an interview could be arranged. Of the 16 foster parents who met this criterion, 12 agreed to be interviewed. All interviews were conducted by a master's-level clinician in the respondent's home, with one interview in an agency office; all interviews occurred between September 24 and October 11, 2004. In homes where there was a spouse, both foster parents were invited to participate in the interview. The interviews were approximately 60 to 90 minutes in length and involved an exploration of the foster parents' experiences, including their perceptions of the benefits and difficulties in providing foster care to children. Several areas related to foster care were discussed, such as why they became foster parents, what they find valuable about being foster parents, struggles or difficulties they experience, and the supports and resources they have used to manage the diffi-

360 culties. All interviews were tape-recorded and transcribed for analysis, and two independent raters reviewed transcripts of the interviews to determine common themes.

## Qualitative Findings

An analysis of the transcripts identified four topical
365 areas relevant to a foster parent's experience: (a) motivation to be a foster provider, (b) values in the provision of foster care services, (c) struggles or difficulties in providing foster care, and (d) issues of resources and supports. Examples of typical reactions in each of these
370 areas are presented.

### Motivation to Be Foster Parents

In discussing the motivation for providing foster care, foster parents tended to express their desire and delight in being around children and wanting to help them. Other times, it was noted that providing foster
375 care involved dealing with the empty nest syndrome or addressing deeper self-actualization needs or fulfilling religious ones. Most of the foster parents were able to recall a specific time in their lives when they were motivated to decide to become a foster parent. What ap-
380 peared to be the motivating factor appeared also to sustain these foster parents to continue to provide care.

*Enjoyment of children.* Mrs. T is a 76-year-old married Caucasian woman who has been providing foster care services for 11 years with her husband, who is 79
385 years old. This couple talked about their love for children and enjoying a home filled with children.

> When my own youngest child, who is now 34, started school I wanted foster care then. We do nothing and we go nowhere. I liked kids all my life. I had my neighbor's
390 kids over all the time. I think I should have children in the house.

Another foster parent, twice-widowed Mrs. B, Caucasian, 63, who started providing foster care at the age of 55, said, "I never enjoyed or found anything more
395 rewarding than having those kids."

Mrs. H, a widowed African American woman of 57, said, "I became a foster parent because I love kids; I got gangs of grandkids, but I just love kids. I'd rather be in a house full of kids than adults." A single African
400 American woman of 66, who has been providing foster care for 4 years, said, "I love kids. I never had none. I figured maybe this is my job to help kids in need, and I enjoy doing it."

*Religious reasons.* Another foster parent, a 79-year-
405 old Caucasian widowed woman, Mrs. S, was motivated by a deal she had made with God when she was going through a medical crisis with her daughter and herself:

> I thought I was pregnant in my 40s and I was tickled to death. I went to the doctor and I wasn't pregnant…. They
410 told me that I had leukemia and I had approximately 9 months to live. My daughter came down with spinal meningitis. They kept her in isolation…I screamed. I didn't pray. I screamed at God above and told him he couldn't do that, take my crippled child and take me. The doctor

415 told me that I couldn't bargain with God. I told him I am not making a bargain. I am telling him that if he doesn't take my kid, I will do anything for his children. I will take care of his children. Dr. Young didn't understand, but my husband did. Kate [her daughter] came out OK
420 with no severe problems. Our church had a foster mother, and she told me to go down to this agency. I went down and I became a foster mother.

Another foster parent, Mrs. C, African American, divorced, 70, phrased it like this, "It is because that is
425 why God has me here. That is the mission that he put me on this earth to do." Mr. and Mrs. D, 68 and 72, Caucasian, said, "It is a wonderful ministry of love. You cannot be a selfish person and do this because if you are, there is no place. So your life, half the time, is
430 put on the back burner."

### Value of Providing Foster Care

The foster parents interviewed identified similar values in providing foster care to those of the foster parents who responded to the questionnaire. Typical responses centered on the desire to make a difference
435 in a child's life and to care for children. Other responses also indicated that the foster parent benefited from the foster care relationship. To some respondents, being a foster parent gives them purpose and adds meaning to their lives.

440 *Contributions to others.* A married couple in their 70s stated the importance of giving something to the child. The wife said, "I think if I can save one child, one is better than none at all. If everybody could just save one of these little kids, that makes a difference."
445 The husband added that it was valuable to "give them something that their own family couldn't give them, which may be love and affection."

A 79-year-old African American foster mother viewed her service of foster care as an opportunity for
450 teaching children. She said, "I teach the kids these things so it will stick with them for the rest of their life. I plant seeds."

*Contributions to self.* A foster mother (age 79) said, "I am not alone in this big house. It gives me some-
455 thing to do. I have to get up in the morning whether I want to or not." A 70-year-old divorced African American woman said, "[Being a foster parent] helped me a lot because it kept me busy after my mother passed. The children…helped keep my mind off of my
460 mother passing. It helped me to keep myself busy." Another single foster mother (age 79, African American) said, "Yes, because I don't want to just sit here and do nothing, worry about just me and get old by myself."

### Struggles or Difficulties in Providing Foster Care

465 The foster parents consistently talked about having difficulties with saying goodbye to the children whom they have cared for when it is time to return them to their birth families. They also noted the difficulties in their relationships with the birth parents; they struggled

470 with the birth parents over parenting issues. They also struggled to manage the child's torn feelings of loyalty between the foster parent and the birth parent.

*Conflict with birth parents.* Widowed foster mother Mrs. C (age 74) said, "The mothers sometimes can be 475 difficult. I got some mothers that have really been a headache. They are mad at the system. They are upset with the foster parent. They blame us that we have their children."

*Child's feelings.* Ms. MJ (age 67) said,

480 They [the children] can be rebellious because they want to be with their mother. It is a struggle to let them know that I am here to help them and give them support and love till they can go back to their mother.

An African American widowed woman of 67 said,

485 It is hard. It is hard. It is hard on them. It is harder on them than you because you are the adult. But the kids, it is a shame that they have to leave, pushed and moved around like that; it is not fair. They are depending all on an adult until they can depend on themselves.

490 A widowed Mrs. S identified the struggle for a child: "But can you imagine the torn morale in this kid—the love for her mother and still the love and respect for the foster mother that raised her."

*Factors Contributing to Success*

The foster parents spoke about the importance of 495 having support and resources available to them from the agency and the community. They appeared willing to acknowledge that they cannot do the work of foster care without assistance from others. It is apparent that when the foster care agency provides the day-to-day 500 assistance for the foster parents, they are appreciative and are able to fulfill their roles. When the children have special needs, assistance from professionals, whether it is from mental health or physical health providers, is necessary to assist these families. Friends and 505 family members also appear to play an important role in providing the social support needed to carry out this challenging work.

Mrs. W, a widowed woman of 71, said, "I have a friend who told me that if I get to the point I obviously 510 need a break, she will watch the kids for me." She went on to explain that she also utilizes the respite services of the agency when she needs a longer break from the "work." Mrs. G stated that she also utilized respite services after an operation when she "just couldn't keep 515 up with them [the children]." Mr. and Mrs. D said, "We left one church and joined another church, which was loving and accepting. This is an absolute must because if you do not have this support, you cannot go out in public."

520 Ms. M, a single African American woman of 67, said,

Oh, I have phone numbers of whom to call. CYF [Children, Youth and Families]…tells me where to go and what to do, and usually they help me to go. Well, CYF

525 and Family Services helps me a whole lot; at least they show me the way to go.

She noted the following about when she cared for a child with behavioral health needs: "The therapist was with him in school during the day, and then he came to 530 the house every evening for 2 hours. So really, I am learning from them; this is teaching me, too."

## Discussion

Older adults can be an important resource for social service agencies by working as foster parents. Their experience and life perspective appear to be advanta- 535 geous qualities for any foster care agency. As many older adults are retired, they may have more time available to devote themselves to the care of children, which is an asset because available time is necessary in completing the many tasks associated with child care, 540 such as attending doctor appointments, enrolling for school, and attending court hearings. Whereas working foster parents often struggle when a new child comes into their home for emergency placement in the middle of the night when there is little time to secure babysit- 545 ting so that they can attend work the following day, a retired adult does not have to grapple with that situation.

The contributions of older adults working as foster parents appear not only to have a beneficial effect for 550 the foster care program but also to enhance the elder's own sense of well-being. It is understood in the literature that older adults who seek work after retirement do so to contribute their experience in a meaningful way and to feel valued. These individuals may seek em- 555 ployment that provides self-actualization as a primary benefit and not for financial rewards. An older adult who provides foster care appears to experience similar benefits of self-actualization.

Older adults serving as foster parents also make an 560 important contribution to society as a whole. An altruistic goal to give of oneself for the benefit of another is a higher-level human experience. Individuals whose work enables them to give profoundly to children who have been neglected or abused find an avenue for 565 achieving this goal. The value of the contribution made by the foster parent is beyond any monetary compensation.

*Limitations*

The ability to generalize the results of this study is limited due to the relatively small agency sample size 570 ($N = 44$) and foster parent sample size ($N = 67$), yielding a relatively modest response rate to the total number of surveys mailed (33% and 26%, respectively). The study was conducted on a very small budget that did not include the possibility of an incentive to either 575 the agency or the foster parents for their participation. The study was limited to only those foster care agencies and foster parents who responded to the request to participate. These factors limit the generalizability and

580 interpretation of the findings. The possibility that the limited results could be attributed to chance cannot be ruled out and thus would need replication before interpretative value can be given. The qualitative study, though yielding a response rate of 75%, also has limited generalizability as the population of foster parents 585 was from Western Pennsylvania and connected with a single provider agency.

*Recommendations for Practice*

The United States currently has the largest older population in its history; this population possesses great potential to continue to contribute to the eco590 nomic and social wealth of the nation and the betterment of conditions for fellow citizens. At the same time, the United States needs older adults' continued contribution. In the social arena, child foster care offers a sterling opportunity for older people to pass the best 595 of their experience to a new generation that needs someone to care for them. To capitalize on this resource, foster care agencies need to consider several recommendations relating to recruitment of older adults as foster parents and tailoring supports for them, 600 as well as boosting public awareness of productive aging alternatives.

*Recruitment.* First, foster care agencies should look at marketing directly to the older population to provide the additional foster care homes that society requires. 605 An important target would be associations where educated and skilled older adults may have natural connections, such as retired nurse or teacher associations. It would also be beneficial to acknowledge directly the benefits the agency and the older person may experi610 ence by forming the foster care relationship. Other marketing tools should depict older adults serving in the capacity of foster parents, and current older foster parents can be utilized directly in recruiting efforts.

*Tailored training and support.* For older adults who 615 decide to become foster parents, foster care agencies may need to provide additional support to help them cope with the stress of caring for young children and to deal with the demands placed on them by the placing agency. Training that acknowledges their unique per620 spectives on parenting should be provided and should include additional lessons on how to manage the complex details of foster parenting. If they are on a limited income and the small stipend that is provided for foster care services causes difficulty, they may face chal625 lenges in managing economics. They also may need to utilize respite services more often as they take time to attend to their own medical or health situations if additional family support is not available. This additional support may also increase the odds that an experienced 630 foster parent who enters older life may continue being a foster parent.

*Productive aging options.* Finally, public information sources need to publicize more comprehensive options for healthy aging. Since the time when the

635 Older Americans Act (1965) was adopted, a great amount of attention to preretirement education programs has developed in the United States. In addition, the popular media frequently feature information related to planning for retirement. Typically, these pro640 grams emphasize the rich potential of leisure activities to fill the retirement years and are based on the notion that older adults want to withdraw from work and relax. Although this is often true, some older adults, for various reasons, would like to continue to work, and 645 some of these would like to enter a second or different type of career. Because this larger, new generation of older adults is so well prepared to continue their contribution to society, it behooves planners of preretirement programs and providers of information on aging 650 in the present and future to make a greater effort to incorporate information on new careers.

## References

Adoption and Foster Care Analysis and Reporting System. (2003). *The AF-CARS Report: Preliminary FY 2001 Estimates as of March 2003 (8).* Retrieved on October 10, 2004, from http://www.acf.hhs.gov/programs/cb/publications/afcars/report8.htm

Adoption and Safe Families Act, 105 U.S.C.§89. (1997).

Adoption Assistance and Child Welfare Act, 96 U.S.C.§272. (1980).

Besl, J. R., & Kale, B. D. (1996, June). Older workers in the 21st century: Active and educated, a case study. *Monthly Labor Review, 119,* 18–28.

Brown, K. (2003). *Staying ahead of the curve 2003: The AARP working in retirement study.* Retrieved April 20, 2005, from http://www.aarp.org/research/reference/publicopinions/aresearch-import-417.html

Child Welfare League of America. (2000). Licensed homes and facilities, 1998. Retrieved March 13, 2001, from http://ndas.cwla.org/data_stats/access/predefined/Report.asp?ReportID=49

Child Welfare League of America. (2002). *Research Roundup: Family Reunification.* Retrieved March 14, 2003, from http://www.cwla.org/programs/r2p/rrnews0203.pdf

Child Welfare Partnership. (1999). *Cohort IV report. An examination of longer-term foster care in Oregon between 1995–1997.* Retrieved August 2, 2004, from www.cwp.pdx.edu/assets/Long_Term_Cohort_IV_Report.pdf

Dahlberg, S. (2004, February). The new elderhood. *Training, 141,* 46–47.

Denby, R., Rindfleisch, N., & Bean, G. (1999). Predictors of foster parents' satisfaction and intent to continue to foster. *Child Abuse & Neglect, 23,* 287–303.

Dulin, P. L., & Hill, R. D. (2003). Relationships between altruistic activity and positive and negative affect among low-income older adult service providers. *Aging & Mental Health, 7,* 294–299.

Dychtwald, K., Erickson, T., & Morison, B. (2004, March). It's time to retire retirement. *Harvard Business Review, 82,* 1.

Ekerdt, D. J. (2004). Born to retire: The foreshortened life course. *The Gerontologist, 44,* 3–9.

Employment Task Force of the European Union. (2003). *Jobs, jobs, jobs: Creating more employment in Europe.* Retrieved April 20, 2005, from http://europa.eu.int/comm/employment_social/employment_strategy/pdf/etf_en.pdf

Hobbs, F. B., & Damon, B. L. (2004). *65+ in the United States.* Retrieved on September 24, 2004, from http://www.census.gov/prod/1/pop/p23-190/p23-190.html

Johnson, R. W. (2004, July). Trends in job demands among older workers. *Monthly Labor Review, 127,* 48–56.

Kleyman, P. (2003, July/August). Phased retirement will ease many into active older years [Electronic version]. *Aging Today: The Bimonthly Newspaper of the American Society for Aging,* 1.

Panek, P. E. (1997). The older worker. In A. D. Fisk & W. A. Rogers (Eds.), *Handbook of human factors and the older adult* (pp. 363–387). New York: Academic.

Pecora, P. J., Whittaker, J. K., Maluccio, A. N., & Barth, R. P. (2000). *The child welfare challenge.* New York: Aldine de Gruyter.

Penner, R. G., Perun, P., & Steuerle, C. E. (2003). *Letting older workers work.* Retrieved April 20, 2005, from http://www.urban.org/url.cfm?ID=310861

Piliavin, J. A. (2003). Doing well by doing good: Benefits for the benefactor. In C. L. M. Keyes & J. Haidt (Eds.), *Flourishing: Positive psychology and the life well lived* (pp. 227–247). Washington, DC: American Psychological Association.

Regier, D. A., Farmer, M. E., Rae, D. S., Locke, B. Z., Keith, S. J., Judd, L. L., & Goodwin, F. K. (1990). Comorbidity of mental disorders with alcohol and other drugs: Results from the Epidemiologic Catchment Area (ECA) Study. *JAMA, 264*, 2511–2518.

Schwartz, C., Meisenhelder, J. B., Ma, Y., & Reed, G. (2003). Altruistic social interest behaviors are associated with better mental health. *Psychosomatic Medicine, 65*, 778–785.

Social Security Act, 42 U.S.C.§1320. (1935).

Steuerle, C. E., & Carasso, A. (2001). *A prediction: Older workers will work more in the future*. Retrieved April 20, 2005, from http://www.urban.org/url.cfm?ID=310258

Strom, R., & Strom, S. (1999). Establishing school volunteer programs. *Child and Youth Services, 20*, 177–188.

Sweeney, A. R. (2000). An evaluation of the foster grandparent program in Fresno, California. Dissertation abstracts international: Section BL the Sciences and Engineering. Vol 61 (1-B), July 2000, 550.

University of Michigan, Institute for Social Research. (2004). *Boomers unexpected ethos: Work until we drop?* Retrieved from http://www.umich.edu/news/index.html?Releases/2004/Jul04/r071504c

U.S. Department of Commerce, Bureau of the Census. (1960). *1960 Census of the population: Vol. 1. Characteristics of the population*. Washington, DC: U.S. Bureau of the Census.

U.S. Department of Commerce, Bureau of the Census. (2002). *Current population Survey*. Retrieved on September 24, 2004, from http://www.census.gov/population/socdemo/age/ppl-167/tab01.txt

Zimmerman, S. L. (2000). A family policy agenda to enhance families' transactional interdependencies over the life span. *Families in Society, 81*, 557–575.

**About the authors**: *Donald H. Goughler*, MSW, is chief executive officer, Family Services of Western Pennsylvania, and part-time faculty member at the University of Pittsburgh, School of Social Work, where he teaches courses in management. *Annette C. Trunzo*, MSW, is director of research and program evaluation, Family Services of Western Pennsylvania.

**Address correspondence to**: Donald H. Goughler at goughlerd@fswp.org or Family Services of Western Pennsylvania, 3230 William Pitt Way, Pittsburgh, PA 15238-1361.

# Exercise for Article 37

## Factual Questions

1. What percentage of the 261 surveys that were distributed to older foster parents were returned to the researchers?

2. What did the researchers do to encourage participation?

3. The researchers used an open-ended question regarding what?

4. How many of the responding agencies specifically focused on recruiting older adults?

5. How many of the 16 foster parents who were contacted by telephone agreed to be interviewed?

6. The mean (*M*) for the first question in Table 2 is 4.71. In light of the measure used, is this a high value?

## Questions for Discussion

7. The literature review in this article is longer than the literature reviews in a number of the other arti-

cles in this book. In your opinion, is this relatively long review a special strength of this article? Explain. (See lines 27–240.)

8. The researchers state that they drew a "stratified random sample." What is your understanding of the meaning of this term? (See lines 243–244.)

9. Of the 132 agencies surveyed, 33% returned the questionnaire. Is this an important weakness of this research? Why? Why not? (See lines 251–253.)

10. The results shown in Table 1 are described in lines 296–314. How helpful is the table in helping you understand these results?

11. The qualitative part of this research was based on interviews. The participants who were interviewed were from one foster care program. In your opinion, does this limit the generalizability of the results? (See lines 337–341.)

12. The researchers present quantitative findings in lines 294–336 and qualitative findings in lines 364–531. In your opinion, are both types of findings equally informative? Is one type more informative than the other? Explain.

13. Unlike most of the other articles in this book, this article is based on both quantitative and qualitative research. Do you believe that this is a strength of this article? Explain.

## Quality Ratings

Directions: Indicate your level of agreement with each of the following statements by circling a number from 5 for strongly agree (SA) to 1 for strongly disagree (SD). If you believe an item is not applicable to this research article, leave it blank. Be prepared to explain your ratings. When responding to criteria A and B, keep in mind that brief titles and abstracts are conventional in published research.

A. The title of the article is appropriate.

SA   5   4   3   2   1   SD

B. The abstract provides an effective overview of the research article.

SA   5   4   3   2   1   SD

C. The introduction establishes the importance of the study.

SA   5   4   3   2   1   SD

D.  The literature review establishes the context for the study.

SA   5   4   3   2   1   SD

E.  The research purpose, question, or hypothesis is clearly stated.

SA   5   4   3   2   1   SD

F.  The method of sampling is sound.

SA   5   4   3   2   1   SD

G.  Relevant demographics (for example, age, gender, and ethnicity) are described.

SA   5   4   3   2   1   SD

H.  Measurement procedures are adequate.

SA   5   4   3   2   1   SD

I.  All procedures have been described in sufficient detail to permit a replication of the study.

SA   5   4   3   2   1   SD

J.  The participants have been adequately protected from potential harm.

SA   5   4   3   2   1   SD

K.  The results are clearly described.

SA   5   4   3   2   1   SD

L.  The discussion/conclusion is appropriate.

SA   5   4   3   2   1   SD

M.  Despite any flaws, the report is worthy of publication.

SA   5   4   3   2   1   SD

# Article 38

# Project D.A.R.E. Outcome Effectiveness Revisited

STEVEN L. WEST
Virginia Commonwealth University

KERI K. O'NEAL
University of North Carolina, Chapel Hill

OBJECTIVES. We provide an updated meta-analysis on the effectiveness of Project D.A.R.E. in preventing alcohol, tobacco, and illicit drug use among school-aged youths.

METHODS. We used meta-analytic techniques to create an overall effect size for D.A.R.E. outcome evaluations reported in scientific journals.

RESULTS. The overall weighted effect size for the included D.A.R.E. studies was extremely small (correlation coefficient = 0.011; Cohen's $d$ = 0.023; 95% confidence interval = −0.04, 0.08) and nonsignificant ($z$ = 0.73, NS).

CONCLUSIONS. Our study supports previous findings indicating that D.A.R.E. is ineffective.

From *American Journal of Public Health*, *94*, 1027–1029. Copyright © 2004 by American Journal of Public Health. Reprinted with permission.

In the United States, Project D.A.R.E. (Drug Abuse Resistance Education) is one of the most widely used substance abuse prevention programs targeted at school-aged youths. In recent years, D.A.R.E. has been the country's largest single school-based prevention program in terms of federal expenditures, with an average of three-quarters of a billion dollars spent on its provision annually.[1] Although its effectiveness in preventing substance use has been called into question, its application in our nation's schools remains very extensive.[2–6]

Given the recent increases in alcohol and other drug use among high school and college students,[7] the continued use of D.A.R.E. and similar programs seems likely. In a meta-analysis examining the effectiveness of D.A.R.E., Ennett et al.[3] noted negligible yet positive effect sizes (ranging from 0.00 to 0.11) when outcomes occurring immediately after program completion were considered. However, this analysis involved 2 major limitations. First, Ennett et al. included research from nonpeer-reviewed sources, including annual reports produced for agencies associated with the provision of D.A.R.E. services. While such an inclusion does not necessarily represent a serious methodological flaw, use of such sources has been called into question.[8]

Second, Ennett and colleagues included only studies in which postintervention assessment was conducted immediately at program termination. As noted by Lynam et al.,[6] the developmental trajectories of drug experimentation and use vary over time. Thus, if individuals are assessed during periods in which rates of experimentation and use are naturally high, any positive effects that could be found at times of lower experimentation will be deflated. Likewise, assessments made during periods in which experimentation and use are slight will exaggerate the overall effect of the intervention.

Ideally, problems such as those just described could be solved by the use of large-scale longitudinal studies involving extensive follow-up over a period of years. There have been several longer-term follow-ups, but the cost of such efforts may limit the number of longitudinal studies that can be conducted. In the present analysis, we attempted to overcome this difficulty by including a wider range of follow-up reports, from immediate posttests to 10-year postintervention assessments, in an updated meta-analysis of all currently available research articles reporting an outcome evaluation of Project D.A.R.E.

## Methods

We conducted computer searches of the *ERIC*, *MEDLINE*, and *PsycINFO* databases in late fall 2002 to obtain articles for the present study. In addition, we reviewed the reference lists of the acquired articles for other potential sources. We initially reviewed roughly 40 articles from these efforts; 11 studies appearing in the literature from 1991 to 2002 met our 3 inclusion criteria, which were as follows:

1. The research was reported in a peer-reviewed journal; reports from dissertations/theses, books, and unpublished manuscripts were not included. We selected this criterion in an attempt to ensure inclusion of only those studies with rigorous methodologies. As noted, a previous meta-analysis of Project D.A.R.E. included research from nonreviewed sources, a fact that critics have suggested may have added error to the reported findings.[8]

2. The research included a control or comparison group (i.e., the research must have involved an experimental or quasi-experimental design).

Table 1
*Primary Articles Included in the Meta-Analysis*

| Study (year) | Sample | $r$ | $d$ | 95% confidence interval |
|---|---|---|---|---|
| Ringwalt et al. (1991)[18] | 5th and 6th graders ($n$ = 1270; 52% female/48% male; 50% African American/40% Anglo/10% other), posttested immediately | 0.025 | 0.056 | –0.06, 0.16 |
| Becker et al. (1992)[19] | 5th graders ($n$ = 2878), posttested immediately | –0.058 | –0.117 | –0.19, –0.04 |
| Harmon (1993)[20] | 5th graders ($n$ = 708), posttested immediately | 0.015 | 0.030 | –0.12, 0.18 |
| Ennett et al. (1994)[21] | 7th and 8th graders ($n$ = 1334; 54% Anglo/22% African American/9% Hispanic/15% other), 2 years post-D.A.R.E. | 0.000 | 0.000[a] | –0.11, 0.11 |
| Rosenbaum et al. (1994)[22] | 6th and 7th graders ($n$ = 1584; 49.7% female/50.3% male; 49.9% Anglo/24.7% African American/8.9% Hispanic/16.5% other), 1 year post-D.A.R.E. | 0.000 | 0.000[a] | –0.10, 0.10 |
| Wysong et al. (1994)[23] | 12th graders ($n$ = 619), 5 years post-D.A.R.E. | 0.000 | 0.000[a] | –0.16, 0.16 |
| Dukes et al. (1996)[24] | 9th graders ($n$ = 849), 3 years post-D.A.R.E. | 0.035 | 0.072 | –0.06, 0.21 |
| Zagumny & Thompson (1997)[25] | 6th graders ($n$ = 395; 48% female/52% male), 4–5 years post-D.A.R.E. | 0.184 | 0.376 | 0.07, 0.68 |
| Lynam et al. (1999)[6] | 6th graders ($n$ = 1002; 57% female/43% male; 75.1% Anglo/20.4% African American/0.5% other), 10 years post-D.A.R.E. | 0.000 | 0.000[a] | –0.15, 0.15 |
| Thombs (2000)[26] | 5th through 10th graders ($n$ = 630; 90.4% Anglo/5.5% African American/4.1% other), posttested at least 1 to 6 years post-D.A.R.E. | 0.025 | 0.038 | –0.15, 0.23 |
| Ahmed et al. (2002)[14] | 5th and 6th graders ($n$ = 236; 50% female/50% male/69% Anglo/24% African American/7% other), posttested immediately | 0.198 | 0.405 | 0.01, 0.80 |

*Note.* $r$ = correlation coefficient; $d$ = difference in the means of the treatment and control conditions divided by the pooled standard deviation. Negative signs for $r$ and $d$ indicate greater effectiveness of control/comparison group.
[a]Assumed effect size.

70 3. The research included both preintervention and postintervention assessments of at least 1 of 3 key variables: alcohol use, illicit drug use, and tobacco use. We chose to include only those effect sizes that concerned actual substance use behaviors, 75 since the true test of a substance use prevention effort is its impact on actual rates of use.

Using these criteria, we refined the original list of studies to 11 studies (Table 1). We calculated effect sizes using the procedures outlined by Rosenthal.[9] 80 Meta-analysis results are commonly presented in the form of either a correlation coefficient ($r$) or the difference in the means of the treatment and control conditions divided by the pooled standard deviation (Cohen's $d$).[10] Since both are ratings of effect size, they 85 can readily be converted to one another, and, if not provided in the original analyses, they can be calculated via F, $t$, and $\chi^2$ statistics as well as means and standard deviations.[9] We calculated both estimations for the individual 90 included studies and for the overall analysis. As discussed by Amato and Keith,[11] tests of significance used in meta-analyses require that effect sizes be independent; therefore, if 2 or more effect sizes were generated within the same outcome category, we used the mean 95 effect size. We also used the procedure for weighting effect sizes suggested by Shadish and Haddock[12] to ensure that all effect sizes were in the form of a com-

mon metric. In addition, we calculated 95% confidence intervals (CIs) for each study and for the overall 100 analysis.

**Results**

The average weighted effect size ($r$) for all studies was 0.011 ($d$ = 0.023; 95% CI = –0.04, 0.08), indicating marginally better outcomes for individuals participating in D.A.R.E. relative to participants in control 105 conditions. The fact that the associated CI included a negative value indicates that the average effect size was not significantly greater than zero at $p < .05$. According to the guidelines developed by Cohen,[13] both of the effect sizes obtained were below the level nor- 110 mally considered small. Four of the included studies noted no effect of D.A.R.E. relative to control conditions, and 1 study noted that D.A.R.E. was less effective than the control condition.

Furthermore, the 6 reports indicating that D.A.R.E. 115 had more positive effects were for the most part small (Figure 1). The largest effect size was found in a report in which the only outcome examined was smoking. Finally, we conducted a test of cumulative significance to determine whether differences existed between 120 D.A.R.E. participants and non-D.A.R.E. participants. This test produced nonsignificant results ($z$ = 0.73, NS).

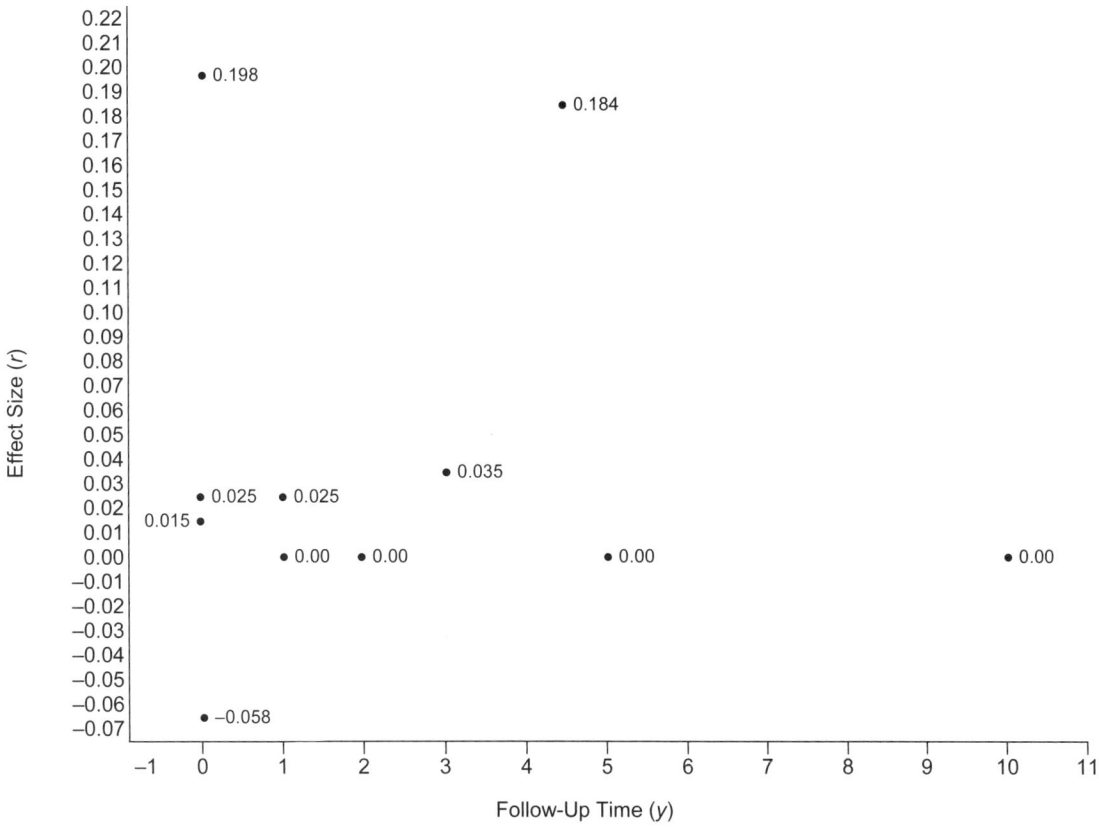

*Figure 1.* Plot of effect sizes, by follow-up time.

## Discussion

Our results confirm the findings of a previous meta-analysis[3] indicating that Project D.A.R.E. is ineffective.
125 This is not surprising, given the substantial information developed over the past decade to that effect. Critics of the present analysis might argue that, despite the magnitude of our findings, the direction of the effect of D.A.R.E. was generally positive. While this is the case,
130 it should be emphasized that the effects we found did not differ significantly from the variation one would expect by chance. According to Cohen's guidelines,[13] the effect size we obtained would have needed to be 20 times larger to be considered even small. Given the
135 tremendous expenditures in time and money involved with D.A.R.E., it would appear that continued efforts should focus on other techniques and programs that might produce more substantial effects.

Our findings also indicate that D.A.R.E. was mini-
140 mally effective during the follow-up periods that would place its participants in the very age groups targeted. Indeed, no noticeable effects could be discerned in nearly half of the reports, including the study involving the longest follow-up period. This is an important con-
145 sideration for those involved in program planning and development.

As noted earlier, progression in regard to experimentation and use varies over time. Use of alcohol and other drugs reaches a peak during adolescence or
150 young adulthood and decreases steadily thereafter.[7,15] Such a developmental path would be expected of all individuals, regardless of their exposure to a prevention effort. Ideally, individuals enrolled in a program such as D.A.R.E. would report limited or no use during their
155 adolescent and young adult years. The fact that half of the included studies reported no beneficial effect of D.A.R.E. beyond what would be expected by chance casts serious doubt on its utility.

One shortcoming of our analysis should be noted.
160 In many of the studies we included, individual students were the unit of analysis in calculating effects. As noted by Rosenbaum and Hanson,[16] this practice tends to lead to overestimates of program effectiveness since the true unit of analysis is the schools in which the stu-
165 dents are "nested." Because our meta-analysis was limited to the types of data and related information available from the original articles, the potential for such inflation of program effectiveness exists. However, the overall effect sizes calculated here were small and non-
170 significant, and thus it is unlikely that inclusion of studies making this error had a significant impact on the current findings.

An additional caveat is that all of the studies included in this analysis represent evaluations of what is
175 commonly referred to as the "old D.A.R.E.": programs generally based on the original formulations of the D.A.R.E. model. In response to the many critiques of

the program, the D.A.R.E. prevention model was substantially revamped in 2001, thanks in part to a $13.6
180  million grant provided by the Robert Wood Johnson Foundation.[17] The revisions to the model have since given rise to programs working under the "new D.A.R.E." paradigm. However, at the time of the writing of this article we were unable to find any major
185  evaluation of the new D.A.R.E. model in the research literature, and the effectiveness of such efforts has yet to be determined.

### References

1. McNeal RB, Hanson WB. An examination of strategies for gaining convergent validity in natural experiments: D.A.R.E. as an illustrative case study. *Eval Rev.* 1995:19:141–158.
2. Donnermeyer J, Wurschmidt T. Educators' perceptions of the D.A.R.E. program. *J Drug Educ.* 1997;27:259–276.
3. Ennett ST, Tobler NS, Ringwalt CL, Flewelling RL. How effective is Drug Abuse Resistance Education? A meta-analysis of Project D.A.R.E. outcome evaluations. *Am J Public Health.* 1994;84:1394–1401.
4. Hanson WB. Pilot test results comparing the All Stars Program with seventh-grade D.A.R.E.: Program integrity and mediating variable analysis. *Subst Use Misuse.* 1996;31:1359–1377.
5. Hanson WB, McNeal RB. How D.A.R.E. works: An examination of program effects on mediating variables. *Health Educ Behav.* 1997;24:165–176.
6. Lynam DR, Milich R, Zimmerman R, et al. Project D.A.R.E: No effects at 10-year follow-up. *J Consult Clin Psychol.* 1999;67:590–593.
7. Johnston LD, O'Malley PM, Bachman JG. *National Survey Results on Drug Use from the Monitoring the Future Study, 1975–1998. Volume 1: Secondary School Students.* Rockville, Md: National Institute on Drug Abuse; 1999. NIH publication 99–4660.
8. Gorman DM. The effectiveness of D.A.R.E. and other drug use prevention programs. *Am J Public Health.* 1995;85:873.
9. Rosenthal R. *Meta-Analytic Procedures for Social Research.* 2nd ed. Thousand Oaks, CA: Sage Publications; 1991.
10. DasEiden R, Reifman A. Effects of Brazelton demonstrations on later parenting: A meta-analysis. *J Pediatr Psychol.* 1996;21:857–868.
11. Amato PH, Keith B. Parental divorce and well-being of children: A meta-analysis. *Psychol Bull.* 1991;110:26–46.
12. Shadish WR, Haddock CK. Combining estimates of effect size. In: Cooper H, Hedges LV, eds. *The Handbook of Research Synthesis.* New York, NY: Russell Sage Foundation; 1994:261–281.
13. Cohen J. *Statistical Power Analysis for the Behavioral Sciences.* 2nd ed. Hillsdale, NJ: Lawrence Erlbaum Associates; 1998.
14. Ahmed NU, Ahmed NS, Bennett CR, Hinds JE. Impact of a drug abuse resistance education (D.A.R.E.) program in preventing the initiation of cigarette smoking in fifth- and sixth-grade students. *J Natl Med Assoc.* 2002;94:249–256.
15. Shedler J, Block J. Adolescent drug use and psychological health: A longitudinal inquiry. *Am Psychol.* 1990;45:612–630.
16. Rosenbaum DP, Hanson GS. Assessing the effects of a school-based drug education: A six-year multilevel analysis of Project D.A.R.E. *J Res Crime Delinquency.* 1998;35:381–412.
17. Improving and evaluating the D.A.R.E. school-based substance abuse prevention curriculum. Available at: http://www.rwjf.org/programs/grantDetail.jsp?id=040371. Accessed January 8, 2003.
18. Ringwalt C, Ennett ST, Holt KD. An outcome evaluation of Project D.A.R.E. (Drug Abuse Resistance Education). *Health Educ Res.* 1991;6:327–337.
19. Becker HK, Agopian MW, Yeh S. Impact evaluation of drug abuse resistance education (D.A.R.E.). *J Drug Educ.* 1992;22:283–291.
20. Harmon MA. Reducing the risk of drug involvement among early adolescents: An evaluation of drug abuse resistance education (D.A.R.E.). *Eval Rev.* 1993;17:221–239.
21. Ennett ST, Rosenbaum DP, Flewelling RL, Bieler GS, Ringwalt CL, Bailey SL. Long-term evaluation of drug abuse resistance education. *Addict Behav.* 1994;19:113–125.
22. Rosenbaum DP, Flewelling RL, Bailey SL, Ringwalt CL, Wilkinson DL. Cops in the classroom: A longitudinal evaluation of drug abuse resistance education (D.A.R.E.). *J Res Crime Delinquency.* 1994;31:3–31.
23. Wysong E, Aniskiewicz R, Wright D. Truth and D.A.R.E.: Tracking drug education to graduation and as symbolic politics. *Soc Probl.* 1994;41:448–472.
24. Dukes RL, Ulllman JB, Stein JA. Three-year follow-up of drug abuse resistance education (D.A.R.E.). *Eval Rev.* 1996;20:49–66.
25. Zagumny MJ, Thompson MK. Does D.A.R.E. work? An evaluation in rural Tennessee. *J Alcohol Drug Educ.* 1997;42:32–41.
26. Thombs DL. A retrospective study of D.A.R.E.: Substantive effects not detected in undergraduates. *J Alcohol Drug Educ.* 2000;46:27–40.

**Acknowledgments**: Portions of this research were presented at the Eighth Annual Meeting of the Society for Prevention Research, Montreal, Quebec, Canada, June 2000.

**About the authors**: *Steven L. West* is with the Department of Rehabilitation Counseling, Virginia Commonwealth University, Richmond. *Keri K. O'Neal* is with the Center for Developmental Science, University of North Carolina, Chapel Hill. Drs. West and O'Neal contributed equally to all aspects of study design, data analysis, and the writing of this article. No protocol approval was needed for this study.

**Address correspondence to**: Steven L. West, Ph.D., Virginia Commonwealth University, Department of Rehabilitation Counseling, 1112 East Clay St., Box 980330, Richmond, VA 23298-0330. E-mail: slwest2@vcu.edu

# Exercise for Article 38

## Factual Questions

1. To identify the articles for this meta-analysis, the researchers conducted computer searches of which three databases?

2. Which study had the largest effect size (*r*)? (Identify it by the name of the author and year of publication.) What was the value of *r* in this study?

3. What was the average weighted effect size (*r*) for all studies included in this meta-analysis?

4. The study with the largest effect size examined only one outcome. What was the outcome?

5. According to Figure 1, the study with the longest follow-up time had what effect size?

6. Were the researchers able to find any major evaluations of the *new* D.A.R.E. paradigm?

## Questions for Discussion

7. The researchers do not describe the D.A.R.E. program components. In your opinion, would it have been desirable for them to do so? Explain.

8. What is your opinion of the researchers' decision to include only research reported in peer-reviewed journals? (See lines 58–66.)

9. What is your opinion of the researchers' decision to include only evaluations that included a control or comparison group? (See lines 67–69.)

10. Does it surprise you that the study by Becker et al. in Table 1 has negative effect sizes? Explain.

11. In Table 1, 95% confidence intervals are reported. What is your understanding of the meaning of these intervals?

12. What is your opinion on the researchers' suggestion in lines 134–138? Is your opinion based on the data in this meta-analysis? Explain.

## *Quality Ratings*

Directions: Indicate your level of agreement with each of the following statements by circling a number from 5 for strongly agree (SA) to 1 for strongly disagree (SD). If you believe an item is not applicable to this research article, leave it blank. Be prepared to explain your ratings. When responding to criteria A and B, keep in mind that brief titles and abstracts are conventional in published research.

A. The title of the article is appropriate.

    SA   5   4   3   2   1   SD

B. The abstract provides an effective overview of the research article.

    SA   5   4   3   2   1   SD

C. The introduction establishes the importance of the study.

    SA   5   4   3   2   1   SD

D. The literature review establishes the context for the study.

    SA   5   4   3   2   1   SD

E. The research purpose, question, or hypothesis is clearly stated.

    SA   5   4   3   2   1   SD

F. The method of sampling is sound.

    SA   5   4   3   2   1   SD

G. Relevant demographics (for example, age, gender, and ethnicity) are described.

    SA   5   4   3   2   1   SD

H. Measurement procedures are adequate.

    SA   5   4   3   2   1   SD

I. All procedures have been described in sufficient detail to permit a replication of the study.

    SA   5   4   3   2   1   SD

J. The participants have been adequately protected from potential harm.

    SA   5   4   3   2   1   SD

K. The results are clearly described.

    SA   5   4   3   2   1   SD

L. The discussion/conclusion is appropriate.

    SA   5   4   3   2   1   SD

M. Despite any flaws, the report is worthy of publication.

    SA   5   4   3   2   1   SD

# Appendix A

# Reading Research Reports: A Brief Introduction

DAVID A. SCHROEDER          DAVID E. JOHNSON          THOMAS D. JENSEN

To many students, the prospect of reading a research report in a professional journal elicits so much fear that no information is, in fact, transmitted. Such apprehension on the part of the reader is not necessary, and we
5 hope that this article will help students understand more clearly what such reports are all about and will teach them how to use these resources more effectively. Let us assure you that there is nothing mystical or magical about research reports, although they may be somewhat
10 more technical and precise in style, more intimidating in vocabulary, and more likely to refer to specific sources of information than are everyday mass media sources. However, once you get beyond these intimidating features, you will find that the vast majority of research
15 reports do a good job of guiding you through a project and informing you of important points of which you should be aware.

A scientific research report has but one purpose: to communicate to others the results of one's scientific
20 investigations. To ensure that readers will be able to appreciate fully the import and implications of the research, the author of the report will make every effort to describe the project so comprehensively that even a naïve reader will be able to follow the logic as he or she
25 traces the author's thinking through the project.

A standardized format has been developed by editors and authors to facilitate effective communication. The format is subject to some modification, according to the specific needs and goals of a particular author for
30 a particular article, but, in general, most articles possess a number of features in common. We will briefly discuss the six major sections of research articles and the purpose of each. We hope that this selection will help you take full advantage of the subsequent articles and to
35 appreciate their content as informed "consumers" of social psychological research.

## Heading

The heading of an article consists of the title, the name of the author or authors, and their institutional affiliations. Typically, the title provides a brief descrip-
40 tion of the primary independent and dependent variables

that have been investigated in the study. This information should help you begin to categorize the study into some implicit organizational framework that will help you keep track of the social psychological material. For
45 example, if the title includes the word *persuasion*, you should immediately recognize that the article will be related to the attitude-change literature, and you should prepare yourself to identify the similarities and differences between the present study and the previous litera-
50 ture.

The names of the authors may also be important to you for at least two reasons. First, it is quite common for social psychologists to use the names of authors as a shorthand notation in referring among themselves to
55 critical articles. Rather than asking, "Have you read 'Videotape and the attribution process: Reversing actors' and observers' points of view'?," it is much easier to say, "Have you read the Storms (1973) article?" In addition, this strategy gives the author(s) credit for the
60 material contained in the article. Second, you will find that most researchers actively pursue programs of research that are specific to a particular area of interest. For example, you will eventually be able to recognize that an article written by Albert Bandura is likely to be
65 about social learning processes, while an article by Leonard Berkowitz is probably going to discuss aggression and violence. Once you begin to identify the major researchers in each area, you will find that you will be able to go beyond the information presented within an
70 article and understand not only how a piece of research fits into a well-defined body of literature but also how it may be related to other less obvious topics.

## Abstract

The Abstract is a short (often less than 150 words) preview of the contents of the article. The Abstract
75 should be totally self-contained and intelligible without any reference to the article proper. It should briefly convey a statement of the problem explored, the methods used, the major results of the study, and the conclusions reached. The Abstract helps to set the stage and to pre-
80 pare you for the article itself. Just as the title helps you place the article in a particular area of investigation, the Abstract helps pinpoint the exact question or questions to be addressed in the study.

## Introduction

The Introduction provides the foundation for the

85 study itself and therefore for the remainder of the article. Thus, it serves several critical functions for the reader. First, it provides a context for the article and the study by discussing past literature that is relevant to and has implications for the present research. Second, it per-
90 mits a thorough discussion of the rationale for the research that was conducted and a full description of the independent and dependent variables that were employed. Third, it allows the hypotheses that were tested to be stated explicitly, and the arguments on which these
95 predictions were based to be elucidated. Each of these functions will be considered in detail.

The literature review that is typically the initial portion of the Introduction is not intended to provide a comprehensive restatement of all the published articles
100 that are tangentially relevant to the present research. Normally, a selective review is presented—one that carefully sets up the rationale of the study and identifies deficiencies in our understanding of the phenomena being investigated. In taking this approach, the author is
105 attempting to provide insights into the thought processes that preceded the actual conducting of the study. Usually, the literature review will begin by discussing rather broad conceptual issues (e.g., major theories, recognized areas of investigation) and will then gradually narrow its
110 focus to more specific concerns (e.g., specific findings from previous research, methods that have been employed). It may be helpful to think of the Introduction as a funnel, gradually drawing one's attention to a central point that represents the critical feature of the article.

115 Following the review of the past literature, the author typically presents the rationale for his or her own research. A research study may have one of several goals as its primary aim: (1) It may be designed to answer a question specifically raised by the previous lit-
120 erature but left unanswered. (2) It may attempt to correct methodological flaws that have plagued previous research and threaten the validity of the conclusions reached. (3) It may seek to reconcile conflicting findings that have been reported in the literature, typically
125 by identifying and/or eliminating confounding variables by exerting greater experimental control. (4) It may be designed to assess the validity of a scientific theory by testing one or more hypotheses that have been deduced or derived from that theory. (5) It may begin a novel
130 line of research that has not been previously pursued or discussed in the literature. Research pursuing any of these five goals may yield significant contributions to a particular field of inquiry.

After providing the rationale for the study, the au-
135 thor properly continues to narrow the focus of the article from broad conceptual issues to the particular variables that are to be employed in the study. Ideally, in experimental studies, the author clearly identifies the independent and dependent variables to be used; in correla-
140 tional studies, the predictor and criterion variables are specified. For those readers who do not have an extensive background in research methodology, a brief ex-

planation of experimental and correlational studies may be in order.

145 *Experimental studies.* An experimental study is designed to identify cause-effect relationships between independent variables that the experimenter systematically manipulates and the dependent variable that is used to measure the behavior of interest. In such a
150 study, the researcher controls the situation to eliminate or neutralize the effects of all extraneous factors that may affect the behavior of interest in order to assess more precisely the impact of the independent variables alone. In most instances, only the tightly controlled ex-
155 perimental method permits valid inferences of cause-effect relationships to be made.

*Correlational studies.* In some circumstances, the researcher cannot exert the degree of control over the situation that is necessary for a true experimental study.
160 Rather than giving up the project, the researcher may explore alternative methods that may still permit an assessment of his or her hypotheses and predictions. One such alternative is the correlational approach. In a correlational study, the researcher specifies a set of
165 measures that should be related conceptually to the display of a target behavior. The measure that is used to assess the target behavior is called the criterion variable; the measure from which the researcher expects to be able to make predictions about the criterion variable is
170 called the predictor variable. Correlational studies permit the researcher to assess the degree of relationship between the predictor variable(s) and the criterion variable(s), but inferences of cause-and-effect cannot be validly made because the effects of extraneous variables
175 have not been adequately controlled. Correlational studies are most frequently used in naturalistic or applied situations in which researchers must either tolerate the lack of control and do the best they can under the circumstances or give up any hope of testing their hy-
180 potheses.

After the discussion of these critical components of the study, the author explicitly states the exact predictions that the study is designed to test. The previous material should have set the stage sufficiently well for
185 you as a reader to anticipate what these hypotheses will be, but it is incumbent on the author to present them nonetheless. The wording of the hypotheses may vary, some authors preferring to state the predictions in conceptual terms (e.g., "The arousal of cognitive disso-
190 nance due to counterattitudinal advocacy is expected to lead to greater attitude change than the presentation of an attitude-consistent argument.") and others preferring to state their predictions in terms of the actual operationalizations that they employed (e.g., "Subjects who
195 received a $1 incentive to say that an objectively boring task was fun are expected to subsequently evaluate the task as being more enjoyable than subjects who were offered a $20 incentive to say that the task was interesting.").

200   In reading a research report, it is imperative that you pay attention to the relationship between the initial literature review, the rationale for the study, and the statement of the hypotheses. In a well-conceived and well-designed investigation, each section will flow logically from the preceding one; the internal consistency of the author's arguments will make for smooth transitions as the presentation advances. If there appear to be discontinuities or inconsistencies throughout the author's presentation, it would be wise to take a more critical view of the study—particularly if the predictions do not seem to follow logically from the earlier material. In such cases, the author may be trying to present as a prediction a description of the findings that were unexpectedly uncovered when the study was being conducted. Although there is nothing wrong with reporting unexpected findings in a journal article, the author should be honest enough to identify them as what they really are. As a reader, you should have much more confidence in the reliability of predictions that obtain than you do in data that can be described by postdictions only.

### Method

To this point, the author has dealt with the study in relatively abstract terms, and has given little attention to the actual procedures used in conducting it. In the Method section, the author at last describes the operationalizations and procedures that were employed in the investigation. There are at least two reasons for the detailed presentation of this information. First, such a presentation allows interested readers to reconstruct the methodology used, so that a replication of the study can be undertaken. By conducting a replication using different subject populations and slightly different operationalizations of the same conceptual variables, more information can be gained about the validity of the conclusions that the original investigator reached. Second, even if a replication is not conducted, the careful description of the method used will permit you to evaluate the adequacy of the procedures employed.

The Method section typically comprises two or more subsections, each of which has a specific function to fulfill. Almost without exception, the Method section begins with a subject subsection, consisting of a complete description of the subjects who participated in the study.[1] The number of subjects should be indicated, and there should be a summary of important demographic information (e.g., numbers of male and female subjects, age) so that you can know to what populations the findings can be reasonably generalized. Sampling techniques that were used to recruit subjects and incentives used to induce volunteering should also be clearly specified. To the extent that subject characteristics are of primary importance to the goals of the research, greater

detail is presented in this subsection, and more attention should be directed to it.

A procedures subsection is also almost always included in the Method section. This subsection presents a detailed account of the subjects' experiences in the experiment. Although other formats may also be effective, the most common presentation style is to describe the subjects' activities in chronological order. A thorough description of all questionnaires administered or tasks completed is given, as well as any other features that might be reasonably expected to affect the behavior of the subjects in the study.

After the procedures have been discussed, a full description of the independent variables in an experimental study, or predictor variables in a correlational study, is typically provided. Verbatim description of each of the different levels of each independent variable is presented, and similar detail is used to describe each predictor variable. This information may be included either in the procedures subsection or, if the description of these variables is quite lengthy, in a separate subsection.

After thoroughly describing these variables, the author usually describes the dependent variables in an experimental study, and the criterion variables in a correlational study. The description of the dependent and/or criterion variables also requires a verbatim specification of the exact operationalizations that were employed. When appropriate and available, information about the reliability and validity of these measures is also presented. In addition, if the investigator has included any questions that were intended to allow the effectiveness of the independent variable manipulation to be assessed, these manipulation checks are described at this point. All of this information may be incorporated in the procedures subsection or in a separate subsection.

After you have read the Method section, there should be no question about what has been done to the subjects who participated in the study. You should try to evaluate how representative the methods that were used were of the conceptual variables discussed in the Introduction. Manipulation checks may help to allay one's concerns, but poorly conceived manipulation checks are of little or no value. Therefore, it is important for you as a reader to remember that you are ultimately responsible for the critical evaluation of any research report.

### Results

Once the full methodology of the study has been described for the reader, the author proceeds to report the results of the statistical analyses that were conducted on the data. The Results section is probably the most intimidating section for students to read, and often the most difficult section for researchers to write. You are typically confronted with terminology and analytical techniques with which you are at best unfamiliar, or at worst totally ignorant. There is no reason for you to feel bad about this state of affairs; as a neophyte in the world of research, you cannot expect mastery of all phases of

---

[1] *Editor's note*: Many researchers prefer the terms *participants* or *respondents* to the term *subjects*.

310 research from the start. Even experienced researchers are often exposed to statistical techniques with which they are unfamiliar, requiring them either to learn the techniques or to rely on others to assess the appropriateness of the procedure. For the student researcher, a little experience and a conscientious effort to learn the basics will lead to mastery of the statistical skills necessary.

315 The author's task is similarly difficult. He or she is attempting to present the findings of the study in a straightforward and easily understood manner, but the presentation of statistical findings does not always lend itself readily to this task. The author must decide
320 whether to present the results strictly within the text of the article or to use tables, graphs, and figures to help convey the information effectively. Although the implications of the data may be clear to the researcher, trying to present the data clearly and concisely so that the
325 reader will also be able to discern the implications is not necessarily assured. In addition, the author is obligated to present all the significant results obtained in the statistical analyses, not just the results that support the hypotheses being tested. Although this may clutter the
330 presentation and detract from the simplicity of the interpretation, it must be remembered that the researcher's primary goal is to seek the truth, not to espouse a particular point of view that may not be supported by the data.

### Discussion

335 The Discussion section is the part of the manuscript in which the author offers an evaluation and interpretation of the findings of the study, particularly as they relate to the hypotheses that were proposed in the Introduction. Typically, the author will begin this section
340 with a brief review of the major findings of the study and a clear statement of whether the data were consistent or inconsistent with the hypotheses. The Discussion will then address any discrepancies between the predictions and the data, trying to resolve these inconsisten-
345 cies and offering plausible reasons for their occurrence. In general, the first portion of the Discussion is devoted to an evaluation of the hypotheses that were originally set forward in the Introduction, given the data that were obtained in the research.

350 The Discussion may be seen as the inverse of the Introduction, paralleling the issues raised in that section in the opposite order of presentation. Therefore, after discussing the relationship of the data with the hypotheses, the author often attempts to integrate the new findings
355 into the body of research that provided the background for the study. Just as this literature initially provided the context within which you can understand the rationale for the study, it subsequently provides the context within which the data can be understood and inter-
360 preted. The author's responsibility at this point is to help you recognize the potential import of the research, without relying on hype or gimmicks to make the point.

The Discussion continues to expand in terms of the breadth of ideas discussed until it reaches the broad,
365 conceptual issues that are addressed by the superordinate theoretical work that originally stimulated the past research literature. If a particular piece of research is to make a significant contribution to the field, its findings must either clarify some past discrepancy in the litera-
370 ture, identify boundary conditions for the applicability of the critical theoretical work, reconcile differences of opinion among the researchers in the field, or otherwise contribute to a more complete understanding of the mechanisms and mediators of important social phenom-
375 ena.

Once the author has reached the goals that are common to most journal articles, attention may be turned to less rigorous ideas. Depending on a particular journal's editorial policy and the availability of additional space,
380 the author may finish the article with a brief section about possible applications of the present work, implications for future work in the area, and with some restraint, speculations about what lies ahead for the line of research. Scientists tend to have relatively little toler-
385 ance for conclusions without foundation and off-the-cuff comments made without full consideration. Therefore, authors must be careful not to overstep the bounds of propriety in making speculations about the future. But such exercises can be useful and can serve a
390 heuristic function for other researchers if the notions stated are well conceived.

Finally, particularly if the article has been relatively long or complex, the author may decide to end it with a short Conclusion. The Conclusion usually simply re-
395 states the major arguments that have been made throughout the article, reminding the reader one last time of the value of the work.

As we suggested earlier, not all articles will follow the format exactly. Some latitude is allowed to accom-
400 modate the particular needs of the author and the quirks of the research being described. Given that the goal is effective communication of information, it would not be reasonable for the format to dictate what could and could not be included in a manuscript. We hope that this
405 introduction will help to demystify research articles and provide you with some insights into what an author is trying to accomplish at various points in the report.

Let us end with a word of encouragement: Your enjoyment of social psychology will be enhanced by your
410 fuller appreciation of the sources of the information to which you are being exposed, and, to the extent that you are able to read and understand these original sources for yourself, your appreciation of this work will be maximized.

### Reference

Storms, M. D. (1973). Videotape and the attribution process: Reversing actors' and observers' points of view. *Journal of Personality and Social Psychology, 27*, 165–175.

# Exercise for Appendix A

## Factual Questions

1. What four elements should the Abstract convey?

2. Which part of a report provides the foundation for the study and the remainder of the article?

3. Normally, should the literature review be selective *or* comprehensive?

4. If there is a research hypothesis, should it be explicitly stated in the Introduction?

5. Are experimental *or* correlational studies better for making inferences about cause-and-effect?

6. What is a *criterion variable* in a correlational study?

7. Which part of a report describes the operationalizations and procedures employed in the investigation?

8. The Method section usually begins with a description of what?

9. According to the authors, what is probably the most intimidating section of a research report for students?

10. Should experienced researchers expect to find statistical techniques with which they are unfamiliar when they read research reports?

11. How should the Discussion section of a research report typically begin?

12. Which part of a report usually simply restates the major arguments that have been made throughout the article?

# Notes

# Notes

# Notes

# Notes

# Notes

# Notes